Optimizing PowerPC Code

Programming the PowerPC Chip in Assembly Language

Gary Kacmarcik

Addison-Wesley Publishing Company

Reading, Massachusetts • Menlo Park, California • New York
Don Mills, Ontario • Wokingham, England • Amsterdam
Bonn • Sydney • Singapore • Tokyo • Madrid • San Juan
Paris • Seoul • Milan • Mexico City • Taipei

Library of Congress Cataloging-in-Publication Data

Kacmarcik, Gary.
    Optimizing PowerPC code / Gary Kacmarcik.
        p. cm.
    Includes index.
    ISBN 0-201-40839-2
    1. PowerPC microprocessors.   I. Title.
QA76.8.P67K33 1995
    005.265—dc20   94-10489
                                                    CIP

Sponsoring Editor: Martha Steffen
Project Manager: Eleanor McCarthy
Production Coordinator: Deborah McKenna
Cover design: Barbara T. Atkinson
Cover art © Michael D. Coe
Set in 10 point Palatino by Michael D. Wile

1 2 3 4 5 6 7 8 9-MA-9998979695
First printing, April 1995

Addison-Wesley books are available for bulk purchases by corporations, institutions, and other organizations. For more information please contact the Corporate, Government, and Special Sales Department at (800) 238-9682.

Tous mes remerciements à ma femme Sylvie Giral, car sans son assistance et sa présence, ce livre aurait été bien difficile à accomplir. Aussi, toute ma gratitude à mes parents pour leur soutien et encouragements continuels: "J'espère qu'ils conserveront ton cerveau au vinaigre après avoir autant investi dans ton éducation."

Thanks are also in order to Tom Pittman of Itty-Bitty Computers for suffering through an earlier draft of this manuscript and suggesting numerous improvements and identifying areas that needed additional clarification.

Special thanks to 鮎川まどか and 音無響子 for providing much needed distractions and helping me maintain my sanity during the creation of this manuscript.

Contents

Introduction | 1

1.1 Purpose of Book

The purpose of this book is simple: to introduce programmers to the concepts of assembly language programming for PowerPC processors. Beyond simply presenting the information required to write functional code, this book presents the information necessary to write *efficient* code, and it also discusses the tricks that compilers use to produce fast code.

The vast majority of people reading this book may have little need to write a significant amount of code in assembly language. But the techniques presented here will be useful to the high-level programmer who needs to read compiler-generated code as part of the debugging process.

1.2 Intended Audience

This book is intended for programmers who have had some sort of experience with high-level languages such as C or Pascal, or with assembly language for another processor.

This book will not spend time defining basic concepts such as hexadecimal notation nor expounding the virtues of null-terminated over length-encoded strings. It will, however, present definitions for any term that is used. For example, concepts like *latency* and *throughput* will be defined before being used.

1.3 Why Assembly Language on a RISC Processor?

The first question that many people ask is something like: "Why would any sane person be interested in learning assembly language for a RISC processor?" The reasoning behind this question is the belief that properly written RISC assembly language routines are significantly more difficult to write than similar CISC assembly routines, and that today's compilers produce far better code than code generated by hand, so why bother?

The question is also valid because the computer industry has been moving away from programming in low-level languages and emphasizing languages that promise robustness, easy verification of correctness, and so on. Assembly language can promise none of those things. So, again, why bother?

The truth of the matter is that there are two major reasons for wanting to be familiar with assembly language for any processor (RISC or not). The first is that you need complete control of all processor resources to make the code as fast or small as possible. The second reason is that you need to debug your code (or someone else's) and see what's really going on. A source-level debugger may not be sufficient (or even available).

The first reason may sound like it's only for anal-retentive speed freaks, but there are reasons for normal human beings to want to hand-code assembly. It is a sad fact that many of the commercially available compilers do not generate highly optimized code. The best-selling compilers are typically those with the fastest *edit-compile-run* times, and a proper optimizer takes a bit of time to run. Thus, while it's true that a *properly written* optimizing compiler *can* generate code that is better than the code an average assembly language programmer would produce, many compilers are not properly written and thus, do not produce properly optimized code.

In addition, a compiler is limited by the source language. As a programmer in assembly language, you know exactly what you need and when you need it (and when you no longer need it). The compiler must try to figure out as much about the program as it can from the source, and when it's in doubt, it must play it safe and produce less efficient code. In the C programming language, the programmer is given such flexibility with addresses and pointers that it becomes extremely difficult for the compiler to determine if a range of memory can be modified by a section of code. Because of the compiler's inability to guarantee that the memory won't be modified, it may not be able to risk applying certain optimizations.

Debugging is another situation that causes programmers to drop down into assembly. Sometimes (one hopes rarely), compilers do not produce correct code. More commonly, you may find that your program works fine in some circumstances, but dies a horrible death when it interacts with other programs. Lacking the source code to the other program, assembly may be the only course of action available.

Of course, there's a reason high-level languages exist. The vast majority of your coding and debugging will be done in some sort of high-level language. You should need to use assembly only when you have a routine that needs to be as fast as possible.

To correctly respond to whether RISC assembly is more difficult than CISC assembly, the terms RISC and CISC must first be discussed in more detail.

CISC versus RISC

There is a lot of confusion surrounding the differences between a RISC and a CISC architecture arising from misuse of the terms and from various marketing departments propagating the "RISC is *always* faster/better than CISC" myth. Unfortunately, part of the confusion also comes from the fact that there is no clear line between the two design philosophies: some architectures are clearly RISC, others are clearly CISC, while still others fall somewhere in between.

The most important thing to note is that RISC ("Reduced Instruction Set Computer") and CISC ("Complex Instruction Set Computer") are terms that are properly applied to an Instruction Set Architecture (ISA) and not to a particular implementation of an ISA. Common usage allows a processor to be called a "RISC processor," but what is really meant is that the processor is an implementation of a RISC architecture.

This difference between an ISA and a hardware implemention of that ISA is fundamental to understanding RISC and CISC.

What RISC Is

The following is a list of features that are commonly associated with RISC ISA's:

- A large uniform register set
- A load/store architecture
- A minimal number of addressing modes
- A simple fixed-length instruction encoding
- No/minimal support for misaligned accesses

This set of "rules" is designed to make fast processors easier to implement. Notice that the list contains no requirements as to the number of instructions, nor does it indicate how the processor should be implemented. These are issues that are commonly mistaken as features required for a RISC processor.

A processor implementing a RISC ISA is not necessarily a fast processor—performance is dependent on how the processor is implemented. However, because the features listed were designed to make it easier to implement fast processors, one can infer that a RISC processor is likely to be faster than a CISC processor of equivalent technology.

As an example to drive this point home, one can imagine two implementations of a particular RISC ISA: one that doesn't use pipelines or superscalar dispatch (these concepts are discussed later in this book); and another one that does. The first processor would perform very poorly when compared to the other processor, and it might even perform worse than many currently available CISC processors. However, just because this processor performs poorly does not mean that it is not a RISC processor.

If you think of RISC as standing for "Reduced Instruction Set Complexity," then you may be less likely to be confused by the term.

What CISC Is

Given the definition of RISC, the original definition of CISC is trivially easy to define: CISC is anything that is not RISC.

When the designers of the first RISC architectures devised the term "RISC," they meant to differentiate their simpler, reduced processor from the current crop of complex processors. Thus, "CISC" was used as a pejorative term that meant non-RISC architectures.

This lack of a real definition has contributed to some of the confusion surrounding RISC and CISC. Today, a CISC architecture typically has:

- Many instruction types that access memory directly
- A large number of addressing modes
- Variable-length instruction encoding
- Support for misaligned accesses,

although architectures vary widely.

What RISC/CISC Are Not

Note that the above lists do not require:

- An instruction pipeline.
- A superscalar instruction dispatch.
- Hardwired or microcoded instructions.

These are all implementation issues that any processor may make use of, regardless of its ISA. RISC processors have become associated with these features because RISC ISAs are designed to facilitate the implementation of these features. However, the presence of these features does not indicate that the processor in question is an implementation of a RISC ISA.

As an example, Intel's Pentium™ processor has an instruction pipeline with a superscalar dispatch. These implementation issues do not change the fact that the Pentium is just another (albeit fast) implementation of a CISC instruction set architecture.

Is RISC Assembly More Difficult than CISC Assembly?

So this brings us back to the original question: Is a RISC processor more difficult to program than a CISC processor? The answer to this question lies somewhere between "There's no way to tell" and "That's a silly question."

It's difficult to answer the question because the programming challenges depend more on the specific processor architecture (that is, 68K, i86, PowerPC) than on the general category (that is, RISC or CISC) of the processor architecture.

An easy way to make this clear is to compare the 68K and the i86 processor families. They are both CISC architectures, but the 68K is widely regarded as being much easier to program in assembly, mostly because of its large store of general purpose registers and flexible addressing modes. The same comparison can be made for RISC architectures: some RISC processor families will be easy to program while others will be more difficult.

In fact, an argument can be made that RISC assembly language programming is *easier* than CISC assembly. The large register store and the fact that most instructions have one cycle throughput reduces some of the complexity of assembly language programming.

For today's processors, the most complicated aspect of programming in assembly language is the instruction scheduling that is necessary on pipelined implementations. Because pipelines can exist on either RISC or CISC processors, this scheduling problem exists on processors of both architecture types. Since RISC simplifies the other aspects of programming, this becomes more manageable.

1.4 PowerPC as a RISC ISA

The preceding sections have spoken in general terms of RISC processors and how they fit into the general scheme of things. This section talks about how the PowerPC fits into the RISC category.

As mentioned earlier, five basic features are commonly found on RISC processors. We'll touch on each one and discuss how the PowerPC fits.

A Large, Uniform Register Set

The PowerPC architecture defines 32 general purpose registers and 32 floating-point registers. All of these registers are general purpose in that any of the registers can be used as arguments to any of the instructions.

The only exception to this is GPR r0. Some instructions (like the non-Update *Load* and *Store* instructions) use a register specification of 0 as a special case to indicate that no register should be used in the calculation.

A Load/Store Architecture

The only instructions that access memory are the *Load* and *Store* instructions. Thus, the PowerPC ISA qualifies as a Load/Store architecture.

A Minimal Number of Addressing Modes

Only two classes of instructions require addressing modes: the load/store instructions and the branch instructions. All other instructions operate on registers or immediate values.

The load/store instructions allow three addressing modes (register indirect, register indirect with register index, or register indirect with immediate index); and the branch instructions allow three modes (absolute, PC relative, or SPR indirect).

Contrast this with the 68000 (a CISC processor), which has a seemingly infinite number of addressing modes, with more coming out with each generation of the processor family.

A Simple Fixed-length Instruction Encoding

Every PowerPC instruction is encoded in 32 bits. There are no exceptions to this rule. Instruction encodings that do not require the full 32 bits are padded with 0 bits so that they fill all 32 bits.

No/Minimal Support for Misaligned Accesses

This is where the PowerPC architecture deviates from the standard RISC design principles. Following the RISC philosophy, misaligned accesses should never occur, so support for them needlessly complicates the implementation.

However, one of the design considerations of the original POWER architecture (the PowerPC's parent) was that it be able to emulate other processors efficiently. Because many of the processors that were likely to be emulated allowed misaligned accesses, it made sense to include support for misaligned accesses in the POWER/PowerPC architecture.

1.5 Overview of this Book

The book is divided conceptually into four parts: an architecture and instruction set description (Chapters 2 through 12), a basic programming section (Chapter 13), an advanced programming section (Chapters 14 through 16), and an instruction set summary (Appendices A and B).

Chapter 2 begins with a basic overview of the PowerPC architecture: the standard data types and the functional units of the processor; and introduces the differences between the 32-bit and 64-bit PowerPC implementations.

Chapter 3 contains a brief summary of the notation used in the remaining instruction set chapters. The following chapters (4 through 9) focus on a specific instruction type, such as floating-point or branch instructions. These are useful chapters to read through at least once, because they give a feel for which operations the PowerPC instruction set provides.

Chapters 10 through 12 provide basic information about memory hierarchies and pipelines.

Chapter 11 describes the standard function-calling mechanism that most PowerPC based systems will use. Note that the information provided in this chapter is not in any way enforced by the processor. It's just a set of conventions that allow routines generated by different compilers to interface consistently. This chapter will be of interest to programmers who need to debug high-level code at the assembly level.

The remaining chapters define more advanced architectural concepts and describe some implementation details for the PowerPC 601 processor. This information is then used in discussions that describe techniques for optimizing code sequences so that they use the processor resources efficiently.

The instruction set summaries in Appendices A and B provide easy-to-use instruction references, alphabetically organized by mnemonic. Appendix A devotes a page to each PowerPC instruction and includes the obsolete POWER instructions found on the 601. Appendix B lists every POWER and PowerPC instruction and all the extended mnemonics, and also gives the mapping of each extended mnemonic into standard instructions. Appendix B is quite useful for reading code that uses the extended mnemonics, because it isn't always apparent from which base instruction the extended form was derived.

PowerPC Architecture Overview | 2

Before the instruction set can be discussed, the basic architecture of the processor must first be defined. This chapter describes the data types and functional units of the PowerPC architecture.

2.1 Data Organization

An understanding of how data is organized is the best place to begin, because everything else in this book assumes you know this. If you are familiar with assembly language for another processor, then nothing in this section should surprise you, and you should be able to quickly skim the information presented here. This section is included for the sake of completeness and to give people completely new to assembly language a good starting point.

Basic Data Types

The PowerPC provides six basic data types: byte, halfword, word, doubleword, and single- and double-precision floating-point. In addition, there is a quadword data type that is useful because quadword alignment is desirable in some circumstances. Table 2-1 summarizes these data types.

Table 2-1 Standard PowerPC Data Types

Data Type	Data Size	Lower 8 Bits of Address[a] (if aligned to this type)
Byte	8-bit	---- ----
Halfword	16-bit	---- ---0
Word	32-bit	---- --00
Doubleword[b]	64-bit	---- -000
Quadword[c]	128-bit	---- 0000
Floating-point single	32-bit	---- --00
Floating-point double	64-bit	---- -000

a. A '−' in the address indicates that the bit may be either a 0 or a 1.

b. Fixed-point instructions that operate directly on doublewords are found on 64-bit PowerPC implementations only.

c. Other than cache instructions, no instructions operate directly on quadwords.

Of these data types, the byte, halfword, word, and the two floating-point types are the most commonly used. The doubleword data type is available only on 64-bit PowerPC implementations. The quadword data type is included for completeness.

Data Alignment

Alignment refers to the placement of a data type in memory. Most processors are designed to operate more efficiently when data is aligned properly, so it is important to be aware of this concept. A data type is considered to be aligned if its address is an integral multiple of the data type size.

Thus, the address of an aligned word value must be a multiple of four. Halfword and doubleword values must have addresses that are multiples of two and eight, respectively, for proper alignment. Because bytes are one byte wide, they are always considered to be aligned.

When the addresses are viewed in binary, it is relatively easy to determine if the quantity is aligned. A multiple of 2 (halfword) always has a low order bit of b0; a multiple of four (word) has b00 for the low order bits; and a multiple of eight (doubleword) has b000.

Byte Ordering

When storing values that require more than one byte, some convention for the order of the bytes must be agreed upon or else the data could potentially be misinterpreted. Figures 2-1 and 2-2 show the two possible organizations for the halfword (2-byte) value 0x0A0B.

Figure 2-1   Big-endian Byte Ordering for 0x0A0B

0A	0B

Figure 2-2   Little-endian Byte Ordering for 0x0A0B

0B	0A

For the four-byte word 0x0A0B0C0D, there are 24 (4! = 24) possible combinations of bytes, but only the two shown in Figures 2-3 and 2-4 make sense.

Figure 2-3   Big-endian Byte Ordering for 0x0A0B0C0D

0A	0B	0C	0D

Figure 2-4   Little-endian Byte Ordering for 0x0A0B0C0D

0D	0C	0B	0A

In both of these figures, the first encoding method stores the most significant byte, or *big*-end, first, and the second encoding stores the least significant byte, or *little*-end, first. Hence, the first method is referred to as *big-endian* and the second is referred to as *little-endian*.

By default, the PowerPC processors operate in big-endian mode, but there are switches to allow user-level or interrupt operations to occur in little-endian mode.

Bit Numbering

Just as the bytes within words are organized using a big-endian scheme, the bits within each byte or word are numbered using a big-endian numbering scheme. Thus, as Figure 2-5 shows, the most significant bit (*msb*) is bit #0 and the least significant bit (*lsb*) is bit #31.

Figure 2-5   Little-endian Bit Numbering for a 32-bit Register

When representing data in registers, the *msb* will always be on the left and the *lsb* will always be on the right so that the displayed data is intelligible.

In general, it doesn't matter how the bits are ordered or numbered within a register, because one typically uses the entire register at a time. However, with the PowerPC, there are instructions that require a starting or ending bit, and for these instructions it is important to be aware of the numbering scheme.

2.2 Functional Units

It is convenient to divide a PowerPC processor into five conceptual units: the Fixed-Point or Integer Unit (IU), the Floating-Point Unit (FPU), the Branch Processor Unit (BPU), the System Register Unit (SRU), and the Load/Store Unit (LSU).

It is important to note that these are conceptual functional units. Although these units will be present in some form on each PowerPC implementation, they will not necessarily be these five particular units. Some units may be combined, or there may be multiple units of the same type. For example, the 601 combines the IU, LSU, and SRU into a unified Integer Unit. Future PowerPC processors will offer multiple IUs to increase integer performance.

Integer Unit (IU)

The Integer Unit performs all of the integer instructions. These instructions include the arithmetic, logical, and shift/rotate instructions.

The IU has a store of General Purpose Registers (GPRs) that are used to perform the calculations. In addition, there is a Fixed-Point Exception Register (XER) that contains status information.

The IU is sometimes called the Fixed-Point Unit (FXU).

Floating-Point Unit (FPU)

The Floating-Point Unit performs all of the floating-point operations that the PowerPC supports. These operations conform to the IEEE 754 floating-point standard for floating-point arithmetic and include all of the required data types (normalized, denormalized, NotANumbers, and others).

The FPU also includes a Floating-Point Status and Control Register (FPSCR) that controls how floating-point operations are performed and provides status information.

Branch Processor Unit (BPU)

The Branch Processor Unit handles all of the predictions and resolutions for the branch instructions. When a branch cannot be completely resolved, the BPU predicts whether or not the branch will be taken and fetches the appropriate instructions.

There are three SPRs associated with the BPU: the Link Register (LR), the Count Register (CTR), and the Condition Register (CR). Both the LR and the CTR can be used to hold target addresses for branching, although this is a secondary function for the CTR. The CR and CTR are used by the conditional branch instructions to hold the conditions that the branch depends on. The CR holds the relational information (*less than*, *greater than*, or *equal*) that is calculated by one of the compare instructions, and the CTR holds a count that can be automatically decremented to facilitate the coding of loop structures.

Load/Store Unit (LSU)

The Load/Store Unit handles all of the load and store instructions executed by the processor. Because these instructions are the only interface between the processor registers and the memory subsystem, the LSU can be considered the data interface for the processor.

System Register Unit (SRU)

The System Register Unit provides access to the various Special Purpose Registers (SPRs) that the PowerPC provides. This unit also implements the various Condition Register logical operations.

2.3 Processor Registers

This section provides an overview of both the user- and supervisor-level registers that the PowerPC specifies. In general, only the user-level registers will be useful to the programmer, but the supervisor-level registers are defined here to give a complete summary.

Remember that bits within registers are numbered using the *big-endian* scheme. That is, the left-most or *most-significant bit* is bit 0, and the right-most or *least significant bit* is bit 31 (or 63). Because some registers can be different widths on different implementations, this can cause some confusion about bit numbering. See §2.4, "32- versus 64-bit Implementations," for more information.

User-Level Registers

The user-level registers are the only registers that most programs are likely to need.

General Purpose Registers (GPRs)

Figure 2-6   General Purpose Register

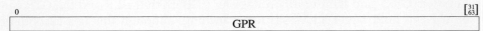

There are 32 general purpose registers. These registers are referred to as GPR0 - GPR31, or simply `r0` - `r31`. The size of these registers depends on the PowerPC implementation: they are 32-bits wide on 32-bit implementations and 64-bits wide on 64-bit implementations.

When instructions that operate on 32-bit data are executed on a 64-bit PowerPC implementation, only the lower (right-most) 32 bits are used.

Floating-Point Registers (FPRs)

Figure 2-7   Floating-Point Register

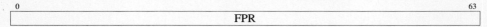

There are 32 floating-point registers. These registers are referred to as FPR0 - FPR31, or simply `fr0` - `fr31`. The floating-point registers are always 64 bits in width and always contain double-precision floating-point values.

Condition Register (CR)

Figure 2-8   Condition Register

0	3	4	7	8	11	12	15	16	19	20	23	24	27	28	31
CR0		CR1		CR2		CR3		CR4		CR5		CR6		CR7	

The Condition Register is a 32-bit-wide register that contains eight 4-bit wide condition fields. These eight fields can be specified as the destination for the result of the comparison operations or as the source for the conditional branch operations.

These eight fields are referred to as `crf0` - `crf7`, or CR{0} - CR{7}. As with the bit numbering, the fields are numbered from left to right. Thus, `crf0` corresponds to CR[0:3], `crf1` = CR[4:7], ... , and `crf7` = CR[28:31].

How the four bits in each field are interpreted depends on the instruction that was used to set the field. Figure 2-9 shows how the bits of the field are set for fixed-point compare operations. In the figure, 0, 1, 2, and 3 specify the corresponding bit within the given CR field.

Figure 2-9   CR Field Bits Resulting from Fixed-Point Compare Operations

LT	GT	EQ	SO

0	LT	Less Than
1	GT	Greater Than
2	EQ	Equal
3	SO	Summary Overflow

Figure 2-10 shows how the bits are set for floating-point compare operations.

Figure 2-10   CR Field Bits Resulting from Floating-Point Compare Operations

FL	FG	FE	FU

0	FL	FP Less Than
1	FG	FP Greater Than
2	FE	FP Equal
3	FU	FP Unordered

CR field 0 is implicitly set by fixed-point instructions and CR field 1 is implicitly set by floating-point instructions that have their Record bit set. Fixed-point instructions with the Record bit set update the CR field 0 as Figure 2-11 shows. In this figure, 0, 1, 2, and 3 are the bits within CR field 0, that is, CR[0:3].

Figure 2-11   CR Field Bits Resulting from Fixed-Point Operations with Record Bit

LT	GT	EQ	SO

0	LT	Negative (Less Than Zero)
1	GT	Positive (Greater Than Zero)
2	EQ	Zero (Equal to Zero)
3	SO	Summary Overflow

Figure 2-12 shows the interpretation of the bits of CR field 1 after a floating-point instruction with the Record bit set has been executed. In this figure, 0, 1, 2, and 3 are the bits within CR field 1, that is, CR[4:7].

Figure 2-12   CR Field Bits Resulting from FP Operations with Record Bit

FX	FEX	VX	OX

0	FX	FP Exception Summary
1	FEX	FP Enabled Exception Summary
2	VX	FP Invalid Operation Exception Summary
3	OX	FP Overflow Exception

Fixed-Point Exception Register (XER)

Figure 2-13   Fixed-Point Exception Register

0 1 2 3	15 16	23 24 25	31
SO OV CA 0 0 0 0 0 0 0 0 0 0 0 0 0	Byte compare value	0	Byte count

The XER (see Figure 2-13) contains information about the operation of integer instructions, such as the Carry bit, the Overflow bit, and a Summary Overflow bit. The XER also contains special-purpose fields that are used by some instructions.

The Summary Overflow (SO) bit is the same as the Overflow (OV) bit except that it is *sticky*. A bit that is sticky is one that will remain set once it has been set—it must be explicitly cleared by using the `mtxer` or `mcrxr` instructions. This is contrasted with the OV bit, which will be updated (cleared or set) by the next instruction that provides overflow information. The SO bit can be used to check if any of a sequence of instructions has caused an overflow, thus eliminating the need to explicitly check after each instruction that could cause an overflow.

The "Byte compare value" and "Byte count" fields of the XER are used by some of the *Load String* and *Store String* instructions. The "Byte compare value" is used only on the 601 to support the obsolete POWER instruction `lscbx`.

A full definition of the XER bits is given in Appendix C.

Floating-Point Status and Control Register (FPSCR)

The FPSCR is a 32-bit register that contains the control and status bits for the FPU (see Figure 2-14). The control bits include enable bits for the various floating-point exceptions and rounding bits for controlling how the FPU performs rounding operations. The status bits record any floating-point exceptions that may have occurred.

Figure 2-14   Floating-Point Status and Control Register

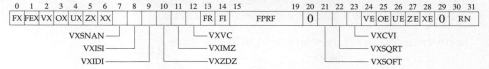

A full definition of the FPSCR bits is given in Appendix C.

Link Register (LR)

The Link Register (see Figure 2-15) is used to hold the target address for a branch. Certain forms of the branch instruction will automatically update the LR with the address of the instruction immediately following the branch. This latter use is well suited for performing subroutine calls: when the branch is taken (that is, the subroutine is called), the LR contains the return address and the subroutine can return to the caller with a simple *Branch to LR* instruction.

Figure 2-15   Link Register

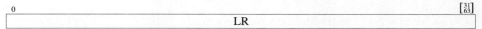

Counter Register (CTR)

The primary function of the Count Register (see Figure 2-16) is to provide a counter that can be set to specify the number of iterations for a loop. Some forms of the conditional branch instructions automatically decrement this counter and use the new counter value as part of the expression to determine if the branch should be taken or not.

Figure 2-16   Count Register

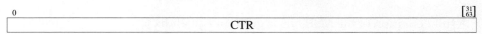

The CTR can also be used to hold branch addresses. By using the CTR, the target address can be calculated and branched to without affecting the contents of the Link Register. It is mostly operating system (OS) glue routines that take advantage of this use of the CTR, although user programs can safely do the same thing.

Supervisor-Level Registers

The supervisor-level registers are registers that contain information that is critical to the proper operation of the system. To help prevent programs from inadvertently accessing one of these registers and causing damage, access to all of these registers is privileged. This means that the program must be running in supervisor mode or a privilege exception will occur.

Fortunately, there is rarely any need to access these registers.

Machine State Register (MSR)

The MSR is a $[\frac{32}{64}]$ bit register that contains the status bits that define the current state of the processor (see Figure 2-17). This includes the bits to indicate if the processor is in 32- or 64-bit mode, if certain interrupts are enabled, if the processor is in big- or little-endian mode, and other bits.

On 32-bit PowerPC implementations, the bits are arranged as shown in Figure 2-17.

Figure 2-17   Machine State Register for 32-bit PowerPC Implementations

0	1			4	5				9	10		12	13	14	15	16	17	18	19	20	21	22	23	24	25	26	27	28	29	30	31
0	0	0	0	0	0	0	0	0	0	0	0	0	POW	0	ILE	EE	PR	FP	ME	FE0	SE	BE	FE1	0	IP	IR	DR	0	0	RI	LE

On 64-bit PowerPC Implementations, there are an additional 32 bits that are part of the MSR, as shown in Figure 2-18. The bits of the 32-bit MSR are mapped into the low-order 32 bits (bits 32 to 63) of the 64-bit MSR. Currently, there is only one bit defined in the upper 32-bits of the 64-bit MSR: the processor mode bit (SF). This bit indicates whether the processor is in 32-bit or 64-bit mode.

Figure 2-18   Machine State Register for 64-bit PowerPC Implementations

0	1																														31
SF	0	0	0	0	0	0	0	0	0	0	0	0	0	0	0	0	0	0	0	0	0	0	0	0	0	0	0	0	0	0	0

32	33			36	37				41	42		44	45	46	47	48	49	50	51	52	53	54	55	56	57	58	59	60	61	62	63
0	0	0	0	0	0	0	0	0	0	0	0	POW	0	ILE	EE	PR	FP	ME	FE0	SE	BE	FE1	0	IP	IR	DR	0	0	RI	LE

A full definition of the MSR bits is given in Appendix C.

Save/Restore Registers (SRR0, SRR1)

The two Save and Restore Registers are used to save the machine status when an interrupt occurs and then to restore the original state when the interrupt has been serviced. Thses two registers are shown in Figure 2-19.

Figure 2-19   Save and Restore Registers

0	$[\frac{31}{63}]$
SRR0	

0	$[\frac{31}{63}]$
SRR1	

SRR0 records the next instruction to be executed after the interrupt has been serviced. SRR1 records the original state of the MSR. When an interrupt occurs, the bits $[\frac{0}{0:32}]$, $[\frac{5:9}{37:41}]$, and $[\frac{16:31}{48:63}]$ are copied from the MSR and placed in the corresponding bit positions of SRR1.

Processor Version Register (PVR)

The PVR is a read-only 32-bit register that provides a processor ID and revision level (see Figure 2-20). The upper 16 bits define the processor (for example, 0x0001 = 601; 0x0003 = 603), and the lower 16 bits define the engineering revision level.

Figure 2-20   Processor Version Register

0   15 16   31

| Version | Revision |

Data Address Register (DAR)

When a Data Storage Interrupt occurs, the DAR is loaded with the effective address of the storage element that caused the access interrupt. Figure 2-21 shows the DAR.

Figure 2-21   Data Address Register

0 $[\frac{31}{63}]$

| DAR |

Data Storage Interrupt Status Register (DSISR)

The DSISR is a 32-bit register that defines the cause of Data Storage and Alignment interrupts (see Figure 2-22).

Figure 2-22   Data Storage Interrupt Status Register

0   31

| DSISR |

This register is sometimes referred to as the DAE/Source Instruction Service Register.

Instruction and Data Block Address Translation Registers (IBAT, DBAT)

The Block Address Translation registers (BATs) are used by the BAT mechanism to record information about the range of memory pages that are considered to be grouped together as a block.

Figure 2-23   Block Address Translation Registers

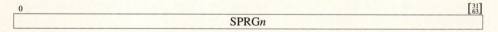

Upper BAT Register

| BEPI | 0 0 0 0 | BL | Vs | Vp |

Lower BAT Register

| BRPN | 0 0 0 0 0 0 0 0 0 0 | WIMG | 0 | PP |

There are four pairs of IBATs and four pairs of DBATs (see Figure 2-23). There are two sets of BAT registers because instruction and data references are handled separately. On PowerPC implementation with unified caches (like the 601), only the IBATs will be implemented.

General SPRs (SPRG0–SPRG3)

The four General SPRs are provided to give the operating system extra registers to store whatever information it needs without tying up GPRs. These registers are 32 bits on 32-bit implementations, and 64 bits on 64-bit implementations. Figure 2-24 shows the format of these four registers.

Figure 2-24   General SPRs

| SPRGn |

Time Base Register (TBU, TBL)

The Time Base Register is a 64-bit register that maintains a counter. The frequency of the counter is system-dependent—to convert the TBR value to calendar values requires the update frequency value that the OS needs to maintain. The two halves of the TBR are shown in Figure 2-25.

Figure 2-25   Time Base Register

| TBU |

| TBL |

The TBR can be accessed as if it were two 32-bit registers by specifying either the upper or lower portion of the register. Read access to the TBR is user-level; write access is supervisor-level.

This register is not defined on the 601.

Decrementer (DEC)

The DEC register is a 32-bit register (see Figure 2-26) that counts down (at the same frequency as the Time Base Register) and generates a Decrementer interrupt when the counter passes 0.

Figure 2-26 Decrementer

0–31
DEC

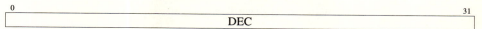

Because the 601 doesn't have a Time Base Register, the frequency of the DEC on the 601 is the same as for the Real-Time Clock (RTC) defined in the next section.

For compatibility with the POWER architecture, the 601 also provides user-level read access to the DEC by using 6 instead of 22 as the SPR ID with the `mfspr` instruction.

External Access Register (EAR)

The EAR is an optional 32-bit SPR that is used to specify the (system specific) resource ID of the target external device that the `eciwx` and `ecowx` instructions can communicate with. The fields of the EAR are given in Figure 2-27.

Figure 2-27 External Access Register

0	1–25	26–31
E	0 0 0 0 0 0 0 0 0 0 0 0 0 0 0 0 0 0 0 0 0 0 0 0 0	RID

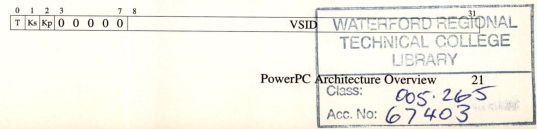

Segment Registers (SRs)

The sixteen 32-bit SRs are used to calculate the virtual address from the 32-bit effective address. These registers are defined for 32-bit implementations only.

The format of the Segment Registers is different depending on if the SR specified an ordinary or a direct-store segment (see Chapter 10, "Memory & Caches," for more information about segments). For ordinary segments, the SR is arranged as shown in Figure 2-28.

Figure 2-28 Segment Register for Ordinary Segments

0	1	2	3–7	8–31
T	Ks	Kp	0 0 0 0 0	VSID

For direct-store segments, the SR is arranged differently, as shown in Figure 2-29.

Figure 2-29   Segment Register for Direct-store Segments

0	1	2	3		11	12		31
T	Ks	Kp		BUID		*controller specific*		

Address Space Register (ASR)

The ASR (Figure 2-30) is a 64-bit SPR that holds the address of the Segment Table. It is defined only for 64-bit implementations.

Figure 2-30   Address Space Register

0		51	52		63
Real Address of Segment Table			*unused*		

Storage Description Register 1 (SDR1)

The SDR1 contains the encoded size and the address of the Page Table. This register is 32 bits wide on 32-bit implementations and 64 bits wide on 64-bit implementations, as shown in Figure 2-31.

Figure 2-31   Storage Description Register

0		45	46		58	59		63
HTABORG			*unused*			HTABSIZE		

This register is also referred to as the Page Table Search Description Register or simply the Table Search Description Register.

Processor Specific Registers

This section discusses the registers that are not part of the PowerPC specification but are defined by some implementation. These registers are provided by the 601 for POWER compatibility.

Multiply-Quotient Register (MQ)

The MQ register (Figure 2-32) is used to emulate the MQ register defined on POWER processors. Certain (non-PowerPC) instructions use this register.

Figure 2-32   Multiply-Quotient Register

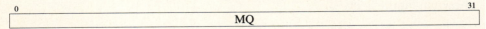

0		31
	MQ	

This register is defined on the 601 only.

Real-Time Clock Registers (RTCU, RTCL)

The RTC registers provide access to the POWER architecture's Real-Time Clock. The upper register (RTCU) keeps track of the number of seconds and the lower register (RTCL) keeps track of the number of nanoseconds since the beginning of the current second. Both halves of this register are shown in Figure 2-33.

Figure 2-33   Real-Time Clock Register

```
0                                                              31
┌──────────────────────────────────────────────────────────────┐
│                            RTCU                                │
└──────────────────────────────────────────────────────────────┘

0  1   2                                    24 25              31
┌──┬──┬────────────────────────────────────┬──────────────────┐
│0 │0 │              RTCL                   │0 0 0 0 0 0 0      │
└──┴──┴────────────────────────────────────┴──────────────────┘
```

This register is defined on the 601 only.

2.4 32- versus 64-bit Implementations

This book describes both the 32-bit and 64-bit versions of the PowerPC architecture. For the most part, the programming model is the same for both versions, but there are some basic differences.

To avoid confusion, it is worth pointing out that the term "64-bit instruction" is used in this section to refer to an instruction that is available on 64-bit implementations only. All of the PowerPC floating-point instructions operate on 64-bit quantities, but are considered 32-bit instructions because they are available on 32-bit PowerPC implementations.

32/64-bit Operating Modes

There are some subtle differences between the 32-bit and 64-bit operating modes for the PowerPC. In general, these differences affect only the instructions that are available for use and the method by which effective addresses are calculated, but in some instances instructions behave differently based on the operating mode.

32-bit Mode on 32-bit Implementations

All 32-bit instructions are available. No 64-bit instructions are available.

64-bit Mode on 32-bit Implementations

Is not allowed. Any attempt to execute a 64-bit instruction on a 32-bit implementation will result in an Illegal Instruction exception.

32-bit Mode on 64-bit Implementations

This compatibility mode for 32-bit implementations behaves just like the 32-bit mode on 32-bit implementations with these exceptions:

- Instructions defined only for 32-bit implementations (for example, `mfsr`, `mtsr`) are not available and will cause an Illegal Instruction exception.

- All effective address calculations are performed using all 64 bits of the source registers. However, the upper 32 bits are set to 0 before accessing data or fetching instructions.

- Instructions that always return a 64-bit result (for example, `mulhd`) will work properly (that is, they will return a 64-bit result as expected) in 32-bit mode.

64-bit Mode on 64-bit Implementations

All instructions operate on all 64 bits of the source registers and produce 64-bit results.

32/64-bit Registers

The most significant difference between 32- and 64-bit implementations is the width of many of the processor registers. These differences are summarized in this section.

GPRs

All of the GPRs are 32 bits wide for 32-bit implementations and 64 bits wide for 64-bit implementations. For 64-bit implementations, all 64 bits of the register are affected, except when executing in 32-bit mode.

Counter Register

The Counter Register (CTR) is 32 or 64 bits wide, depending on the PowerPC implementation. To insure that 64-bit implementations executing in 32-bit mode operate the same as 32-bit implementations, only the low-order 32 bits of the CTR are used when the processor is in 32-bit mode.

Machine State Register

The MSR is 32 bits wide on 32-bit implementations and 64 bits wide on 64-bit implementations. The 32 additional bits for the 64-bit version are used to store the current mode (32- or 64-bit), and to extend the reserved field from the 32-bit MSR.

Save/Restore Registers

These registers (SSR0 and SSR1) are 32 bits on 32-bit implementations and 64 bits on 64-bit implementations. If an interrupt occurs on a 64-bit implementation executing in 32-bit mode, the upper 32 bits of SSR0 (the register that stores the *next instruction address*) are set to 0 because the lower 32 bits are enough to hold the address.

Segment Registers

The sixteen 32-bit SRs are present only on 32-bit implementations. The instructions to access the Segment Registers (`mfsr`, `mfsrin`, `mtsr`, and `mtsrin`) do not exist on 64-bit implementations (not even in 32-bit mode). Trying to execute them will result in an Illegal Instruction exception.

Address Space Register

The ASR is defined only for 64-bit implementations, and thus, does not exist on any 32-bit PowerPC implementation.

Storage Description Register 1

The SDR1 is 32 bits wide on 32-bit implementations and 64 bits wide on 64-bit implementations. Although the SDR1 always contains Page Table information, the format of the information is different for 32- and 64-bit implementations.

Instruction Set Overview | 3

The next few chapters contain an overview of all the instructions and extended instruction forms for the PowerPC ISA. The instructions are grouped according to function under the following headings: Branch and Trap, Load and Store, Integer, Rotate and Shift, Floating-Point, and System Register.

This chapter acts as an introduction to the following chapters. It describes the basic instruction structures and provides a summary of the notation used to describe the instructions and extended forms.

3.1 Instruction Groups

The instructions are grouped according to function within each of the major headings. For example, in Chapter 6, "Integer Instructions," there are subheadings for Addition, Subtraction, Multiplication, and Division. Within these subsections, all relevant instructions are presented along with a short textual description of the instruction operation.

Each section also includes many tables that summarize the operations and the syntax for each instruction form. These tables are meant to make it easy to see the (sometimes subtle) differences between the various instructions of the same type.

3.2 Instruction Suffixes

Many instructions allow standard suffixes to be specified to tell the processor
to perform operations in addition to the basic instruction. For each instruction
that allows suffixes, each valid suffix for the instruction is enclosed in square
brackets ('[' and ']') immediately following the base mnemonic. If there are
multiple suffixes for an instruction, they will each be enclosed in a separate set
of brackets.

Integer Suffixes: 'o' and '.'

For integer instructions, valid suffixes are 'o' and '.'. Appending an 'o' tells the
instruction to update the Fixed-Point Exception Register (XER) to reflect
the Overflow (XER[OV]) and Summary Overflow (XER[SO]) information from
the instruction's operation. Without this option, integer instructions do not sup-
ply the overflow information as part of the result.

When the '.' suffix is appended to integer instructions, it indicates that the condition information should be recorded in field 0 of the Condition Register
(CR{0}). This condition information records whether the result is less than zero,
greater than zero, or equal to zero, and it contains a shadow copy of the Summary Overflow bit in the XER (XER[SO]).

Floating-Point Suffixes: 's' and '.'

Most floating-point instructions allow two types of suffixes to be specified: 's'
and '.'. The 's' suffix indicates that the operation should be performed by interpreting the registers as if they contained single-precision data. If the operand
registers do not truly contain single-precision values, then the result of instructions executed with the 's' option is undefined.

All arithmetic floating-point instructions allow the '.' suffix to be specified. This
suffix tells the instruction to record the condition information in field 1 of the
Condition Register (CR{1}). This keeps track of any floating-point exceptions
that may be caused by the instruction. Floating-point is discussed in detail in
Chapter 8.

Branch Suffixes: 'l' and 'a'

All branch instructions allow an 'l' suffix and some forms also allow an 'a' suffix. The 'l' suffix indicates that the address of the following instruction should
be recorded in the Link Register as part of the instruction operation, and the 'a'
suffix indicates that the specified address is an absolute (instead of a program
counter relative) value. These suffixes are described in greater detail in §4.1,
"Branch Instructions."

3.3 Extended Instruction Forms

Extended instruction forms are extra mnemonics that the assembler accepts and converts into valid instruction forms. These forms are not instructions themselves but are special cases of valid instruction forms. Extended forms are useful when the base form of an instruction is very general, as is the case with the branch and rotate instructions. The special cases provided by the extended forms can render an instruction that is complex and unwieldy (for example, *Rotate Left Word Immediate then AND with Mask*) into something more understandable (for example, *Shift Left Immediate*).

The following chapters present both the standard instruction forms and the extended forms. When an extended form is presented, the base mnemonic from which the form is derived is given, along with a description of how the extended form maps into the base instruction.

3.4 Obsolete Instructions

Obsolete instructions are instructions that were part of the POWER architecture specification but were not included in the PowerPC ISA in an effort to streamline the architecture. All obsolete instructions are clearly marked as being obsolete to eliminate any confusion that might arise from the inclusion of these instructions.

The obsolete instructions listed in the next few chapters are implemented only on the 601, for the purposes of backward compatibility only. New programs should *not* make use of these instructions. No future PowerPC implementation will support these instructions (although a computer system built using a PowerPC processor may trap and emulate them in software).

Wherever possible, a brief explanation is given of why the instruction was removed for the PowerPC architecture. In most cases, the instructions were removed to eliminate bottlenecks caused by seldom-used functionality or to reduce the complexity of PowerPC implementations.

3.5 Optional Instructions

The PowerPC ISA specification defines some instructions to be optional. These instructions may or may not be present on a particular PowerPC implementation. In these chapters, all optional instructions are clearly noted as being optional.

Before using these instructions, the programmer must first verify that the program is running on an implementation that supports the given instruction. To determine which PowerPC processors implement a particular instruction, instructions can be referenced in Appendix A, which contains an alphabetical list of all instructions.

Most of the optional instructions are defined as belonging to one of a variety of instruction groups, for example, the Graphical Group. A processor may implement any or all of the instructions in any of the groups, but if a processor claims to support a given group, it must implement all of the instructions in the given group.

At the moment, there are only two groups of optional instructions defined: the General Purpose Group and the Graphical Group. The General Purpose Group contains the `fsqrt` and `fsqrts` instructions, and the Graphical Group contains `stfiwx`, `fres`, `frsqrte`, and `fsel`.

An optional instruction need not belong to any of the optional groups. For example, `eciwx` and `ecowx` are both optional instructions, but they are not associated with any group.

3.6 Notation

Because of the complexity of most of the instructions, a special notation is needed to properly describe an instruction's operation.

The following notation is used throughout this chapter to describe the operation of instructions.

rT Specifies any of the 32 General Purpose Registers (GPRs) that are part of the Integer Unit. These registers may be 32 or 64 bits wide, depending on the PowerPC implementation: 32 bits wide on 32-bit implementations and 64 bits wide on 64-bit implementations. For example, `r3` specifies GPR 3.

frT Specifies any of the 32 64-bit Floating-Point Registers (FPRs) that are part of the Floating-Point Unit. For example, `fr13` specifies FPR 13.

MQ   Specifies the Multiply-Quotient Register. This register exists only on POWER implementations and is used for multiply, divide and extended shift and rotate operations.

CR   Specifies the Condition Register. This register is commonly divided into eight fields that are specified using CR{0} through CR{7}.

CIP   Current Instruction Pointer. This is not a user-visible register on the PowerPC, but the CIP notation is convenient when describing how an instruction affects the flow of control. For example, CIP ⇐ LR indicates that the next instruction to be executed is at the address contained in the Link Register.

(r*T*)   Specifies the contents of the given register. The specified register may be any GPR, FPR, or Special Purpose Register. For example, (r2) specifies the contents of GPR 2; (fr4), which specifies the contents of FPR 4.

(*x*)   Groups the expressions in *x* so that they are executed before expressions outside of the parentheses.

$[\frac{x1}{x2}]$ Specifies a number *x*. Two values of *x* are given: the top value (*x1*) is the number for 32-bit PowerPC implementations, and the bottom value (*x2*) is the number for 64-bit PowerPC implementations. This notation is used when referring to bits in registers, since the bit numbering is slightly different between the two implementation types.

r*T*[*x*]   Specifies the bit *x* in the given register. The specified register may be any GPR, FPR, or Special Purpose Register. Note that bits are numbered using the big-endian notation, thus bit 0 is the *high-order* or *most-significant bit*, and bit 31 (or 63 for 64-bit implementation) is the *low-order* or *least-significant bit*. For example, r2[4] refers to bit 4 of GPR 2.

r*T* $[\frac{x1}{x2}]$ Specifies the bit *x* in the given register. Two values for *x* are given: the top value (*x1*) specifies the bit for 32-bit PowerPC implementations, and the lower value (*x2*) specifies the bit for 64-bit PowerPC implementations. This is typically used only for GPRs since most other registers are the same size on both implementation types. For example, r3 $[\frac{0}{32}]$ refers to the sign bit of the (low-order) word in GPR 3.

r*T*[*x*:*y*] Specifies the range of bits from *x* to *y* in the given register. The specified register may be any GPR, FPR, or Special Purpose Register. For example, r1[0:7] refers to bits 0 through 7 in GPR 1.

r*T* $[\frac{x1:y1}{x2:y2}]$ Specifies the range of bits from *x* to *y* in the given register. Two ranges of *x* and *y* are given: the upper range (*x1:y1*) for 32-bit PowerPC implementations and the lower range (*x2:y2*) for 64-bit implementations. This is typically used only for GPRs since most other registers are the same size on both implementation types. For example, r3 $[\frac{24:31}{56:63}]$ refers to the least significant byte of GPR 3.

r*T*{*x*}   Specifies the range of bits corresponding to field *x* in the given register. The bits for a field *n* range from bit *n*×4 to bit *n*×4+3, thus, this notation is equivalent to r*T*[(*x* × 4):(*x* × 4) + 3]. The specified register may be any GPR, FPR, or Special Purpose Register. For example, CR{0} refers to field 0 (bits 0:3) of the Condition Register.

X   Where *X* is any number of digits 0-9, specifies a decimal constant, for example, 24.

b*X*   Where *X* is any number of digits 0-1, specifies a binary constant, for example, b0110.

0x*X*   Where *X* is any number of digits 0-9 or letters **A-F**, specifies a hexadecimal constant. Hexadecimal constants will always be specified using uppercase alphabetic characters, for example, 0x**BABE**.

$x \Leftarrow y$ Loads *x* with the value *y*. This is used to identify the value that gets assigned to the instruction's target register. For example, r*T* $\Leftarrow$ 0 means that register r*T* gets assigned a value of 0.

$x := y$ Loads the temporary variable *x* with the value *y*. Temporary variables are used when the instruction operation is too complex to express in a single expression. This separate assignment notation for temporary variables is used to emphasize the fact that the variable *x* is not a processor resource that is being updated. For example, *m* := (r2) means that the temporary variable *m* is set equal to the contents of register r2.

$x = y$ Returns true if *x* is equal to *y*, false otherwise.

$x \neq y$ Returns true if *x* is not equal to *y*, false otherwise.

$x > y$ Returns true if *x* is greater than *y*, false otherwise.

$x < y$ Returns true if *x* is less than *y*, false otherwise.

$x \geq y$ Returns true if *x* is greater than or equal to *y*, false otherwise.

$x \leq y$ Returns true if *x* is less than or equal to *y*, false otherwise.

$\approx x$ Returns a value that is approximately equal to *x*, for example, r*T* $\Leftarrow \approx \sqrt{2}$ assigns r*T* with a value that is close to, but not necessarily equal to, the square root of *x*.

$|x|$ Calculates the absolute value of *x*.

$\sim x$ Calculates the one's complement of *x*. A one's complement operation converts all binary '1's in the source value to binary '0's in the destination value and vice versa. For example, ~b01101010 becomes b10010101.

$-x$ Negates *x*. This is the same as performing the two's complement of *x*. The two's complement of a value is equal to the one's complement plus 1. For example, -b0110 becomes b1010.

\`*x*   Sign-extends the value *x* as appropriate. Sign-extension means that the most significant bit of *x* (also called the *sign bit*) is replicated to the left to fill all available bit positions. For example, \`0x0042 sign-extends to 0x00000000 00000042 on 64-bit implementations; and \`0xFADE sign-extends to 0xFFFFFADE on 32-bit implementations.

°*x*   Zero-extends the value *x* as appropriate. Zero-extension means that 0 bits are used to the left of *x* to fill all available bit positions. For example, °0xDEADF00D zero-extends to 0xDEADF00D on 32-bit implementations and to 0x00000000 DEADF00D on 64-bit implementations.

$x + y$ Adds *x* to *y*.

x - y Subtracts y from x.

$x \times y$ Multiplies x by y.

$x \div y$ Divides x by y.

$x \% y$ Calculates the remainder of x divided by y.

$x \perp y$ Concatenates x with y. For example, `0x5CAB` $\perp$ `0xFACE` becomes `0x5CABFACE`.

$x \,\&\, y$ Logically ANDs x and y. For example, `b0110` & `b1010` becomes `b0010`.

$x \mid y$ Logically ORs x and y. For example, `b0110` | `b1010` becomes `b1110`.

$x \oplus y$ Logically XORs x and y. For example, `b0110` ⊕ `b1010` becomes `b1100`.

$x \equiv y$ Calculates the equivalence of x and y. The result of the equivalence is `1` wherever the bits of x and y are the same and `0` wherever they differ. For example, `b0110` ≡ `b1010` becomes `b0011`.

$x \ll y$ Shifts x left by y bits. For example, `b10101111` « `2` becomes `b10111100`.

$x \gg y$ Shifts x right by y bits. For example, `b10101111` » `2` becomes `b00101011`.

$x \overset{s}{\gg} y$ Shifts x right algebraically by y bits. An algebraic shift duplicates the most significant bit (bit 0 or the *sign* bit) as it shifts the data. For example, `b10101010` $\overset{s}{\gg}$ `4` becomes `b11111010`; `b01110101` $\overset{s}{\gg}$ `4` becomes `b00000111`.

$x \circlearrowleft y$ Rotates x left by y bits. For example, `b11110000` ↺ `2` becomes `b11000011`.

$x \circlearrowright y$ Rotates x right by y bits. For example, `b00001111` ↻ `2` becomes `b11000011`.

$x\,?\,y:z$ Returns either y or z depending on the value of x, where x is a Boolean expression. If x is true, then y is returned, otherwise z is returned. For example, $rT \Leftarrow (rA[26]{=}0)\,?\,0 : (rB)$ means that if bit $rA[26]$ is `0`, rT is set equal to `0`, otherwise it is set equal to the contents of rB.

Branch and Trap Instructions 4

The Branch, Trap, and System Call instructions are the only instructions that change the flow of control of the processor. Since this potential change of control can disrupt the smooth operation of the pipeline, these instructions are handled by a separate branch processor that does its best to remove these instructions from the instruction stream before passing the instructions on to the other execution units.

4.1 Branch Instructions

There are four basic types of branch instructions: *Branch, Branch Conditional*, and *Branch Conditional to* either the *Link Register* or the *Counter Register* (see Table 4.1). The first two of these instructions expect the target address to be encoded in the branch instruction, while the second two branch instructions get the target address from one of the processor's Special Purpose Registers.

All four of the branch instructions allow an optional 'l' suffix to indicate that the address of the instruction following the branch should be stored in the Link Register (LR) as part of the branch operation. This provides a simple way of implementing subroutines, since the return address can be saved in the LR using the 'l' option, and the subroutine can return to the caller by using a *Branch to Link Register* (blr) instruction.

The *Branch* (b) and *Branch Conditional* (bc) instructions have an additional option 'a' that allows the target address to be specified as an absolute value. Usually, the target address is specified relative to the current location counter,

Table 4-1 Basic Branch Instructions

b[l][a] *addr*
Branch
	if(l = 1)
	    LR $\Leftarrow$ CIP + 4
	if(a = 1)
	    CIP $\Leftarrow$ `addr`
	else
	    CIP $\Leftarrow$ CIP + `addr`

bc[l][a] *BO,BI,addr*
Branch Conditional
	if(l = 1)
	    LR $\Leftarrow$ CIP + 4
	if(*condition*)
	    if(a)
	        CIP $\Leftarrow$ `addr`
	    else
	        CIP $\Leftarrow$ CIP + `addr`

bcctr[l] *BO,BI*
Branch Conditional to Count Register
	if(l = 1)
	    LR $\Leftarrow$ CIP + 4
	if(*condition*)
	    CIP $\Leftarrow$ CTR

bclr[l] *BO,BI*
Branch Conditional to Link Register
	oldLR := LR
	if(l = 1)
	    LR $\Leftarrow$ CIP + 4
	if(*condition*)
	    CIP $\Leftarrow$ *oldLR*

that is, as a positive or negative offset from the address of the branch instruction. If the "Absolute Address" option is set by using the 'a' option, then the target address is taken directly from the branch instruction, without adjusting for the current location counter.

As mentioned earlier, the *Branch Conditional to Link Register* (**bclr**) instruction is useful for returning from a subroutine call when the return address is stored in the LR. The *Branch Conditional to Counter Register* (**bcctr**) instruction is also useful for this purpose. Technically, the Counter Register (CTR) is intended to be used only as a counter for loops, and it doesn't make sense to use it as a register to branch through. However, the original system designers of the POWER architecture needed an extra register to branch through when they were implementing the global linkage mechanism, so they added the **bcctr** instruction since the CTR was conveniently available in the branch processor. The global linkage mechanism, which describes this use of the **bcctr** instruction, is discussed in §13.13, "Linking with Global Routines."

One important thing to note about the operation of the branch and link instructions (those with the 'l' option specified) is that the Link Register is updated with the value of the instruction following the branch *even if the branch is not taken*. This shouldn't cause problems if the LR is saved and restored according to standard function calling conventions (see §9.4 "Subroutine Calling Conventions") but may cause problems for programmers who are trying to optimize code by saving and restoring the LR only when necessary.

The *branch-on* (BO) and *bit* (BI) parameters for the conditional branches provide a mechanism for specifying a wide range of conditional branch instructions. The *branch-on* parameter specifies which condition is used as a test for the branch and the *bit* parameter specifies which bit of the Condition Register (0-31) is used in the test.

Table 4-2 contains a list of the valid *branch-on* parameters. The parameters control how the CTR and the bit from the CR work together to determine if the branch should be taken. For example, to encode an instruction that branches to the contents of the LR if the *equal* (EQ) flag in CR{2} is set (ignoring the CTR entirely), the bclr instruction should be used with *BO* equal to b01100 and *BI* set to 10. The *BI* parameter is set to 10 because CR field 2 ranges from bit 8 to bit 11, and the EQ flag is the third bit within a field.

Table 4-2 Branch-On (BO) Parameter for Branch Conditional Instructions

b0000y	Decrement CTR Branch if CTR ≠ 0 AND CR[*BI*] = 0
b0001y	Decrement CTR Branch if CTR = 0 AND CR[*BI*] = 0
b001zy	Branch if CR[*BI*] = 0
b0100y	Decrement CTR Branch if CTR ≠ 0 AND CR[*BI*] = 1
b0101y	Decrement CTR Branch if CTR = 0 AND CR[*BI*] = 1
b011zy	Branch if CR[*BI*] = 1
b1z00y	Decrement CTR Branch if CTR ≠ 0
b1z01y	Decrement CTR Branch if CTR = 0
b1z1zz	Branch Always
z bits are ignored but must be 0 for the instruction to be valid. *y* bits encode hints as to whether the conditional branch is likely to be taken.	

As can be seen from the example given in the preceding paragraph, using the *BO* and *BI* parameters directly can be somewhat confusing and error-prone. For this reason, a large number of extended instruction forms are provided for the most commonly used conditional branches.

The next few sections deal with these extended branch forms. The first section, "Contitional Branch Extended Forms, " presents the extended forms for conditional branch instructions when the target address is encoded in the instruction. The next two sections, "Branch to LR Extended Forms" and "Branch to CTR Extended Forms," present the extended forms for branch instructions to the Link and Counter Registers.

Conditional Branch Extended Forms

The Conditional Branch extended forms are built on top of the *Branch Conditional* (bc) instruction. Because of the large number of extended forms, this section is divided into three parts: the bit test forms, the CTR-dependent forms, and the forms with encoded conditions.

Bit Test Extended Forms

The Bit Test extended forms test a designated bit in the Condition Register and branch to the encoded address depending on if the specified bit is set ('1' or *true*) or clear ('0' or *false*) (see Table 4-3).

Table 4-3 Conditional Branch Extended Instruction Forms with Bit Tests

bt[l][a] *bit,addr* **Branch if Condition True** *extended form for* bc[l][a] 12,*bit,addr*	if(CR[*bit*] = 1) branch to *addr*
bf[l][a] *bit,addr* **Branch if Condition False** *extended form for* bc[l][a] 4,*bit,addr*	if(CR[*bit*] = 0) branch to *addr*

The *Branch if Condition True* (bt) form tests bit *bit* in the Condition Register and branches to the target address *addr* if the bit is '1'.

The *Branch if Condition False* (bf) form tests the bit *bit* in the Condition Register and branches to the target address *addr* if the bit is '0'.

CTR-Dependent Extended Forms

The CTR-Dependent Conditional Branch forms use the predecremented value of the Counter Register to determine if the branch should be taken.

Table 4-4 summarizes the two basic types of CTR Conditional Branches: those that depend solely on the CTR and those that depend on the CTR and a condition in the CR.

The first two CTR extended forms are the *Branch if Decremented CTR is Non-Zero* (bdnz) and the *Branch if Decremented CTR is Zero* (bdz). These instructions depend only on the CTR. They decrement the CTR and then compare the new CTR value with 0 to determine if the branch should be taken. The first form branches if the new CTR is not equal to 0, while the second form branches if it is equal to 0.

The remaining four CTR-based Conditional Branches depend on both the CTR and a specified bit in the Condition Register. The four forms cover all possibilities of the CTR being zero or non-zero and the bit in the CR being '0' or '1'.

Table 4-4 Conditional Branch Extended Forms with CTR Conditions

bdnz[l][a] *addr* **Branch if Decremented CTR is Non-Zero** *extended form for* `bc[l][a]` `16,0,`*addr*	CTR ⟸ CTR - 1 if(CTR ≠ 0) branch to *addr*
bdz[l][a] *addr* **Branch if Decremented CTR is Zero** *extended form for* `bc[l][a]` `18,0,`*addr*	CTR ⟸ CTR - 1 if(CTR = 0) branch to *addr*
bdnzt[l][a] *bit,addr* **Branch if Decremented CTR is Non-Zero and** **Condition True** *extended form for* `bc[l][a]` `8,`*bit,addr*	CTR ⟸ CTR - 1 if((CTR ≠ 0) AND (CR[*bit*] = 1)) branch to *addr*
bdnzf[l][a] *bit,addr* **Branch if Decremented CTR is Non-Zero and** **Condition False** *extended form for* `bc[l][a]` `0,`*bit,addr*	CTR ⟸ CTR - 1 if((CTR ≠ 0) AND (CR[*bit*] = 0)) branch to *addr*
bdzt[l][a] *bit,addr* **Branch if Decremented CTR is Zero and** **Condition True** *extended form for* `bc[l][a]` `10,`*bit,addr*	CTR ⟸ CTR - 1 if((CTR = 0) AND (CR[*bit*] = 1)) branch to *addr*
bdzf[l][a] *bit,addr* **Branch if Decremented CTR is Zero and** **Condition False** *extended form for* `bc[l][a]` `2,`*bit,addr*	CTR ⟸ CTR - 1 if((CTR = 0) AND (CR[*bit*] = 0)) branch to *addr*

The *Branch if Decremented CTR is Non-Zero and Condition True* (`bdnzt`) form decrements the CTR and branches if the new value of the CTR is not equal to 0 *and* the specified bit in the CR is '1' (true). The `bdnzf` form is identical, except that it requires that the bit in the CR be '0' (false) in order for the branch to be taken.

The last two forms, `bdzt` and `bdzf`, are similar to `bdnzt` and `bdnzf`, except that they branch only if the decremented CTR is equal to 0 and the appropriate condition holds.

Extended Forms with Encoded Conditions

Because the Condition Register is divided into eight fields, it is convenient to use instructions which operate on fields in the CR instead of individual bits. The Conditional Branches with Encoded Conditions are extended forms which provide this convenience by building on top of the standard *Branch Conditional* (`bc`) instruction.

The 12 conditional branch forms listed in Table 4-5 have the condition encoded as part of the mnemonic. These forms operate on a field of the CR that is specified as one of the parameters. However, the CR field is an optional parameter. If a CR field isn't specified explicitly, the instruction is assumed to refer to CR{0}.

Table 4-5 Condition Branch Extended Forms with Encoded Conditions

beq[l][a] *[crf,]addr* **Branch if Equal** *extended form for* bc[l][a] 12,*crf**4+2,*addr*	if(CR[*crf**4+2] = 1) branch to *addr*
bne[l][a] *[crf,]addr* **Branch if Not Equal** *extended form for* bc[l][a] 4,*crf**4+2,*addr*	if(CR[*crf**4+2] = 0) branch to *addr*
blt[l][a] *[crf,]addr* **Branch if Less Than** *extended form for* bc[l][a] 12,*crf**4+0,*addr*	if(CR[*crf**4+0] = 1) branch to *addr*
ble[l][a] *[crf,]addr* **Branch if Less Than or Equal** *extended form for* bc[l][a] 4,*crf**4+1,*addr*	if(CR[*crf**4+1] = 0) branch to *addr*
bgt[l][a] *[crf,]addr* **Branch if Greater Than** *extended form for* bc[l][a] 12,*crf**4+1,*addr*	if(CR[*crf**4+1] = 1) branch to *addr*
bge[l][a] *[crf,]addr* **Branch if Greater Than or Equal** *extended form for* bc[l][a] 4,*crf**4+0,*addr*	if(CR[*crf**4+0] = 0) branch to *addr*
bnl[l][a] *[crf,]addr* **Branch if Not Less Than** *extended form for* bc[l][a] 4,*crf**4+0,*addr*	if(CR[*crf**4+0] = 0) branch to *addr*
bng[l][a] *[crf,]addr* **Branch if Not Greater Than** *extended form for* bc[l][a] 4,*crf**4+1,*addr*	if(CR[*crf**4+1] = 0) branch to *addr*
bso[l][a] *[crf,]addr* **Branch if Summary Overflow** *extended form for* bc[l][a] 12,*crf**4+3,*addr*	if(CR[*crf**4+3] = 1) branch to *addr*
bns[l][a] *[crf,]addr* **Branch if Not Summary Overflow** *extended form for* bc[l][a] 4,*crf**4+3,*addr*	if(CR[*crf**4+3] = 0) branch to *addr*
bun[l][a] *[crf,]addr* **Branch if Unordered** *extended form for* bc[l][a] 12,*crf**4+3,*addr*	if(CR[*crf**4+3] = 1) branch to *addr*
bnu[l][a] *[crf,]addr* **Branch if Not Unordered** *extended form for* bc[l][a] 4,*crf**4+3,*addr*	if(CR[*crf**4+3] = 0) branch to *addr*

The beq form branches if the EQ bit (bit 2) of the given CR field is '1'. The bne form is similar, but it branches if that bit is '0'.

The blt and bgt forms check the *less than* (LT) and *greater than* (GT) bits (respectively) of the specified CR field and branch if the bit is set.

The `ble` and `bng` forms are two mnemonics that map to the same instruction. They both check the GT (*greater than*) bit of the specified CR field and branch if that bit is '0'.

The `bge` and `bnl` forms also map to the same instruction. They check the LT (*less than*) bit of CR{*crf*} and branch if the bit is clear.

The last four extended branch forms depend on the state of bit 3 of the designated CR field. This bit has different meanings depending on how the bit was set, and there is a set of extended forms for the two most common of these bit interpretations.

The first set of forms assumes that the CR field was set by an integer arithmetic or compare instruction. For these instructions, bit 3 contains the *summary overflow* (SO) bit that is copied from the XER. The `bso` and `bns` instructions branch if the SO bit is '1' or '0', respectively.

The second set of extended forms assumes that the CR field has been set by a floating-point compare instruction. Floating-point compare instructions set the *unordered* flag (bit 3) of the destination CR field if one or both of the numbers being compared is *Not a Number* (NaN). The `bun` instruction branches if the comparison returned an unordered result, and the `bnu` instruction branches if an unordered result was not returned.

Branch to LR Extended Forms

There are four major types of extended forms for the `bclr` instruction: unconditional branch forms, bit test forms, CTR-dependent forms, and forms with encoded conditions.

Most of these forms are identical to their *Branch Conditional* (`bc`) counterparts, except that the branch destination is taken from the Link Register (LR) instead of encoded directly in the instruction.

Branch Unconditional

There is one extended form that unconditionally branches to the contents of the Link Register (see Table 4-6).

Table 4-6 Unconditional Branch to LR Extended Instruction Form

`blr[l]` **Branch to LR** *extended form for* `bclr[l]` `20,0`	branch via LR

The `blr` instruction branches directly to the address stored in LR. If the '1' option is specified, the LR is updated with the address of the instruction immediately following the branch. The new LR value is stored after the old LR value has been used for the branch operation.

Bit Test Extended Forms

As with the Branch Conditional forms described in the preceding section, the Bit Test extended forms (see Table 4-7) test a given bit in the Condition Register and branch depending on the current value of the specified CR bit. These forms differ in that they branch to the address stored in the LR instead of the address encoded in the branch instruction.

Table 4-7 Branch to LR Extended Instruction Forms with Bit Tests

`btlr[l]` *bit* **Branch to LR if Condition True** *extended form for* `bclr[l]` `12,`*bit*	if(CR[*bit*] = 1) branch via LR
`bflr[l]` *bit* **Branch to LR if Condition False** *extended form for* `bclr[l]` `4,`*bit*	if(CR[*bit*] = 0) branch via LR

The `btlr` form branches to the LR if the specified bit in the CR is '1'. The `bflr` form branches if CR[*bit*] is '0'.

CTR-Dependent Extended Forms

The CTR-dependent *Branch to Link Register* forms (see Table 4-8) use the decremented value of the Counter Register and an optional condition to determine if the branch should be taken.

All six of these forms are identical to the *Branch Conditional* forms described in the previous section, except for the fact that they branch via the LR instead of to the address encoded in the instruction.

The first two CTR extended forms are the *Branch to LR if Decremented CTR is Non-Zero* (`bdnzlr`) and the *Branch to LR if Decremented CTR is Zero* (`bdzlr`). These instructions depend only on the CTR. The `bdnzlr` instruction decrements the CTR and branches if the new value of the CTR is *not* equal to 0. The `bdzlr` instruction performs a similar operation but branches if the CTR is equal to 0.

The remaining four CTR dependent Conditional Branches depend on both the CTR and a specified bit in the Condition Register. These four forms cover all possibilities of the CTR being zero or non-zero, and the bit in the CR being '0' or '1'.

Table 4-8 Branch to LR Extended Instruction Forms with CTR Conditions

bdnzlr[l] **Branch to LR if Decremented CTR is Non-Zero** *extended form for* bclr[l] 16,0	CTR ⇐ CTR - 1 if(CTR ≠ 0) branch via LR
bdzlr[l] **Branch to LR if Decremented CTR is Zero** *extended form for* bclr[l] 18,0	CTR ⇐ CTR - 1 if(CTR = 0) branch via LR
bdnztlr[l] *bit* **Branch to LR if Decremented CTR is Non-Zero** **and Condition True** *extended form for* bclr[l] 8,*bit*	CTR ⇐ CTR - 1 if((CTR ≠ 0) AND (CR[*bit*] = 1)) branch via LR
bdnzflr[l] *bit* **Branch to LR if Decremented CTR is Non-Zero** **and Condition False** *extended form for* bclr[l] 0,*bit*	CTR ⇐ CTR - 1 if((CTR ≠ 0) AND (CR[*bit*] = 0)) branch via LR
bdztlr[l] *bit* **Branch to LR if Decremented CTR is Zero and** **Condition True** *extended form for* bclr[l] 10,*bit*	CTR ⇐ CTR - 1 if((CTR = 0) AND (CR[*bit*] = 1)) branch via LR
bdzflr[l] *bit* **Branch to LR if Decremented CTR is Zero and** **Condition False** *extended form for* bclr[l] 2,*bit*	CTR ⇐ CTR - 1 if((CTR = 0) AND (CR[*bit*] = 0)) branch via LR

The *Branch to LR if Decremented CTR is Non-Zero and Condition True* (bdnztlr) form decrements the CTR and branches if the new value of the CTR is not equal to 0 *and* the specified bit in the CR is '1' (true). The bdnzflr form is identical, except that it requires that the bit in the CR be '0' (false) in order for the branch to be taken.

The last two forms, bdztlr and bdzflr, are similar to bdnztlr and bdnzflr, except that they branch only if the decremented CTR is equal to 0.

Extended Forms with Encoded Conditions

The 12 conditional Branch to LR forms listed in Table 4-9 have the condition encoded as part of the mnemonic. These 12 forms are the same as the 12 Branch Conditional forms described in the previous section and presented in Table 4-5.

All of these forms operate on a field of the CR that is specified as one of the parameters. However, the CR field is an optional parameter. If it isn't specified explicitly, the instruction is assumed to refer to CR{0}.

Table 4-9 Branch to LR Extended Forms with Encoded Conditions

beqlr[l] [crf] **Branch to LR if Equal** *extended form for* bclr[l] 12,*crf**4+2	if(CR[*crf**4+2] = 1) branch via LR
bnelr[l] [crf] **Branch to LR if Not Equal** *extended form for* bclr[l] 4,*crf**4+2	if(CR[*crf**4+2] = 0) branch via LR
bltlr[l] [crf] **Branch to LR if Less Than** *extended form for* bclr[l] 12,*crf**4+0	if(CR[*crf**4+0] = 1) branch via LR
blelr[l] [crf] **Branch to LR if Less Than or Equal** *extended form for* bclr[l] 4,*crf**4+1	if(CR[*crf**4+1] = 0) branch via LR
bgtlr[l] [crf] **Branch to LR if Greater Than** *extended form for* bclr[l] 12,*crf**4+1	if(CR[*crf**4+1] = 1) branch via LR
bgelr[l] [crf] **Branch to LR if Greater Than or Equal** *extended form for* bclr[l] 4,*crf**4+0	if(CR[*crf**4+0] = 0) branch via LR
bnllr[l] [crf] **Branch to LR if Not Less Than** *extended form for* bclr[l] 4,*crf**4+0	if(CR[*crf**4+0] = 0) branch via LR
bnglr[l] [crf] **Branch to LR if Not Greater Than** *extended form for* bclr[l] 4,*crf**4+1	if(CR[*crf**4+1] = 0) branch via LR
bsolr[l] [crf] **Branch to LR if Summary Overflow** *extended form for* bclr[l] 12,*crf**4+3	if(CR[*crf**4+3] = 1) branch via LR
bnslr[l] [crf] **Branch to LR if Not Summary Overflow** *extended form for* bclr[l] 4,*crf**4+3	if(CR[*crf**4+3] = 0) branch via LR
bunlr[l] [crf] **Branch to LR if Unordered** *extended form for* bclr[l] 12,*crf**4+3	if(CR[*crf**4+3] = 1) branch via LR
bnulr[l] [crf] **Branch to LR if Not Unordered** *extended form for* bclr[l] 4,*crf**4+3	if(CR[*crf**4+3] = 0) branch via LR

The beqlr form branches if the EQ bit (bit 2) of the given CR field is '1'. The bnelr form branches if that bit is '0'.

The bltlr and bgtlr forms check the LT and GT bits (respectively) of the specified CR field and branch if the bit is set.

The `blelr` and `bnglr` forms are two mnemonics that map to the same instruction. They both check the GT bit of the specified CR field and branch if the bit is '0'.

The `bgelr` and `bnllr` forms also map to the same instruction. They check the LT bit of CR{*crf*} and branch if the bit is clear.

The last four extended branch forms depend on the state of bit 3 of the designated CR field. The `bsolr` and `bnslr` forms interpret this bit as indicating the CR field's *summary overflow* status, and they indicate that the branch should be taken if the bit is set (`bsolr`) or if it is not set (`bnslr`).

The `bunlr` and `bnulr` extended forms interpret bit 3 of a CR field as containing the *unordered result* flag of a floating-point compare. The `bunlr` and `bnulr` instructions branch if this bit is '1' or '0', respectively.

Branch to CTR Extended Forms

There are three major types of extended forms for the `bcctr` instruction: unconditional branch forms, bit test forms, and forms with encoded conditions. There are no forms that use the CTR as part of the condition since these types of instructions are not sensible.

Branch Unconditional

There is one extended form (see Table 4-10) that provides a simple way of encoding an unconditional branch to the Counter Register.

Table 4-10 Unconditional Branch to CTR Extended Instruction Form

`bctr[l]` **Branch to CTR** *extended form for* `bcctr[l] 20,0`	branch via CTR

The `bctr` instruction branches directly to the address stored in the CTR.

Bit Test Extended Forms

As with the Branch Conditional forms described earlier in "Conditional Branch Extended Forms," the Bit Test extended forms (see Table 4-11) test a given bit in the Condition Register and branch to the address contained in the CTR depending on the current value of the specified CR bit.

Table 4-11 Branch to CTR Extended Instruction Forms with Bit Tests

btctr[l] *bit* **Branch to CTR if Condition True** *extended form for* bcctr[l] 12,*bit*	if(CR[*bit*] = 1) branch via CTR
bfctr[l] *bit* **Branch to CTR if Condition False** *extended form for* bcctr[l] 4,*bit*	if(CR[*bit*] = 0) branch via CTR

The `btctr` form tests CR[*bit*] and branches to the address stored in the CTR if the bit is '1.' The `bfctr` form tests the same bit but branches via the CTR if the bit is '0.'

Extended Forms with Encoded Conditions

The 12 conditional Branch to CTR forms listed in Table 4-12 have the condition encoded as part of the mnemonic. These 12 forms are the same as the 12 Branch Conditional forms described in "Conditional Branch Extended Forms" and presented in Table 4-5.

All of these forms operate on a field of the CR that is specified as one of the parameters. However, the CR field is an optional parameter. If it isn't specified explicitly, the instruction is assumed to refer to CR{0}.

Table 4-12 Branch to CTR Extended Forms with Encoded Conditions

beqctr[l] *[crf]* **Branch to CTR if Equal** *extended form for* bcctr[l] 12,*crf**4+2	if(CR[*crf**4+2] = 1) branch via CTR
bnectr[l] *[crf]* **Branch to CTR if Not Equal** *extended form for* bcctr[l] 4,*crf**4+2	if(CR[*crf**4+2] = 0) branch via CTR
bltctr[l] *[crf]* **Branch to CTR if Less Than** *extended form for* bcctr[l] 12,*crf**4+0	if(CR[*crf**4+0] = 1) branch via CTR
blectr[l] *[crf]* **Branch to CTR if Less Than or Equal** *extended form for* bcctr[l] 4,*crf**4+1	if(CR[*crf**4+1] = 0) branch via CTR
bgtctr[l] *[crf]* **Branch to CTR if Greater Than** *extended form for* bcctr[l] 12,*crf**4+1	if(CR[*crf**4+1] = 1) branch via CTR
bgectr[l] *[crf]* **Branch to CTR if Greater Than or Equal** *extended form for* bcctr[l] 4,*crf**4+0	if(CR[*crf**4+0] = 0) branch via CTR
bnlctr[l] *[crf]* **Branch to CTR if Not Less Than** *extended form for* bcctr[l] 4,*crf**4+0	if(CR[*crf**4+0] = 0) branch via CTR

bngctr[l] [crf] **Branch to CTR if Not Greater Than** *extended form for* bcctr[l] 4,crf*4+1	if(CR[*crf**4+1] = 0) branch via CTR
bsoctr[l] [crf] **Branch to CTR if Summary Overflow** *extended form for* bcctr[l] 12,crf*4+3	if(CR[*crf**4+3] = 1) branch via CTR
bnsctr[l] [crf] **Branch to CTR if Not Summary Overflow** *extended form for* bcctr[l] 4,crf*4+3	if(CR[*crf**4+3] = 0) branch via CTR
bunctr[l] [crf] **Branch to CTR if Unordered** *extended form for* bcctr[l] 12,crf*4+3	if(CR[*crf**4+3] = 1) branch via CTR
bnuctr[l] [crf] **Branch to CTR if Not Unordered** *extended form for* bcctr[l] 4,crf*4+3	if(CR[*crf**4+3] = 0) branch via CTR

The `beqctr` form branches if the EQ bit (bit 2) of the given CR field is '1'. The `bnectr` form branches if that bit is '0'.

The `bltctr` and `bgtctr` forms check the LT and GT bits (respectively) of the specified CR field and branch if the bit is set.

The `blectr` and `bngctr` forms are two mnemonics that map to the same instruction. They both check the GT bit of the specified CR field and branch if the bit is '0'.

The `bgectr` and `bnlctr` forms also map to the same instruction. They check the LT bit of CR{*crf*} and branch if the bit is clear.

The last four extended branch forms depend on the state of bit 3 of the designated CR field. The `bsoctr` and `bnsctr` forms interpret this bit as indicating the CR field's Summary Overflow status, and they indicate that the branch should be taken if the bit is set (`bsoctr`) or if it is not set (`bnsctr`).

The `bunctr` and `bnuctr` extended forms interpret bit 3 of a CR field as containing the *unordered result* flag of a floating-point compare. The `bunctr` and `bnuctr` instructions branch if this bit is '1' or '0', respectively.

4.2 Branch Prediction

Branches present some of the worst pipeline hazards since they disrupt the steady flow of instructions to the rest of the processor. Using a scheme such as Branch Prediction can help alleviate the penalties associated with branches.

Note that the PowerPC architecture does not *require* any sort of branch prediction mechanism, but it does allow implementations of the architecture to provide whatever sort of branch prediction is deemed necessary.

What is Branch Prediction?

Branch Prediction is a mechanism for the processor to guess whether or not a particular branch will be taken. The ability to generate some sort of reasonable prediction is quite useful since the processor is not always able to completely resolve a branch before it needs to be executed.

On heavily pipelined processors, some sort of branch prediction is practically a requirement, because the alternative is to stall the processor until the branch is resolved.

A good prediction scheme is a great benefit to code throughput because of the penalties associated with a mispredicted branch. In the worst case, a mispredicted branch may require that the pipeline be flushed and then stalled while the correct instructions are fetched from memory.

Branch Prediction Types

There are two common types of branch prediction: static branch prediction and dynamic branch prediction.

Static Branch Prediction

Static Branch Prediction has a default prediction for each type of branch based on branch direction and other branch parameters. For example, backward branches are assumed to be taken, and forward branches are assumed to be not taken. Many static prediction schemes also have a *reverse prediction* flag to indicate that the default prediction should be reversed.

The advantages of a static prediction implementation are that it is simple to implement and it is powerful enough to characterize branch behavior in most situations.

The disadvantage is that this system requires the programmer (or compiler) to analyze the branches and set the appropriate instruction bits so that the instruction is predicted as desired.

Dynamic Branch Prediction

Dynamic Branch Prediction uses additional hardware to record whether or not a branch was taken the last few times it was encountered. By analyzing the past operation of the instruction, the processor can formulate a prediction as to whether the branch is likely to be taken.

The benefit of a dynamic prediction scheme is that the programmer or compiler doesn't need to analyze branches and set instruction bits in order to have branches predicted "correctly."

The disadvantages are that this type of system is costly to implement and the benefits are not significantly better than for a simple static prediction mechanism.

Note that Dynamic Branch Prediction still requires some sort of default prediction mechanism to apply when the processor encounters a branch for the first time.

Branch Prediction on PowerPC Processors

The 601 implements a simple static branch prediction that follow these rules:

- If it is a *forward* branch, the branch is assumed to be *not taken*.
- If it is a *backward* branch, the branch is assumed to be *taken*.
- Conditional branches to the LR or CTR are assumed to be *not taken*.

The rational behind these rules is:

- A backward branch is assumed to be the closing instruction of a loop, and since loops are generally executed more than once, the branch should be taken back to the beginning of the loop most of the time.
- A forward branch is assumed to be not taken because forward branches have roughly a 50% likelihood of being taken or not taken and one of these operations had to be chosen as the default.

These assumptions obviously do not apply to every forward or backward branch, so this simple static prediction will make mistakes. The branch predictions were optimized for looping structures, which is presumably where many programs spend a majority of their time.

Branch Prediction Hints

Since the static branch prediction is not always correct, a mechanism for overriding the default prediction is provided. This mechanism is in the form of a branch prediction *reverse* bit, which is encoded in the *BO* parameter of a branch instruction (see §Table 4-2 *"Branch-On (BO) Parameter for Branch Conditional Instructions"*).

The reverse bit in a conditional branch instruction tells the processor that the standard predictions should be reversed for this instruction. Thus, a forward branch is assumed to be taken, and a backward branch is assumed to be not taken.

Note that the setting of this bit does not *guarantee* that the branch will be taken or not taken. It merely provides a hint as to whether or not the branch is *likely* to be taken. The processor can use this hint to pre-fetch instructions, or it can ignore it.

Encoding Branch Predictions

By convention, PowerPC assemblers accept a '+' suffix for conditional branch instructions to indicate that the reverse prediction bit should be set. If this suffix is not provided, the reverse bit is set to '0'.

```
beq      cr0,*-10    # predicted taken
beq      cr0,*+10    # predicted not taken

beq+     cr0,*-10    # predicted not taken
beq+     cr0,*+10    # predicted taken
```

The reverse bit can also be set by directly setting the appropriate bit in the *BO* field for the branch. The *BO* field is described in Table 4-2 "*Branch-On (BO) Parameter for Branch Conditional Instructions.*"

```
bc       0x0C,2,adr  # same as beq cr0,adr
bc       0x0D,2,adr  # same as beq+ cr0,adr
```

4.3 Trap Instructions

The trap instructions listed in Table 4-13 provide a mechanism for invoking the system trap handler based on a comparison between the provided instruction operands.

Table 4-13 Trap Instructions

tw *TO,rA,rB* **Trap Word**	if(*condition*) invoke system trap handler
twi *TO,rA,s16* **Trap Word Immediate**	if(*condition*) invoke system trap handler
td *TO,rA,rB* **Trap Doubleword** *64-bit implementations only*	if(*condition*) invoke system trap handler
tdi *TO,rA,s16* **Trap Doubleword Immediate** *64-bit implementations only*	if(*condition*) invoke system trap handler

For each of the word and doubleword varieties of the trap instruction, there are two instruction forms: one compares two registers, and the other compares a register with an immediate value.

The type of comparison performed depends on the value of the *Trap-On (TO)* parameter (see Table 4-14). Setting any of the five bits means that the trap handler should be invoked if the conditions associated with those bits is satisfied.

Table 4-14 Trap-On (TO) Parameter for Trap Instructions

0b00001	Trap if Less Than
0b00010	Trap if Greater Than
0b00100	Trap if Equal
0b01000	Trap if Logically Less Than
0b10000	Trap if Logically Greater Than

Coding the *TO* parameter, while not nearly as tedious as the *BO* and *BI* parameters for the conditional branch instructions, is not quite as much fun one might initially imagine it to be. To make coding the *Trap* instructions more enjoyable, a set of extended mnemonics that encode the condition as part of the instruction mnemonic is provided.

These 15 extended forms are summarized in Table 4-15 and described in detail in Table 4-16.

Table 4-15 Summary of Extended TO Encodings

0b11111	Trap Unconditionally
0b00100	Trap if Equal
0b11000	Trap if Not Equal
0b10000	Trap if Less Than
0b10100	Trap if Less Than or Equal
	Trap if Not Greater Than
0b01000	Trap if Greater Than
0b01100	Trap if Greater Than or Equal
	Trap if Not Less Than
0b00010	Trap if Logically Less Than
0b00110	Trap if Logically Less Than or Equal
	Trap if Logically Not Greater Than
0b00001	Trap if Logically Greater Than
0b00101	Trap if Logically Greater Than or Equal
	Trap if Logically Not Less Than

Table 4-16 is an overview of the trap extended instruction forms. This table contains summaries of all the trap forms, including the word, doubleword, register, and immediate forms of the instructions.

Table 4-16 Extended Trap Conditional Instructions

Trap Always	word	register	**trap** *extended form for* tw 31,r0,r0
Trap if Equal	word	register	**tweq rA,rB** *extended form for* tw 4,rA,rB
		immediate	**tweqi rA,s16** *extended form for* twi 4,rA,s16
	doubleword *64-bit only*	register	**tdeq rA,rB** *extended form for* td 4,rA,rB
		immediate	**tdeqi rA,s16** *extended form for* tdi 4,rA,s16
Trap if Not Equal	word	register	**twne rA,rB** *extended form for* tw 24,rA,rB
		immediate	**twnei rA,s16** *extended form for* twi 24,rA,s16
	doubleword *64-bit only*	register	**tdne rA,rB** *extended form for* td 24,rA,rB
		immediate	**tdnei rA,s16** *extended form for* tdi 24,rA,s16
Trap if Less Than	word	register	**twlt rA,rB** *extended form for* tw 16,rA,rB
		immediate	**twlti rA,s16** *extended form for* twi 16,rA,s16
	doubleword *64-bit only*	register	**tdlt rA,rB** *extended form for* td 16,rA,rB
		immediate	**tdlti rA,s16** *extended form for* tdi 16,rA,s16
Trap if Less Than or Equal *or* **Trap if Not Greater Than**	word	register	**twle rA,rB** **twng rA,rB** *extended form for* tw 20,rA,rB
		immediate	**twlei rA,s16** **twngi rA,s16** *extended form for* twi 20,rA,s16
	doubleword *64-bit only*	register	**tdle rA,rB** **tdng rA,rB** *extended form for* td 20,rA,rB
		immediate	**tdlei rA,s16** **tdngi rA,s16** *extended form for* tdi 20,rA,s16

Trap if Greater Than	word	register	`twgt rA,rB` *extended form for* `tw 8,rA,rB`
		immediate	`twgti rA,s16` *extended form for* `twi 8,rA,s16`
	doubleword *64-bit only*	register	`tdgt rA,rB` *extended form for* `td 8,rA,rB`
		immediate	`tdgti rA,s16` *extended form for* `tdi 8,rA,s16`

Trap if Greater Than or Equal
 	
or
 	
Trap if Not Less Than
	word	register	`twge rA,rB`
			`twnl rA,rB`
			extended form for `tw 12,rA,rB`

		immediate	`twgei rA,s16`
			`twnli rA,s16`
			extended form for `twi 12,rA,s16`

	doubleword
	64-bit only
		register	`tdge rA,rB`
			`tdnl rA,rB`
			extended form for `td 12,rA,rB`

		immediate	`tdgei rA,s16`
			`tdnli rA,s16`
			extended form for `tdi 12,rA,s16`

Trap if Logically Less Than	word	register	`twllt rA,rB` *extended form for* `tw 2,rA,rB`
		immediate	`twllti rA,s16` *extended form for* `twi 2,rA,s16`
	doubleword *64-bit only*	register	`tdllt rA,rB` *extended form for* `td 2,rA,rB`
		immediate	`tdllti rA,s16` *extended form for* `tdi 2,rA,s16`

Trap if Logically Less Than or Equal
 	
or
 	
Trap if Logically Not Greater Than
	word	register	`twlle rA,rB`
			`twlng rA,rB`
			extended form for `tw 6,rA,rB`

		immediate	`twllei rA,s16`
			`twlngi rA,s16`
			extended form for `twi 6,rA,s16`

	doubleword
	64-bit only
		register	`tdlle rA,rB`
			`tdlng rA,rB`
			extended form for `td 6,rA,rB`

		immediate	`tdllei rA,s16`
			`tdlngi rA,s16`
			extended form for `tdi 6,rA,s16`

Trap if Logically Greater Than	word	register	`twlgt rA,rB` *extended form for* `tw 1,rA,rB`
		immediate	`twlgti rA,s16` *extended form for* `twi 1,rA,s16`
	doubleword *64-bit only*	register	`tdlgt rA,rB` *extended form for* `td 1,rA,rB`
		immediate	`tdlgti rA,s16` *extended form for* `tdi 1,rA,s16`

Trap if Logically Greater Than or Equal
 	
or
 	
Trap if Logically Not Less Than
	word	register	`twlge rA,rB`
			`twlnl rA,rB`
			extended form for `tw 5,rA,rB`

		immediate	`twlgei rA,s16`
			`twlnli rA,s16`
			extended form for `twi 5,rA,s16`

	doubleword
	64-bit only
		register	`tdlge rA,rB`
			`tdlnl rA,rB`
			extended form for `td 5,rA,rB`

		immediate	`tdlgei rA,s16`
			`tdlnli rA,s16`
			extended form for `tdi 5,rA,s16`

4.4 System Linkage Instructions

The system linkage instructions listed in Table 4-17 provide a mechanism so that programs can call on the operating system to perform a function or service.

Table 4-17   System Linkage Instructions

sc
System Call
	$\text{SRR0} \Leftarrow \text{CIP} + 4$
	$\text{SRR1} \Leftarrow \text{MSR} \left[\frac{0, 5:9, 16:31}{0:32, 37:41, 48:63} \right]$
	if(MSR[IP])
	$\qquad \text{CIP} \Leftarrow \text{`0xFFF0 0C00}$
	else
	$\qquad \text{CIP} \Leftarrow \text{°0x0000 0C00}$

rfi **Return From Interrupt**	$\text{MSR} \Leftarrow \text{SRR1} \left[\frac{0, 5:9, 16:31}{0:32, 37:41, 48:63} \right]$ $\text{CIP} \Leftarrow \text{SRR0} \left[\frac{0:29}{0:61} \right] \perp \text{b00}$

The *System Call* (`sc`) instruction saves the current machine state in the SRR*n* registers and passes control to the system handler. This instruction can be used to request that an operation be performed by the operating system (OS). The calling conventions and the services provided are entirely dependent on the structure of the OS. The sc instruction merely provides a standard method of accessing OS functions.

The *Return From Interrupt* (rfi) instruction is used by the system handler to return control to the user level program after the system call or interrupt has been handled. This instruction restores the state of the system to what it was when the system call or interrupt was invoked and then passes control back to the original program.

Load and Store Instructions

5

The transfer of data from the memory store and the processor is handled by the Load and Store instructions. These instructions load data from memory into a register or store the contents of a register out into main memory.

5.1 Loads and Stores

Most of the *Load* and *Store* instructions have the same basic forms. There is a base *Load* and *Store* form for each of the data types supported by the PowerPC, and then there are the combinations of *Indexed* and *Update* forms. This section describes the common forms to eliminate redundancy and so that the later sections can focus on deviations from this standard.

Loads

The four types of *Load* instructions are

- *Load*
- *Load with Update*
- *Load Indexed*
- *Load Indexed with Update*

The *Load* forms are the most basic forms, and they simply load the data from the specified memory location into the designated target register (rT). The memory location is calculated by adding a 16-bit signed offset (d) to the contents of the source register (rA).

The *Load with Update* forms load the data into the target register as the *Load* forms do, but they also update the source register rA by adding the offset d to rA after the memory has been accessed. This can be used to *pre-increment* (or *pre-decrement*) the data pointer in rA if the increment size is stored in d.

The *Load Indexed* forms also load the target register with the data from the specified memory location. However, the *Indexed* forms calculate the address from two registers, rA and rB, instead of from a register and an offset.

The *Load Indexed with Update* forms are a combination of the *Indexed* and the *Update* load forms. These forms load the target register with the data specified by the two source registers and update one of the source registers (rA) by adding the contents of the other (rB) to it after the load has been performed.

For all of the *Load* instructions, if r0 is specified for the source register rA, then the contents of rA (r0) are *not* used in the address calculation. Instead, the constant 0 is used in the address calculation. This allows for the address to be calculated from just an immediate constant or from just the contents of one register (rB). For the *Indexed* forms, if the contents of r0 need to be part of the address calculation, r0 can be specified as rB.

If r0 is specified for rA for any of the *Load with Update* forms, then the instruction is invalid. Instructions are also invalid if the register given for rA is the same as that specified for rT.

For the *Update* forms, the POWER architecture allows r0 to be specified for rA, and it allows rA to be the same register as rT. If r0 is used or if rA is the same as rT, the register is simply not updated with the new address. The PowerPC architecture does not allow these situations to be coded because it is not useful to have an update form that cannot update, and the extra check to see if the register is valid needlessly complicates the hardware.

Stores

As with the standard *Load* instructions, there are also four basic types of *Store* instructions:

- *Store*
- *Store with Update*
- *Store Indexed*
- *Store Indexed with Update*

The *Store* forms take the contents (or part of the contents) of a source register (rS) and write it out to memory. The memory address at which the data is stored is calculated by adding a 16-bit signed offset (d) to the contents of the source register (rA).

The *Store with Update* forms store the contents of the source register and update the source register rA by adding the offset d to rA after the memory has been written. This can be used to *pre-increment* the data pointer in rA if the increment size is stored in d.

The *Store Indexed* forms store the target register contents to the specified memory location. The *Indexed* forms calculate the address from two registers, rA and rB, instead of from a register and an offset.

The *Store Indexed with Update* forms store the contents of the target register out to memory and update one of the source registers (rA) by adding the contents of the other register (rB) to it after the store operation has been performed.

For all of the *Store with Update* instructions, if $r0$ is specified for the source register rA, then the instruction is invalid.

The POWER architecture allowed the update forms of the *Store* instructions to specify $r0$ for rA. In this case, the updated address value would not be written to rA. The PowerPC architecture does not recognize this as a valid form because such an instruction would not be very useful and it would complicate implementations.

5.2 Load and Store Byte

The *Load* and *Store Byte* instructions listed in Tables 5-1 and 5-2 transfer eight bits of information to or from a GPR. The 8-bits are transferred from the least significant byte of the GPR, thus, on 32-bit PowerPC implementations, data is moved to and from bits 24:31. On 64-bit implementations, data is moved between memory and bits 56:63 of the GPR.

Table 5-1 Load Byte Instructions

`lbz rT,d(rA)` **Load Byte and Zero**	$rT \Leftarrow {}^{\circ}\text{Byte}((rA\,|\,0)+{}^{\backprime}d)$
`lbzu rT,d(rA)` **Load Byte and Zero with Update**	$rT \Leftarrow {}^{\circ}\text{Byte}((rA)+{}^{\backprime}d)$ $rA \Leftarrow (rA)+{}^{\backprime}d$
`lbzx rT,rA,rB` **Load Byte and Zero Indexed**	$rT \Leftarrow {}^{\circ}\text{Byte}((rA\,|\,0)+(rB))$
`lbzux rT,rA,rB` **Load Byte and Zero with Update Indexed**	$rT \Leftarrow {}^{\circ}\text{Byte}((rA)+(rB))$ $rA \Leftarrow (rA)+(rB)$

The four types of *Load Byte and Zero* instructions are standard *Load* instructions. The value from the specified memory location is loaded into the low-order byte of the target register rT. The upper bytes of the target register are cleared to 0.

Table 5-2 Store Byte Instructions

stb $rS,d(rA)$ **Store Byte**	$\mathrm{Byte}((rA\,|\,0)+\grave{}d) \Leftarrow rS\ [{}^{24:31}_{56:63}]$
stbu $rS,d(rA)$ **Store Byte with Update**	$\mathrm{Byte}((rA)+\grave{}d) \Leftarrow rS\ [{}^{24:31}_{56:63}]$ $rA \Leftarrow (rA)+\grave{}d$
stbx rS,rA,rB **Store Byte Indexed**	$\mathrm{Byte}((rA\,|\,0)+(rB)) \Leftarrow rS\ [{}^{24:31}_{56:63}]$
stbux rS,rA,rB **Store Byte with Update Indexed**	$\mathrm{Byte}((rA)+(rB)) \Leftarrow rS\ [{}^{24:31}_{56:63}]$ $rA \Leftarrow (rA)+(rB)$

The four *Store Byte* instructions are also modelled after the standard *Store* instructions. These instructions take the low-order byte in the source register rS and store it at the specified memory location.

5.3 Load and Store Halfword

The *Load* and *Store Halfword* instructions listed in Tables 5-3 and 5-4 transfer sixteen bits of information to or from a GPR.

Table 5-3 Load Halfword Instructions

lhz $rT,d(rA)$ **Load Halfword and Zero**	$rT \Leftarrow {}^{\circ}\mathrm{Half}((rA\,|\,0)+\grave{}d)$
lhzu $rT,d(rA)$ **Load Halfword and Zero with Update**	$rT \Leftarrow {}^{\circ}\mathrm{Half}((rA)+\grave{}d)$ $rA \Leftarrow (rA)+\grave{}d$
lhzx rT,rA,rB **Load Halfword and Zero Indexed**	$rT \Leftarrow {}^{\circ}\mathrm{Half}((rA\,|\,0)+(rB))$
lhzux rT,rA,rB **Load Halfword and Zero Indexed with Update**	$rT \Leftarrow {}^{\circ}\mathrm{Half}((rA)+(rB))$ $rA \Leftarrow (rA)+(rB)$
lha $rT,d(rA)$ **Load Halfword Algebraic**	$rT \Leftarrow {}^{\grave{}}\mathrm{Half}((rA\,|\,0)+\grave{}d)$
lhau $rT,d(rA)$ **Load Halfword Algebraic with Update**	$rT \Leftarrow {}^{\grave{}}\mathrm{Half}((rA)+\grave{}d)$ $rA \Leftarrow (rA)+\grave{}d$
lhax rT,rA,rB **Load Halfword Algebraic Indexed**	$rT \Leftarrow {}^{\grave{}}\mathrm{Half}((rA\,|\,0)+(rB))$
lhaux rT,rA,rB **Load Halfword Algebraic Indexed with Update**	$rT \Leftarrow {}^{\grave{}}\mathrm{Half}((rA)+(rB))$ $rA \Leftarrow (rA)+(rB)$

There are two basic types of *Load Halfword* instructions: *Load Halfword and Zero* and *Load Halfword Algebraic*. Both of these types come in the four standard varieties, making a total of eight different *Load Halfword* instructions.

The *Load Halfword and Zero* instructions load the data into the lower two bytes of the target register and zero out the upper bytes.

The *Load Halfword Algebraic* instructions load the halfword data into the lower two bytes of the target register and copy the sign bit from the loaded data into the upper bytes.

There is also a *Load Halfword* instruction that loads the data in byte-reversed order. This is described in §5.6 "Load and Store Byte-Reversed Data."

Table 5-4 Store Halfword Instructions

`sth rS,d(rA)` **Store Halfword**	$\text{Half}((rA\,|\,0)+\grave{}d) \Leftarrow rS\ [\frac{16:31}{48:63}]$
`sthu rS,d(rA)` **Store Halfword with Update**	$\text{Half}((rA)+\grave{}d) \Leftarrow rS\ [\frac{16:31}{48:63}]$ $rA \Leftarrow (rA)+\grave{}d$
`sthx rS,rA,rB` **Store Halfword Indexed**	$\text{Half}((rA\,|\,0)+(rB)) \Leftarrow rS\ [\frac{16:31}{48:63}]$
`sthux rS,rA,rB` **Store Halfword with Update Indexed**	$\text{Half}((rA)+(rB)) \Leftarrow rS\ [\frac{16:31}{48:63}]$ $rA \Leftarrow (rA)+(rB)$

The four *Store Halfword* instructions take the lower two bytes of the source register and store it at the given memory location.

A *Store Halfword* instruction that handles byte-reversed data is also available. It is discussed in §5.6 "Load and Store Byte-Reversed Data."

5.4 Load and Store Word

The *Load* and *Store Word* instructions listed in Tables 5-5 and 5-6 transfer 32 bits of information to and from a GPR. The 64-bit implementations also define an algebraic form which sign-extends the loaded word value.

Table 5-5 Load Word Instructions

`lwz rT,d(rA)` **Load Word and Zero**	$rT \Leftarrow {}^{\circ}\text{Word}((rA\,|\,0)+\grave{}d)$
`lwzu rT,d(rA)` **Load Word and Zero with Update**	$rT \Leftarrow {}^{\circ}\text{Word}((rA)+\grave{}d)$ $rA \Leftarrow (rA)+\grave{}d$
`lwzx rT,rA,rB` **Load Word and Zero Indexed**	$rT \Leftarrow {}^{\circ}\text{Word}((rA\,|\,0)+(rB))$

`lwzux rT,rA,rB` **Load Word and Zero Indexed with Update**	$rT \Leftarrow {}^{\circ}\text{Word}((rA)+(rB))$ $rA \Leftarrow (rA)+(rB)$
`lwa rT,d(rA)` **Load Word Algebraic** *64-bit implementations only*	$rT \Leftarrow {}^{\backprime}\text{Word}((rA\,|\,0)+{}^{\backprime}d)$
`lwax rT,rA,rB` **Load Word Algebraic Indexed** *64-bit implementations only*	$rT \Leftarrow {}^{\backprime}\text{Word}((rA\,|\,0)+(rB))$
`lwaux rT,rA,rB` **Load Word Algebraic Indexed with Update** *64-bit implementations only*	$rT \Leftarrow {}^{\backprime}\text{Word}((rA)+(rB))$ $rA \Leftarrow (rA)+(rB)$

As with the *Load Halfword* instructions, there are two types of *Load Word* instructions: *Load Word and Zero* and *Load Word Algebraic*. The algebraic forms are defined only on 64-bit implementations since the two types perform the same operation when the registers are 32 bits in size.

The *Load Word and Zero* instructions load the word at the specified address into the target register. For 64-bit implementations, these instructions also clear out the upper word of the loaded register.

The *Load Word Algebraic* instructions load the word into the low word of the register and copy the sign bit from the loaded word into the upper bits of the target register. Note that there is no non-Indexed Update form for the *Load Word Algebraic* instruction.

A special instruction is defined for loading words from memory with byte-reversed data. This instruction is defined in §5.6 "Load and Store Byte-Reversed Data."

Table 5-6 Store Word Instructions

`stw rS,d(rA)` **Store Word**	$\text{Word}((rA\,|\,0)+{}^{\backprime}d) \Leftarrow rS\ [\frac{0:31}{32:63}]$
`stwu rS,d(rA)` **Store Word with Update**	$\text{Word}((rA)+{}^{\backprime}d) \Leftarrow rS\ [\frac{0:31}{32:63}]$ $rA \Leftarrow (rA)+{}^{\backprime}d$
`stwx rS,rA,rB` **Store Word Indexed**	$\text{Word}((rA\,|\,0)+(rB)) \Leftarrow rS\ [\frac{0:31}{32:63}]$
`stwux rS,rA,rB` **Store Word with Update Indexed**	$\text{Word}((rA)+(rB)) \Leftarrow rS\ [\frac{0:31}{32:63}]$ $rA \Leftarrow (rA)+(rB)$

The four standard *Store Word* instructions copy a word of data from the given source register into the specified memory address.

One additional *Store Word* instruction is defined to handle byte-reversed data. This instruction is presented in §5.6 "Load and Store Byte-Reversed Data."

5.5 Load and Store Doubleword

The *Load* and *Store Doubleword* instructions listed in Tables 5-7 and 5-8 transfer 64 bits of information to or from a GPR. These instructions are defined only on 64-bit PowerPC implementations. If they are executed on a 32-bit implementation, they will cause the illegal instruction handler to be invoked.

Table 5-7 Load Doubleword Instructions

`ld rT,d(rA)` **Load Doubleword** *64-bit implementations only*	$rT \Leftarrow \text{Doubleword}((rA \mid 0)+`d)$
`ldu rT,d(rA)` **Load Doubleword with Update** *64-bit implementations only*	$rT \Leftarrow \text{Doubleword}((rA)+`d)$ $rA \Leftarrow (rA)+`d$
`ldx rT,rA,rB` **Load Doubleword Indexed** *64-bit implementations only*	$rT \Leftarrow \text{Doubleword}((rA \mid 0)+(rB))$
`ldux rT,rA,rB` **Load Doubleword with Update Indexed** *64-bit implementations only*	$rT \Leftarrow \text{Doubleword}((rA)+(rB))$ $rA \Leftarrow (rA)+(rB)$

The four *Load Doubleword* forms allow a doubleword (eight bytes) of data to be loaded into a register from memory.

Table 5-8 Store Doubleword Instructions

`std rS,d(rA)` **Store Doubleword** *64-bit implementations only*	$\text{Doubleword}((rA \mid 0)+`d) \Leftarrow rS$
`stdu rS,d(rA)` **Store Doubleword with Update** *64-bit implementations only*	$\text{Doubleword}((rA)+`d) \Leftarrow rS$ $rA \Leftarrow (rA)+`d$
`stdx rS,rA,rB` **Store Doubleword Indexed** *64-bit implementations only*	$\text{Doubleword}((rA \mid 0)+(rB)) \Leftarrow rS$
`stdux rS,rA,rB` **Store Doubleword with Update Indexed** *64-bit implementations only*	$\text{Doubleword}((rA)+(rB)) \Leftarrow rS$ $rA \Leftarrow (rA)+(rB)$

The *Store Doubleword* forms store a doubleword of data into the specified memory location.

5.6 Load and Store Byte-Reversed Data

The *Load* and *Store Byte-Reversed* instructions listed in Table 5-9 provide an easy method for accessing data that is stored in the opposite byte-order than the processor expects.

There are two common byte-orderings for halfwords and words: big-endian and little-endian. Big-endian byte-ordering has the *most significant byte* (MSB) in the lowest address position and the *least significant byte* (LSB) in the highest address position. Little-endian is the reverse of big-endian, with the LSB at the lower address and the MSB at the higher address.

If the processor is operating in big-endian mode, then these instructions allow the program to load and store little-endian encoded data. Conversely, if the processor is in little-endian mode, these instructions provide an easy way to access big-endian data.

Table 5-9 Load/Store Byte-Reversed Data Instructions

lhbrx rT, rA, rB **Load Halfword Byte-Reversed Indexed**	$h := \text{Half}((rA\,|\,0)+(rB))$ $rT \Leftarrow {}^{\circ}(h[8:15] \perp h[0:7])$
lwbrx rT, rA, rB **Load Word Byte-Reversed Indexed**	$w := \text{Word}((rA\,|\,0)+(rB))$ $rT \Leftarrow {}^{\circ}(w[24:31] \perp w[16:23]$ $\qquad \perp w[8:15] \perp w[0:7])$
sthbrx rS, rA, rB **Store Halfword Byte-Reversed Indexed**	$h := rS\,[\frac{24:31}{56:63}]\ \ \perp rS\,[\frac{16:23}{48:55}]$ $\text{Half}((rA\,|\,0)+(rB)) \Leftarrow h$
stwbrx rS, rA, rB **Store Word Byte-Reversed Indexed**	$w := rS\,[\frac{24:31}{56:63}]\ \ \perp rS\,[\frac{16:23}{48:55}]$ $\perp rS\,[\frac{8:15}{40:47}]\ \ \perp rS\,[\frac{0:7}{32:39}]$ $\text{Word}((rA\,|\,0)+(rB)) \Leftarrow w$

The load word and halfword byte-reversed instructions (`lhbrx` and `lwbrx`) load the data from the target address into the destination register. If the loaded data doesn't fill the register completely, the data is zero-extended to fill the entire register.

The store word and halfword byte-reversed instructions (`sthbrx` and `stwbrx`) store the lower word or halfword from the source register into memory at the calculated target address.

All of the byte-reversed storage instructions are indexed and expect the memory address to be specified by the sum of the contents of the registers `rA` and `rB`.

The PowerPC architecture does not define instructions to load or store a doubleword of byte-reversed data.

5.7 Load and Store Floating-Point Double-Precision

The Load and Store Floating-Point Double instructions listed in Tables 5-10 and 5-11 transfer 64 bits of data between the floating-point registers and memory. Since the floating-point registers on the PowerPC always store double-precision data, these instructions simply transfer the data back and forth.

Table 5-10 Load Floating-Point Double-Precision Instructions

lfd frT,d(rA) Load FP Double	$frT \Leftarrow \text{FDouble}((rA \mid 0) + \grave{}d)$
lfdu frT,d(rA) Load FP Double with Update	$frT \Leftarrow \text{FDouble}((rA) + \grave{}d)$ $rA \Leftarrow (rA) + \grave{}d$
lfdx frT,rA,rB Load FP Double Indexed	$frT \Leftarrow \text{FDouble}((rA \mid 0) + (rB))$
lfdux frT,rA,rB Load FP Double with Update Indexed	$frT \Leftarrow \text{FDouble}((rA) + (rB))$ $rA \Leftarrow (rA) + (rB)$

The *Load Floating-Point Double* instructions load the specified floating-point register with the 64 bits of data starting at the given address.

Table 5-11 Store Floating-Point Double-Precision Instructions

stfd frS,d(rA) Store FP Double	$\text{FDouble}((rA \mid 0) + \grave{}d) \Leftarrow frS$
stfdu frS,d(rA) Store FP Double with Update	$\text{FDouble}((rA) + \grave{}d) \Leftarrow frS$ $rA \Leftarrow (rA) + \grave{}d$
stfdx frS,rA,rB Store FP Double Indexed	$\text{FDouble}((rA \mid 0) + (rB)) \Leftarrow frS$
stfdux frS,rA,rB Store FP Double with Update Indexed	$\text{FDouble}((rA) + (rB)) \Leftarrow frS$ $rA \Leftarrow (rA) + (rB)$

The four *Store Floating-Point Double* forms provide standard instructions for storing floating-point values out to memory without any modification or translation.

5.8 Load and Store Floating-Point Single-Precision

Since floating-point registers always contain double-precision data, the Load and Store Floating-Point Single instructions listed in Tables 5-12 and 5-13 must translate between the 64-bit data in the floating-point registers and the 32-bit data stored in memory.

The method for converting between the 32-bit and 64-bit forms of single-precision data is discussed in Chapter 8 "Floating-Point Instructions."

Table 5-12 Load Floating-Point Single-Precision Instructions

`lfs frT,d(rA)` **Load FP Single**	$frT \Leftarrow \text{FSingle}((rA\,|\,0)+`d)$
`lfsu frT,d(rA)` **Load FP Single with Update**	$frT \Leftarrow \text{FSingle}((rA)+`d)$ $rA \Leftarrow (rA)+`d$
`lfsx frT,rA,rB` **Load FP Single Indexed**	$frT \Leftarrow \text{FSingle}((rA\,|\,0)+(rB))$
`lfsux frT,rA,rB` **Load FP Single with Update Indexed**	$frT \Leftarrow \text{FSingle}((rA)+(rB))$ $rA \Leftarrow (rA)+(rB)$

The *Load Floating-Point Single* instructions load a 32-bit value from memory, translate it into a 64-bit double-precision floating-point value, and then store the value into the target register.

Table 5-13 Store Floating-Point Single-Precision Instructions

`stfs frS,d(rA)` **Store FP Single**	$\text{FSingle}((rA\,|\,0)+`d) \Leftarrow frS$
`stfsu frS,d(rA)` **Store FP Single with Update**	$\text{FSingle}((rA)+`d) \Leftarrow frS$ $rA \Leftarrow (rA)+`d$
`stfsx frS,rA,rB` **Store FP Single Indexed**	$\text{FSingle}((rA\,|\,0)+(rB)) \Leftarrow frS$
`stfsux frS,rA,rB` **Store FP Single with Update Indexed**	$\text{FSingle}((rA)+(rB)) \Leftarrow frS$ $rA \Leftarrow (rA)+(rB)$

The Store Floating-Point Single instructions convert the double-precision value in the source floating-point register into a 32-bit single-precision value and then store the value into memory at the given location.

If the value in the source floating-point register cannot be represented as a single-precision value, then the value stored in memory is undefined.

5.9 Load and Store Multiple

The *Load* and *Store Multiple* instructions listed in Table 5-14 provide an easy facility for loading and storing multiple words of data between memory and the processor's general purpose registers. With one instruction, from one up to 32 registers can be loaded or stored.

It should be noted, however, that the *multiple* instructions are not favored in the eyes of the PowerPC designers. These instructions are not very RISC-like in that they perform multiple accesses to memory. This deviation from the standard RISC design philosophy makes it a bit easier for the programmer to code register saves and restores but it also complicates the processor implementation.

The warnings that these instructions may take longer to execute than an equivalent series of load or store instructions, and the absence of load and store multiple instructions that support doubleword (or floating-point) transfers between memory and the registers, should both serve as indications to just how little support these instructions are likely to receive in future PowerPC implementations.

It is likely that the only reason that the load and store multiple instructions were carried over from the POWER to the PowerPC architecture is because of the number of old applications that make use of them.

Table 5-14 Load/Store Multiple Instructions

lmw rT,d(rA) **Load Multiple Word**	$ea := (rA\|0) + \grave{}d$ $R := T$ $\text{while}(R \leq 31)$ $\quad rR \Leftarrow {}^\circ\text{Word}(ea)$ $\quad ea := ea + 4$ $\quad R := R + 1$
stmw rS,d(rA) **Store Multiple Word**	$ea := (rA\|0) + \grave{}d$ $R := T$ $\text{while}(R \leq 31)$ $\quad \text{Word}(ea) \Leftarrow rR \left[\frac{0-31}{32-63} \right]$ $\quad ea := ea + 4$ $\quad R := R + 1$

The *Load Multiple Word* instruction loads all of the GPRs from rT up to r31 (inclusive) with the data starting at the memory address calculated from adding the offset d to the contents of rA. If r0 is specified for rA, then the address is simply d.

If rA is in the range of register being loaded, or if rT and rA are both r0, the instruction is considered invalid. The POWER architecture handles the case where rA is in the range to be loaded by skipping rA and discarding the data that would have been loaded into it, but this behavior was not considered useful enough to warrant including it in the PowerPC specification.

The *Store Multiple Word* instruction performs the inverse operation of the *Load Multiple Word*. It takes the low-order word from each of the registers between rS and r31 and stores it into the memory block starting at the calculated address.

For both the *Load* and *Store Multiple* instructions, the address calculated form rA and d should be a multiple of four (for the address to be properly word aligned). If the computed address is not a multiple of four, then one of three things may happen:

- The operation may proceed normally.
- The alignment error handler may be invoked.
- The results may be (boundedly) undefined.

Which of the three occurs depends on the particular PowerPC implementation and whether a page boundary has been crossed. On the 601, misaligned *Load* and *Store Multiple* operations proceed normally unless a page boundary is crossed, in which case the alignment error handler is invoked. Other PowerPC processors will either always invoke the alignment error handler or produce results that are boundedly undefined.

The PowerPC architecture also defines preferred forms for the *Load* and *Store Multiple* instructions. The preferred forms for these instructions are structured so that the last byte to be loaded or stored matches the last byte of an aligned quadword in memory. Thus r31 is loaded from or stored into the low-order word of an aligned quadword. This is shown in Figure 5-1   .

Figure 5-1   Alignment for Preferred Form of Load and Store Multiple

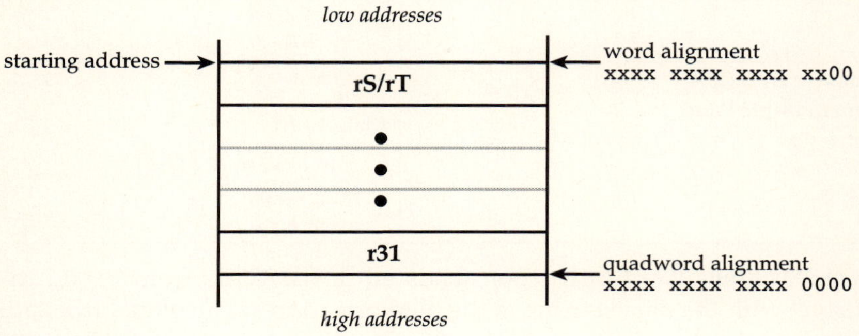

low addresses

starting address ⟶   rS/rT   ⟵ word alignment
xxxx xxxx xxxx xx00

•
•
•

r31   ⟵ quadword alignment
xxxx xxxx xxxx 0000

high addresses

Load and *Store Multiple* operations that do not conform to this preferred form may execute more slowly than forms that do conform.

5.10 Load and Store String

The *Load* and *Store String* instructions listed in Tables 5-15 and 5-16 provide a simple way of accessing unaligned data, like character strings.

These instructions are more properly referred to as *Move Assist* instructions, since they are useful for more than just moving character strings around. These instructions can also be used to copy structures and fields without being concerned about proper data alignment.

Table 5-15 Load String Instructions

`lswi rT,rA,nBytes` **Load String Word Immediate**	$ea := (rA \mid 0)$ $R := T - 1$ $i := \left[\frac{0}{32}\right]$ $\quad$ if(nBytes = 0) $\quad\quad\quad$ nBytes := 32 while($nBytes > 0$) $\quad$ if($i = \left[\frac{0}{32}\right]$) $\quad\quad\quad R := (R + 1) \% 32$ $\quad\quad\quad rR \Leftarrow 0$ $\quad\quad rR[i:(i+7)] \Leftarrow \text{Byte}(ea)$ $\quad\quad i := i + 8$ $\quad$ if($i = \left[\frac{32}{64}\right]$) $\quad\quad\quad i := \left[\frac{0}{32}\right]$ $\quad ea := ea + 1$ $\quad nBytes := nBytes - 1$
`lswx rT,rA,rB` **Load String Word Indexed**	$ea := (rA \mid 0) + (rB)$ $R := T - 1$ $nBytes := \text{XER}[25:31]$ $i := \left[\frac{0}{32}\right]$ while($nBytes > 0$) $\quad$ if($i = \left[\frac{0}{32}\right]$) $\quad\quad\quad R := (R + 1) \% 32$ $\quad\quad\quad rR \Leftarrow 0$ $\quad\quad rR[i:(i+7)] \Leftarrow \text{Byte}(ea)$ $\quad\quad i := i + 8$ $\quad$ if($i = \left[\frac{32}{64}\right]$) $\quad\quad\quad i := \left[\frac{0}{32}\right]$ $\quad ea := ea + 1$ $\quad nBytes := nBytes - 1$

The two *Load String Word* instructions load a number of bytes from memory into a series of GPRs. The two forms, *Load String Word Immediate* (`lswi`) and *Load String Word Indexed* (`lswx`), differ in how the memory address is calculated and where the number of bytes to copy comes from.

For the immediate (non-indexed) form, the number of bytes is specified as an immediate value, *nBytes*, and the memory address where the data to be loaded begins is stored in `rA`. The number of bytes specified in the immediate value can be anywhere from 1 to 32.

The *Indexed* form calculates the memory address from the sum of two registers, ($rA \mid 0$) and `rB`, and gets the number of bytes to copy from bits 25 to 31 of the Fixed-Point Exception Register (XER). This value can be anywhere between 0 and 127, although if the number of bytes to be copied is 0, then the contents of `rT` are undefined.

For both of these instructions, each byte is copied into the register starting with the high-order byte (of the low-order word when in 64-bit mode) and working down to the low-order byte. When each register is full, the next register sequentially is loaded, wrapping around from `r31` to `r0` if necessary.

The last register to be loaded may be only partially filled. In this situation, the lower bytes of that register are cleared to 0.

The *Load String* instructions do not load bytes into the upper word when executing in 64-bit mode. These upper bytes are always set to 0.

If `rA` (or `rB`, for the *Indexed* form) is in the range of the register being loaded, or if `rT` and `rA` are both `r0`, the instruction is considered invalid.

Table 5-16 Store String Instructions

`stswi rS,rA,nBytes` **Store String Word Immediate**	$ea := (rA\|0)$ $R := S - 1$ $i := \left[\frac{0}{32}\right]$ $\quad$ if(nBytes = 0) $\quad\quad$ nBytes := 32 while(*nBytes* > 0) $\quad$ if($i = \left[\frac{0}{32}\right]$) $\quad\quad R := (R + 1) \% 32$ $\quad$ Byte(*ea*) $\Leftarrow$ rR[*i*:(*i*+7)] $\quad i := i + 8$ $\quad$ if($i = \left[\frac{32}{64}\right]$) $\quad\quad i := \left[\frac{0}{32}\right]$ $\quad ea := ea + 1$ $\quad nBytes := nBytes - 1$
`stswx rS,rA,rB` **Store String Word Indexed**	$ea := (rA\|0)+(rB)$ $R := S - 1$ $nBytes := XER[25:31]$ $i := \left[\frac{0}{32}\right]$ while(*nBytes* > 0) $\quad$ if($i = \left[\frac{0}{32}\right]$) $\quad\quad R := (R + 1) \% 32$ $\quad$ Byte(*ea*) $\Leftarrow$ rR[*i*:(*i*+7)] $\quad i := i + 8$ $\quad$ if($i = \left[\frac{32}{64}\right]$) $\quad\quad i := \left[\frac{0}{32}\right]$ $\quad ea := ea + 1$ $\quad nBytes := nBytes - 1$

The two *Store String* instructions perform the opposite operation as the *Load String* instructions: the bytes from the specified registers are written out to memory starting at the given memory address.

Both the *Load* and the *Store String* instructions have preferred forms that may execute more quickly on certain PowerPC implementations. The requirements of the preferred form are

- 32 bytes or less are being transferred.
- The first register (`rS` or `rT`) is `r5`.

These requirements imply that only registers `r5` through `r12` will be used by the operation.

5.11 Load and Store Synchronization

The synchronization forms of the *Load* and *Store* instructions give the programmer control over the order in which storage operations are completed, as they are seen by devices outside the processor. Tables 5-17 and 5-18 list these instructions.

Table 5-17 Load and Reserve Instructions

`lwarx rT,rA,rB` **Load Word and Reserve Indexed**	*Reserve* := 1 *RAddr* := (rA|0)+(rB) rT $\Leftarrow$ °Word((rA|0)+(rB))
`ldarx rT,rA,rB` **Load Doubleword and Reserve Indexed** *64-bit implementations only*	*Reserve* := 1 *RAddr* := (rA|0)+(rB) rT $\Leftarrow$ DoubleWord((rA|0)+(rB))

The *Load and Reserve* instructions load a word from memory and attach a *reservation* to the address from which the data was loaded. If there is a reservation from a previous *Load and Reserve* instruction, the old reservation is replaced with the new one.

Table 5-18 Store Conditional Instructions

stwcx. r*S*,r*A*,r*B*
 Store Word Conditional Indexed
	ea := (r*A* | 0)+(r*B*)'
	 if((*Reserve* = 1) AND (*RAddr* = *ea*))
	     Word(*ea*)⇐r*S* $\left[\frac{0\text{-}31}{32\text{-}63}\right]$
	     Reserve := 0
	     CR{0} ⇐ b001 ⊥ XER[SO]
	 else
	     CR{0} ⇐ b000 ⊥ XER[SO]

stdcx. r*S*,r*A*,r*B*
 Store Doubleword Conditional Indexed
 64-bit implementations only
	ea := (r*A* | 0)+(r*B*)
	 if((*Reserve* = 1) AND (*RAddr* = *ea*))
	     DoubleWord(*ea*)⇐r*S*
	     Reserve := 0
	     CR{0} ⇐ b001 ⊥ XER[SO]
	 else
	     CR{0} ⇐ b000 ⊥ XER[SO]

The *Store Conditional* instructions store the contents of a register to a specified address only if a reservation has been created using a *Load and Reserve* instruction. If a reservation does not exist, then these instructions do nothing.

The EQ bit (bit 2) of Field 0 of the Condition Register can be checked to see if the store operation was completed successfully. This bit will be '1' if the store was performed and '0' if it was not.

5.12 Obsolete Load String

There is only one obsolete load instruction (see Table 5-19), and that is *Load String and Compare Byte Indexed*. This instruction loads bytes from memory and compares each byte with a specified target byte.

Table 5-19 Obsolete String Instructions

lscbx[.] rT,rA,rB
Load String and Compare Byte Indexed
obsolete POWER instruction
	ea := (rA|0)+(rB)
	R := *T* - 1
	nBytes := XER[25:31]
	nBytesCopied := 0
	matchByte := XER[16:23]
	matchFound := 0
	i := 0
	while(*nBytes* > 0)
	    if(*i* = 0)
	            R := (*R* + 1) % 32
	          rR $\Leftarrow$ *undefined*
	    if(*matchFound* = 0)
	          rR[*i*:(*i*+7)] $\Leftarrow$ Byte(*ea*)
	          nBytesCopied := *nBytesCopied* + 1
	    if(Byte(*ea*) = *matchByte*)
	          matchFound := 1
	    i := *i* + 8
	    if(*i* = 32)
	        i := 0
	    ea := *ea* + 1
	    nBytes := *nBytes* - 1
	XER[25:31] $\Leftarrow$ *nBytesCopied*

The *Load String and Compare Byte Indexed* instruction loads bytes into the registers from rT to r31 until one of two conditions is met. These conditions are

- *nBytes* bytes have been loaded, or
- A byte is loaded that matches *matchByte*.

The values for *nBytes* and *matchByte* come from the Fixed-Point Exception Register (XER). *nBytes* is copied from the value in XER[25:31] and the *matchByte* is contained in XER[16:23].

The target registers are loaded starting with the high-order byte and working down to the low-order byte. Registers are not guaranteed to be cleared to 0 before they are loaded. Thus, the lower bytes of the last (partially filled) register are undefined.

This instruction is not part of the PowerPC specification because of its complexity.

Integer Instructions | 6

The integer instructions defined by the PowerPC Architecture include instructions to perform logical (Boolean) operations and integer comparisons in addition to the standard arithmetic operations (add, subtract, multiply, and divide).

6.1 Addition

Addition is performed using variants of the *Add* instruction. The three basic forms of this instruction listed in Table 6-1 allow two registers to be added and provide control over how the Carry bit is affected by the instruction. There are also two other addition instructions that allow the Carry bit to be combined with a register and a constant. All of these instructions have options that allow the overflow ('o') and condition ('.') information to be set based on the result of the operation.

The most basic add instruction is, oddly enough, the *Add* (`add`) instruction. This instruction adds the contents of registers `rA` and `rB` and stores the result in register `rT`. The Carry bit in the XER is neither used nor affected by the execution of this instruction.

The *Add Carrying* (`addc`) instruction performs the same operation as the `add` instruction, but also updates the Carry bit in the XER. The Carry bit is set if there is a carry out of bit $[\frac{0}{32}]$ and is cleared otherwise.

Table 6-1 Add Instructions

add[o][.] rT, rA, rB Add	$rT \Leftarrow (rA) + (rB)$
addc[o][.] rT, rA, rB Add Carrying	$rT \Leftarrow (rA) + (rB)$ update XER[CA]
adde[o][.] rT, rA, rB Add Extended	$rT \Leftarrow (rA) + (rB) + XER[CA]$ update XER[CA]
addme[o][.] rT, rA Add to Minus One Extended	$rT \Leftarrow (rA) + -1 + XER[CA]$ update XER[CA]
addze[o][.] rT, rA Add to Zero Extended	$rT \Leftarrow (rA) + 0 + XER[CA]$ update XER[CA]

The *Add Extended* (`adde`) instruction performs basically the same operation as the `addc` instruction, except that it also adds the Carry bit to the result before storing the result in register `rT` and updates the Carry bit based on the result.

The final two register-based `add` instructions add the contents of `rA` with a constant and the Carry bit and then store the result in `rT`, updating the Carry bit in the process. The constant can be either 0 (for `addze`) or –1 (for `addme`).

There is no `add` instruction which uses the Carry bit but does not update the Carry information.

In addition to the register-based `add` instructions given earlier, the variants listed in Table 6-2 allow 16-bit immediate data (sign-extended to 32 bits) to be specified as one of the operands.

Table 6-2 Add Immediate Instructions

addi rT, rA, s16 Add Immediate	$rT \Leftarrow (rA \mid 0) + \grave{}s16$
addis rT, rA, s16 Add Immediate Shifted	$rT \Leftarrow (rA \mid 0) + \grave{}(s16 \perp 0x0000)$
addic[.] rT, rA, s16 Add Immediate Carrying	$rT \Leftarrow (rA) + \grave{}s16$ update XER[CA]

These instructions are *Add Immediate* (`addi`), *Add Immediate Shifted* (`addis`), and *Add Immediate Carrying* (`addic`). Only the `addic` instruction updates the Carry, and none of these instructions uses the Carry as part of its operation.

On 64-bit implementations, the immediate data is sign-extended to 64 bits before performing the addition operation.

Note that the `addi` and `addis` instructions do not allow the contents of register `r0` to be added with the immediate data. If `r0` is specified as `rA`, then 0 will be added to the sign-extended immediate data and the result will be placed in `rT`.

This provides a convenient method of loading a register with an immediate 16- or 32-bit value, as shown in Table 6-3.

Two extended forms are defined so that it is more readily apparent that the add immediate instructions are being used to load a value into a register. These are the *Load Immediate* and the *Load Immediate Shifted* forms.

Table 6-3 Load Immediate Extended Forms

li rT,s16 **Load Immediate** *extended form for* addi rT,0,s16	$rT \Leftarrow \text{`}s16$
lis rT,s16 **Load Immediate Shifted** *extended form for* addis rT,0,s16	$rT \Leftarrow \text{`}(s16 \perp 0x0000)$

In order to load a 32-bit immediate value into a register, the lis form can be used with the *OR Immediate* instructions:

```
lis     rT,<upper halfword>
ori     rT,<lower halfword>
```

The lis form loads the upper halfword and clears the lower halfword and the ori instruction loads the proper value into the lower halfword.

Note that while it is possible to load a register with an immediate value using extended forms of the *Add Immediate* instruction, the *Add Immediate* instructions should not be used to add an immediate 32-bit value to a value already in a register. This technique is not guaranteed to work since the most significant bit of the lower halfword is (erroneously) interpreted as a sign bit and the value is sign-extended to a word before the addition takes place. Thus, attempting to add 0x0100 8000 with the following sequence:

```
addis   rT,0x0100
addi    rT,0x8000
```

would result in adding 0x00FF 8000 because of the sign-extension of the lower halfword. This method can work if the upper half of the value is adjusted (by adding 1) to compensate for the sign-extension from the lower half. This adjustment should only take place if the sign bit of the lower half is '1'. The following code sequence:

```
addis   rT,0x0101
addi    rT,0x8000
```

would produce the desired result of adding 0x0100 8000 to the value already in rT. In any case, care should be taken when adding immediate 32-bit values.

When loading an address into a register, the *Load Address* (`la`) form of the *Add Immediate* instruction listed in Table 6-4 can be used. This extended form makes more explicit the fact that an address value is being loaded.

Table 6-4 Load Address Extended Forms

la rT,d(rA) **Load Address** *extended form for* `addi` `rT,rA,d`	$rT \Leftarrow (rA \mid 0) + \text{`}s16$
la rT,d **Load Address (with implicit base register)** *extended form for* `addi` `rT,rBase,d`	$rT \Leftarrow (rBase \mid 0) + \text{`}s16$

The two forms of the *Load Address* form allow for the base address to be specified either explicitly by giving `rA` or by allowing the base register to be implicit. An implicit base register is set up using an assembler directive such as the `.using` directive in IBM's AIX assembler.

6.2 Subtraction

The primary instructions for performing subtraction are the variants of the `subf` (*Subtract From*) instruction listed in Table 6-5. The `subf` instruction variants provide control over the use of the Carry bit and allow registers to be subtracted from predefined constants. All of these instructions have options that allow the overflow ('o') and condition ('.') information to be set based on the result of the operation.

Table 6-5 Subtract From Instructions

subf[o][.] rT,rA,rB **Subtract From**	$rT \Leftarrow (rB) - (rA)$
subfc[o][.] rT,rA,rB **Subtract From Carrying**	$rT \Leftarrow (rB) - (rA)$ update XER[CA]
subfe[o][.] rT,rA,rB **Subtract From Extended**	$rT \Leftarrow (rB) - (rA) + \text{XER[CA]} - 1$ update XER[CA]
subfme[o][.] rT,rA **Subtract From Minus One Extended**	$rT \Leftarrow -1 - (rA) + \text{XER[CA]} - 1$ update XER[CA]
subfze[o][.] rT,rA **Subtract From Zero Extended**	$rT \Leftarrow 0 - (rA) + \text{XER[CA]} - 1$ update XER[CA]

The basic form of the *Subtract From* (`subf`) instruction subtracts `rA` from `rB` and stores the result in `rT`. This form of the instruction neither uses nor affects the Carry bit in the XER.

The *Subtract From Carrying* (`subfc`) instruction performs the same operation as the `subf` instruction, except that it updates the Carry bit based on the result of the operation. The Carry bit is normally cleared by this instruction but is set if there is a carry out of bit $[\frac{0}{32}]$.

The *Subtract From Extended* (`subfe`) instruction subtracts rA from rB and then adds the Carry minus 1 to the result before storing it in register rT. The Carry bit is updated based on the result.

The remaining two register based `subf` instructions subtract the contents of rA from a constant and then add the Carry bit minus 1. The result is then stored in the register rT. The constant can be either 0 (for `subfze`) or –1 (for `subfme`).

Because the operation of the `subf` instruction may be confusing given the register order, the extended mnemonics listed in Table 6-6 are provided to allow the programmer to specify the arguments in a more natural order.

Table 6-6 Subtract Extended Forms

sub[o][.] rT,rA,rB **Subtract** *extended form for* `subf[o][.] rT,rB,rA`	$rT \Leftarrow (rA) - (rB)$
subc[o][.] rT,rA,rB **Subtract Carrying** *extended form for* `subfc[o][.] rT,rB,rA`	$rT \Leftarrow (rA) - (rB)$ update XER[CA]

The *Subtract* (`sub`) extended form subtracts rB from rA and places the result in rT. This is the same operation as the `subf` instruction.

The *Subtract Carrying* (`subc`) extended form is identical to `sub`, except that the Carry is updated to reflect the result of the operation. This is the same operation as the `subfc` instruction.

Table 6-7 lists one instruction that allows the contents of a register to be subtracted from a 16-bit sign-extended immediate constant. In addition, the three extended forms listed in Table 6-8 allow a constant to be subtracted from the contents of a register.

Table 6-7 Subtract From Immediate Instruction

subfic rT,rA,s16 **Subtract From Immediate Carrying**	$rT \Leftarrow \text{`}s16 - (rA)$ update XER[CA]

The *Subtract From Immediate Carrying* (`subfic`) instruction subtracts the contents of rA from the specified 16-bit value. The Carry bit in the XER is updated to reflect the result of the operation.

Table 6-8 Subtract Immediate Extended Forms

`subi rT,rA,s16` **Subtract Immediate** *extended form for* `addi rT,rA,-s16`	$rT \Leftarrow (rA\,\vert\,0) - \grave{}s16$
`subis rT,rA,s16` **Subtract Immediate Shifted** *extended form for* `addis rT,rA,-s16`	$rT \Leftarrow (rA\,\vert\,0) - \grave{}(s16 \perp 0x0000)$
`subic[.] rT,rA,s16` **Subtract Immediate Carrying** *extended form for* `addic[.] rT,rA,-s16`	$rT \Leftarrow (rA) - \grave{}s16$ update XER[CA]

The three *Subtract Immediate* (`subi`) extended forms are based on the `addi` instructions: *Add Immediate* (`addi`), *Add Immediate Shifted* (`addis`), and *Add Immediate Carrying* (`addic`). They perform the same operation as the equivalent `addi` instructions with the immediate data negated.

6.3 Multiplication

On 32-bit PowerPC implementations, multiplying two 32-bit quantities has the problem that the result can potentially require 64 bits when only 32 bits are available. A similar situation exists on 64-bit implementations where the result may require 128 bits, thus overflowing the 64-bit registers.

The PowerPC defines instructions to multiply two 32-bit operands and return either the high or the low word of the result. This works similarly on 64-bit implementations when multiplying two 64-bit operands: there are instructions to return either the high or low doubleword of the result. Tables 6-9 and 6-10 list these instructions.

Table 6-9 Multiply Instructions

`mullw[o][.] rT,rA,rB` **Multiply Low Word**	32-bit: $rT \Leftarrow \text{LoWord}((rA) \times (rB))$
	64-bit: $rT \Leftarrow (rA[32:63]) \times (rB[32:63])$
`mulld[o][.] rT,rA,rB` **Multiply Low Doubleword** *64-bit implementations only*	$rT \Leftarrow \text{LoDWord}((rA) \times (rB))$
`mulhw[.] rT,rA,rB` **MultiplyHigh Word (Signed)**	$rT \Leftarrow \text{HiWord}((rA) \times (rB))$
`mulhwu[.] rT,rA,rB` **Multiply High Word Unsigned**	$rT \Leftarrow \text{HiWord}((rA) \times (rB))$

mulhd[.] `rT,rA,rB` **Multiply High Doubleword (Signed)** *64-bit implementations only*	$rT \Leftarrow \text{HiDWord}((rA) \times (rB))$
mulhdu[.] `rT,rA,rB` **Multiply High Doubleword Unsigned** *64-bit implementations only*	$rT \Leftarrow \text{HiDWord}((rA) \times (rB))$

For 32-bit operands, there are three instructions: *Multiply Low Word* (`mullw`), *Multiply High Word* (`mulhw`) and *Multiply High Word Unsigned* (`mulhwu`). Only one instruction is required to return the low word result since it is the same for signed and unsigned multiplication operations.

64-bit implementations define three instructions that are analogous to the 32-bit instructions but perform 64-bit multiplications. These instructions are *Multiply Low Doubleword* (`mulld`), *Multiply High Doubleword* (`mulhd`), and *Multiply High Doubleword Unsigned* (`mulhdu`).

When multiplying two 32-bit numbers on a 64-bit PowerPC implementation, there is no need to calculate the upper and lower half separately since the entire result is guaranteed to fit in 64 bits. For this reason, the `mullw` instruction is defined to return the entire result in rT when executing on 64-bit implementations. The operands are considered to be signed for this calculation.

If the `mulhw` or `mulhwu` instructions are executed on 64-bit implementations, they perform the same operation as on 32-bit implementations. The lower 32 bits of rT contain the result and the upper 32 bits are undefined.

Table 6-10 Multiply Immediate Instructions

mulli `rT,rA,s16` **Multiply Low Immediate**	$rT \Leftarrow \text{LoWord}((rA) \times `s16)$

The *Multiply Low Immediate* (`mulli`) instruction is also provided to allow a register to be multiplied by a sign-extended 16-bit value. The low word of the 48-bit result is returned in rT. On 64-bit implementations, the operation is the same except that the low doubleword of the 80-bit result is returned in rT.

There is no instruction to access the upper word (or doubleword) of the *Multiply Immediate* result.

6.4 Division

The division instructions listed in Table 6-11 divide the contents of one register by the contents of another and store the quotient in a third register. The remainder is not provided as part of the instruction result.

Table 6-11 Divide Instructions

`divw[o][.]  rT,rA,rB` **Divide Word (Signed)**	$rT \Leftarrow {}^\circ rA \left[\frac{0:31}{32:63}\right] \div {}^\circ rB \left[\frac{0:31}{32:63}\right]$
`divwu[o][.]  rT,rA,rB` **Divide Word Unsigned**	$rT \Leftarrow {}^\circ rA \left[\frac{0:31}{32:63}\right] \div {}^\circ rB \left[\frac{0:31}{32:63}\right]$
`divd[o][.]  rT,rA,rB` **Divide Doubleword (Signed)** *64-bit implementations only*	$rT \Leftarrow (rA) \div (rB)$
`divdu[o][.]  rT,rA,rB` **Divide Doubleword Unsigned** *64-bit implementations only*	$rT \Leftarrow (rA) \div (rB)$

The *Divide Word* instructions divide the contents of source register rA by the contents of rB and store the quotient in rT. Normally, the source registers are treated as signed quantities, but the `divwu` instruction interprets the values as unsigned and produces an unsigned result.

On 64-bit implementations, the `divw` and `divwu` instructions use only the lower 32 bits of rA and rB. These 32-bits operands are then zero-extended to 64 bits before the division takes place. The quotient is placed in the lower 32 bits of rT and the upper 32 bits are undefined.

The `divd` and `divdu` instructions perform the same division operation as the word versions, but they use all 64 bits of the source registers and produce a 64-bit result.

Note that there are no instructions to calculate the remainder. The recommended way to calculate the remainder is by dividing to calculate the quotient and then multiplying this quotient by the original divisor. The difference between this value and the original dividend is the remainder. This can be done as follows:

```
divw[u]  rT,rA,rB     # rT = (rA-R)/rB
mullw    rT,rT,rB     # rT = rA-R
subf     rT,rT,rA     # rT = R
```

The expression $rT = (rA-R)/rB$ comes from the fact that the remainder should always be the same sign as rA and the magnitude of the remainder should be less than the magnitude of the divisor (rB). This means that the quotient in rT is always rounded towards 0. When calculating 64-bit remainders, `divd[u]` and `mulld` should be used instead of `divw[u]` and `mullw`.

Even though this requires three instructions to calculate the final result, the penalty for calculating the remainder this way is not unreasonable. First of all, the divide operation is a costly one in terms of execution time (36 cycles in execution on the 601), so adding the extra instructions increases the required number of cycles only by 16 to 30 percent.

Secondly, because the remainder does not need to be supplied as part of the result, the hardware designers can employ different divide algorithms that can be faster than algorithms that provide the remainder. This savings in execution time partially offsets the penalty of requiring two additional instructions and benefits all integer divide operations, whether or not the remainder is needed.

6.5 Miscellaneous Arithmetic Instructions

The three extra arithmetic instructions listed in Table 6-12—*Count Leading Zeros, Extend Sign*, and *Negate*—do not fit neatly into the other categories.

Table 6-12 Miscellaneous Arithmetic Instructions

cntlzw[.] rA,rS **Count Leading Zeros Word**	$rA \Leftarrow \text{LeadingZeros(rS)}$
cntlzd[.] rA,rS **Count Leading Zeros Doubleword** *64-bit implementations only*	$rA \Leftarrow \text{LeadingZeros(rS)}$
extsb[.] rA,rS **Extend Sign Byte**	$rA \Leftarrow \text{`rS } [\frac{24:31}{56:63}]$
extsh[.] rA,rS **Extend Sign Halfword**	$rA \Leftarrow \text{`rS } [\frac{16:31}{48:63}]$
extsw[.] rA,rS **Extend Sign Word** *64-bit implementations only*	$rA \Leftarrow \text{`rS[32:63]}$
neg[o][.] rT,rA **Negate**	$rT \Leftarrow \text{-(rA)}$

The *Count Leading Zeros* instructions count the number of '0' bits that are occupying the high-order bits of rS. This number, which can range from 0 to 32 for cntlzw and 0 to 64 for cntlzd, is then stored in rA.

There are three *Extend Sign* instructions: one extends a byte to a word (extsb), another extends a halfword to a word (extsh), and a third which extends a word to a doubleword (extsw). These instructions take the high-order (or *sign*) bit from the quantity being extended (byte, halfword, or word) and replicate it throughout the upper bits of the destination quantity (word or doubleword) to produce the result.

The *Negate* instruction simply takes the two's complement of the quantity in rA and stores the result in rT.

6.6 Comparison Instructions

The two basic forms of the *Compare* instructions listed in Tables 6-13 through 6-16 are defined in the PowerPC architecture. One form performs a standard signed comparison and the other performs an unsigned or *logical* comparison.

Table 6-13 Compare Instructions (Register Based)

cmp *crfT*, **L**, **rA**, **rB** **Compare**	CR{*crfT*} ⟸ SignedCompare(rA,rB)
cmpl *crfT*, **L**, **rA**, **rB** **Compare Logical**	CR{*crfT*} ⟸ UnsignedCompare(rA,rB)

The *Compare* instruction compares the contents of rA with the contents of rB and sets the bits in the specified CR field appropriately. The bits in the CR field are set as follows:

- LT is set if $(rA) < (rB)$.
- GT is set if $(rA) > (rB)$.
- EQ is set if $(rA) = (rB)$.
- SO is copied from XER[SO].

The *Compare Logical* instruction performs the same operation but treats the contents of rA and rB as unsigned quantities for purposes of the comparison.

The *L* field for each of the *Compare* instructions determines if a 32-bit or a 64-bit comparison should be performed. The *L* field must be 0 for 32-bit implementations.

Table 6-14 Compare Instructions (Immediate Data)

cmpi *crfT*, **L**, **rA**, **s16** **Compare Immediate**	CR{*crfT*} ⟸ SignedCompare(rA,`s16)
cmpli *crfT*, **L**, **rA**, **u16** **Compare Logical Immediate**	CR{*crfT*} ⟸ UnsignedCompare(rA,°u16)

The *Compare Immediate* instruction compares the contents of rA with the sign-extended immediate value and sets the bits in the specified CR field appropriately. The bits in the CR field are set as follows:

- LT is set if $(rA) <$ `s16.
- GT is set if $(rA) >$ `s16.
- EQ is set if $(rA) =$ `s16.
- SO is copied from XER[SO].

The *Compare Logical Immediate* instruction compares the contents of rA with the unsigned immediate value and updates the appropriate CR field. The CR field bits are set as follows:

- LT is set if $(rA) < °u16$.
- GT is set if $(rA) > °u16$.
- EQ is set if $(rA) = °u16$.
- SO is copied from XER[SO].

As with the non-immediate *Compare* instructions, the *L* field is used to switch between 32-bit and 64-bit compares.

Since it soon becomes annoying to have to specify the *L* field for each comparison performed, extended forms are defined to perform word and doubleword compares.

Table 6-15 Compare Word Extended Forms

cmpw crfT,rA,rB **Compare Word** *extended form for* cmp crfT,0,rA,rB	$CR\{crfT\} \Leftarrow$ SignedCompare(rA,rB)
cmplw crfT,rA,rB **Compare Logical Word** *extended form for* cmpl crfT,0,rA,rB	$CR\{crfT\} \Leftarrow$ UnsignedCompare(rA,rB)
cmpwi crfT,rA,SI **Compare Word Immediate** *extended form for* cmpi crfT,0,rA,s16	$CR\{crfT\} \Leftarrow$ SignedCompare(rA,`s16)
cmplwi crfT,rA,UI **Compare Logical Word Immediate** *extended form for* cmpli crfT,0,rA,u16	$CR\{crfT\} \Leftarrow$ UnsignedCompare(rA,°u16)

The four *Compare Word* forms are the same as the four base *Compare* instructions, except that they implicitly set the *L* field to 0 so that 32-bit compares are performed.

The four *Compare Doubleword* forms are the same as the four base *Compare* instructions, except that they implicitly set the *L* field to 1 so that 64-bit compares are performed.

Table 6-16 Compare Doubleword Extended Forms

cmpd *crfT*,*rA*,*rB* **Compare Doubleword** *extended form for* cmp *crfT,1,rA,rB* *64-bit implementations only*	CR{*crfT*} ⇐ SignedCompare(r*A*,r*B*)
cmpld *crfT*,*rA*,*rB* **Compare Logical Doubleword** *extended form for* cmpl *crfT,1,rA,rB* *64-bit implementations only*	CR{*crfT*} ⇐ UnsignedCompare(r*A*,r*B*)
cmpdi *crfT*,*rA*,*SI* **Compare Doubleword Immediate** *extended form for* cmpi *crfT,1,rA,s16* *64-bit implementations only*	CR{*crfT*} ⇐ SignedCompare(r*A*,`s16)
cmpldi *crfT*,*rA*,*UI* **Compare Logical Doubleword Immediate** *extended form for* cmpli *crfT,1,rA,u16* *64-bit implementations only*	CR{*crfT*} ⇐ UnsignedCompare(r*A*,°u16)

6.7 Logical (Boolean) Instructions

The logical instructions listed in Tables 6-17, 6-18, and 6-19 perform bitwise Boolean operations on registers. There are three basic bitwise operations that can be performed: AND, OR, and XOR. By negating or *complementing* one of the source registers or the result, additional logical operations can be constructed. The PowerPC defines five additional operations that are built in this manner: *Equivalent, AND with Complement, OR with Complement, NAND,* and *NOR.*

Table 6-17 Logical Instructions

and[.] *rA*,*rS*,*rB* **AND**	r*A* ⇐ (r*S*) & (r*B*)
andc[.] *rA*,*rS*,*rB* **AND with Complement**	r*A* ⇐ (r*S*) & ~(r*B*)
eqv[.] *rA*,*rS*,*rB* **Equivalent**	r*A* ⇐ (r*S*) ≡ (r*B*)
nand[.] *rA*,*rS*,*rB* **NAND**	r*A* ⇐ ~((r*S*) & (r*B*))
nor[.] *rA*,*rS*,*rB* **NOR**	r*A* ⇐ ~((r*S*) | (r*B*))
or[.] *rA*,*rS*,*rB* **OR**	r*A* ⇐ (r*S*) | (r*B*)
orc[.] *rA*,*rS*,*rB* **OR with Complement**	r*A* ⇐ (r*S*) | ~(r*B*)
xor[.] *rA*,*rS*,*rB* **Exclusive OR**	r*A* ⇐ (r*S*) ⊕ (r*B*)

The *AND* instruction calculates the bitwise AND of the source registers. Each bit in the target register (rA) is set if and only if the corresponding bits in both source registers (rS and rB) are set.

The *AND with Complement* instruction calculates the bitwise AND of the source register rS and the *one's complement* of source register rB. Each bit in the target register (rA) is set if and only if the corresponding bits in rS and ~rB are set.

The *Equivalent* instruction calculates the equivalence of the two source registers. Each bit in the target register (rA) is set if and only if the corresponding bits in the source registers (rS and rB) are equal to each other.

The *NAND* instruction calculates a bitwise AND like the *AND* instruction but takes the ones's complement of the result before storing it in rA.

The *NOR* instruction calculates a bitwise OR like the *OR* instruction but takes the one's complement of the result before storing it in rA.

The *OR* instruction calculates the bitwise OR of the source registers. Each bit in the target register (rA) is set if either of the corresponding bits in the source registers (rS and rB) are set.

The *OR with Complement* instruction calculates the bitwise OR of the source register rS and the *one's complement* of source register rB. Each bit in the target register (rA) is set if either of the corresponding bits in rS and ~rB are set.

The *Exclusive OR* instruction calculates the bitwise XOR of the source registers. Each bit in the target register (rA) is set if the corresponding bit in one of the source registers (either rS or rB) is set. If both source registers have the bit set, or if neither of them do, then the target register bit is cleared. Note that this operation is equivalent to negating the result of the *Equivalent* instruction.

Table 6-18 Logical Immediate Instructions

`andi. rA,rS,u16` **AND Immediate**	$rA \Leftarrow (rS) \; \& \; °u16$
`andis. rA,rS,u16` **AND Immediate Shifted**	$rA \Leftarrow (rS) \; \& \; °(u16 \perp 0x0000)$
`ori rA,rS,u16` **OR Immediate**	$rA \Leftarrow (rS) \; | \; °u16$
`oris rA,rS,u16` **OR Immediate Shifted**	$rA \Leftarrow (rS) \; | \; °(u16 \perp 0x0000)$
`xori rA,rS,u16` **XOR Immediate**	$rA \Leftarrow (rS) \oplus °u16$
`xoris rA,rS,u16` **XOR Immediate Shifted**	$rA \Leftarrow (rS) \oplus °(u16 \perp 0x0000)$

Logical Immediate forms are defined for the three basic Boolean operations: AND, OR, and XOR. For each of these operations, there are two instructions: one instruction zero extends the 16-bit immediate value before performing the logical operation, and the other shifts the immediate value 16 bits to the left (filling with 0's from the right) before performing the logical operation.

On 64-bit implementations, the immediate data is zero-extended to 64 bits before the operation is performed.

The logical instructions allow many simpler instructions to be constructed from them. These three extended forms listed in Table 6-19 are the preferred forms for implementing these operations. Implementations of the PowerPC architecture that provide some sort of run-time optimization for these operations will look for the preferred form to trigger the optimization.

Table 6-19 Extended Forms for Logical Instructions

mr[.] rA,rB **Move Register** *extended form for* or rA,rB,rB	$rA \Leftarrow (rB)$
not[.] rA,rB **Not (One's Complement)** *extended form for* nor rA,rB,rB	$rA \Leftarrow \sim(rB)$
nop **No-operation** *extended form for* ori r0,r0,r0	$r0 \Leftarrow r0$

The *Move Register* form provides an easy way to transfer the contents of one register to another.

The *Not* instruction calculates the one's complement of the source register and stores it in the destination register.

The *No-operation* or *No-op* instruction does nothing. It can be useful as a placeholder instruction that may be overwritten with a "real" instruction.

6.8 Obsolete Arithmetic Instructions

A variety of arithmetic instructions were defined for the POWER architecture but were not included in the PowerPC specification. These instructions were either unnecessarily complicated (as with the *Absolute Value* and *Difference or Zero* instructions), or they made use of the MQ register (as with the *Multiply* and *Divide* instructions).

Obsolete Multiply

The obsolete POWER multiply instructions do not provide separate instructions to return the upper and lower part of a 32-bit × 32-bit multiply result. Instead, a single instruction listed in Table 6-20 is defined to return the 64-bit result split across two registers: rT and MQ.

Table 6-20 Obsolete POWER Multiply Instructions

`mul[o][.] rT,rA,rB` **Multiply** *obsolete POWER instruction*	$rT \Leftarrow \text{HiWord}((rA) \times (rB))$ $MQ \Leftarrow \text{LoWord}((rA) \times (rB))$

Since the MQ register was removed for the PowerPC specification, this instruction has been removed also. Its complete functionality is provided via the `mullw` and `mulhw` instructions.

Obsolete Divide

In contrast to the PowerPC divide instructions, the obsolete POWER divide instructions listed in Table 6-21 provide both the quotient and the remainder as part of the result. The quotient is returned in the specified register, and the remainder is returned in the MQ register. Since the MQ register is not part of the PowerPC specification, these divide instructions needed to be removed.

Table 6-21 Obsolete POWER Divide Instructions

`div[o][.] rT,rA,rB` **Divide** *obsolete POWER instruction*	$rT \Leftarrow ((rA) \perp (MQ)) \div (rB)$ $MQ \Leftarrow ((rA) \perp (MQ)) \% (rB)$
`divs[o][.] rT,rA,rB` **Divide Short** *obsolete POWER instruction*	$rT \Leftarrow (rA) \div (rB)$ $MQ \Leftarrow (rA) \% (rB)$

The two obsolete divide instructions are *Divide* (`div`) and *Divide Short* (`divs`).

The *Divide* instruction divides a 64-bit value by a 32-bit value and returns the quotient and the remainder. The 64-bit dividend is composed of the contents of register rA concatenated with the contents of the MQ register, and the 32-bit divisor is the contents of register rB. The quotient is returned in rT and the remainder is returned in the MQ register.

The *Divide Short* instruction divides the 32-bit dividend in rA by the 32-bit divisor in rB and returns the quotient in rT and the remainder in the MQ register.

For both the `div` and `divs` instructions, the remainder in MQ is guaranteed to have the same sign as the dividend (rA).

Other Obsolete Arithmetic Instructions

The POWER architecture also defines two additional operations listed in Table 6-22 not found in the PowerPC architecture: integer *Absolute Value* and *Difference or Zero*. The instructions implementing these operations were removed for the PowerPC specification in an effort to simplify the design.

These instructions were removed because the operation being performed is *data dependent*. This means that the processor can't simply perform an operation on the data but must first examine the data to determine which operation to perform. For *Absolute Value*, the two operations are either to do nothing (if the source is positive) or negate (if negative); and for the *Difference or Zero* instruction, the two operations are to subtract (if (rA) is less than the other value) or return 0.

This data dependency requires an extra multiplexer in the arithmetic unit to decide which of the two function results to save to the destination register. This multiplexer is likely to be located on the critical execution path of the processor, thus, supporting these instructions is likely to have the effect of slowing down every other instruction while benefitting only these four instructions. Since these instructions are infrequently used, they are not included as part of the PowerPC specification.

Table 6-22 Obsolete POWER Arithmetic Instructions

abs[o][.] rT,rA **Absolute Value** *obsolete POWER instruction*	$rT \Leftarrow |(rA)|$
nabs[o][.] rT,rA **Negative Absolute Value** *obsolete POWER instruction*	$rT \Leftarrow -|(rA)|$
doz[o][.] rT,rA,rB **Difference Or Zero** *obsolete POWER instruction*	$rT \Leftarrow ((rA) > (rB))\ ?\ 0$ $\qquad\qquad : ((rB) - (rA))$
dozi rT,rA,s16 **Difference Or Zero Immediate** *obsolete POWER instruction*	$rT \Leftarrow ((rA) > \text{`}s16)\ ?\ 0$ $\qquad\qquad : (\text{`}s16 - (rA))$

The two absolute value instructions are *Absolute Value* (abs) and *Negative Absolute Value* (nabs). These instructions calculate the absolute value (or its negative) of rA and store the result in rT. Both of these instructions have options which allow the overflow and condition information to be set based on the result of the operation.

The two "difference or zero" instructions are *Difference Or Zero* (doz) and *Difference Or Zero Immediate* (dozi). These instructions compare the two operands and return 0 if rA is greater than the other operand or the difference of the two operands in all other cases. The end result is that the value stored in rT is guaranteed to be non-negative. The doz instruction compares rA with another register, and dozi compares rA with a sign-extended 16-bit quantity.

Rotate and Shift Instructions | 7

The PowerPC architecture defines a complex set of rotate and shift operations that can be used to perform a wide range of operations in one instruction. These operations include

- Rotate the contents of a register to the left or right.
- Shift the register contents to the left or right.
- Extract and shift a range of bits from a register.
- Shift and insert a range of bits into a register.
- Clear a range of bits in a register.

In addition, the rotate instructions' built-in masking operation facilitates the implementation of multiple-precision shifts and rotates.

7.1 Rotation Masks

The rotate instructions have a mask generation facility that allows a mask to be specified. The rotated quantity is ANDed with this mask so that only a portion of the rotated word is copied into the destination register. This allows complex bit manipulation operations to be performed in one instruction by using an appropriate mask.

This facility is limited by the restriction that only certain types of masks are allowed. The valid types of masks vary depending on whether the mask is for a 32-bit or a 64-bit quantity.

Word Masks

When specifying a mask for a word (for example, a 32-bit quantity), a valid mask must be composed of either:

- A contiguous range of '1's surrounded by '0's.
- A contiguous range of '0's surrounded by '1's.
- A contiguous range of '1's followed by '0's.
- A contiguous range of '0's followed by '1's.
- All 1's.

Note that there is no way to specify a mask consisting of all '0's. Such a mask would not be very useful since it would entirely mask out the result of the rotation operation.

Simplifying the acceptable masks in this fashion allows the mask to be encoded by recording the starting bit (*maskBegin*) and the ending bit (*maskEnd*). These mask bit values must be between 0 and 31. Figure 7-1   shows the five types of acceptable word masks.

Figure 7-1   Valid Word Rotation Masks

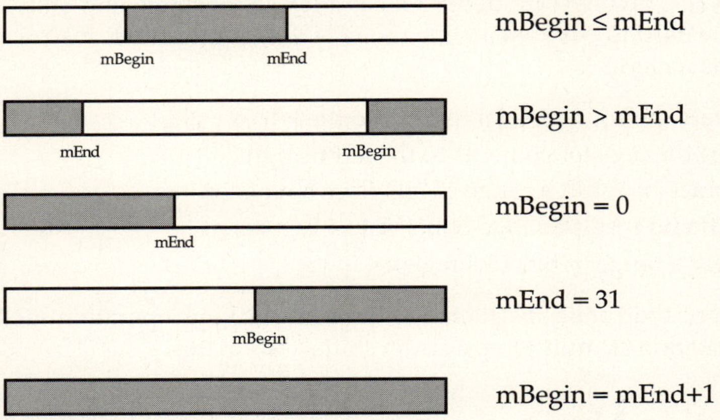

A mask that consists of a contiguous range of '1's surrounded by '0's is encoded by setting *maskBegin* to the bit number of the first '1' bit and *maskEnd* to the bit number of the last '1' bit. Thus, the mask 0x00FF FF00 would be encoded with *maskBegin* = 8 and *maskEnd* = 23 (since the leftmost bit is bit 0). If *maskBegin* = *maskEnd*, then a mask is generated with only one bit set.

A mask that consists of a contiguous range of '0's surrounded by '1's is encoded by setting *maskEnd* to the bit number of the bit immediately before the first '0' bit and *maskBegin* to the bit number of the bit immediately after the last '0' bit. This type of mask is identified by recognizing that *maskBegin* is greater than *maskEnd*.

As an example, the mask 0xFF00 00FF would be encoded with *maskBegin* = 24 and *maskEnd* = 7.

A mask that consists of a contiguous range of '1's followed by a range of '0's is encoded by setting *maskBegin* to bit 0 and *maskEnd* equal to the last bit of the mask. Thus, the mask 0xFFF0 0000 would be encoded as maskBegin = 0 and maskEnd = 11.

A mask that consists of a contiguous range of '0's followed by a range of '1's is encoded by setting *maskBegin* to the first bit of the mask and *maskEnd* to bit 31. Thus, the mask 0x0000 0FFF would be encoded as maskBegin = 20 and maskEnd = 31.

A mask of all '1's is encoded by setting *maskBegin* equal to *maskEnd*+1 (wrapping around to 0 if *maskEnd*+1 = 32). While any values for *maskBegin* and *maskEnd* that satisfy the *maskBegin* = (*maskEnd*+1) % 32 equation define valid mask specifications, by convention the values *maskBegin*=0 and *maskEnd*=31 are used.

When specifying word masks on 64-bit implementations, the *maskBegin* and *maskEnd* values are automatically offset by 32 so that they specify bits in the low-order word of the 64-bit register. Thus, specifying a mask from bit 8 to bit 15 on a 64-bit implementation actually results in a mask from bit 40 to bit 47.

Doubleword Masks

Doubleword masks are used by the doubleword rotate instructions that are available on 64-bit PowerPC implementations. When specifying a mask for a doubleword, the mask must be composed of either

- A series of '1's followed by a series '0's.
- A series of '0's followed by a series '1's.
- All 1's.
- A contiguous range of '1's surrounded by '0's (with restrictions).

Note that there is no way to specify a mask consisting of all '0's. As is the case with word masks, such a mask would not be very useful since it would entirely mask out the result of the rotation operation.

Figure 7-2   shows these four types of acceptable doubleword masks.

Figure 7-2   Valid Doubleword Rotation Masks

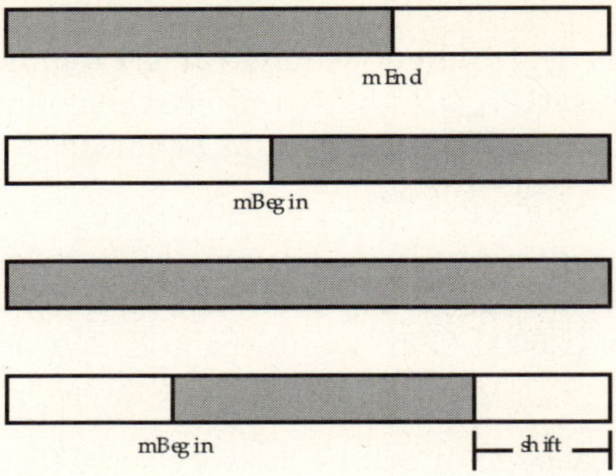

Simplifying the acceptable masks in this fashion allows the mask to be encoded by recording either just the starting bit (*maskBegin*) or just the ending bit (*maskEnd*). These mask bit values must be between 0 and 63. The *maskBegin* and *maskEnd* values cannot both be specified simultaneously because of instruction encoding limitations. It is always clear from the context whether the bit value being specified defines the beginning or the end of the mask.

Some instructions allow *maskBegin* to be specified and use an implicit *maskEnd* that is generated from the instruction's *shift* value. These are the only instructions that allow a range of '1's surrounded by '0's to be used as a mask.

A mask of '1's followed by '0's is encoded by setting *maskEnd* to the bit number of the last '1' bit, using 0 as an implicit *maskBegin*. A mask of '0's followed by '1's is encoded by setting *maskBegin* to the bit number of the first '1' bit, using 63 as an implicit *maskEnd*. A mask of all '1's can be constructed by setting either *maskBegin* to 0 or *maskEnd* to 63, depending on which value is available.

Instructions that permit the last type of mask record the *maskBegin* value and use 63-*shift* as the implicit *maskEnd* value. The *maskEnd* value cannot be controlled independently of the *shift* value.

7.2 How Rotates and Shifts Update the CR

All of the shift and rotate instructions allow the '.' suffix to be appended to the instruction mnemonic to have field 0 of the Condition Register updated to reflect the result of the operation.

For 32-bit PowerPC implementations, these instructions set CR{0} by algebraically comparing the shift or rotate result with 0.

For 64-bit implementations, the comparison is dependent on the mode that the processor is currently in. When executing in 32-bit mode, the low-order word of the result is algebraically compared with a 0 word. In 64-bit mode, the entire doubleword of the result is algebraically compared with a 0 doubleword.

Executing Word Instructions in 64-bit Mode

When the rotate and shift word instructions are executed on a 64-bit PowerPC processor, the upper 32 bits of the result are always 0.

One side-effect of this is that the condition code values returned in CR{0} are dependent on the mode in which the processor is currently executing. If the processor is in 32-bit mode, only the lower 32-bit will be compared, and if the processor is in 64-bit mode, the entire 64-bit result will be involved in the comparison.

As a demonstration of this, consider shifting 0xFFFF FFFF to the left by eight with the Record Bit set. If the processor is in 32-bit mode, the result will be 0xFFFF FF00 and the condition codes will be set to indicate that the result is negative. In 64-bit mode, this same instruction will return 0x0000 0000 FFFF FF00 and the condition codes will indicate a positive result.

Thus, all shift and rotate operations which produce "negative" results in 32-bit mode will produce positive results when executed in 64-bit mode.

7.3 Rotate Instructions

The rotate with mask instructions provide a powerful mechanism for extracting and inserting a range of bits to or from a register. There are only two basic types of rotate instructions: *Rotate Left Word* and *Rotate Left Doubleword*. There is no explicit *Rotate Right* instruction because it is trivial to construct a right rotate operation from a *Rotate Left* instruction (there are extended mnemonics that implement *Rotate Right* functionality).

Even though there are obvious similarities between the word and doubleword rotate instructions, there are significant differences between these two instruction forms. These differences arise from the difficulty of encoding all of the necessary information for a 64-bit rotate instruction in the 32 bits allowed for each instruction. It is these encoding limitations that led to the limited range of mask types for doubleword rotate instructions.

Rotate Word Instructions

The two basic types of rotate word with mask instructions are listed in Table 7-1: *Rotate Left Word then AND with Mask* and *Rotate Left Word then Mask Insert*.

Table 7-1 Rotate Word Instructions

rlwnm[.] rA,rS,rB,mB,mE **Rotate Left Word then AND with Mask**	$r := (rS) \, Q \, rB \, [\frac{27:31}{59:63}]$ $m := \text{Mask}(mB,mE)$ $rA \Leftarrow (r \, \& \, m)$
rlwinm[.] rA,rS,n,mB,mE **Rotate Left Word Immediate then AND with** **Mask**	$r := (rS) \, Q \, n$ $m := \text{Mask}(mB,mE)$ $rA \Leftarrow (r \, \& \, m)$
rlwimi[.] rA,rS,n,mB,mE **Rotate Left Word Immediate then Mask Insert**	$r := (rS) \, Q \, n$ $m := \text{Mask}(mB,mE)$ $rA \Leftarrow (r \, \& \, m) \mid ((rA) \, \& \, {\sim}m)$

The *Rotate Left Word then AND with Mask* instructions take the source register rS
and rotate it by the specified amount. The rotated rS is then ANDed with the
generated mask to produce the result. This is shown in Figure 7-3 .

Figure 7-3   Rotate Left Word then AND with Mask Operation

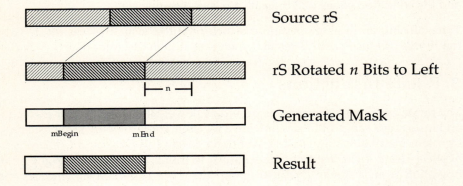

Source rS

rS Rotated *n* Bits to Left

Generated Mask

Result

The rotate amount can either be specified as an immediate value (using
`rlwinm`), or it can be taken from a register (using `rlwnm`). When the rotate
amount is given via a register, only the low order 5 bits of the register are used
to insure that the rotate value lies between 0 and 31.

The *Rotate Left Word then Mask Insert* instruction rotates rS and then inserts a
range of bits from the rotated word into the destination register, rA.

This is basically the same operation as the *Rotate Left Word then AND with Mask*
instruction with the exception of how the mask is used to generate the final
result. Instead of simply ANDing the rotated word and mask to overwrite the
entire destination register, the only bits in the destination register that are overwritten are those where the mask is '1'. This operation is presented in Figure 7-
4

Figure 7-4 Rotate Left Word then Mask Insert Operation

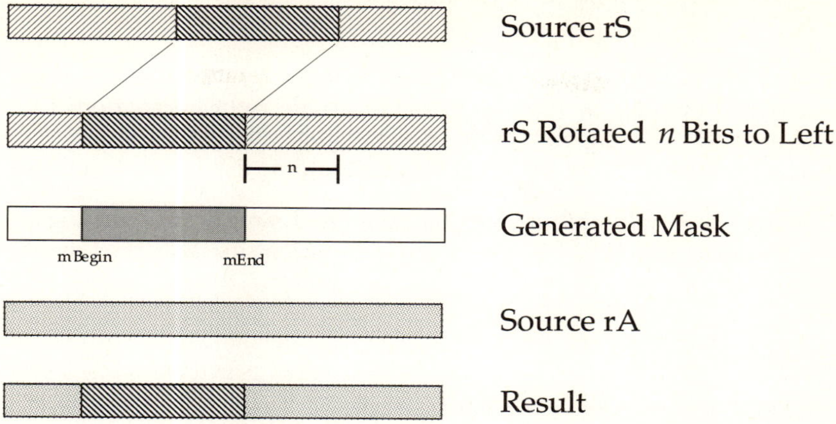

Note that there is no *Rotate Left Word then Mask Insert* form that allows the rotation amount to be specified in a register. This instruction was originally part of the POWER architecture but not included in the PowerPC specification because it would require that the processor be able to read from three source registers (rA, rS, and rB) simultaneously, which would have made implementing the architecture more costly.

Three rotate extended forms are provided to return the rotated contents of a register without masking out any portion of the result. Table 7-2 lists these forms.

Table 7-2 Rotate Word Extended Instruction Forms

rotlw[.] rA,rS,rB **Rotate Left Word** *extended form for* rlwnm rA,rS,rB,0,31	$rA \Leftarrow (rS) \circlearrowleft rB \; [\frac{27:31}{59:63}]$
rotlwi[.] rA,rS,n **Rotate Left Word Immediate** *extended form for* rlwinm rA,rS,n,0,31	$rA \Leftarrow (rS) \circlearrowleft n$
rotrwi[.] rA,rS,n **Rotate Right Word Immediate** *extended form for* rlwinm rA,rS,32−n,0,31	$rA \Leftarrow (rS) \circlearrowleft n$

The *Rotate Left Word* form (rotlw) rotates rS left rB $[\frac{27:31}{59:63}]$ bits and stores the result in rA. *Rotate Left Word Immediate* (rotlwi) performs the same operation but obtains the rotate amount from an immediate value instead of from the lower bits of rB.

To rotate a word right by an immediate amount *n*, the *Rotate Right Word Immediate* form can be used. This extended form rotates rS to the right *n* bits and stores the result in rA. Since there is no primitive right rotate instruction, this form is implemented by rotating left by 32-*n* places, which produces exactly the same result.

A *Rotate Right Word* extended form that accepts the rotate amount in a register is not provided because there is no primitive rotate right instruction. To use the rlwnm instruction to implement this functionality, the rotate amount in r*B* must be subtracted from 32 and then that value should be used as the rotate amount.

Optionally, the rotate amount can be calculated simply by negating r*B*. This works because the PowerPC rotate word instructions use only the lower 5 bits of rotate amount.

Rotate Doubleword

As mentioned earlier, the six *Rotate Doubleword* instructions listed in Table 7-3 differ from the *Rotate Word* instructions in the types of masks that are accepted. The first four of these instructions are similar to the rlwnm and rlwinm instructions for word quantities, except that two doubleword instructions are provided for each of the word instructions: one to mask the right portion and another to mask the left portion. The two remaining doubleword rotate instructions compute the mask from a start bit and the rotate amount.

Table 7-3 Rotate Doubleword Instructions

rldcl[.] rA, rS, rB, mB **Rotate Left Doubleword then Clear Left** *64-bit implementations only*	$r := (rS) \circlearrowleft rB[58{:}63]$ $m := \text{Mask}(mB,63)$ $rA \Leftarrow (r \,\&\, m)$
rldcr[.] rA, rS, rB, mE **Rotate Left Doubleword then Clear Right** *64-bit implementations only*	$r := (rS) \circlearrowleft rB[58{:}63]$ $m := \text{Mask}(0,mE)$ $rA \Leftarrow (r \,\&\, m)$
rldicl[.] rA, rS, n, mB **Rotate Left Doubleword Immediate then Clear Left** *64-bit implementations only*	$r := (rS) \circlearrowleft n$ $m := \text{Mask}(mB,63)$ $rA \Leftarrow (r \,\&\, m)$
rldicr[.] rA, rS, n, mE **Rotate Left Doubleword Immediate then Clear Right** *64-bit implementations only*	$r := (rS) \circlearrowleft n$ $m := \text{Mask}(0,mE)$ $rA \Leftarrow (r \,\&\, m)$
rldic[.] rA, rS, n, mB **Rotate Left Doubleword Immediate then Clear** *64-bit implementations only*	$r := (rS) \circlearrowleft n$ $m := \text{Mask}(mB,63{-}n)$ $rA \Leftarrow (r \,\&\, m)$
rldimi[.] rA, rS, n, mB **Rotate Left Doubleword Immediate then Mask Insert** *64-bit implementations only*	$r := (rS) \circlearrowleft n$ $m := \text{Mask}(mB,63{-}n)$ $rA \Leftarrow (r \,\&\, m) \mid ((rA) \,\&\, {\sim}m)$

The `rldcl` and `rldcr` instructions both rotate the source register rS by an amount stored in the lower six bits of rB. The rotated value is then ANDed with a different mask for each of these instructions: the `rldcl` instruction masks out the high order bits ("clear"ing the left part of the result) and `rldcr` masks out the low order bits ("clear"ing right). The last parameter of these instructions is either the first bit (when clearing to the left in `rldcl`) or the last bit (when clearing to the right in `rldcr`) to be copied to the result.

The `rldicl` and `rldicr` instructions perform the same operation as the `rldcl` and `rldcr` instructions, except that they get the rotate amount n from the immediate value encoded as part of the instruction.

The `rldic` instruction rotates rS and then masks out bits to the left and right of a bit field in the center of the result. The bit field that is copied into rA starts at bit position mB and extends out to the 63-nth bit, where n is the amount of the rotation. This is basically the same operation as the `rlwinm` instruction, except that the mask end bit cannot be specified independently of the rotate amount.

Similar to `rlwimi` except for how the mask is calculated, the `rldimi` instruction merges the rotated contents of rS with the current contents in rA. This instruction allows a right-justified bit field to be inserted into another register as shown in Figure 7-5. The mask is calculated in the same manner as the `rldic` instruction: the mask extends from bit mB to bit 63-n.

Figure 7-5   Rotate Left Doubleword then Insert Operation

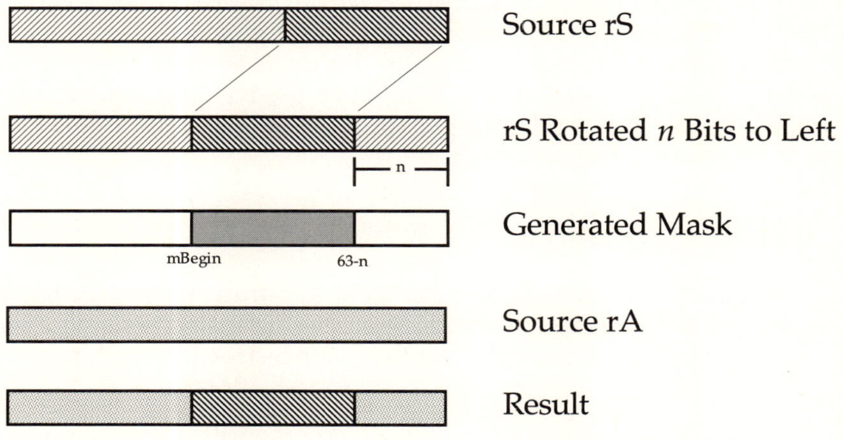

Source rS

rS Rotated n Bits to Left

Generated Mask

mBegin   63-n

Source rA

Result

As with the rotate word instructions, there are three extended forms for rotating a 64-bit quantity without masking out any of the bits. Table 7-4 lists these forms.

Table 7-4 Rotate Doubleword Extended Instruction Forms

`rotld[.] rA,rS,rB` **Rotate Left Doubleword** *extended form for* `rldcl rA,rS,rB,0` *64-bit implementations only*	$rA \Leftarrow (rS) \circlearrowleft rB[58{:}63]$
`rotldi[.] rA,rS,n` **Rotate Left Doubleword Immediate** *extended form for* `rldicl rA,rS,n,0` *64-bit implementations only*	$rA \Leftarrow (rS) \circlearrowleft n$
`rotrdi[.] rA,rS,n` **Rotate Right Doubleword Immediate** *extended form for* `rldicl rA,rS,64-n,0` *64-bit implementations only*	$rA \Leftarrow (rS) \circlearrowleft n$

The *Rotate Left Doubleword* form (`rotld`) rotates rS left $rB[58{:}63]$ bits and stores the result in rA. *Rotate Left Doubleword Immediate* (`rotldi`) performs the same operation, but obtains the rotate amount from an immediate value instead of from rB.

To rotate a doubleword to the right by an immediate amount n, the *Rotate Right Doubleword Immediate* form is defined. This form rotates rS to the right n bits and stores the result in rA. This form is implemented by using the `rldicl` instruction to rotate the doubleword to the left by $64-n$ places, which performs the same operation as rotating right by n bits.

As with the *Rotate Right Word* forms, a *Rotate Right Doubleword* extended form that accepts the rotate amount in a register is not provided. To use the `rldcl` instruction to implement this functionality, the rotate amount in rB must be subtracted from 64 and then that value should be used as the rotate amount. The rotate amount can also be calculated simply by negating rB since only the lower 6 bits of the rotate amount are used.

7.4 Shift Instructions

Considering how powerful the rotate and mask instructions are, it might at first seem somewhat redundant to provide separate shift instructions since the shift functionality can be constructed using the rotate instructions with an appropriate mask.

However, the PowerPC shift instructions differ from the rotate instructions in two significant ways. First, the shift instructions provide a shift operation where the shift amount can be specified in a register, whereas the rotate instructions can only be used to implement shift operations where the shift amount is supplied as an immediate value. Even the `rlwnm` instruction (which allows the rotate amount to be specified in rB) is not useful for this purpose because it requires that the mask be specified using immediate values, thus precluding its use for shift operations.

Secondly, the shift instructions provide additional functionality in that they perform more than just a basic shift around a word (or doubleword) quantity. The shift instructions allow the shift amount to range between $[\frac{0:63}{0:127}]$, which allows the bits to be completely "shifted out" to the right or left (if the shift amount is greater than or equal to $[\frac{32}{64}]$). While this may not seem incredibly useful at first, this feature allows multi-word (or multi-doubleword) shift operations to be constructed easily from a series of *shift*, *add*, and *or* instructions. This technique is described in §7.6 "Multiple-Precision Shifts."

The *Shift Right Algebraic* instructions represent another set of forms that could not be implemented using the rotate and mask instructions without adding a few extra instructions. These shift instructions replicate the sign bit so that the shifted result retains the same sign as the source operand. As with the other shift instructions, the shift amount can be in the range $[\frac{0:63}{0:127}]$ to facilitate multi-word algebraic shifts.

Shift Left

Figure 7-6 shows how the *Shift Left* instructions shift the contents of the source register r S to the left by the amount specified in r B and save the result in r A. '0's are shifted in from the right to fill in the bits as the value is shifted to the left.

Figure 7-6   Shift Left Operation

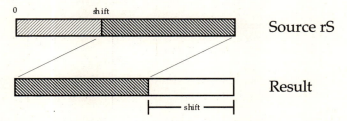

Table 7-5 lists the two types of shift left instructions: the first type operates on words, and the other operates on doublewords.

Table 7-5 Shift Left Instructions

`slw[.] rA,rS,rB` **Shift Left Word**	$rA \Leftarrow (rS) \ll rB \ [\frac{26:31}{58:63}]$
`sld[.] rA,rS,rB` **Shift Left Doubleword** *64-bit implementations only*	$rA \Leftarrow (rS) \ll rB[57:63]$

The *Shift Left Word* instruction shifts the word in rS to the left by the amount specified in $rB[26:31]$. The shift amount can range from 0 to 63; if the shift amount is greater than 31, the quantity in rS is completely shifted out and the value 0 is stored in rA as the result.

The *Shift Left Doubleword* instruction shifts the doubleword quantity in rS to the left by the amount specified in $rB[57:63]$. The shift amount can range from 0 to 127; if the shift amount is greater than 63, rS is completely shifted out and the result of the instruction is 0.

No *Shift Left* instructions accept the shift amount as an immediate value, but the *Shift Left Immediate* forms listed in Table 7-6 can be constructed from the rotate left with mask instructions. Two extended *Shift Left Immediate* forms are defined, one each for words and doublewords. Since these instructions are built from the rotate instructions, the shift amount must range between $[\frac{0:31}{0:63}]$.

Table 7-6 Shift Left Immediate Extended Instruction Forms

`slwi[.] rA,rS,n` **Shift Left Word Immediate** *extended form for* `rlwinm rA,rS,n,0,31-n`	$rA \Leftarrow (rS) \ll n$
`sldi[.] rA,rS,n` **Shift Left Doubleword Immediate** *extended form for* `rldicr rA,rS,n,63-n` *64-bit implementations only*	$rA \Leftarrow (rS) \ll n$

The *Shift Left Word Immediate* (`slwi`) extended form shifts the source register rS to the left by n bits and stores the result in rA.

The *Shift Left Doubleword Immediate* (`sldi`) form performs the same operation as `slwi` but operates on a doubleword quantity instead of a word quantity.

Shift Right

Figure 7-7 shows how the *Shift Right* instructions shift the contents of the source register rS to the right by the amount specified in rB and save the result in rA. '0's are shifted in from the left to fill in the bits as the value is shifted to the right.

Figure 7-7   Shift Right Operation

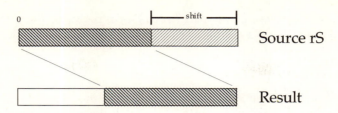

The two forms of the *Shift Right* instruction listed in Table 7-7 operate on word or doubleword quantities. The shift amount is always specified in the lower bits of rB.

Table 7-7 Shift Right Instructions

srw[.] rA,rS,rB **Shift Right Word**	$rA \Leftarrow (rS) \gg rB \ [\frac{26:31}{58:63}]$
srd[.] rA,rS,rB **Shift Right Doubleword** *64-bit implementations only*	$rA \Leftarrow (rS) \gg rB[57:63]$

The *Shift Right Word* instruction shifts the word in rS to the right by the amount specified in rB[26:31]. The shift amount can range from 0 to 63; if the shift amount is greater than 31, the quantity in rS is completely shifted out and the value 0 is stored in rA as the result.

The *Shift Right Doubleword* instruction shifts the doubleword quantity in rS to the right by the amount specified in rB[57:63]. The shift amount can range from 0 to 127 if the shift amount is greater than 63, rS is completely shifted out and 0 is returned as the result.

Two extended forms of the rotate left with mask instructions listed in Table 7-8 are defined to make coding the *Shift Right Immediate* instructions a bit easier. Since these instructions are built from the rotate instructions, the shift amount must range between $[\frac{0:31}{0:63}]$.

Table 7-8 Shift Right Immediate Extended Instruction Forms

srwi[.] rA,rS,n **Shift Right Word Immediate** *extended form for* rlwinm rA,rS,32-n,n,31	$rA \Leftarrow (rS) \gg n$
srdi[.] rA,rS,n **Shift Right Doubleword Immediate** *extended form for* rldicl rA,rS,64-n,n *64-bit implementations only*	$rA \Leftarrow (rS) \gg n$

The *Shift Right Word Immediate* (`srwi`) extended form shifts the source register `rS` to the left by *n* bits and stores the result in `rA`.

The *Shift Right Doubleword Immediate* (`srdi`) form performs the same operation as `srwi` but operates on a doubleword quantity instead of a word.

Shift Right Algebraic

Figure 7-8 shows how an algebraic shift differs from a normal shift in that the sign bit of the source register is replicated so that the result of the operation has the same sign as the source value.

Figure 7-8   Shift Right Algebraic Operation

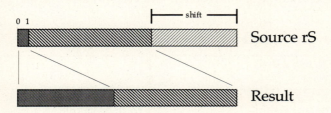

Since the sign is always recorded in the *most significant bit* (MSB), or bit 0, of a register, the sign can be maintained during the operation by shifting copies of the sign bit in from the left. This way, the sign of the result is the same as the sign of the source value.

The algebraic shift instructions listed in Table 7-9 are the only shift operations that affect the Carry bit in the XER. The Carry bit is normally set to '0', but it is set to '1' if the source value is negative and any '1' bits have been shifted out the right side of the register. This carry value is useful when the *Shift Right Algebraic* instructions are being applied to perform division operations as described in §16.3 under "Using Algebraic Right Shifts for Division."

Table 7-9 Shift Right Algebraic Instructions

`sraw[.] rA,rS,rB` **Shift Right Algebraic Word**	$rA \Leftarrow (rS) \overset{s}{\gg} rB \left[\frac{26:31}{58:63}\right]$ update XER[CA]
`srawi[.] rA,rS,n` **Shift Right Algebraic Word Immediate**	$rA \Leftarrow (rS) \overset{s}{\gg} n$ update XER[CA]
`srad[.] rA,rS,rB` **Shift Right Algebraic Doubleword** *64-bit implementations only*	$rA \Leftarrow (rS) \overset{s}{\gg} rB[57:63]$ update XER[CA]
`sradi[.] rA,rS,n` **Shift Right Algebraic Doubleword Immediate** *64-bit implementations only*	$rA \Leftarrow (rS) \overset{s}{\gg} n$ update XER[CA]

The *Shift Right Algebraic* instructions that operate on word quantities are the *Shift Right Algebraic Word* (`sraw`) and *Shift Right Algebraic Word Immediate* (`srawi`) instructions. These instructions accept a shift amount, either as an immediate value or from a register, and algebraically shift register `rS` to the right that many bits, storing the result in `rA`.

The *Shift Right Algebraic Doubleword* (`srad`) and *Shift Right Algebraic Doubleword Immediate* (`sradi`) instructions perform the same operation as their word-sized counterparts, but they operate on doubleword quantities instead of words.

7.5 Extended Rotate Instruction Forms

While the rotate with mask instructions provide a powerful mechanism for performing bit manipulation operations, using the base instruction forms directly can be somewhat confusing and error prone. For this reason, three general types of extended forms are defined that allow extraction, insertion, clearing, and "clear and shift"ing of a range of bits in the source register.

Extract and Justify Extended Instruction Forms

The *Extract and Justify* extended form provides an easy instruction form for extracting a range of bits and then justifying the bits to either the right or the left of the destination register. A *justify* operation involves shifting the bits all the way to the right or left of the register. There are both word and doubleword versions of these forms.

These forms accept a starting bit, b, and a number of bits, n, as parameters. The n-bit field in the source register (`rS`) that starts at bit b is shifted to the right or left and then extracted. The result of this extraction is stored in the destination register (`rA`).

Figure 7-9 shows the operation of this form when performing a left justify. For this form, `rS` is rotated b bits to the left and then ANDed with a mask composed of the high-order n bits (0 to n-1).

Figure 7-9   Extract and Left-Justify Operation

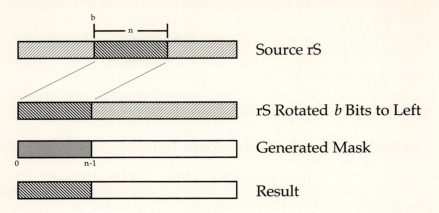

For the right-justify extended forms, rS needs to be rotated to the right $\left[\frac{32}{64}\right]$ - $(b+n)$ bits (or equivalently, left rotated $b+n$ bits) and then ANDed with a mask composed of the low-order n bits. This is shown in Figure 7-10   .

Figure 7-10   Extract and Right-Justify Operation

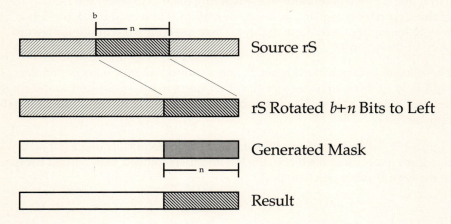

Extract and Justify Word

The word versions of the *Extract and Justify* extended form are based on the `rlwinm` instruction. Table 7-10 summarizes these two forms and shows how they map into the `rlwinm` instruction.

Table 7-10 Extract and Justify Word Extended Instruction Forms

extlwi[.] rA,rS,n,b **Extract and Left Justify Word Immediate** *extended form for* rlwinm rA,rS,b,0,n-1	$m := \mathrm{Mask}(\ [\frac{0}{32}],\ [\frac{0}{32}]+(n\text{-}1))$ $rA \Leftarrow ((rS) \ll b)\ \&\ m$
extrwi[.] rA,rS,n,b **Extract and Right Justify Word Immediate** *extended form for* rlwinm rA,rS,b+n,32-n,31	$m := \mathrm{Mask}(\ [\frac{32}{64}]\text{-}n,\ [\frac{31}{63}]\ )$ $rA \Leftarrow ((rS) \ll (b+n))\ \&\ m$

The extlwi form extracts the *n*-bit field starting at bit *b* in rS and stores the left-justified bit field in rA. The extrwi form performs the same operation, except that the bit field is justified to the right before the value is stored in rA.

To prevent invalid rlwinm instructions from being generated by these extended forms, *n* must be ≥ 1 and ($b+n$) must be ≤ 32.

Extract and Justify Doubleword

The *Extract and Justify* doubleword forms are based on the rldicr and rldicl instructions. Table 7-11 summarizes the two separate instructions that are needed because only the start or the end of the mask can be specified when using 64-bit rotate instructions.

Table 7-11 Extract and Justify Doubleword Extended Instruction Forms

extldi[.] rA,rS,n,b **Extract and Left Justify Doubleword** **Immediate** *extended form for* rldicr rA,rS,b,n-1 *64-bit implementations only*	$m := \mathrm{Mask}(0,n\text{-}1)$ $rA \Leftarrow ((rS) \ll b)\ \&\ m$
extrdi[.] rA,rS,n,b **Extract and Right Justify Doubleword** **Immediate** *extended form for* rldicl rA,rS,b+n,64-n *64-bit implementations only*	$m := \mathrm{Mask}(64\text{-}n,63)$ $rA \Leftarrow ((rS) \ll (b+n))\ \&\ m$

The extldi and extrdi forms are identical to the word-based *Extract and Justify* forms, except that they operate on doubleword quantities. A bit field is extracted from rS and stored in rA after it has been justified to the left or right.

To prevent invalid rldicr or rldicl instructions from being generated by this extended form, *n* must be ≥ 1 and ($b+n$) must be ≤ 64.

Insert Extended Instruction Forms

The *Insert* extended forms can be viewed as the opposite of the *Extract and Justify* forms. These forms take a bit field that is justified to either the left or right of a register and insert that field into another register at a specified bit offset. Figures 7-11 and 7-12 show this operation for the *Insert from Left* and *Insert from Right* forms.

Figure 7-11   Insert from Left Operation

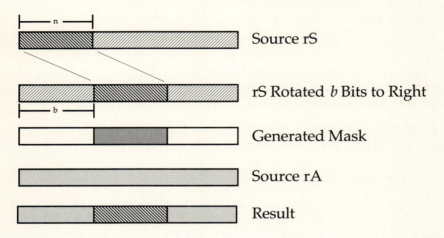

The *Insert from Left* form takes the high-order n bits and inserts them into rA starting at bit position b. This operation is accomplished by rotating the source register to the right b bit positions and then inserting via the appropriate mask.

Figure 7-12   Insert from Right Operation

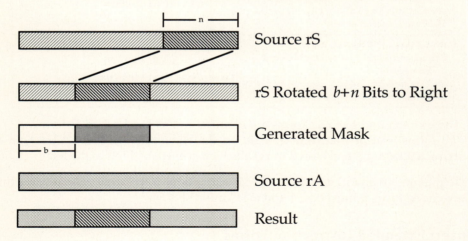

The *Insert from Right* form also inserts a n-bit field into rA starting at bit position b, but the bit field comes from the low-order n bits of rS instead of the high-order bits. This is done by rotating $b+n$ bits to the right before inserting with the mask.

Insert Word

The two *Insert Word* forms listed in Table 7-12 are built from the `rlwimi` instruction.

Table 7-12 Insert Word Extended Instruction Forms

`inslwi[.] rA,rS,n,b`
Insert from Left Word Immediate
extended form for
   `rlwimi rA,rS,32-b,b,(b+n)-1`
	$m := \text{Mask}(\left[\frac{0}{32}\right]+b, \left[\frac{0}{32}\right]+(b+n)-1)$
	
	$rA \Leftarrow ((rS) \ll (\left[\frac{32}{64}\right]-b)) \ \& \ m$

`insrwi[.] rA,rS,n,b`
Insert from Right Word Immediate
extended form for
   `rlwimi rA,rS,32-(b+n),b,(b+n)-1`
	$m := \text{Mask}(\left[\frac{0}{32}\right]+b, \left[\frac{0}{32}\right]+(b+n)-1)$
	
	$rA \Leftarrow ((rS) \ll (\left[\frac{32}{64}\right]-(b+n))) \ \& \ m$

These two forms insert a bit field from either the left (`inslwi`) or right (`insrwi`) of the source register rS and insert it into the destination register rA starting at bit position b.

The parameter n should be ≥ 1 and the inequality $(b+n) \leq 32$ should hold true in order for these extended forms to map into valid `rlwimi` instructions.

Insert Doubleword

The only *Insert Doubleword* form is the *Insert from Right Doubleword Immediate* (`insrdi`) form listed in Table 7-13. Limitations with how masks can be specified for doubleword rotate operations preclude defining an extended form that would implement the *Insert from Left Doubleword Immediate* functionality in one instruction. However, such an operation can be constructed using a `rldicl rS,rS,n,0` instruction to right justify the bit field followed by a `insrdi rA,rS,n,b` instruction.

Table 7-13 Insert Doubleword Extended Instruction Form

`insrdi[.] rA,rS,n,b` **Insert from Right Doubleword Immediate** *extended form for* `rldimi rA,rS,64-(b+n),b` *64-bit implementations only*	$m := \text{Mask}(b,(b+n)-1)$ $rA \Leftarrow ((rS) \ll (64-(b+n))) \ \& \ m$

The `insrdi` form takes an n-bit, right-justified bit field from the source register rS and inserts it at bit position b into rA. For this form to make sense, $(b+n)$ must be ≤ 64, and n must be ≥ 1.

Clear Extended Instruction Forms

The *Clear* extended forms provide a simple method of clearing all of the bits on one side of a given bit in the source register. There are two types of *Clear* extended forms: one clears all bits to the left, and the other clears all bits to the right. Both of these forms come in word and doubleword flavors.

The *Clear Word* and *Doubleword* forms don't perform any sort of rotation on the source register and are considered rotate forms only because they are constructed on top of the standard rotate instructions.

The most useful characteristic of these forms is that they allow a left- or right-justified bit field to be extracted without requiring a complete mask to be specified as an argument. Since such a mask would need to be 32 or 64 bits in size, it would obviously not fit into an instruction encoding (which is limited to 32 bits). The mask would need to be stored elsewhere, and extra instructions would be required to get the mask from memory, resulting in additional memory accesses.

While the *Clear* extended forms do not allow every possible type of mask to be encoded, they do optimize one of the more common types of register mask operation. When the *Clear* forms can be used, they allow the operation to be encoded as one instruction with no unnecessary memory accesses.

The *Clear Left* operation clears out the high-order n bits from the source register and stores the result in the destination register. Figure 7-13   shows this relatively simple operation. Because of the fact that bits in registers are numbered using a big-endian scheme (that is, the most significant bit is bit 0), this operation can be viewed as clearing all the bits to the left of bit position n.

Figure 7-13   Clear Left Operation

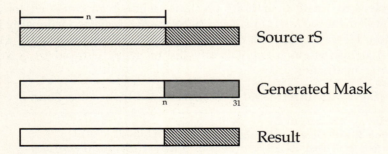

The *Clear Right* operation clears out the low-order n bits from the source register and then copies the result into the destination register. Figure 7-14 shows this operation. It is important to be aware of the fact that n represents the number of bits to be cleared, not an absolute bit position. With the *Clear Left* operation, the programmer can be confused about the true meaning of n and things will work as expected, but this is not the case for the *Clear Right* operation.

Figure 7-14   Clear Right Operation

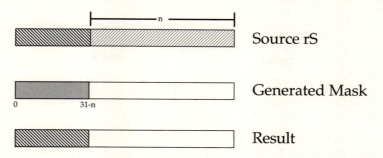

Clear Word

The two versions of the *Clear Word* form listed in Table 7-14 clear the n bits at the extreme left or right of the specified 32-bit register. If these forms are executed on 64-bit PowerPC implementations, only the lower word is affected by this instruction; the upper word of the result is always cleared to zeros.

Table 7-14 Clear Word Extended Instruction Forms

clrlwi[.] rA,rS,n **Clear Left Word Immediate** *extended form for* rlwinm rA,rS,0,n,31	$m := \text{Mask}(\ [\tfrac{0}{32}]+n,\ [\tfrac{31}{63}])$ $rA \Leftarrow (rS) \ \& \ m$
clrrwi[.] rA,rS,n **Clear Right Word Immediate** *extended form for* rlwinm rA,rS,0,0,31−n	$m := \text{Mask}(\ [\tfrac{0}{32}],\ [\tfrac{31}{63}]\ -n)$ $rA \Leftarrow (rS) \ \& \ m$

The *Clear Left Word Immediate* (clrlwi) form accepts the number of bits, n, and generates the appropriate rlwinm instruction so that the left-most n bits of rS are cleared and the result is copied into rA. The clrlri form performs a similar operation, except that it clears out the right-most n bits before copying the result into rA.

Clear Doubleword

The two doubleword versions of the *Clear Left* and *Clear Right* forms listed in Table 7-15 are based on the rldicl and rldicr instructions, respectively. These forms clear the n bits at the extreme left or right of the specified 64-bit register.

Table 7-15 Clear Doubleword Extended Instruction Forms

`clrldi[.] rA,rS,n` **Clear Left Doubleword Immediate** *extended form for* `rldicl rA,rS,0,n` *64-bit implementations only*	$m := \text{Mask}(n,63)$ $rA \Leftarrow (rS) \,\&\, m$
`clrrdi[.] rA,rS,n` **Clear Right Doubleword Immediate** *extended form for* `rldicr rA,rS,0,63-n` *64-bit implementations only*	$m := \text{Mask}(0,63-n)$ $rA \Leftarrow (rS) \,\&\, m$

The `clrldi` and `clrrdi` forms are identical to the *Clear Word* forms, except that they operate on an entire 64-bit register instead of just the low-order word.

Clear Left and Shift Left Extended Instruction Forms

The *Clear Left and Shift Left* forms listed in Table 7-16 provide a simpler interface to the masked rotate instructions for performing an operation to extract a right-justified field and left shift it to a desired bit position.

These forms take two parameters: the first bit of the right-justified field and the number of bits to shift to the right. The first bit of the field can alternatively be viewed as the number of bits to the left that should be cleared before performing the shift.

Figure 7-15 shows the *Clear Left and Shift Left* operation. This is the same operation as the `rlwinm` instruction. The only difference is how the parameters for the shift and mask are specified.

Figure 7-15 Clear Left and Shift Left Operation

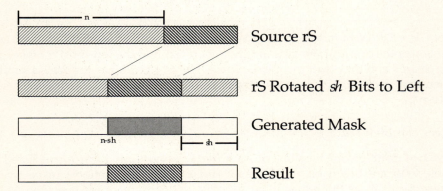

Table 7-16 Clear Left and Shift Left Extended Instruction Forms

clrlslwi[.] rA,rS,n,sh **Clear Left and Shift Left Word Immediate** *extended form for* rlwinm rA,rS,sh,n-sh,31-sh	$r := (rS) \, \mathbb{Q} \, sh$ $m := \text{Mask}(\, [\frac{0}{32}]+n\text{-}sh, \, [\frac{31}{63}]\text{-}sh)$ $rA \Leftarrow r \, \& \, m$
clrlsldi[.] rA,rS,n,sh **Clear Left and Shift Left Doubleword** **Immediate** *extended form for* rldic rA,rS,sh,n-sh *64-bit implementations only*	$r := (rS) \, \mathbb{Q} \, sh$ $m := \text{Mask}(n\text{-}sh,63\text{-}sh)$ $rA \Leftarrow r \, \& \, m$

The two *Clear Left and Shift Left* forms, clrlslwi and clrlsldi, take a right-justified bit field starting at bit *n* from source register rS, shift it to the left *sh* places, and then store the bit field into the destination register rA. The remaining bits in the destination register are cleared to 0. In order for these forms to generate coherent rotate instructions, *n* must be ≥ *sh*.

There is no predefined form to perform a *Clear Right and Shift Right Word Immediate* operation, but one could be constructed by defining clrrsrwi[.] rA,rS,n,sh to map to rlwinm[.] rA,rS,32-sh,sh,31+sh-n.

As with the *Insert* forms, doubleword mask restrictions prevent a similar *Clear Right and Shift Right* form from being defined for doubleword quantities. A rldicl rS,rS,n,0 instruction can be used in conjunction with clrlsldi rA,rS,n,sh to perform this operation.

7.6 Multiple-Precision Shifts

A *multiple-precision shift* is a shift which operates on quantities larger than a word (or doubleword, in the case of processors executing in 64-bit mode) in size.

The best method for performing a multiple-precision shift depends on these factors:

- Whether the shift is being performed on words or doublewords.
- Whether the shift amount is less than $[\frac{32}{64}]$ or less than $[\frac{64}{128}]$.
- Whether the shift amount is an immediate value or from a register.
- Whether the direction of the shift is to the left or right.

Methods for performing shifts greater than $[\frac{64}{128}]$ are not presented in this section, but they can be constructed from the algorithms presented here.

Multiple-Precision Left Shifts

Figure 7-16 shows how a multiple-precision left shift is performed when the shift amount is less than the shift register size (that is, the shift amount is less than 32 for 32-bit implementations or 64-bit implementations in 32-bit mode and less than 64 for 64-bit implementations in 64-bit mode). In this figure, the contents of registers A, B, and C are concatenated together and shifted to the left to produce the result A', B', and C'.

Figure 7-16   Multiple-Precision Left Shifts (shift < 32)

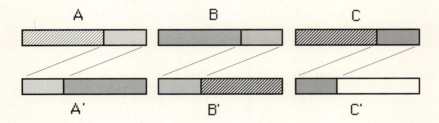

For each register in the shift except the last, the final result is the sum of two quantities: the shifted low-order bits from the current register and the high-order bits from the register immediately to the right. The last register is calculated simply by shifting its low-order bits by the shift amount.

Most of these shift operations are performed inline, that is, the register that contains A on entry will contain A' on exit. In the code examples, rA will be used to denote the register that holds A and A' and likewise with rB and rC.

Multiple-Precision Left Shift

Performing multiple left shifts is a straightforward operation: each half of each register is calculated, and then the halves are merged together to produce the result for each register. Since this operation is basically the same for word and doubleword sized shifts, this section discusses only word shifts and then provides Table 7-17, a summary of both types of shifts.

Before we can begin shifting, we must first calculate and save the *counter shift* amount. This is the amount that we need to shift right to move the high-order bits down into their proper position, and it is equal to $32 - shift$ for word shifts. If register rS contains the shift amount, we can compute the counter shift using

```
subfic  rS1,rS,32
```

where $rS1$ is the register in which we are storing the counter shift.

A' can now be calculated by left shifting the low-order bits in A and right shifting the high-order bits in B. When these two values are ORed together, the result is A'.

```
slw     rA,rA,rS
srw     rT,rB,rS1
or      rA,rA,rT
```

Note that A is shifted to the left by the shift amount and B is shifted to the right by the counter shift amount. rT is just a temporary register used to hold the result of the right shift. This sequence of instructions needs to be repeated for each register being shifted except for the last one.

The last register (C in Figure 7-16) is calculated simply by shifting rC to the left, which can be accomplished by using

```
slw     rC,rC,rS
```

The code sequence for this operation is summarized in Table 7-17.

Table 7-17 Multiple-Precision Left Shift Code Summary (shift < $[\frac{32}{64}]$)

Shift Stage	Word		Doubleword	
Initialization	subfic	$rS1,rS,32$	subfic	$rS1,rS,64$
For each register except the last	slw srw or	rN,rN,rS $rT,r(N+1),rS1$ rN,rN,rT	sld srd or	rN,rN,rS $rT,r(N+1),rS1$ rN,rN,rT
For the last register	slw	rN,rN,rS	sld	rN,rN,rS

Only two changes are needed for handling doubleword shifts. The first is that the counter shift must be based on a shift around 64 bits, and the other change is that the doubleword shift instructions must be used instead of the word shift.

Long Multiple-Precision Left Shift

Long multiple-precision shifts are shifts that are larger than the width of one register. Thus, word shifts that can range from 0 to 63 and doubleword shifts that can range from 0 to 127 are considered to be long shifts. This can be seen in Figure 7-17, where the value being shifted out of C ends up in A' and B'. For the sake of simplicity, shifts greater than two registers (that is, word shifts ≥ 64 and doubleword shifts ≥ 128) are not considered.

To simplify the discussion, long word shifts will be described first, and then the changes necessary for long doubleword shifts will be given.

Figure 7-17   Multiple-Precision Left Shifts (32 ≤ shifts < 64)

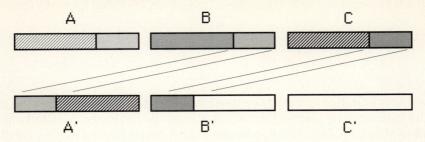

Long shifts need to be able to handle situations where the shift amount is between 0 and 31 and where the shift amount is between 32 and 63. This could be implemented by using a test and a conditional branch, but branches can stall the instruction pipeline and so they should be avoided wherever possible. The technique described in this section takes advantage of the properties of the Shift instructions to eliminate the need for any branches.

The technique that we use to calculate long shifts is to first handle the case where the shift amount is less than 32, making sure that the result is 0 if the shift is greater than or equal to 32. Then we handle the opposite case, where the shift amount is between 32 and 63, and make sure that the result is 0 if the shift amount is less than 32. Once this is done, we can simply OR the two results together and know that every possible shift value is handled correctly.

In order to do this, we need to pre-calculate three counter shift values: 32 - *shift*, *shift* - 32, and 64 - *shift*. These counter shift values will be referred to as *shift1* (for 32 - *shift*), *shift2* (for *shift* - 32), and *shift3* (for 64 - *shift*) to differentiate them from the real `shift` value. These values can be calculated using

```
subfic  rS1,rS,32
subic   rS2,rS,32
subfic  rS3,rS,64
```

For each register that needs to be shifted, we need to handle the two situations where 0 ≤ *shift* < 32 and 32 ≤ *shift* < 64. We'll handle the case where *shift* < 32 by using the same code that we used at the beginning of this section, for shift amounts that are always less than 32.

```
slw     rA,rA,rS
srw     rT,rB,rS1
or      rA,rA,rT
```

Notice that when the shift amount in rS is greater than or equal to 32, two things happen:

- The `slw` instruction returns a result of 0 because the *shift* amount is greater than 31.
- The `srw` instruction returns a result of 0 because the *shift1* amount is a negative number. Since only the low-order six bits from $rS1$ are used for the shift amount, the `srw` instruction interprets this as a very large number and shifts the value completely out.

Thus, we properly handle the case where *shift* < 32 and return a 0 if *shift* ≥ 32. To handle the case where shift is between 32 and 63, we need to get the proper values from the two registers to the right of the current one. That is, in order to calculate the shifted value of A, we need to manipulate the values in B and C.

```
slw     rT,rB,rS2   # get lower bits of B
or      rA,rA,rT
srw     rT,rC,rS3   # get upper bits of C
or      rA,rA,rT
```

This code correctly handles shift values between 32 and 63 and returns 0 if the shift amount is less than 32. Whenever the shift amount is less than 32, *shift2* becomes a negative number (effectively a large positive number), and *shift3* is greater than 32. For both of these shift values, the value in rB and rC is completely shifted out of the register and 0 is returned.

Note that we write the result to a temporary register and OR the value into rA after each stage. We need to do this because we want this result to be merged with the result we calculated earlier. We don't want to overwrite the previous value of rA.

Computing the last two registers of a multiple word shift is the same as for the other registers, except that some of the operations can be omitted because the required registers are not present. To compute the next to last register, we do not need to get the upper bits from the register two places over, thus we have

```
# calculate if shift < 32
slw     rB,rB,rS
srw     rT,rC,rS1
or      rB,rB,rT

# calculate if 32 <= shift < 64
slw     rT,rC,rS2   # get lower bits of C
or      rB,rB,rT
```

The very last register is even easier, since we only need to account for the situation when *shift* is less than 32. We simply have to shift the register value over by the specified shift amount.

```
slw     rC,rC,rS
```

As mentioned earlier in this section, a long doubleword shift is performed in the same manner as the long word shift. Table 7-18 summarizes the code required for long shift operations on word and doubleword quantities.

Table 7-18 Long Multiple-Precision Left Shift Code Summary (shift < $[\frac{64}{128}]$)

Shift Stage	Word		Doubleword	
Initialization	subfic	rS1,rS,32	subfic	rS1,rS,64
	subic	rS2,rS,32	subic	rS2,rS,64
	subfic	rS3,rS,64	subfic	rS3,rS,128
For each register except the last 2	slw	rN,rN,rS	sld	rN,rN,rS
	srw	rT,r(N+1),rS1	srd	rT,r(N+1),rS1
	or	rN,rN,rT	or	rN,rN,rT
	slw	rT,r(N+1),rS2	sld	rT,r(N+1),rS2
	or	rN,rN,rT	or	rN,rN,rT
	srw	rT,r(N+2),rS3	srd	rT,r(N+2),rS3
	or	rN,rN,rT	or	rN,rN,rT
For the next to last register	slw	rN,rN,rS	sld	rN,rN,rS
	srw	rT,r(N+1),rS1	srd	rT,r(N+1),rS1
	or	rN,rN,rT	or	rN,rN,rT
	slw	rT,r(N+1),rS2	sld	rT,r(N+1),rS2
	or	rN,rN,rT	or	rN,rN,rT
For the last register	slw	rN,rN,rS	sld	rN,rN,rS

Note that since the *shift3* counter shift value is not used by the last two registers, the initialization instruction that calculates this value can be omitted when only two registers are being shifted.

Multiple-Precision Immediate Left Word Shift

When the shift amount is an immediate value, multiple-precision left shifts can be rewritten to take advantage of the `rlwimi` instruction, which allows a rotate and an insert operation to be performed in one instruction. One important limitation of the technique presented here is that it can only be used when the shift amount is less than 32. However, supporting shift amounts larger than 32 is trivially handled by applying the shifts to the appropriately selected registers. This is straightforward since the shift amount is an immediate constant.

For example, A′ can be calculated from A and B by using the code:

```
slwi      rA,rA,shift
rlwimi    rA,rB,shift,32-shift,31
```

where *shift* is the shift amount.

The first instruction (`slwi`, an extended form for `rlwinm`) takes the low-order bits of A and shifts them over to the proper position for A'. The second instruction (`rlwimi`) takes the high-order bits of B, shifts them down to the proper position for A', and inserts the bits into A'. The old value of A is overwritten with the new value A' by this operation.

The last register (C in Figure 7-16   ) is calculated simply by shifting C to the left, which can be accomplished by using

```
slwi      rC,rC,shift
```

Table 7-19 summarizes the left word operation when the shift amount is specifed as an immediate value.

Table 7-19 Multiple-Precision Immediate Left Word Shift Code Summary

Shift Stage	Word	
For each register except the last	`slwi`	`rN,rN,shift`
	`rlwimi`	`rN,r(N+1),shift,32-shift,31`
For the last register	`slwi`	`rN,rN,shift`

Multiple-Precision Immediate Left Doubleword Shift

Because of mask limitations in the doubleword rotate instructions, performing shifts on multiple doubleword quantities is more complicated than it is for multiple word quantities.

The major limitation is that the `rldimi` instruction cannot rotate a quantity *and* have a mask that extends all the way to the least significant bit of the register. This is because the *maskEnd* value is automatically calculated from the specified rotate amount.

There are many ways to overcome this limitation, the easiest of which is to simply avoid it by manually building each half of each shifted register and then ORing the results together. This is the same method used to calculate the multiple-precision left shifts when the shift amount is from a register. This is done using the code:

```
sldi      rA,rA,shift
srdi      rT,rB,64-shift
or        rA,rA,rT
```

This method is not as efficient as the word version because it requires more instructions for each register being shifted. It's inefficient because it doesn't take advantage of the `rldimi` instruction's ability to insert into another register. In order to produce a code sequence as efficient as the word version, we need to restructure our shifting algorithm. One way is to work from the low-order register up to the high-order register instead of downwards from the high-order register.

However, working from low-order to high-order means that we can't perform the shift operation inline, that is, we need to store each register result in a different register. This doesn't cause any real problems other than the fact that it becomes slightly more difficult to describe.

Figure 7-18   shows the basic structure of the multiple-precision shift doubleword operation when only two registers are being shifted. The important thing to note in this figure is that each "column" represents a separate register. This means that the register that holds B on entry contains A' of the result on exit. The remaining two registers in this example contain only input values (A) or only output values (B'). To help avoid confusion in this example, $r\alpha$ is used to refer to the register that contains A/-, $r\beta$ refers to B/A', and $r\gamma$ refers to -/B'.

Figure 7-18   Multiple-Precision Immediate Left Doubleword Shifts

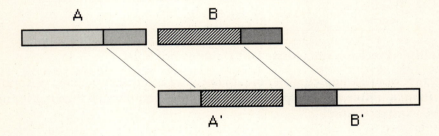

The key to this technique is recognizing that we can take the low-order bits from A (in $r\alpha$), insert them into B (in $r\beta$), and then rotate $r\beta$ to produce A'. Figure 7-19 shows how this technique works. The insert operation doesn't require any shifting of bits, and since we're inserting the low-order bits, we can use the `rldimi` instruction.

Figure 7-19   Calculating Shifted A (A') from A and B

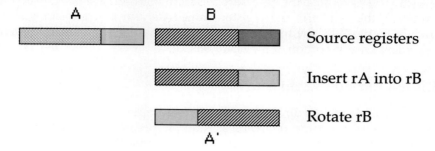

Of course, in order to do this properly, we need to copy the low-order bits of B from rβ into another register before we overwrite them with the bits from A. This is why we use the extra register (rγ) to hold the low-order register of the result.

The low-order register can be calculated with

```
sldi    rγ,rβ,sh      # calculate B' from B
```

The remaining register can now be calculated by inserting and rotating using the code:

```
rldimi  rβ,rα,0,sh   # insert A into B
rotldi  rβ,rβ,sh     # rotate to produce A'
```

The `rldimi` instruction copies the low-order bits in A (rα) from sh to 63 into B (rβ). The `rotldi` operation (an extended form for `rldicl`) takes the value in rβ and rotates it sh places, resulting in A'.

If there are more than two registers being shifted, they can be calculated by applying this technique to each register by working from right to left.

Table 7-20 summarizes the code necessary to implement a multiple-precision left shift on doubleword quantities when the shift amount is an immediate value. Note that the last register must be shifted first, and then the other registers can be shifted from right to left.

Table 7-20 Multiple-Precision Immediate Left Doubleword Shift Summary

Shift Stage	Doubleword	
For the last register	`sldi`	`r(N+1),rN,shift`
For each register except the first	`rldimi` `rotldi`	`rN,r(N-1),0,shift` `rN,rN,shift`

Note that the register containing the first doubleword doesn't need to be shifted explicitly. This is because the necessary bits from this register have already been included in the results in the register immediately to its right. Also, as was shown in Figure 7-18, the register that contains the first doubleword on entry doesn't contain any portion of the result on exit.

Multiple-Precision Right Shift

With the exception of the direction of the shift, multiple-precision right shifts are performed using the same algorithm as multiple-precision left shifts. The most significant difference is that the registers involved in the shift are calculated from right to left instead of from left to right.

Figure 7-20   shows the right shift operation. As with the left shifts, each destination word is composed of an upper and a lower half: one of the halves shifted from the same register and the other half from an adjacent register.

Figure 7-20   Multiple-Precision Right Shifts (shift < 32)

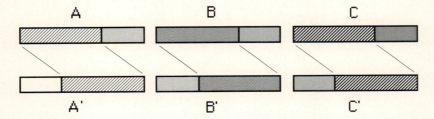

Multiple-Precision Right Shift

When the shift amount is less than $[\frac{32}{64}]$, a multiple-precision right shift is performed using the same algorithm as for a multiple-precision left shift. The only difference is that, for right shifts, the register immediately to the left is merged with the current register instead of the register immediately to the right. This slight modification changes only the arguments to the `srw` (`srd`) and `slw` (`sld`) instructions.

Table 7-21 contains the code necessary to perform both the word and the doubleword versions of the multiple-precision right shift operation. Note that these operations must be performed from the low-order register up to the high-order register.

Table 7-21 Multiple-Precision Right Shift Code Summary

Shift Stage	Word		Doubleword	
Initialization	`subfic`	`rS1,rS,32`	`subfic`	`rS1,rS,64`

For each register except the first	`srw`
	`slw`
	`or`
		`rN,rN,rS`
		`rT,r(N-1),rS1`
		`rN,rN,rT`
			`srd`
			`sld`
			`or`
				`rN,rN,rS`
				`rT,r(N-1),rS1`
				`rN,rN,rT`

For the first register	`srw`	`rN,rN,rS`	`srd`	`rN,rN,rS`

Long Multiple-Precision Right Shift

As with the right shift code described in the previous section, the long versions of the right shift are basically the same as the long versions of the left shift. The only difference is the parameters passed to the Shift Left and Shift Right instructions to account for the changed shift direction.

Table 7-22 summarizes the required code for the long multiple-precision right shift operation. This is the same as the code presented in Table 7-18 for long left shifts except that the code inserts bits from the two registers immediately to the left of the current register.

Table 7-22 Long Multiple-Precision Right Shift Code Summary

Shift Stage	Word		Doubleword	

Initialization	`subfic`
	`subic`
	`subfic`
		`rS1,rS,32`
		`rS2,rS,32`
		`rS3,rS,64`
			`subfic`
			`subic`
			`subfic`
				`rS1,rS,64`
				`rS2,rS,64`
				`rS3,rS,128`

For each register except the first two	`srw`
	`slw`
	`or`
	`srw`
	`or`
	`slw`
	`or`
		`rN,rN,rS`
		`rT,r(N-1),rS1`
		`rN,rN,rT`
		`rT,r(N-1),rS2`
		`rN,rN,rT`
		`rT,r(N-2),rS3`
		`rN,rN,rT`
			`srd`
			`sld`
			`or`
			`srd`
			`or`
			`sld`
			`or`
				`rN,rN,rS`
				`rT,r(N-1),rS1`
				`rN,rN,rT`
				`rT,r(N-1),rS2`
				`rN,rN,rT`
				`rT,r(N-2),rS3`
				`rN,rN,rT`

For the second register	`srw`
	`slw`
	`or`
	`srw`
	`or`
		`rN,rN,rS`
		`rT,r(N-1),rS1`
		`rN,rN,rT`
		`rT,r(N-1),rS2`
		`rN,rN,rT`
			`srd`
			`sld`
			`or`
			`srd`
			`or`
				`rN,rN,rS`
				`rT,r(N-1),rS1`
				`rN,rN,rT`
				`rT,r(N-1),rS2`
				`rN,rN,rT`

For the first register	`srw`	`rN,rN,rS`	`srd`	`rN,rN,rS`

Multiple-Precision Immediate Right Word Shift

Just like left shifts, the multiple-precision immediate right shifts can be rewritten to take advantage of the `rlwimi` instruction. The extended form Insert from

Right Word Immediate (`insrwi`) can be used to take the lower bits of a register and insert them into another register starting at bit position 0. Table 7-23 summarizes this shift operation for word quantities.

Table 7-23 Multiple-Precision Immediate Left Word Shift Code Summary

Shift Stage	Word	
For each register except the first	`srwi`	`rN,rN,`*shift*
	`insrwi`	`rN,r(N-1),`*shift*`,0`
For the first register	`srwi`	`rN,rN,`*shift*

Multiple-Precision Immediate Right Doubleword Shift

The masking limitations that restricted the immediate multi-doubleword left shift operations fortunately do not adversely affect the equivalent right shift operations. The same algorithm can be used, but the shift can be done inline (that is, using the same registers that contain the source values) instead of requiring the result to roll into another register.

As with the left shift equivalent, the key to this technique is recognizing that we can take the low-order bits from A, insert them into B, and then rotate B to produce B'. This is exactly the same operation that we used for the multi-doubleword left shift shown in Figure 7-19 . The only difference is that we're using this operation to calculate B' instead of A'.

All of the registers except the first (that is, the most significant) one can be shifted right using the code:

```
rldimi  rB,rA,0,64-sh # insert A into B
rotrdi  rB,rB,sh      # rotate to produce B'
```

The `rldimi` instruction inserts the bits from A into B, and then the `rotrdi` form rotates the bits into the proper position to produce B'.

The high-order register can be calculated with

```
srdi    rA,rA,sh      # calculate A' from A
```

This multiple-doubleword shift operation is summarized in Table 7-24.

Table 7-24 Multiple-Precision Immediate Right Doubleword Shift Summary

Shift Stage	Doubleword	
For each register except the first	`rldimi`	`rN,r(N-1),0,`*shift*
	`rotrdi`	`rN,rN,`*shift*
For the first register	`srdi`	`rN,rN,`*shift*

Multiple-Precision Right Shift Algebraic

Performing a multiple-precision *algebraic* right shift differs from a normal multiple-precision right shift only in how the upper registers are shifted.

Multiple-Precision Right Shift Algebraic

When the shift amount is less than the size of one register, an algebraic right shift is the same as a normal right shift with the exception of how the high-order register needs to be shifted. For this register, we need to use an algebraic shift instead of a standard shift.

Table 7-25 contains a summary of the code necessary to perform a multiple-precision algebraic right shift for both word and doubleword quantities. The only difference between this table and Table 7-21 is that Shift Right Algebraic instructions (displayed in **boldface** in Table 7-25) are used for the first register instead of Shift Right instructions.

Table 7-25 Multiple-Precision Right Shift Algebraic Code Summary

Shift Stage	Word		Doubleword	
Initialization	`subfic`	`rS1,rS,32`	`subfic`	`rS1,rS,64`

For each register except the first	`srw`
	`slw`
	`or`
		`rN,rN,rS`
		`rT,r(N-1),rS1`
		`rN,rN,rT`
			`srd`
			`sld`
			`or`
				`rN,rN,rS`
				`rT,r(N-1),rS1`
				`rN,rN,rT`

For the first register	**`sraw`**	**`rN,rN,rS`**	**`srad`**	**`rN,rN,rS`**

Long Multiple-Precision Right Shift Algebraic

A long multiple-precision algebraic right shift is similar to the long non-algebraic right shift but has the added concern that the sign from the high-order register may need to be merged with the two high-order registers of the result. This causes problems because of the differences between the Shift Right Algebraic and Shift Right instructions.

The method that we used to support word shifts up to 63 and doubleword shifts up to 127 involved implementing "short" (0-31 or 0-63) and "long" (32-63 or 64-127) shifts separately and then ORing the results together. This works because the code is set up to handle the appropriate case or return a 0 (so that the partial results can be merged easily).

The key feature of the Shift Right instruction that is used to implement the long shift right is the fact that the Shift Right instructions return 0 if the shift amount is greater than the size of one register. This is not the case with the Shift Right Algebraic instructions. The algebraic right shifts return a register full of sign bits, which can be either 0 (all bits set to 0) or -1 (all bits set to 1).

Because one-half of the calculated result can now return a non-zero value when the partial result is not needed, we cannot blindly OR in the value but must branch over the `or` instruction when it doesn't apply. This necessitates two changes to our previous algorithm: we need to determine when we need to branch, and we need to perform a conditional branch over the `or`.

These differences between a long algebraic right shift and a long right shift are summarized as follows:

- The Shift Right Algebraic instructions are used instead of the Shift Right instructions when calculating portions of the high-order register of "short" shifts and the high-order two registers of "long" shifts.
- `subic.` is used instead of `subic` when calculating *shift2*. This is used to determine when the branch should be taken.
- A branch instruction (`ble`) is added to branch over the `sraw` result when it is not applicable. This is only needed when calculating the result from the second register.

The fact that a branch instruction is needed is unfortunate, but the branch can be folded out if the `subic.` instruction is far enough ahead of the branch instruction. This is discussed more in Chapter 16 "Instruction Scheduling."

In Table 7-26, instructions that are different for Algebraic Right Shifts (when compared to the non-algebraic variety of right shift) are displayed in **boldface**.

Table 7-26 Long Multiple-Precision Right Shift Algebraic Code Summary

Shift Stage	Word		Doubleword	
Initialization	subfic	rS1,rS,32	subfic	rS1,rS,64
	subic.	**rS2,rS,32**	**subic.**	**rS2,rS,64**
	subfic	rS3,rS,64	subfic	rS3,rS,128
For each register except the first two	srw	rN,rN,rS	srd	rN,rN,rS
	slw	rT,r(N-1),rS1	sld	rT,r(N-1),rS1
	or	rN,rN,rT	or	rN,rN,rT
	srw	rT,r(N-1),rS2	srd	rT,r(N-1),rS2
	or	rN,rN,rT	or	rN,rN,rT
	slw	rT,r(N-2),rS3	sld	rT,r(N-2),rS3
	or	rN,rN,rT	or	rN,rN,rT
For the second register	srw	rN,rN,rS	srd	rN,rN,rS
	slw	rT,r(N-1),rS1	sld	rT,r(N-1),rS1
	or	rN,rN,rT	or	rN,rN,rT
	sraw	**rT,r(N-1),rS2**	**srad**	**rT,r(N-1),rS2**
	ble	**@nextReg**	**ble**	**@nextReg**
	or	rN,rN,rT	or	rN,rN,rT
For the first register	**sraw**	**rN,rN,rS**	**srad**	**rN,rN,rS**

Multiple-Precision Immediate Right Shift Algebraic

Algebraic immediate right shifts are performed the same way as standard immediate right shifts with the exception of the high-order register. Just like the other algebraic right shift operations, the high-order register must be shifted using one of Shift Right Algebraic instructions.

Table 7-27 shows the instruction sequence required to implement a multiple-precision algebraic right shift with the shift amount specified as an immediate value. The only difference between this code sequence and the code required for a non-algebraic right shift is the *Shift Right Algebraic Immediate* instruction used to calculate the high-order register.

Table 7-27 Multiple-Precision Immediate Right Shift Algebraic Summary

Shift Stage	Word		Doubleword	
For each register except the first	`srwi` `insrwi`	`rN,rN,sh` `rN,r(N-1),sh,0`	`rldimi` `rotrdi`	`rN,r(N-1),0,64-sh` `rN,rN,sh`
For the first register	`srawi`	`rN,rN,sh`	`sradi`	`rN,rN,sh`

7.7 Obsolete Rotate and Shift Instructions

The POWER architecture defines a large number of shift and rotate instructions that are not included in the PowerPC architecture in an effort to reduce the complexity and cost of PowerPC implementations.

The 601 supports all of these instructions in hardware, but no other PowerPC implementation will do so. The instructions listed in this section should not be used, and the descriptions are provided for reference purposes only.

Obsolete Mask Instructions

The POWER architecture defines two mask-related instructions that are not included as part of the PowerPC specification. These instructions, listed in Table 7-28, are *Mask Generate*, which generates a mask from the *maskBegin* and *maskEnd* parameters, and *Mask Insert from Register*, which inserts a register into another based on a specified mask.

Table 7-28 Obsolete Mask Instructions

`maskg[.] rA,rS,rB`
Mask Generate
obsolete POWER instruction
	$mStart := rS[27:31]$
	$mEnd := rB[27:31]$
	if($mStart = mEnd+1$)
	　　　$m := $ 0xFFFF FFFF
	if($mStart < mEnd+1$)
	　　　$m := $ Mask($mStart,mEnd$)
	if($mStart > mEnd+1$)
	　　　$m := $ ~Mask($mEnd+1,mStart-1$)
	$rA \Leftarrow m$

`maskir[.] rA,rS,rB` **Mask Insert from Register** *obsolete POWER instruction*	$rA \Leftarrow ((rB)\ \&\ (rS))\ |\ (\sim(rB)\ \&\ (rA))$

The *Mask Generate* (`maskg`) instruction generates a mask in the same manner as the standard word mask facility described in §7.1 under "Word Masks." The mask begins at the specified start bit and continues to the end bit, wrapping around the word if necessary.

The main difference between this instruction and the mask generation facility found in the rotate instructions is that the *Mask Generate* instruction allows the begin and end bits to be specified in a register. This allows the masks to be specified dynamically during runtime instead of being statically defined once the instruction is assembled. For the PowerPC, the `maskg` instruction was removed in an effort to simplify the mask generation hardware.

The *Mask Insert from Register* (`maskir`) instruction uses the contents of a register (`rB`) as a mask to determine how the remaining two source registers (`rS` and `rA`) should be merged. This instruction is not part of the PowerPC specification because it requires three source registers, which would make implementations more costly.

Obsolete Rotate Instructions

The POWER architecture defines two rotate operations: *Rotate Right and Insert Bit* (`rrib`) and *Rotate Left then Mask Insert* (`rlmi`). Listed in Table 7-29, these instructions are not part of the PowerPC architecture because they both require three source operands.

Table 7-29 Obsolete Rotate Instructions

`rrib[.] rA,rS,rB` **Rotate Right and Insert Bit** *obsolete POWER instruction*	$rA[rB[27:31]] \Leftarrow rS[0]$
`rlmi[.] rA,rS,rB,mB,mE` **Rotate Left then Mask Insert** *obsolete POWER instruction*	$r := (rS)\ Q\ rB[27:31]$ $m := $ Mask(mB,mE) $rA \Leftarrow (r\ \&\ m)\ |\ ((rA)\ \&\ \sim m)$

The *Rotate Right and Insert Bit* instruction rotates bit 0 (the most significant bit or the sign bit) of rS to the right by the amount stored in $rB[27:31]$. This bit is then inserted into rA.

The *Rotate Left then Mask Insert* instruction is identical to the *Rotate Left Word Immediate then Mask Insert* (`rlwimi`) instruction, except that the shift amount is specified in a register instead of as an immediate value. This rotates a source register (rS) and inserts the rotated result into another register (rA) based on a specified mask.

Obsolete Shift Instructions

There are fifteen shift instructions—six left shifts, six right shifts, and three algebraic right shifts—are part of the POWER architecture, but not part of the PowerPC architecture. These instructions are listed in Tables 7-30, 7-31, and 7-32. All of these shift instructions use the MQ register as either a source or destination register (or both). Since the MQ register is not part of the PowerPC specification, all of these instructions needed to be eliminated.

The worst "feature" of these instructions is that the mnemonics are inconsistent and non-intuitive. Since these instructions have been removed, it is probably not worth the effort of remembering (or even trying to figure out) what each of these instructions does.

Table 7-30 Obsolete Shift Left Instructions

`sle[.] rA,rS,rB` **Shift Left Extended** *obsolete POWER instruction*	$rA \Leftarrow (rS) \ll rB[27:31]$ $MQ \Leftarrow (rS) \circlearrowleft rB[27:31]$
`sleq[.] rA,rS,rB` **Shift Left Extended with MQ** *obsolete POWER instruction*	$r := (rS) \circlearrowleft rB[27:31]$ $m := \text{Mask}(0,31\text{-}rB[27:31])$ $rA \Leftarrow (r \mathrel{\&} m) \mid (MQ \mathrel{\&} {\sim}m)$ $MQ \Leftarrow r$
`sliq[.] rA,rS,n` **Shift Left Immediate with MQ** *obsolete POWER instruction*	$rA \Leftarrow (rS) \ll n$ $MQ \Leftarrow (rS) \circlearrowleft n$
`slliq[.] rA,rS,n` **Shift Left Long Immediate with MQ** *obsolete POWER instruction*	$r := (rS) \circlearrowleft n$ $m := \text{Mask}(0,31\text{-}n)$ $rA \Leftarrow (r \mathrel{\&} m) \mid (MQ \mathrel{\&} {\sim}m)$ $MQ \Leftarrow r$

sllq[.] *rA,rS,rB* **Shift Left Long with MQ** *obsolete POWER instruction*	$r := (rS) \: Q \: rB[27{:}31]$ $m := \text{Mask}(0,31{-}rB[27{:}31])$ $\text{if}(rB[26] = 0)$ $\qquad rA \Leftarrow (r \: \& \: m) \mid (MQ \: \& \: {\sim}m)$ else $\qquad rA \Leftarrow (MQ \: \& \: m)$
slq[.] *rA,rS,rB* **Shift Left with MQ** *obsolete POWER instruction*	$\text{if}(rB[26] = 0)$ $\qquad rA \Leftarrow (rS) \ll rB[27{:}31]$ else $\qquad rA \Leftarrow 0$ $MQ \Leftarrow (rS) \: Q \: rB[27{:}31]$

The `sle` instruction left shifts rS by the amount specified by $rB[27{:}31]$ and places the result in rA. The MQ register gets the value of rS left rotated by $rB[27{:}31]$.

The `sleq` instruction is the same as the `sle` instruction, except that the value stored in rA is a combination of the original MQ register and the shifted rS.

The `sliq` instruction is identical to the `sle` instruction, except that the shift amount is specified as an immediate value.

The `slliq` instruction is identical to the `sleq` instruction, except that the shift amount is specified as an immediate value.

The `sllq` instruction is the same as the `sleq` instruction, except that the shift value is specified in $rB[26{:}31]$. This allows the shift value to range from 0 to 63. If the shift value is greater than 31, the value returned in rA is copied from the MQ register. Unlike the `sleq` instruction, this instruction does not update the MQ register.

The `slq` instruction is identical to the `sle` instruction, except that the left shift value is specified in $rB[26{:}31]$, allowing the range of shift values to be between 0 and 63. If the shift value is greater than 31, 0 is returned in rA.

Table 7-31 Obsolete Shift Right Instructions

sre[.] *rA,rS,rB* **Shift Right Extended** *obsolete POWER instruction*	$rA \Leftarrow (rS) \gg rB[27{:}31]$ $MQ \Leftarrow (rS) \: Q \: rB[27{:}31]$
sreq[.] *rA,rS,rB* **Shift Right Extended with MQ** *obsolete POWER instruction*	$r := (rS) \: Q \: rB[27{:}31]$ $m := \text{Mask}(rB[27{:}31],31)$ $rA \Leftarrow (r \: \& \: m) \mid (MQ \: \& \: {\sim}m)$ $MQ \Leftarrow r$
sriq[.] *rA,rS,n* **Shift Right Immediate with MQ** *obsolete POWER instruction*	$rA \Leftarrow (rS) \gg n$ $MQ \Leftarrow (rS) \: Q \: n$

srliq[.] rA,rS,n	$r := (rS) \circlearrowright n$
Shift Right Long Immediate with MQ	$m := \text{Mask}(n,31)$
obsolete POWER instruction	$rA \Leftarrow (r \ \& \ m) \mid (\text{MQ} \ \& \ \sim m)$
	$\text{MQ} \Leftarrow r$
srlq[.] rA,rS,rB	$r := (rS) \circlearrowright rB[27{:}31]$
Shift Right Long with MQ	$m := \text{Mask}(rB[27{:}31],31)$
obsolete POWER instruction	$\text{if}(rB[26] = 0)$
	$\quad\quad rA \Leftarrow (r \ \& \ m) \mid (\text{MQ} \ \& \ \sim m)$
	else
	$\quad\quad rA \Leftarrow (\text{MQ} \ \& \ m)$
srq[.] rA,rS,rB	$\text{if}(rB[26] = 0)$
Shift Right with MQ	$\quad\quad rA \Leftarrow (rS) \gg rB[27{:}31]$
obsolete POWER instruction	else
	$\quad\quad rA \Leftarrow 0$
	$\text{MQ} \Leftarrow (rS) \circlearrowright rB[27{:}31]$

The six obsolete *Shift Right* instructions are analagous to the six obsolete *Shift Left* instructions, and follow the same bizarre naming convention.

The `sre` instruction right shifts rS by the amount specified by rB[27:31] and places the result in rA. The MQ register gets the value of rS right rotated by rB[27:31].

The `sreq` instruction is the same as the `sre` instruction, except that the value stored in rA is a combination of the original MQ register and the shifted rS.

The `sriq` instruction is identical to the `sre` instruction, except that the shift amount is specified as an immediate value.

The `srliq` instruction is identical to the `sreq` instruction, except that the shift amount is specified as an immediate value.

The `srlq` instruction is the same as the `sreq` instruction, except that the shift value is specified in rB[26:31]. This allows the shift value to range from 0 to 63. If the shift value is greater than 31, the value returned in rA is copied from the MQ register. Unlike the `sreq` instruction, this instruction does not update the MQ register.

The `srq` instruction is identical to the `sre` instruction, except that the right shift value is specified in rB[26:31], allowing the range of shift values to be between 0 and 63. If the shift value is greater than 31, 0 is returned in rA.

Table 7-32 Obsolete Shift Right Algebraic Instructions

sraiq[.] rA,rS,n **Shift Right Algebraic Immediate with MQ** *obsolete POWER instruction*	$rA \Leftarrow (rS) \overset{s}{\gg} n$ $MQ \Leftarrow (rS) \circlearrowright n$ update XER[CA]

sraq[.] rA,rS,rB
Shift Right Algebraic with MQ
obsolete POWER instruction
	if(rB[26] = 0)
	      $rA \Leftarrow (rS) \overset{s}{\gg} rB[27{:}31]$
	else
	      $rA \Leftarrow rS[0]$
	$MQ \Leftarrow (rS) \circlearrowright rB[27{:}31]$
	update XER[CA]

srea[.] rA,rS,rB **Shift Right Extended Algebraic** *obsolete POWER instruction*	$rA \Leftarrow (rS) \overset{s}{\gg} rB[27{:}31]$ $MQ \Leftarrow (rS) \circlearrowright rB[27{:}31]$ update XER[CA]

The sraiq instruction is the same as the sriq instruction, except that it performs an algebraic right shift.

The sraq instruction is the same as the srq instructions, except that an algebraic right shift is performed. If the shift amount is greater than 31, the value in rA is a word of sign bits from rS. This can be either 0x0000 0000 or 0xFFFF FFFF.

The srea instruction performs an algebraic right shift operation on rS but is otherwise identical to the sre instruction.

All three of the algebraic shift instructions update the Carry bit in the XER. The Carry is set to '1' if the shifted value is negative and any '1' bits have been shifted out the right side of the register. This is useful when using the algebraic right shift to perform quick divide operations.

Floating-Point Instructions | 8

Floating-point arithmetic operations are significantly more complicated than their fixed-point counterparts. The underlying principles of floating-point are not conceptually difficult, but a lot of background needs to be presented before the floating-point instructions can be understood.

After providing a general introduction to floating-point concepts and data formats, this chapter discusses the instructions that implement the various floating-point operations defined by the IEEE floating-point specification (IEEE-754) as implemented in the PowerPC specification. These include instructions to perform arithmetic, comparison, and conversion operations.

This chapter does not include descriptions of the floating-point load and store instructions. These instructions are discussed in Chapter 5 "Load and Store Instructions."

8.1 Floating-Point Data Representation

Floating-point arithmetic on a computer is performed using a binary floating-point representation. This floating-point format is analogous to the decimal floating-point system commonly known as *scientific notation*.

In scientific notation, a number is represented by allowing the decimal or *radix* point to be variable or "float," and a new number, the *exponent*, is introduced to keep track of where the current radix point is relative to the actual radix point. Thus, a number like 5280 is represented by two numbers: a significand of 5.28

and an exponent of 3 (because the radix point was shifted three places to the left). Since this is a decimal (base 10) number, each shift of the decimal point increases (or decreases) the value of the number by a power of 10, thus, this number is commonly written as 5.28×10^3.

One advantage of this system is that it allows very large and very small numbers to be expressed easily, for example, 2.9979246×10^8 (the speed of light in a vacuum *meters / sec*) and 6.626176×10^{-34} (Planck's constant *Joules×sec*). Numbers like these are unwieldy in a system where the radix point is not allowed to float.

Binary floating-point values are represented in a way that is very similar to scientific notation. The only differences are that the values are binary (base 2) values and that it is a *binary point* that floats to the left or right. As an example, the decimal value 868 is represented in binary as b1101100100. This would be stored as a binary floating-point value as $b1.1011001 \times b10^{b1001}$ or 1.6953125×2^9.

One additional convention that is used for floating-point numbers is the concept of *normalization*. A normalized number is one where there is only one digit to the left of the radix point, and that one digit is non-zero. For example, 2.998 and 6.63 are both normalized numbers. The advantage of using normalized numbers is that it allows two floating-point numbers to be compared by simply comparing the exponents and then, if the exponents are equal, comparing the significands. Other arithmetic operations are also greatly simplified when operating on normalized values.

Floating-Point Formats

A binary floating-point number is represented by recording three values: the *sign*, the *significand* and the *exponent*, which are related in the following manner.

$$(-1)^{sign} \cdot significand \cdot 2^{exponent}$$

The *sign* is a one-bit value that is either 0 (for positive numbers) or 1 (for negative numbers). The *significand* and *exponent* are binary values that are interpreted as described in the previous section.

The PowerPC architecture supports the two basic IEEE-754 floating-point formats: 32-bit single-precision and 64-bit double-precision. For the single-precision format, the *sign* is one bit, the *exponent* is represented in eight bits and the *significand* is represented by a 23-bit value. For double-precision values, the *sign* is one bit, the *exponent* is 11 bits and the *significand* is 52 bits. These formats are shown in Figure 8-1 and Figure 8-2 .

Figure 8-1   Format of Single-PrecisionValues

0	1		8	9		31
s	exponent			significand		

Figure 8-2   Format of Double-Precision Values

0	1		11	12		63
s	exponent			significand		

The fact that there are two precision types may seem to cause a small problem on the PowerPC since the floating-point registers are all 64 bits in width. This width is ideal for double-precision values, but something must be done to handle the single-precision values. The PowerPC architecture eliminates this problem by storing all floating-point values in registers as double-precision.

Single-precision values (when stored in registers) are thus identical to double-precision values with respect to how the bits are interpreted. The only differences between register-based single- and double-precision values are

- The range of the exponent (double-precision allows 11 bits for the exponent; single-precision allows only eight bits).
- The accuracy of the fraction (only the leftmost 23 of the 52 fraction bits are used for single-precision values; the remaining bits should be 0).

Exponent Bias

The *exponent* value is not stored directly in the exponent field. A *bias* term is added to the exponent so that the stored exponent value is always a positive number. This biased value is referred to as the *biased exponent* and is related to the exponent by the equation:

$$biased\ exponent\ =\ exponent + bias$$

The *bias* value is 127 for single-precision values and 1023 for double-precision values. This gives an potential exponent range of 2^{-127} to 2^{128} for single-precision and 2^{-1023} to 2^{1024} for the double-precision format. However, the minimum and maximum exponent values are used to represent special floating-point values (discussed later). This reduces the effective exponent range down to 2^{-126} to 2^{127} for single-precision and 2^{-1022} to 2^{1023} for double-precision. Table 8-1 shows the relationship between the *exponent* and the *biased exponent* values for single- and double-precision numbers.

Table 8-1 Exponent Encodings for Single- and Double-Precision Numbers

exponent	Single-Precision biased exponent		Double-Precision biased exponent
	single[1]	double[2]	
1023	-	-	2046
1022	-	-	2045
...	-	-	...
127	254	1150	1150
126	253	1149	1149
...	...	...	...
0	127	1023	1023
...	...	...	...
-125	2	898	898
-126	1	897	897
...	-	-	...
-1021	-	-	2
-1022	-	-	1

[1] The single-precision biased exponent is used when a single-precision value is stored using the single-precision format (as in when a single-precision value is stored in memory).

[2] The double-precision biased exponent is used when a single-precision value is stored using the double-precision format (as in when a single-precision value is stored in a floating-point register).

In this chapter, the *exponent* value will be used almost exclusively. When a biased exponent value is referred to, it will always be explicitly noted as a *biased exponent* to eliminate any potential ambiguity.

Representing Floating-Point Values

There are five classes of floating-point values:

- Normalized Numbers
- Denormalized Numbers
- Zeros
- Infinities
- Not a Numbers (NaNs)

The first four of these classes represent real numbers, and the last class (NaN) is used to represent invalid numbers (for example, $\sqrt{-1}$ or $\infty \div \infty$).

Normalized numbers are the most prevalent of the number classes. The range of the magnitude of normalized numbers extends to include values that are very small and values that are very large. The range of normalized numbers was chosen to coincide with the range of non-0 values in common use.

Denormalized numbers are used to represent very small non-0 values whose magnitude is below the range of normalized numbers.

Zeros are used to represent zero values. A zero value can be either positive or negative, but most operations treat both forms identically.

Infinities are used to represent values whose magnitude is too large to fit within the range of normalized numbers. Infinities may be positive or negative.

Table 8-2 summarizes these first four classes of floating-point numbers and gives an indication of how they are ordered with respect to each other and what range of values they can accept.

Table 8-2 Allowable Ranges for Floating-Point Numbers

	Approximate Range of Values	
	Single	**Double**
+ Infinity	$+\infty$	$+\infty$
+ Normalized	10^{-38} to 10^{38}	10^{-308} to 10^{308}
+ Denormalized	10^{-45} to 10^{-38}	10^{-324} to 10^{-308}
+ Zero	$+0$	$+0$
- Zero	-0	-0
- Denormalized	-10^{-38} to -10^{-45}	-10^{-308} to -10^{-324}
- Normalized	-10^{38} to -10^{-38}	-10^{308} to -10^{-308}
- Infinity	$-\infty$	$-\infty$

The last class of floating-point numbers are the *Not a Numbers*. There are two types of NaNs: Signalling and Quiet. Signalling NaNs cause an exception to occur when they are used as operands to most floating-point operations while Quiet NaNs do not.

Table 8-3 shows how these numbers are encoded.

Table 8-3 Exponent and Fraction Encodings for Floating-Point Numbers

	Biased Exponent		Fraction
	single	**double**	
Quiet NaN	255	2047	non-0 high-order bit set
Signalling NaN	255	2047	non-0 high-order bit clear
Infinity	255	2047	0
Normalized	1 to 254	1 to 2046	any
Denormalized	0		non-0
Zero	0		0

Normalized Numbers

Binary floating-point values are normalized using the definition of normalized given earlier. All of the bits to the left of the binary point, except for the unit bit, must be '0', and the unit bit must be non-0. The *unit* bit is the bit that is in the unit position, that is, the position immediately to the left of the binary point. Thus, b1.101 is a normalized binary floating-point value while b101.001 and b0.0011 are not.

Since the unit position is forced to be non-'0', the unit position *must* be a '1' (the only other possibility for a binary number). And since the unit position is always a '1', there is no reason for it to be stored explicitly. Hence, all normalized floating-point numbers have an *implicit* unit bit of '1'. This bit is not stored as part of the significand, which gives the significand an extra bit of precision. The portion of the significand without the implicit unit bit is known as the *fraction*.

The relationship given earlier for floating-point values can be modified slightly to account for normalized numbers using the equation:

$$(-1)^{sign} \cdot 1.fraction \cdot 2^{exponent}$$

As an example, the value 0.1875 (binary: 0.0011) is stored in single-precision by converting the value to $b1.1 \times 2^{-3}$ and then storing -3 for the exponent (*biased exponent* = 127 + -3 = 124), and recording b100 0000 0000 0000 0000 0000 (1.1 with the '1' stored implicitly) as the significand.

The range of values representable as normalized numbers is summarized in Table 8-4.

Table 8-4 Range of Values for Normalized Floating-Point Numbers

	Floating-Point Format	
	Single-Precision	**Double-Precision**
Biased exponent range	1 to 254	1 to 2046
Exponent range	-126 to 127	-1022 to 1023
Minimum representable value	1×2^{-126}	1×2^{-1022}
	$\approx 1.18 \times 10^{-38}$	$\approx 2.23 \times 10^{-308}$
Maximum representable value	$\approx 2 \times 2^{127}$	$\approx 2 \times 2^{1023}$
	$\approx 3.40 \times 10^{38}$	$\approx 1.80 \times 10^{308}$

Denormalized Numbers

Denormalized numbers provide a mechanism for representing numbers that are smaller in magnitude than the smallest representable normalized number.

Denormalized values have an exponent value that is always equal to the smallest allowable exponent (1-*bias*) for normalized numbers (corresponding to a biased exponent of 0), but they do not require the significand to be in normalized form. Since the exponent is not allowed to vary, the range of values for denormalized numbers comes from the ability to vary the fraction.

A consequence of a non-normalized fraction is that there is no implict '1' bit in the unit position for denormalized numbers, and there may be any number of '0's immediately to the right of the binary point. Both b0.100 × 2^{-126} and b0.0011 × 2^{-126} are examples of single-precision values in denormalized form.

Denormalized numbers can be interpreted as

$$(-1)^{sign} \cdot 0.fraction \cdot 2^{(1-bias)}$$

The range of values representable as denormalized numbers is summarized in Table 8-5.

Table 8-5 Range of Values for Denormalized Numbers

	Floating-Point Format	
	Single-Precision	**Double-Precision**
Exponent	-126	-1022
Minimum representable value	$1 \times 2^{(-126-23)}$	$1 \times 2^{(-1022-52)}$
	$\approx 1.40 \times 10^{-45}$	$\approx 4.94 \times 10^{-324}$
Maximum representable value	$\approx 1 \times 2^{-126}$	$\approx 1 \times 2^{-1022}$
	$\approx 1.18 \times 10^{-38}$	$\approx 2.23 \times 10^{-308}$

Zero values

Zero values are represented by a biased exponent of 0 (just like denormalized numbers) and a fraction of 0. As with denormalized numbers, there is no implicit "1" bit prefix for the significand.

Note that zero values can be either positive or negative. For most operations, negative zeros are identical to positive zeros. There are, however, cases where a negative zero will be returned as the result of an operation. For example, *x* - *x* when in *Round to -∞* mode and the square root of -0 both return -0 as the result.

Infinities

Infinity values are used to represent values that are greater in magnitude than the largest normalized floating-point value. Infinities can be either positive or negative, with positive infinity defined as being greater than all other representable numbers and negative infinity defined as being less than all other representable numbers.

Infinity values can be generated when certain exceptions are disabled and an overflow or a division by 0 occurs. In the case of divide by 0, the returned infinity value will be of the proper sign.

Not a Numbers (NaNs)

The Not a Number (NaN) values are used to encode values that are not valid floating-point numbers. These values can occur when variables are uninitialized or when certain operations are performed (for example, the square root of a value less than 0).

NaNs do not fit on the number line of valid numbers. If a NaN is compared with a real number, an *unordered* result will be returned since NaNs are neither greater than, less than, or equal to any real value.

There are two types of NaN values: Signalling and Quiet. A Signalling NaN (SNaN) causes an exception if it is used as an operand for a floating-point operation. A Quiet NaN (QNaN) is the most common type and silently propagates through most floating-point operations.

SNaNs are never created by floating-point operations but may be created manually (for example, to identify uninitialized memory).

8.2 Floating-Point Operation

This section discusses some of the general issues that apply to almost all of the floating-point operations. These issues include a description of normalization and rounding and also describe how floating-point exceptions and interrupts are handled by the processor.

Normalization and Denormalization

Values calculated by the floating-point operations are typically not in a normalized form. However, before the result can be stored in a floating-point register, the value must be normalized. The normalization process is quite simple, but it requires that the intermediate value is sufficiently precise so that the normalized result has the required precision.

A number is normalized by shifting the fraction one bit to the left and decrementing the exponent until the unit bit of the significand is '1.' Since normalization involves decrementing the exponent, it is possible that an exponent underflow exception will occur.

A number is denormalized when it is too small (in magnitude) to fit in the normalized representation. Denormalization is performed by shifting the significand to the right while incrementing the exponent. Note that this operation may cause a *loss of accuracy* due to bits dropping off the right side of the fraction. If a loss of accuracy occurs, then the Underflow Exception bit of the FPSCR (FPSCR[UX]) will be set.

Rounding

Rounding is necessary because most of the floating-point operations can produce intermediate results that are more precise than can be represented in single- or double-precision values. Rounding provides a way of generating the "best" representable value and gives the programmer some control over how the best value is determined.

There are four defined rounding modes:

- Round to Nearest
- Round toward Zero
- Round toward +Infinity
- Round toward -Infinity

Rounding is performed by choosing one of two *rounding candidates*. These candidates are the representable numbers immediately above and below (in terms of magnitude) the actual value. The lower value is calculated by truncating the low-order bits of the actual value so that it will fit in the target representation. The upper value is derived from the lower value by incrementing the least significant bit of the fraction. One way of understanding these two values is by noting that the lower candidate is always closer to zero than the actual value, while the upper candidate is further from zero (closer to +/- ∞).

Table 8-6 summarizes how the sign of the result and the rounding mode combine to select one of the two rounding candidates. In this table, 'L' refers to the lower candidate and 'U' refers to the upper candidate.

Table 8-6 Choosing the Best Rounding Candidate

Rounding Mode	Sign of Actual Value	
	+	-
Round to Nearest	choose best approximation	
Round toward Zero	L	L
Round toward +Infinity	U	L
Round toward -Infinity	L	U

For Round to Nearest mode, the candidate closest to the actual value is chosen. In the case of a tie, the *even* candidate (least significant bit of 0) is chosen.

Rounding is further complicated when one of the two rounding candidates does not exist, for example, when there is no number larger than the actual value that will fit in the target representation. In these cases, either an Overflow or an Underflow exception will be signalled. If the upper candidate does not exist, then an Overflow Exception will be signalled. If the lower candidate does not exist, then an Underflow Exception will be signalled. These exceptions are discussed later in the "Exceptions" section.

Interrupts

An interrupt is a mechanism through which the processor can change state to handle abnormal conditions, errors, or external signals. Interrupts are related to exceptions in that an exception may cause an interrupt to be generated.

A floating-point exception does not always result in an interrupt. A floating-point interrupt handler is invoked only when all of the following conditions are met:

- An exception must have occured.
- That type of exception must be enabled. Each exception type has a corresponding enable bit in the FPSCR that must be set to 1 for an interrupt of that type to occur.
- Floating-point exceptions must be enabled by setting the Floating-Point Exception Mode bits in the Machine State Register (MSR[FE0,FE1]) to an appropriate value.

Note that the "Exception Enable" bits in the FPSCR and the "Exception Mode" bits in the MSR do not control whether the corresponding *exception* will occur. The exception will occur and the appropriate bit in the FPSCR will be set regardless of whether the exception is "enabled" or not. The "Exception Enable" bits merely control whether or not an interrupt will be generated in response to the exception. The only exception to this occurs with the Underflow Exception. In this case, the setting of the Underflow Exception Enable bit in the FPSCR affects the conditions under which an Underflow Exception will occur in addition to controlling whether or not an interrupt should be generated.

Interrupts (floating-point and otherwise) are discussed in greater detail in Chapter 12 "Exceptions & Interrupts."

Exceptions

Floating-point exceptions are caused by abnormal circumstances during the execution of a floating-point instruction or through a software request.

When an exception occurs, the processor responds by performing one of three tasks:

- Set a flag in the FPSCR.
- Invoke an interrupt handler.
- Set a flag and invoke an interrupt handler.

Which action the processor performs depends on the type of exception and on the settings of the "Exception Enable" bits in the FPSCR and the "Exception Mode" bits in the MSR.

There are five types of floating-point exceptions that may be generated: Invalid Operation, Zero Divide, Overflow, Underflow, and Inexact.

Invalid Operation Exception

The Invalid Operation Exception is signalled if either of the operands is invalid for the operation being performed. The eight types of operations that cause the Invalid Operation Exception are

- Any arithmetic operation involving a Signalling NaN (Load, Store, Move, and Select operations do not cause this exception.)
- $\infty - \infty$
- $0 \times \infty$
- $0/0$ or ∞/∞
- $\sqrt{x}$, where $x < 0$ (Only on processors that implement one of the square root instructions.)
- Invalid floating-point to integer conversion (A float to int conversion involving overflow, infinity, or NaN.)
- Invalid comparison (Using any sort of NaN as an operand to `fcmpo`.)
- Software request (By setting FPSCR[VXSOFT]).)

The details of how the target and result flags are updated differ for each type of invalid operation. In general, if Invalid Operation Exceptions are enabled (FPSCR[VE]=1), then the result will be unchanged. If Invalid Operation Exceptions are disabled, then the result will be a Quiet NaN.

Zero Divide Exception

The Zero Divide Exception is signalled when a finite, non-0 number is divided by 0. This exception can be generated by the divide instructions or any of the optional reciprocal estimate instructions (`fres`, `frsqrte`).

A Zero Divide Exception always causes the FPSCR to be updated by setting the Zero Divide Exception (ZE) bit and clearing the Fraction Rounded (FR) and Fraction Inexact (FI) bits.

If Zero Divide Exceptions are enabled (FPSCR[ZE]=1), the target register is left unchanged.

If Zero Divide Exceptions are disabled (FPSCR[ZE]=0), the target register is set to a properly signed ∞, and the FP Result Flags (FPRF) are set to indicate that the result is +/- Infinity.

Overflow Exception

The Overflow Exception is signalled whenever the magnitude of the rounded result (assuming the exponent range is unbounded) exceeds the magnitude of the destination format. The Overflow Exception bit (FPSCR[OX]) is always set in response to an overflow exception. Additional actions depend on the current setting of the Overflow Exception Enable bit (FPSCR[OE]).

If FPSCR[OE] = 1, then the overflow interrupt handler is invoked, which adjusts the exponent of the result so that it fits in the range of normalized numbers and then stores the new result in the target register. The exponent is adjusted by subtracting 1536 for double-precision instructions and by subtracting 192 for single-precision instructions and the `frsp` instruction. FPSCR[FPRF] is also set to indicate the class and sign of the result (which will be +/- Normalized Number).

If FPSCR[OE] = 0, then the overflow interrupt handler is not invoked and the result is adjusted based on the current rounding mode before being stored in the target register. The result is adjusted according to Table 8-7.

Table 8-7 Rounded Overflow Result Based on Rounding Mode

Rounding Mode	Sign[1]	Result
Round to Nearest	+	+ Infinity
	-	- Infinity
Round toward Zero	+	+ Largest normalized number
	-	- Largest normalized number
Round toward +Infinity	+	+ Infinity
	-	- Largest normalized number
Round toward -Infinity	+	+ Largest normalized number
	-	- Infinity
[1] Sign is the sign of the intermediate result before rounding		

In addition, the Inexact Exception (XX) and Fraction Inexact (FI) bits of the FPSCR are set and the Fraction Rounded (FR) bit is set to an undefined value. The FP Result Flags (FPSCR[FPRF]) are also set to indicate the class and sign of the result (which will be either +/- Normalized Number or +/- Infinity).

Underflow Exception

The conditions that cause an Underflow Exception are different depending on whether Underflow Exceptions are currently enabled (FPSCR[UE]=1) or disabled (FPSCR[UE]=0). The basic underflow conditions are

- If the intermediate result is *tiny* (a tiny result is a non-0 value that is smaller than the smallest normalized number).
- If there is any *loss of accuracy* (loss of accuracy occurs when fraction bits are shifted out to the right during denormalization).

If FPSCR[UE] = 1, any tiny result will cause underflow. If FPSCR[UE] = 0, then the result must be tiny and there must be a loss of accuracy for underflow to occur.

If underflow occurs, then the Underflow Exception bit in the FPSCR (FPSCR[UX]) is always set. Additional actions depend on whether or not Underflow Exceptions are currently enabled.

If Underflow Exceptions are enabled, then the underflow interrupt handler is invoked, which adjusts the exponent of the result so that it fits in the range of normalized numbers and then stores the new result in the target register. The exponent is adjusted by adding 1536 for double-precision instructions and by adding 192 for single-precision instructions and the `frsp` instruction.

If Underflow Exceptions are disabled, then the underflow interrupt handler is not invoked and the result is rounded and placed in the target register.

Regardless of the current enabled/disabled state of Underflow Exceptions, FPSCR[FPRF] is always set to indicate the class and sign of the result. The value of FPRF will be +/- Normalized Number if exceptions are enabled, and either +/- Denormalized Number or +/- Zero if exceptions are currently disabled.

Inexact Exception

An Inexact Exception occurs whenever the rounded result differs from the calculated intermediate result (assuming that the intermediate result was of unlimited range and precision). An Inexact Exception also occurs when the rounding operation results in an overflow and Overflow Exceptions are disabled (FPSCR[OE] = 0).

An interrupt is not invoked in response to an Inexact Exception. When an Inexact Exception occurs, the result is placed in the target register, the Inexact Exception bit (FPSCR[XX]) is set, and the FP Result Flags (FPSCR[FPRF]) are set to reflect the class and sign of the stored result.

8.3 Floating-Point Instructions

All of the floating-point instructions (except the compare) allow a '.' suffix and many also allow an 's' suffix to be appended to the base mnemonic.

The '.' suffix sets the *record bit* for the instruction. For floating-point instructions, this means that exception information is copied from the FPSCR and placed in field 1 of the Condition Register (CR{1}), after the completion of the operation.

The interpretation of the bits in CR{1} is summarized in Table 8-8.

Table 8-8 CR{1} After Executing an FP Instruction with the Record Bit Set

CR{1} bit	Name	Description
0	FX	**FP Exception Summary** Set whenever any exception bit is set. This bit is the logical OR of all of the other exception bits.
1	FEX	**FP Enabled Exception** Set whenever any *enabled* exception bit is set. This bit is the logical OR of all of the exception bits that are currently enabled.
2	VX	**FP Invalid Operation Exception Summary** Set whenever any sort of invalid operation occurs. This bit is the logical OR of all of the invalid operation exception bits.
3	OX	**FP Overflow Exception** Set whenever the exponent of the rounded result is larger than the largest valid exponent.

The 's' suffix indicates that the operation should be performed by interpreting the values in the operand registers as if they contained single-precision data. Since floating-point registers always contain double-precision data, the 's' suffix more accurately indicates that the double-precision data in the specified source registers is *representable* in the single-precision format. If the input values to a single-precision operation are not representable as single-precision values, then the result is placed in the output register, and the status bits in the FPSCR and CR (if the record bit is set) are undefined.

FP Move Instructions

The four floating-point instructions listed in Table 8-9 move the contents of one floating-point register into another floating-point register. One of these instructions (fmr) moves the data unaltered, while the others modify the sign bit of the value before storing it in the destination register.

These instructions do not interpret the data being moved in any way. Thus, it is possible to perform non-sensible operations such as taking the absolute value of a Signalling NaN and instruction will cause no exceptions will be raised.

In addition, none of these instructions affect the FPSCR.

Table 8-9 Floating-Point Move Instructions

fabs[.] frT,frB FP Absolute Value	$frT \Leftarrow \|(frA)\|$
fmr[.] frT,frB FP Move Register	$frT \Leftarrow (frB)$
fnabs[.] frT,frB FP Negative Absolute Value	$frT \Leftarrow -\|(frB)\|$
fneg[.] frT,frB FP Negate	$frT \Leftarrow -(frB)$

The `fabs` instruction takes the absolute value of frB and places it in frT. The absolute value is calculated by forcing the sign of the result to be 0.

The `fmr` instruction simply copies the contents of frB into frT.

The `fnabs` instruction takes the negative of the absolute value of frB and places it in frT. The negative absolute value is calculated by forcing the sign of the result to be 1.

The `fneg` instruction negates the value of frB and places it in frT. The value is negated by inverting the sign of frB.

FP Arithmetic Instructions

The four basic arithmetic operations listed in Table 8-10 are supported directly by PowerPC instructions. These operations are add, subtract, multiply, and divide.

All of these instructions allow the '**.**' suffix to be specified. This suffix causes the four high-order status bits from the FPSCR to be copied into field 1 of the Condition Register. The copied bits are: FX (FP Exception Summary), FEX (FP Enabled Exception Summary), VX (FP Invalid Operation Summary), and OX (FP Overflow Exception).

There are two variants for each of the instructions: a double-precision version and a single-precision version. Each version operates on operands of the appropriate size and returns a result of the same size. If a single-precision instruction contains data that is not representable as single-precision data, then the results stored in the target register and status register (FPSCR and CR) are undefined.

Table 8-10 Floating-Point Arithmetic Instructions

`fadd[s][.] frT,frA,frB` FP Add [Single-Precision]	$frT \Leftarrow (frA) + (frB)$
`fdiv[s][.] frT,frA,frB` FP Divide [Single-Precision]	$frT \Leftarrow (frA) \div (frB)$
`fmul[s][.] frT,frA,frC` FP Multiply [Single-Precision]	$frT \Leftarrow (frA) \times (frC)$
`fsub[s][.] frT,frA,frB` FP Subtract [Single-Precision]	$frT \Leftarrow (frA) - (frB)$

The *Floating-Point Add* instruction calculates the result of adding the two operands and places the result in the target register. The add operation is implemented by comparing the exponents of the two operands and adding (or subtracting, if the signs of the two operands are not the same) the fractions. If the exponents do not match, the fraction of the operand with the smaller exponent is shifted to the right until the exponents match, and then the fractions are added together and rounded to produce the result in the appropriate format.

The divide operation is performed by subtracting the exponents and dividing the fractions of the operands.

The multiply operation is implemented by adding the exponents of the two operands and multiplying the two fractions to produce the result.

The *Floating-Point Subtract* instruction performs the same operation as the *FP Add* instruction, except that the operands (fractions) are subtracted instead of added.

In addition to the basic arithmetic operations described above, the PowerPC also defines a variety of *Multiply-Add* instructions. Listed in Table 8-11, these instructions provide a multiply and an add as a single operation, without an intermediate rounding step (which would be necessary if the operation was implemented as two separate instructions). This benefits both the speed and the accuracy of the computed result.

Table 8-11 Floating-Point Multiply-Add Instructions

`fmadd[s][.] frT,frA,frC,frB` FP Multiply-Add [Single-Precision]	$frT \Leftarrow (frA) \times (frC) + (frB)$
`fmsub[s][.] frT,frA,frC,frB` FP Multiply-Subtract [Single-Precision]	$frT \Leftarrow (frA) \times (frC) - (frB)$
`fnmadd[s][.] frT,frA,frC,frB` FP Negative Multiply-Add [Single-Precision]	$frT \Leftarrow -((frA) \times (frC) + (frB))$
`fnmsub[s][.] frT,frA,frC,frB` FP Negative Multiply-Subtract [Single-Precision]	$frT \Leftarrow -((frA) \times (frC) - (frB))$

The `fmadd` instruction is the basic *Multiply-Add* instruction: it first multiplies frA with frC, and then it adds frB to the result and stores the final value in frT.

The `fmsub` instruction is the same as the `fmadd` instruction except that the contents of frB are subtracted from the multiplied result.

The remaining two *Multiply-Add* instructions are variants of the first two. These instructions, `fnmadd` and `fnmsub`, negate the result before storing the value in frT.

FP Comparison Instructions

The two instructions listed in Table 8-12 which compare the contents of two floating-point registers and return the result in one of the Condition Register fields. The only difference between these two compare instructions is how they handle NaN operands.

Table 8-12 Floating-Point Compare Instructions

`fcmpo crfT,frA,frB` FP Compare Ordered	$CR\{crfT\} \Leftarrow OFCmp(frA,frB)$
`fcmpu crfT,frA,frB` FP Compare Unordered	$CR\{crfT\} \Leftarrow UFCmp(frA,frB)$

The *FP Compare* instructions compare the contents of the two floating-point registers and place the result of the compare in the specified field of the Condition Register. Table 8-13 tells how the bits of the target CR field are interpreted.

Table 8-13 CR Field Bit Interpretations after Floating-Point Compare

CR{crfT} Bit	Name	Description
0	FL	FP Less Than Set if (frA) < (frB)
1	FG	FP Greater Than Set if (frA) > (frB)
2	FE	FP Equal Set if (frA) = (frB)
3	FU	FP Unordered Set if either of the two values being compared is NaN

The two compare instructions differ in how they handle NaN operands: the `fcmpo` instruction will flag an invalid operation if it encounters any sort of NaN, while the `fcmpu` instruction will only flag Signalling NaNs.

The `fcmpo` instruction reacts in the following manner when NaN operands are encountered. First, if either of the operands is a Signalling NaN, then the VXS-NAN (FP Invalid Operation Exception for Signalling NaN) bit of the FPSCR is set.

Additionally, the VXVC (FP Invalid Operation Exception for Invalid Compare) bit of the FPSCR will be set if either of these conditions are true:

- If either of the two operands is a Signalling NaN and the VE (FP Invalid Operation Exception Enable) bit of the FPSCR is 0 (disabled).
- If at least one of the operands is a Quiet NaN and neither of the operands is a Signalling NaN.

Note that if FPSCR[VE] is enabled and one of the operands is a Signalling NaN, then the Invalid Operation Exception handler will always be invoked (because FPSCR[VXSNAN] will be set). Thus, it is unnecessary to set FPSCR[VXVC] in this case. If FPSCR[VE] is not enabled, then the handler will not be invoked and FPSCR[VXVC] needs to be set to indicate that the compare operation is invalid.

The `fcmpu` instruction will set FPSCR[VXSNAN] if a Signalling NaN is specified as one of the operands, but will never set FPSCR[VXVC].

Table 8-14 summarizes the situations under which the floating-point compare instructions cause exceptions. An 'X' indicates that an Invalid Operation Exception will be invoked, and a '-' indicates that the instruction will complete without causing any exceptions.

Table 8-14 Operands that Cause Exceptions for FP Compare

		fcmpo			fcmpu		
		operand2			operand2		
		SNaN	QNaN	normal	SNaN	QNaN	normal
operand1	SNaN	X	X	X	X	X	X
operand1	QNaN	X	X	X	X	-	-
operand1	normal	X	X	-	X	-	-

FP Conversion Instructions

The floating-point conversion instructions listed in Tables 8-15, 8-16, and 8-17 provide a simple method of converting between the various numeric formats provided for by the PowerPC architecture.

§8.4 "Floating-Point Conversions" provides more information about converting between various number formats.

Table 8-15 Floating-Point Rounding Instruction

frsp[.] frT,frB FP Round to Single-Precision	frT ⇐ Double2Single(frB)

The *FP Round to Single-Precision* instruction takes the double-precision value stored in frB, rounds it to single-precision, and then stores the rounded result in frT. If the value in frB is already in single-precision range, its value is simply copied into frT.

Table 8-16 Floating-Point Convert to Integer Instructions

fctiw[.] frT,frB FP Convert to Integer Word	frT[32:63] ⇐ FPtoInt32(frB)
fctiwz[.] frT,frB FP Convert to Integer Word with Round toward Zero	frT[32:63] ⇐ FPtoInt32Rnd0(frB)
fctid[.] frT,frB FP Convert to Integer Doubleword *64-bit implementations only*	frT ⇐ FPtoInt64(frB)
fctidz[.] frT,frB FP Convert to Integer Doubleword with Round toward Zero *64-bit implementations only*	frT ⇐ FPtoInt64Rnd0(frB)

The `fctiw` instruction converts the double-precision value in frB to an integer word using the current rounding mode (defined by FPSCR[RN]).

The `fctiwz` instruction converts the double-precision value in frB to an integer word using the *Round to Zero* (truncate) rounding mode.

The `fctid` and `fctidz` instructions perform the same operation as `fctiw` and `fctiwz`, but they convert the value to a doubleword.

Table 8-17 Floating-Point Convert from Integer Instruction

fcfid[.] frT,frB FP Convert from Integer Doubleword *64-bit implementations only*	frT ⇐ Int64toFP(frB)

The `fcfid` instruction takes the 64-bit integer stored in frB and converts it to a double-precision floating-point value. The result is stored in frT.

Optional Floating-Point Instructions

Currently, the four floating-point instructions listed in Table 8-18 are defined as optional. Three of these instructions are part of the Graphical Group, and the fourth instruction belongs to the General Group.

Table 8-18 Optional Floating-Point Instructions

fres[.] frT, frB **FP Reciprocal Estimate Single-Precision** *part of the Graphical group of optional instructions*	$frT \Leftarrow\; \approx \dfrac{1}{(frB)}$
frsqrte[.] frT, frB **FP Reciprocal Square Root Estimate** *part of the Graphical group of optional instructions*	$frT \Leftarrow\; \approx \dfrac{1}{\sqrt{(frB)}}$
fsel[.] frT, frA, frC, frB **FP Select** *part of the Graphical group of optional instructions*	$frT \Leftarrow ((frA) \geq 0.0)\ ?\ (frC)$ $: (frB))$
fsqrt[s][.] frT, frB **FP Square Root [Single-Precision]** *part of the General group of optional instructions*	$frT \Leftarrow \sqrt{(frB)}$

The `fres` instruction calculates a single-precision approximation of the reciprocal of the source operand and stores the result in the destination register. The precision of the estimated result is correct to within one part in 256 of the actual value.

The `frsqrte` instruction calculates a double-precision estimate of the reciprocal of the square root of the source operand frB and stores the result in frT. The precision of the estimated result is correct to within one part in 32 of the actual reciprocal-square root value.

The `fsel` instruction provides an operation similar to the conditional operator in the high-level language C. This instruction selects one of the operands based on the value of a third operand. If frA is greater than or equal to 0.0, then frC is returned as the result; otherwise frB is returned. This instruction does not cause exceptions—if frA is NaN, then frB is returned as the result.

Table 8-19 summarizes which of the optional floating-point instructions are implemented on which PowerPC processor.

Table 8-19 Optional Floating-Point Instructions vs. PowerPC Processor

	Graphical			General
	fres	**frsqrt**	**fsel**	**fsqrt[s]**
601	no	no	no	no
603	yes	yes	yes	no

Using one of these instructions on a processor that does not support it will cause an *Illegal Instruction* Program Interrupt to occur.

8.4 Floating-Point Conversions

The PowerPC architecture defines various instructions for converting between different numeric formats. This section summarizes these instructions by conversion type and "fills in the blanks" by providing algorithms for performing conversions that are not directly supported by the instruction set.

Converting Between Single- and Double-Precision

Double-Precision to Single-Precision

Double-precision floating-point values can be converted to single-precision by using the *FP Round to Single-Precision* (`frsp`) or *Store Floating-Point Single-Precision* (`stfs`, `stfsu`, `stfsx`, or `stfsux`) instructions.

The `frsp` instruction converts the double-precision value to single-precision and stores the converted value into a floating-point register.

The *Store Floating-Point Single-Precision* instructions convert the double-precision value to single-precision and store the converted value into memory.

One important difference between these two operations is that the `frsp` instruction will raise an exception if an invalid conversion operation is attempted. The store instructions do not raise any type of floating-point exceptions.

Single-Precision to Double-Precision

There is no need for a register-based single- to double-precision conversion operation since single-precision values are always stored in registers using the double-precision floating-point format.

As a consequence of this, simply loading a single-precision value into a register with one of the *Load Floating-Point Single-Precision* (`lfs`, `lfsu`, `lfsx`, or `lfsux`) instructions will automatically convert a value to double-precision.

Conversion Between Integer Words and Double-Precision

Double-Precision to Integer Word

There are two instructions to convert from floating-point values to integer words: `fctiw` and `fctiwz`. These instructions convert the value to a word by using either the current rounding mode (`fctiw`) or the *Round to Zero* (truncate) rounding mode (`fctiwz`).

One difficulty with these instructions is that they store the integer result in one of the floating-point registers, and there is no simple instruction to move values from the floating-point to the general-purpose registers. The standard way of transferring data between the register sets is to write the value to memory and then read it back. This can be done as

```
# temporary storage for intermediate value
temp:           .word           0x0,0x0

        # f0 <= converted int from fr1
        fctiw   fr0,fr1

        # move the converted result into r3
        stfd    fr0,temp(r1)
        lwz     r3,temp+4(r1)
```

Integer Word to Double-Precision

There is no instruction to easily convert integer words into floating-point values. Assuming that the word to be converted is in register r3, the following sequence of instructions will place the floating-point equivalent value in fr0:

```
# zero value = 2^52 * 0x100000 80000000
# the lower 32-bits of the fraction are equivalent
# to 0 (for signed integer words)
zero:           .word           0x43300000,0x80000000

# a place to build the intermediate fp value
temp:           .word           0x43300000,0x0

        # built the intermediate value by setting it equal
        # to: 0x43300000 <int32-with-inverted-sign>
        # which is: 2^52 * 0x100000 <int32>
        xoris   r3,r3,0x8000 # invert sign of int
        stw     r3,temp+4(r1)

        lfd     f0,temp(r1)
        lfd     f1,zero(r1)
        fsub    f0,f0,f1
```

This works by first inverting the sign of the word that is to be converted. This sign-inversion offsets the value of the word so that the smallest negative number (0x8000 0000) is mapped to 0x0000 0000 and the largest positive number (0x7FFF FFFF) is mapped to 0xFFFF FFFF.

This sign-inverted word is then used as the lower 32 bits of the fraction for a double-precision floating-point value. The magnitude of this number is set so that all 32 bits of the word are to the left of the actual binary point, that is, the exponent is set to 52 (since there are 52 bits in the fraction).

As the final step, a *zero constant* is subtracted from the constructed floating-point value. This constant is set up so that the lower 32 bits of the fraction are equal to the zero-point of the sign-inverted word. By subtracting this constant from the constructed floating-point value, the sign of the original word will be preserved. The subtraction operation also serves to properly normalize the result.

To modify this algorithm so that it works for unsigned integer words, 0x43300000 00000000 should be used as the *zero constant* and the `xoris` instruction should be removed.

Conversion Between Integer Doublewords and Double-Precision

Note: the conversion instructions discussed in this section exist only on 64-bit PowerPC implementations.

Double-Precision to Integer Doubleword

There are two instructions to convert from floating-point values to integer doublewords: `fctid` and `fctidz`. These instructions convert the value to a doubleword by using either the current rounding mode (`fctid`) or the *Round to Zero* (truncate) rounding mode (`fctidz`).

One difficulty with these instructions is that they store the integer result in one of the floating-point registers, and there is no simple instruction to move values from the floating-point to the general-purpose registers. The standard way of transferring data between the register sets is to write the value to memory and then read it back. This can be done as

```
        # temporary storage for intermediate value
temp:           .word       0x0,0x0

        # f0 <= converted int from fr1
        fctid   fr0,fr1

        # move the converted result into r3
        stfd    fr0,temp(r1)
        ld      r3,temp(r1)
```

Integer Doubleword to Double-Precision

The `fcfid` instruction is defined for 64-bit PowerPC implementations to convert a doubleword to a double-precision floating-point value.

As with the conversion from floating-point to fixed-point, this operation is complicated by the lack of an instruction to move values directly between the floating-point and general-purpose registers. This is overcome by writing the value to memory and then reading it back into the proper register set. This can be done as

```
# temporary storage for intermediate value
temp:          .word          0x0,0x0

    # move the contents of r3 into fr0
    std     r3,temp(r1)
    lfd     fr0,temp(r1)

    # convert fr0 to double-precision
    fcfid   fr0,fr0
```

System Register Instructions | 9

A large number of instructions and extended instruction forms can be used to access the various system registers of the PowerPC processors. Other than the Condition Register (CR) instructions, most of these will not be used by normal programs.

9.1 CR Instructions

The Condition Register is the most common of the special-purpose registers and thus, the largest number of instructions operate on it. CR fields 0 or 1 can be set implicitly by instructions that set the record bit; and any CR field can be updated when it is specified as the target of a compare instruction. Otherwise, the only way that the CR field values can be updated is through the *CR Logical* instructions and the *CR Move* instructions.

The CR Logical instructions allow the values in the CR fields to be combined using Boolean logic operations. These permit complex Boolean expressions to be built from the simple operations provided by the compare instructions.

The CR Move instructions provide a mechanism for moving the values in a CR field to other fields in the CR or to other registers. These instructions also allow values to be written into the CR.

Condition Register Logical

The CR Logical instructions provide the basic Boolean operations—AND, OR, and XOR—plus variations involving bit complements. The eight operations provided are *AND, OR,* and *XOR; Not AND, Not OR,* and *Equivalent* (which is the same as *Not XOR*); and *AND with Complement* and *OR with Complement.* Table 9-1 lists these instructions.

Table 9-1 Condition Register Logical Instructions

`crand` *bitT,bitA,bitB* **CR AND**	CR[T] $\Leftarrow$ CR[A] & CR[B]
`crandc` *bitT,bitA,bitB* **CR AND with Complement**	CR[T] $\Leftarrow$ CR[A] & ~CR[B]
`creqv` *bitT,bitA,bitB* **CR Equivalent**	CR[T] $\Leftarrow$ CR[A] $\equiv$ CR[B]
`crnand` *bitT,bitA,bitB* **CR Not AND**	CR[T] $\Leftarrow$ ~(CR[A] & CR[B])
`crnor` *bitT,bitA,bitB* **CR Not OR**	CR[T] $\Leftarrow$ ~(CR[A] | CR[B])
`cror` *bitT,bitA,bitB* **CR OR**	CR[T] $\Leftarrow$ CR[A] | CR[B]
`crorc` *bitT,bitA,bitB* **CR OR with Complement**	CR[T] $\Leftarrow$ CR[A] | ~CR[B]
`crxor` *bitT,bitA,bitB* **CR XOR**	CR[T] $\Leftarrow$ CR[A] $\oplus$ CR[B]

The mapping from the mnemonic to the operation is fairly straightforward. The instructions corresponding to the eight CR Logical instructions operations are `crand`, `cror`, `crxor`; `crnand`, `crnor`, `creqv`, `crandc` and `crorc`.

All of these instructions take three operands, the target bit where the result of the operation should be stored, and the two source bits.

Four additional extended forms listed in Table 9-2 make simple CR bit operations easy to perform. These are `crclr`, `crmove`, `crnot`, and `crset`.

Table 9-2 Condition Register Logical Extended Forms

`crclr` *bitT* **CR Clear** *extended form for* `crxor` *bitT,bitT,bitT*	CR[*bitT*] $\Leftarrow$ 0
`crmove` *bitT,bitA* **CR Move** *extended form for* `cror` *bitT,bitA,bitA*	CR[*bitT*] $\Leftarrow$ CR[*bitA*]

crnot *bitT,bitA* **CR Not** *extended form for* **crnor** *bitT,bitA,bitA*	CR[*bitT*] $\Leftarrow$ ~CR[*bitA*]
crset *bitT* **CR Set** *extended form for* **creqv** *bitT,bitT,bitT*	CR[*bitT*] $\Leftarrow$ 1

These forms can be used to set (**crset**) or clear (**crclr**) a bit in the CR; to copy a CR bit to another bit position (**crmove**); or to negate a CR bit and place the negated bit in another bit in the CR (**crnot**).

Condition Register Move

The CR Move instructions are used to perform three tasks: to move the fields of the CR around within the CR; to copy fields from the CR into a register; or to copy fields into the CR.

There is one instruction for copying CR fields within the CR: **mcrf**, an abbreviation for *Move CR Field* (see Table 9-3).

Table 9-3 Move within Condition Register Instruction

mcrf *crfT, crfA* **Move CR Field**	CR{*crfT*} $\Leftarrow$ CR{*crfA*}

The **mcrf** instruction requires a target CR field *T* and a source CR field *A*. CR field *T* is overwritten with the data from the CR field *A*.

To copy data out of the Condition Register, the only instruction available is **mfcr**, which copies the data into a designated GPR (see Table 9-4).

Table 9-4 Move from Condition Register Instruction

mfcr *rT* **Move from CR to GPR**	r*T* $\Leftarrow$ °(CR)

The entire destination register is overwritten with the contents of the CR. For 64-bit implementations, the upper 32 bits of the register are cleared to 0.

The PowerPC architecture specifies many instructions that move data into the CR. These instructions can be used to conditionally branch based on the value of a bit in the FPSCR, XER, or a GPR. The interesting bits can be first copied into the CR, and then any one of the standard conditional branch instructions can be used.

The three Move to CR instructions listed in Table 9-5 are **mcrfs**, **mcrxr**, and **mtcrf**.

Table 9-5 Move to Condition Register Instruction

`mcrfs crfT,crfA` **Move to CR from FPSCR**	CR{*crfT*} ⟸ FPSCR{*crfA*} FPSCR{*crfA*} ⟸ 0
`mcrxr crfT` **Move to CR from XER**	CR{*crfT*} ⟸ XER{0} XER{0} ⟸ 0
`mtcrf CRmask,rS` **Move to CR Fields from GPR**	CR{T} ⟸ (r*S*) & mask

The `mcrfs` instruction is used to copy a field from the FPSCR to a field in the CR. The `mcrxr` instruction is similar, except that it copies only from field 0 of the XER into a field of the CR. After the execution of a `mcrfs` or `mcrxr` instruction, the bits that were copied out of the FPSCR or XER are cleared to 0. Thus, after execution of a `mcrxr` instruction, XER{0} will always be b0000.

The `mtcrf` instruction can be used to copy CR fields from the given register into the CR. Only the fields specified in the mask are updated by this instructions; the other CR fields are unchanged.

An extended form (`mtcr`) is provided to facilitate restoring the entire CR from a register where it was saved earlier. The `mtcr` form overwrites the entire CR with the data in the given register (see Table 9-6).

Table 9-6 Move to Condition Register Extended Form

`mtcr rS` **Move to CR from GPR** *extended form for* `mtcrf 0xFF,rS`	CR ⟸ r*S* $\left[\frac{0:31}{32:64}\right]$

9.2 FPSCR Instructions

The Floating-Point Status and Control Register also has a set of special instructions devoted to it. These instructions allow the FPSCR to be copied to and from a designated FPR, and they allow specific bits within the FPSCR to be modified.

To move a copy of the FPSCR into a floating-point register, the `mffs` instruction should be used (see Table 9-7).

Table 9-7 Move from FPSCR Instruction

`mffs[.] frT` **Move from FPSCR**	fr*T* ⟸ (FPSCR)

The `mffs` instruction copies the FPSCR into the lower 32 bits of the specified FPR. The upper 32 bits of the FPR are undefined.

Table 9-16 Supervisor-Level Move from SPR Extended Forms

mfasr r*T* **Move from Address Space Register** *extended form for* mfspr r*T*,280 *supervisor-level instruction* *64-bit implementations only*	r*T* ⇐ (ASR)
mfdar r*T* **Move from Data Address Register** *extended form for* mfspr r*T*,19 *supervisor-level instruction*	r*T* ⇐ (DAR)
mfdbatl r*T*,*n* **Move from Data BAT Register Lower** *extended form for* mfspr r*T*,537+2*n* *supervisor-level instruction*	r*T* ⇐ (DBATL[*n*])
mfdbatu r*T*,*n* **Move from Data BAT Register Upper** *extended form for* mfspr r*T*,536+2*n* *supervisor-level instruction*	r*T* ⇐ (DBATU[*n*])
mfdec r*T* **Move from Decrement Register** *extended form for* mfspr r*T*,22 *supervisor-level instruction*	r*T* ⇐ (DEC)
mfdsisr r*T* **Move from DSISR** *extended form for* mfspr r*T*,18 *supervisor-level instruction*	r*T* ⇐ (DSISR)
mfear r*T* **Move from External Access Register** *extended form for* mfspr r*T*,282 *supervisor-level instruction*	r*T* ⇐ (EAR)
mfibatl r*T*,*n* **Move from Instruction BAT Register Lower** *extended form for* mfspr r*T*,529+2*n* *supervisor-level instruction*	r*T* ⇐ (IBATL[*n*])
mfibatu r*T*,*n* **Move from Instruction BAT Register Upper** *extended form for* mfspr r*T*,528+2*n* *supervisor-level instruction*	r*T* ⇐ (IBATU[*n*])
mfpvr r*T* **Move from Processor Version Register** *extended form for* mfspr r*T*,287 *supervisor-level instruction*	r*T* ⇐ (PVR)
mfsdr1 r*T* **Move from Storage Descriptor Register 1** *extended form for* mfspr r*T*,25 *supervisor-level instruction*	r*T* ⇐ (SDR1)

mfsprg r*T*,n **Move from Special Purpose Register G*n*** *extended form for* mfspr r*T*,272+*n* *supervisor-level instruction*	rT ⇐ (SPRG[*n*])
mfsrr0 r*T* **Move from Save/Restore Register 0** *extended form for* mfspr r*T*,26 *supervisor-level instruction*	rT ⇐ (SRR0)
mfsrr1 r*T* **Move from Save/Restore Register 1** *extended form for* mfspr r*T*,27 *supervisor-level instruction*	rT ⇐ (SRR1)

The *Move To SPR* forms listed in Table 9-17 are the same as the *Move From* forms with one exception: there is no instruction provided to write to the PVR. The PVR is a read-only register, so it makes no sense to write to it (processor upgrades cannot be performed in software).

Table 9-17 Supervisor-Level Move to SPR Extended Forms

mtasr r*S* **Move to Address Space Register** *extended form for* mtspr 280,r*S* *supervisor-level instruction* *64-bit implementations only*	ASR ⇐ (rS)
mtdar r*S* **Move to Data Address Register** *extended form for* mtspr 19,r*S* *supervisor-level instruction*	DAR ⇐ (rS)
mtdbatl n,r*S* **Move to Data BAT Register Lower** *extended form for* mtspr 537+2**n*,r*S* *supervisor-level instruction*	DBATL[*n*] ⇐ (rS)
mtdbatu n,r*S* **Move to Data BAT Register Upper** *extended form for* mtspr 536+2**n*,r*S* *supervisor-level instruction*	DBATU[*n*] ⇐ (rS)
mtdec r*S* **Move to Decrement Register** *extended form for* mtspr 22,r*S* *supervisor-level instruction*	DEC ⇐ (rS)
mtdsisr r*S* **Move to DSISR** *extended form for* mtspr 18,r*S* *supervisor-level instruction*	DSISR ⇐ (rS)

mtear r*S* **Move to External Access Register** *extended form for* `mtspr 282,r`*S* *supervisor-level instruction*	EAR $\Leftarrow$ (r*S*)
mtibatl n,r*S* **Move to Instruction BAT Register Lower** *extended form for* `mtspr 529+2*n,r`*S* *supervisor-level instruction*	IBATL[*n*] $\Leftarrow$ (r*S*)
mtibatu n,r*S* **Move to Instruction BAT Register Upper** *extended form for* `mtspr 528+2*n,r`*S* *supervisor-level instruction*	IBATU[*n*] $\Leftarrow$ (r*S*)
mtsdr1 r*S* **Move to Storage Descriptor Register 1** *extended form for* `mtspr 25,r`*S* *supervisor-level instruction*	SDR1 $\Leftarrow$ (r*S*)
mtsprg n,r*S* **Move to Special Purpose Register G*n*** *extended form for* `mtspr 272+n,r`*S* *supervisor-level instruction*	SPRG[*n*] $\Leftarrow$ (r*S*)
mtsrr0 r*S* **Move to Save/Restore Register 0** *extended form for* `mtspr 26,r`*S* *supervisor-level instruction*	SRR0 $\Leftarrow$ (r*S*)
mtsrr1 r*S* **Move to Save/Restore Register 1** *extended form for* `mtspr 27,r`*S* *supervisor-level instruction*	SRR1 $\Leftarrow$ (r*S*)

Obsolete Supervisor-Level SPR Instructions

The two obsolete SPRs listed in Table 9-18 have supervisor write access only—the RTC registers.

Table 9-18 Obsolete Supervisor-Level Move from Extended Forms

mtrtcl r*T* **Move to Real Time Counter Lower** *extended form for* `mtspr r`*T*`,20` *supervisor-level instruction* *defined on POWER and 601 only*	RTCL $\Leftarrow$ (r*T*)
mtrtcu r*T* **Move to Real Time Counter Upper** *extended form for* `mtspr r`*T*`,21` *supervisor-level instruction* *defined on POWER and 601 only*	RTCU $\Leftarrow$ (r*T*)

Note that the SPR ID used for these registers with the `mtspr` instruction is different from that used with the `mfspr` instruction. The IDs 20 and 21 are used with `mtspr`, and IDs 4 and 5 are used with `mfspr`.

9.7 Time Base Register Instructions

Access to the Time Base Register (TBR) is provided by the `mftb` (Table 9-19) and `mtspr` (Table 9-20) instructions. The `mftb` instruction is a user-level instruction that provides read access to the TBR, and `mtspr` can be used at the supervisor level to update the TBR.

Table 9-19 Move from Time Base Instructions

`mftb` rT, **TBR**
Move from Time Base Register
	if(TBR = 268)
	    $rT \Leftarrow$ (TBRL)
	else if(TBR = 269)
	    $rT \Leftarrow$ (TBRU)

The `mftb` instruction requires that a code be provided to specify which half of the TBR is required, the upper or the lower half.

To make the `mftb` instruction easier to use by eliminating the need to remember the code for the upper and lower portion of the TBR, two extended forms are defined.

Table 9-20 Move from Time Base Extended Forms

`mftb` rT **Move from Time Base Register (Lower)** *extended form for* `mftb` rT,268	$rT \Leftarrow$ (TBRL)
`mftbu` rT **Move from Time Base Register Upper** *extended form for* `mftb` rT,269	$rT \Leftarrow$ (TBRU)

The `mftb` form uses the same mnemonic as the instruction from which it is derived. Assemblers differentiate between the two by examining the arguments provided.

The two extended forms (based on `mtspr`) for updating the TBR are privileged (Table 9-21). Given a source GPR, these instructions will copy the contents of the register into the upper or lower portion of the TBR.

Table 9-21 Move to Time Base Extended Forms

`mttbl rS` **Move to Time Base Register Lower** *extended form for* `mtspr 284,rS` *supervisor-level instruction*	$\text{TBRL} \Leftarrow rS\ \left[\frac{0:31}{32:64}\right]$
`mttbu rS` **Move to Time Base Register Upper** *extended form for* `mtspr 285,rS` *supervisor-level instruction*	$\text{TBRU} \Leftarrow rS\ \left[\frac{0:31}{32:64}\right]$

Because each half of the TBR is 32 bits wide, 64-bit PowerPC implementations will only use the low-order 32 bits of the source register.

9.8 Segment Register Instructions

All 32-bit PowerPC implementations use Segment Registers instead of a Segment Table. These registers can be accessed at the supervisor level using the instructions given in this section.

The `mfsr` and `mfsrin` instructions listed in Table 9-22 copy the contents of the specified Segment Register into the specified target GPR. For `mfsr`, the SR is specified by an immediate value, and for `mfsrin`, the SR is specified by the upper four bits (bits 0:3) of the source register rB.

Table 9-22 Move from Segment Register Instructions

`mfsr rT,SR` **Move from Segment Register** *supervisor-level instruction* *32-bit implementations only*	$rT \Leftarrow \text{SR}[SR]$
`mfsrin rT,rB` **Move from Segment Register Indirect** *supervisor-level instruction* *32-bit implementations only*	$rT \Leftarrow \text{SR}[rB[0:3]]$

The `mtsr` and `mtsrin` instructions listed in Table 9-23 copy the contents of the source GPR into the target Segment Register. The SR is selected in the same fashion as the `mfsr`/`mfsrin` instructions: for `mtsr`, the SR is specified by an immediate value, and for `mtsrin`, the SR is specified by the upper four bits (bits 0:3) of the source register rB.

Table 9-23 Move to Segment Register Instructions

mtsr *SR,rS* **Move to Segment Register** *supervisor-level instruction* *32-bit implementations only*	$SR[SR] \Leftarrow (rS)$
mtsrin *rS,rB* **Move to Segment Register Indirect** *supervisor-level instruction* *32-bit implementations only*	$SR[rB[0\text{-}3]] \Leftarrow (rS)$

Memory and Caches | 10

All computer programs and data must be loaded into memory before they can be used. It is important to be aware of the memory structures because they can have a significant effect (both positive and negative) on the performance of a program.

10.1 Introduction

Computer users want an unlimited amount of fast memory. No matter how fast computers may become, users always want something just a bit faster. A memory subsystem that can't keep pace with the processor slows the entire system down.

Unfortunately, even a moderate (much less an *unlimited*) amount of fast memory tends to be quite expensive. These same computer users who want gobs of memory typically don't want to pay a lot of money for it.

This conflict (speed versus $$$) causes a lot of problems for the computer designer. The only good side to all this is that many of these problems have been addressed over the years with a reasonable amount of success. The remainder of this chapter is devoted to describing how memory systems work in general and gives specific information about the PowerPC memory system.

10.2 Memory and Cache Overview

In an ideal computer system, the CPU-memory interaction would be as simple as Figure 10-1. There would be a CPU, and a large store of memory, and they would talk to each other. Whenever the CPU needed to access a storage location, it would send a request to the memory store, which would handle the request directly.

Figure 10-1 Simple Memory Model Showing Basic CPU/Memory Interaction

Many real-world issues, however, make this ideal a naïve expectation. The most important of these real-world issues is cost.

Using the fastest available memory can result in a system that is either very expensive or very limited (due to lack of memory). Using less expensive memory can result in a system too slow to keep pace with the processor. It would be nice if there were some way of using a large amount of slow (and inexpensive) memory that performed as if fast memory were used.

This is where caches come in. A cache provides a mechanism for increasing the apparent speed of slow memory by using a small amount of fast memory. A cache can be used to design a system with a large amount of slow memory that still performs as if it had a much faster memory store available.

The performance of a cache varies greatly. In the best case, a program can run almost entirely from the cache and the memory system will appear to be just as fast as the cache. In the worst case, performance could be slightly worse than if the cache were not present. Fortunately, in most cases, caches perform quite well, and they significantly speed up memory accesses.

Memory Caches

The type of cache that we have been talking about so far is a *memory cache*. This type of cache uses a small store of high-speed memory to cache data from main memory (which is typically much larger and slower).

When the CPU needs to access memory, it sends the request to the cache. If the cache can handle the request by itself, it does so and fulfills the memory request without accessing main memory. If it cannot handle the request, it sends the request to the main memory store and then passes the returned data along to the CPU. Figure 10-2 illustrates this process.

Figure 10-2   Memory Organization with a Cache

Other Types of Caches

Memory caches aren't the only type of caches commonly found in computer systems. Creating a cache is a general technique that can be used to speed up many types of access.

Disk Cache

A disk cache uses the computer's main memory as a cache for a slow I/O device, like a hard disk or a CD-ROM drive.

Instead of the computer accessing the hard disk directly, as shown in Figure 10-3,

Figure 10-3   System with Simple Memory/Disk Interface

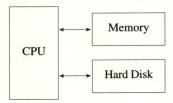

. . . all hard disk accesses are sent to the disk cache, which handles the request from memory (if possible) and only goes to the hard disk if necessary. This is shown in Figure 10-4.

Figure 10-4   System with a Disk Cache between the CPU and Hard Disk

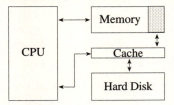

Disk cache architectures typically differ from other types of cache architectures in that the access time between the hard disk and memory is quite large (memory accesses are typically 1000 times faster than hard drive accesses). In this extra time disk caches can utilize more complex (and presumably more accurate) algorithms for deciding what belongs in the cache and what should be removed.

Virtual Memory

Virtual Memory (VM) is similar to a disk cache in that it uses main memory to cache accesses to a hard disk. However, the actual setup and operation of VM differs greatly from a simple disk cache.

The interesting thing about VM is that it applies the concept of a cache in reverse. The goal of VM (at least as originally implemented) was not to make memory accesses faster, but to make more memory available. Using VM is slower than using memory directly, because all accesses must go through the extra stages of address translation, and they may need to access the hard drive.

Figure 10-5 shows VM in its most primitive form. It works by pretending that all (or most) of main memory is actually just a cache for a portion of memory from a secondary storage device like a hard disk.

Figure 10-5   Simplified Virtual Memory Organization

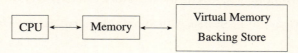

Current virtual memory implementations are actually far more complex than this overview would suggest. More detail is provided later in §10.7, "Virtual Memory."

10.3 Cache Architecture

In computer science, a cache is a *small* area of *fast* storage that is used to temporarily store data that would normally be directly accessed from a *large* area of *slow* storage. The terms small/large and fast/slow are relative terms—there is no requirement that the cache be particularly fast, only that it be faster than the storage area that is being cached. Caches are commonly used to speed up accesses to memory or to secondary storage devices like hard drives. For discussion purposes, this chapter will always refer to a memory cache, that is, a cache that is caching accesses to main memory.

A cache operates by handling all memory-read requests and checking to see if the request can be handled with data in the cache. If so, then the data is returned directly from the cache, without accessing the main memory. This is known as a *cache hit*.

If the memory read request is not located in the cache, then the cache must request the data from main memory. This is known as a *cache miss*. A cache miss is slightly slower than accessing main memory directly because of the overhead of the cache.

Write requests are handled in a slightly different fashion. If the storage location being stored to is already loaded in the cache, the cache updates its local copy and then optionally sends the new data to main memory. If the cache sends the new data to main memory, then the cache is referred to as *write-through*. If the cache does not immediately pass the new data to memory, it is known as a *write back* cache. Write back caches wait and send the updated cache data to memory only when necessary.

If the storage location being stored to is not currently loaded in the cache, the cache again has two options. It can read the requested data from memory and then treat the access as a write hit, or it can send the write request directly to main memory and have it bypass the cache entirely. If the cache fetches the block on a write miss, it is known as a *write allocate* cache. Caches that pass the write directly to memory are known as *write around* caches.

Why Caches Work

There is one small problem with caches: they require that the data already be in the cache for the cache to be of any benefit. The cache needs to have some method for analyzing past memory accesses and predicting future memory accesses. Fortunately the *principle of locality of reference* allows caches to predict reasonably well which data should be kept and which data should be removed from the cache.

The principle of locality of reference states simply that there are two types of reference locality for standard computer programs: locality in time (*temporal locality*) and locality in space (*spacial locality*).

- **Temporal locality** implies that if an item is referenced, then it is likely to be referenced again in the near future.

- **Spacial locality** implies that if an item is referenced, then items close to that item are likely to be referenced again in the near future.

A cache can take advantage of temporal locality by timestamping each memory reference made through the cache and discarding the oldest entry when the cache is full and a new item needs to be added. This is commonly known as the LRU (Least Recently Used) algorithm.

A cache can take advantage of spacial locality by defining a block size that is the smallest unit that the cache will read from main memory. This will force the bytes surrounding each reference to be read into the cache, thus making them available for future accesses to the cache.

How Caches Work

Figure 10-6 shows how a cache is typically arranged as a set of N cache lines, each of which contains M bytes, where M is an integral number of words and N is an integral power of 2. The overall cache size is thus N x M (N lines of M bytes). Additionally, a cache line can be divided into an integral number of cache sectors, although in many cases the line size and the sector size are the same. Cache operations always affect an entire cache sector at a time.

Note that common terminology also includes the terms *cache block* and *cache sub-block*, which are equivalent to the terms *cache line* and *cache sector* defined earlier. To make matters worse, sometimes *block* is used to mean *sector*. To eliminate any confusion about this ambiguous terminology, the terms from the preceding paragraph (*line* and *sector*) will always be used in this book. However, it is important to be aware of these alternate terms because they may be used in other documentation.

Figure 10-6   General Cache Organization

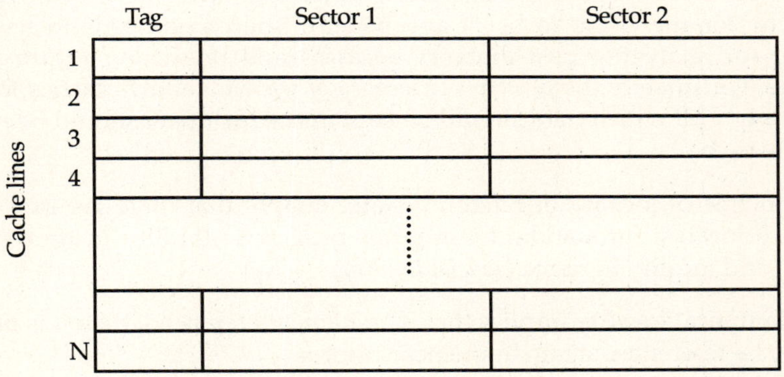

In addition to the data that is being cached, each cache line must also contain some housekeeping information: a cache line tag and a valid bit for each sector in the cache line. The tag identifies the memory location that corresponds to each cache line. The valid bit indicates whether or not the cache sector contains valid data.

Hash Functions

A hash function is a simple algorithm that is used to associate memory addresses with cache lines. When the cache needs to check for the presence of a particular address, it takes the address and applies the hash function to determine which cache lines need to be searched.

Because the hash function must be applied for every memory access, it is essential that it be trivial to compute. The majority of hash functions are simple bit manipulations such as taking the upper or middle n bits of the address.

Figure 10-7   Effective Address Fields, as Interpreted by the Hash Function

tag	hash key	byte offset

The hash function that will be used in most of the following examples divides the effective address into three fields: a *tag*, a *hash key*, and a *byte offset*. The *hash key* is used to determine which cache lines to search and the *tag* is used to determine if the cache line contains the correct data. The *byte offset* is used to identify the correct byte within the cache line after the cache line has been found.

Cache Associativity

The number and size of the cache lines is not enough to fully describe the cache geometry. The associativity of the cache is an important parameter that greatly affects how well the cache performs.

The *associativity* of a cache defines how the lines of the cache are grouped for searching and replacing purposes. This grouping, while not necessary, is useful for implementing high-speed caches because it limits the number of cache line entries that need to be searched.

There are three types of cache line groupings: direct mapped, fully associative, and n-way set associative.

The simplest cache is the *direct mapped cache* shown in Figure 10-8. This type of cache has one cache line in each group, thus, after the hash function is applied to the address, only one cache line needs to be checked. If that cache line contains the address, then the desired data has been found; otherwise, the data is not contained in the cache.

Figure 10-8   Direct Mapped Cache with Simple Hash Function

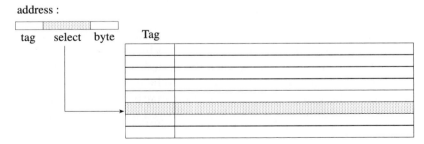

address :

tag   select   byte   Tag

completely occupied. Of the various possible strategies, two are commonly used:

- Least Recently Used (LRU)
- Random

The LRU algorithm checks the timestamps and chooses the cache line that was accessed least recently. The idea for this algorithm is based on the principle of temporal locality mentioned earlier. The more recently used cache lines are more likely to be used again soon, so the cache hit rate should be least affected by removing the least recent cache line.

The Random algorithm merely picks a random cache line to replace. Oddly enough, cache simulations have demonstrated that large caches using the Random algorithm have hit rates almost identical to rates of similar caches using the LRU algorithm. Another benefit of the Random algorithm is that it is far simpler to implement than the LRU algorithm.

Split Caches

When the processor accesses memory, it generally knows whether the memory being accessed is program data or program instructions. It knows the difference because it generates all of the instruction references (when it performs instruction fetches), and it assumes that all program references to memory are data references.

This allows the processor to have two separate caches: one for data and another for instructions. This type of cache organization is known by various names: *split* cache, *dual* cache, or *Harvard architecture* cache. This cache organization is different from the *unified* or *mixed* cache, where all of the memory (whether accessed as instruction or data) is stored in a single cache. In this book, the terms split cache and unified cache refer to these two cache architectures.

The advantage of a split cache is that the instruction cache can be architected to better handle instruction accesses, and the data cache can be architected to better handle data accesses. For example, instructions are read-only, so the instruction cache doesn't need to worry about recording and flushing changes out to the next level of memory, because modifications to instruction data aren't allowed. A processor could also implement a separate data path to each of the caches, so that an instruction and a data access could be handled in parallel.

The disadvantage of split caches is the amount of cache that is allocated for instructions and data is fixed in hardware. A small loop of code that accesses a lot of data will fully utilize the data cache but will underutilize the instruction cache.

Split caches are also bad for self-modifying code. When the program loads the instructions so that it can modify them, the processor treats the memory access as a data access, thus the instructions enter the data cache. This may produce two copies of the instructions: one in the instruction cache (for execution) and another in the data cache (for modification). When the program modifies the instruction, only the data cache is updated. The next time the updated instruction needs to be executed, old data from the instruction cache may be used, producing unexpected results.

Fortunately, this isn't a major concern for most people because self-modifying code is considered a Bad Thing for many other reasons. Hardware checks could be added, but because self-modifying code is frowned upon by the computer science community, it is not worth the effort. A software solution is to flush the instruction cache whenever instructions are modified, but flushing the cache tends to negatively affect performance.

Multiple Cache Levels

Not surprisingly, there can be many levels of caches in a particular system. For example, Figure 10-11 shows how a small amount of very fast memory on the processor could cache data from another cache of fast external memory which, in turn, is caching data from a large store of slow memory.

Figure 10-11   Memory Hierarchy with Multiple Caches

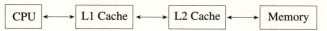

To differentiate between levels of caches, the terms "L1 cache," "L2 cache," and so on, are used. The L1 cache is the cache closest to the processor, and as caches become progressively further away from the processor, their level numbers increase. For split caches, the numbering: "L1I," "L1D," "L2I," "L2D," . . . is commonly used to denote the instruction and data caches at each cache level.

Performance analysis of programs using multi-level caches quickly becomes quite complex. In general, programmers tune their code by conceptualizing a single-level cache, and the results carry over fairly well.

Cache Coherency

One problem with caches arises because multiple copies of the same data are now in memory: the original in main memory and all the copies in the caches.

If the processor is the only device accessing memory, then there is no problem because the processor always accesses memory through the cache. When another device is added that accesses memory, there can be problems with old or *stale* copies of the data sitting in memory or in one of the caches.

Consider an output device like a display which reads the screen image directly from a screen buffer in memory. If the cache uses a *write back* write policy, then new data written to the screen buffer will be stored in the cache and the output device will be reading stale data from memory. *Write through* caches do not exhibit this problem.

An input device causes another problem for caches. If a device is writing new data to an already cached storage location, the cache will have no way of knowing that it contains stale data. A processor read from this location will get the old value from the cache instead of the current value from memory. Solutions to this problem include marking certain memory pages as uncacheable or requiring the input device to flush the cache containing the address that was written to.

Multi-Processor Systems

The cache coherency problem becomes even more acute when multiple processors are accessing the same data. One processor can reach into main memory and get an old data value because another processor has updated the value in its caches, but hasn't yet sent the changes back to main memory.

Two standard mechanisms handle multi-processor coherency. The first, known as *directory based*, involves using a directory that is shared by all of the processors in the system.

The other mechanism for coherency is called *snooping*. This protocol requires that each cache be connected to a common bus so that they can monitor or *snoop* all memory accesses to determine if they have a copy of a shared memory block. Most processors that snoop have an extra read port that is used exclusively for snooping so that the snooping operation does not interfere with the normal cache operation—the processor is interrupted only when a coherency problem needs to be addressed.

The keys to maintaining coherency are that each cache must insure that it has the most recent copy of the data when it needs to perform a read, and each cache must have exclusive write access when it needs to perform a write. On a write, the cache may either broadcast the new data to the other caches, or it may simply inform them that they need to invalidate their local copy of the data. The former technique is known as *write broadcast*, and the latter is called *write invalidate*.

10.4 PowerPC Cache Geometry

The PowerPC ISA does not specify such implementation details as the cache organization, but it does outline a set of assumptions that the programmer may safely make when dealing with the processor's caches. It also provides a set of instructions that provide basic cache control.

According to the PowerPC ISA, the programmer should assume that the processor has a split (instruction/data) cache, and that the processor will *not* automatically keep the instruction cache consistent with data written via the store instructions (that is, with the data cache).

Caches in the PowerPC 601

The 601 has a unified 32K, eight-way set associative cache. The cache geometry is summarized as:

- 64 cache sets with 8 cache lines per set
- $64 \times 8 = 512$ cache lines with 64 bytes per line
- Two 32-byte sectors in each cache line

The main difference between the 601 cache and the "standard" PowerPC cache structure is that the 601 has one unified cache instead of split instruction/data caches.

10.5 PowerPC Cache Coherency

The caches keep track of the data in the cache by recording the *MESI state* for each sector. The term "MESI" comes from the four allowable states for each sector: Modified, Exclusive, Shared, or Invalid. These states are defined as:

- A **Modified** sector contains valid data that has been changed with respect to main memory. The sector is valid only in this cache.
- An **Exclusive** sector is valid in this cache only, and that is consistent with main memory.
- A **Shared** sector is valid in this cache and at least one other cache in the system. Because the sector is shared it must be consistent with main memory.
- An **Invalid** sector does not exist in the current cache.

The MESI information is automatically maintained by the hardware in the PowerPC processors, so there is little need for user-level programs to be aware of it. A supervisor-level program can control the allowable memory accesses by setting the WIMG bits for memory blocks or pages. These bits are described later in §10.9 "PowerPC Memory Access Modes."

10.6 PowerPC Storage Control Instructions

The instructions described in this section give the programmer control over the processor caches and over how loads and stores are seen by external devices. There is also one instruction (not part of the PowerPC specification) that is defined on the 601 for POWER compatibility.

Data Cache

The instructions listed in Table 10-1 provide control over the processor's data caches. If the processor has a unified cache architecture (like the 601), then these instructions apply to the unified data/instruction cache.

The instruction descriptions in this section are simplified. The actual operation of these instructions depends on whether the cache line is in the cache, the current settings for the page containing the cached data, and the current system coherency mode. Appendix A provides more detailed descriptions of these instructions.

Table 10-1 Condition Register Logical Extended Forms

dcbf rA,rB **Data Cache Block Flush**	*flush the data cache line*
dcbi rA,rB **Data Cache Block Invalidate** *supervisor-level instruction*	*invalidate the data cache line*
dcbst rA,rB **Data Cache Block Store**	*store the data cache line to memory*
dcbt rA,rB **Data Cache Block Touch**	*touch the data cache line*
dcbtst rA,rB **Data Cache Block Touch for Store**	*touch (for store) the data cache line*
dcbz rA,rB **Data Cache Block Zero**	*clear the data cache line*

The *Data Cache Block Flush* (dcbf) instruction writes the cache line out to memory if it has been modified and then invalidates the cache line.

The *Data Cache Block Invalidate* (dcbi) instruction invalidates the cache line. If the cache line was modified, the changes are discarded. The dcbi instruction requires that the processor be in supervisor mode.

The *Data Cache Block Store* (dcbst) instruction writes the specified cache line out to main memory.

The *Data Cache Block Touch* (dcbt) instruction gives a hint to the processor that the specified cache line is likely to be loaded from in the near future. The processor may ignore this hint, or it may load the specified cache line.

The *Data Cache Block Touch for Store* (dcbtst) instruction is similar to the dcbt in that it gives a hint to the processor, but it hints that the specified cache line is likely to be stored to in the near future. As with dcbt, the processor may treat this instruction as a no-op, or it may load the specified cache line. In no situation does this instruction perform a store operation.

The *Data Cache Block Zero* (`dcbz`) instruction sets all of the bytes in the specified cache line to 0.

Instruction Cache

If the processor provides a separate instruction cache, the instruction in Table 10-2 can be used to invalidate the cache. As with the data cache descriptions, the description in this section is somewhat simplified. A more thorough description is given in Appendix A.

Table 10-2 Condition Register Logical Extended Forms

`icbi rT,rA` **Instruction Cache Block Invalidate**	*invalidate the instruction cache line*

The *Instruction Cache Block Invalidate* (`icbi`) instruction invalidates the cache line in the instruction cache. On implementations with combined instruction-data caches, this instruction acts as a no-op.

Cache Synchronization

The two instructions listed in Table 10-3 provide a way of insuring that all cache related operations have completed execution before dispatching any subsequent instructions.

Table 10-3 Condition Register Logical Extended Forms

`sync` **Data Cache Synchronize**	*synchronize the data cache*
`isync` **Instruction Cache Synchronize**	*synchronize the instruction cache*

The `sync` instruction makes sure that all instructions that were dispatched before the `sync` instruction appear to complete before the `sync` instruction completes. It also insures that no subsequent instructions are dispatched until after it completes.

The `isync` instruction waits for all previous instructions to complete operation, and then it discards any prefetched instructions. This forces all subsequent instructions to be reloaded from storage.

Enforce In-Order Execution of I/O

The `eieio` instruction (Table 10-4) is used to control the execution of I/O instructions as they are seen by external devices.

Table 10-4 Condition Register Logical Extended Forms

`eieio` **Enforce In-Order Execution of I/O**	*wait for all loads and stores to* *complete execution*

The `eieio` instruction makes sure that all of the load and store instructions that were dispatched before the `eieio` instruction are completed (that is, written out to main storage) before any load or store instruction after the `eieio` instruction is dispatched.

It acts as barrier in the instruction stream, preventing the processor from combining loads or stores that are on different sides of the barrier. This is useful to insure that the processor and the I/O device are executing the storage instruction in the correct order.

Obsolete Cache Instructions

The lone instruction in Table 10-5 is provided for compatibility with the POWER architecture. Only the 601 will implement this instruction.

Table 10-5 Condition Register Logical Extended Forms

`clcs rT,rA` **Cache Line Compute Size** *defined on POWER and 601 only*	$rT \Leftarrow$ *size of requested cache line*

The Cache Line Compute Size instruction returns the size of the cache line specified by rA into rT. The value of rA can specify the data cache line size, the instruction cache line size, or the minimum or maximum cache line size. The 601 returns 64 for all of these cache line sizes.

10.7 Virtual Memory

Virtual memory (VM) has evolved from a simple method of fooling the operating system to increase the address space, into a complex unit that manages memory protection for multiple processes.

If you're comfortable with the concept of caching, then most of the basic underlying principles of virtual memory will be familiar. One potential source of confusion is the difference in terminology between caches and VM. These differences are mostly due to the separate evolution of the two concepts.

In VM, a "cache line" is referred to as a *page* or a *segment*, which is typically not divided into sectors. A "cache miss" is called a *page fault* or *address fault*.

What does VM provide?

Virtual memory was originally developed to provide a larger "virtual" primary memory by using the main memory as a cache for a pre-allocated chunk of storage on a secondary storage device, such as a hard disk.

As computers and operating systems became more complex, the basic goal of VM changed from simply providing additional addressable memory to providing a suite of memory management functions, like memory protection and program relocation.

Current VM systems typically provide:

- A separate virtual address space for each process.
- Demand paged memory so that only memory that is currently being used is loaded.
- Protection to prevent a process from overwriting the memory allocated to another process.

Operating system complexity has grown to the point where most OSs require that these VM services be available.

How VM Works

The basic service of VM is to take a virtual address from an executing process, verify that the address is valid for that process, and then translate the virtual address into a physical address. The physical address can then be used to satisfy the memory request of the process.

A virtual address is an address in the local address space of the process. A physical address is an address in the "real" address space of main memory. Storage can only be accessed by using a real address, so all virtual addresses must be translated to a physical address.

It's important to be aware that the virtual address space for a process doesn't necessarily exist as a contiguous chunk of memory anywhere in the computer. As Figure 10-12 shows, the virtual addresses are used to map the memory accesses to the appropriate place in physical memory.

In the figure, memory is divided into *pages*, simply contiguous chunks of memory that the VM system uses for convenience. The size of a page varies depending on the implementation, but typical values range from 512 bytes to 16 Kb.

Figure 10-12   A Sample Virtual to Physical Address Mapping

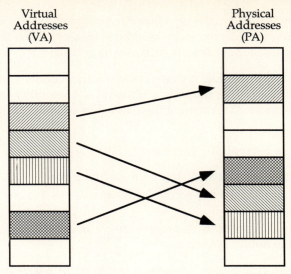

One thing that may not be apparent from Figure 10-12 is how VM uses memory efficiently. Only the pages that are actually being used by this process are loaded into physical memory—when a new page is needed, an unused block is discarded so that the new page can be loaded. Because the new page can be loaded anywhere in physical memory, the VM system is free to choose the page that is least likely to be used.

Note how this also allows the physical address space to be shared by multiple processes. Pages that are not being used by this process can be allocated to other processes so that all of physical memory is being used efficiently.

Missing from Figure 10-12 is the structure that maps the relationship between the virtual and physical pages. This structure is known as a *page table*. A page table takes a virtual address page and translates it into a physical address page. Figure 10-13 shows how the page table is used to arrive at the physical address.

In its simplest form, a page table is simply a large array that is indexed by the upper bits of the virtual address. For example, in Figure 10-13 with 1000-byte pages, the physical address of virtual address 4100 can be found by looking at the fourth (4100 / 1000 = 4) entry in the page table, which in this case contains the value 6000. The offset into the page, 100 can be added to the base address of the physical page to obtain the physical address, 6100.

Figure 10-13   Mapping from a Virtual to a Physical Address via the Page Table

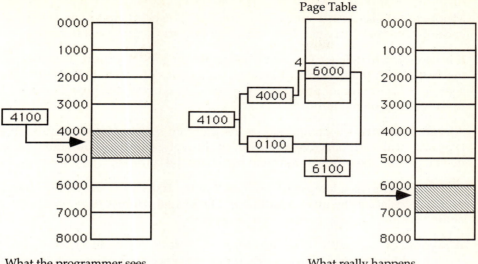

What the programmer sees   What really happens

Translation Lookaside Buffers (TLBs)

One point was glossed over in the previous section: the page table must be stored somewhere in memory. Because the virtual address space (and thus, the page table) can be quite large, it typically isn't feasible to cache the entire table. In most systems, the page table resides in main memory and is paged in and out of the cache like other memory accesses.

This can cause a serious performance problem because now a memory access can potentially require two memory accesses: one to load the relevant portion of the page table, and another to get the requested data. This is known as a *double page fault*, and the double memory access penalty associated with it is generally unacceptable.

Fortunately, the page table accesses can take advantage of the principle of locality of reference by caching recent page table translations in a separate cache, known as a *translation lookaside buffer* or TLB for short.

A TLB is a simple cache that stores associations between the recently used virtual addresses and the corresponding physical address. In addition to the physical address, most TLBs also store information (like protection level) about the page.

10.8 PowerPC Memory Management

Memory is managed in a similar fashion for all PowerPC processors, but differences do exist between the 32-bit and 64-bit PowerPC implementations.

It is necessary to define a few terms before jumping into the address translation mechanisms of the PowerPC. First of all, a *page* is defined as being 4Kb and a *segment* is 256Mb for all processors, regardless of whether the processor is a 32- or 64-bit implementation.

An *effective* address is an address as the program sees it. User-level programs typically deal with effective addresses exclusively, and these programs never need to worry about how the system translates this address.

A *virtual* address is a temporary address that the translation mechanism builds as it is calculating the physical address. The virtual address never exists as an entity because it is only needed for a short time.

A *physical*, or real, address is the address as it really exists in the computer's memory. As mentioned above, a program rarely needs to be aware of the actual storage location in memory, because all accesses are translated automatically.

Address Translation Overview

Two mechanisms present in PowerPC processors handle the translation from an effective to a physical address. These mechanisms are known as *Segmented Address Translation* and *Block Address Translation* (BAT). In addition, there is *Direct Address Translation*, which is used only when the other translations are disabled.

Segmented Address Translation, the translation mechanism most commonly used, supports two types of segments: *direct-store* and *ordinary*. For a direct-store segment, the effective address is directly converted into an I/O address and passed to the I/O subsystem. For an ordinary segment, the effective address is translated into a virtual address, which is then translated into a physical address before being used.

Block Address Translation is used when a range of pages need to be contiguous in physical memory. This grouping of pages is technically known as a *block,* but the term *BAT area* will be used instead to avoid confusion.

Direct Address Translation is used when the other translation mechanisms are disabled. In these "translations," the effective address is the same as the physical address, and no paging is performed.

When the memory management unit on a processor is given an effective address, the address is passed simultaneously to both of the translation mechanisms (if they are enabled), with the assumption that only one of them should

Figure 10-2   Memory Organization with a Cache

Other Types of Caches

Memory caches aren't the only type of caches commonly found in computer systems. Creating a cache is a general technique that can be used to speed up many types of access.

Disk Cache

A disk cache uses the computer's main memory as a cache for a slow I/O device, like a hard disk or a CD-ROM drive.

Instead of the computer accessing the hard disk directly, as shown in Figure 10-3,

Figure 10-3   System with Simple Memory/Disk Interface

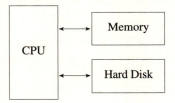

. . . all hard disk accesses are sent to the disk cache, which handles the request from memory (if possible) and only goes to the hard disk if necessary. This is shown in Figure 10-4.

Figure 10-4   System with a Disk Cache between the CPU and Hard Disk

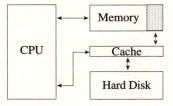

Disk cache architectures typically differ from other types of cache architectures in that the access time between the hard disk and memory is quite large (memory accesses are typically 1000 times faster than hard drive accesses). In this extra time disk caches can utilize more complex (and presumably more accurate) algorithms for deciding what belongs in the cache and what should be removed.

Virtual Memory

Virtual Memory (VM) is similar to a disk cache in that it uses main memory to cache accesses to a hard disk. However, the actual setup and operation of VM differs greatly from a simple disk cache.

The interesting thing about VM is that it applies the concept of a cache in reverse. The goal of VM (at least as originally implemented) was not to make memory accesses faster, but to make more memory available. Using VM is slower than using memory directly, because all accesses must go through the extra stages of address translation, and they may need to access the hard drive.

Figure 10-5 shows VM in its most primitive form. It works by pretending that all (or most) of main memory is actually just a cache for a portion of memory from a secondary storage device like a hard disk.

Figure 10-5   Simplified Virtual Memory Organization

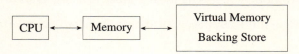

Current virtual memory implementations are actually far more complex than this overview would suggest. More detail is provided later in §10.7, "Virtual Memory."

10.3 Cache Architecture

In computer science, a cache is a *small* area of *fast* storage that is used to temporarily store data that would normally be directly accessed from a *large* area of *slow* storage. The terms small/large and fast/slow are relative terms—there is no requirement that the cache be particularly fast, only that it be faster than the storage area that is being cached. Caches are commonly used to speed up accesses to memory or to secondary storage devices like hard drives. For discussion purposes, this chapter will always refer to a memory cache, that is, a cache that is caching accesses to main memory.

A cache operates by handling all memory-read requests and checking to see if the request can be handled with data in the cache. If so, then the data is returned directly from the cache, without accessing the main memory. This is known as a *cache hit*.

If the memory read request is not located in the cache, then the cache must request the data from main memory. This is known as a *cache miss*. A cache miss is slightly slower than accessing main memory directly because of the overhead of the cache.

Write requests are handled in a slightly different fashion. If the storage location being stored to is already loaded in the cache, the cache updates its local copy and then optionally sends the new data to main memory. If the cache sends the new data to main memory, then the cache is referred to as *write-through*. If the cache does not immediately pass the new data to memory, it is known as a *write back* cache. Write back caches wait and send the updated cache data to memory only when necessary.

If the storage location being stored to is not currently loaded in the cache, the cache again has two options. It can read the requested data from memory and then treat the access as a write hit, or it can send the write request directly to main memory and have it bypass the cache entirely. If the cache fetches the block on a write miss, it is known as a *write allocate* cache. Caches that pass the write directly to memory are known as *write around* caches.

Why Caches Work

There is one small problem with caches: they require that the data already be in the cache for the cache to be of any benefit. The cache needs to have some method for analyzing past memory accesses and predicting future memory accesses. Fortunately the *principle of locality of reference* allows caches to predict reasonably well which data should be kept and which data should be removed from the cache.

The principle of locality of reference states simply that there are two types of reference locality for standard computer programs: locality in time (*temporal locality*) and locality in space (*spacial locality*).

- **Temporal locality** implies that if an item is referenced, then it is likely to be referenced again in the near future.

- **Spacial locality** implies that if an item is referenced, then items close to that item are likely to be referenced again in the near future.

A cache can take advantage of temporal locality by timestamping each memory reference made through the cache and discarding the oldest entry when the cache is full and a new item needs to be added. This is commonly known as the LRU (Least Recently Used) algorithm.

A cache can take advantage of spacial locality by defining a block size that is the smallest unit that the cache will read from main memory. This will force the bytes surrounding each reference to be read into the cache, thus making them available for future accesses to the cache.

How Caches Work

Figure 10-6 shows how a cache is typically arranged as a set of N cache lines, each of which contains M bytes, where M is an integral number of words and N is an integral power of 2. The overall cache size is thus $N \times M$ (N lines of M bytes). Additionally, a cache line can be divided into an integral number of cache sectors, although in many cases the line size and the sector size are the same. Cache operations always affect an entire cache sector at a time.

Note that common terminology also includes the terms *cache block* and *cache sub-block*, which are equivalent to the terms *cache line* and *cache sector* defined earlier. To make matters worse, sometimes *block* is used to mean *sector*. To eliminate any confusion about this ambiguous terminology, the terms from the preceding paragraph (*line* and *sector*) will always be used in this book. However, it is important to be aware of these alternate terms because they may be used in other documentation.

Figure 10-6   General Cache Organization

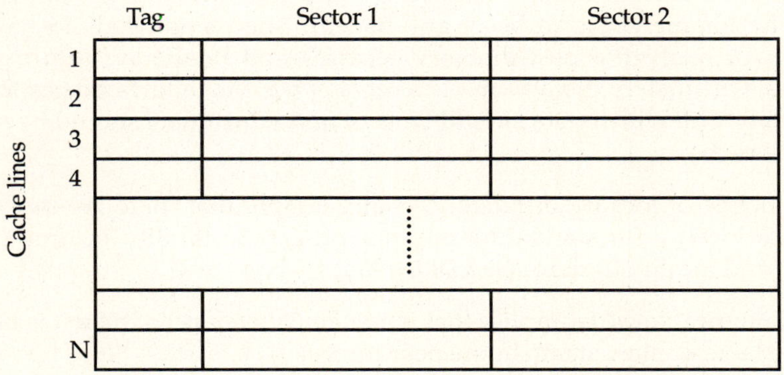

In addition to the data that is being cached, each cache line must also contain some housekeeping information: a cache line tag and a valid bit for each sector in the cache line. The tag identifies the memory location that corresponds to each cache line. The valid bit indicates whether or not the cache sector contains valid data.

Hash Functions

A hash function is a simple algorithm that is used to associate memory addresses with cache lines. When the cache needs to check for the presence of a particular address, it takes the address and applies the hash function to determine which cache lines need to be searched.

Because the hash function must be applied for every memory access, it is essential that it be trivial to compute. The majority of hash functions are simple bit manipulations such as taking the upper or middle *n* bits of the address.

Figure 10-7   Effective Address Fields, as Interpreted by the Hash Function

tag	hash key	byte offset

The hash function that will be used in most of the following examples divides the effective address into three fields: a *tag*, a *hash key*, and a *byte offset*. The *hash key* is used to determine which cache lines to search and the *tag* is used to determine if the cache line contains the correct data. The *byte offset* is used to identify the correct byte within the cache line after the cache line has been found.

Cache Associativity

The number and size of the cache lines is not enough to fully describe the cache geometry. The associativity of the cache is an important parameter that greatly affects how well the cache performs.

The *associativity* of a cache defines how the lines of the cache are grouped for searching and replacing purposes. This grouping, while not necessary, is useful for implementing high-speed caches because it limits the number of cache line entries that need to be searched.

There are three types of cache line groupings: direct mapped, fully associative, and *n*-way set associative.

The simplest cache is the *direct mapped cache* shown in Figure 10-8. This type of cache has one cache line in each group, thus, after the hash function is applied to the address, only one cache line needs to be checked. If that cache line contains the address, then the desired data has been found; otherwise, the data is not contained in the cache.

Figure 10-8   Direct Mapped Cache with Simple Hash Function

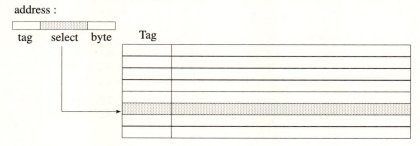

In any case, it only takes a check of one cache line in the cache to determine if the cache contains the address. This makes the direct mapped cache the easiest type of cache to implement.

One potential problem with direct mapped caches is that the cache can be under-utilized if the hash function does not mesh well with the access pattern for the data being cached. If many addresses hash to the same cache line, there can be a large number of cache misses even though there are unused cache lines in the cache. This is a worst-case scenario, and, in general, this type of cache works reasonably well for memory caches.

The opposite end of the spectrum from a simple direct mapped cache is the *fully associative cache* illustrated in Figure 10-9. This organization allows the data for an address to be stored anywhere in the cache. As a result, the cache is completely utilized before it needs to overwrite any of the cache lines.

Figure 10-9   Fully Associative Cache (No Hash Function Necessary)

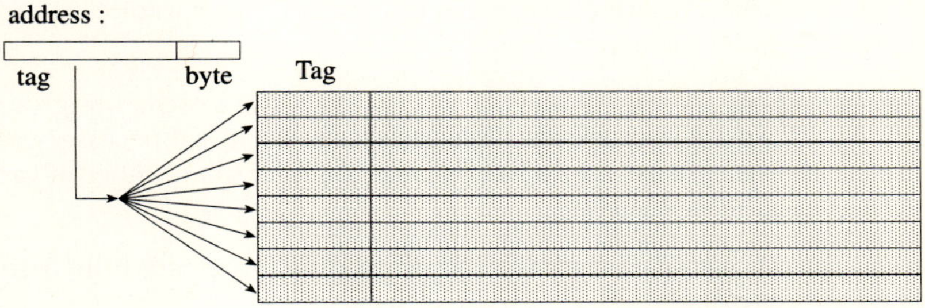

This organization of the fully associative cache implies a few very crucial things. First, because an address can be located anywhere in the cache, the entire cache needs to be searched to determine if the address is in the cache or not. For a disk cache (where there's plenty of time available to implement a complex algorithm), this may be acceptable. For a memory cache, however, there isn't enough time to search sequentially through the cache lines, and the additional hardware necessary to perform a parallel search would quickly become unmanageable for a reasonably-sized cache.

The second important implication for a fully associative cache is that it requires some sort of *line replacement algorithm* to decide which cache line to discard when the cache is full and a new line needs to be added. This algorithm can also cost time because all of the cache lines may need to be analyzed to determine which one is the least likely to be used soon. A direct mapped cache doesn't need a line replacement algorithm because the data is allowed to reside in only one line and that is the line that needs to be replaced.

Because of the additional complexity needed to find and replace the cache lines, fully associative caches are not typically used for memory caches. Fully associative caches are more common with disk caches or virtual memory systems where the difference between the memory and the secondary storage access times is large.

There is fortunately a happy medium between the mindless simplicity of the direct mapped cache and the unmanageable complexity of the fully associative cache. In between these two extremes is the *n-way set associative cache* illustrated in Figure 10-10.

A set associative cache maps the cache into distinct sets, each of which contains *n* cache lines. When data needs to be accessed from a cache, the address is hashed, and then all *n* of the cache lines in the target set are searched in parallel for the address.

Figure 10-10   N-way Set Associative Cache with Simple Hash Function

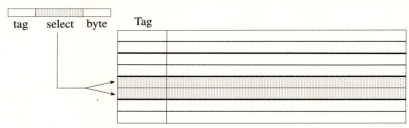

Typical values for *n* are 2 and 4. Studies have shown that increasing *n* above 4 results in small performance benefits and greatly complicates (and thus, tends to slow down) the cache search circuitry.

By reducing the number of cache lines that need to be searched in parallel to 4 or less, the set associative cache organization makes the search circuitry reasonable to implement and allows the cache size to be reasonably large without affecting the search time.

It should be noted that the definition for an *n*-way set associative cache is actually general enough to encompass the direct mapped and fully associative cache organizations. A direct mapped cache is simply a set associative cache with $n = 1$, and a fully associative cache is a set associative cache with $n = N$ (where N is the number of cache lines).

Line Replacement Algorithms

The *n*-way set and fully associative caches require some sort of replacement algorithm to determine which cache line to replace when the cache (or set) is completely occupied. Of the various possible strategies, two are commonly used:

- Least Recently Used (LRU)
- Random

The LRU algorithm checks the timestamps and chooses the cache line that was accessed least recently. The idea for this algorithm is based on the principle of temporal locality mentioned earlier. The more recently used cache lines are more likely to be used again soon, so the cache hit rate should be least affected by removing the least recent cache line.

The Random algorithm merely picks a random cache line to replace. Oddly enough, cache simulations have demonstrated that large caches using the Random algorithm have hit rates almost identical to rates of similar caches using the LRU algorithm. Another benefit of the Random algorithm is that it is far simpler to implement than the LRU algorithm.

Split Caches

When the processor accesses memory, it generally knows whether the memory being accessed is program data or program instructions. It knows the difference because it generates all of the instruction references (when it performs instruction fetches), and it assumes that all program references to memory are data references.

This allows the processor to have two separate caches: one for data and another for instructions. This type of cache organization is known by various names: *split* cache, *dual* cache, or *Harvard architecture* cache. This cache organization is different from the *unified* or *mixed* cache, where all of the memory (whether accessed as instruction or data) is stored in a single cache. In this book, the terms split cache and unified cache refer to these two cache architectures.

The advantage of a split cache is that the instruction cache can be architected to better handle instruction accesses, and the data cache can be architected to better handle data accesses. For example, instructions are read-only, so the instruction cache doesn't need to worry about recording and flushing changes out to the next level of memory, because modifications to instruction data aren't allowed. A processor could also implement a separate data path to each of the caches, so that an instruction and a data access could be handled in parallel.

The disadvantage of split caches is the amount of cache that is allocated for instructions and data is fixed in hardware. A small loop of code that accesses a lot of data will fully utilize the data cache but will underutilize the instruction cache.

Split caches are also bad for self-modifying code. When the program loads the instructions so that it can modify them, the processor treats the memory access as a data access, thus the instructions enter the data cache. This may produce two copies of the instructions: one in the instruction cache (for execution) and another in the data cache (for modification). When the program modifies the instruction, only the data cache is updated. The next time the updated instruction needs to be executed, old data from the instruction cache may be used, producing unexpected results.

Fortunately, this isn't a major concern for most people because self-modifying code is considered a Bad Thing for many other reasons. Hardware checks could be added, but because self-modifying code is frowned upon by the computer science community, it is not worth the effort. A software solution is to flush the instruction cache whenever instructions are modified, but flushing the cache tends to negatively affect performance.

Multiple Cache Levels

Not surprisingly, there can be many levels of caches in a particular system. For example, Figure 10-11 shows how a small amount of very fast memory on the processor could cache data from another cache of fast external memory which, in turn, is caching data from a large store of slow memory.

Figure 10-11   Memory Hierarchy with Multiple Caches

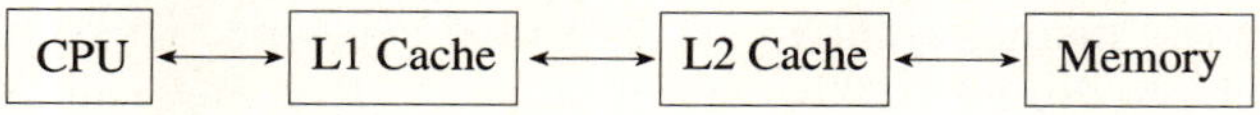

To differentiate between levels of caches, the terms "L1 cache," "L2 cache," and so on, are used. The L1 cache is the cache closest to the processor, and as caches become progressively further away from the processor, their level numbers increase. For split caches, the numbering: "L1I," "L1D," "L2I," "L2D," . . . is commonly used to denote the instruction and data caches at each cache level.

Performance analysis of programs using multi-level caches quickly becomes quite complex. In general, programmers tune their code by conceptualizing a single-level cache, and the results carry over fairly well.

Cache Coherency

One problem with caches arises because multiple copies of the same data are now in memory: the original in main memory and all the copies in the caches.

If the processor is the only device accessing memory, then there is no problem because the processor always accesses memory through the cache. When another device is added that accesses memory, there can be problems with old or *stale* copies of the data sitting in memory or in one of the caches.

Consider an output device like a display which reads the screen image directly from a screen buffer in memory. If the cache uses a *write back* write policy, then new data written to the screen buffer will be stored in the cache and the output device will be reading stale data from memory. *Write through* caches do not exhibit this problem.

An input device causes another problem for caches. If a device is writing new data to an already cached storage location, the cache will have no way of knowing that it contains stale data. A processor read from this location will get the old value from the cache instead of the current value from memory. Solutions to this problem include marking certain memory pages as uncacheable or requiring the input device to flush the cache containing the address that was written to.

Multi-Processor Systems

The cache coherency problem becomes even more acute when multiple processors are accessing the same data. One processor can reach into main memory and get an old data value because another processor has updated the value in its caches, but hasn't yet sent the changes back to main memory.

Two standard mechanisms handle multi-processor coherency. The first, known as *directory based*, involves using a directory that is shared by all of the processors in the system.

The other mechanism for coherency is called *snooping*. This protocol requires that each cache be connected to a common bus so that they can monitor or *snoop* all memory accesses to determine if they have a copy of a shared memory block. Most processors that snoop have an extra read port that is used exclusively for snooping so that the snooping operation does not interfere with the normal cache operation—the processor is interrupted only when a coherency problem needs to be addressed.

The keys to maintaining coherency are that each cache must insure that it has the most recent copy of the data when it needs to perform a read, and each cache must have exclusive write access when it needs to perform a write. On a write, the cache may either broadcast the new data to the other caches, or it may simply inform them that they need to invalidate their local copy of the data. The former technique is known as *write broadcast*, and the latter is called *write invalidate*.

10.4 PowerPC Cache Geometry

The PowerPC ISA does not specify such implementation details as the cache organization, but it does outline a set of assumptions that the programmer may safely make when dealing with the processor's caches. It also provides a set of instructions that provide basic cache control.

According to the PowerPC ISA, the programmer should assume that the processor has a split (instruction/data) cache, and that the processor will *not* automatically keep the instruction cache consistent with data written via the store instructions (that is, with the data cache).

Caches in the PowerPC 601

The 601 has a unified 32K, eight-way set associative cache. The cache geometry is summarized as:

- 64 cache sets with 8 cache lines per set
- $64 \times 8 = 512$ cache lines with 64 bytes per line
- Two 32-byte sectors in each cache line

The main difference between the 601 cache and the "standard" PowerPC cache structure is that the 601 has one unified cache instead of split instruction/data caches.

10.5 PowerPC Cache Coherency

The caches keep track of the data in the cache by recording the *MESI state* for each sector. The term "MESI" comes from the four allowable states for each sector: Modified, Exclusive, Shared, or Invalid. These states are defined as:

- A **Modified** sector contains valid data that has been changed with respect to main memory. The sector is valid only in this cache.
- An **Exclusive** sector is valid in this cache only, and that is consistent with main memory.
- A **Shared** sector is valid in this cache and at least one other cache in the system. Because the sector is shared it must be consistent with main memory.
- An **Invalid** sector does not exist in the current cache.

The MESI information is automatically maintained by the hardware in the PowerPC processors, so there is little need for user-level programs to be aware of it. A supervisor-level program can control the allowable memory accesses by setting the WIMG bits for memory blocks or pages. These bits are described later in §10.9 "PowerPC Memory Access Modes."

10.6 PowerPC Storage Control Instructions

The instructions described in this section give the programmer control over the processor caches and over how loads and stores are seen by external devices. There is also one instruction (not part of the PowerPC specification) that is defined on the 601 for POWER compatibility.

Data Cache

The instructions listed in Table 10-1 provide control over the processor's data caches. If the processor has a unified cache architecture (like the 601), then these instructions apply to the unified data/instruction cache.

The instruction descriptions in this section are simplified. The actual operation of these instructions depends on whether the cache line is in the cache, the current settings for the page containing the cached data, and the current system coherency mode. Appendix A provides more detailed descriptions of these instructions.

Table 10-1 Condition Register Logical Extended Forms

`dcbf rA,rB` **Data Cache Block Flush**	*flush the data cache line*
`dcbi rA,rB` **Data Cache Block Invalidate** *supervisor-level instruction*	*invalidate the data cache line*
`dcbst rA,rB` **Data Cache Block Store**	*store the data cache line to memory*
`dcbt rA,rB` **Data Cache Block Touch**	*touch the data cache line*
`dcbtst rA,rB` **Data Cache Block Touch for Store**	*touch (for store) the data cache line*
`dcbz rA,rB` **Data Cache Block Zero**	*clear the data cache line*

The *Data Cache Block Flush* (`dcbf`) instruction writes the cache line out to memory if it has been modified and then invalidates the cache line.

The *Data Cache Block Invalidate* (`dcbi`) instruction invalidates the cache line. If the cache line was modified, the changes are discarded. The `dcbi` instruction requires that the processor be in supervisor mode.

The *Data Cache Block Store* (`dcbst`) instruction writes the specified cache line out to main memory.

The *Data Cache Block Touch* (`dcbt`) instruction gives a hint to the processor that the specified cache line is likely to be loaded from in the near future. The processor may ignore this hint, or it may load the specified cache line.

The *Data Cache Block Touch for Store* (`dcbtst`) instruction is similar to the `dcbt` in that it gives a hint to the processor, but it hints that the specified cache line is likely to be stored to in the near future. As with `dcbt`, the processor may treat this instruction as a no-op, or it may load the specified cache line. In no situation does this instruction perform a store operation.

The *Data Cache Block Zero* (`dcbz`) instruction sets all of the bytes in the specified cache line to 0.

Instruction Cache

If the processor provides a separate instruction cache, the instruction in Table 10-2 can be used to invalidate the cache. As with the data cache descriptions, the description in this section is somewhat simplified. A more thorough description is given in Appendix A.

Table 10-2 Condition Register Logical Extended Forms

`icbi rT,rA` **Instruction Cache Block Invalidate**	*invalidate the instruction cache line*

The *Instruction Cache Block Invalidate* (`icbi`) instruction invalidates the cache line in the instruction cache. On implementations with combined instruction-data caches, this instruction acts as a no-op.

Cache Synchronization

The two instructions listed in Table 10-3 provide a way of insuring that all cache related operations have completed execution before dispatching any subsequent instructions.

Table 10-3 Condition Register Logical Extended Forms

`sync` **Data Cache Synchronize**	*synchronize the data cache*
`isync` **Instruction Cache Synchronize**	*synchronize the instruction cache*

The `sync` instruction makes sure that all instructions that were dispatched before the `sync` instruction appear to complete before the `sync` instruction completes. It also insures that no subsequent instructions are dispatched until after it completes.

The `isync` instruction waits for all previous instructions to complete operation, and then it discards any prefetched instructions. This forces all subsequent instructions to be reloaded from storage.

Enforce In-Order Execution of I/O

The `eieio` instruction (Table 10-4) is used to control the execution of I/O instructions as they are seen by external devices.

Table 10-4 Condition Register Logical Extended Forms

eieio **Enforce In-Order Execution of I/O**	*wait for all loads and stores to* *complete execution*

The `eieio` instruction makes sure that all of the load and store instructions that were dispatched before the `eieio` instruction are completed (that is, written out to main storage) before any load or store instruction after the `eieio` instruction is dispatched.

It acts as barrier in the instruction stream, preventing the processor from combining loads or stores that are on different sides of the barrier. This is useful to insure that the processor and the I/O device are executing the storage instruction in the correct order.

Obsolete Cache Instructions

The lone instruction in Table 10-5 is provided for compatibility with the POWER architecture. Only the 601 will implement this instruction.

Table 10-5 Condition Register Logical Extended Forms

clcs rT,rA **Cache Line Compute Size** *defined on POWER and 601 only*	rT ⇐ *size of requested cache line*

The Cache Line Compute Size instruction returns the size of the cache line specified by rA into rT. The value of rA can specify the data cache line size, the instruction cache line size, or the minimum or maximum cache line size. The 601 returns 64 for all of these cache line sizes.

10.7 Virtual Memory

Virtual memory (VM) has evolved from a simple method of fooling the operating system to increase the address space, into a complex unit that manages memory protection for multiple processes.

If you're comfortable with the concept of caching, then most of the basic underlying principles of virtual memory will be familiar. One potential source of confusion is the difference in terminology between caches and VM. These differences are mostly due to the separate evolution of the two concepts.

In VM, a "cache line" is referred to as a *page* or a *segment*, which is typically not divided into sectors. A "cache miss" is called a *page fault* or *address fault*.

What does VM provide?

Virtual memory was originally developed to provide a larger "virtual" primary memory by using the main memory as a cache for a pre-allocated chunk of storage on a secondary storage device, such as a hard disk.

As computers and operating systems became more complex, the basic goal of VM changed from simply providing additional addressable memory to providing a suite of memory management functions, like memory protection and program relocation.

Current VM systems typically provide:

- A separate virtual address space for each process.
- Demand paged memory so that only memory that is currently being used is loaded.
- Protection to prevent a process from overwriting the memory allocated to another process.

Operating system complexity has grown to the point where most OSs require that these VM services be available.

How VM Works

The basic service of VM is to take a virtual address from an executing process, verify that the address is valid for that process, and then translate the virtual address into a physical address. The physical address can then be used to satisfy the memory request of the process.

A virtual address is an address in the local address space of the process. A physical address is an address in the "real" address space of main memory. Storage can only be accessed by using a real address, so all virtual addresses must be translated to a physical address.

It's important to be aware that the virtual address space for a process doesn't necessarily exist as a contiguous chunk of memory anywhere in the computer. As Figure 10-12 shows, the virtual addresses are used to map the memory accesses to the appropriate place in physical memory.

In the figure, memory is divided into *pages*, simply contiguous chunks of memory that the VM system uses for convenience. The size of a page varies depending on the implementation, but typical values range from 512 bytes to 16 Kb.

Figure 10-12   A Sample Virtual to Physical Address Mapping

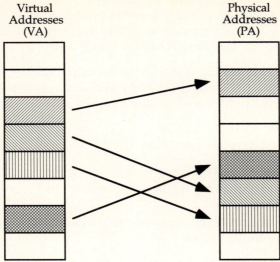

One thing that may not be apparent from Figure 10-12 is how VM uses memory efficiently. Only the pages that are actually being used by this process are loaded into physical memory—when a new page is needed, an unused block is discarded so that the new page can be loaded. Because the new page can be loaded anywhere in physical memory, the VM system is free to choose the page that is least likely to be used.

Note how this also allows the physical address space to be shared by multiple processes. Pages that are not being used by this process can be allocated to other processes so that all of physical memory is being used efficiently.

Missing from Figure 10-12 is the structure that maps the relationship between the virtual and physical pages. This structure is known as a *page table*. A page table takes a virtual address page and translates it into a physical address page. Figure 10-13 shows how the page table is used to arrive at the physical address.

In its simplest form, a page table is simply a large array that is indexed by the upper bits of the virtual address. For example, in Figure 10-13 with 1000-byte pages, the physical address of virtual address 4100 can be found by looking at the fourth (4100 / 1000 = 4) entry in the page table, which in this case contains the value 6000. The offset into the page, 100 can be added to the base address of the physical page to obtain the physical address, 6100.

Figure 10-13 Mapping from a Virtual to a Physical Address via the Page Table

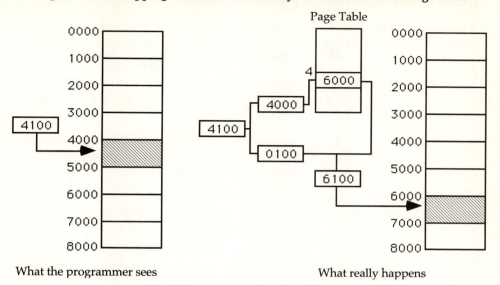

What the programmer sees   What really happens

Translation Lookaside Buffers (TLBs)

One point was glossed over in the previous section: the page table must be stored somewhere in memory. Because the virtual address space (and thus, the page table) can be quite large, it typically isn't feasible to cache the entire table. In most systems, the page table resides in main memory and is paged in and out of the cache like other memory accesses.

This can cause a serious performance problem because now a memory access can potentially require two memory accesses: one to load the relevant portion of the page table, and another to get the requested data. This is known as a *double page fault*, and the double memory access penalty associated with it is generally unacceptable.

Fortunately, the page table accesses can take advantage of the principle of locality of reference by caching recent page table translations in a separate cache, known as a *translation lookaside buffer* or TLB for short.

A TLB is a simple cache that stores associations between the recently used virtual addresses and the corresponding physical address. In addition to the physical address, most TLBs also store information (like protection level) about the page.

10.8 PowerPC Memory Management

Memory is managed in a similar fashion for all PowerPC processors, but differences do exist between the 32-bit and 64-bit PowerPC implementations.

It is necessary to define a few terms before jumping into the address translation mechanisms of the PowerPC. First of all, a *page* is defined as being 4Kb and a *segment* is 256Mb for all processors, regardless of whether the processor is a 32- or 64-bit implementation.

An *effective* address is an address as the program sees it. User-level programs typically deal with effective addresses exclusively, and these programs never need to worry about how the system translates this address.

A *virtual* address is a temporary address that the translation mechanism builds as it is calculating the physical address. The virtual address never exists as an entity because it is only needed for a short time.

A *physical*, or real, address is the address as it really exists in the computer's memory. As mentioned above, a program rarely needs to be aware of the actual storage location in memory, because all accesses are translated automatically.

Address Translation Overview

Two mechanisms present in PowerPC processors handle the translation from an effective to a physical address. These mechanisms are known as *Segmented Address Translation* and *Block Address Translation* (BAT). In addition, there is *Direct Address Translation*, which is used only when the other translations are disabled.

Segmented Address Translation, the translation mechanism most commonly used, supports two types of segments: *direct-store* and *ordinary*. For a direct-store segment, the effective address is directly converted into an I/O address and passed to the I/O subsystem. For an ordinary segment, the effective address is translated into a virtual address, which is then translated into a physical address before being used.

Block Address Translation is used when a range of pages need to be contiguous in physical memory. This grouping of pages is technically known as a *block*, but the term *BAT area* will be used instead to avoid confusion.

Direct Address Translation is used when the other translation mechanisms are disabled. In these "translations," the effective address is the same as the physical address, and no paging is performed.

When the memory management unit on a processor is given an effective address, the address is passed simultaneously to both of the translation mechanisms (if they are enabled), with the assumption that only one of them should successfully translate the address. If neither mechanism succeeds, then a storage exception results. If both succeed, then the Block Address Translation is taken over the Segmented Address Translation.

Segmented Address Translation

The Segmented Address Translation (sometimes referred to as Page Address Translations) mechanism involves translating an effective address into a virtual address, and then converting that virtual address into a physical or *real* address. Figure 10-14 illustrates this process. To simplify the discussion, these addresses will be abbreviated as EA (effective address), VA (virtual address), and RA (real address).

Figure 10-14   Converting EAs into RAs Using Segmented Address Translation

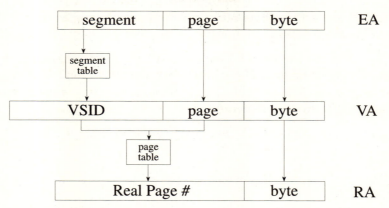

The EA is first divided into three fields: the *segment* portion, the *page* portion, and the *byte* portion. The *page* and *byte* fields specify the page and the byte-offset into the page of the address. These fields are always 16 bits and 12 bits, respectively. The *segment* field occupies the remaining bits of the EA and specifies which 256Mb segment to use. Thus, the segment specification is 4 bits wide on 32-bit implementations and 36 bits wide on 64-bit implementations.

The segment information from the EA is then used to determine the *Virtual Segment ID* (VSID) of the address. The exact mechanism used differs for 32-bit and 64-bit implementations, but the general idea is that the segment specified in the EA is used to index into a Segment Table (or register store), which returns the appropriate VSID. If the segment table identifies the segment as a direct-store segment, then the address translation stops and the processor proceeds as described later in "Direct-store Segments."

Note that a complete VA is never really calculated because it is never needed. If it were needed, a VA could be constructed by concatenating the VSID, the page, and the byte-offset.

The VSID is then concatenated with the page from the EA to form the *virtual page number* (VPN) to use as a look-up key into the Page Table. The page table returns the *real page number* (RPN), which can then be concatenated with the EA's byte field to construct the final RA.

32-bit Implementations

The Segmented Address Translation for 32-bit implementations deviates from the general translation described earlier in two significant ways: the size of the addresses and how the segment information is used to determine the VSID.

The EA is 32 bits wide, with a 4-bit Segment Register specification, a 16-bit page specification, and a 12-bit byte offset. One important thing to note is that the segment specification field contains the ID of a Segment Register (SR).

The 16 Segment Registers store information about the segment. For ordinary segments, the SRs contain a 24-bit *VSID*, and two bits (K_s and K_p) that contain the state storage key. The *T* bit (bit 0) of the SR is always 0 for ordinary segments. Figure 10-15 illustrates this structure.

Figure 10-15   Segment Register Structure

0	1	2	3				7	8		31
T	Ks	Kp	0	0	0	0	0		VSID	

The 24-bit VSID from the Segment Register can then be concatenated with the 16-bit page specification and the 12-bit byte offset to produce the 52-bit virtual address. As mentioned earlier, the VA is never actually built because only its upper portion is needed. The upper portion of the VA is known as the *virtual page number* (VPN) and consists of the VSID and the page.

64-bit Implementations

Not surprisingly, the Segmented Address Translation for 64-bit implementations deviates from the general description similar to how the 32-bit implementations do: by the size of the addresses, and how the segment information is used to determine the VSID.

The EA is 64 bits wide, with a 36-bit *effective segment ID* (ESID) specification, a 16-bit page specification, and a 12-bit byte offset. One important thing to note is that the segment specification field contains the ESID that is used to index into the Segment Table to find the *segment table entry* (STE) corresponding to this segment.

Each STE stores the same information about the segment that a Segment Register would in 32-bit implementations. The only difference is that the stored VSID is 52 bits wide instead of only 24.

The 52-bit VSID from the STE can then be concatenated with the 16-bit page specification and the 12-bit byte offset to produce the 80-bit virtual address. As mentioned earlier, the VA is never actually built because only its upper portion is needed. The upper portion of the VA is known as the *virtual page number* (VPN) and consists of the VSID and the page.

Direct-store Segments

A direct-store segment directly maps effective addresses into an external address space, such as an I/O bus. Direct-store segments are provided mostly for POWER compatibility, and their use is discouraged.

The value sent to the external storage controller depends on the PowerPC implementation. Thirty-two–bit PowerPC implementations send:

- A one-bit field that represents the storage access privilege.
- The low-order 29 bits from the appropriate Segment Register.
- The low-order 28 bits of the EA.

64-bit implementations send:

- A one-bit field that represents the storage access privilege.
- The 32-bit IO field from the appropriate STE.
- The low-order 28 bits of the EA.

Many instructions—`lwarx`, `ldarx`, `eciwx`, `ecowx`, `stwcx`, and `stdcx`—do not make sense for direct-store segments, and will cause a Data Storage interrupt if they are executed with an EA from a direct-store segment. Optionally, these instruction may produce results that are merely boundedly undefined.

Other instructions—`dcbt`, `dcbtst`, `dcbf`, `dcbi`, `dcbst`, `dcbz`, and `icbi`—will simply behave as no-ops if they are used with an EA from a direct-store segment.

Block Address Translation

Block Address Translation is used when a range of virtual addresses need to map into real memory so that the physical addresses are contiguous. If a BAT and a Segmented Address Translation both exist for a particular address, the BAT takes precedence.

Each range of addresses is known as a BAT area and is defined by the special BAT registers. These registers contain the starting address (in both effective and real address space) and the size of each BAT area.

The BAT registers are arranged as shown in Figure 10-16. There are two sets of BAT registers, one set for translating instruction addresses (IBATs) and another for data addresses (DBATs). For implementations with unified caches (like the 601), there is only one set of BAT registers that map to the IBAT registers. Each set consists of four pairs of registers, numbered from 0 to 3. Each pair has an upper and a lower register. The upper register, BAT*n*U, contains the page index of the EA, the length of the BAT area, and some state flags. The lower register, BAT*n*L, contains the real page number of the block, storage access controls, and protection bits.

Figure 10-16 Block Address Translation Register (Upper/Lower) Structure

Upper BAT Register

0 … [14/46]	[15/47] … [18/50]	[19/51] … [29/61]	[30/62]	[31/63]
BEPI	0 0 0 0	BL	Vs	Vp

Lower BAT Register

0 … [14/46]	[15/47] … [24/56]	[25/57] … [28/60]	[29/61]	[30/62] [31/63]
BRPN	0 0 0 0 0 0 0 0 0 0	WIMG	0	PP

Only certain sizes are allowed for BAT areas. The smallest valid size is 128Kb and the largest is 256 Mb. BAT area sizes must be an integral power of 2.

Direct Address Translation

Direct Address Translation is the default translation used when all other address translations are disabled. Direct Address Translation is basically the same as *no* address translation.

When this address translation is used, no paging is performed and all stores to the cache are write-through.

10.9 PowerPC Memory Access Modes

Both Segmented Address Translation and Block Address Translation provide mode control bits that are used to specify the storage mode for all accesses to the page (or block, for BAT).

The PowerPC specification defines four mode control bits: W, I, M, and G. These letters are abbreviations for Write Through, Caching Inhibited, Memory Coherence, and Guarded Storage.

- If the **Write Through** (**W**) control bit is set, then all writes to the page are written directly to main memory also. This forces the cache to be consistent with main memory.
- Pages with the **Caching Inhibited** (**I**) bit set are not cached. All memory accesses are passed through the cache directly to main storage.
- The **Memory Coherence** (**M**) bit controls whether or not the hardware should enforce the memory coherence protocols. It is sometimes desirable to disable this bit when coherence can be enfored more efficiently via software.
- **Guarded Storage** (**G**) is not well behaved with respect to prefetching. For example, the storage could represent an I/O device that changes regularly or has memory gaps that are invalid addresses.

Ignoring the G bit (which may be on or off), Table 10-6 lists the eight possible combinations of the WIM bits. Of these eight modes, only six make sense because the W and I bits may not be set together.

Table 10-6 Interpretation of WIM access modes

W	I	M	Description
0	0	0	*Data from this page may be cached.* *Storage consistency is **not** enforced by hardware.*
0	0	1	*Data from this page may be cached.* *Storage consistency is enforced by hardware.*
0	1	0	*Data from this page may **not** be cached.* *Storage consistency is **not** enforced by hardware.*
0	1	1	*Data from this page may **not** be cached.* *Storage consistency is enforced by hardware.*
1	0	0	*Data from this page may be cached.* *Write operations must be passed to main memory.* *Storage consistency is **not** enforced by hardware.*
1	0	1	*Data from this page may be cached.* *Write operations must be passed to main memory.* *Storage consistency is enforced by hardware.*
1	1	0	*not allowed*
1	1	1	*not allowed*

PowerPC 601 Access Modes

The 601 supports the W, I, and M control modes for pages but does not support guarded storage (G).

10.10 PowerPC Lookaside Buffer Instructions

Most PowerPC implementations will provide lookaside buffers for the common address translation tables. The instructions described in this section provide the programmer with some control over the contents of these buffers.

TLB Instructions

Because most PowerPC implementations will use a TLB to cache Page Table entries, the standard TLB instructions listed in Table 10-7 are defined. Any PowerPC processor that provides a TLB must provide mechanisms for invalidating a TLB entry (`tlbie`) and invalidating the entire TLB (`tlbia`).

If an implementation does not implement a TLB, then these instructions will be treated as no-ops.

Table 10-7 Condition Register Logical Extended Forms

`tlbia` **TLB Invalidate All** *supervisor-level instruction* *this is an optional part of the PowerPC specification*	*Invalidate entire TLB.*
`tlbie rB` **TLB Invalidate Entry** *supervisor-level instruction* *this is an optional part of the PowerPC specification*	*Invalidate TLB entry containing (rB).*
`tlbsync` **TLB Synchronize** *supervisor-level instruction* *this is an optional part of the PowerPC specification*	*Wait for all pending TLB instructions to complete.*

The `tlbia` instruction invalidates the entire contents of the TLB.

The `tlbie` instruction looks up the TLB entry associated with the effective address contained in r*B* and invalidates that entry (if present).

The `tlbsync` instruction forces the processor to wait until all of the previously executed `tlbie` and `tlbia` instructions from this processor have completed execution on all other processors. Thus, this instruction stalls the current processor until the TLBs of all the processors are synchronized.

SLB Instructions

An SLB is defined on 64-bit PowerPC implementations that want to cache entries of the Segment Table. Trying to execute the instructions listed in Table 10-8 on a 32-bit implementation will result in an illegal instruction exception.

If a 64-bit PowerPC implementation does not implement an SLB, then these instructions will be treated as no-ops.

Table 10-8 Condition Register Logical Extended Forms

`slbia` **SLB Invalidate All** *supervisor-level instruction* *64-bit implementations only* *this is an optional part of the PowerPC specification*	*Invalidate entire SLB.*
`slbie rB` **SLB Invalidate Entry** *supervisor-level instruction* *64-bit implementations only* *this is an optional part of the PowerPC specification*	*Invalidate SLB entry containing (rB).*

The `slbia` instruction invalidates the entire contents of the SLB.

The `slbie` instruction looks up the SLB entry associated with the effective address contained in rB and invalidates that entry (if present).

Pipelining | 11

Although nothing in the PowerPC specification *requires* a pipeline, a pipeline is an architectural feature commonly used to achieve high processor throughput. It is important to understand the fundamentals of pipelining because many advanced optimization techniques are based on taking advantage of pipeline architecture to avoid pipeline conflicts.

11.1 What is a Pipeline?

A pipeline is an implementation technique that allows the execution of multiple instructions to be overlapped in the processor. This means that at any time, the processor may be in the middle of processing many instructions instead of just one.

Pipelines take advantage of the fact that the execution of any instruction can be broken into a set of stages that must be performed sequentially. For example, instead of executing an instruction as one unit, a hypothetical processor could divide instruction execution into five distinct stages, named simply *stage 1* through *stage 5* to avoid introducing unnecessary complexity and terminology at this time. Figure 11-1 shows these stages.

**Figure 11-1   The Execution of an Instruction (at top) Can Be Conceptually
Broken Up into Distinct Stages (shown at bottom)**

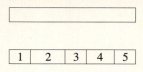

To execute an instruction, the instruction must pass through each of the stages in
order. Thus, the instruction passes from *stage1* → *stage2* → ... → *stage5*, at which
point the instruction has completed execution and all the results have been written to the proper places.

It's important to note in this execution scheme that after one stage of an instruction has completed execution, the instruction no longer needs the portion of the
processor dedicated to executing that stage. This means that stage is free for the
next instruction to use; the next instruction can begin execution before the first
instruction has completed. This *overlapped execution* is shown in Figure 11-2.

Figure 11-2   Overlapped Instruction Execution in a Pipeline

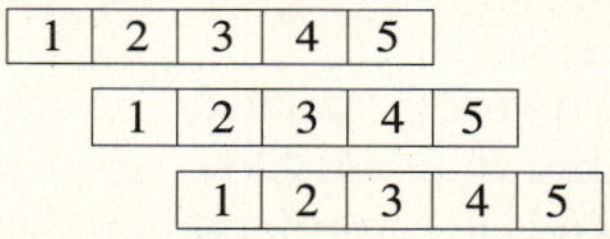

| 1 | 2 | 3 | 4 | 5 |

| 1 | 2 | 3 | 4 | 5 |

| 1 | 2 | 3 | 4 | 5 |

11.2 Basic Pipeline Functions

This section describes a simple pipeline and its operation. It introduces various
terms and concepts that you need to understand before jumping in and tackling
a real-world pipeline implemented for various PowerPC processors.

The first step in implementing a pipeline is dividing the instruction execution
into discrete stages. This division doesn't come free; a certain amount of overhead associated with the extra logic is required to control the flow of instructions
through the pipeline stages. The end result is that it actually takes longer for any
one particular instruction to execute from start to finish (commonly referred to
as the instruction *latency*) than it would on a properly implemented non-pipelined implementation. However, this minor detriment is more than offset by the
overall increase in instruction throughput.

This comparison is shown in Figure 11-3.

Figure 11-3   To Keep the Stages Synchronized, the Longest Stage (Stage 2 in this Figure) Defines How Wide All the Stages Must Be

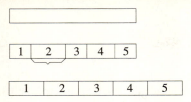

Note that the longest stage determines the length of time taken to execute each stage. Stages that require less time finish early and waste time, so that all of the stages remain synchronized.

Consider three instructions executing on a non-pipelined processor and a pipelined procession. Instruction 1 is *dispatched* (that is, execution begins) at the same time on both systems. Because of the reduced latency of the non-pipelined system, the first instruction *retires* (completes) before the same instruction on the pipelined system.

However, the second (and subsequent) instructions show the real advantage of the pipelined architecture. In the non-pipelined system, the second instruction must wait until the first one is completely done before it can begin execution, as illustrated in Figure 11-4.

Figure 11-4   Three Sample Instructions in a Non-pipelined (above) and Pipelined System (below)

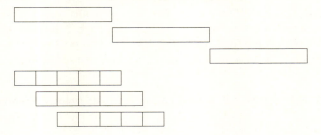

The pipelined system doesn't need to wait before dispatching the second instruction. It dispatches one instruction per cycle (ideally) and retires one instruction per cycle after the pipeline has been filled, in a situation known as "one instruction per cycle throughput." The term *throughput* refers to the number of instructions completed per cycle, ignoring the set-up time required to fill the processor pipelines.

Not surprisingly, the situation is actually more complicated than suggested so far. Consider this code fragment:

```
add     r3,r2,r1
add     r3,r3,r4
```

In this case, we have a data dependency: the second instruction ($r3 = r3 + r4$) depends on the result of the first instruction ($r3 = r2 + r1$). This is not a problem in non-pipelined systems because we don't dispatch the second instruction until the first instruction is completed. However, a pipelined implementation will have to handle this condition gracefully or an incorrect value of r3 will be added to r4.

One simple way to handle this case is to stall the second instruction in the pipe until the results of the first instruction are available, as shown in Figure 11-5. This is less than ideal, but it's more important that the instructions execute properly than execute quickly (imagine a very fast divide operation that only sometimes gave the correct answer).

Figure 11-5   A Data Dependency Causing Two Stall Cycles

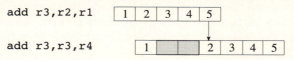

To minimize the impact of the stall, the pipeline can be set up so that it forwards the results of the first instruction to the second instruction as soon as they are available. The results of an instruction are typically calculated a few cycles before the instruction is complete, so this can save a few cycles. The second instruction doesn't have to wait for the results to be written to the register store before continuing. This technique, known as data *feed-forwarding,* is illustrated in Figure 11-6.

Figure 11-6   Data Feed-forwarding Can Eliminate Many Dependency Stalls

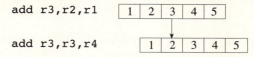

Of course, the best way to eliminate the stalls due to data dependencies is by rescheduling the code so that there are independent instructions between the load and use of the register. Known as *instruction scheduling,* this is covered later in the chapters on instruction timing and resource scheduling.

11.3 PowerPC 601 Pipeline Description

The 601's pipeline is, of course, much more complicated than a simple pipeline with a few stages. The three basic pipelines in the 601 each handle a specific class of instructions. In addition, a dispatcher takes the instructions to be executed and passes them along to the appropriate pipeline for execution.

Coordinating and synchronizing these three pipelines complicates the simple pipeline model considerably.

Functional Units of the 601

There are seven basic units in the 601's processor core:

- Fetch Arbitration Unit (FAU)
- Cache Access Unit (CAU)
- Dispatch Unit (DU)
- Integer Unit (IU)
- Floating-Point Unit (FPU)
- Branch Processing Unit (BPU)
- Data Access Queueing Unit (DAQU)

All instructions that are executed pass through the FA, CAU, and DU before they are passed to the appropriate pipeline: BPU for branches, IU for integer and load/store instructions, and FPU for floating-point instructions. The DAQU is a special queueing unit that is used only by the store instructions.

The flow of instructions through the pipeline units is shown in Figure 11-7. Note that the DAQU does not directly process instructions and is not in this figure.

Figure 11-7   Instruction Path through the 601's Pipeline

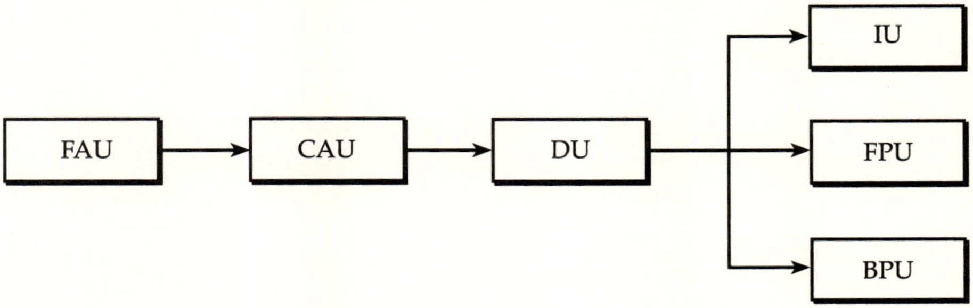

The flow of data through the pipeline units is shown in Figure 11-8. This figure also includes the instruction flow from the previous figure. Here the DAQU has been added to the data path between the IU and the CAU.

Figure 11-8   Instruction (Thick Lines) and Data (Thin Lines) Paths in the 601

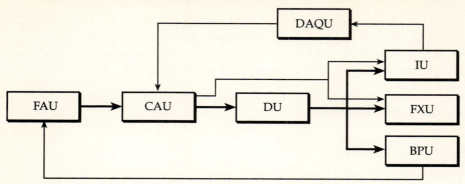

Fetch Arbitration Unit (FAU)

The FAU is responsible for determining which instructions need to be fetched from memory. After the address of the next fetch group is generated, it is sent to the CAU so that the instructions can be fetched from memory.

Cache Access Unit (CAU)

The CAU provides an interface between the processor core units and the memory system. The CAU responds to requests from both the FAU (for instruction fetches) and the IU (for instructions that access memory).

Requests from the FAU are instruction groups that need to be loaded and dispatched. The results of these accesses are sent directly to the DU.

Requests from the IU are data load/store requests. Store requests are sent to the memory system, and load requests are sent to either the IU or FPU, as appropriate.

Dispatch Unit (DU)

The DU is an eight-instruction queue from which instructions are dispatched to the BPU, FPU, or IU. Up to three instructions (one to each unit) can be dispatched each cycle.

Integer Unit (IU)

The integer unit executes these instruction types:

- Integer arithmetic and logical instructions
- All load and store instructions (integer and floating-point)
- Condition Register instructions

- Special Purpose Register instructions
- Memory management instructions

The IU consists of a four-stage pipeline with an extra writeback stage for integer load instructions.

Floating-Point Unit (FPU)

The FPU executes these instruction types:

- Floating-point arithmetic and compare instructions
- Floating-point store instructions

The FPU consists of a five-stage pipeline with an extra writeback stage for floating-point load instructions.

Note that the FPU and the IU both handle floating-point store instructions. The instructions must pass through both pipelines simultaneously.

Branch Processing Unit (BPU)

The BPU executes branch instructions by either resolving the branch and sending the target address to the FAU, or by predicting the branch (using a static prediction scheme), sending the address to the FAU, and then waiting until the branch is resolved.

If the branch prediction is incorrect, the BPU is responsible for cancelling the invalid instructions and initiating the fetch of the correct instructions.

Data Access Queueing Unit (DAQU)

The DAQU contains an Integer Buffer and a Floating-Point Store Buffer (ISB and FPSB) that are used to buffer accesses to the memory unit when the cache is busy or the data to be stored is not yet available. Each of these queues is one element deep.

The 601 Fetch Arbitration Unit (FAU)

The FAU is responsible for determining the address of the next instruction group to load from memory. This address is then sent to the CAU so that the instructions can be loaded and executed.

The address is calculated from either the:

- Mispredict Recovery address (from the MR stage of the BPU)
- Branch target address (from the branch in the BE stage of the BPU)
- Next sequential address

These sources are listed in order of priority, so an MR address takes precedence over a branch target address, and the next sequential address is only used as a last resort.

There is only one stage in the FAU, the Fetch Arbitrate (FA) stage.

The 601 Cache Access Unit (CAU)

The CAU consists of the two stages, Cache Arbitration (CARB) and Cache Access (CACC), shown in Figure 11-9. The CARB stage queues up all the cache access requests and decides which one gets passed along to the CACC stage. The CACC stage performs the cache access.

Figure 11-9   The Two Stages of the Cache Access Unit

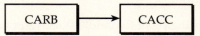

Cache Arbitration (CARB)

During the CARB stage, all of the pending cache requests fight it out to determine which request gets sent to the CACC stage. The winner of this battle is determined by choosing the request with the highest priority, because each type of cache request has a different priority. These priorities are discussed in §12.6 "Cache Access Timings."

Cache Access (CACC)

The CACC stage is where the cache is accessed and the requested data is sent to or retrieved from the cache.

After the data is loaded from the cache, it is forwarded to the appropriate part of the processor. Instruction fetches are passed on to the Dispatch Unit, and load operations are passed directly to the appropriate unit (either the IU or the FPU).

The 601 Dispatch Unit (DU)

The Dispatch Unit illustrated in Figure 11-10 is an Instruction Queue that can hold up to eight instructions that are waiting to be dispatched. Each element in this queue is considered a different stage of the DU, so there are effectively eight stages, named IQ7 through IQ0.

Figure 11-10   The Eight IQ Stages of the Dispatch Unit

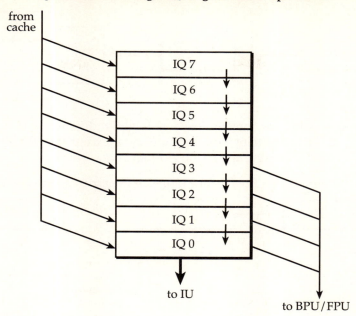

The DU analyzes the instructions in the bottom half of the instruction queue (IQ3 - IQ0) and identifies the instruction type (branch, integer, or floating-point) for each instruction. After the instruction types have been identified, the DU can then dispatch one of each instruction type to the respective units.

The only restriction is that an integer instruction can only be dispatched from the IQ0 position. This restriction simplifies the task of synchronizing the various pipelines.

The 601 Integer Unit (IU)

The Integer Unit consists of five stages, only four of which are considered part of the primary pipeline. The fifth stage is only used by integer load instructions.

Figure 11-11 shows the conceptual arrangement of the four primary stages and the primary path most integer instructions use.

Figure 11-11   The Primary Pipeline of the Integer Unit

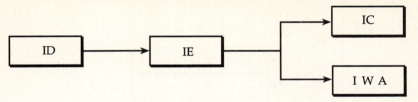

The pipeline path for integer loads is slightly different and is shown in Figure 11-12. Floating-point loads are the same except that the FWL stage in the FPU is used instead of the IU's IWL stage.

Figure 11-12   The Pipeline Usage for Integer Load Instructions

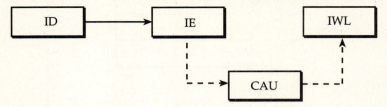

Integer Decode (ID)

The ID stage is where the integer instructions are decoded and the operands are fetched from the GPRs. This stage is typically entered in the same cycle that the instruction enters the IQ0 stage of the DU.

Integer Execute (IE)

The IE stage is where all of the arithmetic integer instructions are executed and where the effective address for loads and stores is calculated.

The results of an instruction in IE can be forwarded to the instruction currently in ID to prevent data dependency stalls in the IU.

Integer Completion (IC)

The IC stage indicates that the instruction has been committed, even though it is not yet complete. This signals other execution units that the instruction is essentially complete and needs only to write the results in the proper place.

The IC stage is always executed in parallel with another stage, usually the IWA or CACC stages.

Integer Arithmetic Writeback (IWA)

The IWA stage is used by the arithmetic instructions to perform the writeback of the calculated results into the GPRs.

Integer Load Writeback (IWL)

The IWL stage is used by the integer load instructions to write the loaded data into the GPRs.

The 601 Floating-Point Unit (FPU)

There are six stages in the Floating-Point Unit, four of which are considered part of the primary floating-point pipeline. One of the remaining two stages is an additional instruction buffer, and the other is only used by floating-point load instructions.

The four primary stages, and the buffer, are conceptually arranged as shown in Figure 11-13. This figure shows the primary path that the majority of the floating-point instructions use. Note that the buffer stage (F1) is only used if necessary. If the FD stage is available, instructions skip F1 and go directly to FD.

Figure 11-13   The Primary Floating-Point Pipeline

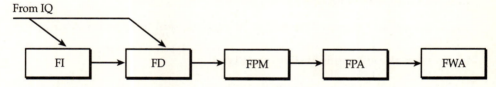

Figure 11-14 shows the pipeline path for floating-point loads. It's completely different from other floating-point operations because all load instructions (including floating-point loads) are handled by the Integer Unit. The only FPU stage used by floating-point loads is the FWL stage, which is used in much the same way as the IWL stage is used for integer load operations.

Figure 11-14   Pipeline Flow for Floating-Point Load Instructions

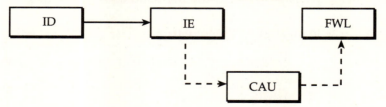

Floating-Point Instruction Queue (F1)

The FP1 stage is a one-instruction buffer used only if the FD stage is currently occupied by a previous floating-point instruction. If the FD stage is available, the instruction skips this stage and proceeds directly to FD.

Floating-Point Decode (FD)

The FD stage is where the floating-point instructions are decoded and any required operands are fetched from the FP register store.

Floating-Point Multiply (FPM)

The FPM stage is where the Floating-Point Unit performs a 27×53 bit multiply operation.

Double-precision floating-point instructions that involve multiplication (`fmul`, `fmadd`, `fmsub`, `fnmadd`, `fnmsub`) require two cycles in this stage and may stall subsequent floating-point instructions.

Floating-point divide operations require 16/30 cycles (for single-/double-precision) in this stage.

Floating-Point Add (FPA)

The FPA stage is where the floating-point addition/subtraction is performed.

Floating-Point Arithmetic Writeback (FWA)

The FWA stage is when most of the floating-point instructions write their results back into the FPRs. The results are also made available to the instruction currently in FD, if necessary.

Floating-Point Load Writeback (FWL)

The FWL stage is used only by the floating-point load instructions to write the data into the FPRs. If this data is required by the instruction currently in FD, then the data is made available to that instruction simultaneously with the writeback.

The 601 Branch Processing Unit (BPU)

The BPU has a simple three-stage pipeline that is arranged as shown in Figure 11-15.

Figure 11-15   Stages of the Branch Processing Unit

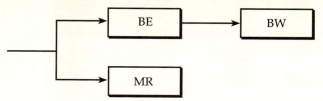

It's important to note that while all the branch instructions need to use the BE stage, the MR and BW stages are only used if necessary. A non-conditional branch that doesn't need to update the LR or CTR requires only one stage of execution in BE.

Branch Execute (BE)

During the BE stage, the branch target address is calculated and conditional branches are predicted (if necessary). If the branch is determined or predicted to be taken, the branch also initiates a fetch for the instructions at the target address. The FA stage for this fetch occurs in parallel with the BE stage.

Mispredict Recovery (MR)

The MR stage is when all conditional branches that needed to be predicted remain until the branch is resolved. After the branch is resolved, the prediction is determined to be either correct or incorrect.

Correct predictions require no action other than allowing the branch to leave the MR stage.

An incorrect prediction requires that the MR stage purge all the incorrectly dispatched instructions and initiate a fetch of the correct instructions so that they can be dispatched.

Branch Writeback (BW)

The BW stage is when the branch instructions stay until they are able to write results back into the LR or CTR.

Not all branch instructions need to writeback results. Those that don't need to update the LR or CTR skip the BW stage entirely.

The 601 Data Access Queueing Unit (DAQU)

The DAQU contains two buffers used to queue store instructions that have been committed by the IU, but can't yet be written to memory because either the cache is busy handling other requests, or the required data is not available from the FPU. These buffers are quite useful because they free the IE stage in the IU and allow additional integer instructions to be processed.

There are only two stages in the DAQU; the Floating-Point Store Buffer (FPSB) and the Integer Store buffer (ISB).

Floating-Point Store Buffer (FPSB)

The FPSB is used to queue one outstanding floating-point store instruction that has completed in the IU but is either waiting for data from the FPU or waiting to gain access to the processor cache.

Integer Store Buffer (ISB)

The ISB stage is used to queue one integer store instruction that has completed in IU but is waiting to gain access to the processor cache so that it can write the data to memory.

PowerPC 601 Instruction Timing | 12

This chapter gives an overview of the instruction timings for the PowerPC 601 processor. It's important to note that the timings given here do not take into account the conflicts that might arise when multiple instructions need to use the same processor resource. This resource conflict problem is covered in Chapter 15, "Resource Scheduling."

12.1 Reading the Timing Tables

Two types of timing tables will be used in this chapter. The first type shows the timing for a single instruction and identifies the number of cycles that the instruction will spend in each pipeline stage. Here's an example of a timing table for a generic integer instruction.

# of Cycles	1	1	1
Stages	ID	IE	IC IWA

This instruction spends one cycle in ID, followed by one cycle in IE, and then another one cycle simultaneously in both the IC and IWA stages. The overall latency (from start to finish) for this instruction is three cycles.

The second type of timing table shows the timing for a sequence of instructions to demonstrate how the instructions interact with each other. Here's an example of this type of timing table.

Cycle #:	1	2	3	4	5	6	7
cmp crf0,r30,r31	FA CARB	CACC	IQ0 ID	IE	IC IWA	-	-
beq crf0,target	FA CARB	CACC	IQ1 BE MR	MR	-	-	-
and r0,r0,r1	FA CARB	CACC	IQ2	IQ0 ID	IE	IC IWA	-
nand r2,r2,r3	FA CARB	CACC	IQ3	IQ1	IQ0 ID	IE	IC IWA

In this table, each row represents a different instruction and each column represents successive cycles. This makes it easy to identify which stage each instruction is in for each cycle of execution.

12.2 Instruction Dispatch Timing

All instructions that are executed must pass from the processor caches into the dispatch buffers.

Retrieving Instructions from the Cache

The first stage of instruction execution is determining which instructions need to be executed next. This task is accomplished by the Fetch Arbitration (FA) stage of the Fetch Arbitration Unit (FAU).

After the address has been generated by FA, it is passed to the Cache Access Unit (CAU), which arbitrates for the cache and then retrieves the data from the cache. This is done in two stages, with Cache Arbitration (CARB) stage arbitrating, and the Cache Access (CACC) stage retrieving data.

After the instruction reaches the Dispatch Unit, it is placed in one of the eight Instruction Queue entries (IQ7 - IQ0). The term Dispatch Stage, or DS, is sometimes used to refer to an instruction in the IQ buffer.

Thus, the timing for an instruction passing through the initial pipeline stages would be:

# of Cycles:	1	1	1
Stages:	FA CARB	CACC	DS

As with most of the cache timings in this chapter, the CARB takes one cycle executed in parallel with another pipeline stage (in this case, FA). The CACC stage also takes only one cycle. Both of these are ideal timings that do not always hold true. A complete discussion of Cache Access timings is in §12.6, "Cache Access Timings."

Instruction Dispatching

From the DS stage, the instruction is then dispatched to the appropriate execution unit: branches to the BPU, integer instructions to the IU, and floating-point instructions to the FPU. Because the 601 supports out-of-order dispatch, this dispatch process is more interesting than it may initially appear.

First of all, there are eight IQ buffer entries, but instructions can only be dispatched from the lower four IQ entries, IQ3 - IQ0. After an instruction enters the lower half of the IQ buffer, it is a candidate for dispatch. Dispatching follows these rules:

- One integer instruction can be dispatched to the IU from IQ0.
- One floating-point instruction can be dispatched to the FPU from IQ0-IQ3. If there are multiple floating-point instructions in the lower half of the IQ buffer, the lowest one (closest to IQ0) is dispatched.
- One branch instruction can be dispatched to the BPU from IQ0-IQ3. If there are multiple branch instructions in the lower half of the IQ buffer, the one closest to IQ0 is dispatched.

A graphic representation of these rules is given in Figure 12-1.

Figure 12-1 Dispatching from the Lower Four of the Eight IQ Buffers

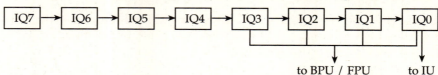

This gives a best case dispatch of three instructions per cycle. Note that these dispatch rules are such that instructions are always executed in order with respect to each execution unit. This means that all instructions from a particular execution unit are executed in order with respect to other instructions from that same unit. However, instructions from other execution units may be executed out of order with respect to these instructions.

A good way to demonstrate this is to analyze a sequence of instructions and track which IQ stage they are in during each cycle. (The other pipeline stages are omitted for clarity.) To help simplify this example, both of the branches in the code sequence are assumed to be fully resolved and not-taken.

Cycle #:	1	2	3	4
fsub1	**(IQ0)**	-	-	-
branch1	**(IQ1)**	-	-	-
add1	IQ2	**(IQ0)**	-	-
add2	IQ3	IQ1	**(IQ0)**	-
fsub2	IQ4	**(IQ2)**	-	-
fsub3	IQ5	IQ3	**(IQ1)**	-
add3	IQ6	IQ4	IQ2	**(IQ0)**
branch2	IQ7	IQ5	**(IQ3)**	-

During the first cycle, the fsub1 and the branch1 instructions (shown in **bold** with parentheses) are dispatched. The integer instruction add1 cannot be dispatched because it is not in the IQ0 position.

In the second cycle, all the instructions shift down as far as they can. Now the add1 instruction is in IQ0, so it can be dispatched. Two floating-point instruction candidates, fsub2 in IQ2 and fsub3 in IQ3, could be dispatched. The fsub2 instruction is dispatched because it is in the lower IQ entry.

In the third cycle, all the instructions shift down again. The fsub3 instruction shifts down two entries because fsub2 has been removed from the IQ. This brings branch2 into the IQ3 position so that it can be dispatched. The add2 and fsub3 instructions are also dispatched at this time.

In the fourth cycle, add3 enters IQ0 and is dispatched. Presumably, the instructions following branch2 would be in the lower half of the IQ buffer by now and, thus, would also be candidates for dispatch.

Another way of viewing this same sequence of instructions is to watch the IQ stages as the instructions pass through them.

Cycle #:	1	2	3	4
IQ7:	branch2	-	-	-
IQ6:	add3	-	-	-
IQ5:	fsub3	branch2	-	-
IQ4:	fsub2	add3	-	-
IQ3:	add2	fsub3	(branch2)	-
IQ2:	add1	(fsub2)	add3	-
IQ1:	(branch1)	add2	(fsub3)	-
IQ0:	(fsub1)	(add1)	(add2)	(add3)

The instruction dispatching is identical to the earlier example, but here it is more apparent that the instructions are being dispatched from the bottom half of the IQ and that the integer instructions are dispatched only from the bottom (IQ0) position.

12.3 Fixed-Point Instruction Timings

The fixed-point, or integer, instructions are the easiest to time because the integer pipeline is simple and almost all of the instructions have the same timing.

Of the five stages in the IU pipeline, one (the IWL stage) is used only by integer load instructions. This leaves four stages that are commonly used by integer instructions: Integer Decode (ID), Integer Execute (IE), Integer Completion (IC), and Integer Arithmetic Writeback (IWA).

Of these remaining four stages, the ID stage is almost always executed in parallel with the IQ0 stage in the Dispatch Unit. The only time that integer instructions are not passed directly from IQ0 to ID is when the ID stage is currently occupied by a previous instruction due to a pipeline stall.

The IC and IWA stages are also executed in parallel. As a result, the integer pipeline is effectively only three stages from decode to writeback. Almost all of the integer instructions spend only one cycle in each stage, resulting in a three-cycle latency for most instructions.

Integer Add and Subtract Instructions

All of the add and subtract instructions require one cycle in ID, IE, IC, and IWA. The IC and IWA stages are executed in parallel so that the total latency is only three cycles.

# of Cycles	1	1	1
Stages	ID	IE	IC IWA

The *Negate, Absolute Value,* and *Difference or Zero* instructions are commonly grouped with the add and subtract instructions because they all allow the Overflow Exception and Record bits to be set in the instruction encoding. These instructions have the same timing as the add and subtract instructions.

Integer Multiply Instructions

The integer multiply instructions require one cycle in ID, either five, nine, or ten cycles in IE, and a shared cycle in IC/IWA. The number of cycles spent in IE depends on the instruction and the data that is being multiplied.

The *Multiply Low Immediate* (`mulli`) instruction always takes five cycles in IE.

# of Cycles	1	5	1
Stages	ID	IE	IC IWA

The length of time that the other multiply instructions spend in IE is dependent on the data contained in rB. If the upper 16 bits of rB are all sign bits, then the instruction spends five cycles in IE, otherwise it spends nine cycles. This means that the lesser (in magnitude) of the two arguments should be placed in rB because there is a potential savings of four cycles if $-2^{15} \le (rB) < 2^{15}-1$.

# of Cycles	1	5/9	1
Stages	ID	IE	IC IWA

For the *Multiply High Word Unsigned* instruction, the timing is the same except that ten cycles will be spent in IE if the high-order bit of rB is a '1'.

# of Cycles	1	5/9/10	1
Stages	ID	IE	IC IWA

Integer Divide Instructions

The integer divide instructions require one cycle in ID, 36 cycles in IE, and a shared cycle in IC/IWA.

# of Cycles	1	36	1
Stages	ID	IE	IC IWA

From this information, it should be apparent that the integer divide instructions should be avoided whenever possible.

Integer Boolean Instructions

The Boolean logic instructions (and the extend sign and count leading zeros instructions) need one cycle in each of the ID, IE, and IC/IWA stages.

# of Cycles	1	1	1
Stages	ID	IE	IC IWA

Shift, Rotate, and Mask Instructions

All the shift, rotate and mask instructions require the standard one cycle in the ID, IE, and IC/IWA stages.

# of Cycles	1	1	1
Stages	ID	IE	IC IWA

Integer Compare Instructions

All integer compare instructions spend one cycle in ID, one cycle in IE, and a shared cycle in IC/IWA. The results of the compare are written into the CR and forwarded to the BPU during the IE stage.

# of Cycles	1	1	1
Stages	ID	IE	IC IWA

Integer Load Instructions

The Integer Unit handles all of the load instructions, including the floating-point load instructions. For the simple case where the operand being loaded does not cross a doubleword boundary, only one cycle in IE/CARB is required.

# of Cycles	1	1	1	1
Stages	ID	CARB IE	CACC IC	IWL

The *Load with Update* forms have similar timings, except that the instruction must also spend a cycle in IWA, which is in parallel with the cycle spent in IC.

# of Cycles	1	1	1	1
Stages	ID	CARB IE	CACC IC IWA	IWL

Timings for misaligned data loads are given in §12.8, "Abnormal Integer Conditions."

Timings for the floating-point load instructions are the same as given above, except that the FWL stage (in the FPU) is used for writeback instead of the IWL stage. Timings for misaligned floating-point loads are given in §12.9, "Abnormal Floating-Point Conditions."

Load Multiple and Load String Instructions

The *Load Multiple* and *Load String* instructions require one cycle in IE for each register of data that is being loaded. If n registers are being loaded and the data is word-aligned, then the instruction timing is:

# of Cycles	1	1	1	n-2	1	1
Stages	ID	CARB IE	CARB CACC IE IC	CARB CACC IE IWL	CACC IWL	IWL

Timings for misaligned *Load Multiple* and *Load String* accesses are given in §12.8, "Abnormal Integer Conditions."

Integer Store Instructions

The Integer Unit also handles all of the store instructions, including all of the floating-point store instructions. For the simple case where the operand being stored does not cross a doubleword boundary, only one cycle in IE/CARB is required.

The primary difference between the store and the load instructions (which were discussed earlier) is that the store instructions do not need to write the results into registers during a IWL stage.

# of Cycles	1	1	1
Stages	ID	CARB IE	CACC IC

The *Store with Update* forms have similar timings, except that the instruction must also spend a cycle in IWA, which is in parallel with the cycle spent in IC.

# of Cycles	1	1	1
Stages	ID	CARB IE	CACC IC IWA

Timings for misaligned data stores are given in §12.8, "Abnormal Integer Conditions."

Timings for the floating-point store instructions are significantly different and are given later in §12.4, "Floating-Point Instruction Timings."

Store Conditional Word Instruction

The Store Conditional Word (`stwcx.`) is a special case of the integer store instructions because it needs to update the EQ bit of CR field 0 to indicate whether or not the store was successfully performed.

If the store is performed, then the timing is:

# of Cycles	1	1	1	1
Stages	ID	CARB IE	CACC (IE) IC IWA	(IE) IWA

If the store is not performed, the timing is:

# of Cycles	1	1	1
Stages	ID	CARB IE	CACC (IE) IC IWA

In these timing tables, note that the `stwcx.` instruction makes use of the resources in the IE stage while it is in IWA—this is how the instruction updates the CR. This is indicated in the timing tables by placing the IE stage in parentheses for these cycles. The store conditional instruction isn't technically occupying the IE stage, but it is preventing another instruction from performing useful work in IE.

While the `stwcx.` instruction is in IWA, another instruction may be in IE, but it will be stalled there until `stwcx.` leaves IWA and frees the IE resources.

Store Multiple and Store String Instructions

The *Store Multiple* and *Store String* instructions require one cycle in IE for each register of data that is being stored. If n registers are being stored and the data is word-aligned, then the instruction timing is:

# of Cycles	1	1	1	n-2	1
Stages	ID	CARB IE	CARB CACC IE IC	CARB CACC IE	CACC

Timings for misaligned *Store Multiple* and *Store String* accesses are given in §12.8, "Abnormal Integer Conditions."

Move to/from SPR Instructions

The timings for instructions that move data to and from SPRs depend on the SPR being accessed or updated.

# of Cycles	1	n	m
Stages	ID	IE	IC IWA

The values for n and m are determined by using the SPR as an index into this table:

# of Cycles		Move	Special Purpose Registers
n	m		
1	1	to/from	CR, LR, CTR, MQ, XER, PIR, DABR, EAR, RTCL, DEC, SDR1, SR
2	1	to	SPRGn, DSISR, DAR, RTCU, SRR0, SRR1
2	2	from	MSR
2	4	from	SPRGn, DSISR, DAR, HID0, HID1, HID2, RTCU, SRR0, SRR1
2	7	from	PVR
2	11	to	HID0
2	12	to	HID1
2	17	to	HID2, MSR (when FPSCR[FEX]=0)
2	20	to	MSR (when FPSCR[FEX]=1)

Of these SPR instructions, the `mtmsr` instruction is unique in that it stalls in ID until all previous instructions (in program order) have completed execution.

Cache Instructions

The timings for the cache instructions depend on many factors, including the current MESI state for the block being operated on, the current state of the processor bus, and the speed of the bus (relative to the processor speed).

When the `dcbf`, `dcbst`, or `dcbz` instructions are used on a block in the MESI "Modified" (M) state (for all three instructions) or the MESI "Exclusive" (E) state (`dcbz` only), they do not require access to the processor bus. The timings for these operations are thus very similar to that of the load instructions. The only difference is the absence of the IWL stage.

# of Cycles	1	1	1
Stages	ID	CARB IE	CACC IC

The cache instructions that require access to the processor bus must spend at least six cycles in the CACC/IC stage. These instructions are `tlbi`, `sync`, `dcbi`, and `dcbf` and `dcbst` (when operating on E, S, and I blocks), and `dcbz` (when operating on S and I blocks).

# of Cycles	1	1	≥6
Stages	ID	CARB IE	CACC IC

Trap Instructions

The trap instructions spend one cycle in ID and IE and then spend either one cycle or 22 cycles in IC/IWA, depending on whether or not the trap is taken. If the trap is not taken (the common case), then the instruction takes one cycle in IC/IWA; otherwise it requires 22 cycles.

# of Cycles	1	1	1/22
Stages	ID	IE	IC IWA

System Call/Return from Interrupt Instructions

Both of these instructions take two cycles in IE and either 13 or 16 cycles in IC/IWA. The `sc` instruction requires 16 cycles in IC/IWA.

# of Cycles	1	2	16
Stages	ID	IE	IC IWA

The `rfi` instruction requires 13 cycles in IC/IWA.

# of Cycles	1	2	13
Stages	ID	IE	IC IWA

12.4 Floating-Point Instruction Timings

The floating-point pipeline is somewhat more complex than the integer pipeline due to both the increased number of stages and the inherent complexity of floating-point calculations.

In general, there are four basic stages in the floating-point pipeline: FP Decode (FD), FP Multiply (FPM), FP Add (FPA), and FP Arithmetic Writeback (FWA). One additional stage, FP Load Writeback (FWL), is only used by floating-point load instructions.

Also, a special, one-entry, Floating-point Instruction Queue (F1) stage is used only when an instruction needs to be dispatched to the FPU and the FD stage is already occupied (because a previous instruction is stalling the pipeline).

Unlike the integer instructions, floating-point instructions do not enter FD (or F1) simultaneously with the cycle spent in the IQ buffer. The FD stage is not entered until the cycle after the instruction has been dispatched, as the timing for the `fadd` instruction shows.

Cycles:	1	2	3	4	5	6	7
fadd fr1,fr1,fr2	FA CARB	CACC	IQ0	FD	FPM	FPA	FWA

Note that all of the timings given in this chapter assume that the instructions are being used under "normal circumstances": the instruction operands and results are valid floating-point values that do not require pre-normalization or denormalization. For floating-point timings under these conditions see §12.9, "Abnormal Floating-Point Conditions."

Floating-Point Add and Subtract Instructions

All the floating-point add and subtract instructions require one cycle in each of the FD, FPM, FPA, and FWA stages. This is true for both single- and double-precision operations.

# of Cycles	1	1	1	1
Stages	FD	FPM	FPA	FWA

Floating-Point Multiply/Multiply-Accumulate Instructions

The floating-point multiply and the multiply-accumulate (such as `fmadd` and `fmsub`) operations have a latency of either four or five cycles, depending on whether the calculation is single- or double-precision.

Single-precision multiplies/multiply-accumulates are similar to floating-point adds in that they require one cycle in each of the four major FPU stages.

# of Cycles	1	1	1	1
Stages	FD	FPM	FPA	FWA

Double-precision multiplies/multiply-accumulates require two cycles in each of the FD, FPM, and FPA stages. This means that the next floating-point instruction cannot enter FD immediately after the multiply (it must stall for one cycle). The instruction is "self-pipelining," so that many of the stages overlap in execution and the resulting latency is only five cycles.

# of Cycles	1	1	1	1	1
Stages	FD	FD FPM	FPM FPA	FPA	FWA

Floating-Point Divide Instructions

The floating-point divide instructions have very large latencies and stall the FPU until the operation reaches the last cycle of FWA stage.

Single-precision divides have a latency of 18 cycles; in 14 of these cycles the FD, FPM, FPA, and FWA stages are all occupied. A floating-point instruction immediately following a divide instruction must stall for 16 cycles.

# of Cycles	1	1	1	14	1
Stages	FD	FD FPM	FD FPM FPA	FD FPM FPA FWA	FWA

Double-precision divides are just like single-precision divides except that they hog up all four pipeline stages twice as long.

# of Cycles	1	1	1	28	1
Stages	FD	FD FPM	FD FPM FPA	FD FPM FPA FWA	FWA

Floating-Point Load Instructions

Floating-point load instructions are primarily handled by the Integer Unit, except the load writeback stage is handled by the FWL stage of the FPU instead of the IWL stage in the IU.

When the loaded operand does not cross a doubleword boundary, only one cycle in IE/CARB is required.

# of Cycles	1	1	1	1
Stages	ID	CARB IE	CACC IC	FWL

The floating-point *Load with Update* forms have similar timings, except that the instruction must also spend a cycle in IWA, which is in parallel with the cycle spent in IC.

# of Cycles	1	1	1	1
Stages	ID	CARB IE	CACC IC IWA	FWL

Timings for misaligned floating-point loads are given in §12.9, "Abnormal Floating-Point Conditions."

Floating-Point Store Instructions

Even though the Integer Unit handles most of the work for the floating-point store instructions, the FPU must provide the properly formatted data that is to be stored. For this reason, all floating-point store instructions propagate through both the IU and the FPU pipelines.

If the operand being stored does not cross a doubleword boundary, only one cycle in IE is required.

# of Cycles	1	1	1	1	1	1
Stages (IU/CAU/DAQU)	ID	IE	IC FPSB	FPSB	CARB FPSB	CACC
Stages (FPU)	-	FD	FPM	FPA	FWA	-

Note that the store instruction finishes in the integer pipeline first and then waits in the Floating-Point Store Buffer (FPSB) until the data to be stored is ready in the FWA stage of the floating-point pipeline. When the data is ready, the instruction arbitrates for the cache (CARB) and then stores the data.

The *Store with Update* forms have similar timings, except that the instruction must also spend a cycle in IWA, which is in parallel with the cycle spent in IC.

# of Cycles	1	1	1	1	1	1
Stages (IU/CAU/DAQU)	ID	IE	IC IWA FPSB	FPSB	CARB FPSB	CACC
Stages (FPU)	-	FD	FPM	FPA	FWA	-

Timings for misaligned floating-point stores are given in §12.9, "Abnormal Floating-Point Conditions."

Move to FPSCR Instructions

The *Move to FPSCR* instructions (`mtfsfi`, `mtfsf`, `mtfsb0`, and `mrfsb1`) cause the FPU pipeline to stall in FD for three cycles.

# of Cycles	1	1	1	1
Stages	FD	FD FPM	FD FPM FPA	FD FPM FPA FWA

Note that the *Move from FPSCR* instructions (`mffs` and `mcrfs`) do not stall in FD and progress through the pipeline as normal floating-point instructions should.

Other Floating-Point Instructions

All other floating-point instructions require one cycle in each of the FD, FPM, FPA, and FWA stages.

# of Cycles	1	1	1	1
Stages	FD	FPM	FPA	FWA

12.5 Branch Instruction Timings

Timing branch instructions is more difficult because it is very dependent on the instructions around the branch. Because of this, the timings presented in this section will involve not only the branch in question, but also some surrounding instructions to provide some context for the branch.

Simple Branches

Because describing the timing for branch instructions is complicated, it is best to start with a simple (non-conditional) branch that is always taken. Later sections will deal with the more complicated conditional branches.

Branch, Branch Absolute

For simple (non-conditional) branches, the timing chart is quite simple. After the instruction enters one of the lower four stages of dispatch (IQ3 - IQ0), it enters BE and is complete.

# of Cycles	1
Stages	DS BE

However, this simple timing chart only gives a (very small) part of the picture. Because the branch is passing control from one part of the code to another, the timing of the surrounding instructions is also significant.

The timing chart is also misleading because it implies that the branch instruction requires one cycle, which is not exactly the case. If the branch is executed early enough, it is likely to take zero cycles because the branch can be completely "folded" out of the instruction stream.

For example, consider this sequence of instructions:

```
        and     r0,r0,r1
        nand    r2,r2,r3
        b       target
        or      r4,r4,r5
        ...
target:
        nor     r6,r6,r7
        xor     r8,r8,r9
```

Some Boolean instructions have been added to this sequence to provide context and to fill up the pipeline to demonstrate the zero cycle branching. The register assignments for these instructions can be ignored—they were chosen simply to avoid resource conflicts.

This instruction sequence would have the following timing:

Cycle #:	1	2	3	4	5	6	7	8
and r0,r0,r1	FA CARB	CACC	IQ0 ID	IE	IC IWA	-	-	-
nand r2,r2,r3	FA CARB	CACC	IQ1	IQ0 ID	IE	IC IWA	-	-
b target	FA CARB	CACC	IQ2 BE	-	-	-	-	-
or r4,r4,r5	FA CARB	CACC	IQ3	-	-	-	-	-
...	-	-	-	-	-	-	-	-
nor r6,r6,r7	-	-	FA CARB	CACC	IQ0 ID	IE	IC IWA	-
xor r8,r8,r9	-	-	FA CARB	CACC	IQ1	IQ0 ID	IE	IC IWA

In this example, the *And* and *Branch* instructions are executed simultaneously in the third cycle. When the branch is executed (during cycle 3), the target instructions enter the FA stage so that they will be fetched into the dispatch queue.

The end result is that the processor completes one Boolean instruction per cycle starting with cycle 5: and, nand, nor, and then xor. The branch instruction has been effectively removed from the instruction stream.

Branch with Link, Branch with Link Absolute

When the Link bit of a simple branch is set, the LR needs to be updated in the BW stage. This takes a variable number of cycles because the writeback cannot occur until all fixed-point instructions before the branch have completed.

# of Cycles	1	n
Stages	DS BE	BW

As is the case with non-Link branches, this table doesn't give the full picture.

Consider the same code sequence given above with a *Branch with Link* instruction used instead of a *Branch* instruction.

Cycle #:	1	2	3	4	5	6	7	8
and r0,r0,r1	FA CARB	CACC	IQ0 ID	IE	IC IWA	-	-	-
nand r2,r2,r3	FA CARB	CACC	IQ1	IQ0 ID	IE	IC IWA	-	-
LR tag = nand	-	-	-	ID	IE	IC	-	-
bl target	FA CARB	CACC	IQ2 BE	BW	BW	BW	-	-
or r4,r4,r5	FA CARB	CACC	IQ3	-	-	-	-	-
...	-	-	-	-	-	-	-	-
nor r6,r6,r7	-	-	FA CARB	CACC	IQ0 ID	IE	IC IWA	-
xor r8,r8,r9	-	-	FA CARB	CACC	IQ1	IQ0 ID	IE	IC IWA

In this case the branch instruction needs to stay in BW until the LR can be updated, which can't occur until after the nand instruction completes. After the nand instruction reaches the IC stage (cycle 6), the proper value can be written into the LR (during the same cycle).

The mechanism for properly updating the LR involves tagging the branch instruction to the previous integer instruction (in this case, nand), and temporarily writing the LR value into one of the two shadow LRs created for just this purpose.

The interesting thing to note about this timing is that the non-branch instructions are not affected by the extra stages branch instruction requires to perform the writeback.

Branch Tags & Bubbles

Before continuing with the timings for conditional branches, it is worth stepping aside and covering *branch tags* and *bubbles* because they play a very important role in branch timings.

Branch tags are carried through the integer pipeline by either an integer instruction or a pipeline bubble. These tags synchronize the different pipelines so that the instructions appear to complete in sequential order even though they are dispatched out of order for performance reasons. Not every type of branch needs to use tags: only conditional branches and branches that need to update the LR or CTR generate tags.

In general, the branch tag is placed on the last integer instruction before the branch, but there are situations when this is not possible and an imaginary integer instruction (called a *bubble*) must be created to carry the tag through the integer pipeline.

In this code sample:

```
and     r0,r0,r1
nand    r2,r2,r3
fadd    fr0,fr0,fr1
bl      target
```

the tag for the branch instruction is carried by the `nand` instruction because it is the last integer instruction before the branch.

Types of Branch Tags

There are three different types of branch tags:

- LR tags for branch instructions that update the LR.
- CTR tags for branch instructions that update the CTR.
- Predicted branch tags for conditional branches that are unresolved.

An integer instruction can carry only one of each type of tag. If a branch instruction needs to tag an integer instruction that already has a tag of that type, a bubble will be created to carry the tag. The bubble will be placed between the integer instruction and the branch.

LR/CTR Tags

LR and CTR branch tags are synchronization tags that tell the branch instruction when it's time to update the LR or CTR, respectively. The tag is placed on the last instruction that needs to execute before the register should be "officially" updated by the branch processor.

To understand how the LR and CTR tags are used, consider the following nonsensical code fragment, which uses LR tags (CTR tags are identical):

```
and     r0,r0,r1
nand    r2,r2,r3
```

```
        bl          target1
        ...
target1:
        bl          target2
        ...
target2:
        or          r4,r4,r5
```

The timing for this code would be:

Cycle #:	1	2	3	4	5	6	7	8
and r0,r0,r1	FA CARB	CACC	IQ0 ID	IE	IC IWA	-	-	-
nand r2,r2,r3	FA CARB	CACC	IQ1	IQ0 ID	IE	IC IWA	-	-
LR tag = nand	-	-	-	ID	IE	IC	-	-
bl target1	FA CARB	CACC	IQ2 BE	BW	BW	BW	-	-
...	-	-	-	-	-	-	-	-
LR tag =bubble	-	-	-	-	-	IE	IC	-
bl target2	-	-	FA CARB	CACC	IQ0 BE	BW	BW	-
...	-	-	-	-	-	-	-	-
or r4,r4,r5	-	-	-	-	FA CARB	CACC	ID0 ID	IE

The first branch instruction enters BE during cycle 3. At this time, it adds an LR tag to the `nand` instruction currently in IQ1 so that it knows when it's safe to update the LR.

In cycle 5, when the second `bl` instruction tries to enter IQ0, the processor realizes that there is no integer instruction to accept this instruction's LR tag (since the `nand` instruction already has one). A bubble is created to float through the integer pipeline (with the tag) while the branch enters BE. When the bubble reaches IC, the second branch instruction updates the LR.

Predicted Branch Tags

Predicted branch tags are completely different from the LR/CTR tags in that they are not pipeline synchronization tags. Rather, they are tags used internally by the branch processor so that it can keep track of instructions before and after a conditional branch.

These tags are used as a barrier in the pipeline between the *nonspeculative* instructions before the branch (the instructions that must be executed regardless of whether or not the branch is taken) and the *speculative* instructions after the branch (the instructions that may need to be purged if the branch prediction is incorrect). After the branch is resolved, the tag is removed along with any incorrectly dispatched instructions.

The predicted branch tags are special because they are not allowed to progress beyond the IE stage of the IU. This stalls all of the speculative integer instructions in the ID stage. The BPU and FPU are a little more flexible because they allow speculative instructions to progress through the pipeline.

It should be noted that, although a predicted branch tag is not allowed to progress beyond the IE stage, the instruction that is carrying the tag can. In this case, the tag will separate from the instruction so that the tag remains in IE while the instructions continues through the pipeline.

Another implication of the fact that the branch tags stalls in IE is that there can only be one unresolved conditional branch at a time. A second conditional branch will stall in the IQ buffer.

Also, after an instruction is given a predicted branch tag, it is not allowed to accept any other tags. This makes sense because tags for speculative instructions (after the branch) should not be placed on nonspeculative instructions (the instruction or bubble holding the predicted branch tag).

The next section covers conditional branches and uses these branch tags extensively.

Conditional Branches

Conditional branches complicate matters because the branch instructions are executed out of program order, and many times the processor is unable to determine if the branch will be taken or if it will fall through.

If the processor cannot figure out if the branch is going to be taken or not, the branch is considered to be *unresolved* and must be *predicted*. The prediction involves deciding whether or not the branch is likely to be taken. Because this prediction is simply a guess, it may be correct or incorrect. Correct guesses are useful because the processor doesn't have to wait for the branch to be resolved before continuing. However, the processor must have some way of cancelling incorrectly dispatched instructions due to misprediction.

Of course, if the processor has enough information to *resolve* the branch, then a prediction is not necessary and the branch timing is the same as for nonconditional branches.

The simple timing chart for conditional branch instructions is:

# of Cycles	1	k
Stages	DS BE MR	MR

where k is the number of cycles necessary to resolve the branch. The additional stage is the Mispredict Recovery (MR) stage that the branch must stay in until the branch is resolved.

As mentioned earlier, if $k=0$ (that is, if the branch can be resolved during BE), then this table simplifies to that for a non-conditional branch.

For conditional branches that need to update the LR or CTR, the branch waits for two external events: the branch to be resolved and the previous instruction to complete (for writeback). If the number of cycles required for the branch to be resolved is k and the number of cycles until writeback can be performed is n, then if $n > k$ the timing will be:

# of Cycles	1	k	n-k
Stages	DS BE MR	MR BW	BW

and if $k > n$:

# of Cycles	1	n	k-n
Stages	DS BE MR	MR BW	MR

In short, the branch will stay in whatever stages it needs for however long it needs to.

Branch Prediction

By default, forward conditional branches are predicted to be *not-taken* and backward conditional branches are predicted to be *taken* (because they are assumed to be loop-closing branches). Also, an encoding bit in each branch instruction reverses the default prediction.

As suggested earlier, this leads to four situations that can occur for conditional branches:

- predicted not-taken correctly—the branch is predicted not-taken and the branch is not-taken.
- predicted not-taken incorrectly—the branch is predicted not-taken and the branch is taken.
- predicted taken correctly—the branch is predicted taken and the branch is taken.
- predicted taken incorrectly—the branch is predicted taken and the branch is not-taken.

In the next few sections, the following code sample will be examined under each of the situations listed. Each situation must be treated separately because the timing characteristics are significantly different.

```
        cmp       crf0,r30,r31
        beq       crf0,target
        and       r0,r0,r1
        nand      r2,r2,r3
        ...
target:
        or        r4,r4,r5
        nor       r6,r6,r7
```

The important aspect of this code sample is that the branch is dependent on the results of the compare operation immediately preceding it. The surrounding instructions are just for context.

The beq instruction will be given a '+' or '−' suffix as a reminder that the branch is being predicted taken ('+') or not-taken ('−'). Since the target address of the beq instruction is after the branch, the '+' suffix corresponds to setting the reverse-prediction bit in the branch instruction. The '−' suffix is not used by assemblers but is used here to make the branch prediction explicit.

Predicted Not-taken Correctly

The timing table for the predicted not-taken correctly case is quite simple:

Cycle #:	1	2	3	4	5	6	7
cmp crf0,r30,r31	FA CARB	CACC	IQ0 ID	IE	IC IWA	-	-
pbr tag = cmp	-	-	-	IE	-	-	-
beq- crf0,target	FA CARB	CACC	IQ1 BE MR	MR	-	-	-
and r0,r0,r1	FA CARB	CACC	IQ2	IQ0 ID	IE	IC IWA	-
nand r2,r2,r3	FA CARB	CACC	IQ3	IQ1	IQ0 ID	IE	IC IWA
...	-	-	-	-	-	-	-
or r4,r4,r5	-	-	-	-	-	-	-
nor r6,r6,r7	-	-	-	-	-	-	-

During cycle 3, the branch instruction is executed. Because it can't be resolved, it must be predicted. It is predicted as being not-taken because it is a forward branch. In the next cycle, the information from the cmp instruction is made available to the MR stage of the BPU, which determines that the branch was predicted correctly. The predicted branch tag is purged, and the remaining instructions proceed through execution as they would if the branch was not present.

Predicted Not-taken Incorrectly

If the branch is predicted as not-taken, but later determined to be taken, then the timing changes:

Cycle #:	1	2	3	4	5	6	7
cmp crf0,r30,r31	FA CARB	CACC	IQ0 ID	IE	IC IWA	-	-
pbr tag = cmp	-	-	-	IE	-	-	-
beq- crf0,target	FA CARB	CACC	IQ1 BE MR	MR	-	-	-
and r0,r0,r1	FA CARB	CACC	IQ2	IQ0 ID	-	-	-
nand r2,r2,r3	FA CARB	CACC	IQ3	IQ1	-	-	-
...	-	-	-	-	-	-	-
or r4,r4,r5	-	-	-	FA CARB	CACC	IQ0 ID	IE
nor r6,r6,r7	-	-	-	FA CARB	CACC	IQ1	IQ0 ID

Here, the first three cycles are identical to the previous case. In the fourth cycle, the BPU figures out that the prediction was wrong, and it begins fetching the correct instructions. The incorrect instructions are discarded in the next cycle. In this case, two cycles are "lost."

The statement that the two cycles are "lost" is somewhat misleading. In this branching case, the two cycles can easily be "regained" if we can assume that there are two independent instructions between the compare and the branch. This is known as code scheduling to make maximal use of the pipeline resources and is covered in Chapter 15, "Resource Scheduling."

Predicted Taken Correctly

If the above branch is encoded to reverse the default prediction, then the timing will obviously be different. For the case where the branch is correctly predicted to be taken, the timing chart is:

Cycle #:	1	2	3	4	5	6	7
cmp crf0,r30,r31	FA CARB	CACC	IQ0 ID	IE	IC IWA	-	-
pbr tag = cmp	-	-	-	IE	-	-	-
beq+ crf0,target	FA CARB	CACC	IQ1 BE MR	MR	-	-	-
and r0,r0,r1	FA CARB	CACC	IQ2	IQ0 ID	-	-	-
nand r2,r2,r3	FA CARB	CACC	IQ3	IQ1	-	-	-

...	-	-	-	-	-	-	-
or r4,r4,r5	-	-	FA CARB	CACC	IQ0 ID	IE	IC IWA
nor r6,r6,r7	-	-	FA CARB	CACC	IQ1	IQ0 ID	IE

As usual, the branch is predicted during cycle 3. Because the branch is predicted as being taken, the target instructions enter FA during this cycle. The sequential instructions (and and nand) are left in the Instruction Queue until either the branch has been resolved or the target instructions have been fetched. This gives the processor the opportunity to correct a misprediction if it can catch it early enough. In this case, however, the branch is resolved to be correct in cycle 4 and the instructions and tags are removed or overwritten with the target instructions in cycle 5.

Similar to the situation with the predicted not-taken incorrectly example, the lost cycle can be "regained" if we simply include a few extra instructions before the compare in our timing sample. This is not a scheduling optimization, but is actually a timing problem that is discussed in the subsection "Timing an Instruction Sample That Is Too Small" in §12.10, "Timing Pitfalls."

Predicted Taken Incorrectly

If the branch is predicted to be taken, but later discovered to be not-taken, the timing would be:

Cycle #:	1	2	3	4	5	6	7
cmp crf0,r30,r31	FA CARB	CACC	IQ0 ID	IE	IC IWA	-	-
pbr tag = cmp	-	-	-	IE	-	-	-
beq+ crf0,target	FA CARB	CACC	IQ1 BE MR	MR	-	-	-
and r0,r0,r1	FA CARB	CACC	IQ2	IQ0 ID	IE	IC IWA	-
nand r2,r2,r3	FA CARB	CACC	IQ3	IQ1	IQ0 ID	IE	IC IWA
...	-	-	-	-	-	-	-
or r4,r4,r5	-	-	FA CARB	CACC	-	-	-
nor r6,r6,r7	-	-	FA CARB	CACC	-	-	-

Here again the branch is predicted in cycle 3 and resolved in cycle 4, but in this case the branch was predicted incorrectly so the target instructions (or and nor) must be purged and replaced with the correct instructions.

Fortunately, the misprediction is caught early enough so that sequential instructions (and and nand) are still in the IQ buffer when the branch is resolved. The target instructions are purged, and the sequential instructions are allowed to continue.

If the misprediction couldn't be caught until the next cycle, then the target instructions would have overwritten the sequential instructions before the misprediction was recognized. The sequential instructions would have to be refetched from the cache, causing a significant delay.

12.6 Cache Access Timings

To make the timings in this chapter manageable, the examples ignore the effects of cache misses. However, it should come as no surprise that cache misses can profoundly affect code performance. In addition to simple cache misses, some other features of the Cache Access Unit (CAU) can also subtly affect instruction timings.

Cache Priorities

If there are multiple cache access requests during Cache Arbitration (CARB), the CAU decides which cache access request to grant. It uses a simple priority scheme, listed from highest priority to lowest priority:

- Cache Maintenance Requests
- Data Load Requests
- Data Store Requests
- Instruction Fetch Requests

The Cache Maintenance Requests come from the memory subsystem and include operations like cache line reloads due to a cache miss.

Note that the instruction fetch request is a relatively low priority operation. This is why the IQ buffer can store up to eight instructions. When the instruction fetch request gains access to the cache, it needs to utilize it fully because it may have to wait a while before another request is granted.

Cache Timings

Timing cache hits and misses can be quite complicated. However, a few rules of thumb that can be used to get a general idea of how these accesses will affect instruction timing.

Cache Hits

Cache hits are simple to time because there are basically three cycles of operation for a cache hit. The first two cycles are the CARB and CACC stages of the CAU pipeline. What happens during the third cycle depends on the type of cache access.

For instruction fetch accesses, the timing is:

Cycle #:	1	2	3
instruction fetch	FA CARB	CACC	DS

This should look familiar because it is the timing used for instruction fetches in all of the timing examples in this chapter. Here, the cache arbitration (CARB) occurs in cycle 1 and the cache is accessed (CACC) in cycle 2. The data from the cache hit is returned during cycle 2, and the instructions are available for dispatch in cycle 3.

For data load accesses, the timing is:

Cycle #:	1	2	3
data load	CARB	CACC	IWL

As above, the CARB and CACC stages occur in cycles 1 and 2. If an instruction in IE is waiting for the loaded data, it is forwarded to the IE during cycle 2. The standard writeback (in IWL or FWL) occurs during the third cycle.

Cache Misses

Cache misses are horrible, difficult-to-time events. Part of the difficulty arises because the number of cycles that the cache miss will take depends on both the clock frequency of the system bus, which is obviously system dependent, and the current state of the bus, which may be difficult to keep track of.

The best case situation occurs when the system bus clock frequency is the same as the processor clock frequency. This is known as a 1:1 bus-to-processor clock frequency ratio.

Cycle #:	1	2	3	4	5	6	7	8
fetch/load	CARB	CACC	CACC	CACC	CACC	CACC	CACC	DS IWL

There are (at least) six cycles between entering CACC and the data being available in the IQ buffer or for writeback. As with the cache hit case, if the data is needed it will be forwarded to IE in the cycle before the data is available for writeback, cycle 7 for this example.

But the diagram doesn't tell the entire story. Even after the required data has been delivered, the cache is still busy servicing the request for two additional cycles. This means that a new cache request cannot be granted until cycle 10 at the earliest.

To reiterate, the above cycle count represents a best case situation for a 1:1 bus-to-processor clock ratio. Even on systems with a 1:1 ratio, the actual timings may be worse than these timings would suggest. When the bus clock is slower than the processor clock, the timings become progressively worse.

Some simple formulæ for calculating the best case timings for systems with different bus-to-processor clock ratios are:

$$\text{\# of cycles until data is available } = \ 3 + \left(3 \times \frac{processor\ clock}{memory\ bus\ clock} \right)$$

and:

$$\text{\# of cycles until cache operation is complete } = \ 3 + \left(5 \times \frac{processor\ clock}{memory\ bus\ clock} \right)$$

So a 1:2 bus-to-processor clock ratio will require nine cycles until the data is available for writeback and 13 cycles until the CAU is finished servicing the memory request. A 1:3 ratio would require 12 and 18 cycles for these operations.

These cycle counts are not terribly accurate because they ignore all of the cycles lost due to bus synchronization and memory wait states. However, it is much more accurate to use these numbers than to blindly assume that all cache accesses require only one cycle.

12.7 Pipeline Synchronization

Because it is important that the instructions appear to complete in the order that they occur in the program (program order), some sort of mechanism is needed to insure that the different pipelines are synchronized.

To keep the three pipelines in sync, the integer pipeline is considered the "reference pipeline" and the other two pipelines keep track of their instructions relative to the instructions in the integer pipeline. They do this using tags.

Two (LR and CTR) of the three types of synchronization tags were discussed in the section describing the timing of branch instructions. The third tag type is the *floating-point tag*, which is used to synchronize the floating-point and integer pipelines.

A fourth type of tag, the predicted branch tag, is not discussed here because it isn't a synchronization tag.

LR and CTR Tags

The LR and CTR tags are used to synchronize the BPU and the IU. These tags are discussed earlier in "Branch Tags & Bubbles."

Floating-Point Tags

Every floating-point instruction generates a floating-point tag to the previous integer instruction or to a bubble if no integer instruction is available to accept the tag.

The exact operation of the floating-point tags depends on the current Floating-Point Exception mode, which may be either enabled or disabled.

Floating-Point Precise Exceptions Disabled

When floating-point precise exceptions are disabled, the processor is allowed to complete instructions out of order. For example, multiple integer instructions could complete before a floating-point instruction even though the floating-point instruction occurs first in program order.

If the floating-point instruction causes an exception, these integer instructions will have already completed execution before the interrupt handler is invoked. This is what is meant by "precise exceptions" being "disabled."

However, the ability to dispatch and complete instructions out of order can be a significant benefit to processor throughput. Consider this example:

```
and      r0,r0,r1
nand     r2,r2,r3
fadd     fr0,fr0,fr1
fsub     fr2,fr2,fr3
bl       target
```

The timing for this fragment is:

Cycle #:	1	2	3	4	5	6	7	8
and r0,r0,r1	FA CARB	CACC	IQ0 ID	IE	IC IWA	-	-	-
nand r2,r2,r3	FA CARB	CACC	IQ1	IQ0 ID	IE	IC IWA	-	-
fp tag = nand	-	-	-	IQ0 ID	IE	IC	-	-
fadd fr0,fr0,fr1	FA CARB	CACC	IQ2	FD	FPM	FPA	FWA	-
fp tag = bubble1	-	-	-	-	IQ0 ID	IE	IC	-
fsub fr2,fr2,fr3	FA CARB	CACC	IQ3	IQ1	FD	FPM	FPA	FWA
LR tag = bubble1	-	-	-	-	IQ0 ID	IE	IC	-
bl target	FA CARB	CACC	IQ4	IQ2 BE	BW	BW	BW	-

When the fadd instruction is dispatched to the FPU in cycle 3, the nand instruction is available to hold the floating-point tag. The second floating-point instruction, fsub, is dispatched on the next cycle. It would also like to place a tag on the nand instruction, but it must create a bubble because nand already has a floating-point tag.

The branch instruction also needs to add a tag to a previous integer instruction. In this case, the bubble created by the fsub instruction is the closest integer "instruction," so it accepts the LR tag (remember, instructions can have multiple tags as long as they are of different types).

When the floating-point tags reach the IC stage, the IU records that the associated floating-point instruction is allowed to complete. The tag for the fadd instruction completes in cycle 6, which allows the fadd instruction to complete as soon as it is finished in cycle 7. The Integer Unit can keep track of up to three outstanding floating-point instructions that have not entered FP Writeback, even though their tags have completed IC. If a fourth floating-point instruction has a tag that enters IC, the tag stalls the integer pipeline until the floating-point pipeline catches up.

Floating-Point Precise Exceptions Enabled

When floating-point precise exceptions are enabled, the processor is not allowed to complete instructions out of order. This is because the processor needs to insure that if an exception occurs, it is generated before any instructions following the exception-causing instruction are completed. It can only do this is by requiring that all integer and floating-point instructions are dispatched and completed strictly in order. Branch instructions, however, are still allowed to be executed out of order.

To enforce this in-order execution, all floating-point instructions are tagged to bubbles in the IU pipeline (even if there is a valid integer instruction to accept the floating-point tag). In addition, this tag is not allowed to leave the IC stage until the floating-point instruction has entered the FWA or FWL stage.

Not surprisingly, all this extra synchronization can slow down the processor.

The previous code sample would be timed as follows if it were executed with precise floating-point exceptions enabled.

Cycle #:	1	2	3	4	5	6	7	8
and r0,r0,r1	FA CARB	CACC	IQ0 ID	IE	IC IWA	-	-	-
nand r2,r2,r3	FA CARB	CACC	IQ1	IQ0 ID	IE	IC IWA	-	-
fp tag = bubble1	-	-	-	IQ1	IQ0 ID	IE	IC	-
fadd fr0,fr0,fr1	FA CARB	CACC	IQ2	FD	FPM	FPA	FWA	-

fp tag = bubble2	-	-	-	-	IQ1	IQ0 ID	IE	IC
fsub fr2,fr2,fr3	FA CARB	CACC	IQ3	IQ1	FD	FPM	FPA	FWA
LR tag = bubble2	-	-	-	-	IQ1	IQ0 ID	IE	IC
bl target	FA CARB	CACC	IQ4	IQ2 BE	BW	BW	BW	BW

In this example, the floating-point performance was not greatly affected. However, the two tags occupying stages in the integer pipeline are likely to delay the dispatch of subsequent instructions.

12.8 Abnormal Integer Conditions

All of the timings given in this chapter for integer load and store instructions assume that the data being loaded or stored is properly aligned. If this assumption is not valid, then pipeline stalls may occur.

Misaligned Data Accesses

A misaligned data access occurs when the data being loaded or stored crosses a doubleword boundary. How this affects instruction timings depends on the instruction in question.

Integer Load Instructions

If the operand for an integer load instruction crosses a doubleword boundary, two cycles (instead of one) are needed in the IE/CARB stage. Thus, for the non-update load forms, the timing chart becomes:

# of Cycles	1	1	1	1	1
Stages	ID	IE CARB	IE CARB CACC IC	CACC	IWL

The integer *Load with Update* form timing is the same, except for the addition of the IWA stage, which is executed in parallel with the IC stage.

# of Cycles	1	1	1	1	1
Stages	ID	IE CARB	IE CARB CACC IC IWA	CACC	IWL

Timings for the floating-point load instructions are also the same, except that the FWL stage (in the FPU) is used for writeback instead of the IWL stage.

Load Multiple and Load String Instructions

If the data for a *Load Multiple* or *Load String* instruction is not word-aligned, significant delays occur because every other load operation is loading data that crosses a doubleword boundary and requires two cycles in IE instead of one.

# of Cycles	1	1	1	$(n-2)/2$		1	1
Stages	ID	IE CARB	IE CARB CACC IC	IE CARB CACC	IE CARB CACC IWL	IE CARB CACC IWL	CACC IWL	IWL

Integer Store Instructions

If the operand being stored crosses a doubleword boundary, two cycles are needed in IE/CARB stage. The timing table for the non-update store forms becomes:

# of Cycles	1	1	1	1
Stages	ID	IE CARB	IE CARB CACC IC	CACC

The timing for the integer *Store with Update* form (when the data crosses a doubleword boundary) is the same as above, except for addition of the IWA stage, which is executed in parallel with the IC stage.

# of Cycles	1	1	1	1
Stages	ID	IE CARB	IE CARB CACC IC IWA	CACC

Store Multiple and Store String Instructions

If the data for a *Store Multiple* or *Store String* instruction is not word-aligned, significant delays occur because every other store operation is storing data that crosses a doubleword boundary and requires two cycles in IE instead of one.

# of Cycles	1	1	1	$(n-2)/2$			1
Stages	ID	IE CARB	IE CARB CACC IC	IE CARB CACC	IE CARB CACC	IE CARB CACC	CACC

12.9 Abnormal Floating-Point Conditions

All of the floating-point timings given so far in this chapter assume that the processor is executing the floating-point instructions under "normal" conditions. Abnormal conditions like misaligned data accesses are likely to have an adverse effect on the instruction timings.

For floating-point instructions, "normal" operating conditions also means that the source operands and the result are all normalized values. If they are not, or if the processor predicts that they will not be, then considerable pipeline stalls can occur.

Misaligned Data Accesses

A misaligned data access occurs when the data being loaded or stored crosses a doubleword boundary. How this affects instruction timings depends on the instruction in question.

Floating-Point Load Instructions

If the operand for a floating-point load instruction crosses a doubleword boundary, two cycles (instead of one) are needed in IE/CARB stage. Thus, for the non-update load forms, the timing chart becomes:

# of Cycles	1	1	1	1	1
Stages	ID	IE CARB	IE CARB CACC IC	CACC	FWL

The floating-point *Load with Update* form timing is the same, except for the addition of the IWA stage, which is executed in parallel with the IC stage.

# of Cycles	1	1	1	1	1
Stages	ID	IE CARB	IE CARB CACC IC IWA	CACC	FWL

Floating-Point Store Instructions

If the data for a floating-point store instruction is being written to an address that causes the store to cross a doubleword boundary, the store must first be broken into two separate store requests. This means that the instruction stalls in IE for *at least* four cycles because the FP store buffer (FPSB) can only handle one outstanding store request at a time.

# of Cycles	1	1	1	1	1	1	1	1
Stages (IU/CAU/DAQU)	ID	IE	IE FPSB IC	IE FPSB	IE FPSB CARB	IE FPSB CARB CACC	FPSB	FPSB CACC
Stages (FPU)	-	FD	FPM	FPA	FWA	-	-	-

The timing for the store with update form (when the data crosses a doubleword boundary) is the same except for the extra IWA stage, which is executed in parallel with the IC stage.

# of Cycles	1	1	1	1	1	1	1	1
Stages (IU/CAU/DAQU)	ID	IE	IE FPSB IC IWA	IE FPSB	IE FPSB CARB	IE FPSB CARB CACC	FPSB	FPSB CACC
Stages (FPU)	-	FD	FPM	FPA	FWA	-	-	-

Prenormalization

Prenormalization is required if any of the source operands are not normalized. Because all normalization is performed in the FWA stage, any non-normalized operands must flow through the pipeline to the FWA stage and be normalized before the instruction can begin execution.

If only one of the operands requires normalization, then the timing for the instruction (shown here for `fadd`) is:

Cycle #:	1	2	3	4	5	6	7	8
operand prenorm	FD	FPM	FPA	FWA	-	-	-	-
fadd	-	FD	FD	FD	FD	FPM	FPA	FWA

In this situation, the operand requiring normalization passes through the pipeline before the `fadd` instruction. Because the `fadd` instructions needs this operand before it can leave FD, it stalls in FD. After the operand completes FWA, the normalized operand is available for the `fadd` instruction to begin in FD, which it does in cycle 5.

If two source operands require normalization, the timing is:

Cycle #:	1	2	3	4	5	6	7	8	9
operand1 prenorm	FD	FPM	FPA	FWA	-	-	-	-	-
operand2 prenorm	-	FD	FPM	FPA	FWA	-	-	-	-
fadd	-	-	FD	FD	FD	FD	FPM	FPA	FWA

Here, both operands need to pass through the pipeline before the `fadd` instruction can begin execution. This costs only one additional cycle because of the pipelining.

The timings are similar for the case where all three operands (for the multiply-accumulate instructions) require normalization.

Underflow

If the floating-point unit predicts that the result of a floating-point operation will produce a denormalized result, it will keep the instruction in FD until it has completed the FW stage. This prevents any subsequent floating-point instruction from entering FD and effectively stalls the FPU.

Stalling the instruction in FD is necessary because, if the result does cause an underflow, the result must be passed again through the floating-point pipeline (starting at FPM) so that the value can be properly denormalized.

The timing of this condition is:

Cycle #:	1	2	3	4	5	6	7
fadd	FD	FD FPM	FD FPA	FD FW	-	-	-
denormalize	-	-	-	-	FPM	FPA	FW

In this case, the final result of the `fadd` instruction is available during cycle 7, after it has been denormalized.

Note that the instruction may not, in fact, require any sort of denormalization. The processor stalls the instruction if it thinks that it *might* require denormalization. This prediction could be incorrect.

The timing for the case where no denormalization is required (even though the FPU thought that it might be) is:

Cycle #:	1	2	3	4	5	6	7
fadd	FD	FD FPM	FD FPA	FD FW	-	-	-
denormalize	-	-	-	-	-	-	-

Here, the results of the `fadd` instruction are available during cycle 4. The next floating-point instruction still cannot enter FD until cycle 5, but the results of the `fadd` are available three cycles earlier (which may benefit dependent instructions).

Normalization

For most floating-point values, the result normalization that takes place in the FPA/FWA stage isn't likely to require more than one cycle in FWA. However, under some conditions the normalization will take longer.

Remember that normalization is performed by shifting the bits of the result to the left until the most significant bit is a 1. The FPA can perform a one-time shift of up to 48 bits before passing the result to the FWA, and the FWA can shift up to 16 bits per cycle.

Because the intermediate result in the FPU is 161 bits in width, a worst-case scenario would be when this result needed to be shifted over 160 bits to normalize the result. This would require $(160 - 48)/16 = 7$ cycles in the FWA stage.

The exact number of cycles required to normalize a value has to be calculated case-by-case by examining the intermediate result and determining how many bits need to be shifted for it to be normalized.

12.10 Timing Pitfalls

Generating timing diagrams for a sequence of instructions can be quite complex. Some of the complications are removed by the assumptions with cache hits and instruction fetches. However, it is important to be aware of these assumptions because they can, at times, significantly affect timings.

Timing an Instruction Sample That Is Too Small

One easy-to-make mistake is to time a code sequence without taking into account the instructions executing before the "interesting" code. These instructions set the stage for the instructions that follow them, and it is important to make sure that any timings account for the pipeline stages that they occupy.

Incorporating the information about previous instructions doesn't always adversely affect the timing for the code that follows. In fact, because instructions are fetched earlier, it is likely to benefit the timings.

Consider an example presented earlier and reproduced here for convenience where a branch is correctly predicted to be taken :

Cycle #:	1	2	3	4	5	6	7
cmp crf0,r30,r31	FA CARB	CACC	IQ0 ID	IE	IC IWA	-	-
pbr tag = cmp	-	-	IQ0 ID	IE	-	-	-
beq crf0,target	FA CARB	CACC	IQ1 BE MR	MR	-	-	-

and r0,r0,r1	FA CARB	CACC	IQ2	IQ0 ID	-	-	-
nand r2,r2,r3	FA CARB	CACC	IQ3	IQ1	-	-	-
...	-	-	-	-	-	-	-
or r4,r4,r5	-	-	FA CARB	CACC	IQ0 ID	IE	IC IWA
nor r6,r6,r7	-	-	FA CARB	CACC	IQ1	IQ0 ID	IE

It might at first seem as if a cycle is wasted between the cmp and the or instructions, and it would be if execution began with the cmp instruction. However, when an instruction is added before the compare instruction, the situation doesn't seem so bad:

Cycle #:	1	2	3	4	5	6	7
xor r8,r8,r9	FA CARB	CACC	IQ0 ID	IE	IC IWA		
cmp crf0,r30,r31	FA CARB	CACC	IQ1	IQ0 ID	IE	IC IWA	-
pbr tag = cmp	-	-	IQ1	IQ0 ID	IE	-	
beq crf0,target	FA CARB	CACC	IQ2 BE MR	MR	MR	-	-
and r0,r0,r1	FA CARB	CACC	IQ3	IQ1	-	-	-
nand r2,r2,r3	FA CARB	CACC	IQ4	IQ2	-	-	-
...	-	-	-	-	-	-	-
or r4,r4,r5	-	-	FA CARB	CACC	IQ0 ID	IE	IC IWA
nor r6,r6,r7	-	-	FA CARB	CACC	IQ1	IQ0 ID	IE

That extra instruction at the beginning causes the branch to be dispatched one cycle earlier so no cycles are wasted.

Fetching too Many Instructions

During the CACC stage, somewhere between one and eight instructions are returned to the Dispatch Unit. The exact number returned depends on many things, including the alignment of the address at which the instructions are being fetched.

This may seem like a strange thing to affect timing, but the address affects where the data will be stored in the cache, and the cache timing is different when the request is from the upper or lower part of a cache line. If your timings always assume that you'll receive four or eight instructions at a time, you may be surprised when the code is timed on a real system.

In general, it is difficult to account for this in timings, but it is important to be aware of it. For a critical loop, it might be worthwhile to place a few no-operations *before* the loop so that it fits nicely into a cache line. However, these situations need to be timed and considered case-by-case.

Not Considering Instruction Fetch Delays

Instruction fetches are the lowest priority cache access requests. Because of this, the CARB stage for an instruction fetch will take more than one cycle if the Cache Access Unit is servicing another request or receives one simultaneously with the instruction fetch.

A good test for code is to see how it is affected by instruction fetches that require more than one cycle in the CARB stage. This test is especially important for code that is moving a lot of data since the cache collisions can seriously degrade performance.

Ignoring Cache Misses

Cache misses (both for instruction fetches and data accesses) can cause a well optimized code fragment to perform horribly when it encounters a worst-case memory situation.

Cache misses can't be accounted for entirely (because they sometimes result from external events). It is a good idea (and unfortunately a lot of work) to map out critical sections of memory and assume that the first access into each block of memory will be a cache miss while subsequent accesses to the same block will be hits.

Odd as it may seem, in some situations a cache miss will cause a sequence of code to perform better. If a branch is incorrectly predicted to be taken, a cache miss on the target instruction fetch will give the processor more time to resolve the branch before the sequential instructions (in this case, the correct instructions) are purged from the IQ buffer. Thus, the delay in fetching the (incorrect) target instructions gives the processor enough time to realize that the correct instructions are already in the Dispatch Unit.

Of course, the proper way of addressing an incorrectly predicted branch is to correct the prediction. This example points out the potentially bizarre effects that memory can have on instruction timings.

Programming Model | 13

Although the PowerPC processor does not enforce any particular programming model, a variety of programming conventions that IBM devised for the POWER architecture have become the standard for the PowerPC. These conventions are part of the PowerOpen Application Binary Interface (ABI) and Application Programming Interface (API) that formalize the standard to make compliant systems binary and source-code compatible. These same conventions are also used on Apple's PowerPC-based Macintosh computers.

13.1 Register Usage Conventions

All of the registers that the PowerPC provides are defined as being either *volatile* or *non-volatile*. A volatile register can be freely used by any routine—a volatile register does not need to be saved and restored. A non-volatile register needs to be saved and restored if it is used.

Additionally, a few of the registers are defined as *dedicated*. A dedicated register is used for one very well-defined purpose and shouldn't be used for anything else. There are only two dedicated registers: the stack pointer (r1) and the TOC pointer (r2). Both of these registers are discussed in detail later in this chapter.

GPR Usage

The PowerPC has 32 GPRs, which may be either 32 or 64 bits (depending on the implementation). Table 13-1 summarizes the standard register usage conventions.

Table 13-1   GPR Register Usage Conventions

GPR	Type	Must be Preserved?	Usage
r0	volatile	no	used in prolog/epilog code
r1	dedicated	yes	stack pointer
r2			table of contents (TOC) pointer
r3	volatile	no	1st fixed-point parameter 1st word of return value
r4			2nd fixed-point parameter 2nd word of return value
r5	volatile	no	3rd fixed-point parameter
...			...
r10			8th fixed-point parameter
r11	volatile	no	environment pointer (if needed)
r12			used by global linkage routines
r13	non-volatile	yes	general registers that must be preserved across function calls
...			
r31			

Two of the GPRs (r1 and r2) are dedicated for use with OS-related tasks, three (r0, r11 and r12) are used by compiler, linkage, or glue routines, and eight more (r3 through r10) are allocated for passing parameters into a function (see §13.5, "Subroutine Calling Conventions," for more information). This leaves 19 GPRs (r13 through r31) which are available for general use, but which must be saved and restored if used.

By convention, a routine should use the volatile registers first because they do not need to be saved and restored. Thus, a routine should first use GPR0 and any of the registers GPR3 through GPR12 that are not already being used by the routine for parameters.

If a routine needs to use still more registers, the non-volatile GPRs should be used from highest numbered to lowest numbered. That is, GPR31 is used first, followed by GPR30, and so on. Using the non-volatile registers in this fashion allows the stmw and lmw instructions to be used to save and restore the registers in the function prolog/epilog code. However, some important issues are involved with using the load and store multiple instructions. These issues are discussed later in §13.8, "Saving Registers on the Stack."

FPR Usage

The PowerPC defines thirty-two 64-bit floating point registers. Of these registers, one (`fr0`) is set aside as a scratch register, 13 (`fr1` through `fr13`) are used for passing parameters to subroutines, and the remaining 18 (`fr14` through `fr31`) are available for general use. Table 13-2 summarizes the floating-point register usage conventions.

Table 13-2   FPR Register Usage Conventions

FPR	Type	Must be preserved?	Usage
fr0	volatile	no	scratch register
fr1			1st floating-point parameter 1st 8-bytes of return value
...	volatile	no	...
fr4			4th floating-point parameter 4th 8-bytes of return value
fr5			5th floating-point parameter
...	volatile	no	...
fr13			13th floating-point parameter
fr14			scratch registers that must be preserved across function calls
...	non-volatile	yes	
fr31			

As with the GPRs, a routine that needs to use floating-point registers should first use the volatile registers, `fr0` and any of the registers `fr1` through `fr13` that are not being used to hold parameters. The remaining 18 FPRs can be used if there are not enough volatile registers to hold the required values.

The non-volatile registers should be used from the highest to the lowest (that is, from `fr31` down to `fr14`) so that the FPR and GPR register save methods follow the same basic conventions. (See §13.8, "Saving Registers on the Stack," later in this chapter.)

SPR Usage

Table 13-3 summarizes the standard usage conventions for the common SPRs available on PowerPC implementations. In general, the system registers do not need to be preserved across function calls. The only exceptions are that some of the fields within the CR must always be preserved, and the FPSCR should be preserved under certain circumstances.

Table 13-3   SPR Register Usage Conventions

SPR		Type	Must be Preserved?	Usage
CR	0	volatile	no	general use; implicitly used by integer instructions with the Record bit set
	1			general use; implicitly used by floating-point instructions with the Record bit set
	2	non-volatile	yes	general use; must be preserved
	3			
	4			
	5	volatile	no	general use
	6			
	7			
LR		volatile	no	branch target address subroutine return address
CTR				loop counter branch address (goto, case, system glue)
XER				fixed point exceptions
FPSCR				floating-point exceptions
MQ		volatile	no	obsolete; exists on the 601 only

Note that even though the FPSCR is listed as a volatile register that doesn't need to be preserved, it is considered rude for a routine to change the floating-point exception *enable* bits in the FPSCR without restoring them to their original state. The only exceptions are routines defined to modify the floating-point execution state.

It is unnecessary to restore the FPSCR if it was only used to record the exception information as set by the standard arithmetic floating-point instructions.

13.2 Table of Contents (TOC)

Each program module (collection of routines) has associated with it a Table of Contents (TOC) area that identifies imported symbols and also provides a reference point for accessing the module's static storage area. A register is (by convention) reserved to always point to the current TOC area. This register is r2, but it is also referred to as rTOC.

For the most part, TOC maintenance is not something you need to worry about because all of the functions in the same module will share the same TOC. However, when calling routines in other modules (for example, the standard library routines), care must be taken so that the TOC for the called routine is set up properly, and so that the TOC of the caller is restored before control returns to the caller. Examples of how this transition is accomplished are given later in §13.13, "Linking with Global Routines."

A routine accesses its global variables (including external routine descriptors) by recording the variable's offset from the routine's TOC. This allows the variable to be accessed by simply adding the offset to the current TOC value in rTOC:

```
lwz     r3,offset(rTOC)
```

The data referenced from the TOC typically isn't the actual global data—it is usually just a pointer to the data. In the above example, the actual data would then be accessed via the pointer that has been loaded into r3.

The reason pointers are stored in the TOC area instead of the actual data is that 64K is the maximum size for the TOC area (because *offset* is a signed 16-bit quantity). If all of the program data needed to be directly accessible from the TOC, then the global static data would have an obviously unacceptable 64K limit.

By storing only pointers in the TOC area, the 64K limit applies only to the number of pointers that can be stored. Because each pointer is four bytes in size, the maximum of 16,384 global data pointers isn't a practical limitation for most applications.

Initializing the TOC

There is no need for a routine or module to initialize its TOC pointer. In fact, it is allowed to assume that the TOC has already been set up before it is given control. However, the TOC must be initialized *somewhere*. Fortunately, that somewhere is in the system loader, so most programmers do not need to worry about it.

The system loader handles the TOC initialization because it is in control of where the program's code and data are loaded. After the loader has decided where the program should be loaded, it knows the location of the TOC and can set up the TOC and update any portions of the code or data that need to be initialized with its value.

13.3 The Stack Pointer

By convention, GPR 1 contains a 16-byte aligned value that *always* points to the top of the stack, and the top of the stack *always* contains a valid *stack frame* for the current routine. The stack frame for a routine identifies the routine's execution context—it contains the register save area, local storage area, and a few other bits of information for the given routine. The information in the stack frame allows the entire calling chain to be examined at any time, because each stack frame also contains a pointer to the stack frame of the routine that called it. Figure 13-1 shows a sample stack with the call-chain pointers to the previous stack frame made explicit.

Figure 13-1   Sample Stack Showing Multiple Stack Frames

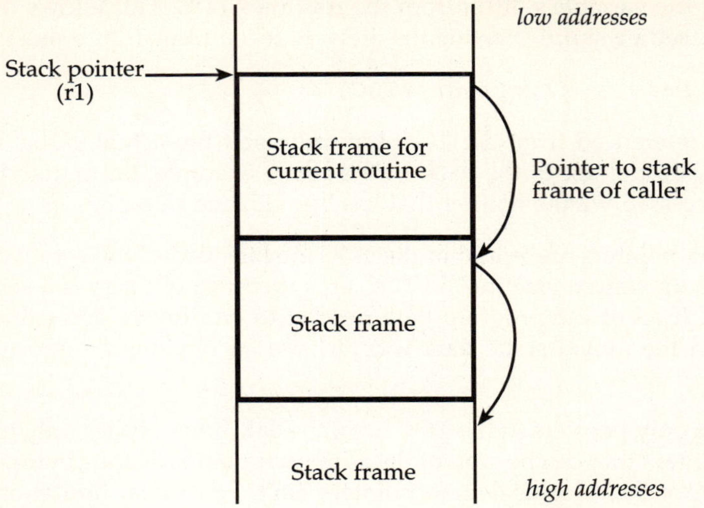

It's nice to be able to assume that the stack pointer always points to a valid stack frame, because interrupt-level code doesn't need to worry about the stack being in an inconsistent state. However, it does require a little bit of effort on the part of the program to insure that the stack pointer does, indeed, always identify a valid stack frame.

Basically, this effort amounts to making sure that the stack pointer update operation is atomic (that is, it is accomplished in one instruction). This means that the stack frame cannot be built by using a series of small steps that each allocate a small area on the stack—the entire stack frame size must be allocated at once, and the offsets to each area within the frame must be calculated. These calculations can become quite cumbersome because of multiple variable-sized areas in a stack frame. Efforts to simplify these calculations have led to some rather bizarre stack frame building conventions, which are covered later in "Building Stack Frames."

Updating the Stack Pointer

Because the stack pointer must always point to a valid stack frame at the top of the stack, the only time the stack pointer should be updated is when the flow of control is entering or exiting a function.[1]

---

1.   Actually, the C library routine `alloca()`, which dynamically allocates storage on the stack, also updates the stack pointer. This special case is discussed later in §13.12, "Stack Frames and alloca()."

When a function is entered, it needs to create a new stack frame above the current one on the stack and update r1 to point to the new frame, saving the address of the previous stack frame in the process. When a function exits, it simply needs to restore the previous stack frame.

Figure 13-2 shows this for the simple case of the routine foo() calling the routine bar(). At point (A), foo() has initialized itself but has not yet called another routine. During (B), foo() has called bar(), and bar() has set itself up with its own stack frame. A pointer back to foo()'s stack frame is recorded as part of bar()'s initialization process. After the call to bar() is complete (C), the stack pointer once again points to foo()'s stack frame.

Figure 13-2 Stack When foo() Calls bar()

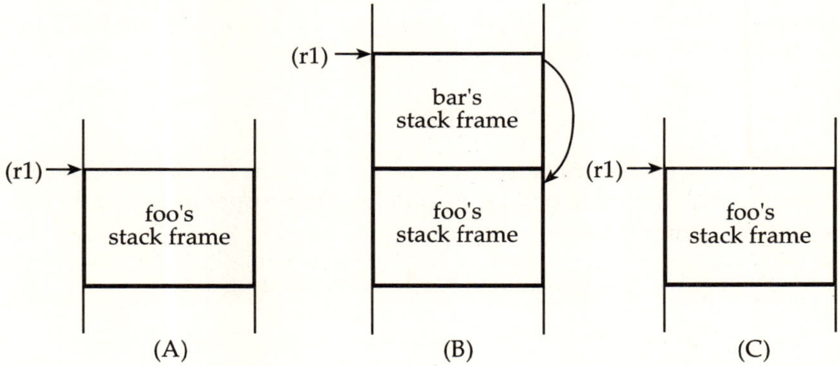

The three states shown in Figure 13-2 are the only states that the stack pointer has during the subroutine call. There are no intermediate states where bar()'s stack frame is only partially built.

Stack Pointer Maintenance on Function Entry

When the size of the stack frame is less than 32K, the stack pointer update that is required when a function is entered can be accomplished with a single instruction:

```
stwu    r1,–frame_size(r1)
```

This instruction calculates the address of the new stack frame from (r1)-*frame_size* and stores the old value of r1 (which points to the current stack frame) at that address. The calculated address is then stored in r1. The first part of this operation saves a pointer to the old stack frame in the first word of the new stack frame, and the second part updates the stack pointer to point to the new stack frame.

Stack Pointer Maintenance on Function Exit

For functions with stack frames less than 32K in size, the code required to update the stack pointer on function exit is also quite simple:

```
addi      r1,r1,frame_size
```

All that is required is that the stack be adjusted down by the same amount that it was adjusted up during function entry.

Alternatively, because a pointer to the previous stack frame was saved at offset 0 of the current stack frame, the stack pointer could be updated as:

```
lwz       r1,0(r1)
```

However, this method is less efficient because it requires a load from memory that the `addi` method avoids.

Handling Stack Frames ≥ 32K in Size

Handling stack frames that are 32K or larger in size is not difficult, but care must be taken so that the stack pointer is updated in one operation and not in a series of small adjustments.

On function entry, this operation should be performed as:

```
# load the 32-bit -frame_size value into r12
lis       r12,<upper 16 bits of -frame_size>
ori       r12,<lower 16 bits of -frame_size>

# update the stack pointer
stwux     r1,r1,r12
```

On function exit, the same technique is used as with small stack frames, but the `addi` instruction cannot be used (because it only handles 16-bit values). The *frame_size* value can be placed in a register and then added to the stack pointer, like this:

```
# load the 32-bit frame_size value into r12
lis       r12,<upper 16 bits of frame_size>
ori       r12,<lower 16 bits of frame_size>

# update the stack pointer
add       r1,r1,r12
```

As in the small stack frame case, the previous stack frame can be restored using a load from offset 0 of the current stack frame, as:

```
lwz       r1,0(r1)
```

Which of the two methods is more efficient depends on the particular routine since the three-instruction sequence provides more opportunities for scheduling the instructions.

Building Stack Frames

This section discusses the steps necessary to build a stack frame as they relate to the stack pointer. It does not provide all the details and the structure of stack frames (these will be given later in the sections detailing the subroutine calling conventions), but rather it discusses the order in which the components of the stack frame should be built.

The values in the stack frame can be initialized during two periods: before the frame is built and after it has been created. Both of these periods are shown in Figure 13-3.

After the stack frame is built the stack pointer (r1) points to the newly created stack frame. At this time, the area in the stack frame can be initialized by using a positive offset from the stack pointer (which is also a pointer to this stack frame). This period is typically when most stack frame initialization is performed.

Figure 13-3   Periods When Stack Frame Values Can Be Initialized

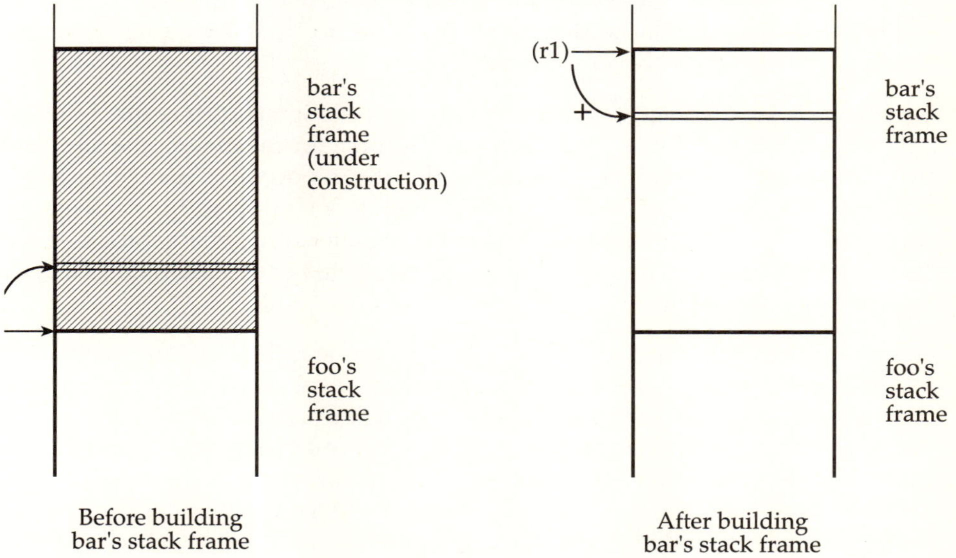

bar's stack frame (under construction)

foo's stack frame

Before building bar's stack frame

(r1)

bar's stack frame

foo's stack frame

After building bar's stack frame

Before the frame is built, r1 points to the stack frame of the previous routine, which is conveniently located immediately below where the new stack frame is going to be built. The new stack frame areas can be initialized at this point by using a negative offset from r1 to write values *above* the top of the stack.

Writing *Above* the Stack Pointer... *ick*!

The calling conventions for most well-designed systems involve initializing the stack frame values *after* the frame has been built and consider it a bad idea to write values above the current stack pointer. There's a very good reason for this: if an interrupt comes along, it may need to allocate some temporary storage on the stack for itself. Although it will free the space and return the stack pointer to its original value, any data that was above the stack pointer is likely to be trashed.

The PowerPC calling conventions are no exception: it is still considered bad form to write data above the stack pointer—with this one exception of building stack frames. Two things make this exception acceptable. First, the only values written above the stack are the GPR and FPR save areas, guaranteed to be no larger than a certain maximum size (because only a certain number of registers will ever need to be saved). Second, interrupts and other system-level code are aware of this maximum size and skip over that many bytes before they allocate any space on the stack.

Now, this may seem like too much effort just to write values safely above the stack, and, to a certain extent, it is. The GPR and FPR save areas could have been written using offsets from the new stack frame after it had been built. However, because many areas in the stack frame are of variable width and need to be properly aligned, the formula to determine the offset to these two areas from the frame pointer is relatively complicated.

So, it's basically a choice between complicating the interrupt handlers (which very few people write) or complicating the formula for calculating the offsets to these areas (which would affect more people). It's important to note that neither option affects performance. The interrupt handlers simply add the maximum save area size to the amount of space that they're allocating on the stack, and the "more complex offset formula" is statically computed at assembly time doesn't generate any extra code.

The end result is that it doesn't really matter. The standard calling convention involves writing above the stack, and the system-level code is designed to handle this. If writing above the stack offends you as a programmer, you can simply not do it. It is perfectly acceptable to save the GPR and FPR values after the stack frame has been built because the only code that uses them is the function that owns the stack frame (no one else *can* use them since the number of registers saved isn't even recorded unless debugging information (*à la* traceback table) is present).

It's interesting to note that because the size of the GPR and FPR save areas is dependent on the size and number of registers being saved, the maximum save area size will change for 64-bit PowerPC implementations. In order to make room for the nineteen 64-bit GPRs and eighteen 64-bit FPRs, 296 bytes (instead of the 220 required for nineteen 32-bit GPRs and eighteen 64-bit FPRs) will need to be "reserved" above the stack.

13.4 Brief Interlude: Naming Conventions

In the remainder of this chapter, three routine names will be used in the examples: `sna()`, `foo()`, and `bar()`. Of these three routines, `foo()` and `bar()` will commonly be used in the examples. The relationship between these routines is that `foo()` calls `bar()`. The `sna()` routine is only used to refer to the routine that originally called `foo()`. This calling order will always hold true for all the examples given here: `sna()` always calls `foo()`, which always calls `bar()`.

The terms *caller/callee* or *pitcher/catcher* can also be used when describing how the functions are interacting with the surrounding routines. However, a routine is never referred to as simply a caller or a callee—these terms are always used with respect to some other function. For example, `foo()` is the *caller* of `bar()`, but is a *callee* of `sna()`—how it's referred to depends on the context. Most of the time, this caller/callee relationship will not be used because using these terms can lead to confusion when the context of the discussion changes.

13.5 Subroutine Calling Conventions

A subroutine call requires that the caller and the callee both agree on a protocol for passing data and control back and forth. As mentioned earlier, these conventions are not enforced by the processor. These conventions are instead "enforced" by the operating system and the libraries, because a program must follow these conventions in order to access the system-provided routines.

According to these calling conventions, the calling routine has the responsibility of setting up the parameters, passing the return address, and then handing off control to the subroutine.

The called routine has the responsibility of saving the return address and any non-volatile register that it modifies, setting up any stack structures that it requires, and then cleaning everything up and restoring registers before returning to the calling routine. These two tasks (set up and clean up) are performed by code fragments known as prologs and epilogs.

Prologs and Epilogs

Prologs and epilogs are little code snippets at the beginning (prologs) or ending (epilogs) of a function. The purpose of these `logs is to set up the proper environment for the routine and then restore the original environment when the routine is finished.

Function Prologs

When a function is called, it must set up the stack properly so that it creates room for all local and register-save storage, and so that it sets up a proper back chain. The portion of a function that does this is known as the function prolog.

Function Epilogs

The function epilog undoes the work of the prolog. It restores the registers that were saved and makes sure that the stack pointer once again points to the stack frame of the routine that originally called this routine.

13.6 A Simple Subroutine Call

The easiest way to describe a function call is to step through a very basic subroutine call and explain what is happening along the way. For this example, the routine `foo()` (which is assumed to have already been set up) is calling the routine `bar()`, using a standard *Branch with Link* instruction:

```
bl      bar
```

The parameters being passed are not important for this general discussion, so they are not specified.

Before Calling `bar()`

As mentioned earlier, `foo()` is assumed to have been set up properly already. This means that the stack pointer currently points to `foo()`'s stack frame. This is shown in Figure 13-4.

There are five areas in this stack frame: the *link area*, the *argument area*, the *local storage area*, the *GPR save area*, and the *FPR save area*. The last two areas are sometimes collectively referred to as the *register save area* or simply the *save area*. These areas are briefly described in the next few paragraphs and more completely described in §13.9, "Stack Frames."

The *link area* is used to save the back-chain (the pointer to the previous function's stack frame) and to provide space to store a few special registers: the Table Of Contents, the Condition Register, and the Link Register.

Figure 13-4   The Stack Frame of `foo()`

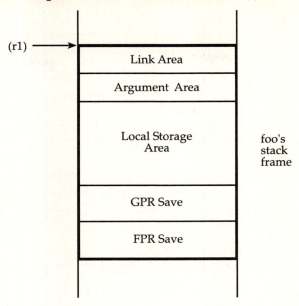

(r1) →

| Link Area |
| Argument Area |
| Local Storage Area |
| GPR Save |
| FPR Save |

foo's stack frame

The *argument area* is where the arguments are placed if there isn't enough room to store all of them in the registers. This area is always at least eight words in size and is left unused most of the time (because the arguments are stored in registers if possible). The arguments stored here are the arguments that `foo()` (in this example) is sending to another routine (`bar()`). These are *not* the arguments that were passed to `foo()`.

The *local storage area* is where `foo()` stores whatever it likes. Its size is determined by `foo()` when it creates the stack frame.

The *register save area* is where `foo()` stores the original contents of any of the non-volatile GPRs or FPRs that it needs to use. This way it can restore them to their original values before returning. If no non-volatile registers are used by `foo()`, then this area will be zero bytes in size.

Prolog for `bar()`

After control is passed to `bar()`, its prolog code is executed, which performs these tasks:

- Saves any non-volatile registers that are used by `bar()`.
- Creates `bar()`'s stack frame (saving a pointer to the previous frame).

After `bar ()` has accomplished these tasks, the stack looks like Figure 13-5.

Figure 13-5   The Stack after `bar( )` Has Built Its Stack Frame.

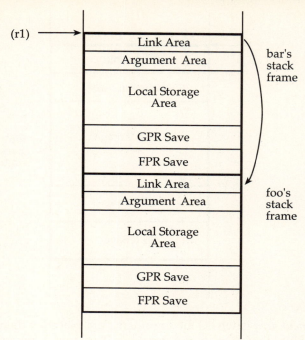

Saving the Non-volatile Registers

The following registers are non-volatile and must be saved if `bar( )` uses them: GPRs 13 through 31, FPRs 14 through 31, and the Condition Register. In addition, the Link Register (technically a volatile register) should be saved and restored.

As mentioned earlier, the GPRs and FPRs are saved in `bar( )`'s stack frame before the stack frame is built. First, the FPRs are stored immediately above `foo( )`'s stack frame, and then the GPRs are written above the FPRs. A simplified diagram showing only the GPR and FPR save areas is given in Figure 13-6.

Figure 13-6   Saving the GPRs and FPRs above the Stack Pointer

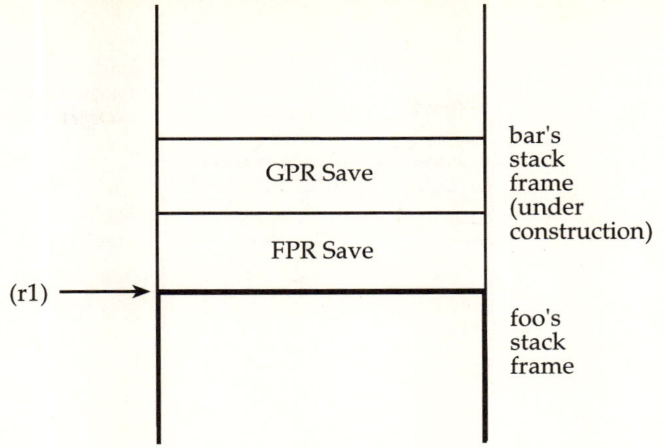

Because of the register usage convention of starting from register 31 and working down, each routine will have a contiguous range of registers (r*N* through r31) that need to be saved. This simplifies the save/restore code and allows the *Load* and *Store Multiple* instructions to be used for this purpose. In reality, the process of saving and restoring registers ends up being a little more complicated, but these complications don't affect the fact that the registers are stored in the *register save area* in ascending order. Register saving is treated in more detail later in §13.8, "Saving Registers on the Stack."

For the CR and LR, storage space is set aside in foo()'s stack frame to save these values. The CR is saved at offset 4 from the start of foo()'s stack frame, and the LR is stored at offset 8. Figure 13-7 shows this operation. In this figure, the highlighted area in foo()'s stack frame is the area in the Link Area where the register is being stored.

The code to save the CR and LR is:

```
# save the Link Register
mflr   r0
stw    r0,8(r1)

# save the Condition Register
mfcr   r0
stw    r0,4(r1)
```

Figure 13-7   Saving Values into foo( )'s Stack Frame

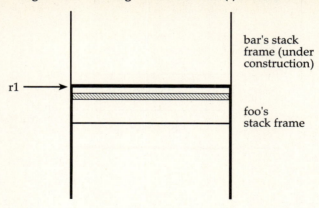

bar's stack
frame (under
construction)

r1

foo's
stack frame

One additional register, the FPSCR, is a special case because it generally doesn't
need to be saved and restored, but there are situations where it should be. If any
of the *enable* (VE, OE, UE, ZE, or XE) or *mode* (NI or RN) bits of the FPSCR are
changed, then the routine should save and restore the FPSCR, because it is impo-
lite for a routine to globally change the floating-point model. The other bits of
the FPSCR, which may be set as a side effect of executing floating-point instructions, are volatile, and the FPSCR does not need to be saved if they are modified.

No special storage location is set aside for the FPSCR. If a routine needs to save
and restore it, the routine must allocate space in its *local storage area*.

Creating the Stack Frame

After all the registers have been saved, the stack frame for bar( ) can be created.
This is usually a single instruction:

```
stwu    r1,-frame_size(r1)
```

where the *frame_size* value is calculated from the sum of the sizes of the five areas
comprising the stack frame, plus some padding bytes to insure that the stack
frame always starts on a quadword boundary. Hence:

$$frame\_size = link\_size + arg\_size + local\_size + gpr\_size + fpr\_size + padding$$

where:

link_size is always six words (24 bytes) in length.

arg_size is large enough to hold all arguments needed for any function that
bar( ) calls. Note that this is *not* related to the arguments that are passed

into `bar()`. This area is for the arguments that `bar()` will (possibly) pass to another routine. This is always at least eight words (64 bytes) in length.

local_size is the size of the local storage area that `bar()` needs, or 0 if it doesn't need any local storage.

gpr_size is large enough to hold all of the GPRs that `bar()` is saving and restoring. This can range from 0 to 19 words (76 bytes).

fpr_size is large enough to hold all of the FPRs that `bar()` is saving and restoring. This can range from 0 to 18 doublewords (144 bytes).

padding is the number of extra bytes needed to insure that the stack pointer is always quadword (16-byte) aligned.

Because the *link, argument,* and *local storage area* are allocated from the top of the stack frame, and the *FPR* and *GPR save area*s are allocated from the bottom, the padding bytes fall between the *local storage area* and the *GPR save area*.

It is important to note that this one *Store with Update* instruction performs two critical functions: it allocates the new stack frame on the stack, and it saves the back chain (pointer to the previous stack frame) at offset 0 into the newly created stack frame.

Execution of `bar()`

Finally, `bar()` can execute its code and accomplish the tasks that it needs to, including calling other routines.

Epilog of `bar()`

During the epilog, `bar()` must restore the registers, restore `foo()`'s stack frame, and then return control to `foo()`.

Restoring the Non-volatile Registers

The FPRs and GPRs can be restored by loading from the values stored in the *register save area*. For GPRs, the *Load Multiple* instruction can be used, but since there is no equivalent instruction for FPRs, some other method must be used. The problems associated with saving and restoring registers are covered later in §13.8, "Saving Registers on the Stack."

Restoring the CR and LR is just as easy as saving them. The code to restore these registers is:

```
# restore the Link Register
lwz     r0,frame_size+8(r1)
```

```
        mtlr    r0

        # restore the Condition Register
        lwz     r0,frame_size+4(r1)
        mtcr    r0
```

Technically, only the CR fields that have changed need to be restored, but some PowerPC implementations may execute a complete CR restore instruction significantly faster than they would execute a partial CR restore.

Restoring the Stack Frame

To restore `foo()`'s stack frame, we add the size of `bar()`'s stack frame to the stack pointer:

```
        addi    r1,r1,frame_size
```

Returning Control to `foo()`

Because the LR has been restored, it now holds the return address in `foo()`. This means that control can be returned to `foo()` by simply executing a *Branch to Link Register* instruction:

```
        blr
```

Return to `foo()`

At this point, control has been returned to `foo()`, and the stack and all of the non-volatile registers have been restored. Execution in `foo()` continues.

13.7 An Even Simpler Subroutine Call

One thing was not made explicit in the simple subroutine call: it was assumed that the routine `bar()` needed a stack frame. A routine needs a stack frame only:

- If `bar()` calls another routine. A stack frame is needed because the arguments for the routine being called must be stored in the argument area for `bar()`. `foo()`'s argument area holds the arguments for `bar()` and cannot be reused to also hold the arguments for another routine.

- if `bar()` requires more than 220 bytes of storage area. The magical "220 byte" value comes from the maximum size of the GPR and FPR save area that all interrupt level code will skip over before allocating space on the stack. If `bar()` can fit its register save area and its local storage area into 220 bytes, then it can get away without having a stack frame.

If a routine doesn't require a stack frame, then there's no sense in creating one. This section will step through the subroutine call where is it assumed that `bar()` does not need a stack frame.

Before Calling bar()

The frameless routine is called like an ordinary routine, through a `blr` instruction. The stack for `foo()` is set up just as it was in the previous section. Basically, `foo()` doesn't know (or care) if any routine it calls has a stack frame or not. It just passes control to the routine and waits for control to return.

Prolog of bar()

The only task that the prolog needs to perform is saving the non-volatile registers that `bar()` needs to use. This is done above the stack pointer (where `bar()`'s stack frame would be if it were to build one). §13.8, "Saving Registers on the Stack," discusses in detail how this is done.

The CR and LR should also be saved. Because space has been allocated for them in `foo()`'s stack frame, they can be saved using the same code given in the previous section:

```
# save the Link Register
mflr    r0
stw     r0,8(r1)

# save the Condition Register
mfcr    r0
stw     r0,4(r1)
```

In general, the LR should be saved even though it may seem unneeded (because `bar()` doesn't call any functions). There are two reasons for this. First, there may be some constructs (like case statements) that use the LR; and, second, some system-level routines are branched to (saving the LR), but are not considered real subroutines because they do not require a stack frame (see §13.8, "Saving Registers on the Stack").

Execution of bar()

As in the previous description, the execution of `bar()` continues as it normally would. The only differences are that `bar()` is not allowed to call any other routines, and any of `bar()`'s local variables must be accessed using a positive offset from the top of the stack.

Epilog of `bar()`

Because there is no stack frame to restore, the epilog code just restores the non-volatile registers that were used by `bar()` and then returns control to `foo()`.

For the GPRs and FPRs, the original values are pulled from above the stack and stuffed into the appropriate registers. See §13.8, "Saving Registers on the Stack," for a full discussion of how this should be done.

For the CR and LR, the original values were stored at offsets 4 and 8 of `foo()`'s stack frame. This is the same code used in the previous section, with the simplification that the *frame_size* is known to be 0.

```
# restore the Link Register
lwz     r0,8(r1)
mtlr    r0

# restore the Condition Register
lwz     r0,4(r1)
mtcr    r0
```

Not surprisingly, the instruction to return to `foo()` is the standard:

```
blr
```

13.8 Saving Registers on the Stack

The previous sections hinted that saving the GPRs and FPRs on the stack was not quite as straightforward as it might seem. This section finally explains the complications surrounding the seemingly simple task of saving and restoring registers.

Using the Load and Store Multiple Instructions

For two really good reasons, the *Load* and *Store Multiple* routines are *not* encouraged as part of the standard register saving mechanism.

The first is the ominous hint in the PowerPC Architecture manual that the *Load* and *Store Multiple* instructions may (on some PowerPC implementations) execute significantly slower than an equivalent series of loads or stores. Basically, this means that the hardware designers aren't going to bother wasting transistors on these instructions—if it's easy to add support for them, then it might be thrown in, but otherwise it'll be emulated in software. Note that this doesn't mean that a series of loads or stores will *always* be faster than the analagous *Load* or *Store Multiple* instruction. On processors with unified caches (like the 601), the instruction fetches from the series of loads/stores can collide with the data cache accesses and thus be less efficient than the *Load* or *Store Multiple*.

The second reason is that equivalent instructions do not exist for the FPRs, and there are no planned instructions to support 64-bit GPRs. This means that the only time these instructions can be used is with the GPRs on 32-bit PowerPC implementations, *and* they might be horribly inefficient.

So, because a mechanism is needed for the FPRs anyway, it might as well be generalized to handle the GPRs.

Saving GPRs Only

The easiest case to describe is where a series of GPRs need to be saved, but no FPRs. In this case, the GPR save area is located immediately above the stack frame for the previous routine. Figure 13-8 shows the save area when only the GPRs need to be saved.

Figure 13-8 Saving GPRs into bar ( )'s Soon-to-be-constructed Stack Frame

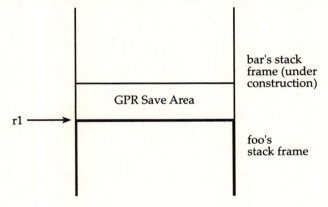

There are three common ways of accomplishing this. The first is to use the *Store Multiple* instruction, which has already been presented as a potentially bad idea. However, it doesn't hurt to show how it *would* be done. The second and third methods both involve using a series of *Store* instructions. The second method has these instructions inline, and the third branches to a system routine that performs the appropriate register saves.

Using the Store Multiple Instruction

The stmw instruction automatically stores all of the registers, from a specified starting register up to r31, at a specified effective address. By specifying the appropriate offset above the current stack pointer as the effective address, the GPRs can be saved above the stack using one instruction.

There is really only one variable here, the number of registers that need to be saved. If this variable is called N, and it is allowed to range from one (only r31 is saved) to 19 (r13 through r31 are saved), then the instruction needed to save this number of registers above the stack pointer would be:

```
stmw    32-N,-4*N(r1)
```

So, for $N = 1$, this would be:

```
stmw    r31,-4(r1)
```

For $N = 19$, it would be:

```
stmw    r13,-76(r1)
```

Using a Series of Store Instructions

After the formula for the *Store Multiple* instruction is known, the *Store* instructions are easy to generate because the arguments are basically the same. To save five registers, this series of stores would be used:

```
stw     r27,-20(r1)
stw     r28,-16(r1)
stw     r29,-12(r1)
stw     r30,-8(r1)
stw     r31,-4(r1)
```

To save all the GPRs, a series of 19 stw instructions would be used:

```
stw     r13,-76(r1)
stw     r14,-72(r1)
...                     # 15 more stw instructions
stw     r30,-8(r1)
stw     r31,-4(r1)
```

Branching to System-Provided GPR Save Routine

Because the stw instructions are always the same series of instructions, it makes sense to put the instructions in a system-level routine that any routine can branch to. If the system provides this, then the registers can be stored by branching to the appropriate entry point in this system routine.

As an example, consider the following (abbreviated) implementation of such a system routine with the listed entry points:

```
_savegpr13:     stw         r13,-76(r1)
_savegpr14:     stw         r14,-72(r1)
_savegpr15:     stw         r15,-68(r1)
                ...
_savegpr30:     stw         r30,-8(r1)
_savegpr31:     stw         r31,-4(r1)
                blr
```

In order to save nine registers (r23 through r31), a routine could branch to the "gpr23" entry point:

```
        mflr        r0
        bla         _savegpr23
```

Note that the LR must be saved (in this case, in r0) before the save routine is called.

The bla (*Branch with Link Absolute*) instruction is used to call the save routine because it is assumed that the routine is at a fixed location determined by the OS. If the routine is *not* at a fixed location, then the bl (*Branch with Link*) instruction would be used instead.

Restoring GPRs Only

Just as there are three ways to save the GPRs, there are three ways to restore the registers: using a *Load Multiple* instruction; using a series of loads; or using a system-provided routine to load the registers.

It is important to note that these methods must be applied *after* the original routine's stack pointer has been restored in r1.

Using the Load Multiple Instruction

A *Load Multiple* instruction with the same parameters as the Store Multiple instruction used to save the registers, restores all the GPRs in one instruction.

To summarize, this instruction should be used:

```
lmw     32-N,-4*N(r1)
```

where N is the number of registers to be saved, ranging from 1 to 19.

Using a Series of Load Instructions

Because this series of load instructions is exactly the same sequence provided in the system GPR load routine described in the next section, it isn't necessary to go into detail here—the same information would be duplicated.

However, it is perfectly valid to take this system GPR load routine and copy it inline into a routine.

Branching to System-Provided GPR Restore Routine

The standard GPR restore routine is a series of load instructions that are analogous to the store instructions in the GPR save routine:

```
_restgpr13:     lwz       r13,-76(r1)
_restgpr14:     lwz       r14,-72(r1)
_restgpr15:     lwz       r15,-68(r1)
                ...
_restgpr30:     lwz       r30,-8(r1)
_restgpr31:     lwz       r31,-4(r1)
                blr
```

A routine can restore the registers by branching to the appropriate entry point. For example, to restore registers r23 to r31, this branch would be used:

```
                bla       _restgpr23
```

Saving FPRs Only

Now that the save procedure for the GPRs has been discussed, it is much easier to describe the save procedure for the 18 FPRs. There are two options: the provided FPR save routine or an inline copy of this routine. Because these are both the same code, only the system FPR save routine will be discussed.

A system FPR save routine might look like this:

```
_savefpr14:     stfd      fr14,-144(r1)
_savefpr15:     stfd      fr15,-136(r1)
_savefpr16:     stfd      fr16,-128(r1)
                ...
_savefpr30:     stfd      fr30,-16(r1)
_savefpr31:     stfd      fr31,-8(r1)
                blr
```

In order to save nine floating-point registers (`fr23` through `fr31`), a routine could branch to the "fpr23" entry point:

```
mflr    r0
bla     _savefpr23
```

As with the GPR case, the LR must be saved before the save routine is called.

Restoring FPRs Only

Not surprisingly, the standard FPR restore routine is just a series of floating-point load instructions that follow the same pattern as the store instructions in the FPR save routine:

```
_restfpr14:    lfd     fr14,-144(r1)
_restfpr15:    lfd     fr15,-136(r1)
_restfpr16:    lfd     fr16,-128(r1)
               ...
_restfpr30:    lfd     fr30,-16(r1)
_restfpr31:    lfd     fr31,-8(r1)
               blr
```

A routine to restore floating-point registers `fr23` to `fr31` would use this branch instruction:

```
bla     _restfpr23
```

Saving Both GPRs and FPRs

Restoring both GPRs and FPRs gets somewhat messy because the FPRs get stored first and the GPRs must be stored immediately above them. Where the GPRs get stored now depends on the number of FPRs saved, so a simple scheme of storing them at a constant offset from the current stack pointer (as was done above) won't work anymore.

The way around this is to calculate and use a GPR base address instead of the stack pointer, as shown in Figure 13-9. This base address is easy to calculate from the current stack pointer and the number of FPRs being saved:

```
subi    r12,r1,8*number_of_FPRs
```

Figure 13-9   The GPRs Save Area Is Immediately above the FPR Save Area.

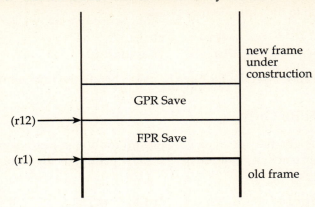

If the standard GPR save routines are rewritten to use `r12` instead of `r1`, then this code can be used to save six GPRs and five FPRs:

```
mflr    r0
subi    r12,r1,8*5
bla     _savegpr26
bla     _savefpr27
```

Restoring Both GPRs and FPRs

Restoring GPRs and FPRs is done the same way as the GPR/FPR save—an extra register is used to calculate the GPR base address. As with the save routine, the GPR restore routine must be rewritten to use this new base register.

To continue the example, this code could be used to restore the six GPRs and five FPRs saved:

```
subi    r12,r1,8*5
bla     _restgpr26
bla     _restfpr27
```

System Save/Restore Routine in Practice

In practice, the GPR/FPR save and restore routines can be slightly different than the examples. These differences arise because some systems provide two types of GPR save and restore routines (one based on `r1` and another based on `r12`), and because the routines are sometimes expanded to perform duties in addition to saving and restoring GPRs or FPRs.

Multiple GPR Save/Restore Routines

Because it is convenient to have GPR save and restore routines based on both r1 and r12, many systems provide both. These routines are identical except for the base register used.

To differentiate between these two versions, the standard name of the routines are changed: _savegpr0_XX and _restgpr0_XX reference the save/restore off of r1, and _savegpr1_XX and _restgpr1_XX reference the save/restore off of r12.

Note that the '0' variant is used when only the GPRs are being saved, and the '1' variant is used when both GPRs and FPRs are being saved.

Additional Functionality

Because these routines are always part of a function's prolog or epilog, it makes sense to include some other prolog/epilog tasks in their code.

Additional Functionality for Save Routines

For the save routines, it's easy to add the store of the original LR into the caller's stack frame because it is something that the function prolog needs to do anyway. If the LR is saved in r0 before calling the save routine (as it should be), the LR can be saved in the proper place using:

```
stw        r0,8(r1)
```

For the GPR save routine, this instruction only needs to be added to the '0' variant because the '1' variant is always used with the FPR save routine, which will presumably handle the LR save.

The FPR save routine that includes an LR save is differentiated from the standard FPR save routine by adding an underscore between the 'fpr' and the register number. Thus, _savefpr_29 would be used instead of _savefpr29.

Additional Functionality for Restore Routines

The restore routines can restore the saved LR value and return directly to the value stored there, eliminating the need to return back to the function performing the restore. This is done by adding code to the end of the restore routine:

```
lwz        r0,8(r1)
mtlr       r0
blr
```

When this version of a restore routine is used, it isn't necessary to use the *Branch with Link* form to call the restore routine (no damage will occur if it is used). Only the non-Link branch form is needed because the restore routine will return directly to the caller.

Rewriting the example that restores six GPRs and five FPRs, the restore routines would be called as:

```
subi      r12,r1,8*5
bla       _restgpr1_26
ba        _restfpr_27
```

As with the save routines, this extra functionality only needs to be added to the '0' variant of the GPR save routines. The FPR restore routine that restores the LR adds an underscore to the name just like the FPR save routine does. Thus, `_restfpr_27` is used in the above example instead of `_restfpr27`.

13.9 Stack Frames

Stack frames have been discussed throughout this chapter, but not thoroughly, so that other, more interesting topics could be discussed sooner. This section provides a detailed analysis of the structures that comprise a routine's stack frame.

A stack frame is composed of five basic areas as shown in Figure 13-10. To help speed up data accesses, stack frames are always quadword aligned and the areas within the frame are either doubleword or word aligned. The required alignment for the stack frame areas is also shown in Figure 13-10. Quadword boundaries are marked with a 'Q', doubleword boundaries with a 'D', and word boundaries with a 'W'.

Because the Link, Argument, and Local Storage areas grow down from the top of the frame, and the FPR and GPR save areas grow up from the bottom of the frame, some unused "padding" bytes may be left between the Local Storage Area and GPR Save Area.

As in the previous sections, the routines in this discussion will be referred to by name instead of usage (because usage may change with the context). Thus, the routine that owns the stack frame will be known as `foo()`, and `bar()` will be used as an example routine that is called by `foo()`. The routine that originally called `foo()` will be referred to as `sna()`. Hence, the complete calling chain is `sna()` ⇒ `foo()` ⇒ `bar()`. This terminology helps simplify the discussion by eliminating some unwieldy phrases needed to identify each routine properly.

Figure 13-10   Stack Frame Structure Showing the Required Alignment

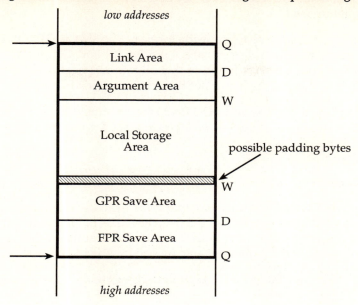

Link Area

The Link Area is a 24-byte area that is used by both `foo()` (the stack frame owner) and `bar()`. Table 13-4 lists the area's fields.

Table 13-4   Link Area fields

Offset	Size	Description	Set/Used by
0	W	back chain to sna()'s stack frame	foo()
4	W	saved CR	bar()
8	W	saved LR	bar()
12	W	reserved (used by compilers)	-
16	W	reserved (used by binders)	-
20	W	saved TOC	bar()

The first word (at offset 0) contains a pointer to the stack frame of the routine that called `foo()`, in this case `sna()`. This field is initialized by `foo()` as part of its function prolog and is used by `foo()`'s epilog to restore the original stack frame when the routine is complete.

The next two fields are used by routines that `foo()` calls, in this case `bar()`, so that they have a place to store the LR and CR. These values are stored here because it is possible that `bar()` will not need to create a stack frame and it is convenient to always save these register values in the same place.

The next two fields are reserved for use by compilers and binders, but they are generally left unused.

The last field is a storage space set aside for bar() to save its TOC pointer when it makes out-of-module function calls. Like the LR and CR storage areas, this area is part of foo()'s stack frame so that all routines have a common place to store their TOC value, whether or not they create a stack frame.

Because the Saved CR, LR, and TOC fields are presumed to be available to any routine that foo() calls, foo() *must* create a stack frame if it calls any other routine.

Argument Area

The Argument Area is a storage place that foo() can use to hold arguments that are being passed to bar(). Table 13-5 lists the area's fields. Note that this is not where the arguments to foo() are stored. The arguments being passed to foo() are stored in the Argument area owned by sna().

Table 13-5   Argument Area Fields

Offset	Size	Description	GPR
0	W	1st parameter word	3
4	W	2nd parameter word	4
...	...	...	...
24	W	7th parameter word	9
28	W	8th parameter word	10
32	-	additional parameters (if necessary)	-

Because the Argument Area is used to hold the arguments that foo() is passing to bar(), it must be large enough to hold all the arguments that bar() expects. If foo() calls multiple routines, then this area must be large enough to hold all the arguments for the routine that requires the most argument space.

One restriction on the size of the Argument Area is that it is always at least eight words in size. The first eight words of arguments would be placed in these eight words if they weren't placed in GPRs 3 through 10. These eight words are always allocated because it may be necessary for bar() to take the address of one of the arguments. In this case, the value would be written from the GPR into the analogous slot in the Argument Area and the address into the Argument Area would be used.

Local Storage Area

The Local Storage Area is a free-form data area that begins immediately below the Argument Area. Its size is determined by the amount of stack space that `foo()` allocates for its stack frame.

GPR Save Area

The GPR Save Area is an area set aside for storing the original values of the non-volatile GPRs so that they can be restored before `foo()` returns control to `sna()`.

The number of registers saved here depends on the number of non-volatile registers that `foo()` uses. This can vary from zero to 19 registers, which results in this area's size varying from zero to 76 bytes. The position depends on the size of the FPR Save Area because the GPR Save Area is defined to be placed immediately above the FPR Save Area.

FPR Save Area

The FPR Save Area is where the original values of the non-volatile FPRs are stored so that `foo()` can restore them when it exits. The size of this area varies from 0 to 144 bytes, depending on the number of FPRs (0 through 19) that need to be saved.

13.10 Passing Arguments to Routines

The subroutine calling convention used on most PowerPC systems is register-based. This means the parameters are passed to the routine using agreed-upon registers. This scheme works very well in most cases. However, in some situations, this simple scheme breaks down, for example:

- When there are >8 words of fixed-point arguments.
- When there are >13 doublewords of floating-point arguments.
- When there are a large number of both fixed- and floating-point arguments.
- When passing structures or other complex data types into a routine.

The best way of describing the parameter passing scheme is to formalize the basic system and then to extend it to handle the situations listed. This section includes many examples that demonstrate how the function parameters are assigned to the registers.

Arguments for Simple Routines

A simple routine (as far as this section is concerned) has a small number of parameters, all of which are basic types. For example, the following routine has four fixed-point parameters:

```
void f1(int a,char b,short c,long d)
```

These four parameters are assigned to the GPRs from left to right, starting with GPR 3 (the first GPR available for use as a parameter). Thus, the register assignments listed in Table 13-6 are made.

Table 13-6   **Arguments for** `void f1(int a,char b,short c,long d)`

Arg	1	2	3	4
Type	int	char	short	long
Offset	(0)	(4)	(8)	(12)
GPR	3	4	5	6
FPR	-	-	-	-
		char in low-order byte of register	short in low-order halfword of register	

Because this table format will be used throughout this section to describe the argument-passing conventions, it is worthwhile to spend a few paragraphs to describe how the data is arranged in the table.

First of all, each argument is described in a separate column. Since there are four arguments, there are four columns numbered 1 through 4. This numbering is useful because it is convenient to refer to arguments by number instead of name or type.

For each argument, the argument type, an offset, and a GPR/FPR allocation will be given. In addition, sometimes notes on the bottom describe some special feature of the argument.

The argument type is simply the type originally defined for the variable, to typically something like *int*, *char*, or *long*.

The offset for each argument is the offset into the Argument Area that is being used to hold the arguments. In many cases, the arguments are passed in registers and the space left in the Argument Area is unused. In these cases, the offset will be displayed in parentheses.

The last two rows are the GPR or FPR assignment for this argument. For GPRs, this ranges between 3 and 10, and for FPRs it ranges from 1 to 13. Not all arguments have register assignments, and it is possible for an argument to be assigned to both a GPR and an FPR.

Routines with Integer Arguments

Routines with only integer arguments are the most basic in terms of how the data is allocated.

A couple of things are important to note about the example arguments described in Table 13-6. The first item of note is that each argument is assigned to a different register in order starting with GPR 3. The arguments are not combined in any way to save registers (as could possibly have been done with arguments 2 and 3). The second is that the data is always placed in the low-order (rightmost) bits of the register. This second rule is true even when the data is allocated in the Argument Area.

Routines with Floating-Point Arguments

Floating-point arguments are allocated to floating-point registers in the same manner that integer arguments are allocated to GPRs.

In Table 13-7 the four floating-point values are assigned to the first four available FPRs. Each value is also mapped into an appropriate number of bytes in the Argument Area: eight bytes for double-precision values and four bytes for single-precision values.

Table 13-7   Arguments for `void f2(double a,double b,float c,double d)`

Arg	1	2	3	4
Type	*double*	*double*	*float*	*double*
Offset	(0)	(8)	(16)	(20)
GPR	-	-	-	-
FPR	1	2	3	4

Routines with Both Integer and Floating-point Arguments

When both integer and floating-point arguments are being passed to a routine, things become somewhat complicated. The problem stems from the fact that the eight words in the argument area are assigned to GPRs 3-10, and now some floating-point values may need to be mapped into that area.

The conflict is resolved by not using the GPRs that would be assigned to the same area in the Argument Area as the FPRs that need to be mapped into that area. The tables show this by allocating the GPRs to the floating-point values and listing the GPR numbers in parentheses.

Table 13-8 shows how GPRs 4 and 5 are set aside to eliminate any conflict with the double-precision value stored in FPR 1, and GPR 7 is set aside for FPR 2 (which contains only a single-precision value). These three GPRs are not used for argument passing, but they can be used by the called routine for any other purpose.

Table 13-8   Arguments for `void f3(int a,double b,char c,float d,int e)`

Arg	1	2	3	4	5
Type	*int*	*double*	*char*	*float*	*int*
Offset	(0)	(4)	(12)	(16)	(20)
GPR	3	(4,5)	6	(7)	8
FPR	-	1	-	2	-

Routines with More than 32 Bytes of Arguments

If there are more than 32 bytes of arguments, then some arguments will not fit into the GPRs and must be stored directly in the Argument Area. Whenever there are more than 32 bytes of arguments, all of the argument bytes beyond the 32nd must be stored in the Argument Area.

In Table 13-9, the first six parameters fill up the entire 32 bytes of the Argument Area, so it must be expanded to 44 bytes to hold all of the arguments.

Table 13-9   Arguments for `void f4(int a,double b,double c,`
`single d,int e,int f,int g,double h)`

Arg	1	2	3	4	5	6	7	8
Type	*int*	*double*	*double*	*single*	*int*	*int*	*int*	*double*
Offset	(0)	(4)	(12)	(20)	(24)	(28)	32	36
GPR	3	(4,5)	(6,7)	(8)	9	10	-	-
FPR	-	1	2	3	-	-	-	4

Another interesting aspect of this example is that even though the GPRs have all been expended and the Argument Area has been partially used, the FPRs can continue to be allocated as long as they are available. In this case, the floating-point values must still be passed in the Argument Area, but they may also be passed in the appropriate FPRs.

Routines without Prototypes

The only difference between routines with and without prototypes is how the floating-point parameters are handled. If a called routine does not have a prototype, then the floating-point values are passed in both the GPRs and the FPRs.

The mapping follows the same technique used when there were mixed integer and floating-point arguments. The difference is that now the GPRs aren't just being allocated. They are actually being used to store the floating-point value (in addition to the FPR, which stores the same value).

To show some of these register assignments, routines with floating-point arguments are revisited in Tables 13-10 and 13-11 to show the GPR allocation.

Table 13-10   Arguments for `void f2(double a,double b,float c,double d)`

Arg	1	2	3	4
Type	*double*	*double*	*float*	*double*
Offset	(0)	(8)	(16)	(20)
GPR	3,4	5,6	7	8,9
FPR	1	2	3	4

Table 13-11   Arguments for `void f3(int a,double b,char c,float d,int e)`

Arg	1	2	3	4	5
Type	*int*	*double*	*char*	*float*	*int*
Offset	(0)	(4)	(12)	(16)	(20)
GPR	3	4,5	6	7	8
FPR	-	1	-	2	-

Routines with an Ellipsis

An ellipsis indicates that the routine can have a variable number of unspecified arguments, which is very similar to a routine that doesn't have a prototype.

If a routine prototype has an ellipsis, then it is treated as if the prototype didn't exist, and the arguments are passed in both the GPRs and FPRs.

Passing Complex Arguments

Complex arguments like structures are passed using the registers just as if the elements of the structure were passed to the routine individually. The only exception to this rule is that arguments that do not require the entire register word (like *chars* and *shorts*) are *left* justified in the register instead of right justified. The reason for this difference is to match the way the structure is stored in memory.

The example routine in Table 13-12 assumes the definition of the structure:

```
typedef struct {
    int a;
    short b;
    double c;
} data;
```

Table 13-12   Arguments for `void f5(data abc,double d,int e)`

Arg	data			4	5
	1	2	3		
Type	*int*	*short*	*double*	*double*	*int*
Offset	(0)	(4)	(8)	(16)	(24)

GPR	3	4	(5,6)	(7,8)	9
FPR	-	-	1	2	-
		short in high-order halfword of register			

13.11 Retrieving Results from Routines

Like arguments that are passed to routines, the results returned to the calling routine are all register based.

Integer Results

Integer function results are returned in registers `r3` and `r4`. The rules governing the use of these registers are:

- int, long, and pointer values are returned in `r3`.
- Unsigned char and short values are returned in `r3`, where the value is right justified in the register and zero-extended.
- Signed char and short values are returned in `r3`, where the value is right justified in the register and sign-extended.
- Bit fields of 32 bits or less are returned right justified in `r3`.
- 64-bit fixed-point values are returned in `r3:r4`, where `r3` contains the high-order portion of the value and `r4` contains the low-order portion.

Floating-Point Results

Floating-point function results are returned in registers `fr1` through `fr4`, according to these rules:

- Single-precision (32-bit) values are returned in `fr1`.
- Double-precision (64-bit) values are returned in `fr1`.
- Long double-precision (128-bit) values are returned in `fr1:fr2`, where `fr1` contains the high-order 64 bits and `fr2` contains the low-order 64 bits.
- Single- or double-precision complex values are returned in `fr1:fr2`, where `fr1` contains the real single- or double-precision portion, and `fr2` contains the imaginary single- or double-precision portion.
- Long double-precision complex values are returned in `fr1:fr4`, where `fr1:fr2` contain the high- and low-order bits of the real portion, and `fr3:fr4` contain the high- and low-order bits of the imaginary portion.

Complex Results

When complex data types like structures or strings (of greater than four characters) need to be returned as a function result, the caller must first allocate a buffer large enough to hold the result. A pointer to this buffer is passed to the routine as its first argument and occupies GPR 3 (and the first four bytes of the Argument Area).

The first user-visible argument to the routine is passed in GPR 4.

13.12 Stack Frames and `alloca()`

The C library routine `alloca()` causes a small problem with the requirement that the stack pointer always be a valid stack frame. Since `alloca()` is defined to allocate storage space dynamically on the stack, it must update the stack pointer. The trick is to make sure that it allocates the needed storage while keeping the current stack frame intact.

This is done by maintaining two pointers into the stack: the stack pointer and a *local storage area* pointer for this routine. The stack pointer is always `r1` and the *local storage area* pointer can be any register chosen by the routine. By using these two pointers, the *link area* and the *argument area* can be copied to the top of the newly expanded stack frame and the new storage space is taken from the area between the *argument area* and the *local storage area*. As Figure 13-11 shows, this results in the new storage area partially overlapping the area on the stack that used to contain the *link area* and *argument area*.

The *local storage area* pointer can be any available GPR and must be initialized and maintained by the routine.

Routines that do *not* use `alloca()` do not need to use a separate pointer for local storage because the top of the local storage area is trivially calculated from the stack pointer and guaranteed not to change.

In their epilog code, routines that use `alloca()` must restore the previous stack frame using the value stored at offset 0 from the current stack frame. This must be done because there is no easy way to calculate the current size of the stack frame because the values passed to `alloca()` are presumably runtime dependent.

Figure 13-11   Stack Frame before and after Call to `alloca()`

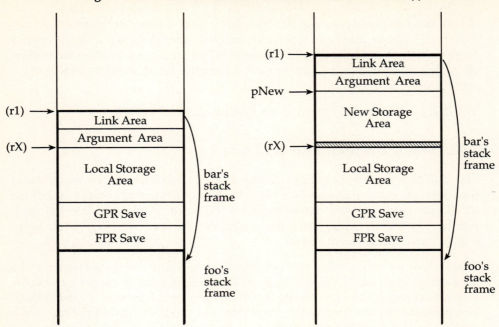

13.13 Linking with Global Routines

Subroutine calls are complicated when the routine being called is not located in the same module as the routine making the subroutine call. Routines located in different modules are likely to have different TOC environments, and each routine needs to have the proper environment to function properly.

Consider the arrangement of routines shown in Figure 13-12.

Two modules are defined, each with a different TOC environment. As far as the routine `foo()` is concerned, the routine `bar()` is a local routine because it is located in `foo()`'s local module. A call to `bar()` from `foo()` can be accomplished by simply using the *Branch with Link* instruction to the address of `bar()`. This is acceptable because both share the same TOC environment.

Figure 13-12   Two Sample Modules with Different TOC Environments

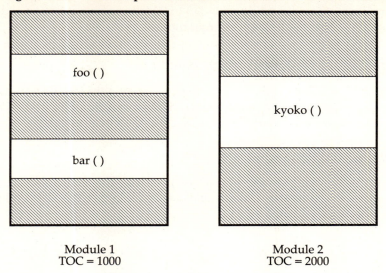

Module 1
TOC = 1000

Module 2
TOC = 2000

The kyoko() routine is located in a module that is foreign to foo()'s module, so kyoko() has a different TOC environment. If foo() were to simply *Branch with Link* to the address of kyoko(), kyoko() would inherit the wrong TOC environment, which would probably cause bad things to happen.

To prevent them from happening, there must be some mechanism for switching TOC environments whenever an "out-of-module" routine is called.

Function Descriptors

One way of handling the necessary TOC context switch is to use a structure called a *function descriptor* (sometimes called a *transition vector*) instead of just a simple pointer. A function descriptor is a pointer to the structure described in Table 13-13.

Table 13-13   Structure of a Function Descriptor

Offset	Description
0	routine address
4	TOC
8	environment pointer

The first word of this structure contains the address of the routine, and the second word contains the TOC pointer. Following words can contain data such as an environment pointer, but anything beyond the TOC pointer is optional and depends on the development environment originally used to create the routine. In many cases, these following words are zero or are not present.

Using this structure, an external routine can be called by passing the function descriptor to a special routine provided to take the information in the descriptor and properly pass control to the target routine.

Pointer Global Linkage (.ptrgl) Routines

A *pointer global linkage* (`.ptrgl`) routine is a small glue routine whose purpose is to pass control to a routine defined by a given function descriptor. Part of the routine's operation is to handle the TOC context switch properly.

Using the .ptrgl Routine

The method of using a `.ptrgl` routine is exactly the same as using a normal routine call, except that the *Branch with Link* to the target routine is replaced with these actions:

- Load the function descriptor into `r11`.
- *Branch with Link* to the `.ptrgl` routine.
- Restore the current routine's TOC (if necessary).

Some development environments use `r12` instead of `r11`, but the general idea is still the same.

Loading the address of the function descriptor and the branch are both straightforward, but the TOC restoration might seem a bit tricky because the current TOC doesn't seem to have been saved anywhere. The part that is not apparent from the bulleted list is that part of the `.ptrgl` routine's responsibility is to save the TOC in the Link Area of the stack frame before setting up the target routine's TOC environment. This allows the TOC to be restored using a simple load instruction:

```
lwz     rTOC,20(r1)
```

The "20" value is the magic offset from the top of the stack frame to the TOC storage area in the Link Area. This is where the `.ptrgl` routine will save the current TOC.

If it is known that the source and target routines both share the same TOC environment, then the `lwz` instruction is not necessary. In this case, a standard no-op instruction will be added in place of the load. This no-op is commonly encoded as a `ori  r0,r0,0`, but some older development environments used `cror 31,31,31` or `cror 15,15,15`.

This no-op reflects the fact that the compiler is generally unable to tell if the target routine will be in the same module as the source (the calling) routine. The compiler cannot figure this out because module assignments are not made until the object code is linked by the linker. When the compiler encounters a subroutine call to a routine that is not defined in the same source file, it must assume that the linker could place the routine in another module. To support this potential out-of-module call, a no-op placeholder instruction is placed after the subroutine call. This gives the linker a place to write the required load instruction. If the two routines are in the same module, the linker doesn't add the load instruction and the no-op instruction remains.

Of course, if the compiler has enough information available to determine if the called routine is in the same TOC environment, then the placeholder no-op instruction is unnecessary and is not generated.

How the .ptrgl Routine Works

The actions performed by the .ptrgl routine are best described by examining the code:

```
lwz     r0,0(r11)    # r0 <= routine address
stw     rTOC,20(r1)  # save current TOC
mtctr   r0           # ctr <= routine address
lwz     rTOC,4(r11)  # setup proper TOC
lwz     r11,8(r11)   # setup proper env ptr
bctr                 # call routine
```

Because this is a short routine, each of its instructions will be examined in turn.

The lwz r0,0(r11) instruction gets the address of the target routine from the function descriptor and stores it in r0. This value will later be stored in the CTR so that the bctr instruction can be used to jump to the routine.

The stw rTOC,20(r1) instruction saves the current TOC in the Link Area of the current routine's stack frame. The value stored here will be restored by the lwz instruction, which follows the branch to the .ptrgl routine.

The mtctr r0 instruction takes the target routine address and places it in the CTR register so that it can be jumped to easily.

The lwz rTOC,4(r11) instruction gets the target routine's TOC pointer and stores it in the TOC register.

The optional lwz r11,8(r11) instruction sets up the target routine's environment pointer. Because the environment pointer isn't used by all development systems, this instruction may not be necessary.

The bctr instruction actually (finally) calls the target routine.

Note that the code does not touch the LR. The calling routine calls the .ptrgl glue using a *Branch with Link* instruction that sets the LR to hold the address (in the original routine) where control should return. Since the LR hasn't been modified, the target routine can return control using the standard `blr` instruction.

Global Linkage (.glink) Routines

Global Linkage (`.glink`) routines are similar to `.ptrgl` routines except in usage. A `.glink` routine is created for every external routine that a module imports, so there would be a separate `.glink` routine for every system or library routine that a program calls.

The main difference between a `.glink` routine and the `.ptrgl` routine is where the function descriptor originates. The `.ptrgl` routine is a general routine that is passed a function descriptor; the `.glink` routines are specific to a particular target routine.

This does not mean that the function descriptors for `.glink` routines are encoded in the `.glink` routine itself. A separate function descriptor is still stored in the TOC area for the module. Each `.glink` routine encodes only the offset from the TOC to the function descriptor. This method gives both the linker and the `.glink` routine easy access to the descriptor.

Using the .glink Routines

Other than this difference in the source of the function descriptor, `.glink` routines are used like `.ptrgl` routines, except the function descriptor (obviously) needn't be passed in `r11`. All `.glink` routines are called using a *Branch with Link* instruction, and they are always followed by a `lwz` or no-op instruction.

How the .glink Routines Work

The code for the standard `.glink` routine is:

```
lwz     r12,offset(rTOC)  # r12 <= f() desc
stw     rTOC,20(r1) # save current TOC
lwz     r0,0(r12)   # r0 <= routine address
lwz     rTOC,4(r12) # set up routine's TOC
mtctr   r0          # ctr <= routine address
bctr                # call routine
```

As with the `.ptrgl` code, it is useful to describe the routine instruction by instruction.

The first instruction, `lwz r12,offset(rTOC)`, gets a pointer to the target routine's function descriptor and places it in `r12`. The offset to the function descriptor from the module's TOC is hard-coded into this instruction.

The `stw rTOC,20(r1)` instruction saves the current TOC in the Link Area of the current routine's stack frame.

The next two instructions, `lwz r0,0(r12)` and `lwz rTOC,4(r12)`, get the target routine's address and TOC pointer and load them into `r0` and `rTOC`, respectively.

The last two instructions put the target routine's address into the CTR register and then call the routine.

Function Pointers in High-Level Languages

In high-level languages, function pointers are always implemented as function descriptors. However, these descriptors are never directly visible to the programmer—the compiler handles all necessary descriptor magic so the programmer only deals with (apparent) function pointers.

Function descriptors are necessary because there is no way for the compiler to know what the program plans to do with the "function pointer." If it is going to be used as a callback function for a system routine, then the routine must be passed along with its TOC environment as a function descriptor.

Because the compiler can't know if a descriptor is needed, it plays it safe and always creates one.

Introduction to Optimizing | 14

Until this point, the chapters in this book have been concerned with describing how the instructions work at a functional level so that conceptually correct fragments of code can be written. Starting with this chapter, the book switches gears and concentrates on taking these working code fragments and modifying them so that they execute more efficiently.

Note that these optimization techniques are very important for programs written in assembly language. In general, RISC processors require that the programmer (or compiler) have a large store of knowledge about the processor. It requires a lot of effort to produce an assembly language routine that is more efficient than one produced by a properly written compiler. If you are not willing to apply these techniques, then you are most likely better off using a high-level language and letting the compiler handle all these issues.

14.1 When to Optimize

Optimizing is a trade-off between code that executes quickly and code that is easy to write and maintain. This is true from both the high-level language and the assembly language points of view, although the problem is more acute for the assembly language programmer.

Because it's more time-consuming to write and maintain optimized code, it's important to invest the effort spent optimizing code wisely. Many times this comes down to simply applying common sense, for example, recognizing that certain routines are less likely to benefit from optimization.

Thus, the key to optimizing effectively has less to do with scheduling instructions and more to do with identifying what needs to be optimized and understanding how to rewrite the code. Any person (or compiler) can learn to schedule instructions optimally, but identifying the code that should be optimized requires skill and intelligence.

This, coupled with the fact that the human programmer actually understands the program that is being written at a conceptual level, is why properly optimized hand-assembled code is almost guaranteed to be superior to properly optimized compiled code.

Pre-Optimization Steps

Four basic steps to writing optimized code should be taken *before* any low-level optimizations should even be considered:

- Make sure that the program is written correctly.
- Profile the code to identify which routines will benefit most from optimizing.
- Optimize the high-level algorithm and data structures.
- Apply standard high-level optimizations.

Only after all of these steps have been taken (and perhaps applied iteratively) should assembly-level optimizations be considered. Many times, these steps are all that is necessary.

Profiling Code

One of the first steps involves using a *profiler*. Although profiler features vary widely, it is worthwhile to take time to discuss them briefly.

A profiler is a utility program that "watches" the execution of another program (the *target application*) and produces a summary of how much time each of the target application's routines takes. Depending on the profiler, the target application may need to be recompiled, or it may be able to get all the required information from the debugging symbols.

The information returned by the profiler can be quite useful because it gives a reasonably good summary of where a program is spending most of its time. For example, a profiler may return some summary information like this:

```
%Time   Name
47.2%   foo
28.7%   bar
14.1%   sna
```

```
8.1%    init
1.9%    main
```

This information indicates that almost half of the execution time was spent in the `foo()` routine, which means that `foo()` is a potential candidate for optimization.

Of course, this is just the first step. After the routines that require the most CPU time have been identified, they need to be evaluated to see if optimization is worthwhile. In some cases, the routine may not be easily optimizable. In other cases, the routine may not be the proper place to expend effort.

As an example of the latter situation, consider the time percentage distribution where the `sna()` routine is basically a loop that calls the `foo()` routine repeatedly. This could quite easily lead to the situation where `foo()` takes 47.2% of the CPU time and `sna()` takes only 14.1%. In this case, it is possible that a small change in `sna()` could reduce the number of times that it calls `foo()`. This optimization could possibly affect program execution speed more greatly than any optimizations applied to `foo()`.

Most profilers provide more information than the example gives. Some profilers record the number of times that each routine was called, and others record the entire call-chain to determine how much time a particular routine spent in execution when called by each routine. Profiler feature sets vary widely, so it is best to familiarize yourself with whatever profiler you have and learn to use the information that it provides.

14.2 Examining Compiled Code

In a chapter devoted to writing optimized code, it may at first seem strange to have a section on reading compiled code. There are two really good reasons that directly relate to optimizing, and a third reason that doesn't directly apply to writing optimized code, but is a good reason nonetheless.

First, only by reviewing the compiler output will a programmer get an idea of how intelligent the compiler is with respect to optimization. Only when you know the capabilities (and limitations) of the compiler can you take advantage of them (or work around them).

The second reason for looking at compiler-generated output is to learn how the compiler optimizes so you can apply similar techniques when hand-coding in assembly. At first glance, this reason may seem a bit silly: if the compiler is better at optimizing than a particular programmer, it makes sense for that programmer to simply use the compiler and not bother with assembly language. This is somewhat true, but the programmer is bringing to this picture a high level knowledge of what is being accomplished (something the compiler isn't likely to have). Many times, this gives the programmer a significant advantage over the compiler.

The final reason for wanting to be able to read compiler-generated output is that it is sometimes necessary to debug at that level. Most debugging is, of course, done at the source-code level, but at times the source is not available or subtle interactions between the system and the program cause the source-level debugger to be inadequate.

Disassemblers

One of the most important tools used when decompiling is the disassembler. When choosing a disassembler, it is important that you find one that disassembles the instructions into their most readable forms.

Surprisingly, a number of disassemblers disassemble instructions improperly. "Improperly," does not mean that instructions are disassembled incorrectly; they are just not disassembled as well as they could be.

Consider these instruction disassemblies:

```
bc      12,10,addr
rlwinm  0,0,4,0,27
mfspr   0,8
```

While these disassemblies are technically correct, compare them to the following disassemblies of the same instructions:

```
beq     crf2,addr
slwi    r0,r0,4
mflr    r0
```

Using a disassembler that disassembles properly makes the code easier to follow and understand. It also reduces the likelihood that the instruction will be misinterpreted because you won't have to remember details like "the 10 means bit 2 (the EQ bit) of CR field 2," and "the 12 means the branch occurs if the bit is set." You see the instruction as `beq crf2`, and you know right away what operation it's performing.

This is especially important for the complex *Rotate and Insert with Mask* instructions that the PowerPC provides. In the example, it's not readily apparent that the `rlwinm 0,0,4,0,27` instruction is performing a left shift of four bits, whereas the `slwi r0,r0,4` instruction is less opaque.

Difficulties with Reading Compiled Code

The biggest problem with reading compiled (or even hand-assembled) code is that it quickly becomes confusing. Sequences of instructions that are part of the same conceptual "operation" are spread out and intertwined as part of the instruction scheduling optimization.

Take, for example, this simple sequence of instructions:

```
# ptr(r2) contains a pointer to a word
# load that word into r6
lwz     r5,ptr(r2)  # get the ptr
lwz     r6,0(r5)    # get the data

# get the return address and exit
lwz     r0,8(r1)    # get rtn addr
mtlr    r0          # move it into LR
blr                 # exit
```

This would typically be written as:

```
lwz     r0,8(r1)
lwz     r5,ptr(r2)
mtlr    r0
lwz     r6,0(r5)
blr
```

Even with comments added, the rewritten code would be harder to follow. The real problem is that it's hard to add comments to the rewritten code because the instructions performing the two different operations are intertwined. Of course, the example is simplified. Most real-world examples are much worse.

Good Things about Compiled Code

On the other hand, compilers have a wonderful tendency to use standard templates for most operations. Functions are almost guaranteed to begin and end with the standard routine prolog and epilog code. A sequence of code like this:

```
mflr    r0
stmw    r22,-40(r1)
stw     r0,0x8(r1)
stwu    r1,-120(r1)
```

only occurs at the beginning of a routine, because it is saving registers and creating a new stack frame.

A large number of these code templates are used by compilers. When you know and recognize these standard templates, reading compiled code becomes much easier.

Conclusions

Overall, compiler-generated code is sort of a mixed blessing. On one hand, the code can be somewhat confusing because compilers can be quite good at instruction scheduling, but there are also a lot of commonly used templates that can also be used as landmarks for identifying code.

Half the battle of reading compiled code is knowing the basics—what the individual instructions do and how the GPR and FPR usage conventions are applied. The previous chapters in this book have attempted to address this need.

The rest of the skills required come from examining real-world code samples and knowing how the code is typically optimized, both at the high level and at the assembly level. The remainder of this book tries to form a good foundation upon which these skills can be built.

14.3 Standard Optimizations

Before covering the specific optimizations for the PowerPC processor, it is probably worthwhile to quickly review some standard optimization techniques commonly used to improve code performance. This section does not attempt to cover all compiler optimization techniques. Such a task is beyond its scope.

Instruction Strength Reduction

This technique involves replacing "strong" (more complex) instructions with "weak" (simpler) instructions. The criterion by which an instruction is judged either strong or weak can be a measure of its execution speed or its object code size.

A commonly used strength reduction is substituting algebraic shift instructions for multiply and divide operations. This optimization can only be applied when the value is being multiplied (or divided) by a power of 2, but the savings in execution time can be substantial.

Common Subexpression Elimination (CSE)

A common subexpression is an expression or portion of an expression that occurs more than once in one or more statements. In the examples:

```
c = (a+b) + (b/(a+b));
```

and

```
q = (a+b) * (3*2);
r = (c+3) + (a+b);
```

the subexpression (a+b) is common because it occurs more than once.

A subexpression can be common across statements or across compiler blocks. When elimination is being performed across compiler blocks, the technique is termed "Global Common Subexpression Elimination." Note that this use of the term "global" refers to CSE across basic compiler blocks and not across function boundaries.

Implementing global CSE can be tricky because sometimes the compiler must insert extra copy statements to apply the CSE. This is shown below, where the e=a+b statement cannot be simply replaced with either e=c or e=d.

```
if(x)
      c = a + b;
else
      d = a + b;
e = a + b;
```

The code must first be transformed so that the final assignment statement can be replaced with e=t:

```
t = a + b;
if(x)
      c = t;
else
      d = t;
e = t;
```

Code Motion of Loop Invariants

Loop invariants are computations whose values do not change within the body of a loop. These computations can be moved outside (preferably before) the loop, thus reducing the time that must be spent within the loop. This optimization (along with the elimination of a common subexpression) can be used to change:

```
while(i>(x-1))
      a[i++] = y+(x-1);
```

to:

```
t1 = x-1;
t2 = y+t1;
while(i>t1)
    a[i++] = t2;
```

These optimizations reduce the number of arithmetic operations (not including the expression to increment i) from 3×(x-1-$i1$) down to only 2, where $i1$ is the value of i when the loop is entered.

Function Inlining

Small functions are many times ideal candidates to be compiled "inline." A function compiled inline is simply expanded and placed at the point of the function call. Inline functions take more space than the function calls because the code must be repeated at each point where the function is "called." However, because the function calling overhead is eliminated, the typical result is faster code.

Loop Unrolling

Loop unrolling is the process of reducing the number of loop iterations by repeating the loop code multiple times. This speed optimization increases code size. By reducing the number of loop iterations, the code reduces the impact of the overhead associated with the branch back to the head of the loop. This optimization is especially useful for pipelined processors, because each branch reduces the effectiveness of the pipeline.

This loop:

```
for(i=0;i<100;)
    a[i++] = 0;
```

can be unrolled once to produce:

```
for(i=0;i<50;) {
    a[i++] = 0;
    a[i++] = 0;
}
```

or twice to produce:

```
for(i=0;i<25;) {
    a[i++] = 0;
    a[i++] = 0;
    a[i++] = 0;
    a[i++] = 0;
}
```

or it could even be completely unrolled. The speed of the loop tends (although it is not guaranteed) to increase as the loop is unrolled further.

One potential problem with loop unrolling is that the overall performance can *decrease* if the loop is unrolled so far that cache misses on the instruction fetches offset performance gains. Take care when unrolling a loop more than once or twice.

Resource Scheduling | **15**

Every CPU has a limited number of processor resources that programs can use. When optimizing code, it is important to maximize the use of all of resources while minimizing conflicts that may arise from multiple parts of the processor trying to use the same resource at the same time.

To simplify matters, most modern processors seek to minimize the number of special resources in the CPU. This is why recent processors tend to have a large store of general purpose registers instead of special purpose registers, like looping and branching registers.

In spite of this trend, the PowerPC has a variety of special purpose registers, namely, the LR, CTR, and CR. However, certain POWER SPRs (like the MQ register) are *not* part of the PowerPC specification because they can become resource bottlenecks.

The LR, CTR, and CR were included because they permit certain types of hardware optimizations to be implemented. However, care must be taken when using these registers or they may lead to resource conflicts that can adversely affect performance.

15.1 Types of Processor Resources

Three types of processor resources can lead to conflicts: the pipeline stages, the processor registers, and the memory subsystem. Each of these resource types will be discussed.

Pipeline Stages

The pipeline stages are the most obvious timing-related resources. For the most part, the processor has one copy of each pipeline stage and only one instruction can be in each stage at any time.

There are some exceptions to this "rule." Certain simple pipeline stages (like the writeback stages) allow multiple instructions to be in the stage simultaneously. Also, some future implementations of the PowerPC are likely to implement duplicate pipelines so that there would be multiple copies of the "same" pipeline stage.

Processor Registers

There is only one copy of each of the registers in the processor. This means multiple instructions that need to access the same register must have some mechanism for arbitrating and sharing the resource.

For the GPRs and FPRs, the programmer has some control over which specific register to use. Arranging instructions so that they use different registers (if possible) can help avoid conflicts.

With the SPRs, the programmer doesn't have much choice—there's only one of each. However, many techniques can be applied to avoid stalls due to these unique resources.

Memory Subsystem and Cache

The memory and cache conflicts are the most interesting to discuss because they require that the discussion be held at a level much higher than the assembly language level.

These conflicts arise because the processor uses caches to increase performance, and these caches are limited in size. Since a cache miss can stall the processor for many cycles, it is important to arrange the memory accesses to minimize the likelihood of a cache miss.

15.2 Pipeline Conflicts

The pipeline conflicts were discussed earlier at a simple level in Chapter 12, which covered instruction timings. That chapter only covered the basics of pipeline timings and showed the stages each instruction required.

This section will go into more detail, discussing each processor stage and outlining the specific conflicts that can arise in each stage.

Fetch Arbitration Unit (FAU) Stages

The FAU consists of only one "stage," the Fetch Arbitrate (FA) stage. However, the FA stage of the FAU differs from other pipeline stages because instructions do not really pass through the FAU. The job of the FAU is to generate the address of the next instruction group to be loaded from the cache into the Dispatch Unit. Instruction execution technically doesn't begin until the instructions are loaded into the IQ buffer in the DU.

Referring to an instruction as being in the "FA stage" is simply a convenient way of noting that the instruction in question is one that *will be* loaded into the Dispatch Unit after the cache is accessed.

The end result is that the FA stage can never cause a pipeline stall because it is not really a pipeline stage. If a stall occurs during the instruction fetch process, it occurs during the CARB stage of the CAU.

Cache Access Unit (CAU) Stages

Because the CAU provides the only interface between the execution units of the processor and the cache, there are plenty of opportunities for pipeline stalls to occur. Two major types of stalls are caused by different units of the processor trying to access memory simultaneously and by the requested block of memory not being present in the cache. These cases are handled by the CARB and CACC stages, respectively.

This section reviews the potential stalls that can occur in the CAU. A more thorough treatment of this topic is given in §12.6, "Cache Access Timings."

Cache Arbitration (CARB)

The CARB stage decides which cache request gets passed along to the CACC stage. Because of this, lower priority cache access will stall in CARB if another cache access of higher priority is in CARB. Cache accesses are prioritized as:

- Cache Maintenance Requests
- Data Load Requests
- Data Store Requests
- Instruction Fetch Requests

where *Cache Maintenance Requests* from the memory subsystem have the highest priority and the *Instruction Fetch Requests* have the lowest priority.

Cache Access (CACC)

After a cache access has been initiated, the access requires one cycle in CACC if the data is present in the cache. If the data is not present, then *at least* six cycles will be spent waiting for the cache to get the data from the main memory store. After the data is forwarded to the proper place, the CACC stage will be occupied for *at least* another two cycles while it completes the cache update operation.

To summarize, this means that at least six cycles are spent waiting for the data, and that the CACC stage cannot be used by another instruction until at least two more cycles have gone by. §12.6, "Cache Access Timings," provides more details about cache miss timings.

Dispatch Unit (DU) Stages

The Dispatch Unit consists of only an eight-entry Instruction Queue. The only stalls that can arise in this unit are due to stalls in the IU, FPU, or BPU that prevent an instruction from being dispatched.

Integer Unit (IU) Stages

Almost all integer instructions require one cycle in each of the primary IU stages, some of which can be overlapped. Exceptions to this are well defined and are presented below.

The IWL stage is the only IU stage that is not considered a "primary stage." This stage is used only by the integer load instructions.

Integer Decode (ID)

Only two situations cause an instruction to stall in the ID stage. The first condition is when the instruction needs to read the CR or XER and that resource is currently being updated by an instruction currently in IE. This causes the instruction to stall in ID until the previous instruction moves into IWA and updates the appropriate register.

The second situation is when a previous instruction occupies the IE stage of the IU pipeline for more than one cycle. In this case, the instruction must wait in ID until the IE stage is available.

When an instruction stalls in ID, a new instruction can enter the IQ0 stage of the DU. However, when the ID stage is vacated, this instruction occupies the IQ0 *and* ID stages for one cycle instead of moving on to just the ID stage so that a new instruction can enter IQ0.

The following timing table shows this, where the `nand` instruction stalls in IQ0 until the `and` instruction can vacate the ID stage. After the ID stage is free (cycle 7), the `nand` instruction occupies both the IQ0 and ID stages for a cycle before continuing to the IE stage.

Cycle #:	1	2	3	4	5	6	7	8	9
mulli r9,r9,5	IQ0 ID	IE	IE	IE	IE	IE	IC IWA	-	-
and r0,r0,r1	IQ1	IQ0 ID	ID	ID	ID	ID	IE	IC IWA	-
nand r2,r2,r3	IQ2	IQ1	IQ0	IQ0	IQ0	IQ0	IQ0 ID	IE	IC IWA

Integer Execute (IE)

All instructions spend one cycle in IE except:

- Multiply instructions.
- Divide instructions.
- Load and store multiple (including string) instructions.
- *Move to/from SPR* instructions for certain SPRs.
- *System Call* and *Return from Interrupt* instructions.

The multiply instructions require five, nine, or ten cycles, depending on the data being multiplied. The divide operation always takes 36 cycles in IE. The load/store multiple and string operations require one cycle in IE for each register of data being transferred.

The SPR and *System Call* instructions listed above all require two cycles in IE. Note that not all *Move to/from SPR* instructions require two cycles—all the commonly used SPRs (CR, CTR, LR, and XER) require only one cycle in IE.

Another situation that causes an instruction in IE to stall is when a `stwcx.` instruction is in IWA. See the timing for the *Store Conditional Word* instruction in §12.3, "Fixed-Point Instruction Timings," for an explanation of this stalling condition.

Integer Completion (IC)

The IC stage is always executed in parallel with another stage, and it is used to notify the other stages that the instruction is *committed*, even though it may not yet be complete. Because this stage performs no calculations, it doesn't generate any stalls.

However, the IC stage can inherit a stall from the IWA stage. Almost all instructions spend one cycle in IWA and, thus, require only one cycle in IC. The *Trap*, *System Call*, and some *Move to/from SPR* instructions are exceptions because they require multiple cycles in IWA and IC.

Integer Arithmetic Writeback (IWA)

As in IC, most instructions require only one cycle in IWA. The exceptions to this are the same as noted for the IC stage: *Trap*, *System Call*, and some *Move to/from SPR* instructions.

Integer Load Writeback (IWL)

The IWL stage is the writeback stage for integer load instructions. All integer load instructions require one cycle in this stage. This stage is completely independent of the IWA stage (the writeback stage for non-load integer instructions). Both the IWL and IWA can writeback to the GPRs during the same cycle, provided that they both don't need to update the same GPR.

Floating-Point Unit (FPU) Stages

Timing for the FPU is more complex than for the IU because the FPU can handle both single- and double-precision operations.

The simple floating-point instructions require one cycle in each of the four primary FPU stages: FD, FPM, FPA, and FWA. Exceptions are noted in the next section.

FP Instruction Queue (F1)

The F1 stage is simply an instruction queueing stage used when the FD stage is full. Because this stage is just a queue that doesn't perform calculations, it doesn't generate stalls.

FP Decode (FD)

Instructions typically require one cycle in this stage, although an instruction will stall in this stage for any of these reasons:

- A multi-cycle floating-point operation is currently executing in the FPM stage.
- One of the source operands is a target of an outstanding load, or an operand of an instruction in the FPM, FPA, or FWA stages.
- One of the source operands requires prenormalization, or the FPU predicts that the result will be a denormalized number.

The first case is a simple pipeline stall, where the instruction spends time in both the FD and FPM stages. Instructions that require multiple cycles in FD are the same instructions that require multiple cycles in FPM, namely, the double-precision multiply (two cycles), single- and double-precision divide (17/31 cycles), and the *Move to FPSCR* (four cycles) instructions.

The second case, a register conflict, is discussed in the next section.

Instruction timings for situations when the operand/result requires prenormalization/denormalization are covered in §12.9, "Abnormal Floating-Point Conditions."

FP Multiply (FPM)

In general, most floating-point instructions require only one cycle in FPM. The double-precision multiply, single- and double-precision divide, and the *Move to FPSCR* instructions are the only exceptions.

The double-precision multiplies (and multiply-accumulates) require two cycles in FPM. The first FPM cycle is overlapped with the second FD cycle for these instructions.

The divide instructions require either 16 cycles (single-precision) or 30 cycles (double-precision). These cycles are completely overlapped with the last 16/30 cycles that the instructions spends in FD.

The *Move to FPSCR* family of instructions all require three cycles in FPM. These three cycles are required because the *Move to FPSCR* instructions can potentially change the floating-point execution model, so no new floating-point instructions should be dispatched until the FPSCR has been updated.

FP Add (FPA)

In general, most floating-point instructions require only one cycle in FPA. The double-precision multiply, single- and double-precision divide, and the *Move to FPSCR* instructions are the only exceptions.

The double-precision multiplies (and multiply-accumulates) require two cycles in FPA. The first FPA cycle is overlapped with the second FPM cycle for these instructions.

The single-precision divide instructions require 15 cycles (overlapped with the last 15 cycles in FPM). The double-precision divide instructions require 29 cycles (also overlapped with the last 29 cycles of FPM).

The *Move to FPSCR* family of instructions all require two cycles in FPM. These two cycles are required because the *Move to FPSCR* instructions can potentially change the floating-point execution model, so no new floating-point instructions should be dispatched until the FPSCR has been updated.

FP Arithmetic Writeback (FWA)

Because the FWA stage performs normalization in addition to writeback, stalls can occur if the result requires excessive normalization. The exact details of this are given in §12.9, "Abnormal Floating-Point Conditions."

FP Load Writeback (FWL)

The FWL stage is the writeback stage for floating-point load instructions. All of the floating-point load instructions require one cycle in this stage. This stage is completely independent of the FWA stage (the writeback stage for arithmetic floating-point instructions). Both the FWL and FWA can writeback to the FPRs during the same cycle, provided that they both don't need to update the same FPR.

Branch Processing Unit (BPU) Stages

Of the three BPU stages, only the MR stage requires that branches be scheduled around it.

Branch Execute (BE)

Only one branch instruction can be in BE at any time, but this is not a problem because the Dispatch Unit can only dispatch one branch per cycle and branches never need more than one cycle in BE.

Mispredict Recovery (MR)

The MR stage is where all conditional branches stay until they are resolved. There can only be one branch in MR at any time, so there can only be one outstanding conditional branch at any time.

The next code sample shows a basic MR stall. It is a simple two-instruction loop that *should* require two cycles per loop iteration. Note that the branch is a backward branch (to the beginning of the loop); it is predicted to be taken.

```
start:
        add     r0,r0,r1
        cmp     crf0,r0,r2
        beq     crf0,start
```

The timing for the first iteration of this loop is:

Cycle #:	1	2	3	4	5	6	7
add r0,r0,r1	FA CARB	CACC	IQ0 ID	IE	IC IWA	-	-
cmp crf0,r0,r2	FA CARB	CACC	IQ1	IQ0 ID	IE	IC IWA	-
pbr tag = cmp	-	-	-	ID	IE	-	-
beq crf0,start	FA CARB	CACC	IQ2 BE MR	MR	MR	-	-

and for the second iteration is:

Cycle #:	1	2	3	4	5	6	7
add r0,r0,r1	-	-	FA CARB	CACC	IQ0 ID	IE	IC IWA
cmp crf0,r0,r2	-	-	FA CARB	CACC	IQ1	IQ0 ID	IE
pbr tag = cmp	-	-	-	-	-	-	IE
beq crf0,start	-	-	FA CARB	CACC	IQ2	IQ1 BE MR	MR

During cycle 3, the first branch needs to be predicted because it needs the result from the `cmp` instruction, which hasn't finished execution yet. In this case, the branch is predicted to be taken, and the first `beq` instruction enters the MR stage. This branch causes the instructions for the second iteration of the loop to be fetched.

During cycle 5, the second iteration of the loop reaches the same point that the first iteration reached in cycle 3—the branch needs to be predicted because the results of the `cmp` aren't available yet. However, the first branch still occupies the MR stage of the pipeline, so this branch must stay in the DU.

Also during cycle 5, the results of the first compare are forwarded to the first branch instruction. In this example, the prediction is confirmed, and the first branch leaves the MR stage.

In cycle 6, because the MR stage is now free, the second branch can be executed and predicted. The instructions for the third iteration (not shown) are fetched at this time.

The result is that every odd-numbered loop (including the first) requires two cycles, and every even-numbered loop requires three cycles. The "three-cycle" value comes from the two cycles spent executing the loop plus an extra cycle spent waiting for the next set of instructions. This wasted cycle is present because the branch was executed (and thus, the instructions were fetched) a cycle late.

Branch Writeback (BW)

The BW stage doesn't typically lead to pipeline stalls because up to nine branch instructions can be in BW simultaneously. However, only two branch instructions are allowed to writeback during each cycle—one can update the LR, and another can update the CTR.

Data Access Queueing Unit (DAQU) Stages

The stages of the DAQU are queueing stages for store instructions rather than execution stages. As such, they do not cause stalls themselves, but they may cause a stall in IE if the CAU doesn't grant access to the cache or if the floating-point unit doesn't provide the store data in a reasonable time.

A common example is when floating-point data is being stored to a location that crosses a doubleword boundary. This effectively results in two back-to-back store operations that both need to use the FPSB. Because the FPSB is only one element deep, the second half of the store operation stalls the IU in IE until the first half can be written. This results in at least four additional cycles spent in IE for the store instruction because the data must come from the FWA stage of the FPU pipeline.

15.3 Register Usage Dependencies

Register usage dependencies can very easily turn into register usage conflicts because the pipelined architecture allows multiple instructions to be executing simultaneously.

Types of Dependencies

Four different situations can occur when two sequential instructions need to access the same register resource.

Read after Read (RAR)

A RAR dependency does not cause problems because neither of the two instructions needs to change the value of the register. Both reads will read the same (correct) value.

Read after Write (RAW)

With a RAW dependency, care must be taken so that the write operation completes (or appears to complete) before the read operation takes place. If the read operation occurs too early, it will read the register value *before* the write occurs, which is obviously incorrect.

This, the most common type of data dependency, is sometimes referred to as *true data dependency*.

Write after Read (WAR)

While rare, a WAR dependency can lead to a conflict when store operations are allowed to occur before all previous read operations are handled. In this case, the read may get the new value instead of the old value. The 601 doesn't have this type of conflict because all instructions write back in program order.

WAR dependencies are sometimes referred to as *anti-dependencies*.

Write after Write (WAW)

Also rare, a WAW dependency can cause problems if the stores are allowed to complete out of order. The 601 doesn't have this type of conflict because all stores are performed in order (as far as the processor is concerned).

WAW dependencies are sometimes referred to as *output dependencies*.

Handling Conflicts Due to Dependencies

The processor can choose to handle the conflicts that arise from data dependencies in many ways. For each dependency, it is important to know what the processor will do, because this will affect execution time.

Ignore the Conflict

The easiest thing for the processor to do is to ignore the conflict and expect the programmer to arrange the instructions so that conflicts do not occur. In many cases, explicit no-op instructions must be added to pad the pipeline.

Stall the Pipeline

Another easy way of handling data conflicts is to stall the pipeline whenever conflicts are detected. This has an advantage: code will work as expected even if no-ops are not inserted.

Feed-forward the Required Data

Feed-forwarding is useful for some RAW conflicts because the data being calculated can be passed back to other instructions in the pipeline before the results are officially available in the register.

Feed-forwarding is generally used only between instructions executing in the same processor unit, for example, between two integer instructions or between two floating-point instructions.

Shadow the Register

Register shadowing is a simple case of providing a small pool of registers that can be used whenever a register needs to be updated. If an instruction needs to update the register, and it's possibile that another instruction may need to read the register value, the instruction writes the value into a shadow register until it is safe to update the real register.

Shadowing is typically limited to a few shadow registers all associated with one real register.

Remap the Register

A more general case of shadowing, register remapping has a large pool of registers (called physical registers) shared by a number of user-visible registers (called architected registers). Remapping is typically used on general purpose registers, like the GPRs and FPRs in the PowerPC.

This can be quite useful for processors that have WAR and WAW conflicts. For WAR conflicts, the architected register in conflict can be mapped into two separate physical registers: one before the write and one after. For WAW conflicts, the architected register can be mapped into three physical registers: one before the first write, one between the two writes, and one after the second write. When the architected register no longer needs to be mapped into multiple physical registers, the older physical registers are recycled to restore a 1:1 correspondence between architected and physical registers.

Link Register (LR)

The LR, a special register, holds an address that can be used as a target branch address. Other than the *Move to/from LR* instructions, only the branch instructions affect the LR.

Having the BPU entirely in control of the LR allows the BPU to implement some optimizations for the LR which prevents BPU stalls. This optimization is implemented using two LR *shadow registers* that hold temporary LR values. Using these shadow registers is discussed in the next sections.

LR-Branch / LR-Branch Dependencies

If a branch instruction uses the LR following a branch that updates the LR, there is potential for a RAW conflict. The BPU avoids stalls by having the first branch write the new LR value into one of the LR shadow registers until the value can be written to the real LR. The second branch can now read the new LR value from the shadow LR and continue execution without stalling.

The timing diagram shows an example of this. Note that the order of execution is and, nand, bl, followed by nor, xor, blr, and then execution returns to the or instruction.

Cycle #:	1	2	3	4	5	6	7
and r0,r0,r1	IQ0 ID	IE	IC IWA	-	-	-	-
nand r2,r2,r3	IQ1	IQ0 ID	IE	IC IWA	-	-	-
LR tag	-	IQ0 ID	IE	IC	-	-	-
bl target	IQ2 BE	BW	BW	BW	-	-	-
or r4,r4,r5	IQ3	-	FA CARB	CACC	IQ0 ID	IE	IC IWA
...	-	-	-	-	-	-	-
nor r6,r6,r7	FA CARB	CACC	IQ0 ID	IE	IC IWA	-	-
xor r8,r8,r9	FA CARB	CACC	IQ1	IQ0 ID	IE	IC IWA	-
blr	FA CARB	CACC	IQ2/BE	-	-	-	-

The blr instruction reads the new value of LR from the appropriate shadow LR during cycle 3. The LR is updated during cycle 4. In this case, the processor completes and, nand, nor, xor, and then or in five subsequent cycles—both of the branches have been removed from the instruction stream without causing any stalls.

Note that, in this example, two instructions were needed between the two branch instructions so that there would be no stalls while the new instructions (starting at or) were fetched from memory. This "two-instruction" value is not a magic number that is always needed between 2 LR-dependent branches—the number of instructions required depends on the surrounding instructions. However, it is a good rule of thumb to place at least two independent instructions between branches of this sort.

mtlr / LR-Branch Dependencies

When the write operation of a RAW dependency comes from the mtlr instruction, the processor must stall the branch in dispatch until the mtlr reaches the integer readback stage (IWA). This is necessary because the mtlr instruction is handled by the IU instead of the BPU, so the data can't simply be forwarded to the branch.

Two situations need to be examined here: the case where the branch is taken, and the case where the branch is not-taken. Note that branch prediction doesn't come into play here because the branch stalls in the IQ because of the dependency on the LR.

The code sample that will be examined is:

```
        mtlr    r0
        beqlr   crf0
        and     r0,r0,r1
        ...
target:
        or      r2,r2,r3
```

where `r0` initially contains the address of `target`. The timing for this code snippet when the branch is not-taken is:

Cycle #:	1	2	3	4	5	6	7	8
mtlr r0	FA CARB	CACC	IQ0 ID	IE	IC IWA	-	-	-
beqlr crf0	FA CARB	CACC	IQ1	IQ0	IQ0 BE	-	-	-
and r0,r0,r1	FA CARB	CACC	IQ2	IQ1	IQ1	IQ0 ID	IE	IC IWA
...	-	-	-	-	-	-	-	-
or r2,r2,r3	-	-	-	-	-	-	-	-

The branch instruction stalls in IQ until the `mtlr` instruction reaches IWA in cycle 5. During this same cycle, the branch is executed, freeing up the IQ and allowing the subsequent instructions to be executed. Two wasted cycles in ID between the `mtlr` and the branch instruction could have been filled with independent integer instructions.

If the branch is taken or if `blr` is used instead of a conditional branch, the timing is:

Cycle #:	1	2	3	4	5	6	7	8
mtlr r0	FA CARB	CACC	IQ0 ID	IE	IC IWA	-	-	-
beqlr crf0	FA CARB	CACC	IQ1	IQ0	IQ0 BE	-	-	-
and r0,r0,r1	FA CARB	CACC	IQ2	IQ1	IQ1	-	-	-
...	-	-	-	-	-	-	-	-
or r2,r2,r3	-	-	-	-	FA CARB	CACC	IQ0 ID	IE

As with the branch not-taken example, the branch stalls until cycle 5. At this time, the branch is executed and the target instructions are fetched. In this case, three wasted cycles in ID could have been used if there were independent integer instructions between the `mtlr` and branch instructions.

It's important to be aware of this dependency because most function calls end with a `mtlr-blr` instruction pair.

Link Shadow Overflow

The 601 only provides two Link shadow registers, used to hold the temporary LR values until they can be written back to the "real" LR. Because there are only two shadow registers, pipeline stalls can occur when all of the shadow registers are currently being used.

One situation that can lead to stalls is when a series of conditional *Branch with Link* instructions are not-taken, like this example:

```
and     r0,r0,r1
beql    crf0,target1
beql    crf1,target2
beql    crf2,target3
```

The code timing diagram assumes that the CR is coherent so the branches do not need to be predicted:

Cycle #:	1	2	3	4	5	6	7	8
and r0,r0,r1	FA CARB	CACC	IQ0 ID	IE	IC IWA	-	-	-
LR tag = and	-	-	-	IE	IC	-	-	-
beql crf0,target1	FA CARB	CACC	IQ1 BE	BW	BW	-	-	-
LR tag = bubble1	-	-	-	-	IE	IC	-	-
beql crf1,target1	FA CARB	CACC	IQ2	IQ0 BE	BW	BW	-	-
LR tag = bubble2	-	-	-	-	-	-	IE	IC
beql crf2,target1	FA CARB	CACC	IQ3	IQ1	IQ0	IQ0 BE	BW	BW

In this example, the first shadow LR is used when the first branch enters BE during cycle 3, and the second shadow LR is used when the second branch enters BW on the following cycle. When the third branch tries to enter BE during cycle 5, it cannot because a shadow LR isn't available for it to use. However, it can be dispatched during the next cycle because the first branch completes its writeback and frees up one of the shadow LRs.

Another situation can lead to this—when a long-latency integer instruction (like multiply or divide) precedes a *Branch with Link* (`bl`) instruction. Because the branch stays in BW (occupying a shadow LR) until this instruction is complete, it only takes one more `bl` instruction to use all the shadow registers. A third `bl` instruction stalls in the Dispatch Unit until a shadow LR is freed by the first branch.

The following (contrived) example demonstrates this:

```
        mulli   r9,r9,5
        bl      target1
        ...
target1:
```

```
        and     r0,r0,r1
        bl      target2
    ...
    target2:
        nand    r2,r2,r3
        bl      target3
```

which has the timing:

Cycle #:	1	2	3	4	5	6	7	8	9	10
mulli r9,r9,5	FA CARB	CACC	IQ0 ID	IE	IE	IE	IE	IE	IC IWA	-
LR tag = mulli	-	-	-	IE	IE	IE	IE	IE	IC	-
bl target1	FA CARB	CACC	IQ1 BE	BW	BW	BW	BW	BW	BW	-
...	-	-	-	-	-	-	-	-	-	-
and r0,r0,r1	-	-	FA CARB	CACC	IQ0 ID	ID	ID	ID	IE	IC IWA
LR tag = and	-	-	-	-	-	ID	ID	ID	IE	IC
bl target2	-	-	FA CARB	CACC	IQ1 BE	BW	BW	BW	BW	BW
...	-	-	-	-	-	-	-	-	-	-
nand r2,r2,r3	-	-	-	-	FA CARB	CACC	IQ0	IQ0	IQ0 ID	IE
LR tag	-	-	-	-	-	-	-	-	-	-
bl target3	-	-	-	-	FA CARB	CACC	IQ1	IQ1	IQ1	IQ0 BE

Here, the first branch takes the first shadow LR during cycle 3 when it enters BE, but it can't writeback (and free the shadow LR) until the multiply instruction enters IC during cycle 9. The second branch instruction takes the second shadow LR, but it is forced to wait for the and instruction, which stalled because of the multiply instruction. This results in the second shadow LR being occupied until cycle 10.

When the third branch comes along, it must wait in IQ until cycle 10 because a shadow LR isn't available for the branch to use. During cycle 10, the branch can use the shadow LR that was freed by the first branch during cycle 9.

In general, this is not a common resource conflict, although care should be taken when a branch follows a multiply or divide instruction.

Counter Register (CTR)

The CTR was originally simply a register in the BPU used to hold the counter for loops. It became a branching register (similar to the LR) when some glue routines needed an extra branch register and the CTR was conveniently available in the BPU. This is another example of how the POWER software model affected the POWER hardware design which, in turn, affected the PowerPC design.

Like the LR, this SPR was deemed useful because it separated the registers being used by the BPU from those used by the Integer Unit. This allowed the processor to make certain optimizations to increase performance, resulting in features like zero-cycle branching for CTR loops.

In real-world code, CTR conflicts are not a major concern because the BPU handles the feed-forwarding of the appropriate CTR value.

CTR-Branch / CTR-Branch Dependencies

Branches that depend only on the CTR are a special case because the BPU can always resolve the branch (because the CTR is part of the BPU). For this reason, it is convenient to consider this type of conditional branch as an unconditional branch for timing purposes. Like all branches that require a writeback, the branch instruction stays in BW until the previous integer instructions have completed so that the CTR can be updated at the proper time.

The next loop example demonstrates a common use for CTR branches, where the CTR controls the number of loop iterations:

```
start:
        and     r0,r0,r1
        nand    r2,r2,r3
        ...
        or      r4,r4,r5
        nor     r6,r6,r7
        bdnz    start
```

The timing for the interesting part of this loop, where control passes from the bottom back to the top, is (note that execution starts at the or instruction):

Cycle #:	1	2	3	4	5	6	7	8
and r0,r0,r1	-	-	FA CARB	CACC	IQ0 ID	IE	IC IWA	-
nand r2,r2,r3	-	-	FA CARB	CACC	IQ1	IQ0 ID	IE	IC IWA
...	-	-	-	-	-	-	-	-
or r4,r4,r5	FA CARB	CACC	IQ0 ID	IE	IC IWA	-	-	-
nor r6,r6,r7	FA CARB	CACC	IQ1	IQ0 ID	IE	IC IWA	-	-
bdnz start	FA CARB	CACC	IQ2 BE	BW	BW	BW	-	-

Here the branch instruction stays in BW until the previous integer instruction (nor) completes (cycle 6); then it updates the CTR with the newly decremented value.

However, if the loop is small enough, then the second CTR-branch may be executed while the first CTR-branch is still waiting in BW to update the CTR. This situation is handled (without stalling) by having the BPU automatically feed-forward the proper CTR value from the first branch to the second branch.

Consider this code snippet. It demonstrates a small loop that exhibits these properties:

```
start:
        and     r0,r0,r1
        nand    r2,r2,r3
        bdnz    start
```

This loop simply repeats the two-instruction loop and decrements the CTR to 0.

After the instructions have entered dispatch, the timing is as diagrammed. Here the timing has been broken into separate tables for each iteration of the loop so that it is easier to see what is going on. The first iteration of this loop is timed:

Cycle #:	1	2	3	4	5	6	7	8
and r0,r0,r1	FA CARB	CACC	IQ0 ID	IE	IC IWA	-	-	-
nand r2,r2,r3	FA CARB	CACC	IQ1	IQ0 ID	IE	IC IWA	-	-
bdnz start	FA CARB	CACC	IQ2 BE	BW	BW	BW	-	-

and the second iteration is:

Cycle #:	1	2	3	4	5	6	7	8
and r0,r0,r1	-	-	FA CARB	CACC	IQ0 ID	IE	IC IWA	-
nand r2,r2,r3	-	-	FA CARB	CACC	IQ1	IQ0 ID	IE	IC IWA
bdnz start	-	-	FA CARB	CACC	IQ2 BE	BW	BW	BW

Two additional iterations (which begin FA/CARB during cycles 5 and 7) are not shown because they simply repeat the timings in the diagram shifted over a few cycles.

In this example, the second-iteration bdnz has the correct CTR value fed to it from the first-iteration bdnz instruction during cycle 5. The first bdnz instruction doesn't actually update the CTR until cycle 6 when nand reaches IC.

Note that two branch instructions are waiting in WB at the same time during cycle 6 and again during cycle 8 (not shown).

mtctr / CTR-Branch Dependencies

This situation is identical to the timings given in the previous section, "mtlr/LR-Branch Dependencies," except that the CTR is used instead of the LR.

Nested CTR Loops

With only one CTR register, nested loops that want to use the CTR have to save and restore the appropriate CTR value manually. In general, this extra save/ restore step is not worthwhile because it can cost more than a conditional branch that depends on a counter stored in a GPR.

Condition Register (CR) Fields

The Condition Register is divided into eight 4-bit fields used to store the result of arithmetic and compare operations. Because instructions operate on individual fields, it is useful to consider the CR as eight independent resources.

The first rule of thumb is that a series of instructions that need to use the CR should use different CR fields whenever possible. By using different CR fields, the instructions can be scheduled more easily. Care must be taken to include instructions that have the Record bit set because they will implicitly update CR field 0 (integer instructions) or CR field 1 (floating-point instructions).

Compare / Conditional Branch Dependencies

The four tables in this section show the timings for a conditional branch that follows a compare instruction. The important feature of these timing tables is that the results of the compare operation are forwarded to the BPU during the compare's IE stage. This allows the branch to recover quickly from a misprediction.

The timings for this section are basically the same as those presented in §12.5, "Branch Instruction Timings."

Predicted Not-taken Correctly:

Cycle #:	1	2	3	4	5	6	7
cmp crf0,r30,r31	FA CARB	CACC	IQ0 ID	IE	IC IWA	-	-
pbr tag = cmp	-	-	-	IE	-	-	-
beq- crf0,target	FA CARB	CACC	IQ1 BE MR	MR	-	-	-
and r0,r0,r1	FA CARB	CACC	IQ2	IQ0 ID	IE	IC IWA	-
...	-	-	-	-	-	-	-
or r4,r4,r5	-	-	-	-	-	-	-

Predicted Not-taken Incorrectly:

Cycle #:	1	2	3	4	5	6	7
cmp crf0,r30,r31	FA CARB	CACC	IQ0 ID	IE	IC IWA	-	-
pbr tag = cmp	-	-	-	IE	-	-	-
beq- crf0,target	FA CARB	CACC	IQ1 BE MR	MR	-	-	-
and r0,r0,r1	FA CARB	CACC	IQ2	IQ0 ID	-	-	-
...	-	-	-	-	-	-	-
or r4,r4,r5	-	-	-	FA CARB	CACC	IQ0 ID	IE

Predicted Taken Correctly:

Cycle #:	1	2	3	4	5	6	7
cmp crf0,r30,r31	FA CARB	CACC	IQ0 ID	IE	IC IWA	-	-
pbr tag = cmp	-	-	-	IE	-	-	-
beq+ crf0,target	FA CARB	CACC	IQ1 BE MR	MR	-	-	-
and r0,r0,r1	FA CARB	CACC	IQ2	IQ0 ID	-	-	-
...	-	-	-	-	-	-	-
or r4,r4,r5	-	-	FA CARB	CACC	IQ0 ID	IE	IC IWA

Predicted Taken Incorrectly:

Cycle #:	1	2	3	4	5	6	7
cmp crf0,r30,r31	FA CARB	CACC	IQ0 ID	IE	IC IWA	-	-
pbr tag = cmp	-	-	-	IE	-	-	-
beq+ crf0,target	FA CARB	CACC	IQ1 BE MR	MR	-	-	-
and r0,r0,r1	FA CARB	CACC	IQ2	IQ0 ID	IE	IC IWA	-
...	-	-	-	-	-	-	-
or r4,r4,r5	-	-	FA CARB	CACC	-	-	-

Integer-Record / Conditional Branch Dependencies

The four tables in this section show the timings for the conditional branch that follows an integer instruction that has the Record bit set. The major difference between these tables and the tables in the previous section is that branch prediction cannot be confirmed until the results of the integer instruction have been written back to the appropriate registers (during cycle 5). This causes a one-cycle stall because the *predicted branch tag* prevents instructions past the branch from entering IE.

Predicted Not-taken Correctly:

Cycle #:	1	2	3	4	5	6	7
add. r30,r30,r31	FA CARB	CACC	IQ0 ID	IE	IC IWA	-	-
pbr tag = add.	-	-	-	IE	IE	-	-
beq- crf0,target	FA CARB	CACC	IQ1 BE MR	MR	MR	-	-
and r0,r0,r1	FA CARB	CACC	IQ2	IQ0 ID	IQ0 ID	IE	IC IWA
...	-	-	-	-	-	-	-
or r4,r4,r5	-	-	-	-	-	-	-

Predicted Not-taken Incorrectly:

Cycle #:	1	2	3	4	5	6	7
add. r30,r30,r31	FA CARB	CACC	IQ0 ID	IE	IC IWA	-	-
pbr tag = add.	-	-	-	IE	IE	-	-
beq- crf0,target	FA CARB	CACC	IQ1 BE MR	MR	MR	-	-
and r0,r0,r1	FA CARB	CACC	IQ2	IQ0 ID	IQ0 ID	-	-
...	-	-	-	-	-	-	-
or r4,r4,r5	-	-	-	-	FA CARB	CACC	IQ0 ID

Predicted Taken Correctly:

Cycle #:	1	2	3	4	5	6	7
add. r30,r30,r31	FA CARB	CACC	IQ0 ID	IE	IC IWA	-	-
pbr tag = add.	-	-	-	IE	IE	-	-
beq+ crf0,target	FA CARB	CACC	IQ1 BE MR	MR	MR	-	-
and r0,r0,r1	FA CARB	CACC	IQ2	IQ0 ID	-	-	-
...	-	-	-	-	-	-	-
or r4,r4,r5	-	-	FA CARB	CACC	IQ0 ID	IE	IC IWA

Predicted Taken Incorrectly:

Cycle #:	1	2	3	4	5	6	7
add. r30,r30,r31	FA CARB	CACC	IQ0 ID	IE	IC IWA	-	-
pbr tag = add.	-	-	-	IE	IE	-	-
beq+ crf0,target	FA CARB	CACC	IQ1 BE MR	MR	MR	-	-
and r0,r0,r1	FA CARB	CACC	IQ2	IQ0 ID	FA CARB	CACC	IQ0 ID
...	-	-	-	-	-	-	-
or r4,r4,r5	-	-	FA CARB	CACC	IQ0 ID	-	-

Floating-Point Record / Conditional Branch Dependencies

The four tables in this section show the timings for the conditional branch that follows a floating-point instruction that has its Record bit set. The key difference between these tables and the tables for integer-record (other than the fact that the FPU is being used) is that the results of the floating-point instruction aren't available in the BPU until the cycle *after* the FPU's FWA stage. This prevents the branch from being resolved until cycle 8, effectively stalling the pipeline until that time.

Predicted Not-taken Correctly:

Cycle #:	1	2	3	4	5	6	7	8	9	10	11
fp tag = bubble1	-	-	-	IE	IC	IC	IC	-	-	-	-
fadds. fr1,fr1,fr2	FA CARB	CACC	IQ0	FD	FPM	FPA	FWA	-	-	-	-
pbr tag = bubble1	-	-	-	IE	IE	IE	IE	IE	-	-	-
beq- crf0,target	FA CARB	CACC	IQ1 BE MR	MR	MR	MR	MR	MR	-	-	-
and r0,r0,r1	FA CARB	CACC	IQ2	IQ0 ID	ID	ID	ID	ID	IE	IC IWA	-
...	-	-	-	-	-	-	-	-	-	-	-
or r4,r4,r5	-	-	-	-	-	-	-	-	-	-	-

Predicted Not-taken Incorrectly:

Cycle #:	1	2	3	4	5	6	7	8	9	10	11
fp tag = bubble1	-	-	-	IE	IC	IC	IC	-	-	-	-
fadds. fr1,fr1,fr2	FA CARB	CACC	IQ0	FD	FPM	FPA	FWA	-	-	-	-
pbr tag = bubble1	-	-	-	IE	IE	IE	IE	IE	-	-	-
beq- crf0,target	FA CARB	CACC	IQ1 BE MR	MR	MR	MR	MR	MR	-	-	-
and r0,r0,r1	FA CARB	CACC	IQ2	IQ0 ID	ID	ID	ID	ID	-	-	-
...	-	-	-	-	-	-	-	-	-	-	-
or r4,r4,r5	-	-	-	-	-	-	-	FA CARB	CACC	IQ0 ID	IE

Predicted Taken Correctly:

Cycle #:	1	2	3	4	5	6	7	8	9	10	11
fp tag = bubble1	-	-	-	IE	IC	IC	IC	-	-	-	-
fadds. fr1,fr1,fr2	FA CARB	CACC	IQ0	FD	FPM	FPA	FWA	-	-	-	-
pbr tag = bubble1	-	-	-	IE	IE	IE	IE	IE	-	-	-
beq+ crf0,target	FA CARB	CACC	IQ1 BE MR	MR	MR	MR	MR	MR	-	-	-
and r0,r0,r1	FA CARB	CACC	-	-	-	-	-	-	-	-	-
...	-	-	-	-	-	-	-	-	-	-	-
or r4,r4,r5	-	-	FA CARB	CACC	IQ0 ID	ID	ID	ID	IE	IC IWA	-

Predicted Taken Incorrectly:

Cycle #:	1	2	3	4	5	6	7	8	9	10	11
fp tag = bubble1	-	-	-	IE	IC	IC	IC	-	-	-	-
fadds. fr1,fr1,fr2	FA CARB	CACC	IQ0	FD	FPM	FPA	FWA	-	-	-	-
pbr tag = bubble1	-	-	-	IE	IE	IE	IE	IE	-	-	-
beq+ crf0,target	FA CARB	CACC	IQ1 BE MR	MR	MR	MR	MR	MR	-	-	-
and r0,r0,r1	FA CARB	CACC	-	-	-	-	-	FA CARB	CACC	IQ0 ID	IE
...	-	-	-	-	-	-	-	-	-	-	-
or r4,r4,r5	-	-	FA CARB	CACC	IQ0 ID	ID	ID	ID	-	-	-

CR-write / CR-read Dependencies

Two dependent arithmetic Condition Register instructions can generally follow one another without causing stalls in the IU pipeline. This is possible because all arithmetic CR instructions are handled by the IU, and the data can be forwarded directly to the dependent instruction in ID.

In this example, the `crand` instruction immediately follows the `add.` instruction, implicitly updating CR field 0.

Cycle #:	1	2	3	4	5	6
add. r0,r1,r2	FA CARB	CACC	IQ0 ID	IE	IC IWA	-
crand crf1,crf0,crf2	FA CARB	CACC	IQ1	IQ0 ID	IE	IC IWA

In this case, the proper CR value is passed along from the `add.` instruction's IE stage to the `crand` instruction's ID stage.

The timing chart in this section is valid for any combination of CR Boolean, integer arithmetic with record, `mtcrf`, and `mcrxr` instructions. It is also valid for the `mcrf` instruction followed by any of these instructions.

stwcx. / CR-read Dependencies

The `stwcx.` instruction has special timing considerations because it updates the CR during its IWA, using some of the resources in the IE stage. This means that the instruction currently in IE must stall while the `stwcx.` instruction is in IWA. This stall cycle cannot be avoided.

When the store is successfully performed (because the reservation for the address was set), the timing is in the next table. Here the integer instruction following `stwcx.` stalls in IE because `stwcx.` is using the IE stage. These stalls occur in cycles 5 and 6, then the instruction is allowed to execute normally in IE.

Cycle #:	1	2	3	4	5	6	7	8
stwcx. r0,r1,r2	FA CARB	CACC	IQ0 ID	CARB IE	CACC (IE) IC IWA	(IE) IWA	-	-
and r4,r4,r5	FA CARB	CACC	IQ1	IQ0 ID	IE	IE	IE	IC IWA

If the store is not performed (because the reservation was not set for this address), the timing changes because the IE is only occupied for one cycle instead of two.

Cycle #:	1	2	3	4	5	6	7
stwcx. r0,r1,r2	FA CARB	CACC	IQ0 ID	CARB IE	CACC (IE) IC IWA	-	-
and r4,r4,r5	FA CARB	CACC	IQ1	IQ0 ID	IE	IE	IC IWA

CR-write / mcrf Dependencies

When the `mcrf` instruction immediately follows a CR Boolean or integer arithmetic with record instruction, the `mcrf` instruction stalls in ID for one cycle after the CR is updated. In most cases (as in the next example), this update occurs during the CR instruction's IE stage (cycle 5).

Cycle #:	1	2	3	4	5	6	7
add. r0,r1,r2	FA CARB	CACC	IQ0 ID	IE	IC IWA	-	-
mcrf crf3,crf4	FA CARB	CACC	IQ1	IQ0 ID	ID	IE	IC IWA

Because the `stwcx.` instruction doesn't update the CR until its IWA stage, the timing for a `stwcx.`/`mcrf` pair is slightly different. The next timing example shows the case where the store is performed. The CR is updated in cycle 6, so the `mcrf` must stall in ID for one more cycle and then enter IE in cycle 8.

Cycle #:	1	2	3	4	5	6	7	8	9
stwcx. r0,r1,r2	FA CARB	CACC	IQ0 ID	CARB IE	CACC (IE) IC IWA	(IE) IWA	-	-	-
mcrf crf3,crf4	FA CARB	CACC	IQ1	IQ0 ID	ID	ID	ID	IE	IC IWA

If the `stwcx.` instruction does not perform a store (because the reservation wasn't set for this location), the timing changes because the CR is updated one cycle earlier (in cycle 5), allowing the `mcrf` to leave ID one cycle sooner.

Cycle #:	1	2	3	4	5	6	7	8	9
stwcx. r0,r1,r2	FA CARB	CACC	IQ0 ID	CARB IE	CACC (IE) IC IWA	-	-	-	-
mcrf crf3,crf4	FA CARB	CACC	IQ1	IQ0 ID	ID	ID	IE	IC IWA	-

Note that this stall occurs even though the `mcrf` instruction is not reading or writing the CR field that is being updated.

Multiply-Quotient Register (MQ)

No resource conflict stalls are associated with the MQ register. The IU makes sure that the proper MQ value is feed-forwarded whenever it is needed.

Fixed-Point Exception Register (XER)

The XER is mainly used to record the overflow and carry information for integer arithmetic and shift instructions. Some additional fields are also used by the load and store string instructions.

The XER dependencies are checked based on any part of the register being read from or written to. Thus, an instruction that reads any part of the XER depends on a previous instruction that updates any part of the XER.

XER-write / XER-read Dependencies

RAW conflicts typically do not cause stalls in the integer pipeline, although some cases do. Whether or not a stall occurs depends on the instructions being used to read and write the XER.

If the XER is written to by:

- Arithmetic instructions with the OE bit set
- Arithmetic instructions that set the CA
- Shift instructions that set the CA
- `lscbx`, `mcrxr`, or `mtxer`

and it is read by:

- Arithmetic instructions that use the CA
- `mfxer`

then there will be no stall even if the read occurs immediately after the write operation. This is demonstrated in the timing table:

Cycle #:	1	2	3	4	5	6
addo r0,r0,r1	FA CARB	CACC	IQ0 ID	IE	IC IWA	-
addme r2,r2	FA CARB	CACC	IQ1	IQ0 ID	IE	IC IWA

XER-write / String Dependencies

The non-immediate forms of the *Load* and *Store String* instructions (`lscbx`, `lswx`, and `stswx`) need to read the XER during their ID stage in the IU. Because of this, if they follow an instruction that updates the XER, they stall until the previous instruction updates the XER during its IWA stage (for one cycle).

In the next timing example, the `lswx` instruction must stall in ID for cycle 5 while the XER is being updated. After this one-cycle stall, the instruction continues normally. In this example, only two registers are loaded by the `lswx` instruction.

Cycle #:	1	2	3	4	5	6	7	8	9
addo r0,r0,r1	FA CARB	CACC	IQ0 ID	IE	IC IWA	-	-	-	-
lswx r3,r4,r5	FA CARB	CACC	IQ1	IQ0 ID	ID	CARB IE	CARB CACC IE IC	CACC IWL	IWL

This stall can be avoided by placing an independent instruction between the XER update and the string instruction.

XER-write / mcrxr Dependencies

Like the Load and Store String instructions above, the mcrxr needs to read the XER during its ID stage. It exhibits the same (avoidable) one-cycle stall that the string instructions do.

Cycle #:	1	2	3	4	5	6	7
addo r0,r0,r1	FA CARB	CACC	IQ0 ID	IE	IC IWA	-	-
mcrxr crf3	FA CARB	CACC	IQ1	IQ0 ID	ID	IE	IC IWA

General Purpose Registers (GPRs)

Although the large number of GPRs permits many register dependencies to be avoided, plenty of RAW conflicts still can arise. Fortunately, the feed-forward mechanism in the Integer Units handles most of these conflicts without stalls.

GPR-write / GPR-read Dependencies

The 601's IU is capable of feed-forwarding data from the IE and IWA stages into the ID stage. This means that all RAW conflicts involving arithmetic instructions are handled without causing pipeline stalls.

When there are no instructions between the write and read, the dependent read (sub r4,r0,r3) has the operand passed directly from the IE stage of the write (add r0,r1,r2) into its ID stage (cycle 4).

Cycle #:	1	2	3	4	5	6
add r0,r1,r2	FA CARB	CACC	IQ0 ID	IE	IC IWA	-
sub r4,r0,r3	FA CARB	CACC	IQ1	IQ0 ID	IE	IC IWA

If one independent instruction is between the two instructions, the data is passed from the IWA stage of the write to the ID stage of the read (cycle 5).

Cycle #:	1	2	3	4	5	6	7
add r0,r1,r2	FA CARB	CACC	IQ0 ID	IE	IC IWA	-	-
or r29,r30,r31	FA CARB	CACC	IQ1	IQ0 ID	IE	IC IWA	-
sub r4,r0,r3	FA CARB	CACC	IQ2	IQ1	IQ0 ID	IE	IC IWA

If more than one independent instruction is between the write and the read, then there is no data conflict because the data can simply be read from the register store.

Note that this feed-forwarding also occurs if there is a dependency on the update register of the *Load* or *Store with Update* instructions, for example, with the code:

```
lwzu    r3,4(r9)
addi    r10,r9,24
```

The update register (r9) is updated by the load instruction and read by the addi instruction. This instruction sequence causes no stalls due to GPR resource conflicts. Dependencies on the GPR that is loaded (r3, in this case) are much different and are covered next.

GPR-load / GPR-read Dependencies

If an instruction that uses a particular GPR immediately follows a load of that same register, the instruction must stall in IE until the load enters IWL. Ideally, this takes only one cycle, but if there is a cache miss, the delay could be quite lengthy.

In the next example, the add instruction stalls in IE during cycle 5 while it waits for the results of the load to be written back.

Cycle #:	1	2	3	4	5	6	7
lwzx r3,0,r2	FA CARB	CACC	IQ0 ID	CARB IE	CACC IC	IWL	-
add r3,r3,r4	FA CARB	CACC	IQ1	IQ0 ID	IE	IE	IC IWA

This pipeline stall can be eliminated by placing independent instructions between the load and the use of the GPR in question.

GPR-load / GPR-load Dependencies

Two sequential load operations will cause a GPR resource stall only when the destination of the first load is used by the second load. If the two loads are independent, then no GPR resource stalls occur.

This is similar to the previous case, where the second instruction needs to wait for the results of the load to be written back during the IWL stage. Also, as with the previous case, the one-cycle stall shown here (in cycle 5) is a best case situation. If there is a cache miss, the stall in IE will be for more than one cycle.

Cycle #:	1	2	3	4	5	6	7	8
lwz r3,0(r2)	FA CARB	CACC	IQ0 ID	CARB IE	CACC IC	IWL	-	-
lwzx r4,0(r3)	FA CARB	CACC	IQ1	IQ0 ID	CARB IE	CARB IE	CACC IC	IWL

This stall can also be avoided by inserting independent instructions between the two load instructions.

Load Multiple / GPR-read Dependencies

Because the Load Multiple instruction remains in IE for one cycle per register being loaded, the only possible GPR resource conflict that can arise is with the last register being loaded, always r31. If a Load Multiple instruction is followed by an instruction that uses r31, there is at least a one-cycle delay due to the GPR-load/GPR-read dependency described in an earlier section.

Like all GPR load/use dependencies, the stalls can be avoided by inserting independent instructions between the load and the instruction that needs to read the GPR.

GPR-store Dependencies

Store instructions do not need to update any registers, so they do not cause GPR resource conflicts as the GPR-load instructions do.

The one exception is the *Store with Update* forms. Timings for dependency conflicts caused by this type of instruction are covered earlier in the "GPR-write/GPR-read Dependencies" section.

mtspr / GPR Dependencies

Some `mtspr` instructions are special because they require access to the source GPR during the IWA stage in addition to the IE stage. SPRs that require this additional GPR access are SPRGn, DSISR, DAR, HID0, HID1, HID2, RTCU, SRR0, and SRR1.

If an instruction following a `mtspr` instruction uses the same GPR, then the following instruction will stall in IE until the `mtspr` instruction releases the GPR. The exact number of cycles that this instruction will stall depends on the number of cycles that the `mtspr` instruction needs to spend in IWA. A table in "Move to/from SPR Instructions" in Chapter 12 summarizes the number of cycles required in IWA for each SPR.

mfspr / GPR Dependencies

Like `mtspr`, some of the `mfspr` instructions require access to the target GPR during the IWA stages of the `mfspr` instruction. These SPRs are SPRGn, DSISR, HID0, HID1, HID2, MSR, PVR, RTCU, SDR1, SR, SRR0, and SRR1.

If an instruction following a `mfspr` instruction uses the same GPR, then the following instruction will stall in IE until the `mfspr` instruction releases the GPR. The exact number of cycles that this instruction will stall depends on the number of cycles that the `mfspr` instruction needs to spend in IWA. See "Move to/from SPR Instructions" in Chapter 12 for a summary of the `mfspr` instruction timings.

Floating-Point Registers (FPRs)

The 601's FPU does not support feed-forwarding of data between dependent floating-point instructions. This causes a variety of dependency stalls that the IU is able to avoid.

FPR-write / FPR-read Dependencies

Because of the lack of feed-forwarding, a floating-point instruction that requires the result of a previous instruction must wait in FD until after the previous instruction has completed writeback in FWA.

This situation is diagrammed next, where the stages before the FD stage have been omitted. The second `fadds` instruction must wait until cycle 5 before it can begin executing in FD because not all of the operands are ready.

Cycle #:	1	2	3	4	5	6	7	8
fadds fr0,fr0,fr1	FD	FPM	FPA	FWA	-	-	-	-
fadds fr2,fr2,fr0	DS	FD	FD	FD	FD	FPM	FPA	FWA

FPR-write / FPR-store Dependencies

In many cases, an FPR-write/FPR-store dependency is like standard FPR-write/ FPR-read dependencies, where the read (or in this case, the store) cannot execute in FD until the write operation has left the FWA stage.

The one exception is when the store *immediately* follows the write. The FPU detects this case and allows the store to continue without stalling. When the write operation is in the FWA stage (cycle 4 in the diagram below), it knows about the store instruction following it in FPA and automatically forwards the data to the cache.

Cycle #:	1	2	3	4	5
fadds fr0,fr0,fr1	FD	FPM	FPA	FWA	-
	IQ0	FD	FPM	FPA	FWA
stfs fr0,0(r2)	IQ0	IE	IC	CARB	CACC
	ID		FPSB	FPSB	

15.4 Memory Dependencies

Two types of memory dependencies can occur. The first type is the true memory dependency, where the same address is being accessed by different instructions. These types of dependencies are easy to detect and work around (as with the register dependencies). The other type of memory dependency is the cache dependency. It's far more difficult to detect, but can impact performance tremendously.

Load and Store Dependencies

Load and Store dependencies are the basic types of memory dependencies, and they come in two exciting varieties: the load after store dependency and the store after load dependency.

Load / Store Dependencies

A load/store dependency occurs when a store instruction follows a load instruction that uses the same effective address. On the 601, this does not cause a dependency stall although there may be pipeline stalls due to a cache miss.

Cycle #:	1	2	3	4	5	6
lwz r0,0(r2)	FA CARB	CACC	IQ0 ID	CARB IE	CACC IC	IWL
stw r3,0(r2)	FA CARB	CACC	IQ1	IQ0 ID	CARB IE	CACC IC

Store / Load Dependencies

A store/load dependency occurs when a load instruction follows a store instruction to the same effective address. As with the load/store dependency, this does not cause a stall in the pipeline.

Cycle #:	1	2	3	4	5	6	7
stw r3,0(r2)	FA CARB	CACC	IQ0 ID	CARB IE	CACC IC	-	-
lwz r0,0(r2)	FA CARB	CACC	IQ1	IQ0 ID	CARB IE	CACC IC	IWL

Cache Dependencies

A cache dependency occurs when multiple load or store instructions access the same cache line. There are three major differences between cache dependencies and the other dependencies described in this chapter.

Cache Dependencies Are Good

The first difference between cache dependencies and other dependencies is that cache dependencies are *good* because they tend to improve performance.

As mentioned earlier when discussing caches, a cache miss can have a very large negative effect on code performance. When there is a cache dependency, the second cache access is almost guaranteed a cache hit. Thus, cache dependencies improve performance by reducing the likelihood that the dependent accesses will have a cache miss.

Note the use of the phrases "almost guaranteed" and "reducing the likelihood." The dependent access is not guaranteed a cache hit because other (unpredictable) external events may come into play and affect the data in the cache. However, this is unlikely, and, in most cases, it is safe to assume that the second and subsequent accesses will in fact be cache hits.

Cache Dependencies Are Long Term

All of the dependencies discussed previously are relatively short-term in nature. This means that the dependency is important only if the instructions are close to each other (within a few instructions). Cache dependencies, in contrast, are long term. Depending on memory usage, a cache dependency can cross hundreds of instructions.

Cache Dependencies Are Difficult to Control

Alas, the downside of cache dependencies is that they are difficult to control. Other than the ability to clear cache entries or flush the cache (which does not result in increased cache hits), the programmer has little direct control of the cache. The only way to "control" the cache is to control the memory access pattern or use the cache "touch" instructions.

Increasing Cache Dependencies

Even though cache dependencies are difficult to control, some techniques can be used to increase the number of cache dependencies. These techniques are inspired by the principles that led to the development of caches in the first place—the principles of locality.

To reiterate, these principles state that:

- If an item is referenced, then it is likely to be referenced again in the near future (*temporal locality*).
- If an item is referenced, then the items surrounding this item are likely to be referenced again in the near future (*spacial locality*).

Most programs naturally exhibit these characteristics; that's why caches work at all. However, a program can use the cache more effectively if it is written so that it increases the temporal and spacial locality of its memory accesses. This works because caches are designed to take advantage of that sort of locality.

So, the principles of locality can be transformed into these programming guidelines:

- If an item is referenced, it is good to reference it again soon.
- If an item is referenced, it is good to reference the items surrounding it soon.

For most code, not much can be done to follow the first guideline. If the data needs to be used again, that's good, but if it isn't needed anymore, it doesn't make sense to access it again. The most useful conclusion is that after a memory location has been accessed, the programmer shouldn't be overly concerned about accessing that location again.

The second guideline, however, *can* be applied in a wide variety of coding situations. Memory should be accessed as sequentially as possible (either forward or backward from the current position). Large jumps in memory accesses should be avoided whenever possible.

One-Dimensional Arrays

Single-dimensional arrays are the most obvious cases where the sequential access guideline can be applied. If the elements of a single-dimensional array need to be processed, then they should be processed in order whenever possible. If this is done, then the cache will be used as efficiently as possible.

The worst practice with single-dimensional arrays is bouncing around the array and accessing elements at different parts of the array. Unfortunately, this is the access pattern for many searching algorithms, such as binary searches.[1]

N-Dimensional Arrays

Multi-dimensional arrays are special cases of single-dimensional arrays. When multi-dimensional arrays are stored in memory, they are mapped into a large single-dimensional array. Consider this two-dimensional array:

	Columns			
	0,0	0,1	0,2	0,3
Rows	1,0	1,1	1,2	1,3
	2,0	2,1	2,2	2,3
	3,0	3,1	3,2	3,3

When stored in *row-major* order, the elements of this array are stored in memory in this order:

0,0	0,1	0,2	0,3	1,0	1,1	1,2	1,3	2,0	2,1	2,2	2,3	3,0	3,1	3,2	3,3

Thus, in order to access the elements of this array sequentially, each row should be processed in order before proceeding to the next row, as this code fragment does:

```
for(row=0; row<MAX_ROWS; row++)
    for(col=0; col<MAX_COLUMNS; col++)
        data[row][col]++;
```

For each row, all the columns are processed in order before continuing to the next row.

If the loops are changed, as in this example:

```
for(col=0; col<MAX_COLUMNS; col++)
    for(row=0; row<MAX_ROWS; row++)
        data[row][col]++;
```

---

1. This statement should **not** be taken as a call to use sequential search algorithms instead of binary (or other) searches. These algorithms have other benefits that outweigh the penalties associated with cache misses, and a certain amount of cache misses are to be expected during searches.

the array elements are processed in an order that skips around in memory. This uses the cache less efficiently and increases the likelihood of cache misses for cache lines that have already been accessed.

Of course, if the language being used happens to store arrays using *column-major* ordering (the columns are stored as units instead of the rows), then the loops in the example would have to be reversed. However, most commonly used languages (except FORTRAN) use row-major ordering for arrays.

Note that these concerns are valid only if the size of each element in the array is small (less than the cache sector size for the processor). If the element size is larger than this, then each element requires at least one cache sector, so there is no cache benefit to ordering the access pattern.

Array Blocking

One problem with the array example is that it assumes that the array loops could be ordered so that the inner-most loop was stepping through the array sequentially. When this assumption is not valid, some memory accesses will not be sequential, leading to inefficient use of the cache.

If the array is excessively large, then another problem arises: the inefficient use of the cache mentioned earlier leads to a large number of cache lines being loaded. Because the number of cache lines in the cache is limited, room for the new cache lines must be made by purging lines currently in the cache, often before the looping code finishes using the data in the cache line. This situation, in which the cache loads and purges the same cache lines repeatedly, is known as *cache thrashing*.

Figure 15-1 shows one way of addressing this problem is to divide the array into a collection of smaller arrays, called *blocks*. Because only a small part of the original array is being processed at a time, the number of cache lines needed to store the required data is reduced, which also reduces the likelihood of cache thrashing.

The loop from the previous example can be rewritten to implement blocking:

```
for(row=0; row<MAX_ROWS; row+=ROW_BLOCK)
    for(col=0; col<MAX_COLUMNS; col+=COL_BLOCK)
        for(i=0; i<ROW_BLOCK; i++)
            for(j=0; j<COL_BLOCK; j++)
                data[row+i][col+j]++;
```

Here, the inner two loops implement the blocking. The original array has been divided into a set of blocks that are ROW_BLOCK rows high and COL_BLOCK columns wide.

Figure 15-1 A Large Array before and after It Has Been Divided into Four Blocks

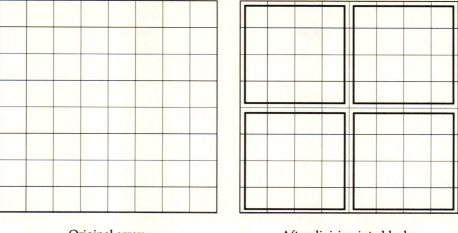

Original array   After division into blocks

Data Structures

Not surprisingly, the data structures used play an important role in how memory is accessed. Consider this structure:

```
struct {
    int tag;
    int data[16];
} array[MAX_ELEMENTS];
```

where the important field is `tag`, and the `data` field is just a generic data field.

Now, if there is an array of these structures, imagine a loop that steps through each element of the array to perform an operation on each element that has a certain type of tag. Using the earlier suggestion of sequentially stepping through the array returns the code:

```
for(i=0; i<MAX_ELEMENTS; i++)
    if(array[i].tag == MAGIC_TAG)
        mangle(&array[i].data);
```

There's a problem with this: while the code is sequentially stepping through the elements of the array, it isn't sequentially stepping through memory. This is because of the size of each element in the array.

One way of working around this is to break up the array so that the tags (which are processed sequentially) are in a separate array. If this can be done so that multiple array elements fit into a single cache line, then sequential access will be a performance gain; otherwise it will be just as inefficient as accessing the array at random.

The previous structure could be divided:

```
int tag[MAX_ELEMENTS];

struct {
     int data[16];
} array[MAX_ELEMENTS];
```

and the looping code would change to:

```
for(i=0; i<MAX_ELEMENTS; i++)
    if(tag[i] == MAGIC_TAG)
        mangle(&array[i].data);
```

There is one caveat with this example. The original structure/loop loaded the tag and part of the array data, while the modified structure/loop loads only the tags. If most elements in the array need to be processed, then the original loop *may* be more efficient because it will have already loaded part of the data that needs to be processed when it loaded the tag. This needs to be analyzed case-by-case.

More Optimization Techniques | 16

Chapter 15 covered a variety of important optimizations but left out one very important aspect of optimization. It talked about the processor resources and discussed how to avoid resource conflicts. While this is important, it is the easy part of the optimization process because it involves taking a set of well-defined rules and applying them to the code in question.

One important thing omitted from the previous chapter was a discussion of maximal resource utilization. This is partly because this topic is difficult to formalize—it depends so much on the nature of the program being optimized.

In spite of the difficulties, this chapter attempts to describe some common techniques used to make as much use of the processor resources as possible. This chapter is, of course, incomplete because it cannot present *every* possible technique. But one hopes it will provide enough information for you to evaluate your own code and devise your own techniques.

16.1 Keeping the Processor Busy

The 601 consists of three different processing units: the BPU, the IU, and the FPU. The processor works most efficiently when all three of these units are busy.

Instruction Mixing

To keep all three execution units busy, one branch, one integer instruction, and one floating-point instruction should be dispatched each cycle. Also, to prevent data dependency stalls, these instructions should be independent of each other. Unfortunately, most real-world code has a dispatch pattern that is nothing like this.

The majority of real-world code tends to be either integer-intensive or floating-point intensive, with a small percentage of branches thrown in. These situations fully utilize one of the arithmetic execution units, leaving the other relatively unused. Floating-point code is more balanced in this respect because all floating-point load and store instructions are handled (at least partially) by the IU. Integer code doesn't use the FPU at all.

However, it's not good enough to evenly distribute the overall percentage of code among these three units. The code must be evenly distributed throughout the program.

For example, the code in the next example has an even distribution of floating-point to integer instructions. There are four floating-point instructions and four integer instructions for a nice 50-50 distribution.

```
fadds    fr0,fr0,fr1
fadds    fr2,fr2,fr3
fadds    fr4,fr4,fr5
fadds    fr6,fr6,fr7
add      r0,r0,r1
add      r2,r2,r3
add      r4,r4,r5
add      r6,r6,r7
```

However, the dispatch unit can only dispatch one instruction of each type per cycle and integer instructions must be dispatched from the IQ0 position. It would take the dispatcher eight cycles to dispatch this code because it can only dispatch one instruction per cycle.

If the sequence of instructions were rearranged:

```
add      r0,r0,r1
fadds    fr0,fr0,fr1
add      r2,r2,r3
fadds    fr2,fr2,fr3
add      r4,r4,r5
fadds    fr4,fr4,fr5
add      r6,r6,r7
fadds    fr6,fr6,fr7
```

the dispatcher could dispatch two instructions (one integer and one floating-point) during each cycle. Four cycles have been saved before the instructions even begin executing.

Note that because the PowerPC supports out-of-order dispatch, the code doesn't have to be perfectly distributed in order to get the best dispatch timing. This code:

```
add     r0,r0,r1
add     r2,r2,r3
fadds   fr0,fr0,fr1
add     r4,r4,r5
fadds   fr2,fr2,fr3
fadds   fr4,fr4,fr5
add     r6,r6,r7
fadds   fr6,fr6,fr7
```

also results in two instructions being dispatched per cycle.

Unit Conversion

If your code is biased towards one unit or the other, it might be worthwhile to analyze your code to determine if it is possible to distribute the integer and floating-point computations more evenly by converting code from one execution unit to the other. If this is possible, then the original and the converted code can be compared to see if an advantage can be gained by splitting the code.

Memory Copy

One common example of this is the simple memory copy. A straightforward way of writing this code would be:

```
int i;
long *pSource, *pDest

for(i=0; i<nBytes/4; i++)
    *pDest = *pSource;
```

This code copies the block of memory four bytes at a time so that it uses the GPRs efficiently. In this situation, no computation is being performed, so the FPRs could just as easily have been used:

```
int i;
double *pSource, *pDest

for(i=0; i<nBytes/8; i++)
    *pDest = *pSource;
```

This could be transformed into PowerPC assembly as follows:

```
        li      r0,nBytes/8
        mtctr   r0
loop:
        lfdu    fr0,8(rSource)
        stfdu   fr0,8(rDest)
        bdnz    loop
```

Here, the IU still does most of the work because it handles all of the loads and stores, but now the FPU is helping out with the stores so that 8 bytes can be transferred at a time instead of only 4.

This technique could also be used to clear a block of memory by initializing an FPR with 0 and clearing out 8 bytes at a time.

Multiplication and Division

Another situation where switching from one unit to the other can be advantageous is with the multiplication and division operations. In the IU, these operations (especially division) are quite costly; in the FPU, they are somewhat less costly.

Whether or not this is a useful transformation to apply depends on a wide variety of factors. The two most important are the number of multiplies/divides and the type of data conversion required.

If only a small number of multiplies or divides are needed, then it isn't likely that the overhead of the transformation will be worthwhile. On the other hand, if there are a large number of these expensive operations, then the performance gains from the conversion can offset the required setup penalty.

This setup penalty can be quite large if a lot of data conversion is necessary from the IU to the FPU. Although data conversion from the FPU to the IU can be handled by the `fctiw` or `fctiwz` instructions, no instruction converts from integer to floating-point—the conversion must be performed manually and requires *at least* three instructions per word being converted, as described in Chapter 8, "Floating-Point Instructions."

16.2 Increasing Scheduling Opportunities

In order to prevent pipeline stalls, a lot of code rescheduling may be necessary. The problem with scheduling code is that often there aren't enough independent instructions to fill the delay slots. This section discusses a few techniques for increasing the number of independent instructions by changing the code structure.

Loop Unrolling

The basics of loop unrolling were discussed in Chapter 14, where it was implied that loop unrolling was less useful on PowerPC processors because the branch penalty could be eliminated if the compare and branch were far enough apart.

However, many small loops can benefit from loop unrolling for another reason. If each loop iteration is relatively independent of other iterations (as is the case for many loops), then loop unrolling increases the number of independent instructions available for scheduling. This increase in scheduling opportunities can significantly impact the performance of small loops.

Copying and Pasting Code

Instruction scheduling is typically done within a *basic block*. A basic block is simply a consecutive sequence of code that has only one entry point and one exit point. For example, in this code, there are four blocks:

```
if(condition)
     then-clause
else
     else-clause
next-instruction
```

The condition, then-clause, else-clause, and the next-instruction are all separate blocks. Figure 16-1 shows their relationship.

Figure 16-1   Basic Block Diagram for the If-Then-Else Structure

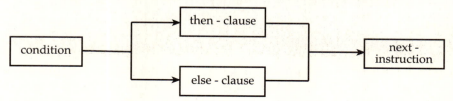

If the basic blocks are small, then there may not be many opportunities for scheduling. A technique to increase the size of critical basic blocks is known as *code pasting*.

Code pasting involves removing code from one block and adding it to another. Typically code is removed from a large block and added to a small block that is having scheduling problems.

For the above *if-then-else* example, code pasting can be applied by taking code from after the *if-then-else* and appending it to the bottom of the *then-* and *else-*

clauses. The code must be added to both clauses; otherwise the overall program structure will be changed, generally a bad thing for an optimization to do.

Of course, it's silly to paste the entire sequence of following instructions into each clause of the *if-then-else* statement. Only a portion of the *next-instruction* sequence is needed so that the clauses have enough instructions to perform whatever scheduling they need.

So, by breaking up the instructions following the *if-then-else* into two smaller blocks (zzz' and zzz''), the first block can be appended to each of the clauses while the second block stays after the *if-then-else*. The transformation shows this:

```
if(ccc)              if(ccc)
    xxx                  xxx
                         zzz'
else                 else
    yyy                  yyy
                         zzz'
zzz'                 zzz''
zzz''
```

Of course, these transformations are useful for structures other than *if-then-else* statements. This technique can be applied whenever a basic block is too small to perform effective rescheduling and there are surrounding blocks with available instructions.

Care must be taken when applying this technique so that the meaning of the program isn't inadvertently changed. The code removed must be pasted to *every* block that passes control to the modified block.

16.3 Strength Reduction

Strength reduction is the process of using simple instructions to replace more complex (or more powerful) instructions. This is a worthwhile technique only when there are instructions that require multiple cycles to execute. On the PowerPC, the only fixed-point arithmetic instructions likely to require multiple cycles are the multiply and divide instructions.

Using Left Shifts for Multiplication

Multiplying by a power of 2 can be accomplished quickly using shift left instructions. For example, multiplying r3 by 4 (2^2) can be accomplished using:

```
slwi    r3,r3,2
```

In general, to multiply the contents of a register rX by 2^n, use:

```
slwi    rX,rX,n
```

Multiplying by a number that is not a power of 2 is a little more complicated, but can be done by adding or subtracting powers of 2. In this case and in Table 16-1, one instruction is being replaced with multiple simpler instructions, but the end result is code that executes faster.

Table 16-1 Left Shift Equivalents for Non-integral Powers of 2

Multiply by	Equivalent to	Transformation	
$3 \times n$	$(2 \times n) + n$	slwi	rT,rN,1
		add	rT,rT,rN
	$(4 \times n) - n$	slwi	rT,rN,2
		sub	rT,rT,rN
$5 \times n$	$(4 \times n) + n$	slwi	rT,rN,2
		add	rT,rT,rN
$6 \times n$	$(4 \times n) + (2 \times n)$	slwi	rN,rN,1
		slwi	rT,rN,1
		add	rT,rT,rN
	$(8 \times n) - (2 \times n)$	slwi	rN,rN,1
		slwi	rT,rN,2
		sub	rT,rT,rN
$7 \times n$	$(8 \times n) - n$	slwi	rT,rN,3
		sub	rT,rT,rN
$9 \times n$	$(8 \times n) + n$	slwi	rT,rN,3
		add	rT,rT,rN
$10 \times n$	$(8 \times n) + (2 \times n)$	slwi	rN,rN,1
		slwi	rT,rN,2
		add	rT,rT,rN

It should be apparent that a large number of possible combinations are not presented in Table 16-1, some of which involve using many more than two or three instructions.

On the PowerPC 601, the multiply instruction takes five cycles when multiplying small values. It should be apparent that replacing the multiply instruction with five or fewer instructions would be a benefit (or at least it would break even assuming there aren't any instruction fetch or cache collision delays). However, this doesn't take into account the fact that the multiply instruction is *guaranteed* to stall in the execute stage of the pipeline for five cycles, whereas the five separate instructions could be scheduled to use the pipeline efficiently.

In some situations, it is advantageous to replace a multiply with *more* than five separate instructions because proper scheduling can result in some of the instructions being executed "for free."

Using Algebraic Right Shifts for Division

Dividing a number (the *dividend*) by a power of 2 (the *divisor*) can be accomplished using variants of the *Shift Right* instructions.

Unsigned values can be divided using one of the non-algebraic *Shift Right* instructions (`srw` or `srd`) or the *Shift Right Immediate* extended forms (`srwi` or `srdi`).

When dealing with a signed value as the dividend, a *Shift Right Algebraic* instruction (`sraw`, `srawi`, `srad`, or `sradi`) should be used instead of a *Shift Right* instruction of the non-algebraic variety. These instructions properly handle the sign of the dividend when generating the result. To insure that the result is rounded properly when the dividend is negative, an `addze` instruction should follow the shift instruction:

```
sraw    rT,rA,rB
addze   rT,rT
```

The `addze` instruction adds the Carry bit to the shifted result. Because the Carry bit is set to 1 only if the value in rA is negative and a '1' bit has been shifted out, this has the effect of adjusting negative values so that the result is rounded toward zero. For example, if rA=-9 and rB=2 (to divide -9 by 4), the result of the `sraw` instruction is -3. The `addze` instruction adds 1 to correct the result and produce -2. The `addze` instruction has no effect when dividing positive values because the Carry bit is always 0 for positive dividends.

Using a shift instruction differs from using a divide instruction in these ways:

- The divisor must be an integral power of 2.
- The divisor cannot be a negative number.
- The Overflow bits (XER[OV], XER[SO]) are not set.
- The operation takes roughly 3 to 6 percent of the time required by the divide instruction (on the 601).

For division by non-integral powers of 2, there is no easy method of combining shifts, adds, and subtracts to replace the division as there was with the multiply operation. However, considering how costly divide instructions are (36 cycles on the 601), it may be worthwhile to apply some other optimization technique to speed up the calculations (like setting up a lookup table).

Using Multiplication for Division

Division is a painfully slow operation. Single-precision floating-point division takes 18 cycles to execute and double-precision division takes 32 cycles.

If the division operation is being applied many times, it becomes beneficial to pre-calculate the reciprocal using a single divide instruction and then perform multiplication using the reciprocal. An example of this sort of situation is:

```
float x[50],d;
int i;

for(i=0;i<50;i++)
    x[i] /= d;
```

In this example, an array of floating-point values are all being divided by the same divisor. The assembly code for the loop portion of this code (before any optimizations have been applied) is shown next. This code assumes that r31 contains a pointer to the floating-point array and that fr30 contains the divisor d.

```
loop:
    lfs     fr31,4(r31)     # load x[i]

    # x[i] /= d
    fdivs   fr31,fr31,fr30

    stfsu   fr31,4(r31)     # save x[i]
    bdn     loop
```

This loop can be rewritten to pre-calculate the reciprocal so that a multiply instruction can be used in the body of the loop instead of the divide instruction. The transformed code would be (where fr1 contains the constant 1.0):

```
    # fr29 = 1.0 / fr30
    fdivs   fr29,fr1,fr30

loop:
    lfs     fr31,4(r31)     # load x[i]

    # x[i] *= (1/d)
    fmuls   fr31,fr29,fr31

    stfsu   fr31,4(r31)     # save x[i]
    bdn     @0
```

The problem with this transformed loop is that it introduces some floating-point round-off errors. In many cases, these round-off errors are acceptable, but the PowerPC's floating-point multiply-accumulate pipeline can be exploited to eliminate the round-off errors at the cost of a few more cycles of execution.

The (re-)transformed code would be:

```
        # fr29 = 1.0 / fr30
        fdivs   fr29,fr1,fr30

loop:
        lfs     fr31,4(r31)     # load x[i]

        # temp = x[i] * (1/d)
        fmuls   fr28,fr31,fr29
        # remainder = temp*d - x[i]
        fmsubs  fr27,fr30,fr28,fr31
        # x[i] = temp + (rem * 1/d))
        fmadds  fr31,fr29,fr27,fr28

        stfsu   fr31,4(r31)     # save x[i]
        bdn     loop
```

This code calculates the error introduced by the multiply and incorporates that value into the result. This adjustment works because the multiply-accumulate instructions (`fmsubs` and `fmadds`) perform the multiply and the add before any rounding takes place.

16.4 Load/Store Ordering

Loads and stores are special cases because they require access to the processor caches, which may cause delays if a cache miss occurs or if the data being stored is not available.

For this reason, loads are typically moved earlier in the instruction stream and stores are commonly moved later in the instruction stream. This code:

```
        lwz     r3,4(r2)
        addi    r3,r3,12
        stw     r3,4(r2)
        lwz     r4,8(r2)
        addi    r4,r4,16
        stw     r4,8(r2)
```

would typically be sequenced as:

```
        lwz     r3,4(r2)
        lwz     r4,8(r2)
        addi    r3,r3,12
        addi    r4,r4,16
        stw     r3,4(r2)
        stw     r4,8(r2)
```

16.5 Software Pipelining

Software pipelining is a way of merging the ideas of load/store ordering and pipelining together and applying them to program loops.

If load/store ordering is applied to the body of a loop, there will be three parts to the code: the load (L) portion, the execute (E) portion, and the store (S) portion. Each part can be considered a stage in a pipeline, where the pipeline is processing entire loop iterations instead of simple instructions.

To compare, consider the diagrammed instruction pipeline, which uses an imaginary three-stage pipeline with stages labelled A, B, and C. Here six instructions are completed in eight cycles:

Cycle #:	1	2	3	4	5	6	7	8
instruction 1	A	B	C	-	-	-	-	-
instruction 2	-	A	B	C	-	-	-	-
instruction 3	-	-	A	B	C	-	-	-
instruction 4	-	-	-	A	B	C	-	-
instruction 5	-	-	-	-	A	B	C	-
instruction 6	-	-	-	-	-	A	B	C

A software pipeline can be viewed the same way, but instead of instructions versus cycles, the table shows original loop iterations versus transformed loop iterations. Here the three stages are labelled L, E, and S:

"Cycle" #:	1	2	3	4	5	6	7	8
iteration 1	L	E	S	-	-	-	-	-
iteration 2	-	L	E	S	-	-	-	-
iteration 3	-	-	L	E	S	-	-	-
iteration 4	-	-	-	L	E	S	-	-
iteration 5	-	-	-	-	L	E	S	-
iteration 6	-	-	-	-	-	L	E	S

Because we're looking at original iterations versus transformed iterations, this can quickly become quite confusing. In this case, the original six loop iterations are accomplished in eight transformed iterations, or "cycles." Note that the term "cycle" is used simply for convenience—these cycles have nothing to do with the processor cycles in the instruction pipeline.

During the first two cycles, the software pipeline is still being filled. It isn't until the third cycle that the pipeline is fully loaded. During this third cycle, the transformed loop performs the S stage for the first iteration, the E stage for the second iteration, and the L stage for the third iteration. The pipeline stays full until cycle 7, when it needs to ramp down and execute the cleanup code for the last two loop iterations.

To put this into practice, a loop like this:

```
for(i=0; i<N; i++)
     L(i)
     E(i)
     S(i)
```

can be transformed into this loop:

```
L(1)
E(1)
L(2)
for(i=1; i<N-1; i++)
    S(i)
    E(i+1)
    L(i+2)
S(N-1)
E(N)
S(N)
```

Or, as it is commonly structured in assembly:

```
# initialize loop counter
li      r0,N-1
mtctr   r0

# handle cycle 1
L(1)
b       start

# execute S,E,L N-2 times
loop:
    S(i-1)
start:
    E(i)
    L(i+1)
    bdnz    loop

# ramp down
S(N-1)
E(N)
S(N)
```

Note that in order for this to work, the results of each stage must be stored in different registers. Thus, a set of registers chosen as the output registers for the Load stage is also used as the input registers for the Execute stage. Likewise, there is another set of registers for communication between the Execute and Store stages.

Instruction Set Summary

This appendix contains an alphabetically sorted list of all PowerPC instructions. This includes all 32-bit and 64-bit instructions plus all optional instructions. In addition, all of the POWER instructions that are provided on the 601 are included in this appendix.

At the head of each main entry is the standard instruction mnemonic along with the instruction description. In general, the mnemonics are displayed in boldface, but obsolete POWER instructions (which are implemented only on the 601), are displayed using an outline font to serve as a reminder that these are not standard PowerPC instructions and that they will not be implemented on future PowerPC processors.

Immediately beneath the instruction title is a summary of the processors on which the instruction is implemented. The value here can be any combination of the following:

- POWER—The instruction is defined on POWER processors.

- 601—The instruction is defined on the PowerPC 601.

- 603—The instruction is defined on the PowerPC 603.

- PowerPC32—The instruction is defined on 32-bit PowerPC implementations only.

- PowerPC64—The instruction is defined on 64-bit PowerPC implementations only.

- PowerPC32/64—The instruction is defined for both 32-bit and 64-bit Power-PC implementations.

- Optional32/64—The instruction is an optional instruction that may be defined on 32-bit and 64-bit implementations.

The **Operation** provides a concise description of the instruction operation using the operators described in Chapter 3.

The **Syntax** area shows all of the valid syntax forms for the instruction.

The register area will show which of the Special Purpose Registers are modified by this instruction. For fixed-point instructions, this section is titled **Condition Register/Fixed-Point Exception Register** and for floating-point instructions it is entitled **Condition Register/Floating-Point Status and Control Register.**

The **Description** field provides a textual description of the instruction's operation and notes any idiosyncracies.

For instructions with extended forms, the **Extended Forms** section provides a summary of all of the valid extended forms that are based on the instruction. Instructions without extended forms will not have this section.

The final section is the **Instruction Encoding** area. This section shows how the instruction and its operands are encoded into a 32-bit word.

Absolute Value

POWER • 601

Operation: $rT \Leftarrow |rA|$

Syntax:

abs	rT,rA	(Rc = 0, OE = 0)
abs.	rT,rA	(Rc = 1, OE = 0)
abso	rT,rA	(Rc = 0, OE = 1)
abso.	rT,rA	(Rc = 1, OE = 1)

Condition Register/Fixed-Point Exception Register:

CR Field 0:   LT,GT,EQ,SO updated if Rc = 1, otherwise not affected
CR Fields 1-7:   not affected

XER[CA]:   not affected
XER[OV,SO]:   updated if OE=1, otherwise not affected

Description:

The **abs** instruction calculates the absolute value of the contents of GPR rA, and stores the result in GPR rT.

If GPR rA contains the largest negative number (0x80000000), then the result in rT will be the largest negative number and, if the OE bit is set, the OV and SO bits of the XER will be set to 1.

This instruction is not part of the PowerPC architecture.

Instruction Encoding:

0					5	6			10	11				15	16				20	21	22								30	31
0	1	1	1	1	1		T				A				0	0	0	0	0	OE	1	0	1	1	0	1	0	0	0	Rc

T   Target GPR rT where result of operation is stored
A   Source GPR rA
OE   Overflow Exception bit
Rc   Record bit

add   Add   add

POWER • 601 • 603 • PowerPC32/64

Operation: $rT \Leftarrow (rA) + (rB)$

Syntax:

add	rT,rA,rB	(Rc = 0, OE = 0)
add.	rT,rA,rB	(Rc = 1, OE = 0)
addo	rT,rA,rB	(Rc = 0, OE = 1)
addo.	rT,rA,rB	(Rc = 1, OE = 1)

Condition Register / Fixed-Point Exception Register:

CR Field 0:   LT,GT,EQ,SO updated if Rc = 1, otherwise not affected
CR Fields 1-7:   not affected

XER[CA]:   not affected
XER[OV,SO]:   updated if OE=1, otherwise not affected

Description:

The **add** instruction adds the contents of GPR rA and GPR rB as signed quantities and places the result in GPR rT.

The archaic POWER mnemonic for this instruction is **cax[o][.]** (Compute Address Indexed).

Instruction Encoding:

0	5	6	10	11	15	16	20	21	22	30	31
0 1 1 1 1 1		T		A		B		OE	1 0 0 0 0 1 0 1 0		Rc

T	Target GPR rT where result of operation is stored
A	Source GPR rA
B	Source GPR rB
OE	Overflow Exception bit
Rc	Record bit

addc   Add Carrying   addc

POWER • 601 • 603 • PowerPC32/64

Operation: $rT \Leftarrow (rA) + (rB)$

Syntax:

addc	rT,rA,rB	(Rc = 0, OE = 0)
addc.	rT,rA,rB	(Rc = 1, OE = 0)
addco	rT,rA,rB	(Rc = 0, OE = 1)
addco.	rT,rA,rB	(Rc = 1, OE = 1)

Condition Register / Fixed-Point Exception Register:

CR Field 0:   LT,GT,EQ,SO updated if Rc = 1, otherwise not affected
CR Fields 1-7:   not affected

XER[CA]:   always updated
XER[OV,SO]:   updated if OE=1, otherwise not affected

Description:

The **addc** instruction adds the contents of GPR r*A* and GPR r*B* as signed quantities and places the result in GPR r*T*, updating the Carry bit of the XER.

The archaic POWER mnemonic for this instruction is **a[o][.]**.

Instruction Encoding:

0 5	6 10	11 15	16 20	21	22 30	31
0 1 1 1 1 1	T	A	B	OE	0 0 0 0 0 1 0 1 0	Rc

T   Target GPR rT where result of operation is stored
A   Source GPR rA
B   Source GPR rB
OE   Overflow Exception bit
Rc   Record bit

adde

Add Extended

adde

POWER • 601 • 603 • PowerPC32/64

Operation: $rT \Leftarrow (rA) + (rB) + XER[CA]$

Syntax:

adde	rT,rA,rB	(Rc = 0, OE = 0)
adde.	rT,rA,rB	(Rc = 1, OE = 0)
addeo	rT,rA,rB	(Rc = 0, OE = 1)
addeo.	rT,rA,rB	(Rc = 1, OE = 1)

Condition Register/Fixed-Point Exception Register:

CR Field 0:   LT,GT,EQ,SO updated if Rc = 1, otherwise not affected
CR Fields 1-7:   not affected

XER[CA]:   always updated
XER[OV,SO]:   updated if OE=1, otherwise not affected

Description:

The **adde** instruction adds the contents of GPR rA and GPR rB as signed quantities with the Carry bit of the XER and places the result in GPR rT, updating the Carry bit.

The archaic POWER mnemonic for this instruction is **ae[o][.]**.

Instruction Encoding:

0	5 6	10 11	15 16	20 21 22	30 31
0 1 1 1 1 1	T	A	B	OE 0 1 0 0 0 1 0 1 0	Rc

T	Target GPR rT where result of operation is stored
A	Source GPR rA
B	Source GPR rB
OE	Overflow Exception bit
Rc	Record bit

addi   Add Immediate   addi

POWER • 601 • 603 • PowerPC32/64

Operation: $rT \Leftarrow (rA | 0) + \grave{}s16$

Syntax: **addi**   rT,rA,s16

Condition Register/Fixed-Point Exception Register:

CR Fields 0-7:   not affected

XER: not affected

Description:

If A≠0, the **addi** instruction adds the sign-extended quantity specified by *s16* with the contents of GPR rA and places the result in GPR rT.

If A=0, the **addi** instruction simply places the sign-extended quantity *s16* in GPR rT.

The archaic POWER mnemonic for this instruction is **cal** (Compute Address Lower). Note that even though the instruction encoding is identical, the assembler parses the parameters for the **cal** instruction as rT,d(rA) instead of rT,rA,s16.

Extended Forms:

la	rT,d(rA)	is equivalent to	**addi**	rT,rA,d
li	rT,s16	is equivalent to	**addi**	rT,0,s16
subi	rT,rA,s16	is equivalent to	**addi**	rT,rA,-s16

Instruction Encoding:

0 5	6 10	11 15	16 31
0 0 1 1 1 0	T	A	SI

     T   Target GPR rT where result of operation is stored
     A   Source GPR rA or 0
     SI   Signed 16-bit integer

addic   Add Immediate Carrying   addic

POWER • 601 • 603 • PowerPC32/64

Operation: $rT \Leftarrow (rA) + \text{`}s16$

Syntax:
addic	$rT,rA,s16$	(Rc = 0)
addic.	$rT,rA,s16$	(Rc = 1)

Condition Register/Fixed-Point Exception Register:

CR Field 0:   LT,GT,EQ,SO updated if Rc = 1, otherwise not affected
CR Fields 1-7:   not affected

XER[CA]:   always updated
XER[OV,SO]:   not affected

Description:

The **addic** instruction adds the contents of GPR r*A* to the 32-bit sign-extended quantity specified by *s16* and places the result in GPR r*T*, updating the Carry bit.

The archaic POWER mnemonic for this instruction is **ai**[.].

Instruction Encoding:

0 4	5 6		10 11		15 16		31
0 0 1 1 0	Rc	T		A		SI	

Rc   Record bit
T   Target GPR rT where result of operation is stored
A   Source GPR rA
SI   Signed 16-bit integer

addis   Add Immediate Shifted   addis

POWER • 601 • 603 • PowerPC32/64

Operation: $rT \Leftarrow (rA \,|\, 0) + \,`(s16 \perp 0x0000)$

Syntax: **addis**   rT,rA,s16

Condition Register/Fixed-Point Exception Register:

CR Fields 0-7:   not affected

XER: not affected

Description:

If A≠0, the **addis** instruction takes the value calculated by concatenating *s16* with 0x0000, adds it to the contents of GPR rA, and then places the result in GPR rT.

If A=0, the **addis** instruction simply places the concatenated value directly in GPR rT.

On 64-bit PowerPC implementations, the 32-bit result of the concatenation is sign-extended to 64 bits before the result is placed in rT.

The archaic POWER mnemonic for this instruction is **cau** (Compute Address Upper). Note that the **cau** instruction accepts an unsigned 16-bit quantity instead of a signed 16-bit quantity as the immediate value. While this difference will not affect the operation of this instruction in 32-bit mode, POWER code that is migrated to 64-bit PowerPC implementations will notice that the upper word of the target register will be filled with sign bits instead of 0.

Instruction Encoding:

0 5	6 10	11 15	16 31
0 0 1 1 1 1	T	A	SI

     T   Target GPR rT where result of operation is stored
     A   Source GPR rA or 0
     SI   Signed 16-bit integer

addme   Add to Minus One Extended   addme

POWER • 601 • 603 • PowerPC32/64

Operation: $rT \Leftarrow (rA) + -1 + XER[CA]$

Syntax:

addme	rT,rA	(Rc = 0, OE = 0)
addme.	rT,rA	(Rc = 1, OE = 0)
addmeo	rT,rA	(Rc = 0, OE = 1)
addmeo.	rT,rA	(Rc = 1, OE = 1)

Condition Register / Fixed-Point Exception Register:

CR Field 0:   LT,GT,EQ,SO updated if Rc = 1, otherwise not affected
CR Fields 1-7: not affected

XER[CA]:   always updated
XER[OV,SO]:   updated if OE=1, otherwise not affected

Description:

The **addme** instruction adds the contents of GPR rA, -1 (0xFFFFFFFF), and the Carry bit, and places the result in GPR rT, updating the Carry bit in the XER.

The archaic POWER mnemonic for this instruction is **ame[o][.]**.

Instruction Encoding:

0 5	6 10	11 15	16 20	21	22 30	31
0 1 1 1 1 1	T	A	0 0 0 0 0	OE	0 1 1 1 0 1 0 1 0	Rc

T	Target GPR rT where result of operation is stored
A	Source GPR rA
OE	Overflow Exception bit
Rc	Record bit

addze   Add to Zero Extended   addze

POWER • 601 • 603 • PowerPC32/64

Operation: $rT \Leftarrow (rA) + 0 + XER[CA]$

Syntax:

addze	rT,rA	(Rc = 0, OE = 0)
addze.	rT,rA	(Rc = 1, OE = 0)
addzeo	rT,rA	(Rc = 0, OE = 1)
addzeo.	rT,rA	(Rc = 1, OE = 1)

Condition Register/Fixed-Point Exception Register:

CR Field 0:   LT,GT,EQ,SO updated if Rc = 1, otherwise not affected
CR Fields 1-7:   not affected

XER[CA]:   always updated
XER[OV,SO]:   updated if OE=1, otherwise not affected

Description:

The **addze** instruction adds the contents of GPR rA, 0 and the Carry bit and places the result in GPR rT, updating the Carry bit in the XER.

The archaic POWER mnemonic for this instruction is **aze[o][.]**.

Instruction Encoding:

0				5	6				10	11				15	16				20	21	22									30	31
0	1	1	1	1	1		T				A				0	0	0	0	0	OE	0	1	1	0	0	1	0	1	0	Rc

T   Target GPR rT where result of operation is stored
A   Source GPR rA
OE   Overflow Exception bit
Rc   Record bit

and   AND   and

POWER • 601 • 603 • PowerPC32/64

Operation: $rA \Leftarrow (rS) \,\&\, (rB)$

Syntax:

and	rA,rS,rB	(Rc = 0)
and.	rA,rS,rB	(Rc = 1)

Condition Register/Fixed-Point Exception Register:

CR Field 0:   LT,GT,EQ,SO updated if Rc = 1, otherwise not affected
CR Fields 1-7:   not affected

XER: not affected

Description:

The **and** instruction logically ANDs the contents of GPR rS and GPR rB and places the result in GPR rA.

Instruction Encoding:

0	5	6	10	11	15	16	20	21	30	31
0 1 1 1 1 1		S		A		B		0 0 0 0 0 1 1 1 0 0		Rc

S	Source GPR rS
A	Target GPR rA where result of operation is stored
B	Source GPR rB
Rc	Record bit

andc   AND with Complement   andc
POWER • 601 • 603 • PowerPC32/64

Operation: $rA \Leftarrow (rS)\ \&\ {\sim}(rB)$

Syntax:

andc	rA,rS,rB	(Rc = 0)
andc.	rA,rS,rB	(Rc = 1)

Condition Register / Fixed-Point Exception Register:

CR Field 0:   LT,GT,EQ,SO updated if Rc = 1, otherwise not affected
CR Fields 1-7:   not affected

XER: not affected

Description:

The **andc** instruction logically ANDs the contents of GPR rS with the one's complement of the contents of GPR rB and places the result in GPR rA.

Instruction Encoding:

0 1 1 1 1 1	S	A	B	0 0 0 0 1 1 1 1 0 0	Rc

Positions: 0 ... 5 | 6 ... 10 | 11 ... 15 | 16 ... 20 | 21 ... 30 | 31

S	Source GPR rS
A	Target GPR rA where result of operation is stored
B	Source GPR rB
Rc	Record bit

andi.   AND Immediate   andi.

POWER • 601 • 603 • PowerPC32/64

Operation: $rA \Leftarrow (rS)$ & $°u16$

Syntax: **andi.** $rA, rS, u16$

Condition Register / Fixed-Point Exception Register:

CR Field 0:   LT,GT,EQ,SO always updated
CR Fields 1-7:   not affected

XER: not affected

Description:

The **andi.** instruction logically ANDs the contents of GPR rS and the value calculated by zero-extending $u16$ and places the result in GPR rA.

The archaic POWER mnemonic for this instruction is **andil.** (AND Immediate Lower).

Instruction Encoding:

0 5	6 10	11 15	16 31
0 1 1 1 0 0	S	A	UI

S   Source GPR rS
A   Target GPR rA where result of operation is stored
UI   Unsigned 16-bit integer

andis.   AND Immediate Shifted   andis.

POWER • 601 • 603 • PowerPC32/64

Operation: $rA \Leftarrow (rS) \mathrel{\&} {}^{\circ}(u16 \perp 0x0000)$

Syntax: **andis.**   rA,rS,u16

Condition Register/Fixed-Point Exception Register:

CR Field 0:   LT,GT,EQ,SO always updated
CR Fields 1-7:   not affected

XER: not affected

Description:

The **andis.** instruction logically ANDs the contents of GPR rS and the value calculated by concatenating *u16* with 0x0000, and places the result in GPR rA. On 64-bit PowerPC implementations, the calculated value is zero-extended to 64 bits before performing the AND operation.

The archaic POWER mnemonic for this instruction is **andiu.** (AND Immediate Upper).

Instruction Encoding:

0 5	6 10	11 15	16 31
0 1 1 1 0 1	S	A	UI

S   Source GPR rS
A   Target GPR rA where result of operation is stored
UI   Unsigned 16-bit integer

POWER • 601 • 603 • PowerPC32/64

Operation:

if (Lk = 1)

$\quad\quad$ LR ⟸ IP + 4

if (AA = 1)

$\quad\quad$ IP ⟸ `(LI ⊥ b00)

else

$\quad\quad$ IP ⟸ IP + `(LI ⊥ b00)

Syntax:

b	*address*	(AA = 0, Lk = 0)
ba	*address*	(AA = 1, Lk = 0)
bl	*address*	(AA = 0, Lk = 1)
bla	*address*	(AA = 1, Lk = 1)

Condition Register/Fixed-Point Exception Register:

CR Fields 0-7:$\quad$ not affected

XER:$\quad\quad\quad\quad$ not affected

Description:

The **b** instruction passes control to the instruction specified by the target *address*. The target address is calculated as follows:

• If the Absolute Address (AA) bit is set, then the target address is simply the contents of the 24-bit LI field concatenated with b00 and sign-extended to 32 bits.

• If the AA bit is clear, then the target address is the sum of the 24-bit LI field concatenated with b00 and sign-extended to 32 bits and the address of the branch instruction.

If the Lk bit is set, the address of the instruction following the branch instruction is saved in the Link Register (LR).

Instruction Encoding:

0 5	6 LI 29	30	31
0 1 0 0 1 0	LI	AA	Lk

LI	24-bit signed offset to (or absolute) target address
AA	Absolute Address bit
Lk	Link bit

bc

Branch Conditional

bc

POWER • 601 • 603 • PowerPC32/64

Operation: if(Lk = 1)
        $LR \Leftarrow IP + 4$
    if (condition is TRUE)
        if (AA = 1)
            $IP \Leftarrow \ `(BD \perp b00)$
        else
            $IP \Leftarrow IP + \ `(BD \perp b00)$

Syntax: **bc**   *BO,BI,address*   (AA = 0, Lk = 0)
           bca   *BO,BI,address*   (AA = 1, Lk = 0)
           bcl   *BO,BI,address*   (AA = 0, Lk = 1)
           bcla *BO,BI,address*   (AA = 1, Lk = 1)

Condition Register/Fixed-Point Exception Register:

CR Fields 0-7: not affected

XER: not affected

Description:

The **bc** instruction passes control to the instruction specified by the target *address* if the condition specified by *BO* and *BI* is true. The target address is calculated as follows:

- If the Absolute Address (AA) bit is set, then the target address is simply the contents of the 14-bit BD field concatenated with b00 and sign-extended to 32 bits.

- If the AA bit is clear, then the target address is the sum of the 14-bit BD field concatenated with b00 and sign-extended to 32 bits and the address of the branch instruction.

If the Link (Lk) bit is set, the address of the instruction following the branch instruction is saved in the Link Register (LR). This will occur even if the branch is not taken.

The Branch Option (*BO*) field of the instruction is used in conjunction with the specified Condition Register bit (*BI*) to determine if the branch should be taken. The *BO* field can be any one of the values listed in the table.

BO	Action
0000*y*	decrement CTR; branch if CTR $\neq$ 0 and CR[*BI*] = 0
0001*y*	decrement CTR; branch if CTR = 0 and CR[*BI*] = 0
001*xy*	branch if CR[*BI*] = 0
0100*y*	decrement CTR; branch if CTR $\neq$ 0 and CR[*BI*] = 1
0101*y*	decrement CTR; branch if CTR = 0 and CR[*BI*] = 1
011*xy*	branch if CR[*BI*] = 1
1*x*00*y*	decrement CTR; branch if CTR $\neq$ 0
1*x*01*y*	decrement CTR; branch if CTR = 0
1*x*1*xx*	branch always

In the table, the *x*'s denote bits that are ignored (but should remain 0 for future compatibility), and the *y*'s denote bits that are used to encode branch prediction information. For the **bc** instruction, this prediction information is:

• If *y* = 0, then forward branches are predicted not-taken and backward branches are predicted taken.

• If *y* = 1, then forward branches are predicted taken and backward branches are predicted not-taken.

Extended Forms:

There are a large number of extended forms for the **bc** instruction, all of which are summarized in the following list. In this list, *BIF* stands for the bit field of the CR that is used for the test. The *BIF* value must range between 0 and 7, inclusive. If the branch is dependent on CR field 0, then the *BIF* parameter may be omitted.

bdnz[l][a]	*addr*	is equivalent to	**bc[l][a]**	0x10,0,*addr*
bdnzf[l][a]	*BI,addr*	is equivalent to	**bc[l][a]**	0x00,*BI,addr*
bdnzt[l][a]	*BI,addr*	is equivalent to	**bc[l][a]**	0x08,*BI,addr*
bdz[l][a]	*addr*	is equivalent to	**bc[l][a]**	0x12,0,*addr*
bdzf[l][a]	*BI,addr*	is equivalent to	**bc[l][a]**	0x02,*BI,addr*
bdzt[l][a]	*BI,addr*	is equivalent to	**bc[l][a]**	0x0A,*BI,addr*
beq[l][a]	*[BIF,]addr*	is equivalent to	**bc[l][a]**	0x0C,*BIF**4+2,*addr*
bf[l][a]	*BI,addr*	is equivalent to	**bc[l][a]**	0x04,*BI,addr*
bge[l][a]	*[BIF,]addr*	is equivalent to	**bc[l][a]**	0x04,*BIF**4+0,*addr*
bgt[l][a]	*[BIF,]addr*	is equivalent to	**bc[l][a]**	0x0C,*BIF**4+1,*addr*
ble[l][a]	*[BIF,]addr*	is equivalent to	**bc[l][a]**	0x04,*BIF**4+1,*addr*
blt[l][a]	*[BIF,]addr*	is equivalent to	**bc[l][a]**	0x0C,*BIF**4+0,*addr*

bne[l][a]	*[BIF,]addr*	is equivalent to	**bc[l][a]**	0x04,*BIF**4+2,*addr*	
bng[l][a]	*[BIF,]addr*	is equivalent to	**bc[l][a]**	0x04,*BIF**4+1,*addr*	
bnl[l][a]	*[BIF,]addr*	is equivalent to	**bc[l][a]**	0x04,*BIF**4+0,*addr*	
bns[l][a]	*[BIF,]addr*	is equivalent to	**bc[l][a]**	0x04,*BIF**4+3,*addr*	
bnu[l][a]	*[BIF,]addr*	is equivalent to	**bc[l][a]**	0x04,*BIF**4+3,*addr*	
bso[l][a]	*[BIF,]addr*	is equivalent to	**bc[l][a]**	0x0C,*BIF**4+3,*addr*	
bt[l][a]	*BI,addr*	is equivalent to	**bc[l][a]**	0x0C,*BI,addr*	
bun[l][a]	*[BIF,]addr*	is equivalent to	**bc[l][a]**	0x0C,*BIF**4+3,*addr*	

Instruction Encoding:

0 5	6 10	11 15	16 29	30	31
0 1 0 0 0 0	BO	BI	BD	A A	Lk

BO	Branch Option
BI	Bit number (0-31) of CR to check
BD	14-bit signed offset to (or absolute) target address
AA	Absolute Address bit
Lk	Link bit

bcctr   Branch Conditional to CTR   bcctr

POWER • 601 • 603 • PowerPC32/64

Operation: if (Lk=1)
       LR $\Leftarrow$ IP + 4
    if (condition is TRUE)
       IP $\Leftarrow$ CTR[0:29] $\perp$ b00

Syntax: **bcctr**   *BO,BI*   (Lk = 0)
            bcctrl   *BO,BI*   (Lk = 1)

Condition Register/Fixed-Point Exception Register:
CR Fields 0-7:   not affected

XER: not affected

Description:
The **bcctr** instruction passes control to the instruction at the address specified in the Count Register (CTR) if the condition specified by *BO* and *BI* is true.

The target address is calculated by concatenating the upper 30 bits of the CTR with b00. This insures that the IP contains a valid word-aligned address.

If the Link (Lk) bit is set, the address of the instruction following the branch instruction is saved in the Link Register (LR).

The archaic POWER mnemonic for this instruction is **bcc[l]**.

The Branch Option (*BO*) field of the instruction is used in conjunction with the specified Condition Register bit (*BI*) to determine if the branch should be taken. The *BO* field can be any one of the following values (although the Branch Options involving decrementing the CTR do not produce sensible instructions):

BO	Action
0000*y*	decrement CTR; branch if CTR $\neq$ 0 and CR[*BI*] = 0
0001*y*	decrement CTR; branch if CTR = 0 and CR[*BI*] = 0
001*xy*	branch if CR[*BI*] = 0
0100*y*	decrement CTR; branch if CTR $\neq$ 0 and CR[*BI*] = 1
0101*y*	decrement CTR; branch if CTR = 0 and CR[*BI*] = 1
011*xy*	branch if CR[*BI*] = 1
1*x*00*y*	decrement CTR; branch if CTR $\neq$ 0
1*x*01*y*	decrement CTR; branch if CTR = 0
1*x*1*xx*	branch always

In the table, the x's denote bits that are ignored (but should remain 0 for future compatibility), and the y's denote bits that are used to encode branch prediction information. For the **bcctr** instruction, this prediction is:

- If $y = 0$, the branch is predicted not-taken.

- If $y = 1$, the branch is predicted taken.

Extended Forms:

There are a large number of extended forms for the **bcctr** instruction, all of which are summarized in the following list. In this list, *BIF* stands for the bit field of the CR that is used for the test. The *BIF* value must range between 0 and 7, inclusive. If the branch is dependent on CR field 0, then the *BIF* parameter may be omitted.

bctr[l]		is equivalent to	**bcctr[l]**	0x14,0
beqctr[l]	[*BIF*]	is equivalent to	**bcctr[l]**	0x0C,*BIF**4+2
bfctr[l]	*BI*	is equivalent to	**bcctr[l]**	0x04,*BI*
bgectr[l]	[*BIF*]	is equivalent to	**bcctr[l]**	0x04,*BIF**4+0
bgtctr[l]	[*BIF*]	is equivalent to	**bcctr[l]**	0x0C,*BIF**4+1
blectr[l]	[*BIF*]	is equivalent to	**bcctr[l]**	0x04,*BIF**4+1
bltctr[l]	[*BIF*]	is equivalent to	**bcctr[l]**	0x0C,*BIF**4+0
bnectr[l]	[*BIF*]	is equivalent to	**bcctr[l]**	0x04,*BIF**4+2
bngctr[l]	[*BIF*]	is equivalent to	**bcctr[l]**	0x04,*BIF**4+1
bnlctr[l]	[*BIF*]	is equivalent to	**bcctr[l]**	0x04,*BIF**4+0
bnsctr[l]	[*BIF*]	is equivalent to	**bcctr[l]**	0x04,*BIF**4+3
bnuctr[l]	[*BIF*]	is equivalent to	**bcctr[l]**	0x04,*BIF**4+3
bsoctr[l]	[*BIF*]	is equivalent to	**bcctr[l]**	0x0C,*BIF**4+3
btctr[l]	*BI*	is equivalent to	**bcctr[l]**	0x0C,*BI*
bunctr[l]	[*BIF*]	is equivalent to	**bcctr[l]**	0x0C,*BIF**4+3

Instruction Encoding:

0				5	6				10	11				15	16					20	21									30	31
0	1	0	0	1	1		BO					BI			0	0	0	0	0	1	0	0	0	0	1	0	0	0	0	Lk

BO   Branch Option
BI   Bit number (0-31) of CR to check
Lk   Link bit

bclr   Branch Conditional to LR   bclr

Operation: $oldLR := LR$
                   if (Lk=1)
                       $LR \Leftarrow IP + 4$
                   if (condition is TRUE)
                       $IP \Leftarrow oldLR[0:29] \perp b00$

Syntax: **bclr**   *BO,BI*   (Lk = 0)
                bclrl   *BO,BI*   (Lk = 1)

Condition Register/Fixed-Point Exception Register:

CR Fields 0-7:   not affected

XER: not affected

Description:

The **bclr** instruction passes control to the instruction at the address specified in the Link Register (LR) if the condition specified by *BO* and *BI* is true.

The target address is calculated by concatenating the upper 30 bits of the LR with b00. This insures that the IP contains a valid word-aligned address.

If the Link (Lk) bit is set, the address of the instruction following the branch instruction is saved in the Link Register (LR).

The archaic POWER mnemonic for this instruction is **bcr[l]**.

The Branch Option (*BO*) field of the instruction is used in conjunction with the specified Condition Register bit (*BI*) to determine if the branch should be taken. The *BO* field can be any one of the values listed in the next table.

BO	Action
0000*y*	decrement CTR; branch if CTR ≠ 0 and CR[*BI*] = 0
0001*y*	decrement CTR; branch if CTR = 0 and CR[*BI*] = 0
001*xy*	branch if CR[*BI*] = 0
0100*y*	decrement CTR; branch if CTR ≠ 0 and CR[*BI*] = 1
0101*y*	decrement CTR; branch if CTR = 0 and CR[*BI*] = 1
011*xy*	branch if CR[*BI*] = 1
1*x*00*y*	decrement CTR; branch if CTR ≠ 0
1*x*01*y*	decrement CTR; branch if CTR = 0
1*x*1*xx*	branch always

In the table, the x's denote bits that are ignored (but should remain 0 for future compatibility), and the y's denote bits that are used to encode branch prediction information. For the **bclr** instruction, this prediction is:

- If $y = 0$, the branch is predicted not-taken.

- If $y = 1$, the branch is predicted taken.

Extended Forms:

There are a large number of extended forms for the **bclr** instruction, all of which are summarized in the following list. In this list, *BIF* stands for the bit field of the CR that is used for the test. The *BIF* value must range between 0 and 7, inclusive. If the branch is dependent on CR field 0, then the *BIF* parameter may be omitted.

blr[l]		is equivalent to	**bclr[l]**	0x14,0
bdnzflr[l]	*BI*	is equivalent to	**bclr[l]**	0x00,*BI*
bdnzlr[l]		is equivalent to	**bclr[l]**	0x10,0
bdnztlr[l]	*BI*	is equivalent to	**bclr[l]**	0x08,*BI*
bdzflr[l]	*BI*	is equivalent to	**bclr[l]**	0x02,*BI*
bdzlr[l]		is equivalent to	**bclr[l]**	0x12,0
bdztlr[l]	*BI*	is equivalent to	**bclr[l]**	0x0A,*BI*
beqlr[l]	[*BIF*]	is equivalent to	**bclr[l]**	0x0C,*BIF**4+2
bflr[l]	*BI*	is equivalent to	**bclr[l]**	0x04,*BI*
bgelr[l]	[*BIF*]	is equivalent to	**bclr[l]**	0x04,*BIF**4+0
bgtlr[l]	[*BIF*]	is equivalent to	**bclr[l]**	0x0C,*BIF**4+1
blelr[l]	[*BIF*]	is equivalent to	**bclr[l]**	0x04,*BIF**4+1
bltlr[l]	[*BIF*]	is equivalent to	**bclr[l]**	0x0C,*BIF**4+0
bnelr[l]	[*BIF*]	is equivalent to	**bclr[l]**	0x04,*BIF**4+2
bnglr[l]	[*BIF*]	is equivalent to	**bclr[l]**	0x04,*BIF**4+1
bnllr[l]	[*BIF*]	is equivalent to	**bclr[l]**	0x04,*BIF**4+0
bnslr[l]	[*BIF*]	is equivalent to	**bclr[l]**	0x04,*BIF**4+3
bnulr[l]	[*BIF*]	is equivalent to	**bclr[l]**	0x04,*BIF**4+3
bsolr[l]	[*BIF*]	is equivalent to	**bclr[l]**	0x0C,*BIF**4+3
btlr[l]	*BI*	is equivalent to	**bclr[l]**	0x0C,*BI*
bunlr[l]	[*BIF*]	is equivalent to	**bclr[l]**	0x0C,*BIF**4+3

Instruction Encoding:

0 1 0 0 1 1	BO	BI	0 0 0 0 0	0 0 0 0 0 1 0 0 0 0	Lk
0 5	6 10	11 15	16 20	21 30	31

BO	Branch Option
BI	Bit number (0-31) of CR to check
Lk	Link bit

Cache Line Compute Size

POWER • 601

Operation: $rT \Leftarrow$ *cache line specified by* rA

Syntax: **clcs**   rT,rA

Condition Register/Fixed-Point Exception Register:

CR Field 0:   undefined if Rc = 1
CR Fields 1-7:   not affected

XER: not affected

Description:

The **clcs** instruction places the cache line size specified by GPR rA into GPR rT. Valid values for rA are listed in the table.

(rA)	Line Size
00xxx	Undefined
010xx	Undefined
01100	Instruction Cache Line Size
01101	Data Cache Line Size
01110	Minimum Line Size
01111	Maximum Line Size
1xxxx	Undefined

The value returned in rT must be between 64 and 4096 (inclusive). The 601 returns 64 as the line size for all valid values of rA.

This instruction is not part of the PowerPC architecture.

Instruction Encoding:

0 5	6 10	11 15	16 20	21 30	31
0 1 1 1 1 1	T	A	0 0 0 0 0	1 0 0 0 0 1 0 0 1 1	Rc

T   Target GPR rT where result of operation is stored
A   GPR rA which contains cache line code
Rc   Record bit

cmp

Compare

cmp

POWER • 601 • 603 • PowerPC32/64

Operation: $CR\{crT\} \Leftarrow$ Signed Compare(rA,rB)

Syntax: **cmp** crT,L,rA,rB

Condition Register/Fixed-Point Exception Register:

CR Field T: LT,GT,EQ,SO always updated
other fields: not affected

XER: not affected

Description:

The **cmp** instruction compares the contents of the two source registers rA and rB and stores the result of the compare in field crT of the Condition Register. The contents of the source registers are interpreted as containing signed values for purposes of the compare.

On 32-bit PowerPC implementations, the L operand must be 0 or else the instruction form is invalid. The 601 ignores the value of L and always operates as if it were 0.

On 64-bit PowerPC implementations, the L operand is used to select a 32-bit or a 64-bit compare. If L is 1, then all 64 bits of the source registers are used for the compare; if L is 0, then only the low-order 32-bits from each register (sign-extended to 64 bits) are used.

Extended Forms:

cmpd	crT,rA,rB	is equivalent to	**cmp**	crT,1,rA,rB
cmpw	crT,rA,rB	is equivalent to	**cmp**	crT,0,rA,rB

Instruction Encoding:

0 5	6 8	9	10	11 15	16 20	21 30	31
0 1 1 1 1 1	T	0	L	A	B	0 0 0 0 0 0 0 0 0 0	0

T   Bit field of CR where result of compare is stored
L   Selector to determine 32/64-bit operands
A   Source GPR rA
B   Source GPR rB

cmpi   Compare Immediate   cmpi

POWER • 601 • 603 • PowerPC32/64

Operation: CR{crT} ⇐ Signed Compare(rA,s16)

Syntax: **cmpi**   crT,L,rA,s16

Condition Register/Fixed-Point Exception Register:

CR Field T: LT,GT,EQ,SO always updated
other fields: not affected

XER: not affected

Description:

The **cmpi** instruction compares the contents of the source register rA and the sign-extended immediate value s16 and stores the result of the compare in field crT of the Condition Register. The contents of the source register are interpreted as containing a signed value for purposes of the compare.

On 32-bit PowerPC implementations, the L operand must be 0 or else the instruction form is invalid. The 601 ignores the value of L and always operates as if it were 0.

On 64-bit PowerPC implementations, the L operand is used to select a 32-bit or a 64-bit compare. If L is 1, then all 64 bits of the source register are compared with the immediate value sign-extended to 64 bits; if L is 0, then the low-order 32-bits of the source register are compared with the immediate value sign-extended to 32 bits.

Extended Forms:

cmpdi	crT,rA,s16	is equivalent to	**cmpi**	crT,1,rA,s16
cmpwi	crT,rA,s16	is equivalent to	**cmpi**	crT,0,rA,s16

Instruction Encoding:

0 5	6 8	9	10	11 15	16 31
0 0 1 0 1 1	T	0	L	A	SI

T   Bit field of CR where result of compare is stored
L   Selector to determine 32/64-bit operands
A   Source GPR rA
SI   Signed 16-bit integer

cmpl   Compare Logical   cmpl

POWER • 601 • 603 • PowerPC32/64

Operation: $CR\{crT\} \Leftarrow$ Unsigned Compare(rA,rB)

Syntax: **cmpl** crT,L,rA,rB

Condition Register/Fixed-Point Exception Register:

CR Field T: LT,GT,EQ,SO always updated
other fields: not affected

XER: not affected

Description:

The **cmpl** instruction compares the contents of the two source registers rA and rB and stores the result of the compare in field crT of the Condition Register. The contents of the source registers are interpreted as containing unsigned values for purposes of the compare.

On 32-bit PowerPC implementations, the L operand must be 0 or else the instruction form is invalid. The 601 ignores the value of L and always operates as if it were 0.

On 64-bit PowerPC implementations, the L operand is used to select a 32-bit or a 64-bit compare. If L is 1, then all 64 bits of the source registers are used for the compare; if L is 0, then only the low-order 32-bits from each register (sign-extended to 64 bits) are used.

Extended Forms:

cmpld	crT,rA,rB	is equivalent to	**cmpl**	$crT,1,rA,rB$
cmplw	crT,rA,rB	is equivalent to	**cmpl**	$crT,0,rA,rB$

Instruction Encoding:

0 1 1 1 1 1	T	0	L	A	B	0 0 0 0 1 0 0 0 0 0	0

Bit positions: 0 ... 5 6 ... 8 9 10 11 ... 15 16 ... 20 21 ... 30 31

T   Bit field of CR where result of compare is stored
L   Selector to determine 32/64-bit operands
A   Source GPR rA
B   Source GPR rB

cmpli   Compare Logical Immediate   cmpli

POWER • 601 • 603 • PowerPC32/64

Operation: $CR\{crT\} \Leftarrow$ Unsigned Compare($rA,u16$)

Syntax: **cmpli** $crT,L,rA,u16$

Condition Register/Fixed-Point Exception Register:

CR Field T: LT,GT,EQ,SO always updated
other fields: not affected

XER: not affected

Description:

The **cmpli** instruction compares the contents of the source register rA and the zero-extended immediate value $u16$ and stores the result of the compare in field crT of the Condition Register. The contents of the source register are interpreted as containing an unsigned value for purposes of the compare.

On 32-bit PowerPC implementations, the L operand must be 0 or else the instruction form is invalid. The 601 ignores the value of L and always operates as if it were 0.

On 64-bit PowerPC implementations, the L operand is used to select a 32-bit or a 64-bit compare. If L is 1, then all 64 bits of the source register are compared with the immediate value zero-extended to 64 bits; if L is 0, then the low-order 32 bits of the source register are compared with the immediate value zero-extended to 32 bits.

Extended Forms:

cmpldi	$crT,rA,u16$	is equivalent to	**cmpli**	$crT,1,rA,u16$
cmplwi	$crT,rA,u16$	is equivalent to	**cmpli**	$crT,0,rA,u16$

Instruction Encoding:

```
0         5 6    8 9 10 11      15 16                          31
 0 0 1 0 1 0   T   0 L     A                  UI
```

T   Bit field of CR where result of compare is stored
L   Selector to determine 32/64-bit operands
A   Source GPR rA
UI   Unsigned 16-bit integer

cntlzd Count Leading Zeros Doubleword cntlzd

PowerPC64

Operation: $numZeros := 0$
while ($numZeros < 64$ && $rS[numZeros] = 0$)
$\qquad numZeros := numZeros + 1$
$rA \Leftarrow numZeros$

Syntax:

cntlzd	rA,rS	(Rc = 0)
cntlzd.	rA,rS	(Rc = 1)

Condition Register / Fixed-Point Exception Register:

CR Field 0:   LT,GT,EQ,SO updated if Rc = 1, otherwise not affected
CR Fields 1-7: not affected

XER: not affected

Description:

The **cntlzd** instruction examines the contents of the source register rS and counts the number of zero bits contiguous with the left side of the register. This value is then stored in rA.

All 64 bits of the source register are used for this computation. The returned value ranges from 0 to 64. A return value between 0 and 63 indicates the bit number of the left-most '1' bit in the source register. A return value of 64 indicates that all of the bits of the source register are 0.

This instruction exists on 64-bit PowerPC implementations only.

Instruction Encoding:

0				5	6			10	11			15	16				20	21									30	31
0	1	1	1	1	1		S				A		0	0	0	0	0	0	0	0	0	1	1	1	0	1	0	Rc

A   Target GPR rA where result of operation is stored
S   Source GPR rS

cntlzw   Count Leading Zeros Word   cntlzw

POWER • 601 • 603 • PowerPC32/64

Operation: $numZeros := 0$
while ($numZeros < 32$ && $rS[numZeros] = 0$)
          $numZeros := numZeros + 1$
$rA \Leftarrow numZeros$

Syntax: **cntlzw** rA,rS (Rc = 0)
          cntlzw. rA,rS (Rc = 1)

Condition Register/Fixed-Point Exception Register:

CR Field 0:   LT,GT,EQ,SO updated if Rc = 1, otherwise not affected
CR Fields 1-7:   not affected

XER: not affected

Description:

The **cntlzw** instruction examines the contents of the source register rS and counts the number of zero bits contiguous with the left side of the register. This value is then stored in rA.

On 32-bit PowerPC implementations, all 32 bits of the source register are used for this computation. The returned value ranges from 0 to 32. A return value between 0 and 31 indicates the bit number of the left-most "1" bit in the source register. A return value of 32 indicates that all of the bits of the source register are 0.

On 64-bit PowerPC implementations, only the low-order 32 bits of the source register are used for this computation. The returned value ranges from 0 to 32. A return value between 0 and 31 indicates the bit number of the left-most '1' bit in the low-order word of the source register. A return value of 32 indicates that the low-order 32 bits of the source are all 0.

The archaic POWER mnemonic for this instruction is **cntlz[.]**.

Instruction Encoding:

0	5 6	10 11	15 16	20 21	30 31
0 1 1 1 1 1	S	A	0 0 0 0 0	0 0 0 0 1 1 0 1 0	Rc

          A   Target GPR rA where result of operation is stored
          S   Source GPR rS

crand

Condition Register AND

crand

POWER • 601 • 603 • PowerPC32/64

Operation: $CR[bitT] \Leftarrow CR[bitA] \ \& \ CR[bitB]$

Syntax: **crand** $bitT, bitA, bitB$

Condition Register/Fixed-Point Exception Register:

CR bit T:	set equal to $CR[bitA] \ \& \ CR[bitB]$
other bits:	not affected
XER:	not affected

Description:

The **crand** instruction ANDs bit $bitA$ of the Condition Register with bit $bitB$ of the Condition Register and stores the result of the operation in bit $bitT$ of the Condition Register.

Instruction Encoding:

0 5	6 10	11 15	16 20	21 30	31
0 1 0 0 1 1	T	A	B	0 1 0 0 0 0 0 0 1 0	0

T	Bit of CR where result of operation is stored
A	Source bit A of CR
B	Source bit B of CR

crandc   Condition Register AND   **crandc**
with Complement
POWER • 601 • 603 • PowerPC32/64

Operation: $CR[bitT] \Leftarrow CR[bitA] \;\&\; {\sim}CR[bitB]$

Syntax: **crandc**   *bitT,bitA,bitB*

Condition Register/Fixed-Point Exception Register:

CR bit T:	set equal to $CR[bitA] \;\&\; {\sim}CR[bitB]$
other bits:	not affected
XER:	not affected

Description:

The **crandc** instruction ANDs bit *bitA* of the Condition Register with the complement of bit *bitB* of the Condition Register and stores the result of the operation in bit *bitT* of the Condition Register.

Instruction Encoding:

0 1 0 0 1 1	T	A	B	0 0 1 0 0 0 0 0 0 1	0

0   5   6   10   11   15   16   20   21   30   31

T	Bit of CR where result of operation is stored
A	Source bit A of CR
B	Source bit B of CR

creqv   Condition Register Equivalent   **creqv**

POWER • 601 • 603 • PowerPC32/64

Operation: $CR[bitT] \Leftarrow CR[bitA] \equiv CR[bitB]$

Syntax: **creqv**   *bitT,bitA,bitB*

Condition Register/Fixed-Point Exception Register:

CR bit T: set equal to $CR[bitA] \equiv CR[bitB]$
other bits: not affected

XER: not affected

Description:

The **creqv** instruction calculates the equivalence bit *bitA* of the Condition Register and bit *bitB* of the Condition Register and stores the result of the operation in bit *bitT* of the Condition Register. The equivalence operation returns 1 if the two source bits are equal and 0 if they are not equal.

Extended Forms:

crset   *bit*   is equivalent to   **creqv**   *bit,bit,bit*

Instruction Encoding:

0					5	6				10	11				15	16				20	21									30	31
0	1	0	0	1	1		T					A					B				0	1	0	0	1	0	0	0	0	1	0

T   Bit of CR where result of operation is stored
A   Source bit A of CR
B   Source bit B of CR

crnand   Condition Register NAND   crnand

POWER • 601 • 603 • PowerPC32/64

Operation: $CR[bitT] \Leftarrow \sim(CR[bitA] \text{ \& } CR[bitB])$

Syntax: **crnand**   *bitT,bitA,bitB*

Condition Register/Fixed-Point Exception Register:

CR bit T: set equal to $\sim(CR[bitA] \text{ \& } CR[bitB])$
other bits: not affected

XER: not affected

Description:

The **crnand** instruction ANDs bit *bitA* of the Condition Register with bit *bitB* of the Condition Register and stores the complement of the result of the operation in bit *bitT* of the Condition Register.

Instruction Encoding:

0	5	6	10	11	15	16	20	21	30	31
0 1 0 0 1 1		T		A		B		0 0 1 1 0 0 0 0 1 0		0

T   Bit of CR where result of operation is stored
A   Source bit A of CR
B   Source bit B of CR

crnor   Condition Register NOR   crnor

POWER • 601 • 603 • PowerPC32/64

Operation: $CR[bitT] \Leftarrow \sim(CR[bitA] \mid CR[bitB])$

Syntax: **crnor** $bitT,bitA,bitB$

Condition Register/Fixed-Point Exception Register:

CR bit T: set equal to $\sim(CR[bitA] \mid CR[bitB])$
other bits: not affected

XER: not affected

Description:

The **crnor** instruction ORs bit $bitA$ of the Condition Register with bit $bitB$ of the Condition Register and stores the complement of the result of the operation in bit $bitT$ of the Condition Register.

Extended Forms:

crnot $bitT,bitA$ is equivalent to   **crnor** $bitT,bitA,bitA$

Instruction Encoding:

0					5	6				10	11				15	16				20	21									30	31
0	1	0	0	1	1			T					A					B			0	0	0	0	1	0	0	0	0	1	0

T   Bit of CR where result of operation is stored
A   Source bit A of CR
B   Source bit B of CR

cror   Condition Register OR   cror

POWER • 601 • 603 • PowerPC32/64

Operation: $CR[bitT] \Leftarrow CR[bitA] \mid CR[bitB]$

Syntax: **cror** $bitT,bitA,bitB$

Condition Register/Fixed-Point Exception Register:

CR bit T: set equal to $CR[bitA] \mid CR[bitB]$
other bits: not affected

XER: not affected

Description:

The **cror** instruction ORs bit $bitA$ of the Condition Register with bit $bitB$ of the Condition Register and stores the result of the operation in bit $bitT$ of the Condition Register.

Extended Forms:

crmove $bitT,bitA$ is equivalent to   **cror** $bitT,bitA,bitA$

Instruction Encoding:

0					5	6			10	11			15	16		20	21									30	31
0	1	0	0	1	1		T				A				B		0	1	1	1	0	0	0	0	1	0

    T   Bit of CR where result of operation is stored
    A   Source bit A of CR
    B   Source bit B of CR

crorc Condition Register OR crorc
with Complement
POWER • 601 • 603 • PowerPC32/64

Operation: $CR[bitT] \Leftarrow CR[bitA] \mid {\sim}CR[bitB]$

Syntax: **crorc** $bitT,bitA,bitB$

Condition Register/Fixed-Point Exception Register:
CR bit T: set equal to $CR[bitA] \mid {\sim}CR[bitB]$
other bits: not affected

XER: not affected

Description:
The **crorc** instruction ORs bit *bitA* of the Condition Register with the complement of bit *bitB* of the Condition Register and stores the result of the operation in bit *bitT* of the Condition Register.

Instruction Encoding:

0 5	6 10	11 15	16 20	21 30	31
0 1 0 0 1 1	T	A	B	0 1 1 0 1 0 0 0 0 1	0

T   Bit of CR where result of operation is stored
A   Source bit A of CR
B   Source bit B of CR

crxor   Condition Register XOR   crxor

POWER • 601 • 603 • PowerPC32/64

Operation: $CR[bitT] \Leftarrow CR[bitA] \oplus CR[bitB]$

Syntax: **crxor** $bitT,bitA,bitB$

Condition Register/Fixed-Point Exception Register:

CR bit T: set equal to $CR[bitA] \oplus CR[bitB]$
other bits: not affected

XER: not affected

Description:

The **crxor** instruction XORs bit $bitA$ of the Condition Register with bit $bitB$ of the Condition Register and stores the result of the operation in bit $bitT$ of the Condition Register.

Extended Forms:

crclr bit is equivalent to   **crxor** bit,bit,bit

Instruction Encoding:

0					5	6				10	11				15	16				20	21									30	31
0	1	0	0	1	1			T					A					B			0	0	1	1	0	0	0	0	1	0

T   Bit of CR where result of operation is stored
A   Source bit A of CR
B   Source bit B of CR

dcbf   Data Cache Block Flush   dcbf

601 • 603 • PowerPC32/64

Operation: *flush the specified block to storage*

Syntax: **dcbf**   r*A*,r*B*

Condition Register/Fixed-Point Exception Register:

CR Fields 0-7:   not affected

XER: not affected

Description:

The **dcbf** instruction flushes the data cache block specified by the given effective address (calculated from (r*A*|0) + (r*B*)) out to main storage. The details of the operation depend on the storage mode associated with the effective address and on the state of the block.

On PowerPC implementations with unified caches (like the 601), this instruction flushes the unified cache.

When the storage mode requires coherency (WIM = xx1), the instruction is implemented as follows:

- *Unmodified block*—All copies of this block are invalidated in the caches of all processors.
- *Modified block*—The block is copied out to storage and all copies of this block in the caches of other processors are invalidated.
- *Absent block*—Force all copies of this block to be invalidated in the caches of all other processors. If any of these are modified copies, then force them to be written to storage before invalidating them.

When coherency is not required (WIM = xx0), **dcbf** acts as follows:

- *Unmodified block*—The block is invalidated.
- *Modified block*—The block is copied out to storage and invalidated.
- *Absent block*—No action is required.

This instruction is treated as a load from the effective address for purposes of address translation and protection.

If the calculated effective address specifies an address belonging to a direct-store segment, then this instruction will operate as a no-op.

Instruction Encoding:

0					5	6				10	11			15	16			20	21										30	31
0	1	1	1	1	1	0	0	0	0	0		A				B			0	0	0	1	0	1	0	1	1	0	0	0

A   Source GPR rA
B   Source GPR rB

dcbi   Data Cache Block Invalidate   dcbi

601 • 603 • PowerPC32/64 • Privileged

Operation: *invalidate the specified block*

Syntax: **dcbi**   r*A*,r*B*

Condition Register/Fixed-Point Exception Register:

CR Fields 0-7:   not affected

XER: not affected

Description:

The **dcbi** instruction invalidates the data cache block specified by the given effective address (calculated from (r*A*|0) + (r*B*)). The details of the operation depend on the storage mode associated with the effective address and on the state of the block.

When the storage mode requires coherency (WIM = xx1), the instruction is implemented as follows:

- *Unmodified block*—All copies of this block are invalidated in the caches of all processors.
- *Modified block*—All copies of this block are invalidated in the caches of all processors. The modifications are discarded.
- *Absent block*—All copies of this block are invalidated in the caches of all other processors. Any modifications are discarded.

When coherency is not required (WIM = xx0), **dcbi** acts as follows:

- *Unmodified block*—The block is invalidated.
- *Modified block*—The block is invalidated. The modications are discarded.
- *Absent block*—No action is required.

This instruction is treated as a store from the effective address for purposes of address translation and protection.

If the calculated effective address specifies an address belonging to a direct-store segment, then this instruction will operate as a no-op.

Instruction Encoding:

0					5	6				10	11		15	16		20	21									30	31
0	1	1	1	1	1	0	0	0	0	0	A			B			0	1	1	1	0	1	0	1	1	0	0	0

A   Source GPR rA
B   Source GPR rB

dcbst   Data Cache Block Store   dcbst

601 • 603 • PowerPC32/64

Operation: *write the specified block to storage*

Syntax: **dcbst**   r*A*,r*B*

Condition Register / Fixed-Point Exception Register:

CR Fields 0-7:   not affected

XER: not affected

Description:

The **dcbst** instruction writes the data cache block specified by the given effective address (calculated from (r*A*|0) + (r*B*)) out to main storage. The details of the operation depend on the storage mode associated with the effective address and on the state of the block.

When the storage mode requires coherency (WIM = xx1), the instruction causes the block to be written if any processor has a modified copy of the block.

When coherency is not required (WIM = xx0), **dcbst** causes the block to be written if the local processor has a modified copy of the block.

If the block has not been modified, then the block is not written.

This instruction is treated as a load from the effective address for purposes of address translation and protection.

If the calculated effective address specifies an address belonging to a direct-store segment, then this instruction will operate as a no-op.

Instruction Encoding:

0					5	6					10	11				15	16				20	21										30	31
0	1	1	1	1	1	0	0	0	0	0		A					B					0	0	0	0	1	1	0	1	1	0	0	0

A   Source GPR rA
B   Source GPR rB

dcbt   Data Cache Block Touch   dcbt

601 • 603 • PowerPC32/64

Operation: *give hint that the address may soon be loaded from*

Syntax: **dcbt**   r*A*,r*B*

Condition Register/Fixed-Point Exception Register:
CR Fields 0-7:   not affected

XER: not affected

Description:

The **dcbt** instruction tells the processor that the effective address (calculated from (r*A* | 0) + (r*B*)) will be loaded from in the near future. The processor can use this hint and attempt to improve performance by preloading the block that contains that address into the data cache. However, the processor is not required to load the addressed block.

This instruction is treated as a load from the effective address for purposes of address translation and protection. The system error handler is never invoked by this instruction.

If the calculated effective address specifies an address belonging to a direct-store segment, then this instruction will operate as a no-op.

Instruction Encoding:

0					5	6					10	11				15	16				20	21									30	31
0	1	1	1	1	1	0	0	0	0	0		A					B					0	1	0	0	0	1	0	1	1	0	0

A   Source GPR rA
B   Source GPR rB

dcbtst Data Cache Block Touch for Store dcbtst

601 • 603 • PowerPC32/64

Operation: *give hint that the address may soon be stored to*

Syntax: **dcbtst** rA,rB

Condition Register/Fixed-Point Exception Register:

CR Fields 0-7: not affected

XER: not affected

Description:

The **dcbtst** instruction tells the processor that the effective address (calculated from (rA | 0) + (rB)) will be stored to in the near future. The processor can use this hint and attempt to improve performance by preloading the block that contains that address into the data cache. However, the processor is not required to load the addressed block.

This instruction is treated as a load from the effective address for purposes of address translation and protection. The system error handler is never invoked by this instruction. Note that this instruction cannot be treated as a store since it does not modify storage.

If the calculated effective address specifies an address belonging to a direct-store segment, then this instruction will operate as a no-op.

Instruction Encoding:

0					5	6					10	11				15	16				20	21									30	31
0	1	1	1	1	1	0	0	0	0	0		A					B					0	0	1	1	1	1	0	1	1	0	0

A	Source GPR rA
B	Source GPR rB

dcbz   Data Cache Block Zero   dcbz

POWER • 601 • 603 • PowerPC32/64

Operation: *set the cache block to contain all zeros*

Syntax: **dcbz**   r*A*,r*B*

Condition Register/Fixed-Point Exception Register:

CR Fields 0-7:   not affected

XER: not affected

Description:

The **dcbz** instruction clears the contents of the data cache block specified by the given effective address (calculated from (rA|0) + (rB)). Any existing modifications to the block are discarded.

If the block is not currently loaded in the cache (and the block is cacheable), then a block of all zeros is established in the cache for this block (the previous block data is not fetched from memory).

If the block is not allowed to be cached (Caching Inhibited) or if stores to this block must be write-through (Write Through Required), then a block of zeros is written out to storage. This operation may be handled by the system alignment interrupt handler.

If the block is in Coherency Required mode and the block exists in the caches of other processors, then the block is kept coherent in those caches.

This instruction is treated as a store from the effective address for purposes of address translation and protection.

If the calculated effective address specifies an address belonging to a direct-store segment, then this instruction will operate as a no-op.

The archaic POWER mnemonic for this instruction is **dclz**.

Instruction Encoding:

0 5	6 10	11 A 15	16 B 20	21 30	31
0 1 1 1 1 1	0 0 0 0 0	A	B	1 1 1 1 1 1 0 1 1 0	0

    A   Source GPR rA
    B   Source GPR rB

POWER • 601

Operation: $rT \Leftarrow ((rA) \perp (MQ)) \div (rB)$

                $MQ \Leftarrow ((rA) \perp (MQ)) \% (rB)$

Syntax:

div	rT,rA,rB	(Rc = 0, OE = 0)
div.	rT,rA,rB	(Rc = 1, OE = 0)
divo	rT,rA,rB	(Rc = 0, OE = 1)
divo.	rT,rA,rB	(Rc = 1, OE = 1)

Condition Register / Fixed-Point Exception Register:

CR Field 0:   LT,GT,EQ,SO updated if Rc = 1, otherwise not affected
CR Fields 1-7:   not affected

XER[CA]:   not affected
XER[OV,SO]:   updated if OE=1, otherwise not affected

Description:

The **div** instruction concatenates the contents of GPR rA and the MQ register and divides that quantity by the contents of GPR rB. The quotient from this operation is placed in GPR rT, and the remainder is placed in the MQ register. All source registers are assumed to contain signed values.

The instruction results will always satisfy the equality:

$$dividend = (divisor \cdot quotient) + remainder$$

where the *dividend* is $(rA) \perp (MQ)$ and the *divisor* is (rB). The remainder is always less than the absolute value of the divisor and has the same sign as the dividend (except that a 0 quotient or remainder will always be positive).

An overflow occurs when the quotient cannot be represented in 32 bits. If the quantity -2^{31} is divided by -1, then the MQ register is cleared and GPR rT is set to -2^{31}. For overflows other than this case, MQ, rT, and CR{0} (if Rc=1) are undefined. If the Record bit is set, then the LT, GT, and EQ bits of CR{0} are updated to reflect the remainder (stored in MQ).

This instruction is not part of the PowerPC architecture.

Instruction Encoding:

0	5 6	10 11	15 16	20 21 22	30 31
0 1 1 1 1 1	T	A	B	OE 1 0 1 0 0 1 0 1 1	Rc

T	Target GPR rT where result of operation is stored
A	Source GPR rA
B	Source GPR rB
OE	Overflow Exception bit
Rc	Record bit

divd   Divide Doubleword   divd

PowerPC64

Operation: $rT \Leftarrow (rA) \div (rB)$

Syntax:

divd	rT,rA,rB	(Rc = 0, OE = 0)
divd.	rT,rA,rB	(Rc = 1, OE = 0)
divdo	rT,rA,rB	(Rc = 0, OE = 1)
divdo.	rT,rA,rB	(Rc = 1, OE = 1)

Condition Register / Fixed-Point Exception Register:

CR Field 0:   LT,GT,EQ,SO updated if Rc = 1, otherwise not affected
CR Fields 1-7:   not affected

XER[CA]:   not affected
XER[OV,SO]:   updated if OE=1, otherwise not affected

Description:

The **divd** instruction divides the contents of GPR rA by the contents of GPR rB and places the quotient from this operation in GPR rT. The source registers are assumed to contain signed values.

The instruction results will always satisfy the equality:

$$dividend = (divisor \cdot quotient) + remainder$$

where the *dividend* is (rA) and the *divisor* is (rB). The remainder is always less than the absolute value of the divisor and has the same sign as the dividend (except that a 0 quotient or remainder will always be positive).

An overflow occurs when the signed quotient cannot be represented in 64 bits. If the quantity -2^{63} is divided by -1 or if any quantity is divided by 0, then rT is undefined. If the Record bit is set, then the LT, GT, and EQ bits of CR{0} are undefined also.

This instruction exists on 64-bit PowerPC implementations only.

Instruction Encoding:

0	5	6	10	11	15	16	20	21	22	30	31
0 1 1 1 1 1		T		A		B		OE	1 1 1 1 0 1 0 0 1		Rc

T	Target GPR rT where result of operation is stored
A	Source GPR rA
B	Source GPR rB
OE	Overflow Exception bit
Rc	Record bit

divdu   Divide Doubleword Unsigned   **divdu**

PowerPC64

Operation: $rT \Leftarrow (rA) \div (rB)$

Syntax:

divdu	rT,rA,rB	(Rc = 0, OE = 0)
divdu.	rT,rA,rB	(Rc = 1, OE = 0)
divduo	rT,rA,rB	(Rc = 0, OE = 1)
divduo.	rT,rA,rB	(Rc = 1, OE = 1)

Condition Register/Fixed-Point Exception Register:

CR Field 0:   LT,GT,EQ,SO updated if Rc = 1, otherwise not affected
CR Fields 1-7:   not affected

XER[CA]:   not affected
XER[OV,SO]:   updated if OE=1, otherwise not affected

Description:

The **divdu** instruction divides the contents of GPR rA by the contents of GPR rB and places the quotient from this operation in GPR rT. The source registers are assumed to contain unsigned values.

The instruction results will always satisfy the equality:

$$dividend = (divisor \cdot quotient) + remainder$$

where the *dividend* is (rA) and the *divisor* is (rB). The remainder is always less than the absolute value of the divisor and is always a positive value.

An overflow occurs when the unsigned quotient cannot be represented in 64 bits. If any quantity is divided by 0, then rT is undefined. If the Record bit is set, then the LT, GT, and EQ bits of CR{0} are undefined also.

This instruction exists on 64-bit PowerPC implementations only.

Instruction Encoding:

0					5	6				10	11				15	16				20	21	22								30	31
0	1	1	1	1	1			T					A					B			OE	1	1	1	0	0	1	0	0	1	Rc

T	Target GPR rT where result of operation is stored
A	Source GPR rA
B	Source GPR rB
OE	Overflow Exception bit
Rc	Record bit

Divide Short

POWER • 601

Operation: $rT \Leftarrow (rA) \div (rB)$

                $MQ \Leftarrow (rA) \% (rB)$

Syntax:

divs	rT,rA,rB	(Rc = 0, OE = 0)
divs.	rT,rA,rB	(Rc = 1, OE = 0)
divso	rT,rA,rB	(Rc = 0, OE = 1)
divso.	rT,rA,rB	(Rc = 1, OE = 1)

Condition Register / Fixed-Point Exception Register:

CR Field 0:	LT,GT,EQ,SO updated if Rc = 1, otherwise not affected
CR Fields 1-7:	not affected
XER[CA]:	not affected
XER[OV,SO]:	updated if OE=1, otherwise not affected

Description:

The **divs** instruction divides the contents of GPR rA by the contents of GPR rB. The quotient from this operation is placed in GPR rT, and the remainder is placed in the MQ register. All source registers are assumed to contain signed values.

The instruction results will always satisfy the equality:

$$dividend = (divisor \cdot quotient) + remainder$$

where the *dividend* is (rA) and the *divisor* is (rB). The remainder is always less than the absolute value of the divisor and has the same sign as the dividend (except that a 0 quotient or remainder will always be positive).

An overflow occurs when the quotient cannot be represented in 32 bits. If the quantity -2^{31} is divided by -1, then the MQ register is cleared and GPR rT is set to -2^{31}. For overflows other than this case, MQ, rT, and CR{0} (if Rc=1) are undefined.

If the Record bit is set, then the LT, GT, and EQ bits of CR{0} are updated to reflect the remainder (stored in MQ).

This instruction is not part of the PowerPC architecture.

Instruction Encoding:

0					5	6				10	11				15	16				20	21	22								30	31
0	1	1	1	1	1			T					A					B			OE	1	0	1	1	0	1	0	1	1	Rc

T	Target GPR rT where result of operation is stored
A	Source GPR rA
B	Source GPR rB
OE	Overflow Exception bit
Rc	Record bit

divw

Divide Word

601 • 603 • PowerPC32/64

divw

Operation: $rT \Leftarrow {}^\circ rA \left[\frac{0:31}{32:63}\right] \div {}^\circ rB \left[\frac{0:31}{32:63}\right]$

Syntax:

divw	r*T*,r*A*,r*B*	(Rc = 0, OE = 0)
divw.	r*T*,r*A*,r*B*	(Rc = 1, OE = 0)
divwo	r*T*,r*A*,r*B*	(Rc = 0, OE = 1)
divwo.	r*T*,r*A*,r*B*	(Rc = 1, OE = 1)

Condition Register/Fixed-Point Exception Register:

CR Field 0:	LT,GT,EQ,SO updated if Rc = 1, otherwise not affected
CR Fields 1-7:	not affected
XER[CA]:	not affected
XER[OV,SO]:	updated if OE=1, otherwise not affected

Description:

The **divw** instruction divides the contents of GPR r*A* by the contents of GPR r*B* and places the quotient from this operation in GPR r*T*. The source registers are assumed to contain signed values.

On 64-bit PowerPC implementations, only the low-order word from each of the source operands participates in the division operation. The result is returned in the low-order word of the target register, and the high-order word is undefined.

The instruction results will always satisfy the equality:

$$dividend = (divisor \cdot quotient) + remainder$$

where the *dividend* is (r*A*) and the *divisor* is (r*B*). The remainder is always less than the absolute value of the divisor and has the same sign as the dividend (except that a 0 quotient or remainder will always be positive).

If the quantity -2^{31} is divided by -1 or if any quantity is divided by 0, then r*T* is undefined. If the Record bit is set, then the LT, GT, and EQ bits of CR{0} are undefined also.

Instruction Encoding:

0	5	6	10	11	15	16	20	21	22	30	31
0 1 1 1 1 1		T		A		B		OE	1 1 1 1 0 1 0 1 1		Rc

T	Target GPR rT where result of operation is stored
A	Source GPR rA
B	Source GPR rB
OE	Overflow Exception bit
Rc	Record bit

divwu   Divide Word Unsigned   divwu

601 • 603 • PowerPC32/64

Operation: $rT \Leftarrow {}^\circ rA \left[\frac{0:31}{32:63}\right] \div {}^\circ rB \left[\frac{0:31}{32:63}\right]$

Syntax:

divwu	rT,rA,rB	(Rc = 0, OE = 0)
divwu.	rT,rA,rB	(Rc = 1, OE = 0)
divwuo	rT,rA,rB	(Rc = 0, OE = 1)
divwuo.	rT,rA,rB	(Rc = 1, OE = 1)

Condition Register / Fixed-Point Exception Register:

CR Field 0:	LT,GT,EQ,SO updated if Rc = 1, otherwise not affected
CR Fields 1-7:	not affected
XER[CA]:	not affected
XER[OV,SO]:	updated if OE=1, otherwise not affected

Description:

The **divwu** instruction divides the contents of GPR rA by the contents of GPR rB and places the quotient from this operation in GPR rT. The source registers are assumed to contain unsigned values.

On 64-bit PowerPC implementations, only the low-order word from each of the source operands participates in the division operation. The result is returned in the low-order word of the target register, and the high-order word is undefined.

The instruction results will always satisfy the equality:

$$dividend = (divisor \cdot quotient) + remainder$$

where the *dividend* is (rA) and the *divisor* is (rB). The remainder is always less than the absolute value of the divisor and is always a positive value.

If any quantity is divided by 0, then rT is undefined. If the Record bit is set, then the LT, GT, and EQ bits of CR{0} are undefined also. If OE=1, the overflow bits in the XER are set.

Instruction Encoding:

0					5	6				10	11				15	16				20	21	22									30	31
0	1	1	1	1	1			T					A					B			OE	1	1	1	0	0	1	0	1	1	Rc

T	Target GPR rT where result of operation is stored
A	Source GPR rA
B	Source GPR rB
OE	Overflow Exception bit
Rc	Record bit

Difference or Zero

POWER • 601

Operation: if ((rA) > (rB))

rT $\Leftarrow$ 0

else

rT $\Leftarrow$ (rB) - (rA)

Syntax:

doz	rT,rA,rB	(Rc = 0, OE = 0)
doz.	rT,rA,rB	(Rc = 1, OE = 0)
dozo	rT,rA,rB	(Rc = 0, OE = 1)
dozo.	rT,rA,rB	(Rc = 1, OE = 1)

Condition Register / Fixed-Point Exception Register:

CR Field 0:   LT,GT,EQ,SO updated if Rc = 1, otherwise not affected
CR Fields 1-7: not affected

XER[CA]:   not affected
XER[OV,SO]:   updated if OE=1, otherwise not affected

Description:

The **doz** instruction performs a signed compare of the contents of GPR rA and GPR rB. If (rA) > (rB), then 0 is placed in GPR rT, otherwise the result of subtracting (rA) from (rB) is placed in GPR rT. This operation can be viewed as subtracting (rA) from (rB), where the result is never allowed to become negative.

An overflow will occur if (rA) < (rB) and the result of subtracting (rA) from (rB) cannot fit in 32 bits. That implies that only positive overflows can occur.

This instruction is not part of the PowerPC architecture.

Instruction Encoding:

0	5	6	10	11	15	16	20	21	22	30	31
0 1 1 1 1 1		T		A		B		OE	1 0 0 0 0 1 0 0 0		Rc

T	Target GPR rT where result of operation is stored
A	Source GPR rA
B	Source GPR rB
OE	Overflow Exception bit
Rc	Record bit

Difference or Zero Immediate

POWER • 601

Operation: if ((rA) > `s16)
        rT ⇐ 0
   else
        rT ⇐ `s16 - (rA)

Syntax: **dozi**   rT,rA,s16

Condition Register/Fixed-Point Exception Register:

CR Fields 0-7:   not affected

XER: not affected

Description:

The **doz** instruction performs a signed compare of the contents of GPR rA and the sign-extended immediate value s16. If (rA) > `s16, then 0 is placed in GPR rT, otherwise the result of subtracting (rA) from `s16 is placed in GPR rT. This operation can be viewed as subtracting (rA) from `s16, where the result is never allowed to become negative.

An overflow will occur if (rA) < `s16 and the result of subtracting (rA) from `s16 cannot fit in 32 bits. That implies that only positive overflows can occur.

This instruction is not part of the PowerPC architecture.

Instruction Encoding:

0 5	6 10	11 15	16 31
0 0 1 0 0 1	T	A	SI

T   Target GPR rT where result of operation is stored
A   Source GPR rA or 0
SI   Signed 16-bit integer

eciwx   External Control   eciwx
Input Word Indexed
601 • 603 • Optional32/64

Operation: *get word from external device*

Syntax: **eciwx**   rT,rA,rB

Condition Register/Fixed-Point Exception Register:
CR Fields 0-7:   not affected

XER: not affected

Description:

The **eciwx** instruction calculates the real address from the specified effective address $((rA|0) + rB)$ and requests that an external device return (in target register rT) the word of data at that address. The cache is bypassed by this operation. On 64-bit implementations, the returned word is loaded into the low-order word of the register and the upper word is cleared.

The target device is specified by a *Resource ID* stored in EAR[RID]. How these resource IDs map into external devices is system dependent.

Before being translated to a real address, the effective address is validated as if a load were taking place to that address for purposes of protection, reference, and change recording.

For most PowerPC processors, if the address references a *direct-store* storage segment, then a Data Storage interrupt occurs or the results are boundedly undefined. If data address translations are disabled (MSR[DR] = 0), then the results are boundedly undefined. The 601 is unique in that it operates whether or not the data address translations are enabled, and it acts as a no-op if the EA specifies an address in a direct-store segment.

If external accesses are not enabled (that is, EAR[E] is 0), then this instruction will set DSISR[11] and cause a Data Storage interrupt to be taken.

This instruction is an optional part of the PowerPC architecture.

Instruction Encoding:

0 1 1 1 1 1	T	A	B	0 1 0 0 1 1 0 1 1 0	0

Bit positions: 0 ... 5 6 ... 10 11 ... 15 16 ... 20 21 ... 30 31

T	Target GPR rT where result of operation is stored
A	Source GPR rA
B	Source GPR rB

ecowx   External Control   ecowx
Output Word Indexed
601 • 603 • Optional32/64

Operation: send word to external device

Syntax: **ecowx**   rS,rA,rB

Condition Register/Fixed-Point Exception Register:
CR Fields 0-7:   not affected

XER: not affected

Description:

The **ecowx** instruction calculates the real address from the specified effective address ((rA|0) + rB) and sends the real address and the contents of GPR rS to an external device. The cache is bypassed by this operation. On 64-bit implementations, only the low-order word of rS is sent to the device.

The target device is specified by a *Resource ID* stored in EAR[RID]. How these resource IDs map into external devices is system dependent.

Before being translated to a real address, the effective address is validated as if a store were taking place to that address for purposes of protection, reference, and change recording.

For most PowerPC processors, if the address references a *direct-store* storage segment, then a Data Storage interrupt occurs or the results are boundedly undefined. If data address translations are disabled (MSR[DR] = 0), then the results are boundedly undefined. The 601 is unique in that it operates whether or not the data address translations are enabled, and it acts as a no-op if the EA specifies an address in a direct-store segment.

If external accesses are not enabled (that is, EAR[E] is 0), then this instruction will set DSISR[11] and cause a Data Storage interrupt to be taken.

This instruction is an optional part of the PowerPC architecture.

Instruction Encoding:

0					5	6				10	11				15	16				20	21										30	31
0	1	1	1	1	1			S					A					B			0	1	1	0	1	1	0	1	1	0	0	0

S   Source GPR rS
A   Source GPR rA
B   Source GPR rB

eieio   Enforce In-Order Execution of I/O   eieio

601 • 603 • PowerPC32/64

Operation: force all loads and stores to complete

Syntax: eieio

Condition Register/Fixed-Point Exception Register:

CR Fields 0-7:   not affected

XER: not affected

Description:

The **eieio** instruction orders the effects of the load and store instructions executed by the processor. All load and store instructions that were initiated by this processor *before* the **eieio** instruction are guaranteed to be completed before any of the loads and stores initiated by this processor *after* the **eieio** instruction.

This instruction is intended for use with memory-mapped I/O. The **eieio** instruction insures that loads and stores on opposite sides of the instruction will not combine in main memory and produce load/store combining errors.

Load operations are ordered if they are to storage that is

- *Caching Inhibited* and *Guarded*

Store operations are ordered if they are to storage that is one of these:

- *Caching Inhibited* and *Guarded*
- *Write Through Required*

This instruction does not order loads and stores with respect to other processors.

On the 601, this instruction is functionally identical to the **sync** instruction.

Instruction Encoding:

0					5	6					10	11					15	16					20	21									30	31
0	1	1	1	1	1	0	0	0	0	0	0	0	0	0	0	0	0	0	0	0	0	1	1	0	1	0	1	0	1	0	1	1	0	0

eqv   Equivalent   eqv

POWER • 601 • 603 • PowerPC32/64

Operation: $rA \Leftarrow (rS) \equiv (rB)$

Syntax:

eqv	rA,rS,rB	(Rc = 0)
eqv.	rA,rS,rB	(Rc = 1)

Condition Register / Fixed-Point Exception Register:

CR Field 0:   LT,GT,EQ,SO updated if Rc = 1, otherwise not affected
CR Fields 1-7:   not affected

XER: not affected

Description:

The **eqv** instruction calculates the equivalence of the contents of GPR rS and GPR rB and places the result in GPR rA. The equivalence operation sets the bits in the result where the corresponding bits in the two source registers are equal and clears all the bits where corresponding bits in the source registers are not equal. This operation is equivalent to taking the complement of the XOR of the two source registers.

Instruction Encoding:

0 5	6 10	11 15	16 20	21 30	31
0 1 1 1 1 1	S	A	B	0 1 0 0 0 1 1 1 0 0	Rc

S	Source GPR rS
A	Target GPR rA where result of operation is stored
B	Source GPR rB
Rc	Record bit

extsb   Extend Sign Byte   extsb

601 • 603 • PowerPC32/64

Operation: $rA\ [\frac{24:31}{56:63}] \Leftarrow rS\ [\frac{24:31}{56:63}]$

$rA\ [\frac{0:23}{0:55}] \Leftarrow rS\ [\frac{24}{56}]$

Syntax:

extsb	rA,rS	(Rc = 0)
extsb.	rA,rS	(Rc = 1)

Condition Register/Fixed-Point Exception Register:

CR Field 0:   LT,GT,EQ,SO updated if Rc = 1, otherwise not affected

CR Fields 1-7:   not affected

XER: not affected

Description:

The **extsb** instruction extends the sign of the low-order byte in GPR rS so that all the bits in the upper bytes of the destination GPR rA contain a copy of the low-order byte's sign.

On 32-bit PowerPC implementations, the sign bit for the low-order byte is bit number 24. This bit is copied into the high-order 24 bits of the destination register to produce a 32-bit result.

On 64-bit PowerPC implementations, the sign bit for the low-order byte is bit number 56. This bit is copied into the high-order 56 bits of the destination register to produce a 64-bit result.

Instruction Encoding:

0 5	6 10	11 15	16 20	21 30	31
0 1 1 1 1 1	S	A	0 0 0 0 0	1 1 1 0 1 1 1 0 1 0	Rc

S   Source GPR rS

A   Target GPR rA where result of operation is stored

Rc   Record bit

extsh   Extend Sign Halfword   extsh

POWER • 601 • 603 • PowerPC32/64

Operation: $rA\ [\frac{16:31}{48:63}] \Leftarrow rS\ [\frac{16:31}{48:63}]$

$rA\ [\frac{0:15}{0:47}] \Leftarrow rS\ [\frac{16}{48}]$

Syntax:

extsh	r*A*,r*S*	(Rc = 0)
extsh.	r*A*,r*S*	(Rc = 1)

Condition Register/Fixed-Point Exception Register:

CR Field 0:   LT,GT,EQ,SO updated if Rc = 1, otherwise not affected

CR Fields 1-7:   not affected

XER: not affected

Description:

The **extsh** instruction extends the sign of the low-order halfword in GPR r*S* so that all the bits in the upper bytes of the destination GPR r*A* contain a copy of the low-order halfword's sign.

On 32-bit PowerPC implementations, the sign bit for the low-order halfword is bit number 16. This bit is copied into the high-order 16 bits of the destination register to produce a 32-bit result.

On 64-bit PowerPC implementations, the sign bit for the low-order halfword is bit number 48. This bit is copied into the high-order 48 bits of the destination register to produce a 64-bit result.

The archaic POWER mnemonic for this instruction is **exts**[.].

Instruction Encoding:

0 5	6 10	11 15	16 20	21 30	31
0 1 1 1 1 1	S	A	0 0 0 0 0	1 1 1 0 0 1 1 0 1 0	Rc

S   Source GPR rS

A   Target GPR rA where result of operation is stored

Rc   Record bit

extsw   Extend Sign Word   extsw

PowerPC64

Operation: $rA[32:63] \Leftarrow rS[32:63]$
$rA[0:31] \Leftarrow rS[32]$

Syntax:

extsw	rA,rS	(Rc = 0)
extsw.	rA,rS	(Rc = 1)

Condition Register/Fixed-Point Exception Register:

CR Field 0:   LT,GT,EQ,SO updated if Rc = 1, otherwise not affected
CR Fields 1-7:   not affected

XER: not affected

Description:

The **extsw** instruction extends the sign of the low-order word in GPR rS so that all the bits in the upper bytes of the destination GPR rA contain a copy of the low-order word's sign.

The sign bit for the low-order word is bit number 32. This bit is copied into the high-order 32 bits of the destination register to produce a 64-bit result.

This instruction exists on 64-bit PowerPC implementations only.

Instruction Encoding:

0 5	6 10	11 15	16 20	21 30	31
0 1 1 1 1 1	S	A	0 0 0 0 0	1 1 1 0 1 1 0 1 0	Rc

S   Source GPR rS
A   Target GPR rA where result of operation is stored
Rc   Record bit

fabs

FP Absolute Value

fabs

POWER • 601 • 603 • PowerPC32/64

Operation: $frT \Leftarrow |(frB)|$

Syntax:

fabs	frT,frB	(Rc = 0)
fabs.	frT,frB	(Rc = 1)

Condition Register/Floating-Point Status and Control Register:

CR Field 1:   FX,FEX,VX,OX updated if Rc = 1, otherwise not affected

CR Fields 0,2-7: not affected

FPSCR: not affected

Description:

The **fabs** instruction takes the contents of frB, sets the sign bit to 0, and stores the result in frT.

This instruction will operate on NaNs without raising an exception.

Instruction Encoding:

0 5	6 10	11 15	16 20	21 30	31
1 1 1 1 1 1	T	0 0 0 0 0	B	0 1 0 0 0 0 1 0 0 0	Rc

T	Target FPR frT where result of operation is stored
A	Source FPR frA
Rc	Record bit

fadd   FP Add   fadd
POWER • 601 • 603 • PowerPC32/64

Operation: $frT \Leftarrow (frA) + (frB)$

Syntax:

fadd	frT,frA,frB	(Rc = 0)
fadd.	frT,frA,frB	(Rc = 1)

Condition Register / Floating-Point Status and Control Register:

CR Field 1:   FX,FEX,VX,OX updated if Rc = 1, otherwise not affected
CR Fields 0,2-7: not affected

FPSCR: FX, FEX, VX, OX, UX, XX, VSNAN, VXISI, FR, FI, FPRF

Description:

The **fadd** instruction adds the contents of frA with the contents of frB. This result is then normalized (if necessary) and rounded to double-precision (according to the current rounding mode) and then stored in frT.

The Invalid Operation Exception will be invoked if either of the operands is a Signalling NaN (VXSNAN) or if the operation is equivalent to ∞ - ∞ (VXISI).

FPSCR[FPRF] is updated to reflect the sign and class of the result, except in the case where an Invalid Operation Exception occurs and this type of exception is enabled (FPSCR[VE] = 1).

The archaic POWER mnemonic for this instruction is **fa[.]**.

Instruction Encoding:

0 5	6 10	11 15	16 20	21 25	26 30	31
1 1 1 1 1 1	T	A	B	0 0 0 0 0	1 0 1 0 1	Rc

T	Target FPR frT where result of operation is stored
A	Source FPR frA
B	Source FPR frB
Rc	Record bit

fadds   FP Add Single   fadds

601 • 603 • PowerPC32/64

Operation: $frT \Leftarrow (frA) + (frB)$

Syntax:

fadds	frT,frA,frB	(Rc = 0)
fadds.	frT,frA,frB	(Rc = 1)

Condition Register/Floating-Point Status and Control Register:

CR Field 1:   FX,FEX,VX,OX updated if Rc = 1, otherwise not affected

CR Fields 0,2-7: not affected

FPSCR: FX, FEX, VX, OX, UX, XX, VSNAN, VXISI, FR, FI, FPRF

Description:

The **fadds** instruction adds the contents of frA with the contents of frB. This result is then normalized (if necessary) and rounded to single-precision (according to the current rounding mode) and then stored in frT.

The Invalid Operation Exception will be invoked if either of the operands is a Signalling NaN (VXSNAN) or if the operation is equivalent to $\infty - \infty$ (VXISI).

FPSCR[FPRF] is updated to reflect the sign and class of the result, except in the case where an Invalid Operation Exception occurs and this type of exception is enabled (FPSCR[VE] = 1).

Instruction Encoding:

0 5	6 10	11 15	16 20	21 25	26 30	31
1 1 1 0 1 1	T	A	B	0 0 0 0 0	1 0 1 0 1	Rc

T	Target FPR frT where result of operation is stored
A	Source FPR frA
B	Source FPR frB
Rc	Record bit

fcfid FP Convert from Integer Doubleword fcfid

PowerPC64

Operation: $frT \Leftarrow (frA) + (frB)$

Syntax:

fcfid	frT,frB	(Rc = 0)
fcfid.	frT,frB	(Rc = 1)

Condition Register / Floating-Point Status and Control Register:
  CR Field 1:   FX,FEX,VX,OX updated if Rc = 1, otherwise not affected
  CR Fields 0,2-7: not affected

  FPSCR: FX, FEX, XX, FR, FI, FPRF

Description:

The **fcfid** instruction takes the 64-bit signed integer value in frB, converts it to a floating-point number, rounds it to double-precision using the current rounding mode (if necessary), and stores the result in frT.

FPSCR[FPRF] is updated to reflect the sign and class of the result. FPSCR[FR] is set if the result was incremented during the rounding process. FPSCR[FI] is set if the result is inexact.

This instruction exists on 64-bit PowerPC implementations only.

Instruction Encoding:

0	5 6	10 11	15 16	20 21	30 31
1 1 1 1 1 1	T	0 0 0 0 0	B	1 1 0 1 0 0 1 1 1 0	Rc

  T   Target FPR frT where result of operation is stored
  B   Source FPR frB
  Rc   Record bit

fcmpo   FP Compare Ordered   fcmpo

POWER • 601 • 603 • PowerPC32/64

Operation: CR{T} $\Leftarrow$ Ordered FP Compare(frA,frB)

Syntax: **fcmpo**   crT,frA,frB

Condition Register / Floating-Point Status and Control Register:

CR Field T: FL,FG,FE,FU always updated
other fields: not affected

FPSCR: FX, FEX, VX, VXSNAN, VXVC, FPCC

Description:

The **fcmpo** instruction compares the contents of frA with the contents of frB, and the result of the compare is stored in field crT of the Condition Register. The compare result is also copied into FPSCR[FPCC]. If either of the operands is a NaN, then the compare result is set to *unordered*.

If either of the operands is a Signalling NaN, then FPSCR[VXSNAN] is set, and, if Invalid Operation Exceptions are disabled, then the Invalid Compare flag (FPSCR[VXVC]) is set.

If either of the operands is a Quiet NaN (and neither operand is a Signalling NaN), then FPSCR[VXVC] is set.

Instruction Encoding:

0					5	6		8	9	10	11				15	16				20	21										30	31
1	1	1	1	1	1	T		0	0		A					B					0	0	0	0	1	0	0	0	0	0	0	0

    T   Bit field of CR where result of compare is stored
    A   Source FPR frA
    B   Source FPR frB

fcmpu   FP Compare Unordered   fcmpu

POWER • 601 • 603 • PowerPC32/64

Operation: CR{BF} $\Leftarrow$ Unordered FP Compare(fr$A$,fr$B$)

Syntax: **fcmpu**   cr$T$,fr$A$,fr$B$

Condition Register/Floating-Point Status and Control Register:

CR Field T: FL,FG,FE,FU always updated
other fields: not affected

FPSCR: FX, FEX, VX, VXSNAN, FPCC

Description:

The contents of fr$A$ are compared with the contents of fr$B$, and the result of the compare is stored in field cr$T$ of the Condition Register. The compare result is also copied into FPSCR[FPCC]. If either of the operands is a NaN, then the compare result is set to *unordered*.

If either of the operands is a Signalling NaN, then FPSCR[VXSNAN] is set.

Instruction Encoding:

0				5	6		8	9	10	11			15	16			20	21										30	31
1	1	1	1	1	1	T		0	0		A				B			0	0	0	0	0	0	0	0	0	0		0

T   Bit field of CR where result of compare is stored
A   Source FPR frA
B   Source FPR frB

fctid   FP Convert to Integer Doubleword   fctid
PowerPC64

Operation: $frT \Leftarrow Double2Int64(frB)$

Syntax:

fctid	frT,frB	(Rc = 0)
fctid.	frT,frB	(Rc = 1)

Condition Register/Floating-Point Status and Control Register:
CR Field 1:   FX,FEX,VX,OX updated if Rc = 1, otherwise not affected
CR Fields 0,2-7: not affected

FPSCR: FX, FEX, VX, XX, VSNAN, VXCVI, FR, FI, FPRF

Description:

The **fctid** instruction takes the value in frB, converts it into a signed 64-bit fixed-point integer using the current rounding mode, and stores the result in frT.

If the contents of frB are greater than $2^{63} - 1$, then frT is set to the largest positive 64-bit integer (0x7FFF FFFF FFFF FFFF). If the contents of frB are less than -2^{63}, then frT is set to the most negative 64-bit number (0x8000 0000 0000 0000).

After this instruction completes execution, the contents of FPSCR[FPRF] are undefined, except in the case where an Invalid Operation Exception occurs and this type of exception is enabled (FPSCR[VE] = 1).

FPSCR[FR] is set if the result was incremented during the rounding process. FPSCR[FI] is set if the result is inexact.

This instruction exists on 64-bit PowerPC implementations only.

Instruction Encoding:

0 5	6 T 10	11 0 0 0 0 0 15	16 B 20	21 1 1 0 0 1 0 1 1 1 0 30	31 Rc
1 1 1 1 1 1	T	0 0 0 0 0	B	1 1 0 0 1 0 1 1 1 0	Rc

T	Target FPR frT where result of operation is stored
B	Source FPR frB
Rc	Record bit

fctidz   FP Convert to Integer   fctidz
Doubleword with Round to Zero
PowerPC64

Operation: $frT \Leftarrow Double2Int64\_Rnd0(frB)$

Syntax:

fctidz	frT,frB	(Rc = 0)
fctidz.	frT,frB	(Rc = 1)

Condition Register/Floating-Point Status and Control Register:

CR Field 1:   FX,FEX,VX,OX updated if Rc = 1, otherwise not affected
CR Fields 0,2-7: not affected

FPSCR: FX, FEX, VX, XX, VSNAN, VXCVI, FR, FI, FPRF

Description:

The **fctidz** instruction takes the value in frB, converts it into a signed 64-bit fixed-point integer using the *Round to Zero* rounding mode, and stores the result in frT.

If the contents of frB are greater than $2^{63} - 1$, then frT is set to the largest positive 64-bit integer (0x7FFF FFFF FFFF FFFF). If the contents of frB are less than -2^{63}, then frT is set to the most negative 64-bit number (0x8000 0000 0000 0000).

After this instruction completes execution, the contents of FPSCR[FPRF] are undefined, except in the case where an Invalid Operation Exception occurs and this type of exception is enabled (FPSCR[VE] = 1).

FPSCR[FR] is set if the result was incremented during the rounding process. FPSCR[FI] is set if the result is inexact.

This instruction exists on 64-bit PowerPC implementations only.

Instruction Encoding:

0 5	6 10	11 15	16 20	21 30	31
1 1 1 1 1 1	T	0 0 0 0 0	B	1 1 0 0 1 0 1 1 1 1	Rc

     T   Target FPR frT where result of operation is stored
     B   Source FPR frB
     Rc   Record bit

fctiw   FP Convert to Integer Word   fctiw

601 • 603 • PowerPC32/64

Operation: frT[32:63] $\Leftarrow$ Double2Int32(frB)

Syntax:

fctiw	frT,frB	(Rc = 0)
fctiw.	frT,frB	(Rc = 1)

Condition Register / Floating-Point Status and Control Register:
CR Field 1:   FX,FEX,VX,OX updated if Rc = 1, otherwise not affected
CR Fields 0,2-7: not affected

FPSCR: FX, FEX, VX, XX, VSNAN, VXCVI, FR, FI, FPRF

Description:

The **fctiw** instruction takes the value in frB, converts it into a signed 32-bit fixed-point integer using the current rounding mode, and stores the result in the low-order word of frT. The high-order word of frT is undefined.

If the contents of frB are greater than 2^{31} - 1, then frT is set to the largest positive 32-bit integer (0x7FFF FFFF). If the contents of frB are less than -2^{31}, then frT is set to the most negative 32-bit number (0x8000 0000).

After this instruction completes execution, the contents FPSCR[FPRF] are undefined, except in the case where an Invalid Operation Exception occurs and this type of exception is enabled (FPSCR[VE] = 1).

FPSCR[FR] is set if the result was incremented during the rounding process. FPSCR[FI] is set if the result is inexact.

Instruction Encoding:

0 5	6 T 10	11 0 0 0 0 0 15	16 B 20	21 0 0 0 0 0 1 1 1 0 30	31 Rc
1 1 1 1 1 1	T	0 0 0 0 0	B	0 0 0 0 0 0 1 1 1 0	Rc

T	Target FPR frT where result of operation is stored
B	Source FPR frB
Rc	Record bit

fctiwz   FP Convert to Integer   fctiwz
Word with Round to Zero
601 • 603 • PowerPC32/64

Operation: $frT[32:63] \Leftarrow Double2Int32\_Rnd0(frB)$

Syntax: **fctiwz** frT,frB (Rc = 0)
          fctiwz. frT,frB (Rc = 1)

Condition Register/Floating-Point Status and Control Register:
  CR Field 1:   FX,FEX,VX,OX updated if Rc = 1, otherwise not affected
  CR Fields 0,2-7: not affected

  FPSCR: FX, FEX, VX, XX, VSNAN, VXCVI, FR, FI, FPRF

Description:

The **fctiwz** instruction takes the value in frB, converts it into a signed 32-bit fixed-point integer using the *Round to Zero* rounding mode, and stores the result in the low-order word of frT. The high-order word of frT is undefined.

If the contents of frB are greater than $2^{31} - 1$, then frT is set to the largest positive 32-bit integer (0x7FFF FFFF). If the contents of frB are less than -2^{31}, then frT is set to the most negative 32-bit number (0x8000 0000).

After this instruction completes execution, the contents FPSCR[FPRF] are undefined, except in the case where an Invalid Operation Exception occurs and this type of exception is enabled (FPSCR[VE] = 1).

FPSCR[FR] is set if the result was incremented during the rounding process. FPSCR[FI] is set if the result is inexact.

Instruction Encoding:

0 5	6 10	11 15	16 20	21 30	31
1 1 1 1 1 1	T	0 0 0 0 0	B	0 0 0 0 0 0 1 1 1 1	Rc

          T   Target FPR frT where result of operation is stored
          B   Source FPR frB
          Rc   Record bit

fdiv   FP Divide   fdiv

POWER • 601 • 603 • PowerPC32/64

Operation: $frT \Leftarrow (frA) \div (frB)$

Syntax:

fdiv	frT, frA, frB	(Rc = 0)
fdiv.	frT, frA, frB	(Rc = 1)

Condition Register / Floating-Point Status and Control Register:

CR Field 1:   FX,FEX,VX,OX updated if Rc = 1, otherwise not affected

CR Fields 0,2-7: not affected

FPSCR: FX, FEX, VX, OX, UX, ZX, XX, VSNAN,VXIDI,VXZDZ, FR,FI,FPRF

Description:

The **fdiv** instruction divides the contents of frA by the contents of frB. This result is then normalized (if necessary) and rounded to double-precision (according to the current rounding mode) and then stored in frT.

The Invalid Operation Exception will be invoked if either of the operands is a Signalling NaN (VXSNAN) or if the operation is equivalent to $\infty \div \infty$ (VXIDI). The Zero Divided by Zero Exception will be invoked if the operation is equivalent to $0 \div 0$ (VXZDZ).

FPSCR[FPRF] is updated to reflect the sign and class of the result, except in the case where an Invalid Operation or Zero Divided by Zero Exception occurs and the appropriate type of exception is enabled.

The archaic POWER mnemonic for this instruction is **fd[.]**.

Instruction Encoding:

0 5	6 10	11 15	16 20	21 25	26 30	31
1 1 1 1 1 1	T	A	B	0 0 0 0 0	1 0 0 1 0	Rc

      T   Target FPR frT where result of operation is stored

      A   Source FPR frA

      B   Source FPR frB

      Rc   Record bit

fdivs FP Divide Single fdivs

601 • 603 • PowerPC32/64

Operation: $frT \Leftarrow (frA) \div (frB)$

Syntax:

fdivs	frT,frA,frB	(Rc = 0)
fdivs.	frT,frA,frB	(Rc = 1)

Condition Register/Floating-Point Status and Control Register:

CR Field 1: FX,FEX,VX,OX updated if Rc = 1, otherwise not affected
CR Fields 0,2-7: not affected

FPSCR: FX, FEX, VX, OX, UX, ZX, XX, VSNAN,VXIDI,VXZDZ,
FR,FI,FPRF

Description:

The **fdivs** instruction divides the contents of frA by the contents of frB. This result is then normalized (if necessary) and rounded to single-precision (according to the current rounding mode) and then stored in frT.

The Invalid Operation Exception will be invoked if either of the operands is a Signalling NaN (VXSNAN) or if the operation is equivalent to $\infty \div \infty$ (VXIDI). The Zero Divide Exception will be invoked if the operation is equivalent to $0 \div 0$ (VXZDZ).

FPSCR[FPRF] is updated to reflect the sign and class of the result, except in the case where an Invalid Operation or Zero Divide Exception occurs and the appropriate type of exception is enabled.

Instruction Encoding:

0				5	6			10	11			15	16			20	21				25	26				30	31
1	1	1	0	1	1		T			A				B			0	0	0	0	0	1	0	0	1	0	Rc

T	Target FPR frT where result of operation is stored
A	Source FPR frA
B	Source FPR frB
Rc	Record bit

fmadd   FP Multiply-Add   fmadd

POWER • 601 • 603 • PowerPC32/64

Operation: $frT \Leftarrow (frA) \times (frC) + (frB)$

Syntax:

fmadd	frT,frA,frC,frB	(Rc = 0)
fmadd.	frT,frA,frC,frB	(Rc = 1)

Condition Register/Floating-Point Status and Control Register:

CR Field 1:   FX,FEX,VX,OX updated if Rc = 1, otherwise not affected
CR Fields 0,2-7: not affected

FPSCR: FX, FEX, VX, OX, UX, XX, VSNAN,VXISI,VXIMZ, FR,FI,FPRF

Description:

The **fmadd** instruction multiplies the contents of frA by the contents of frC and then adds frB to compute the final result. This result is then normalized (if necessary) and rounded to double-precision (according to the current rounding mode) and then stored in frT.

The Invalid Operation Exception will be invoked if either of the operands is a Signalling NaN (VXSNAN) or if the operation involves $\infty - \infty$ (VXISI) or $\infty \times 0$ (VXIMZ).

FPSCR[FPRF] is updated to reflect the sign and class of the result, except in the case where an Invalid Operation Exception occurs and this type of exception is enabled (FPSCR[VE] = 1).

The archaic POWER mnemonic for this instruction is **fma**[.].

Instruction Encoding:

0 5	6 10	11 15	16 20	21 25	26 30	31
1 1 1 1 1 1	T	A	B	C	1 1 1 0 1	Rc

T   Target FPR frT where result of operation is stored
A   Source FPR frA
B   Source FPR frB
C   Source FPR frC
Rc   Record bit

fmadds   FP Multiply-Add Single   **fmadds**

601 • 603 • PowerPC32/64

Operation: $frT \Leftarrow (frA) \times (frC) + (frB)$

Syntax:

fmadds	frT,frA,frC,frB	(Rc = 0)
fmadds.	frT,frA,frC,frB	(Rc = 1)

Condition Register/Floating-Point Status and Control Register:
CR Field 1:   FX,FEX,VX,OX updated if Rc = 1, otherwise not affected
CR Fields 0,2-7: not affected

FPSCR: FX, FEX, VX, OX, UX, XX, VSNAN,VXISI,VXIMZ, FR,FI,FPRF

Description:

The **fmadds** instruction multiplies the contents of frA by the contents of frC and then adds frB to compute the final result. This result is then normalized (if necessary) and rounded to single-precision (according to the current rounding mode) and then stored in frT.

The Invalid Operation Exception will be invoked if either of the operands is a Signalling NaN (VXSNAN) or if the operation involves $\infty - \infty$ (VXISI) or $\infty \times 0$ (VXIMZ).

FPSCR[FPRF] is updated to reflect the sign and class of the result, except in the case where an Invalid Operation Exception occurs and this type of exception is enabled (FPSCR[VE] = 1).

The archaic POWER mnemonic for this instruction is **fma[.]**.

Instruction Encoding:

0	5	6	10	11	15	16	20	21	25	26	30	31
1 1 1 0 1 1		T		A		B		C		1 1 1 0 1		Rc

T	Target FPR frT where result of operation is stored
A	Source FPR frA
B	Source FPR frB
C	Source FPR frC
Rc	Record bit

fmr   FP Move Register   fmr

POWER • 601 • 603 • PowerPC32/64

Operation: $frT \Leftarrow (frB)$

Syntax: **fmr**   frT,frB   (Rc = 0)
           fmr.   frT,frB   (Rc = 1)

Condition Register/Floating-Point Status and Control Register:
CR Field 1:   FX,FEX,VX,OX updated if Rc = 1, otherwise not affected
CR Fields 0,2-7: not affected

FPSCR: not affected

Description:

The **fmr** instruction takes the contents of frB and copies it into frT.

This instruction will operate on NaNs without raising an exception.

Instruction Encoding:

0 5	6 10	11 15	16 20	21 30	31
1 1 1 1 1 1	T	0 0 0 0 0	B	0 0 0 1 0 0 1 0 0 0	Rc

T   Target FPR frT where result of operation is stored
B   Source FPR frB
Rc   Record bit

fmsub   FP Multiply-Subtract   fmsub

POWER • 601 • 603 • PowerPC32/64

Operation: $frT \Leftarrow (frA) \times (frC) - (frB)$

Syntax:

fmsub	frT,frA,frC,frB	(Rc = 0)
fmsub.	frT,frA,frC,frB	(Rc = 1)

Condition Register/Floating-Point Status and Control Register:

CR Field 1:   FX,FEX,VX,OX updated if Rc = 1, otherwise not affected

CR Fields 0,2-7: not affected

FPSCR: FX, FEX, VX, OX, UX, XX, VSNAN,VXISI,VXIMZ, FR,FI,FPRF

Description:

The **fmsub** instruction multiplies the contents of frA by the contents of frC and then subtracts frB to compute the final result. This result is then normalized (if necessary) and rounded to double-precision (according to the current rounding mode) and then stored in frT.

The Invalid Operation Exception will be invoked if either of the operands is a Signalling NaN (VXSNAN) or if the operation involves $\infty - \infty$ (VXISI) or $\infty \times 0$ (VXIMZ).

FPSCR[FPRF] is updated to reflect the sign and class of the result, except in the case where an Invalid Operation Exception occurs and this type of exception is enabled (FPSCR[VE] = 1).

The archaic POWER mnemonic for this instruction is **fms[.]**.

Instruction Encoding:

0 5	6 10	11 15	16 20	21 25	26 30	31
1 1 1 1 1 1	T	A	B	C	1 1 1 0 0	Rc

T	Target FPR frT where result of operation is stored
A	Source FPR frA
B	Source FPR frB
C	Source FPR frC
Rc	Record bit

fmsubs FP Multiply-Subtract Single fmsubs

601 • 603 • PowerPC32/64

Operation: $frT \Leftarrow (frA) \times (frC) - (frB)$

Syntax:

fmsubs	frT,frA,frC,frB	(Rc = 0)
fmsubs.	frT,frA,frC,frB	(Rc = 1)

Condition Register/Floating-Point Status and Control Register:

CR Field 1:   FX,FEX,VX,OX updated if Rc = 1, otherwise not affected
CR Fields 0,2-7: not affected

FPSCR: FX, FEX, VX, OX, UX, XX, VSNAN,VXISI,VXIMZ, FR,FI,FPRF

Description:

The **fmsubs** instruction multiplies the contents of frA by the contents of frC and then subtracts frB to compute the final result. This result is then normalized (if necessary) and rounded to single-precision (according to the current rounding mode) and then stored in frT.

The Invalid Operation Exception will be invoked if either of the operands is a Signalling NaN (VXSNAN) or if the operation involves $\infty - \infty$ (VXISI) or $\infty \times 0$ (VXIMZ).

FPSCR[FPRF] is updated to reflect the sign and class of the result, except in the case where an Invalid Operation Exception occurs and this type of exception is enabled (FPSCR[VE] = 1).

Instruction Encoding:

0 1 1 0 1 1	T	A	B	C	1 1 1 0 0	Rc

T	Target FPR frT where result of operation is stored
A	Source FPR frA
B	Source FPR frB
C	Source FPR frC
Rc	Record bit

fmul   FP Multiply   fmul

POWER • 601 • 603 • PowerPC32/64

Operation: $frT \Leftarrow (frA) \times (frC)$

Syntax: **fmul** frT,frA,frC (Rc = 0)
                   fmul. frT,frA,frC (Rc = 1)

Condition Register/Floating-Point Status and Control Register:
CR Field 1:   FX,FEX,VX,OX updated if Rc = 1, otherwise not affected
CR Fields 0,2-7:   not affected

FPSCR: FX, FEX, VX, OX, UX, XX, VSNAN, VXIMZ, FR, FI, FPRF

Description:
The **fmul** instruction multiplies the contents of frA by the contents of frC. This result is normalized (if necessary) and rounded to double-precision (according to the current rounding mode) and then stored in frT.

The Invalid Operation Exception will be invoked if either of the operands is a Signalling NaN (VXSNAN) or if the operation is equivalent to $\infty \times 0$ (VXIMZ).

FPSCR[FPRF] is updated to reflect the sign and class of the result, except in the case where an Invalid Operation Exception occurs and this type of exception is enabled (FPSCR[VE] = 1).

The archaic POWER mnemonic for this instruction is **fm[.]**.

Instruction Encoding:

0	5 6	10 11	15 16	20 21	25 26	30 31
1 1 1 1 1 1	T	A	0 0 0 0 0	C	1 1 0 0 1	Rc

T   Target FPR frT where result of operation is stored
A   Source FPR frA
C   Source FPR frC
Rc   Record bit

fmuls

FP Multiply Single

601 • 603 • PowerPC32/64

fmuls

Operation: $frT \Leftarrow (frA) \times (frC)$

Syntax:

fmuls	frT,frA,frC	(Rc = 0)
fmuls.	frT,frA,frC	(Rc = 1)

Condition Register/Floating-Point Status and Control Register:

CR Field 1:   FX,FEX,VX,OX updated if Rc = 1, otherwise not affected

CR Fields 0,2-7: not affected

FPSCR: FX, FEX, VX, OX, UX, XX, VSNAN, VXIMZ, FR, FI, FPRF

Description:

The **fmuls** instruction multiplies the contents of frA by the contents of frC. This result is normalized (if necessary) and rounded to single-precision (according to the current rounding mode) and then stored in frT.

The Invalid Operation Exception will be invoked if either of the operands is a Signalling NaN (VXSNAN) or if the operation is equivalent to $\infty \times 0$ (VXIMZ).

FPSCR[FPRF] is updated to reflect the sign and class of the result, except in the case where an Invalid Operation Exception occurs and this type of exception is enabled (FPSCR[VE] = 1).

Instruction Encoding:

0 5	6 10	11 15	16 20	21 25	26 30	31
1 1 1 0 1 1	T	A	0 0 0 0 0	C	1 1 0 0 1	Rc

T	Target FPR frT where result of operation is stored
A	Source FPR frA
C	Source FPR frC
Rc	Record bit

fnabs   FP Negative Absolute Value   fnabs

POWER • 601 • 603 • PowerPC32/64

Operation: $frT \Leftarrow -|(frB)|$

Syntax:

fnabs	frT,frB	(Rc = 0)
fnabs.	frT,frB	(Rc = 1)

Condition Register/Floating-Point Status and Control Register:

CR Field 1:   FX,FEX,VX,OX updated if Rc = 1, otherwise not affected

CR Fields 0,2-7: not affected

FPSCR: not affected

Description:

The **fnabs** instruction takes the contents of frB, sets the sign bit to 1, and stores the result in frT.

This instruction will operate on NaNs without raising an exception.

Instruction Encoding:

0	5	6	10	11	15	16	20	21	30	31
1 1 1 1 1 1		T		0 0 0 0 0		B		0 0 1 0 0 0 1 0 0 0		Rc

T   Target FPR frT where result of operation is stored

B   Source FPR frB

Rc   Record bit

fneg   FP Negate   fneg

Operation: $frT \Leftarrow -(frB)$

Syntax:

fneg	frT,frB	(Rc = 0)
fneg.	frT,frB	(Rc = 1)

Condition Register/Floating-Point Status and Control Register:

CR Field 1:   FX,FEX,VX,OX updated if Rc = 1, otherwise not affected

CR Fields 0,2-7: not affected

FPSCR: not affected

Description:

The **fneg** instruction takes the contents of frB, inverts the sign bit, and stores the result in frT.

This instruction will operate on NaNs without raising an exception.

Instruction Encoding:

0	5	6	10	11	15	16	20	21	30	31
1 1 1 1 1 1		T		0 0 0 0 0		B		0 0 0 0 1 0 1 0 0 0		Rc

T   Target FPR frT where result of operation is stored

B   Source FPR frB

Rc   Record bit

fnmadd FP Negative Multiply-Add fnmadd

POWER • 601 • 603 • PowerPC32/64

Operation: $frT \Leftarrow -((frA) \times (frC) + (frB))$

Syntax:

fnmadd	frT,frA,frC,frB	(Rc = 0)
fnmadd.	frT,frA,frC,frB	(Rc = 1)

Condition Register/Floating-Point Status and Control Register:

CR Field 1:   FX,FEX,VX,OX updated if Rc = 1, otherwise not affected

CR Fields 0,2-7: not affected

FPSCR: FX, FEX, VX, OX, UX, XX, VSNAN,VXISI,VXIMZ, FR,FI,FPRF

Description:

The **fnmadd** instruction multiplies the contents of frA by the contents of frC and then adds frB to compute the result. This intermediate result is negated to produce the final result. The final result is then normalized (if necessary), rounded to double-precision (according to the current rounding mode), and stored in frT.

This operation is equivalent to a **fmadd/fneg** pair of instructions, except for how the sign of NaNs is handled:

• QNaNs propagating through the instruction retain their original sign.

• QNaNs that result from disabled Invalid Operation Exceptions have a sign of 0.

• QNaNs that are converted from SNaNs because of disabled Invalid Operation Exceptions retain the sign of the original SNaN.

The Invalid Operation Exception will be invoked if either of the operands is a Signalling NaN (VXSNAN) or if the operation involves ∞ - ∞ (VXISI) or ∞ × 0 (VXIMZ).

FPSCR[FPRF] is updated to reflect the sign and class of the result, except in the case where an Invalid Operation Exception occurs and this type of exception is enabled (FPSCR[VE] = 1).

The archaic POWER mnemonic for this instruction is **fnma[.]**.

Instruction Encoding:

0					5	6				10	11				15	16				20	21				25	25					30	31
1	1	1	1	1	1			T					A					B					C			1	1	1	1	1	Rc

T	Target FPR frT where result of operation is stored
A	Source FPR frA
B	Source FPR frB
C	Source FPR frC
Rc	Record bit

fnmadds   FP Negative   fnmadds
Multiply-Add Single
601 • 603 • PowerPC32/64

Operation: $frT \Leftarrow -((frA) \times (frC) + (frB))$

Syntax:

fnmadds	frT,frA,frC,frB	(Rc = 0)
fnmadds.	frT,frA,frC,frB	(Rc = 1)

Condition Register/Floating-Point Status and Control Register:
CR Field 1:   FX,FEX,VX,OX updated if Rc = 1, otherwise not affected
CR Fields 0,2-7: not affected

FPSCR: FX, FEX, VX, OX, UX, XX, VSNAN,VXISI,VXIMZ, FR,FI,FPRF

Description:
The **fnmadds** instruction multiplies the contents of frA by the contents of frC and then adds frB to compute the result. This intermediate result is negated to produce the final result. The final result is then normalized (if necessary), rounded to single-precision (according to the current rounding mode), and stored in frT.

This operation is equivalent to a **fmadds**/**fneg** pair of instructions, except for how the sign of NaNs is handled:

- QNaNs propagating through the instruction retain their original sign.

- QNaNs that result from disabled Invalid Operation Exceptions have a sign of 0.

- QNaNs that are converted from SNaNs because of disabled Invalid Operation Exceptions retain the sign of the original SNaN.

The Invalid Operation Exception will be invoked if either of the operands is a Signalling NaN (VXSNAN) or if the operation involves ∞ - ∞ (VXISI) or ∞ × 0 (VXIMZ).

FPSCR[FPRF] is updated to reflect the sign and class of the result, except in the case where an Invalid Operation Exception occurs and this type of exception is enabled (FPSCR[VE] = 1).

Instruction Encoding:

0	5	6	10	11	15	16	20	21	25	26	30	31
1 1 1 0 1 1		T		A		B		C		1 1 1 1 1		Rc

T   Target FPR frT where result of operation is stored

A   Source FPR frA

B   Source FPR frB

C   Source FPR frC

Rc   Record bit

fnmsub   FP Negative   fnmsub
Multiply-Subtract
POWER • 601 • 603 • PowerPC32/64

Operation: $frT \Leftarrow -((frA) \times (frC) - (frB))$

Syntax:

fnmsub	frT,frA,frC,frB	(Rc = 0)
fnmsub.	frT,frA,frC,frB	(Rc = 1)

Condition Register/Floating-Point Status and Control Register:

CR Field 1:   FX,FEX,VX,OX updated if Rc = 1, otherwise not affected
CR Fields 0,2-7: not affected

FPSCR: FX, FEX, VX, OX, UX, XX, VSNAN,VXISI,VXIMZ, FR,FI,FPRF

Description:

The **fnmsub** instruction multiplies the contents of frA by the contents of frC and then subtracts frB to compute the result. This intermediate result is negated to produce the final result. The final result is then normalized (if necessary), rounded to double-precision (according to the current rounding mode), and stored in frT.

This operation is equivalent to a **fmsub**/**fneg** pair of instructions, except for how the sign of NaNs is handled:

- QNaNs propagating through the instruction retain their original sign.

- QNaNs that result from disabled Invalid Operation Exceptions have a sign of 0.

- QNaNs that are converted from SNaNs because of disabled Invalid Operation Exceptions retain the sign of the original SNaN.

The Invalid Operation Exception will be invoked if either of the operands is a Signalling NaN (VXSNAN) or if the operation involves $\infty - \infty$ (VXISI) or $\infty \times 0$ (VXIMZ).

FPSCR[FPRF] is updated to reflect the sign and class of the result, except in the case where an Invalid Operation Exception occurs and this type of exception is enabled (FPSCR[VE] = 1).

The archaic POWER mnemonic for this instruction is **fnms[.]**.

Instruction Encoding:

0					5	6				10	11				15	16				20	21				25	26				30	31
1	1	1	1	1	1			T					A					B					C			1	1	1	1	0	Rc

T	Target FPR frT where result of operation is stored
A	Source FPR frA
B	Source FPR frB
C	Source FPR frC
Rc	Record bit

fnmsubs   FP Negative   fnmsubs
Multiply-Subtract Single
601 • 603 • PowerPC32/64

Operation: $frT \Leftarrow -((frA) \times (frC) - (frB))$

Syntax: **fnmsubs**   frT,frA,frC,frB   (Rc = 0)
              fnmsubs. frT,frA,frC,frB   (Rc = 1)

Condition Register/Floating-Point Status and Control Register:
CR Field 1:   FX,FEX,VX,OX updated if Rc = 1, otherwise not affected
CR Fields 0,2-7: not affected

FPSCR: FX, FEX, VX, OX, UX, XX, VSNAN,VXISI,VXIMZ, FR,FI,FPRF

Description:

The **fnmsubs** instruction multiplies the contents of frA by the contents of frC and then subtracts frB to compute the result. This intermediate result is negated to produce the final result. The final result is then normalized (if necessary), rounded to single-precision (according to the current rounding mode), and stored in frT.

This operation is equivalent to a **fmsubs/fneg** pair of instructions, except for how the sign of NaNs is handled:

- QNaNs propagating through the instruction retain their original sign.

- QNaNs that result from disabled Invalid Operation Exceptions have a sign of 0.

- QNaNs that are converted from SNaNs because of disabled Invalid Operation Exceptions retain the sign of the original SNaN.

The Invalid Operation Exception will be invoked if either of the operands is a Signalling NaN (VXSNAN) or if the operation involves $\infty - \infty$ (VXISI) or $\infty \times 0$ (VXIMZ).

FPSCR[FPRF] is updated to reflect the sign and class of the result, except in the case where an Invalid Operation Exception occurs and this type of exception is enabled (FPSCR[VE] = 1).

Instruction Set Summary   447

Instruction Encoding:

0				5	6		10	11		15	16		20	21		25	26			30	31
1	1	1	0	1	1	T		A		B		C		1	1	1	1	0	Rc

T	Target FPR frT where result of operation is stored
A	Source FPR frA
B	Source FPR frB
C	Source FPR frC
Rc	Record bit

fres   FP Reciprocal Estimate Single   fres

603 • Optional32/64

Operation: $frT \Longleftarrow \approx \dfrac{1}{(frB)}$

Syntax:

fres	frT,frB	(Rc = 0)
fres.	frT,frB	(Rc = 1)

Condition Register/Floating-Point Status and Control Register:

CR Field 1:   FX,FEX,VX,OX updated if Rc = 1, otherwise not affected

CR Fields 0,2-7: not affected

FPSCR: FX, FEX, VX, OX, UX, ZX, VSNAN, FR, FI, FPRF

Description:

The **fres** instruction calculates a single-precision estimate of the reciprocal of frB and stores the result in frT. The precision of the calculated result is correct to within 1 part in 256 of the actual reciprocal of frB, that is, the following equation is satisfied:

$$\left| \frac{estimated - actual}{actual} \right| \leq \frac{1}{256}$$

where *estimated* is the estimated value returned by the instruction and *actual* is the actual value of $1 \div (frB)$.

The table summarizes the results for special values of frB.

Operand	Result	Exception	Notes
+∞	+0	none	-
+0	+∞	ZX	no result if FPSCR[ZE]=1
-0	-∞	ZX	no result if FPSCR[ZE]=1
-∞	-0	none	-
SNaN	QNaN	VXSNAN	no result if FPSCR[VE]=1
QNaN	QNaN	none	-

FPSCR[FPRF] is updated to reflect the sign and class of the result, except in the case where an Invalid Operation or Zero Divide Exception occurs and the appropriate type of exception is enabled. FPSCR[FR] and FPSCR[FI] are set to undefined values.

This instruction is an optional part of the PowerPC architecture.

Instruction Encoding:

0					5	6			10	11					15	16				20	21										30	31
1	1	1	0	1	1		T			0	0	0	0	0			B				0	0	0	0	0	1	1	0	0	0	Rc

T   Target FPR frT where result of operation is stored
B   Source FPR frB
Rc   Record bit

frsp   FP Round to Single-Precision   frsp

POWER • 601 • 603 • PowerPC32/64

Operation: $frT \Leftarrow \text{Double2Single}(frB)$

Syntax:

frsp	frT,frB	(Rc = 0)
frsp.	frT,frB	(Rc = 1)

Condition Register/Floating-Point Status and Control Register:

CR Field 1:   FX,FEX,VX,OX updated if Rc = 1, otherwise not affected
CR Fields 0,2-7: not affected

FPSCR: FX, FEX, VX, OX, UX, XX, VSNAN, FR, FI, FPRF

Description:

The **frsp** instruction takes the value in frB, rounds it down to single-precision range using the current rounding mode, and stores the result in frT. If the value in frB is already within single-precision range, then the value is simply copied into frT.

FPSCR[FPRF] is updated to reflect the sign and class of the result, except in the case where an Invalid Operation Exception occurs and this type of exception is enabled (FPSCR[VE] = 1).

Instruction Encoding:

0 5	6 10	11 15	16 20	21 30	31
1 1 1 1 1 1	T	0 0 0 0 0	B	0 0 0 0 0 0 1 1 0 0	Rc

T   Target FPR frT where result of operation is stored
B   Source FPR frB
Rc   Record bit

frsqrte

FP Reciprocal Square Root Estimate

frsqrte

603 • Optional32/64

Operation: $frT \Longleftarrow \approx \dfrac{1}{\sqrt{(frB)}}$

Syntax:

frsqrte	frT,frB	(Rc = 0)
frsqrte.	frT,frB	(Rc = 1)

Condition Register / Floating-Point Status and Control Register:

CR Field 1:   FX,FEX,VX,OX updated if Rc = 1, otherwise not affected
CR Fields 0,2-7: not affected

FPSCR: FX, FEX, VX, ZX, VSNAN, VXSQRT, FR, FI, FPRF

Description:

The **frsqrte** instruction calculates a double-precision estimate of the reciprocal of the square root of frB and stores the result in frT. The precision of the calculated result is correct to within 1 part in 32 of the actual reciprocal of frB, that is, the following equation is satisfied:

$$\left| \frac{estimated - actual}{actual} \right| \leq \frac{1}{32}$$

where *estimated* is the estimated value returned by the instruction and *actual* is the actual value of $1 \div \sqrt{(frB)}$.

The table summarizes the results for special values of frB.

Operand	Result	Exception	Notes
+∞	+0	none	-
+0	+∞	ZX	no result if FPSCR[ZE]=1
-0	-∞	ZX	no result if FPSCR[ZE]=1
< 0	QNaN	VXSQRT	no result if FPSCR[VE]=1
-∞	QNaN	VXSQRT	no result if FPSCR[VE]=1
SNaN	QNaN	VXSNAN	no result if FPSCR[VE]=1
QNaN	QNaN	none	-

FPSCR[FPRF] is updated to reflect the sign and class of the result, except in the case where an Invalid Operation or Zero Divide Exception occurs and the appropriate type of exception is enabled. FPSCR[FR] and FPSCR[FI] are set to undefined values.

This instruction is an optional part of the PowerPC architecture.

Instruction Encoding:

0 5	6 10	11 15	16 20	21 30	31
1 1 1 1 1 1	T	0 0 0 0 0	B	0 0 0 0 0 1 1 0 1 0	Rc

T	Target FPR frT where result of operation is stored
B	Source FPR frB
Rc	Record bit

fsel

fsel

603 • Optional32 / 64

Operation: if ((frA) ≥ 0.0)
                    frT ⇐ (frC)
                else
                    frT ⇐ (frB)

Syntax: **fsel**   frT,frA,frC,frB   (Rc = 0)
            fsel.   frT,frA,frC,frB   (Rc = 0)

Condition Register/Floating-Point Status and Control Register:

CR Field 1:   FX,FEX,VX,OX updated if Rc = 1, otherwise not affected
CR Fields 0,2-7: not affected

FPSCR: not affected

Description:

The **fsel** instruction compares the contents of frA with 0.0. If the value in frA is greater than or equal to 0.0, then the contents of frC are copied into the target register frT. If frA is less than 0.0 or if frA is NaN, then the contents of frB are copied into frT.

The comparison operation does not generate any exceptions. If frA contains -0, it is treated the same as +0.

This instruction is an optional part of the PowerPC architecture.

Instruction Encoding:

0	5 6	10 11	15 16	20 21	25 26	30 31
1 1 1 1 1 1	T	A	B	C	1 0 1 1 1	Rc

T   Target FPR frT where result of operation is stored
A   Source FPR frA
B   Source FPR frB
C   Source FPR frC
Rc   Record bit

fsqrt

FP Square Root

fsqrt

Optional32/64

Operation: frT $\Leftarrow$ $\sqrt{(frB)}$

Syntax:

fsqrt	frT,frB	(Rc = 0)
fsqrt.	frT,frB	(Rc = 1)

Condition Register / Floating-Point Status and Control Register:

CR Field 1:   FX,FEX,VX,OX updated if Rc = 1, otherwise not affected
CR Fields 0,2-7: not affected

FPSCR: FX, FEX, VX, XX, VSNAN, VXSQRT, FR, FI, FPRF

Description:

The **fsqrt** instruction calculates the double-precision square root of frB and stores the result in frT. The table summarizes the results for special values of frB.

Operand	Result	Exception	Notes
+∞	+∞	none	-
+0	+0	none	-
-0	-0	none	-
< 0	QNaN	VXSQRT	no result if FPSCR[VE]=1
-∞	QNaN	VXSQRT	no result if FPSCR[VE]=1
SNaN	QNaN	VXSNAN	no result if FPSCR[VE]=1
QNaN	QNaN	none	-

FPSCR[FPRF] is updated to reflect the sign and class of the result, except in the case where an Invalid Operation Exception occurs and FPSCR[VE]=1.

This instruction is an optional part of the PowerPC architecture.

Instruction Encoding:

0	5	6	10	11	15	16	20	21	30	31
1 1 1 1 1 1		T		0 0 0 0 0		B		0 0 0 0 0 1 0 1 1 0		Rc

T   Target FPR frT where result of operation is stored
B   Source FPR frB
Rc   Record bit

fsqrts   FP Square Root Single   fsqrts

Optional32 / 64

Operation: $frT \Leftarrow \sqrt{(frB)}$

Syntax:

fsqrts	frT,frB	(Rc = 0)
fsqrts.	frT,frB	(Rc = 1)

Condition Register / Floating-Point Status and Control Register:

CR Field 1:   FX,FEX,VX,OX updated if Rc = 1, otherwise not affected

CR Fields 0,2-7: not affected

FPSCR: FX, FEX, VX, XX, VSNAN, VXSQRT, FR, FI, FPRF

Description:

The **fsqrt** instruction calculates the single-precision square root of frB and stores the result in frT. The table summarizes the results for special values of frB.

Operand	Result	Exception	Notes
+∞	+∞	none	-
+0	+0	none	-
-0	-0	none	-
< 0	QNaN	VXSQRT	no result if FPSCR[VE]=1
-∞	QNaN	VXSQRT	no result if FPSCR[VE]=1
SNaN	QNaN	VXSNAN	no result if FPSCR[VE]=1
QNaN	QNaN	none	-

FPSCR[FPRF] is updated to reflect the sign and class of the result, except in the case where an Invalid Operation Exception occurs and FPSCR[VE]=1.

This instruction is an optional part of the PowerPC architecture.

Instruction Encoding:

0					5	6			10	11					15	16				20	21									30	31
1	1	1	0	1	1		T			0	0	0	0	0			B				0	0	0	0	1	0	1	1	0		Rc

T   Target FPR frT where result of operation is stored

B   Source FPR frB

Rc   Record bit

fsub   FP Subtract   fsub

POWER • 601 • 603 • PowerPC32/64

Operation: $frT \Leftarrow (frA) - (frB)$

Syntax:

fsub	frT, frA, frB	(Rc = 0)
fsub.	frT, frA, frB	(Rc = 1)

Condition Register/Floating-Point Status and Control Register:
CR Field 1:   FX,FEX,VX,OX updated if Rc = 1, otherwise not affected
CR Fields 0,2-7: not affected

FPSCR: FX, FEX, VX, OX, UX, XX, VSNAN, VXISI, FR, FI, FPRF

Description:
The **fsub** instruction subtracts the contents of frB from the contents of frA. This result is then normalized (if necessary) and rounded to double-precision (according to the current rounding mode) and then stored in frT.

The Invalid Operation Exception will be invoked if either of the operands is a Signalling NaN (VXSNAN) or if the operation is equivalent to ∞ - ∞ (VXISI).

FPSCR[FPRF] is updated to reflect the sign and class of the result, except in the case where an Invalid Operation Exception occurs and this type of exception is enabled (FPSCR[VE] = 1).

The archaic POWER mnemonic for this instruction is **fs[.]**.

Instruction Encoding:

0 5	6 10	11 15	16 20	21 25	26 30	31
1 1 1 1 1 1	T	A	B	0 0 0 0 0	1 0 1 0 0	Rc

T   Target FPR frT where result of operation is stored
A   Source FPR frA
B   Source FPR frB
Rc   Record bit

fsubs   FP Subtract Single   fsubs

601 • 603 • PowerPC32/64

Operation: frT $\Leftarrow$ (frA) − (frB)

Syntax: **fsubs**   frT,frA,frB   (Rc = 0)
           fsubs.   frT,frA,frB   (Rc = 1)

Condition Register/Floating-Point Status and Control Register:
CR Field 1:   FX,FEX,VX,OX updated if Rc = 1, otherwise not affected
CR Fields 0,2-7: not affected

FPSCR: FX, FEX, VX, OX, UX, XX, VSNAN, VXISI, FR, FI, FPRF

Description:
The **fsubs** instruction subtracts the contents of frB from the contents of frA. This result is then normalized (if necessary) and rounded to single-precision (according to the current rounding mode) and then stored in frT.

The Invalid Operation Exception will be invoked if either of the operands is a Signalling NaN (VXSNAN) or if the operation is equivalent to ∞ - ∞ (VXISI).

FPSCR[FPRF] is updated to reflect the sign and class of the result, except in the case where an Invalid Operation Exception occurs and this type of exception is enabled (FPSCR[VE] = 1).

Instruction Encoding:

0 5	6 10	11 15	16 20	21 25	26 30	31
1 1 1 0 1 1	T	A	B	0 0 0 0 0	1 0 1 0 0	Rc

T   Target FPR frT where result of operation is stored
A   Source FPR frA
B   Source FPR frB
Rc   Record bit

icbi   Instruction Cache Block Invalidate   icbi

601 • 603 • PowerPC32/64

Operation: *invalidate the specified instruction cache block*

Syntax: **icbi**   r*A*,r*B*

Condition Register/Fixed-Point Exception Register:

CR Fields 0-7:   not affected

XER: not affected

Description:

The **icbi** instruction invalidates the instruction cache block specified by the given effective address (calculated from $(rA\,|\,0) + (rB)$). The details of the operation depend on the storage mode associated with the effective address.

When the storage mode requires coherency (WIM = xx1), this instruction causes all copies of this block in any processor to be made invalid, so that the next reference from any processor causes the block to be reloaded.

When coherency is not required (WIM = xx0), this instruction invalidates the block in the instruction cache of the current processor only.

If the calculated effective address specifies an address belonging to a direct-store segment, then this instruction will operate as a no-op.

This instruction is treated as a load from the effective address for purposes of address translation and protection.

On PowerPC processors with unified caches (such as the 601), this instruction is treated as a no-op. In this case, the effective address is not validated.

Instruction Encoding:

0	5	6	10	11	15	16	20	21	30	31
0 1 1 1 1 1		0 0 0 0 0		A		B		1 1 1 1 0 1 0 1 1 0		0

A   Source GPR rA
B   Source GPR rB

isync   Instruction Cache Synchronize   isync

POWER • 601 • 603 • PowerPC32/64

Operation: *synchronize the instruction cache*

Syntax: **isync**

Condition Register/Fixed-Point Exception Register:

CR Fields 0-7:   not affected

XER: not affected

Description:

The **isync** instruction causes the processor to wait until all previous instructions have completed execution before discarding any prefetched instructions and continuing execution. This forces all subsequent instructions to be (re-)fetched from storage so that they execute in the context extablished by the previously executed instructions.

This instruction is context synchronizing and affects the current processor only.

The archaic POWER mnemonic for this instruction is **ics**.

Instruction Encoding:

0 5	6 10	11 15	16 20	21 30	31
0 1 0 0 1 1	0 0 0 0 0	0 0 0 0 0	0 0 0 0 0	0 0 1 0 0 1 0 1 1 0	0

lbz   Load Byte and Zero   lbz

POWER • 601 • 603 • PowerPC32/64

Operation: $rT \Leftarrow °Byte ((rA \mid 0) + \grave{}d)$

Syntax: **lbz** $rT,d(rA)$

Condition Register / Fixed-Point Exception Register:
CR Fields 0-7:   not affected

XER: not affected

Description:
The **lbz** instruction loads the byte that is stored at the effective address calculated from $(rA \mid 0) + \grave{}d$ and places the byte into the low-order byte of the target
register rT. The upper bytes of rT are cleared.

Instruction Encoding:

0 5	6 10	11 15	16 31
1 0 0 0 1 1	T	A	d

T	Target GPR rT where result of operation is stored
A	Source GPR rA
d	Signed 16-bit displacement

lbzu   Load Byte and Zero with Update   lbzu

POWER • 601 • 603 • PowerPC32/64

Operation: $rT \Leftarrow {}^{\circ}Byte\ ((rA) + `d)$
               $rA \Leftarrow (rA) + `d$

Syntax: **lbzu** $rT,d(rA)$

Condition Register/Fixed-Point Exception Register:
CR Fields 0-7:   not affected

XER: not affected

Description:

The **lbzu** instruction loads the byte that is stored at the effective address calculated from $(rA) + `d$ and places the byte into the low-order byte of the target register rT. The upper bytes of rT are cleared.

After the load is performed, the effective address is stored in rA.

The instruction form is invalid if GPR 0 is used for rA or if rA and rT specify the same register. However, the 601 permits these invalid forms for backward compatibility with the POWER architecture. On the 601, if r0 is specified for rA, then the effective address for the load is calculated from $`d$ and the rA is not updated with the effective address. If rA=rT, then rT is updated with the loaded data instead of the effective address.

Instruction Encoding:

0 5	6 10	11 15	16 31
1 0 0 0 1 1	T	A	d

     T   Target GPR rT where result of operation is stored
     A   Source GPR rA
     d   Signed 16-bit displacement

lbzux   Load Byte and Zero   lbzux
with Update Indexed
POWER • 601 • 603 • PowerPC32/64

Operation: $rT \Leftarrow °Byte\,((rA) + (rB))$
                 $rA \Leftarrow (rA) + (rB)$

Syntax: **lbzux**   rT,rA,rB

Condition Register / Fixed-Point Exception Register:
CR Fields 0-7:   not affected

XER: not affected

Description:
The **lbzux** instruction loads the byte that is stored at the effective address calculated from (rA) + (rB) and places the byte into the low-order byte of the target register rT. The upper bytes of rT are cleared.

After the load is performed, the effective address is stored in rA.

The instruction form is invalid if GPR 0 is used for rA or if rA and rT specify the same register. However, the 601 permits these invalid forms for backward compatibility with the POWER architecture. On the 601, if r0 is specified for rA, then the effective address for the load is calculated from (rB) and the rA is not updated with the effective address. If rA=rT, then rT is updated with the loaded data instead of the effective address.

Instruction Encoding:

0					5	6				10	11				15	16				20	21										30	31
0	1	1	1	1	1		T					A					B				0	0	0	1	1	1	0	1	1	1	0

      T   Target GPR rT where result of operation is stored
      A   Source GPR rA
      B   Source GPR rB

lbzx   Load Byte and Zero Indexed   lbzx

POWER • 601 • 603 • PowerPC32/64

Operation: $rT \Leftarrow {}^{\circ}\text{Byte} ((rA \mid 0) + (rB))$

Syntax: **lbzx** rT,rA,rB

Condition Register/Fixed-Point Exception Register:

CR Fields 0-7:   not affected

XER: not affected

Description:

The **lbzx** instruction loads the byte that is stored at the effective address calculated from $(rA \mid 0) + (rB)$ and places the byte into the low-order byte of the target register rT. The upper bytes of rT are cleared.

Instruction Encoding:

0 5	6 10	11 15	16 20	21 30	31
0 1 1 1 1 1	T	A	B	0 0 0 1 0 1 0 1 1 1 0	0

T   Target GPR rT where result of operation is stored
A   Source GPR rA
B   Source GPR rB

ld

Load Doubleword

PowerPC64

ld

Operation: $rT \Leftarrow \text{Doubleword} ((rA \mid 0) + \grave{}(ds \perp b00))$

Syntax: **ld** $rT,ds(rA)$

Condition Register/Fixed-Point Exception Register:

CR Fields 0-7:   not affected

XER: not affected

Description:

The **ld** instruction loads the doubleword that is stored at the effective address calculated from $(rA \mid 0) + \grave{}(ds \perp b00)$ and places it into the target register rT.

This instruction exists on 64-bit PowerPC implementations only.

Instruction Encoding:

0 5	6 10	11 15	16 29	30 31
1 1 1 0 1 0	T	A	ds	0 0

T   Target GPR rT where result of operation is stored
A   Source GPR rA
ds   Signed 14-bit word displacement

ldarx Load Doubleword Indexed ldarx

PowerPC64

Operation: $rT \Leftarrow {}^\circ\text{Doubleword} ((rA \mid 0) + (rB)$
create a reservation on $((rA \mid 0) + (rB)$

Syntax: **ldarx** rT,rA,rB

Condition Register / Fixed-Point Exception Register:

CR Fields 0-7:   not affected

XER: not affected

Description:

The **ldarx** instruction loads the doubleword that is stored at the effective address calculated from $(rA \mid 0) + (rB)$ and places the doubleword into the target register rT. A *reservation* is placed on this effective address, which can be used by the **stdcx.** instruction. Any existing reservation is replaced.

The calculated effective address must specify an aligned doubleword (that is, it must be a multiple of 8). If the address does not specify an aligned doubleword, the alignment exception handler may be invoked (if the load crosses a page boundary) or the results may be boundedly undefined.

If the address references a *direct-store* storage segment, then a Data Storage interrupt occurs or the results are boundedly undefined.

This instruction exists on 64-bit PowerPC implementations only.

Instruction Encoding:

0	5 6	10 11	15 16	20 21	30 31
0 1 1 1 1 1	T	A	B	0 0 0 1 0 1 0 1 0 0 0	0

T   Target GPR rT where result of operation is stored
A   Source GPR rA
B   Source GPR rB

ldu   Load Doubleword with Update   ldu

PowerPC64

Operation: $rT \Leftarrow$ Doubleword $((rA) + {}^\backprime(ds \perp b00))$

$rA \Leftarrow (rA) + {}^\backprime(ds \perp b00)$

Syntax: **ldu** $rT,ds(rA)$

Condition Register/Fixed-Point Exception Register:

CR Fields 0-7:   not affected

XER: not affected

Description:

The **ldu** instruction loads the doubleword that is stored at the effective address calculated from $(rA \mid 0) + {}^\backprime(ds \perp b00)$ and places it into the target register rT.

After the load is performed, the effective address is stored in rA.

The instruction form is invalid if GPR 0 is used for rA, or if rA and rT specify the same register.

This instruction exists on 64-bit PowerPC implementations only.

Instruction Encoding:

0 5	6 10	11 15	16 29	30 31
1 1 1 0 1 0	T	A	ds	0 1

      T   Target GPR rT where result of operation is stored

      A   Source GPR rA

      ds   Signed 14-bit word displacement

ldux

ldux
Load Doubleword
with Update Indexed
PowerPC64

Operation: $rT \Leftarrow$ Doubleword $((rA) + (rB))$
$rA \Leftarrow (rA) + (rB)$

Syntax: **ldux**   rT,rA,rB

Condition Register/Fixed-Point Exception Register:
CR Fields 0-7:   not affected

XER: not affected

Description:

The **ldux** instruction loads the doubleword that is stored at the effective address calculated from $(rA) + (rB)$ and places it into the target register rT.

After the load is performed, the effective address is stored in rA.

The instruction form is invalid if GPR 0 is used for rA or if rA and rT specify the same register.

This instruction exists on 64-bit PowerPC implementations only.

Instruction Encoding:

0 1 1 1 1 1	T	A	B	0 0 0 0 1 1 0 1 0 1 0	0

0 ..... 5 6 ..... 10 11 ..... 15 16 ..... 20 21 ..... 30 31

T   Target GPR rT where result of operation is stored
A   Source GPR rA
B   Source GPR rB

ldx   Load Doubleword Indexed   ldx

PowerPC64

Operation: $rT \Leftarrow Doubleword((rA \mid 0) + (rB))$

Syntax: **ldx** rT,rA,rB

Condition Register / Fixed-Point Exception Register:

CR Fields 0-7:   not affected

XER: not affected

Description:

The **ldx** instruction loads the doubleword that is stored at the effective address calculated from $(rA \mid 0) + (rB)$ and places it into the target register rT.

This instruction exists on 64-bit PowerPC implementations only.

Instruction Encoding:

0 5	6 10	11 15	16 20	21 30	31
0 1 1 1 1 1	T	A	B	0 0 0 0 0 1 0 1 0 1 0	0

     T   Target GPR rT where result of operation is stored
     A   Source GPR rA
     B   Source GPR rB

lfd   Load Floating-Point Double-Precision   lfd

POWER • 601 • 603 • PowerPC32/64

Operation: $frT \Leftarrow FDouble\ ((rA\,|\,0) + \grave{}d)$

Syntax: **lfd** $frT,d(rA)$

Condition Register/Fixed-Point Exception Register:

CR Fields 0-7:   not affected

XER: not affected

Description:

The **lfd** instruction loads the doubleword that is stored at the effective address calculated from $(rA\,|\,0) + \grave{}d$ and places it into the target register frT.

Instruction Encoding:

0 5	6 10	11 15	16 31
1 1 0 0 1 0	T	A	d

T   Target FPR frT where result of operation is stored
A   Source GPR rA
d   Signed 16-bit displacement

lfdu   Load Floating-Point   lfdu
Double-Precision with Update
POWER • 601 • 603 • PowerPC32/64

Operation: fr$T \Leftarrow$ FDouble ((rA) + `d)

                 r$A \Leftarrow$ (rA) + `d

Syntax: **lfdu**   fr$T$,d(rA)

Condition Register/Fixed-Point Exception Register:

CR Fields 0-7:   not affected

XER: not affected

Description:

The **lfdu** instruction loads the doubleword that is stored at the effective address calculated from (rA) + `d and places it into the target register fr$T$.

After the load is performed, the effective address is stored in rA.

The instruction form is invalid if GPR 0 is used for rA. However, the 601 permits this invalid form for backward compatability with the POWER architecture. On the 601, if A=0, then the effective address for the load is calculated from `d and rA is not updated with the effective address.

Instruction Encoding:

0 5	6 10	11 15	16 31
1 1 0 0 1 1	T	A	d

     T   Target FPR frT where result of operation is stored

     A   Source GPR rA

     d   Signed 16-bit displacement

lfdux   Load Floating-Point Double-   lfdux
Precision with Update Indexed
POWER • 601 • 603 • PowerPC32/64

Operation: $frT \Leftarrow FDouble\ ((rA) + (rB))$

                $rA \Leftarrow (rA) + (rB)$

Syntax: **lfdux** frT,rA,rB

Condition Register/Fixed-Point Exception Register:
CR Fields 0-7:   not affected

XER: not affected

Description:

The **lfdux** instruction loads the doubleword that is stored at the effective address calculated from $(rA) + (rB)$ and places it into the target register frT.

After the load is performed, the effective address is stored in rA.

The instruction form is invalid if GPR 0 is used for rA. However, the 601 permits this invalid form for backward compatability with the POWER architecture. On the 601, if A=0, then the effective address for the load is calculated from (rB) and rA is not updated with the effective address.

Instruction Encoding:

0 5	6 10	11 15	16 20	21 30	31
0 1 1 1 1 1	T	A	B	1 0 0 1 1 1 0 1 1 1	0

     T   Target FPR frT where result of operation is stored

     A   Source GPR rA

     B   Source GPR rB

lfdx

Load Floating-Point
Double-Precision Indexed

lfdx

POWER • 601 • 603 • PowerPC32/64

Operation: $frT \Leftarrow \text{FDouble}((rA|0) + (rB))$

Syntax: **lfdx**   frT,rA,rB

Condition Register/Fixed-Point Exception Register:

CR Fields 0-7:   not affected

XER: not affected

Description:

The **lfdx** instruction loads the doubleword that is stored at the effective address calculated from $(rA|0) + (rB)$ and places it into the target register frT.

Instruction Encoding:

0	5 6	10 11	15 16	20 21	30 31
0 1 1 1 1 1	T	A	B	1 0 0 1 0 1 0 1 1 1 0	0

    T   Target FPR frT where result of operation is stored
    A   Source GPR rA
    B   Source GPR rB

lfs   Load Floating-Point Single-Precision   lfs

POWER • 601 • 603 • PowerPC32/64

Operation: $frT \Leftarrow \text{FSingle} ((rA \mid 0) + {}^\backprime d)$

Syntax: **lfs** $frT,d(rA)$

Condition Register/Fixed-Point Exception Register:

CR Fields 0-7:   not affected

XER: not affected

Description:

The **lfs** instruction loads the word that is stored at the effective address calculated from $(rA \mid 0) + {}^\backprime d$, converts the value to double-precision (by interpreting the word as a single-precision value), and places the converted doubleword into the target register frT.

Instruction Encoding:

0 5	6 10	11 15	16 31
1 1 0 0 0 0	T	A	d

T	Target FPR frT where result of operation is stored
A	Source GPR rA
d	Signed 16-bit displacement

lfsu

lfsu

Load Floating-Point
Single-Precision with Update
POWER • 601 • 603 • PowerPC32/64

Operation: $frT \Leftarrow FSingle((rA) + \grave{}d)$

$rA \Leftarrow (rA) + \grave{}d$

Syntax: **lfsu** $frT,d(rA)$

Condition Register/Fixed-Point Exception Register:

CR Fields 0-7:   not affected

XER: not affected

Description:

The **lfsu** instruction loads the word that is stored at the effective address calculated from $(rA) + \grave{}d$, converts the value to double-precision (by interpreting the word as a single-precision value), and places the converted doubleword into the target register frT.

After the load is performed, the effective address is stored in rA.

The instruction form is invalid if GPR 0 is used for rA. However, the 601 permits this invalid form for backward compatability with the POWER architecture. On the 601, if A=0, then the effective address for the load is calculated from $\grave{}d$ and rA is not updated with the effective address.

Instruction Encoding:

0	5	6	10	11	15	16	31
1 1 0 0 0 1		T		A		d	

T   Target FPR frT where result of operation is stored
A   Source GPR rA
d   Signed 16-bit displacement

lfsux   Load Floating-Point Single-   lfsux
Precision with Update Indexed
POWER • 601 • 603 • PowerPC32/64

Operation: $frT \Leftarrow FSingle((rA) + (rB))$
                 $rA \Leftarrow (rA) + (rB)$

Syntax: **lfsux** frT,rA,rB

Condition Register/Fixed-Point Exception Register:
CR Fields 0-7:   not affected

XER: not affected

Description:
The **lfsux** instruction loads the word that is stored at the effective address calculated from $(rA) + (rB)$, converts the value to double-precision (by interpreting the word as a single-precision value), and places the converted doubleword into the target register frT.

After the load is performed, the effective address is stored in rA.

The instruction form is invalid if GPR 0 is used for rA. However, the 601 permits this invalid form for backward compatability with the POWER architecture. On the 601, if A=0, then the effective address for the load is calculated from (rB) and rA is not updated with the effective address.

Instruction Encoding:

0 5	6 10	11 15	16 20	21 30	31
0 1 1 1 1 1	T	A	B	1 0 0 0 1 1 0 1 1 1 0	0

     T   Target FPR frT where result of operation is stored
     A   Source GPR rA
     B   Source GPR rB

lfsx

Load Floating-Point
Single-Precision Indexed
POWER • 601 • 603 • PowerPC32/64

lfsx

Operation: $frT \Leftarrow FSingle\ ((rA\,|\,0) + (rB))$

Syntax: **lfsx** frT,rA,rB

Condition Register/Fixed-Point Exception Register:
CR Fields 0-7:   not affected

XER: not affected

Description:
The **lfsx** instruction loads the word that is stored at the effective address calculated from $(rA\,|\,0) + (rB)$, converts the value to double-precision (by interpreting the word as a single-precision value), and places the converted doubleword into the target register frT.

Instruction Encoding:

0 5 6	T 10 11	A 15 16	B 20 21	1 0 0 0 0 1 0 1 1 1 30 0 31
0 1 1 1 1 1	T	A	B	1 0 0 0 0 1 0 1 1 1 0

T   Target FPR frT where result of operation is stored
A   Source GPR rA
B   Source GPR rB

lha   Load Halfword Algebraic   lha

POWER • 601 • 603 • PowerPC32/64

Operation: $rT \Leftarrow$ `Halfword $((rA \,|\, 0) +$ `$d)$

Syntax: **lha** $rT,d(rA)$

Condition Register/Fixed-Point Exception Register:

CR Fields 0-7:   not affected

XER: not affected

Description:

The **lha** instruction loads the halfword that is stored at the effective address calculated from $(rA \,|\, 0) +$ `d and places the halfword into the low-order two bytes of the target register rT. The upper bytes of rT are copied from the sign bit of the loaded halfword.

Instruction Encoding:

0 5	6 10	11 15	16 31
1 0 1 0 1 0	T	A	d

T   Target GPR rT where result of operation is stored
A   Source GPR rA
d   Signed 16-bit displacement

lhau Load Halfword Algebraic with Update lhau

POWER • 601 • 603 • PowerPC32/64

Operation: $rT \Leftarrow \text{`Halfword} ((rA) + \text{`}d)$

$rA \Leftarrow (rA) + \text{`}d$

Syntax: **lhau** $rT,d(rA)$

Condition Register/Fixed-Point Exception Register:

CR Fields 0-7:   not affected

XER: not affected

Description:

The **lhau** instruction loads the halfword that is stored at the effective address calculated from $(rA) + \text{`}d$ and places the halfword into the low-order two bytes of the target register rT. The upper bytes of rT are copied from the sign bit of the loaded halfword.

After the load is performed, the effective address is stored in rA.

The instruction form is invalid if GPR 0 is used for rA or if rA and rT specify the same register. However, the 601 permits these invalid forms for backward compatibility with the POWER architecture. On the 601, if r0 is specified for rA, then the effective address for the load is calculated from `d and the rA is not updated with the effective address. If $rA=rT$, then rT is updated with the loaded data instead of the effective address.

Instruction Encoding:

0	5	6	10	11	15	16	31
1 0 1 0 1 1		T		A		d	

T   Target GPR rT where result of operation is stored
A   Source GPR rA
d   Signed 16-bit displacement

lhaux   Load Halfword Algebraic   lhaux
with Update Indexed
POWER • 601 • 603 • PowerPC32/64

Operation: $rT \Leftarrow$ `Halfword $((rA) + (rB))$
              $rA \Leftarrow (rA) + (rB)$

Syntax: **lhaux**   rT,rA,rB

Condition Register/Fixed-Point Exception Register:
CR Fields 0-7:   not affected

XER: not affected

Description:
The **lhaux** instruction loads the halfword that is stored at the effective address calculated from $(rA) + (rB)$ and places the halfword into the low-order two bytes of the target register rT. The upper bytes of rT are copied from the sign bit of the loaded halfword.

After the load is performed, the effective address is stored in rA.

The instruction form is invalid if GPR 0 is used for rA or if rA and rT specify the same register. However, the 601 permits these invalid forms for backward compatibility with the POWER architecture. On the 601, if r0 is specified for rA, then the effective address for the load is calculated from (rB) and the rA is not updated with the effective address. If rA=rT, then rT is updated with the loaded data instead of the effective address.

Instruction Encoding:

0	5	6	10	11	15	16	20	21	30	31
0 1 1 1 1 1		T		A		B		0 1 0 1 1 1 0 1 1 1		0

T   Target GPR rT where result of operation is stored
A   Source GPR rA
B   Source GPR rB

lhax   Load Halfword Algebraic Indexed   lhax

POWER • 601 • 603 • PowerPC32/64

Operation: $rT \Leftarrow$ `Halfword $((rA \mid 0) + (rB))$

Syntax: **lhax**   rT,rA,rB

Condition Register/Fixed-Point Exception Register:

CR Fields 0-7:   not affected

XER: not affected

Description:

The **lhax** instruction loads the halfword that is stored at the effective address calculated from $(rA \mid 0) + (rB)$ and places the halfword into the low-order two bytes of the target register rT. The upper bytes of rT are copied from the sign bit of the loaded halfword.

Instruction Encoding:

0 5	6 10	11 15	16 20	21 30	31
0 1 1 1 1 1	T	A	B	0 1 0 1 0 1 0 1 1 1 0	0

T   Target GPR rT where result of operation is stored
A   Source GPR rA
B   Source GPR rB

lhbrx

Load Halfword
Byte-Reversed Indexed
POWER • 601 • 603 • PowerPC32/64

lhbrx

Operation: $h := \text{Halfword} ((rA \,|\, 0) + (rB))$
$rT \Leftarrow {}^{\circ}(h[8:15] \perp h[0:7])$

Syntax: **lhbrx** rT, rA, rB

Condition Register / Fixed-Point Exception Register:
CR Fields 0-7:   not affected

XER: not affected

Description:
The **lhbrx** instruction loads the halfword that is stored at the effective address calculated from $(rA \,|\, 0) + (rB)$, swaps the two bytes of the halfword, and then places this *byte-reversed* halfword into the low-order two bytes of the target register rT. The upper bytes of rT are cleared.

For some PowerPC implementations, this byte-reversed load instruction may have a greater latency than other load instructions. On the 601 and 603, the latency for this instruction is the same as for a normal load instruction.

Instruction Encoding:

0	5	6	10	11	15	16	20	21	30	31
0 1 1 1 1 1		T		A		B		1 1 0 0 0 1 0 1 1 0	0	

T   Target GPR rT where result of operation is stored
A   Source GPR rA
B   Source GPR rB

lhz   Load Halfword and Zero   lhz

POWER • 601 • 603 • PowerPC32/64

Operation: $rT \Leftarrow °Halfword\ ((rA\,|\,0) + `d)$

Syntax: **lhz** $rT,d(rA)$

Condition Register/Fixed-Point Exception Register:

CR Fields 0-7:   not affected

XER: not affected

Description:

The **lhz** instruction loads the halfword that is stored at the effective address calculated from $(rA\,|\,0) + `d$ and places the halfword into the low-order two bytes of the target register rT. The upper bytes of rT are cleared.

Instruction Encoding:

0 5	6 10	11 15	16 31
1 0 1 0 0 0	T	A	d

T   Target GPR rT where result of operation is stored
A   Source GPR rA
d   Signed 16-bit displacement

lhzu   Load Halfword and Zero with Update   lhzu

POWER • 601 • 603 • PowerPC32/64

Operation: $rT \Leftarrow {}^{\circ}\text{Halfword}\,((rA) + {}^{\backprime}d)$
                $rA \Leftarrow (rA) + {}^{\backprime}d$

Syntax: **lhzu** $rT,d(rA)$

Condition Register/Fixed-Point Exception Register:

CR Fields 0-7:   not affected

XER: not affected

Description:

The **lhzu** instruction loads the halfword that is stored at the effective address calculated from $(rA) + {}^{\backprime}d$ and places the halfword into the low-order two bytes of the target register rT. The upper bytes of rT are cleared.

After the load is performed, the effective address is stored in rA.

The instruction form is invalid if GPR 0 is used for rA or if rA and rT specify the same register. However, the 601 permits these invalid forms for backward compatibility with the POWER architecture. On the 601, if r0 is specified for rA, then the effective address for the load is calculated from `d and the rA is not updated with the effective address. If rA=rT, then rT is updated with the loaded data instead of the effective address.

Instruction Encoding:

0 5	6 10	11 15	16 31
1 0 1 0 0 1	T	A	d

        T   Target GPR rT where result of operation is stored
        A   Source GPR rA
        d   Signed 16-bit displacement

484   Appendix A

lhzux   Load Halfword and Zero   lhzux
with Update Indexed
POWER • 601 • 603 • PowerPC32/64

Operation: $rT \Leftarrow {}^{\circ}\text{Halfword}((rA)+(rB))$

                  $rA \Leftarrow (rA)+(rB)$

Syntax: **lhzux** rT,rA,rB

Condition Register/Fixed-Point Exception Register:
CR Fields 0-7:   not affected

XER: not affected

Description:
The **lhzux** instruction loads the halfword that is stored at the effective address calculated from $(rA)+(rB)$ and places the halfword into the low-order two bytes of the target register rT. The upper bytes of rT are cleared.

After the load is performed, the effective address is stored in rA.

The instruction form is invalid if GPR 0 is used for rA or if rA and rT specify the same register. However, the 601 permits these invalid forms for backward compatibility with the POWER architecture. On the 601, if r0 is specified for rA, then the effective address for the load is calculated from (rB) and the rA is not updated with the effective address. If rA=rT, then rT is updated with the loaded data instead of the effective address.

Instruction Encoding:

0 5	6 10	11 15	16 20	21 30	31
0 1 1 1 1 1	T	A	B	0 1 0 0 1 1 0 1 1 1 0	0

T   Target GPR rT where result of operation is stored

A   Source GPR rA

B   Source GPR rB

lhzx   Load Halfword and Zero Indexed   lhzx

POWER • 601 • 603 • PowerPC32/64

Operation: $rT \Leftarrow {}^{\circ}\text{Halfword} ((rA \mid 0) + (rB))$

Syntax: **lhzx** rT,rA,rB

Condition Register/Fixed-Point Exception Register:

CR Fields 0-7:   not affected

XER: not affected

Description:

The **lhzx** instruction loads the halfword that is stored at the effective address calculated from $(rA \mid 0) + (rB)$ and places the halfword into the low-order two bytes of the target register rT. The upper bytes of rT are cleared.

Instruction Encoding:

0	5 6	10 11	15 16	20 21	30 31
0 1 1 1 1 1	T	A	B	0 1 0 0 0 1 0 1 1 1 0

T   Target GPR rT where result of operation is stored
A   Source GPR rA
B   Source GPR rB

lmw   Load Multiple Word   lmw

POWER • 601 • 603 • PowerPC32/64

Operation:
$$ea := (rA | 0) + `d$$
$$R := T$$
$$\text{while } (R \leq 31)$$
$$\quad rR \Leftarrow °Word (ea)$$
$$\quad ea := ea + 4$$
$$\quad R := R + 1$$

Syntax: **lmw**   rT,d(rA)

Condition Register/Fixed-Point Exception Register:

CR Fields 0-7:   not affected

XER: not affected

Description:

The **lmw** instruction loads words from memory into a set of the GPRs. The first word to be loaded is specified by the effective address calculated from $(rA | 0) +$ `d. Consecutive words are loaded from this address into registers starting with register rT and continuing up to register r31.

On 64-bit PowerPC implementations, each word is loaded into the low-order word of the target register and the upper word is cleared.

The calculated effective address must specify an aligned word (that is, it must be a multiple of 4). If the address does not specify an aligned word, the alignment exception handler may be invoked (if the load crosses a page boundary), or the results may be boundedly undefined.

The preferred form for this instruction is when the effective address and rT are chosen so that the low-order byte that is loaded into r31 is the last byte of an aligned quadword in memory. It is possible that some PowerPC implementations will execute non-preferred forms more slowly than the preferred forms. On future implementations, this instruction may execute more slowly than a series of instructions that perform the same operation.

If rA is in the range of registers to be loaded, then the instruction form is invalid. However, the 601 permits these invalid forms for backward compatability with the POWER architecture. On the 601, if rA is in the range to be loaded, then rA is skipped and the data that would have been written into rA is discarded. If rA = rT = 0, then rA is not being used for addressing and will be loaded with data.

Executing this instruction when the processor is operating in *little-endian* byte-order mode will cause the system alignment error handler to be invoked.

The archaic POWER mnemonic for this instruction is **lm**.

Instruction Encoding:

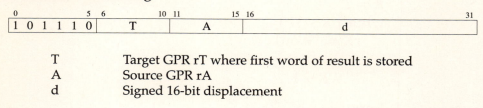

T	Target GPR rT where first word of result is stored
A	Source GPR rA
d	Signed 16-bit displacement

lscbx   Load String and Compare   lscbx
Byte Indexed
POWER • 601

Operation: *load bytes into registers from memory until match*

Syntax:

lscbx	rT,rA,rB	(Rc = 0)
lscbx.	rT,rA,rB	(Rc = 1)

Condition Register/Fixed-Point Exception Register:

CR Field 0:   LT,GT,EQ,SO updated if Rc = 1, otherwise not affected
CR Fields 1-7: not affected

XER: XER[25:31] updated with number of bytes copied

Description:

The **lscbx** instruction loads bytes from memory into a set of GPRs until a matching byte is found or a maximum byte count is reached. The byte-to-match is stored in XER[16:23], and the maximum number of bytes to copy is specified in XER[25:31]. Upon completion, this instruction returns the number of bytes copied in XER[25:31].

The bytes are loaded starting from the effective address (calculated from (rA|0)) and stored into as many registers as are needed, starting with register rT. The register sequence wraps from r31 to r0 if necessary.

Bytes are loaded from left to right into the low-order word of the target registers. If a matching byte is found, that byte is copied into the appropriate register before the instruction terminates.

If the last register to be loaded is only partially filled, then the value stored in the remaining bytes is undefined. If a matching byte was found, then the remaining bytes of all of the registers that would have been loaded are undefined.

The operation of this instruction can be summarized as:

```
ea := (rA | 0) + (rB)
R := T - 1
nBytes := XER[25:31]
nBytesCopied := 0
matchByte := XER[16:23]
matchFound := 0
i := 0
while ( nBytes > 0 )
```

$$\begin{aligned}
&\text{if } (\,i = 0\,) \\
&\qquad R := (R + 1) \,\% \, 32 \\
&\qquad rR \Leftarrow \textit{undefined} \\
&\text{if } (\textit{matchFound} = 0\,) \\
&\qquad rR[i\!:\,(i{+}7)] \Leftarrow \text{Byte}(\,ea\,) \\
&\qquad \textit{nBytesCopied} := \textit{nBytesCopied} + 1 \\
&\text{if } (\,\text{Byte}(\,ea\,) = \textit{matchByte}\,) \\
&\qquad \textit{matchFound} := 1 \\
&i := i + 8 \\
&\text{if } (\,i = 32\,) \\
&\qquad i := 0 \\
&ea := ea + 1 \\
&\textit{nBytes} := \textit{nBytes} - 1 \\
&\text{XER}[25\!:\!31] \Leftarrow \textit{nBytesCopied}
\end{aligned}$$

If XER[25:31] is 0 (indicating that no bytes should be copied from memory), then the contents of rT are undefined. Note that this differs from the POWER architecture where rT is not altered if XER[25:31] = 0.

If rA or B are in the range of registers to be loaded, then the instruction form is invalid. However, the 601 permits these invalid forms for backward compatability with the POWER architecture. On the 601, if rA or B are in the range to be loaded, then they will be skipped and the data that would have been written into the registers will be discarded. If A= 0, then rA is not being used for addressing and will be loaded with data if necessary.

This instruction is not part of the PowerPC architecture.

Instruction Encoding:

0	5 6	10 11	15 16	20 21	30 31
0 1 1 1 1 1	T	A	B	0 1 0 0 0 1 0 1 0 1 0	0

T	Target GPR rT where first 4 bytes of result are stored
A	Source GPR rA
B	Source GPR rB

lswi   Load String Word Immediate   lswi

POWER • 601 • 603 • PowerPC32/64

Operation: *load nBytes bytes into registers from memory*

Syntax: **lswi**   rT,rA,nBytes

Condition Register/Fixed-Point Exception Register:

CR Fields 0-7:   not affected

XER: not affected

Description:

The **lswi** instruction loads bytes from memory into a set of GPRs. The number of bytes (specified by the immediate *nBytes* value) are loaded from the effective address (calculated from (rA|0)) and stored into as many registers as are needed, starting with register rT. The register sequence wraps from r31 to r0 if necessary.

Bytes are loaded from left to right into the low-order word of the target registers. If the last register to be loaded is only partially filled, the remaining bytes will be set to 0. On 64-bit PowerPC implementations, the upper word of each register is cleared.

The operation of this instruction can be summarized as

$$ea := (rA | 0)$$
$$R := T - 1$$
$$i := [\tfrac{0}{32}]$$
if (nBytes = 0)
    nBytes := 32
while ($nBytes > 0$)
    if ($i = [\tfrac{0}{32}]$)
        $R := (R + 1) \% 32$
        $rR \Leftarrow 0$
    $rR[i : (i+7)] \Leftarrow \text{Byte}(ea)$
    $i := i + 8$
    if ($i = [\tfrac{32}{64}]$)
        $i := [\tfrac{0}{32}]$
    $ea := ea + 1$
    $nBytes := nBytes - 1$

The preferred form for this instruction is when the starting register rT is r5. It is possible that some PowerPC implementations will execute non-preferred forms more slowly than the preferred forms. Because of the complexity of this instruction, it is also possible that, on some implementations, this instruction may execute slower than a series of instructions that perform the same operation.

If rA is in the range of registers to be loaded, then the instruction form is invalid. However, the 601 permits these invalid forms for backward compatability with the POWER architecture. On the 601, if rA is in the range to be loaded, then rA is skipped and the data that would have been written into rA is discarded. If A= 0, then rA is not being used for addressing and will be loaded with data if necessary.

Executing this instruction when the processor is operating in *little-endian* byte-order mode will cause the system alignment error handler to be invoked.

The archaic POWER mnemonic for this instruction is **lsi**.

Instruction Encoding:

0	5 6	10 11	15 16	20 21	30 31
0 1 1 1 1 1	T	A	nBytes	1 0 0 1 0 1 0 1 0 1	0

T	Target GPR rT where first 4 bytes of result are stored
A	Source GPR rA
nBytes	Number of bytes to load

lswx   Load String Word Indexed   lswx

POWER • 601 • 603 • PowerPC32/64

Operation: *load XER[25:31] bytes into registers from memory*

Syntax: **lswx**   rT,rA,rB

Condition Register/Fixed-Point Exception Register:

CR Fields 0-7:   not affected

XER: not affected

Description:

The **lswx** instruction loads bytes from memory into a set of GPRs. The number of bytes (specified by bits 25 to 31 of the XER) are loaded from the effective address (calculated from $(rA \mid 0) + (rB)$) and stored into as many registers as are needed, starting with register rT. The register sequence wraps from r31 to r0 if necessary.

Bytes are loaded from left to right into the low-order word of the target registers. If the last register to be loaded is only partially filled, the remaining byte will be set to 0. On 64-bit PowerPC implementations, the upper word of each register is cleared.

The operation of this instruction can be summarized as

$ea := (rA \mid 0) + (rB)$
$R := T - 1$
$nBytes := XER[25:31]$
$i := [\frac{0}{32}]$
while ($nBytes > 0$)
    if ($i = [\frac{0}{32}]$)
        $R := (R + 1) \% 32$
        $rR \Leftarrow 0$
    $rR[i:(i+7)] \Leftarrow Byte(ea)$
    $i := i + 8$
    if ($i = [\frac{32}{64}]$)
        $i := [\frac{0}{32}]$
    $ea := ea + 1$
    $nBytes := nBytes - 1$

If XER[25:31] is 0 (indicating that no bytes should be copied from memory), then the contents of rT are undefined.

The preferred form for this instruction is when the starting register rT is r5 and the total number of registers being loaded is less than or equal to 12. It is possible that some PowerPC implementations will execute non-preferred forms more slowly than the preferred forms. Because of the complexity of this instruction, it is also possible that, on some implementations, this instruction may execute slower than a series of instructions that perform the same operation.

If rA or B are in the range of registers to be loaded, then the instruction form is invalid. However, the 601 permits these invalid forms for backward compatability with the POWER architecture. On the 601, if rA or B are in the range to be loaded, then they will be skipped and the data that would have been written into the registers will be discarded. If A=0, then rA is not being used for addressing and will be loaded with data if necessary.

Executing this instruction when the processor is operating in *little-endian* byte-order mode will cause the system alignment error handler to be invoked.

The archaic POWER mnemonic for this instruction is **lsx**.

Instruction Encoding:

0 5	6 10	11 15	16 20	21 30 31
0 1 1 1 1 1	T	A	B	1 0 0 0 0 1 0 1 0 1 0

T	Target GPR rT where first 4 bytes of result are stored
A	Source GPR rA
B	Source GPR rB

lwa　　　Load Word Algebraic　　　lwa

PowerPC64

Operation:　　$rT \Leftarrow \text{`Word} ((rA | 0) + \text{`}(ds \perp b00)$

Syntax:　　　**lwa**　　　$rT,d(rA)$

Condition Register / Fixed-Point Exception Register:

CR Fields 0-7:　not affected

XER:　　　　　not affected

Description:

The **lwa** instruction loads the word that is stored at the effective address calculated from $(rA | 0) + \text{`}(ds \perp b00)$ and places it into the low-order word of the target register rT. The upper word of rT is copied from the sign bit of the loaded word.

This instruction exists on 64-bit PowerPC implementations only.

Instruction Encoding:

0　　　　5	6　　10	11　　15	16　　　　　　29	30 31
1 1 1 0 1 0	T	A	ds	1 0

T　　　　　Target GPR rT where result of operation is stored
A　　　　　Source GPR rA
ds　　　　　Signed 14-bit word displacement

lwarx   Load Word and Reserve Indexed   lwarx

601 • 603 • PowerPC32/64

Operation: $rT \Leftarrow {}^{\circ}\text{Word}\,((rA\,|\,0) + (rB))$
create a reservation on $((rA\,|\,0) + (rB))$

Syntax: **lwarx** rT,rA,rB

Condition Register/Fixed-Point Exception Register:

CR Fields 0-7:   not affected

XER: not affected

Description:

The **lwarx** instruction loads the word that is stored at the effective address calculated from $(rA\,|\,0) + (rB)$ and places the word into the target register rT. A *reservation* is placed on this effective address, which can be used by the **stwcx.** instruction. Any existing reservation is replaced.

The calculated effective address must specify an aligned word (that is, it must be a multiple of 4). If the address does not specify an aligned word, the alignment exception handler may be invoked (if the load crosses a page boundary) or the results may be boundedly undefined.

If the address references a *direct-store* storage segment, then a Data Storage interrupt occurs or the results are boundedly undefined.

On 64-bit PowerPC implementations, the word is loaded into the low-order word of rT and the upper word of rT is cleared.

Instruction Encoding:

0					5	6			10	11			15	16			20	21									30	31
0	1	1	1	1	1	T		A		B				0	0	0	0	0	1	0	1	0	0	0	0

T   Target GPR rT where result of operation is stored
A   Source GPR rA
B   Source GPR rB

lwaux   Load Word Algebraic   lwaux
with Update Indexed
PowerPC64

Operation: $rT \Leftarrow$ `Word $((rA) + (rB))$

                $rA \Leftarrow (rA) + (rB)$

Syntax: **lwaux** rT, rA, rB

Condition Register / Fixed-Point Exception Register:

CR Fields 0-7:   not affected

XER: not affected

Description:

The **lwaux** instruction loads the word that is stored at the effective address calculated from $(rA) + (rB)$ and places it into the low-order word of the target register rT. The upper word of rT is copied from the sign bit of the loaded word.

After the load is performed, the effective address is stored in rA.

The instruction form is invalid if GPR 0 is used for rA or if rA and rT specify the same register.

This instruction exists on 64-bit PowerPC implementations only.

Instruction Encoding:

0 5	6 10	11 15	16 20	21 30	31
0 1 1 1 1 1	T	A	B	0 1 0 1 1 1 0 1 0 1	0

     T   Target GPR rT where result of operation is stored

     A   Source GPR rA

     B   Source GPR rB

lwax   Load Word Algebraic Indexed   lwax

PowerPC64

Operation: $rT \Leftarrow$ `Word $((rA \mid 0) + (rB))$

Syntax: **lwax** rT, rA, rB

Condition Register / Fixed-Point Exception Register:

CR Fields 0-7:   not affected

XER: not affected

Description:

The **lwax** instruction loads the word that is stored at the effective address calculated from $(rA \mid 0) + (rB)$ and places it into the low-order word of the target register rT. The upper word of rT is copied from the sign bit of the loaded word.

This instruction exists on 64-bit PowerPC implementations only.

Instruction Encoding:

0 5	6 10	11 15	16 20	21 30	31
0 1 1 1 1 1	T	A	B	0 1 0 1 0 1 0 1 0 1 0	0

T	Target GPR rT where result of operation is stored
A	Source GPR rA
B	Source GPR rB

lwbrx
Load Word
Byte-Reversed Indexed
POWER • 601 • 603 • PowerPC32/64

lwbrx

Operation: $w := \text{Word} ((rA \mid 0) + (rB))$
$rT \Leftarrow {}^\circ(w[24:31] \perp w[16:23] \perp w[8:15] \perp w[0:7])$

Syntax: **lwbrx** rT, rA, rB

Condition Register/Fixed-Point Exception Register:
CR Fields 0-7:   not affected

XER: not affected

Description:
The **lwbrx** instruction loads the word that is stored at the effective address calculated from $(rA \mid 0) + (rB)$, reverses the four bytes of the word, and then places this *byte-reversed* word into target register rT.

On 64-bit PowerPC implementations, the word is loaded into the low-order word of rT and the upper word of rT is cleared.

For some PowerPC implementations, this byte-reversed load instruction may have a greater latency than other load instructions. On the 601 and 603, the latency for this instruction is the same as for a normal load instruction.

Instruction Encoding:

0				5	6				10	11				15	16				20	21									30	31
0	1	1	1	1	1		T				A					B				1	0	0	0	0	1	0	1	1	0	0

T	Target GPR rT where result of operation is stored
A	Source GPR rA
B	Source GPR rB

lwz   Load Word and Zero   lwz

POWER • 601 • 603 • PowerPC32/64

Operation: $rT \Leftarrow \,^{\circ}Word\,((rA \,|\, 0) + \,`d)$

Syntax: **lwz** $rT,d(rA)$

Condition Register/Fixed-Point Exception Register:
CR Fields 0-7:   not affected

XER: not affected

Description:

The **lwz** instruction loads the word that is stored at the effective address calculated from $(rA \,|\, 0) + \,`d$ and places the word into the target register rT.

On 64-bit PowerPC implementations, the word is loaded into the low-order word of rT and the upper word of rT is cleared.

The archaic POWER mnemonic for this instruction is l.

Instruction Encoding:

0 5	6 10	11 15	16 31
1 0 0 0 0 0	T	A	d

T	Target GPR rT where result of operation is stored
A	Source GPR rA
d	Signed 16-bit displacement

lwzu   Load Word and Zero with Update   lwzu

POWER • 601 • 603 • PowerPC32/64

Operation: $rT \Leftarrow {}^{\circ}Word ((rA) + {}^{\backprime}d)$

$rA \Leftarrow (rA) + {}^{\backprime}d$

Syntax: **lwzu** $rT,d(rA)$

Condition Register/Fixed-Point Exception Register:

CR Fields 0-7:   not affected

XER: not affected

Description:

The **lwzu** instruction loads the word that is stored at the effective address calculated from $(rA) + {}^{\backprime}d$ and places the word into the target register rT.

On 64-bit PowerPC implementations, the word is loaded into the low-order word of rT and the upper word of rT is cleared.

After the load is performed, the effective address is stored in rA.

The instruction form is invalid if GPR 0 is used for rA or if rA and rT specify the same register. However, the 601 permits these invalid forms for backward compatibility with the POWER architecture. On the 601, if r0 is specified for rA, then the effective address for the load is calculated from ${}^{\backprime}d$ and the rA is not updated with the effective address. If $rA=rT$, then rT is updated with the loaded data instead of the effective address.

The archaic POWER mnemonic for this instruction is **lu**.

Instruction Encoding:

0 5	6 10	11 15	16 31
1 0 0 0 0 1	T	A	d

T   Target GPR rT where result of operation is stored
A   Source GPR rA
d   Signed 16-bit displacement

lwzux   Load Word and Zero   lwzux
with Update Indexed
POWER • 601 • 603 • PowerPC32/64

Operation: $rT \Leftarrow {}^{\circ}Word\ ((rA) + (rB))$
$rA \Leftarrow (rA) + (rB)$

Syntax: **lwzux**   rT,rA,rB

Condition Register/Fixed-Point Exception Register:
CR Fields 0-7:   not affected

XER: not affected

Description:

The **lwzux** instruction loads the word that is stored at the effective address calculated from (rA) + (rB) and places the word into the target register rT.

On 64-bit PowerPC implementations, the word is loaded into the low-order word of rT and the upper word of rT is cleared.

After the load is performed, the effective address is stored in rA.

The instruction form is invalid if GPR 0 is used for rA or if rA and rT specify the same register. However, the 601 permits these invalid forms for backward compatibility with the POWER architecture. On the 601, if r0 is specified for rA, then the effective address for the load is calculated from (rB) and the rA is not updated with the effective address. If rA=rT, then rT is updated with the loaded data instead of the effective address.

The archaic POWER mnemonic for this instruction is **lux**.

Instruction Encoding:

0	5	6	10	11	15	16	20	21	30	31
0 1 1 1 1 1		T		A		B		0 0 0 0 1 1 0 1 1 1 0		0

T   Target GPR rT where result of operation is stored
A   Source GPR rA
B   Source GPR rB

lwzx   Load Word and Zero Indexed   lwzx

POWER • 601 • 603 • PowerPC32/64

Operation: $rT \Leftarrow {}^{\circ}Word ((rA \mid 0) + (rB))$

Syntax: **lwzx**   rT,rA,rB

Condition Register/Fixed-Point Exception Register:

CR Fields 0-7:   not affected

XER: not affected

Description:

The **lwzx** instruction loads the word that is stored at the effective address calculated from $(rA \mid 0) + (rB)$ and places the word into the target register rT.

On 64-bit PowerPC implementations, the word is loaded into the low-order word of rT and the upper word of rT is cleared.

The archaic POWER mnemonic for this instruction is **lx**.

Instruction Encoding:

0 5	6 10	11 15	16 20	21 30	31
0 1 1 1 1 1	T	A	B	0 0 0 0 0 1 0 1 1 1	0

T   Target GPR rT where result of operation is stored
A   Source GPR rA
B   Source GPR rB

Operation:

$mStart := rS[27{:}31]$

$mEnd := rB[27{:}31]$

$if(mStart = mEnd+1)$

    $m := \text{0xFFFF FFFF}$

$if(mStart < mEnd+1)$

    $m := \text{Mask}(mStart, mEnd)$

$if(mStart > mEnd+1)$

    $m := {\sim}\text{Mask}(mEnd+1, mStart-1)$

$rA \Leftarrow m$

Syntax:

maskg	rA, rS, rB	(Rc = 0)
maskg.	rA, rS, rB	(Rc = 1)

Condition Register / Fixed-Point Exception Register:

CR Field 0:   LT,GT,EQ,SO updated if Rc = 1, otherwise not affected

CR Fields 1-7:   not affected

XER: not affected

Description:

The **maskg** instruction generates a mask from the starting bit to the ending bit and places the calculated mask into rA. The starting bit (*mStart*) for the mask is specified in rS[27:31] and the ending bit (*mEnd*) is in rB[27:31].

If *mStart* = *mEnd* + 1, then a mask of all 1's is generated.

If *mStart* < *mEnd* + 1, then a mask with 1's starting at *mStart* and continuing up to (and including) *mEnd* will be generated. All remaining bits of the mask are 0.

If *mStart* > *mEnd* + 1, then a mask with 1's from bit 0 to *mEnd*, and from *mStart* up to bit 31 will be generated. All remaining bits of the mask are 0.

This instruction is not part of the PowerPC architecture.

Instruction Encoding:

0 5	6 10	11 15	16 20	21 30	31
0 1 1 1 1 1	S	A	B	0 0 0 0 0 1 1 1 0 1	Rc

S   Source GPR rS

A   Target GPR rA where result of operation is stored

B   Source GPR rB

Rc   Record bit

maskir Mask Insert from Register maskir

POWER • 601

Operation: $rA \Leftarrow ((rB) \& (rS)) \mid (\sim(rB) \& (rA))$

Syntax:

maskir	rA,rS,rB	(Rc = 0)
maskir.	rA,rS,rB	(Rc = 1)

Condition Register / Fixed-Point Exception Register:

CR Field 0: LT,GT,EQ,SO updated if Rc = 1, otherwise not affected
CR Fields 1-7: not affected

XER: not affected

Description:

The **maskir** instruction inserts the contents of rS into rA using rB as a control mask. Wherever a bit in rB is 1, the corresponding bit from rS will overwrite the bit in rA. Whereever a bit in rB is 0, the corresponding bit in rA will remain untouched.

This instruction is not part of the PowerPC architecture.

Instruction Encoding:

0 5	6 10	11 15	16 20	21 30	31
0 1 1 1 1 1	S	A	B	1 0 0 0 0 1 1 1 0 1	Rc

S	Source GPR rS
A	Target GPR rA where result of operation is stored
B	Source GPR rB
Rc	Record bit

mcrf   Move CR Field   mcrf

POWER • 601 • 603 • PowerPC32/64

Operation: $CR\{crfT\} \Leftarrow CR\{crfS\}$

Syntax: **mcrf**   *crfT,crfS*

Condition Register/Fixed-Point Exception Register:

CR Field T: LT,GT,EQ,SO always updated
other fields: not affected

XER: not affected

Description:

The **mcrf** instruction copies the contents of CR field *crfS* into CR field *crfT*.

The 601 allows the form where bit 31 (the Link bit) of the instruction's encoding is set to 1. If this instruction form is executed, the contents of the LR are undefined.

Instruction Encoding:

0 5	6 8	9 10	11 13	14 15	16 20	21 30	31
0 1 0 0 1 1	T	0 0	S	0 0	0 0 0 0 0	0 0 0 0 0 0 0 0 0 0	0

T   Target CR Field T where result of operation is stored
S   Source CR Field S

506   Appendix A

mcrfs

Move to CR from FPSCR

POWER • 601 • 603 • PowerPC32/64

mcrfs

Operation: CR{*crfT*} ⟸ FPSCR{*crfS*}
FPSCR{*crfS*} ⟸ 0

Syntax: **mcrfs** *crfT,crfS*

Condition Register/Floating-Point Status and Control Register:

CR Field T: always updated with value from FPSCR{*crfs*}
other fields: not affected

FPSCR: field S is set to 0 (except FEX and VX)

Description:

The **mcrfs** instruction copies the contents of FPSCR field *crfS* into CR field *crfT*. All of the bits that are copied from the FPSCR field (except FEX and VX) are reset to 0.

Instruction Encoding:

0					5	6		8	9	10	11		13	14	15	16				20	21								30	31
1	1	1	1	1	1	T		0	0		S		0	0	0	0	0	0	0	0	0	1	0	0	0	0	0	0	0	0

T   Target CR Field T where result of operation is stored
S   Source FPSCR Field S

mcrxr   Move to CR from XER   mcrxr

POWER • 601 • 603 • PowerPC32/64

Operation: $CR\{crfT\} \Leftarrow XER\{0\}$
$XER\{0\} \Leftarrow 0$

Syntax: **mcrxr**   *crfT*

Condition Register / Fixed-Point Exception Register:

CR Field T: always updated with value from XER{0}
other fields: not affected

XER: bits 0:3 are cleared

Description:

The **mcrxr** instruction copies XER[0:3] into CR field *crfT*. Bits 0-3 of the XER are cleared as a result of this instruction.

Instruction Encoding:

0				5	6		8	9 10 11					15	16			20	21									30	31

0 1 1 1 1 1 | T | 0 0 | 0 0 0 0 0 | 0 0 0 0 0 | 1 0 0 0 0 0 0 0 0 0 | 0

T   Target CR Field T where result of operation is stored

mfcr mfcr

Move from CR

POWER • 601 • 603 • PowerPC32/64

Operation: $rT \Leftarrow {}°(CR)$

Syntax: **mfcr** rT

Condition Register/Fixed-Point Exception Register:

CR Fields 0-7: not affected

XER: not affected

Description:

The **mfcr** instruction copies the entire contents of the CR into rT.

For 64-bit PowerPC implementations, the CR is loaded into the low-order word of the target register and the high-order word is cleared.

Instruction Encoding:

0	5	6	10	11	15	16	20	21	30	31
0 1 1 1 1 1		T		0 0 0 0 0		0 0 0 0 0		0 0 0 0 0 1 0 0 1 1		0

T   Target GPR rT where result of operation is stored

mffs   Move from FPSCR   mffs

POWER • 601 • 603 • PowerPC32/64

Operation: $\text{fr}T \Leftarrow (\text{FPSCR})$

Syntax:

mffs	frT	(Rc = 0)
mffs.	frT	(Rc = 1)

Condition Register/Floating-Point Status and Control Register:

CR Fields 0-7:   not affected

FPSCR: not affected

Description:

The **mffs** instruction copies the contents of the FPSCR into the low-order word of frT. The high-order word of the target register is undefined.

For compatibility with the POWER architecture, the 601 sets the high-order word of the target register to 0xFFF8 0000.

Instruction Encoding:

0 5	6 10	11 15	16 20	21 30	31
1 1 1 1 1 1	T	0 0 0 0 0	0 0 0 0 0	1 0 0 1 0 0 0 1 1 1	Rc

T   Target FPR frT where result of operation is stored
Rc   Record bit

mfmsr   Move from MSR   mfmsr

POWER • 601 • 603 • PowerPC32/64

Operation: $rT \Leftarrow (MSR)$

Syntax: **mfmsr** rT

Condition Register/Fixed-Point Exception Register:

CR Fields 0-7:   not affected

XER: not affected

Description:

The **mfmsr** instruction copies the entire contents of the MSR into rT.

This is a supervisor-level instruction.

Instruction Encoding:

0					5	6				10	11					15	16					20	21									30	31
0	1	1	1	1	1			T			0	0	0	0	0		0	0	0	0	0		0	0	0	1	0	1	0	0	1	1	0

T   Target GPR rT where result of operation is stored

mfspr   Move from SPR   mfspr

POWER • 601 • 603 • PowerPC32/64

Operation: $rT \Leftarrow °(SPR)$

Syntax: **mfspr** rT,SPR

Condition Register/Fixed-Point Exception Register:

CR Fields 0-7:   not affected

XER: not affected

Description:

The **mfspr** instruction copies the entire contents of the specified Special Purpose Register (SPR) into rT.

When loading 32-bit registers on 64-bit PowerPC implementations, the 32-bit register is loaded into the low-order word of the target register and the high-order word is cleared.

The SPR returned depends on the value of *SPR* which is used in the instruction. Valid values are given in the following table:

SPR	Register Name	Access	Notes
1	XER	user	
8	LR	user	
9	CTR	user	
18	DSISR	supervisor	
19	DAR	supervisor	
22	DEC	supervisor	
25	SDR1	supervisor	
26	SRR0	supervisor	
27	SRR1	supervisor	
272-275	SPRG0-SPRG3	supervisor	
280	ASR	supervisor	64-bit only
282	EAR	supervisor	
287	PVR	supervisor	
528,530,532,534	IBAT0U - IBAT3U	supervisor	
529,531,533,535	IBAT0L-IBAT3L	supervisor	
536,538,540,542	DBAT0U-DBAT3U	supervisor	
537,539,541,543	DBAT0L-DBAT3L	supervisor	

Attempting to read a register that requires supervisor-level access will result in a Privileged Instruction interrupt unless the processor is in supervisor mode.

In addition to the above-mentioned *SPR* encodings, the 601 provides access to the following implementation-specific registers:

SPR	Register Name	Access	Notes
0	MQ	user	These registers are provided for POWER compatibility.
4	RTCU	user	
5	RTCL	user	
6	DEC	user	
1008	HID0 (Checkstop)	supervisor	
1009	HID1 (Debug Mode)	supervisor	
1010	HID2 (IABR)	supervisor	
1013	HID5 (DABR)	supervisor	
1023	HID15 (PIR)	supervisor	

Extended Forms:

The following extended forms provide access to the user-level SPRs.

mfctr	rT	is equivalent to	**mfspr**	rT,9
mflr	rT	is equivalent to	**mfspr**	rT,8
mfxer	rT	is equivalent to	**mfspr**	rT,1

In addition, there are also a few obsolete forms which provide access to obsolete user-level registers. These forms are available only on the 601.

mfdec	rT	is equivalent to	**mfspr**	rT,6
mfmq	rT	is equivalent to	**mfspr**	rT,0
mfrtcl	rT	is equivalent to	**mfspr**	rT,5
mfrtcu	rT	is equivalent to	**mfspr**	rT,4

There are also a variety of supervisor-level SPRs which have extended forms. Note that **mfdec** appears again in this list since it was originally a user-level register but has been changed to a supervisor-level SPR.

mfasr	rT	is equivalent to	**mfspr**	rT,280
mfdar	rT	is equivalent to	**mfspr**	rT,19
mfdbatl	rT,n	is equivalent to	**mfspr**	rT,537+2*n
mfdbatu	rT,n	is equivalent to	**mfspr**	rT,536+2*n
mfdec	rT	is equivalent to	**mfspr**	rT,22
mfdsisr	rT	is equivalent to	**mfspr**	rT,18
mfear	rT	is equivalent to	**mfspr**	rT,282
mfibatl	rT,n	is equivalent to	**mfspr**	rT,529+2*n
mfibatu	rT,n	is equivalent to	**mfspr**	rT,528+2*n

mfpvr	r*T*	is equivalent to	**mfspr**	r*T*,287
mfsdr1	r*T*	is equivalent to	**mfspr**	r*T*,25
mfsprg	r*T*,*n*	is equivalent to	**mfspr**	r*T*,272+*n*
mfsrr0	r*T*	is equivalent to	**mfspr**	r*T*,26
mfsrr1	r*T*	is equivalent to	**mfspr**	r*T*,27

Instruction Encoding:

0 5	6 10	11 15	16 20	21 30	31
0 1 1 1 1 1	T	SPR - 2	SPR - 1	0 1 0 1 0 1 0 0 1 1	0

Note that the 10-bit SPR parameter is divided into two 5-bit fields: SPR-1 and SPR-2 which are stored in reverse order in the instruction encoding. This is necessary for compatibility with the POWER **mfspr** encodings.

T	Target GPR rT where result of operation is stored
SPR-2	Lower half of SPR specification
SPR-1	Upper half of SPR specification

mfsr   Move from SR   mfsr

POWER • 601 • 603 • PowerPC32

Operation: $rT \Leftarrow SR[SR]$

Syntax: **mfsr** rT,SR

Condition Register/Fixed-Point Exception Register:

CR Fields 0-7:   not affected

XER: not affected

Description:

The **mfsr** instruction copies the entire contents of the Segment Register specified by the immediate value *SR* into rT.

This is a supervisor-level instruction.

This instruction exists on 32-bit PowerPC implementations only.

Instruction Encoding:

0					5	6				10	11	12				15	16					20	21										30	31
0	1	1	1	1	1			T			0			SR			0	0	0	0	0		1	0	0	1	0	1	0	0	1	1	0

T   Target GPR rT where result of operation is stored
SR   Segment Register ID

mfsrin   Move from SR Indirect   **mfsrin**

POWER • 601 • 603 • PowerPC32

Operation: $rT \Leftarrow SR[rB[0:3]]$

Syntax: **mfsrin** rT,rB

Condition Register / Fixed-Point Exception Register:

CR Fields 0-7:   not affected

XER: not affected

Description:

The **mfsrin** instruction copies the entire contents of the Segment Register specified by $rB[0:3]$ into rT.

This is a supervisor-level instruction.

This instruction exists on 32-bit PowerPC implementations only.

The archaic POWER mnemonic for this instruction is **mfsri.** Note that the **mfsri** instruction calculates the effective address from (rA | 0) + (rB) so A must equal 0 for **mfsrin** to be equivalent to **mfsri.**

Instruction Encoding:

0	5	6		10	11			15	16		20	21									30	31
0 1 1 1 1 1		T			0 0 0 0 0				B			1 0 1 0 0 1 0 0 1 1										0

T   Target GPR rT where result of operation is stored
B   Source GPR rB which contains SR specification

mftb   Move from Time Base Register   mftb

603 • PowerPC32/64

Operation: if($TBR = 268$)
    $rT \Leftarrow (TBRL)$
    else if($TBR = 269$)
    $rT \Leftarrow °(TBRU)$

Syntax: **mftb** rT,TBR

Condition Register / Fixed-Point Exception Register:
CR Fields 0-7:   not affected

XER: not affected

Description:
The **mftb** instruction copies the contents of either the upper or lower half of the Time Base Register (TBR) into rT. The half of the TBR is specified by the *TBR* parameter: a value of 268 specifies the lower half of the TBR and 269 specifies the upper half.

On 64-bit PowerPC implementations, a *TBR* value of 268 will cause the entire 64-bit TBR to be loaded into the target register (instead of just the lower word). A *TBR* value of 269 will load the upper word of the TBR into the low-order word of the target register and clear the high-order word.

Even though this is a standard PowerPC instruction, this instruction is not implemented on the PowerPC 601.

Extended Forms:
mftb	rT	is equivalent to	**mftb**	$rT,268$
mftbu	rT	is equivalent to	**mftb**	$rT,269$

Instruction Encoding:

0 5	6 10	11 15	16 20	21 30	31
0 1 1 1 1 1	T	TBR - 2	TBR - 1	0 1 0 1 1 1 0 0 1 1	0

Note that the 10-bit TBR parameter is divided into two 5-bit fields: TBR-1 and TBR-2 which are stored in reverse order in the instruction encoding. This is necessary for consistency with the **mfspr** encodings.

T	Target GPR rT where result of operation is stored
TBR-2	Lower half of TBR specification
TBR-1	Upper half of TBR specification

mtcrf   Move to CR Fields   mtcrf

POWER • 601 • 603 • PowerPC32/64

Operation: $CR \Leftarrow (rS) \ \& \ mask$

Syntax: **mtcrf**   *crfMask,rS*

Condition Register/Fixed-Point Exception Register:

CR Fields 0-7:   updated as specified by mask

XER: not affected

Description:

The **mtcrf** instruction copies r*S* into the Condition Register (CR) under the control of the given mask. Each bit in the 8-bit *crfMask* value represents a 4-bit field in the CR. Thus, a mask value of b0010 1000 would update fields 2 and 4 of the CR. To update the entire CR, use an *crfMask* of b1111 1111.

On some PowerPC implementations, updating fewer than all 8 of the CR fields may result in poorer performance than updating all 8 fields.

Extended Forms:

The following extended form is provided for the **mtcrf** instruction:

    mtcr   r*S*   is equivalent to   **mtcrf**   0xFF,r*S*

Instruction Encoding:

0				5	6			10	11	12			19	20	21									30	31
0	1	1	1	1	1		S		0		CR Mask			0	0	0	1	0	0	1	0	0	0	0	0

S   Source GPR r*S*
CR Mask   Bit mask identifying which CR fields to update

mtfsb0   Move 0 to FPSCR   mtfsb0

POWER • 601 • 603 • PowerPC32/64

Operation: FPSCR[$bitT$] $\Leftarrow$ 0

Syntax:

mtfsb0	$bitT$	(Rc = 0)
mtfsb0.	$bitT$	(Rc = 1)

Condition Register/Floating-Point Status and Control Register:

CR Field 1:   LT,GT,EQ,SO updated if Rc = 1, otherwise not affected
CR Fields 0,2-7: not affected

FPSCR: bit T is cleared to 0

Description:

The **mtfsb0** instruction clears bit $bitT$ of the FPSCR. The FEX and VX bits are the only bits of the FPSCR that cannot be explicitly cleared.

Instruction Encoding:

0 5	6 10	11 15	16 20	21 30	31
1 1 1 1 1 1	T	0 0 0 0 0	0 0 0 0 0	0 0 0 1 0 0 0 1 1 0	Rc

T   Target bit of FPSCR which is cleared
Rc   Record bit

mtfsb1   Move 1 to FPSCR   mtfsb1

POWER • 601 • 603 • PowerPC32/64

Operation: $FPSCR[bitT] \Leftarrow 1$

Syntax:

mtfsb1	*bitT*	(Rc = 0)
mtfsb1.	*bitT*	(Rc = 1)

Condition Register/Floating-Point Status and Control Register:

CR Field 1:   LT,GT,EQ,SO updated if Rc = 1, otherwise not affected
CR Fields 0,2-7: not affected

FPSCR: bit T is set to 1

Description:

The **mtfsb1** instruction sets bit *bitT* of the FPSCR. The FEX and VX bits are the only bits of the FPSCR that cannot be explicitly set.

Instruction Encoding:

0 5	6 10	11 15	16 20	21 30	31
1 1 1 1 1 1	T	0 0 0 0 0	0 0 0 0 0	0 0 0 1 0 0 1 1 0	Rc

T   Target bit of FPSCR which is set
Rc   Record bit

mtfsf   Move to FPSCR Fields   mtfsf

POWER • 601 • 603 • PowerPC32/64

Operation: $FPSCR \Leftarrow frB[32:63] \, \& \, mask$

Syntax:

mtfsf	*fpscrMask,frB*	(Rc = 0)
mtfsf.	*fpscrMask,frB*	(Rc = 1)

Condition Register/Floating-Point Status and Control Register:
CR Field 1:   LT,GT,EQ,SO updated if Rc = 1, otherwise not affected
CR Fields 0,2-7: not affected

FPSCR: updated as specified by mask

Description:
The **mtfsf** instruction copies the low-order 32-bits from *frB* into the FPSCR under the control of the given mask. Each bit in the 8-bit *fpscrMask* value represents a 4-bit field in the FPSCR. Thus, a mask value of b0010 1000 would update fields 2 and 4 of the FPSCR. To update the entire FPSCR, use an *fpscrMask* of b1111 1111.

The FEX and VX bits of the FPSCR will not be updated if they are in the range specified by the mask.

On some PowerPC implementations, updating fewer than all 8 of the FPSCR fields may result in poorer performance than updating all 8 fields.

Extended Forms:
The following extended form is provided for the **mtfsf** instruction:

    mtfs[.]   frB   is equivalent to   **mtfsf[.]**   0xFF,frB

Instruction Encoding:

0 5	6	7 14	15	16 20	21 30	31
1 1 1 1 1 1	0	FPSCR Mask	0	B	1 0 1 1 0 0 0 1 1 1	Rc

FPSCR Mask   Bit mask identifying which FPSCR fields to update
B   Source FPR frB
Rc   Record bit

mtfsfi   Move to FPSCR Field Immediate   mtfsfi

POWER • 601 • 603 • PowerPC32/64

Operation: $FPSCR\{fpscrfT\} \Leftarrow IMM$

Syntax: **mtfsfi**   *crfT,IMM*   (Rc = 0)
                mtfsfi.   *crfT,IMM*   (Rc = 1)

Condition Register / Floating-Point Status and Control Register:

CR Field 1:   LT,GT,EQ,SO updated if Rc = 1, otherwise not affected
CR Fields 0,2-7: not affected

FPSCR: field T updated with immediate value

Description:

The **mtfsfi** instruction copies the immediate value *IMM* into field *fpscrfT* of the FPSCR. The FEX and VX bits are the only bits of the FPSCR that cannot be explicitly set. If FPSCR{0} is specified as the target field, then only the FX and OX bits will be updated.

Instruction Encoding:

0					5	6		8	9	10	11					15	16			19	20	21								30	31
1	1	1	1	1	1	T		0	0	0	0	0	0	0			IMM			0	0	0	1	0	0	0	0	1	1	0	Rc

T   Bit field of FPSCR to be updated
IMM   Immediate 4-bit value to load into FPSCR field
Rc   Record bit

Appendix A

mtmsr   Move to MSR   mtmsr
POWER • 601 • 603 • PowerPC32/64

Operation: MSR ⇐ (rS)

Syntax: **mtmsr**   rS

Condition Register / Fixed-Point Exception Register:
CR Fields 0-7:   not affected

XER: not affected

Description:
The **mfmsr** instruction copies the entire contents of rS into the Machine State Register (MSR).

This is a supervisor-level instruction. This instruction is execution synchronizing.

Instruction Encoding:

0 5	6 10	11 15	16 20	21 30	31
0 1 1 1 1 1	S	0 0 0 0 0	0 0 0 0 0	0 0 1 0 0 1 0 0 1 0	0

    S   Source GPR rS

mtspr   Move to SPR   mtspr

POWER • 601 • 603 • PowerPC32/64

Operation: $SPR \Leftarrow (rS)$

Syntax: **mtspr**   SPR,rS

Condition Register/Fixed-Point Exception Register:

CR Fields 0-7:   not affected

XER: not affected

Description:

The **mtspr** instruction copies the entire contents of rS into the specified Special Purpose Register (SPR).

When updating 32-bit registers on 64-bit PowerPC implementations, the 32-bit register is updated from the low-order word of the source register.

The source SPR depends on the value of SPR which is used in the instruction. Valid values are given in the following table:

SPR	Register Name	Access	Notes
1	XER	user	
8	LR	user	
9	CTR	user	
18	DSISR	supervisor	
19	DAR	supervisor	
22	DEC	supervisor	
25	SDR1	supervisor	
26	SRR0	supervisor	
27	SRR1	supervisor	
272-275	SPRG0-SPRG3	supervisor	
280	ASR	supervisor	64-bit only
282	EAR	supervisor	
284	TBL	supervisor	not on 601
285	TBU	supervisor	not on 601
528,530,532,534	IBAT0U - IBAT3U	supervisor	
529,531,533,535	IBAT0L-IBAT3L	supervisor	
536,538,540,542	DBAT0U-DBAT3U	supervisor	not on 601
537,539,541,543	DBAT0L-DBAT3L	supervisor	not on 601

Attempting to update a register that requires supervisor-level write access will result in a Privileged Instruction interrupt unless the processor is in supervisor mode.

In addition to the above-mentioned *SPR* encodings, the 601 provides access to the following implementation-specific registers:

SPR	Register Name	Access	Notes
0	MQ	user	These registers are provided for POWER compatibility.
4	RTCU	supervisor	
5	RTCL	supervisor	
1008	HID0 (Checkstop)	supervisor	
1009	HID1 (Debug Mode)	supervisor	
1010	HID2 (IABR)	supervisor	
1013	HID5 (DABR)	supervisor	
1023	HID15 (PIR)	supervisor	

Extended Forms:

The following extended forms provide access to the user-level SPRs.

mtctr	rT	is equivalent to	**mtspr**	9,rT
mtlr	rT	is equivalent to	**mtspr**	8,rT
mtxer	rT	is equivalent to	**mtspr**	1,rT

In addition, the obsolete MQ register also allows user-level write access. This form is available only on the 601.

mtmq	rT	is equivalent to	**mtspr**	0,rT

There are also a variety of supervisor-level SPRs which have extended forms.

mtasr	rT	is equivalent to	**mtspr**	280,rT
mtdar	rT	is equivalent to	**mtspr**	19,rT
mtdbatl	rT,n	is equivalent to	**mtspr**	537+2*n,rT
mtdbatu	rT,n	is equivalent to	**mtspr**	536+2*n,rT
mtdec	rT	is equivalent to	**mtspr**	22,rT
mtdsisr	rT	is equivalent to	**mtspr**	18,rT
mtear	rT	is equivalent to	**mtspr**	282,rT
mtibatl	rT,n	is equivalent to	**mtspr**	529+2*n,rT
mtibatu	rT,n	is equivalent to	**mtspr**	528+2*n,rT
mtsdr1	rT	is equivalent to	**mtspr**	25,rT
mtsprg	rT,n	is equivalent to	**mtspr**	272+n,rT
mtsrr0	rT	is equivalent to	**mtspr**	26,rT
mtsrr1	rT	is equivalent to	**mtspr**	27,rT

Instruction Encoding:

0					5	6				10	11				15	16				20	21									30	31
0	1	1	1	1	1			S					SPR - 2					SPR - 1			0	1	1	1	0	1	0	0	1	1	0

Note that the 10-bit SPR parameter is divided into two 5-bit fields: SPR-1 and SPR-2 which are stored in reverse order in the instruction encoding. This is necessary for compatibility with the POWER **mtspr** encodings.

S	Source GPR rS
SPR-2	Lower half of SPR specification
SPR-1	Upper half of SPR specification

mtsr   Move to SR   mtsr

POWER • 601 • 603 • PowerPC32

Operation: $SR[SR] \Leftarrow (rS)$

Syntax: **mtsr**   *SR,rS*

Condition Register/Fixed-Point Exception Register:

CR Fields 0-7:   not affected

XER: not affected

Description:

The **mtsr** instruction copies the contents of r*S* into the Segment Register specified by the immediate value *SR*.

This is a supervisor-level instruction.

This instruction exists on 32-bit PowerPC implementations only.

Instruction Encoding:

0 5	6 10	11	12 15	16 20	21 30	31
0 1 1 1 1 1	S	0	SR	0 0 0 0 0	0 0 1 1 0 1 0 0 1 0	0

S   Source GPR rS

SR   Segment Register ID

mtsrin   Move to SR Indirect   mtsrin

POWER • 601 • 603 • PowerPC32

Operation: $SR[rB[0:3]] \Leftarrow (rS)$

Syntax: **mtsrin** rS,rB

Condition Register/Fixed-Point Exception Register:

CR Fields 0-7:   not affected

XER: not affected

Description:

The **mtsrin** instruction copies the contents of rS into the Segment Register specified by $rB[0:3]$.

This is a supervisor-level instruction.

This instruction exists on 32-bit PowerPC implementations only.

The archaic POWER mnemonic for this instruction is **mtsri.** Note that the **mtsri** instruction calculates the effective address from $(rA | 0) + (rB)$ so A must equal 0 for **mtsrin** to be equivalent to **mtsri.**

Instruction Encoding:

0					5	6				10	11					15	16				20	21									30	31
0	1	1	1	1	1			S			0	0	0	0	0			B				0	0	1	1	1	1	0	0	1	0	0

S   Source GPR rS

B   Source GPR rB which contains the Segment Register ID

Multiply

POWER • 601

Operation: $rT \Leftarrow \text{HiWord}((rA) \times (rB))$
$MQ \Leftarrow \text{LoWord}((rA) \times (rB))$

Syntax:	**mul**	rT,rA,rB	(Rc = 0, OE = 0)
	mul.	rT,rA,rB	(Rc = 1, OE = 0)
	mulo	rT,rA,rB	(Rc = 0, OE = 1)
	mulo.	rT,rA,rB	(Rc = 1, OE = 1)

Condition Register / Fixed-Point Exception Register:

CR Field 0:   LT,GT,EQ,SO updated if Rc = 1, otherwise not affected
CR Fields 1-7: not affected

XER[CA]:   not affected
XER[OV,SO]:   updated if OE=1, otherwise not affected

Description:

The **mul** instruction multiplies the contents of GPR rA and GPR rB as signed quantities and places the high-order 32 bits of the result in GPR rT, and the low-order 32 bits of the result in the MQ register.

The multiply algorithm used on the 601 will execute more quickly if the smaller (in terms of absolute value) of the two operands is placed in rB.

This instruction is not part of the PowerPC architecture.

Instruction Encoding:

0 5	6 10	11 15	16 20	21	22 30	31
0 1 1 1 1 1	T	A	B	OE	0 0 1 1 0 1 0 1 1	Rc

T	Target GPR rT where result of operation is stored
A	Source GPR rA
B	Source GPR rB
OE	Overflow Exception bit
Rc	Record bit

mulhd   Multiply High Doubleword   mulhd
PowerPC64

Operation: $rT \Leftarrow \text{HiDWord}((rA) \times (rB))$

Syntax:

mulhd	rT,rA,rB	(Rc = 0)
mulhd.	rT,rA,rB	(Rc = 1)

Condition Register/Fixed-Point Exception Register:
CR Field 0:   LT,GT,EQ,SO updated if Rc = 1, otherwise not affected
CR Fields 1-7:   not affected

XER: not affected

Description:

The **mulhd** instruction multiplies the contents of GPR rA and GPR rB as signed quantities and places the high-order 64 bits of the 128-bit result in GPR rT. The low-order 64 bits of the result are not returned as a result of this instruction (the **mulld** instruction can be used to calculate the low-order bits).

The multiply algorithm used for many of the PowerPC implementations will execute more quickly if the smaller (in terms of absolute value) of the two operands is placed in rB.

This instruction exists on 64-bit PowerPC implementations only.

Instruction Encoding:

0					5	6				10	11				15	16				20	21	22									30	31
0	1	1	1	1	1		T					A				B				0	0	0	1	0	0	1	0	0	1	Rc

T	Target GPR rT where result of operation is stored
A	Source GPR rA
B	Source GPR rB
Rc	Record bit

mulhdu   Multiply High   mulhdu
Doubleword Unsigned
PowerPC64

Operation: $rT \Leftarrow \text{HiDWord}((rA) \times (rB))$

Syntax: **mulhdu** rT,rA,rB (Rc = 0)
           mulhdu. rT,rA,rB (Rc = 1)

Condition Register / Fixed-Point Exception Register:
CR Field 0:   LT,GT,EQ,SO updated if Rc = 1, otherwise not affected
CR Fields 1-7:   not affected

XER: not affected

Description:
The **mulhdu** instruction multiplies the contents of GPR rA and GPR rB as unsigned quantities and places the high-order 64 bits of the 128-bit result in GPR rT. The low-order 64 bits of the result are not returned as a result of this instruction (the **mulld** instruction can be used to calculate the low-order bits).

The multiply algorithm used for many of the PowerPC implementations will execute more quickly if the smaller (in terms of absolute value) of the two operands is placed in rB.

This instruction exists on 64-bit PowerPC implementations only.

Instruction Encoding:

0 5	6 10	11 15	16 20	21 22 30	31
0 1 1 1 1 1	T	A	B	0 0 0 0 0 0 1 0 0 1	Rc

T   Target GPR rT where result of operation is stored
A   Source GPR rA
B   Source GPR rB
Rc   Record bit

mulhw   Multiply High Word   mulhw

601 • 603 • PowerPC32/64

Operation: $rT \Leftarrow \text{HiWord}((rA) \times (rB))$

Syntax:

mulhw	rT,rA,rB	(Rc = 0)
mulhw.	rT,rA,rB	(Rc = 1)

Condition Register/Fixed-Point Exception Register:

CR Field 0:   LT,GT,EQ,SO updated if Rc = 1, otherwise not affected
CR Fields 1-7:   not affected

XER: not affected

Description:

The **mulhw** instruction multiplies the contents of GPR rA and GPR rB as signed quantities and places the high-order 32 bits of the 64-bit result in GPR rT. The low-order 32 bits of the result are not returned as a result of this instruction (the **mullw** instruction can be used to calculate the low-order bits).

On 64-bit PowerPC implementations, the high-order word of the target register is undefined.

The multiply algorithm used for many of the PowerPC implementations will execute more quickly if the smaller (in terms of absolute value) of the two operands is placed in rB.

Instruction Encoding:

0					5	6				10	11				15	16				20	21	22								30	31
0	1	1	1	1	1			T					A					B			0	0	0	1	0	0	1	0	0	1	Rc

T   Target GPR rT where result of operation is stored
A   Source GPR rA
B   Source GPR rB
Rc   Record bit

mulhwu   Multiply High Word   **mulhwu**
Unsigned
601 • 603 • PowerPC32/64

Operation: $rT \Leftarrow \text{HiWord}((rA) \times (rB))$

Syntax:

mulhwu	rT,rA,rB	(Rc = 0)
mulhwu.	rT,rA,rB	(Rc = 1)

Condition Register/Fixed-Point Exception Register:

CR Field 0:   LT,GT,EQ,SO updated if Rc = 1, otherwise not affected
CR Fields 1-7:   not affected

XER: not affected

Description:

The **mulhwu** instruction multiplies the contents of GPR rA and GPR rB as unsigned quantities and places the high-order 32 bits of the 64-bit result in GPR rT. The low-order 32 bits of the result are not returned as a result of this instruction (the **mullw** instruction can be used to calculate the low-order bits).

On 64-bit PowerPC implementations, the high-order word of the target register is undefined.

The multiply algorithm used for many of the PowerPC implementations will execute more quickly if the smaller (in terms of absolute value) of the two operands is placed in rB.

Instruction Encoding:

0 5	6 10	11 15	16 20	21	22 30	31
0 1 1 1 1 1	T	A	B	0	0 0 0 0 0 1 0 1 1	Rc

T   Target GPR rT where result of operation is stored
A   Source GPR rA
B   Source GPR rB
Rc   Record bit

mulld   Multiply Low Doubleword   mulld

PowerPC64

Operation: $rT \Leftarrow \text{LoDWord}((rA) \times (rB))$

Syntax:

mulld	rT,rA,rB	(Rc = 0, OE = 0)
mulld.	rT,rA,rB	(Rc = 1, OE = 0)
mulldo	rT,rA,rB	(Rc = 0, OE = 1)
mulldo.	rT,rA,rB	(Rc = 1, OE = 1)

Condition Register/Fixed-Point Exception Register:

CR Field 0:   LT,GT,EQ,SO updated if Rc = 1, otherwise not affected
CR Fields 1-7:   not affected

XER[CA]:   not affected
XER[OV,SO]:   updated if OE=1, otherwise not affected

Description:

The **mulld** instruction multiplies the contents of GPR rA and GPR rB and places the low-order 64 bits of the 128-bit result in GPR rT. The high-order 64 bits of the result are not returned as a result of this instruction (the **mulhd** or **mulhdu** instructions can be used to calculate the high-order bits).

This instruction treats the operands as signed quantities but it can be used for both signed and unsigned 64-bit multiply operations since the low-order 64 bits are independent of whether the operands are considered to be signed or unsigned.

The multiply algorithm used for many of the PowerPC implementations will execute more quickly if the smaller (in terms of absolute value) of the two operands is placed in rB.

This instruction exists on 64-bit PowerPC implementations only.

Instruction Encoding:

0 5	6 10	11 15	16 20	21	22 30	31
0 1 1 1 1 1	T	A	B	OE	0 1 1 1 0 1 0 0 1	Rc

T	Target GPR rT where result of operation is stored
A	Source GPR rA
B	Source GPR rB
OE	Overflow Exception bit
Rc	Record bit

mulli   Multiply Low Immediate   mulli

POWER • 601 • 603 • PowerPC32/64

Operation: $rT \Leftarrow \text{LoWord}((rA) \times \text{'}s16)$

Syntax: **mulli** $rT,rA,s16$

Condition Register/Fixed-Point Exception Register:

CR Fields 0-7:   not affected

XER: not affected

Description:

The **mulli** instruction multiplies the contents of GPR rA (interpreted as a signed quantity) and the sign-extended 16-bit immediate quantity and places the low-order 32 bits of the 48-bit result in GPR rT. The high-order 16 bits of the result are not returned as a result of this instruction.

On 64-bit PowerPC implementations, this instruction multiplies the 64-bit signed value in rA by the sign-extended 16-bit immediate value and returns the low-order 64 bits of the resulting 80-bit product. As with the 32-bit version of this instruction, the low-order 64 bits are independent of whether the operands are treated as signed or unsigned quantities.

The archaic POWER mnemonic for this instruction is **muli**.

Instruction Encoding:

0 5	6 10	11 15	16 31
0 0 0 1 1 1	T	A	SI

T   Target GPR rT where result of operation is stored
A   Source GPR rA or 0
SI   Signed 16-bit integer

mullw   Multiply Low Word   **mullw**

POWER • 601 • 603 • PowerPC32/64

Operation: $rT \Leftarrow LoWord((rA) \times (rB))$

Syntax:

mullw	rT,rA,rB	(Rc = 0, OE = 0)
mullw.	rT,rA,rB	(Rc = 1, OE = 0)
mullwo	rT,rA,rB	(Rc = 0, OE = 1)
mullwo.	rT,rA,rB	(Rc = 1, OE = 1)

Condition Register/Fixed-Point Exception Register:

CR Field 0:   LT,GT,EQ,SO updated if Rc = 1, otherwise not affected
CR Fields 1-7: not affected

XER[CA]:   not affected
XER[OV,SO]:   updated if OE=1, otherwise not affected

Description:

The **mullw** instruction multiplies the contents of GPR r*A* and GPR r*B* and places the low-order 32 bits of the 64-bit result in GPR r*T*. The high-order 32 bits of the result are not returned as a result of this instruction (the **mulhw** or **mulhwu** instructions can be used to calculate the high-order bits).

This instruction treats the operands as signed quantities but it can be used for both signed and unsigned 32-bit multiply operations since the low-order 32-bits are independent of whether the operands are considered to be signed or unsigned.

On 64-bit PowerPC implementations, the entire 64-bit result is stored in the target register.

The archaic POWER mnemonic for this instruction is **muls[0][.]**.

Instruction Encoding:

0					5	6				10	11				15	16				20	21	22									30	31
0	1	1	1	1	1		T					A					B				OE	0	1	1	1	0	1	0	1	1	Rc

T	Target GPR rT where result of operation is stored
A	Source GPR rA
B	Source GPR rB
OE	Overflow Exception bit
Rc	Record bit

Negative Absolute Value

POWER • 601

Operation: $rT \Leftarrow - | rA |$

Syntax:

nabs	rT,rA	(Rc = 0, OE = 0)
nabs.	rT,rA	(Rc = 1, OE = 0)
nabso	rT,rA	(Rc = 0, OE = 1)
nabso.	rT,rA	(Rc = 1, OE = 1)

Condition Register/Fixed-Point Exception Register:

CR Field 0:   LT,GT,EQ,SO updated if Rc = 1, otherwise not affected
CR Fields 1-7:   not affected

XER[CA]:   not affected
XER[OV,SO]:   updated if OE=1, otherwise not affected (see below)

Description:

The **nabs** instruction calculates the absolute value of the contents of GPR rA, and stores the negation of this result in GPR rT.

Since this instruction never causes an overflow, if the Overflow Exception (OE) bit is set, the Overflow (OV) bit of the XER is cleared and the Summary Overflow (SO) bit of the XER is not affected.

This instruction is not part of the PowerPC architecture.

Instruction Encoding:

0					5	6			10	11			15	16				20	21	22								30	31
0	1	1	1	1	1		T				A			0	0	0	0	0	OE	1	1	1	1	0	1	0	0	0	Rc

T   Target GPR rT where result of operation is stored
A   Source GPR rA
OE   Overflow Exception bit
Rc   Record bit

nand   NAND   nand

POWER • 601 • 603 • PowerPC32/64

Operation: $rA \Leftarrow \sim((rS) \& (rB))$

Syntax:

nand	rA,rS,rB	(Rc = 0)
nand.	rA,rS,rB	(Rc = 1)

Condition Register/Fixed-Point Exception Register:

CR Field 0:   LT,GT,EQ,SO updated if Rc = 1, otherwise not affected
CR Fields 1-7:   not affected

XER: not affected

Description:

The **nand** instruction logically ANDs the contents of GPR rS and GPR rB and places the one's complement of the result in GPR rA.

Instruction Encoding:

0	5 6	10 11	15 16	20 21	30 31
0 1 1 1 1 1	S	A	B	0 1 1 1 0 1 1 1 0 0	Rc

S	Source GPR rS
A	Target GPR rA where result of operation is stored
B	Source GPR rB
Rc	Record bit

neg   Negate   **neg**

POWER • 601 • 603 • PowerPC32/64

Operation: $rT \Leftarrow -rA$

Syntax:

neg	rT,rA	(Rc = 0, OE = 0)
neg.	rT,rA	(Rc = 1, OE = 0)
nego	rT,rA	(Rc = 0, OE = 1)
nego.	rT,rA	(Rc = 1, OE = 1)

Condition Register/Fixed-Point Exception Register:

CR Field 0:   LT,GT,EQ,SO updated if Rc = 1, otherwise not affected
CR Fields 1-7:   not affected

XER[CA]:   not affected
XER[OV,SO]:   updated if OE=1, otherwise not affected

Description:

The **neg** instruction negates the contents of GPR r*A*, and stores the result in GPR r*T*. This operation is the same as taking the one's complement of r*A* and then adding 1 to the result.

If GPR r*A* contains the largest negative number (0x8000 0000 for 32-bit mode and 0x8000 0000 0000 0000 for 64-bit mode), then the result in r*T* will be the largest negative number and, if the OE bit is set, the OV and SO bits of the XER will be set to 1.

Instruction Encoding:

0	5	6	10	11	15	16	20	21	22	30	31
0 1 1 1 1 1		T		A		0 0 0 0 0		OE	0 0 1 1 0 1 0 0 0		Rc

T   Target GPR rT where result of operation is stored
A   Source GPR rA
OE   Overflow Exception bit
Rc   Record bit

nor   NOR   nor

Operation: $rA \Leftarrow \sim((rS) \mid (rB))$

Syntax: **nor** rA,rS,rB $(Rc = 0)$
              nor. rA,rS,rB $(Rc = 1)$

Condition Register/Fixed-Point Exception Register:

CR Field 0:   LT,GT,EQ,SO updated if Rc = 1, otherwise not affected
CR Fields 1-7:   not affected

XER: not affected

Description:

The **nor** instruction logically ORs the contents of GPR rS and GPR rB and places the one's complement of the result in GPR rA.

Extended Forms:

not[.] rA,rS is equivalent to   **nor**[.] rA,rS,rS

Instruction Encoding:

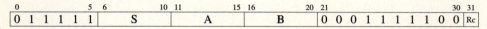

| 0 1 1 1 1 1 | S | A | B | 0 0 0 1 1 1 1 1 0 0 | Rc |

S	Source GPR rS
A	Target GPR rA where result of operation is stored
B	Source GPR rB
Rc	Record bit

or   OR   or

Operation: $rA \Leftarrow (rS) \mid (rB)$

Syntax:

or	rA,rS,rB	$(Rc = 0)$
or.	rA,rS,rB	$(Rc = 1)$

Condition Register/Fixed-Point Exception Register:

CR Field 0:   LT,GT,EQ,SO updated if Rc = 1, otherwise not affected

CR Fields 1-7:   not affected

XER: not affected

Description:

The **or** instruction logically ORs the contents of GPR rS and GPR rB and places the result in GPR rA.

Extended Forms:

mr[.] rA,rS is equivalent to   **or[.]** rA,rS,rS

Instruction Encoding:

0 5	6 10	11 15	16 20	21 30	31
0 1 1 1 1 1	S	A	B	0 1 1 0 1 1 1 1 0 0	Rc

S   Source GPR rS

A   Target GPR rA where result of operation is stored

B   Source GPR rB

Rc   Record bit

orc   OR with Complement   orc

POWER • 601 • 603 • PowerPC32/64

Operation: $rA \Leftarrow (rS) \mid \sim(rB)$

Syntax:

orc	rA,rS,rB	(Rc = 0)
orc.	rA,rS,rB	(Rc = 1)

Condition Register/Fixed-Point Exception Register:

CR Field 0:   LT,GT,EQ,SO updated if Rc = 1, otherwise not affected
CR Fields 1-7:   not affected

XER: not affected

Description:

The **orc** instruction logically ORs the contents of GPR rS with the one's complement of the contents of GPR rB and places the result in GPR rA.

Instruction Encoding:

0 5	6 10	11 15	16 20	21 30	31
0 1 1 1 1 1	S	A	B	0 1 1 0 0 1 1 1 0 0	Rc

S   Source GPR rS
A   Target GPR rA where result of operation is stored
B   Source GPR rB
Rc   Record bit

ori OR Immediate ori

POWER • 601 • 603 • PowerPC32/64

Operation: $rA \Leftarrow (rS) \mid {}^{\circ}u16$

Syntax: **ori** $rA,rS,u16$

Condition Register/Fixed-Point Exception Register:
CR Fields 0-7: not affected

XER: not affected

Description:
The **ori.** instruction logically ORs the contents of GPR rS and the zero-extended immediate value *u16*, and places the result in GPR rA.

The archaic POWER mnemonic for this instruction is **oril**. (OR Immediate Lower).

Extended Forms:
nop is equivalent to **ori** r0,r0,0

Instruction Encoding:

0	5	6	10	11	15	16	31
0 1 1 0 0 0		S		A		UI	

S   Source GPR rS
A   Target GPR rA where result of operation is stored
UI   Unsigned 16-bit integer

oris   OR Immediate Shifted   oris

POWER • 601 • 603 • PowerPC32/64

Operation: $rA \Leftarrow (rS) \mid °(u16 \perp 0x0000)$

Syntax: **oris**   rA,rS,u16

Condition Register/Fixed-Point Exception Register:

CR Fields 0-7:   not affected

XER: not affected

Description:

The **oris.** instruction logically ORs the contents of GPR rS and the value calculated by concatenating *u16* with 0x0000, and places the result in GPR rA.

The archaic POWER mnemonic for this instruction is **oriu**. (OR Immediate Upper).

Instruction Encoding:

0 5	6 10	11 15	16 31
0 1 1 0 0 1	S	A	UI

S   Source GPR rS
A   Target GPR rA where result of operation is stored
UI   Unsigned 16-bit integer

rfi   Return from Interrupt   rfi

POWER • 601 • 603 • PowerPC32/64

Operation: $MSR \Leftarrow SRR1 \left[\frac{0,\, 5:9,\, 16:31}{0:32,\, 37:41,\, 48:63} \right]$

               $CIP \Leftarrow SRR0 \left[\frac{0:29}{0:61} \right] \perp b00$

Syntax: **rfi**

Condition Register/Fixed-Point Exception Register:

CR Fields 0-7:   not affected

XER: not affected

Description:

The **rfi** instruction is used to return control to the original code after the interrupt-servicing code has completed. The instruction restores the original value of the MSR and gets the address of the next instruction to execute from the SRR0 register.

Instruction Encoding:

0				5	6				10	11				15	16				20	21								30	31
0	1	0	0	1	1	0	0	0	0	0	0	0	0	0	0	0	0	0	0	0	0	0	0	1	1	0	0	1	0	0

rldcl Rotate Left Doubleword then Clear Left rldcl

PowerPC64

Operation:

$r := (rS) \circlearrowright rB[58{:}63]$

$m := \text{Mask}(mB,63)$

$rA \Leftarrow (r \,\&\, m)$

Syntax:

rldcl	rA,rS,rB,mB	(Rc = 0)
rldcl.	rA,rS,rB,mB	(Rc = 1)

Condition Register/Fixed-Point Exception Register:

CR Field 0: LT,GT,EQ,SO updated if Rc = 1, otherwise not affected
CR Fields 1-7: not affected

XER: not affected

Description:

The **rldcl** instruction rotates the contents of rS to the left by the number of bits specified in $rB[58{:}63]$, and then ANDs this result with a mask that is composed of 1's from bit position mB up to 63 and 0's everywhere else. The final result is then stored in rA.

The end result of the mask operation is that the leftmost mB bits of the rotated result are cleared before they are stored into the destination register rA. Only the rightmost 63-mB bits are copied into rA.

This instruction exists on 64-bit PowerPC implementations only.

Extended Forms:

rotld[.] rA,rS,rB is equivalent to   **rldcl[.]** $rA,rS,rB,0$

Instruction Encoding:

0	5	6	10	11	15	16	20	21	26	27	30	31
0 1 1 1 1 0		S		A		B		mBegin		1 0 0 0		Rc

S	Source GPR rS
A	Target GPR rA where result of operation is stored
B	Source GPR rB
mBegin	Bit position where mask is to start
Rc	Record bit

rldcr

Rotate Left Doubleword then Clear Right

rldcr

PowerPC64

Operation:

$r := (rS) \, Q \, rB[58:63]$

$m := \text{Mask}(0, mE)$

$rA \Leftarrow (r \, \& \, m)$

Syntax:

rldcr	rA,rS,rB,mE	(Rc = 0)
rldcr.	rA,rS,rB,mE	(Rc = 1)

Condition Register / Fixed-Point Exception Register:

CR Field 0:   LT,GT,EQ,SO updated if Rc = 1, otherwise not affected

CR Fields 1-7:   not affected

XER: not affected

Description:

The **rldcr** instruction rotates the contents of rS to the left by the number of bits specified in rB[58:63], and then ANDs this result with a mask that is composed of 1's from bit position 0 up to mE and 0's everywhere else. The final result is then stored in rA.

The end result of the mask operation is that the rightmost 63-mE bits of the rotated result are cleared before they are stored into the destination register rA. Only the leftmost mE bits are copied into rA.

This instruction exists on 64-bit PowerPC implementations only.

Instruction Encoding:

0 5	6 10	11 15	16 20	21 26	27 30	31
0 1 1 1 1 0	S	A	B	mBegin	1 0 0 1	Rc

S   Source GPR rS

A   Target GPR rA where result of operation is stored

B   Source GPR rB

mEnd   Bit position where mask is to end

Rc   Record bit

rldic   Rotate Left Doubleword   rldic
Immediate then Clear
PowerPC64

Operation: $r := (rS) \circlearrowleft n$

$m := \text{Mask}(mB, 63-n)$

$rA \Leftarrow (r \,\&\, m)$

Syntax:

rldic	rA, rS, n, mB	(Rc = 0)
rldic.	rA, rS, n, mB	(Rc = 1)

Condition Register / Fixed-Point Exception Register:

CR Field 0:   LT,GT,EQ,SO updated if Rc = 1, otherwise not affected

CR Fields 1-7:   not affected

XER: not affected

Description:

The **rldic** instruction rotates the contents of rS to the left by the number of bits specified by the immediate value n, and then ANDs this result with a mask that is composed of 1's from bit position mB up to 63-n and 0's everywhere else. The final result is then stored in rA.

This instruction exists on 64-bit PowerPC implementations only.

Extended Forms:

clrlsldi[.] rA, rS, nb, sh is equivalent to   **rldic[.]** rA, rS, sh, nb-sh

Instruction Encoding:

0	5	6	10	11	15	16	20	21	26	27	29	30	31
0 1 1 1 1 0		S		A		shift - 2		mBegin		0 1 0	sh	Rc

Note that the shift value is split into 2 fields in the encoding: the high-order bit is stored in *sh* and the low-order bits are stored in *shift-2*. This is necessary because a 5-bit field isn't large enough to hold a 64-bit shift value.

S	Source GPR rS
A	Target GPR rA where result of operation is stored
shift-2	Low-order bits of shift value
mBegin	Bit position where mask is to start
sh	High-order bit of shift value
Rc	Record bit

rldicl

Rotate Left Doubleword

rldicl

Immediate then Clear Left
PowerPC64

Operation: $r := (rS) \circlearrowleft n$

$m := \text{Mask}(mB,63)$

$rA \Leftarrow (r \mathbin{\&} m)$

Syntax:

rldicl	rA,rS,n,mB	(Rc = 0)
rldicl.	rA,rS,n,mB	(Rc = 1)

Condition Register / Fixed-Point Exception Register:

CR Field 0:   LT,GT,EQ,SO updated if Rc = 1, otherwise not affected

CR Fields 1-7: not affected

XER: not affected

Description:

The **rldicl** instruction rotates the contents of rS to the left by the number of bits specified by the immediate value n, and then ANDs this result with a mask that is composed of 1's from bit position mB up to 63 and 0's everywhere else. The final result is then stored in rA.

The end result of the mask operation is that the leftmost mB bits of the rotated result are cleared before they are stored into the destination register rA. Only the rightmost $63\text{-}mB$ bits are copied into rA.

This instruction exists on 64-bit PowerPC implementations only.

Extended Forms:

clrldi[.]	rA,rS,nb	is equivalent to	**rldicl[.]**	$rA,rS,0,nb$
extrdi[.]	rA,rS,nb,st	is equivalent to	**rldicl[.]**	$rA,rS,st+nb,64\text{-}nb$
rotldi[.]	rA,rS,nb	is equivalent to	**rldicl[.]**	$rA,rS,nb,0$
rotrdi[.]	rA,rS,nb	is equivalent to	**rldicl[.]**	$rA,rS,64\text{-}nb,0$
srdi[.]	rA,rS,nb	is equivalent to	**rldicl[.]**	$rA,rS,64\text{-}nb,nb$

Instruction Encoding:

0					5	6				10	11				15	16				20	21					26	27			29	30	31
0	1	1	1	1	0		S					A					shift - 2					mBegin				0	0	0	sh	Rc

Note that the shift value is split into 2 fields in the encoding: the high-order bit is stored in *sh* and the low-order bits are stored in *shift-2*. This is necessary because a 5-bit field isn't large enough to hold a 64-bit shift value.

S	Source GPR rS
A	Target GPR rA where result of operation is stored
shift-2	Low-order bits of shift value
mBegin	Bit position where mask is to start
sh	High-order bit of shift value
Rc	Record bit

rldicr   Rotate Left Doubleword   rldicr
Immediate then Clear Right
PowerPC64

Operation: $r := (rS) \circlearrowleft n$

$m := \text{Mask}(0, mE)$

$rA \Leftarrow (r \ \& \ m)$

Syntax:

rldicr	rA, rS, n, mE	(Rc = 0)
rldicr.	rA, rS, n, mE	(Rc = 1)

Condition Register / Fixed-Point Exception Register:
CR Field 0:   LT,GT,EQ,SO updated if Rc = 1, otherwise not affected
CR Fields 1-7:   not affected

XER: not affected

Description:
The **rldicr** instruction rotates the contents of rS to the left by the number of bits specified by the immediate value n, and then ANDs this result with a mask that is composed of 1's from bit position 0 up to mE and 0's everywhere else. The final result is then stored in rA.

The end result of the mask operation is that the rightmost 63-mE bits of the rotated result are cleared before they are stored into the destination register rA. Only the leftmost mE bits are copied into rA.

This instruction exists on 64-bit PowerPC implementations only.

Extended Forms:

clrrdi[.]	rA, rS, nb	is equivalent to	**rldicr[.]**	$rA, rS, 0, 63$-nb
extldi[.]	rA, rS, nb, st	is equivalent to	**rldicr[.]**	rA, rS, st, nb-1
sldi[.]	rA, rS, nb	is equivalent to	**rldicr[.]**	$rA, rS, nb, 63$-nb

Instruction Encoding:

0					5	6				10	11				15	16				20	21					26	27			29	30	31
0	1	1	1	1	0			S					A				shift - 2					mEnd					0	0	1	sh	Rc

Note that the shift value is split into 2 fields in the encoding: the high-order bit is stored in *sh* and the low-order bits are stored in *shift-2*. This is necessary because a 5-bit field isn't large enough to hold a 64-bit shift value.

S	Source GPR rS
A	Target GPR rA where result of operation is stored
shift-2	Low-order bits of shift value
mEnd	Bit position where mask is to end
sh	High-order bit of shift value
Rc	Record bit

rldimi   Rotate Left Doubleword   rldimi
Immediate then Mask Insert
PowerPC64

Operation: $r := (rS) \circlearrowright n$

$m := \text{Mask}(mB, 63\text{-}n)$

$rA \Leftarrow (r \mathbin{\&} m) \mid ((rA) \mathbin{\&} \sim\! m)$

Syntax: **rldimi** rA, rS, n, mB (Rc = 0)

rldimi. rA, rS, n, mB (Rc = 1)

Condition Register / Fixed-Point Exception Register:

CR Field 0:   LT,GT,EQ,SO updated if Rc = 1, otherwise not affected

CR Fields 1-7:   not affected

XER: not affected

Description:

The **rldimi** instruction rotates the contents of rS to the left by the number of bits specified by the immediate value n. This rotated result is then inserted into the destination register rA under the control of a mask that is composed of of 1's from bit position mB up to 63-n and 0's everywhere else.

The final result is an ORing of the original value of rA (wherever the mask bits are 0) and the newly calculated rotated result (whereever the mask bits are 1).

This instruction exists on 64-bit PowerPC implementations only.

Extended Forms:

insrdi[.] rA, rS, nb, st is equivalent to   **rldimi**[.] $rA, rS, 64\text{-}(st+nb), st$

Instruction Encoding:

0				5	6				10	11				15	16				20	21					26	27			29	30	31
0	1	1	1	1	0		S					A				shift - 2					mBegin				0	1	1		sh	Rc

Note that the shift value is split into 2 fields in the encoding: the high-order bit is stored in *sh* and the low-order bits are stored in *shift*-2. This is necessary because a 5-bit field isn't large enough to hold a 64-bit shift value.

S	Source GPR rS
A	Target GPR rA where result of operation is stored
shift-2	Low-order bits of shift value
mBegin	Bit position where mask is to start
sh	High-order bit of shift value
Rc	Record bit

Rotate Left then Mask Insert

POWER • 601

Operation: $r := (rS) \circlearrowleft rB[27:31]$

$m := \text{Mask}(mB,mE)$

$rA \Leftarrow (r \And m) \mid ((rA) \And \sim m)$

Syntax:

rlmi	rA,rS,rB,mB,mE	(Rc = 0)
rlmi.	rA,rS,rB,mB,mE	(Rc = 1)

Condition Register / Fixed-Point Exception Register:

CR Field 0:   LT,GT,EQ,SO updated if Rc = 1, otherwise not affected

CR Fields 1-7:   not affected

XER: not affected

Description:

The **rlmi** instruction rotates the contents of rS to the left by the number of bits specified by rB[27:31]. This rotated result is then inserted into the destination register rA under the control of a mask that is created from *mB* and *mE* as described under the **maskg** instruction.

The final result is an ORing of the original value of rA (wherever the mask bits are 0) and the newly calculated rotated result (wherever the mask bits are 1).

This instruction is not part of the PowerPC architecture.

Instruction Encoding:

0 5	6 10	11 15	16 20	21 25	26 30	31
0 1 0 1 1 0	S	A	B	mBegin	mEnd	Rc

S	Source GPR rS
A	Target GPR rA where result of operation is stored
B	Source GPR rB
mBegin	Bit position where mask is to start
mEnd	Bit position where mask is to end
Rc	Record bit

rlwimi   Rotate Left Word   rlwimi

Immediate then Mask Insert
POWER • 601 • 603 • PowerPC32/64

Operation: $r := (rS) \circlearrowleft n$

$m := \text{Mask}(mB, mE)$

$rA \Leftarrow (r \,\&\, m) \mid ((rA) \,\&\, {\sim}m)$

Syntax:

rlwimi	rA,rS,n,mB,mE	(Rc = 0)
rlwimi.	rA,rS,n,mB,mE	(Rc = 1)

Condition Register/Fixed-Point Exception Register:
CR Field 0:   LT,GT,EQ,SO updated if Rc = 1, otherwise not affected
CR Fields 1-7:   not affected

XER: not affected

Description:
The **rlwimi** instruction rotates the contents of rS to the left by the number of bits specified by the immediate value n. This rotated result is then inserted into the destination register rA under the control of a mask that is composed of of 1's from bit position mB up to mE and 0's everywhere else.

The final result is an ORing of the original value of rA (wherever the mask bits are 0) and the newly calculated rotated result (wherever the mask bits are 1).

The archaic POWER mnemonic for this instruction is **rlimi[.]**.

Extended Forms:

inslwi[.]	rA,rS,nb,st	is equivalent to	**rlwimi[.]** rA,rS,32-st,st,(st+nb)-1
insrwi[.]	rA,rS,nb,st	is equivalent to	**rlwimi[.]** rA,rS,32-(st+nb), st,(st+nb)-1

Instruction Encoding:

0 5	6 10	11 15	16 20	21 25	26 30	31
0 1 0 1 0 0	S	A	shift	mBegin	mEnd	Rc

S   Source GPR rS
A   Target GPR rA where result of operation is stored
shift   Number of bits to rotate
mBegin   Bit position where mask is to start
mEnd   Bit position where mask is to end
Rc   Record bit

rlwinm   Rotate Left Word   rlwinm

Immediate then AND with Mask
POWER • 601 • 603 • PowerPC32/64

Operation: $r := (rS) \circlearrowleft n$

$m := \text{Mask}(mB,mE)$

$rA \Leftarrow (r \ \& \ m)$

Syntax:

rlwinm	rA,rS,n,mB,mE	(Rc = 0)
rlwinm.	rA,rS,n,mB,mE	(Rc = 1)

Condition Register / Fixed-Point Exception Register:
CR Field 0:   LT,GT,EQ,SO updated if Rc = 1, otherwise not affected

CR Fields 1-7:   not affected

XER: not affected

Description:

The **rlwinm** instruction rotates the contents of rS to the left by the number of bits specified by the immediate value n, and then ANDs this result with a mask that is composed of 1's from bit position mB up to mE and 0's everywhere else. The final result is then stored in rA.

The archaic POWER mnemonic for this instruction is **rlinm[.]**.

Extended Forms:

clrslwi[.]	rA,rS,nb,sh	is equivalent to	**rlwinm[.]** $rA,rS,sh,nb\text{-}sh,31\text{-}sh$
clrlwi[.]	rA,rS,nb	is equivalent to	**rlwinm[.]** $rA,rS,0,nb,31$
clrrwi[.]	rA,rS,nb	is equivalent to	**rlwinm[.]** $rA,rS,0,0,31\text{-}nb$
extlwi[.]	rA,rS,nb,st	is equivalent to	**rlwinm[.]** $rA,rS,st,0,nb\text{-}1$
extrwi[.]	rA,rS,nb,st	is equivalent to	**rlwinm[.]** $rA,rS,st+nb,32\text{-}nb,31$
rotlwi[.]	rA,rS,nb	is equivalent to	**rlwinm[.]** $rA,rS,nb,0,31$
rotrwi[.]	rA,rS,nb	is equivalent to	**rlwinm[.]** $rA,rS,32\text{-}nb,0,31$
slwi[.]	rA,rS,nb	is equivalent to	**rlwinm[.]** $rA,rS,nb,0,31\text{-}nb$
srwi[.]	rA,rS,nb	is equivalent to	**rlwinm[.]** $rA,rS,32\text{-}nb,nb,31$

Instruction Encoding:

0				5	6				10	11				15	16				20	21				25	26				30	31
0	1	0	1	0	1		S					A				shift				mBegin				mEnd				Rc

S	Source GPR rS
A	Target GPR rA where result of operation is stored
shift	Number of bits to rotate
mBegin	Bit position where mask is to start
mEnd	Bit position where mask is to end
Rc	Record bit

rlwnm

Rotate Left Word then AND with Mask

rlwnm

POWER • 601 • 603 • PowerPC32/64

Operation: $r := (rS) \circlearrowleft rB \ [\frac{27:31}{59:63}]$

$m := \text{Mask}(mB,mE)$

$rA \Leftarrow (r \ \& \ m)$

Syntax:

rlwnm	rA,rS,rB,mB,mE	(Rc = 0)
rlwnm.	rA,rS,rB,mB,mE	(Rc = 1)

Condition Register / Fixed-Point Exception Register:

CR Field 0:   LT,GT,EQ,SO updated if Rc = 1, otherwise not affected
CR Fields 1-7:   not affected

XER: not affected

Description:

The **rlwnm** instruction rotates the contents of rS to the left by the number of bits specified by $rB \ [\frac{27:31}{59:63}]$, and then ANDs this result with a mask that is composed of 1's from bit position mB up to mE and 0's everywhere else. The final result is then stored in rA.

The archaic POWER mnemonic for this instruction is **rlnm[.]**.

Extended Forms:

rotlw[.] rA,rS,rB is equivalent to   **rlwnm[.]** $rA,rS,rB,0,31$

Instruction Encoding:

0 1 0 1 1 1	S	A	B	mBegin	mEnd	Rc
0–5	6–10	11–15	16–20	21–25	26–30	31

S	Source GPR rS
A	Target GPR rA where result of operation is stored
B	Source GPR rB
mBegin	Bit position where mask is to start
mEnd	Bit position where mask is to end
Rc	Record bit

Rotate Right And Insert Bit

POWER • 601

Operation: $rA[rB[27:31]] \Leftarrow rS[0]$

Syntax:

rrib	rA,rS,rB	(Rc = 0)
rrib.	rA,rS,rB	(Rc = 1)

Condition Register / Fixed-Point Exception Register:

CR Field 0:   LT,GT,EQ,SO updated if Rc = 1, otherwise not affected

CR Fields 1-7:   not affected

XER: not affected

Description:

The **rrib** instruction rotates bit 0 of rS to the right by the number of bits specified in rB[27:31]. This bit is then inserted into that position in rA.

This instruction is not part of the PowerPC architecture.

Instruction Encoding:

0 5	6 10	11 15	16 20	21 30	31
0 1 1 1 1 1	S	A	B	1 0 0 0 0 1 1 0 0 1	Rc

S	Source GPR rS
A	Target GPR rA where result of operation is stored
B	Source GPR rB
Rc	Record bit

POWER • 601 • 603 • PowerPC32/64

Operation:

$$SRR0 \Leftarrow CIP + 4$$

$$SRR1 \Leftarrow MSR \left[\frac{0,\ 5:9,\ 16:31}{0:32,\ 37:41,\ 48:63} \right]$$

if(MSR[IP])

    $CIP \Leftarrow \ `0xFFF0\ 0C00$

else

    $CIP \Leftarrow \ °0x0000\ 0C00$

Syntax: **sc**

Condition Register/Fixed-Point Exception Register:

CR Fields 0-7:   not affected

XER: not affected

Description:

The **sc** instruction is used to pass control to the operating system so that it can perform a service. The details of these services depend on the operating system.

Before passing control to the servicing routine, the address of the next instruction to execute (calculated from the Current Instruction Pointer (CIP) + 4) and selected bits from the current MSR are saved in the SRR0 and SRR1 registers, respectively. This allows the **rfi** instruction to restore these values to their original state before returning control to the program.

This instruction is context-synchronizing.

The 601 differs from the PowerPC specification in how the low-order halfword of the SRR1 register is used. In the 601, bits 16 to 31 of the **sc** instruction are copied to SRR1[0:15].

The archaic POWER mnemonic for this instruction is **svca**. Note that there are many significant differences between the POWER **svc[l][a]** instructions and the PowerPC **sc** instruction.

Instruction Encoding:

0					5	6				10	11				15	16														29	30	31
0	1	0	0	0	1	0	0	0	0	0	0	0	0	0	0	0	0	0	0	0	0	0	0	0	0	0	0	0	0	0	1	0

slbia

SLB Invalidate All

slbia

PowerPC64

Operation: *invalidate all SLB entries*

Syntax: **slbia**

Condition Register / Fixed-Point Exception Register:

CR Fields 0-7: not affected

XER: not affected

Description:

The **slbia** instruction invalidates all of the entries currently in the SLB, regardless of the current setting of the instruction and data translation bits in the MSR (MSR[IT] and MSR[DT]).

This is a supervisor-level instruction.

This instruction exists on 64-bit PowerPC implementations only.

Instruction Encoding:

0					5	6				10	11				15	16				20	21								30	31
0	1	1	1	1	1	0	0	0	0	0	0	0	0	0	0	0	0	0	0	0	0	1	1	1	1	1	0	0	1	0	0

slbie SLB Invalidate Entry slbie

PowerPC64

Operation: *invalidate the specified SLB entry*

Syntax: **slbie**   r*B*

Condition Register/Fixed-Point Exception Register:
CR Fields 0-7:   not affected

XER: not affected

Description:

The **slbie** instruction invalidates the SLB entry which corresponds to the effective address stored in r*B*. The invalidation is performed regardless of the current setting of the instruction and data translation bits in the MSR (MSR[IT] and MSR[DT].

This is a supervisor-level instruction.

This instruction exists on 64-bit PowerPC implementations only.

Instruction Encoding:

0					5	6					10	11					15	16				20	21									30	31
0	1	1	1	1	1	0	0	0	0	0		0	0	0	0	0			B				0	1	1	0	1	1	0	0	1	0	0

B   Source GPR rB

sld   Shift Left Doubleword   sld

PowerPC64

Operation: $rA \Leftarrow (rS) \ll rB[57{:}63]$

Syntax: **sld** rA,rS,rB (Rc = 0)

             sld. rA,rS,rB (Rc = 1)

Condition Register/Fixed-Point Exception Register:

CR Field 0:   LT,GT,EQ,SO updated if Rc = 1, otherwise not affected

CR Fields 1-7:   not affected

XER: not affected

Description:

The **sld** instruction shifts the source register rS to the left by the number of bits specified in $rB[57{:}63]$, and places the shifted result into rA. If the shift amount is greater than 63, then the shifted result will be 0.

This instruction exists on 64-bit PowerPC implementations only.

Instruction Encoding:

0 1 1 1 1 1	S	A	B	0 0 0 0 0 1 1 0 1 1	Rc

| 0 | 5 | 6 | 10 | 11 | 15 | 16 | 20 | 21 | 30 | 31 |

S   Source GPR rS

A   Target GPR rA where result of operation is stored

B   Source GPR rB

Rc   Record bit

Shift Left Extended

POWER • 601

Operation: $rA \Leftarrow (rS) \ll rB[27:31]$

$MQ \Leftarrow (rS) \circlearrowleft rB[27:31]$

Syntax:

sle	rA,rS,rB	(Rc = 0)
sle.	rA,rS,rB	(Rc = 1)

Condition Register/Fixed-Point Exception Register:

CR Field 0:   LT,GT,EQ,SO updated if Rc = 1, otherwise not affected

CR Fields 1-7:   not affected

XER: not affected

Description:

The **sle** instruction shifts the contents of rS to the left by the number of bits specified by rB[27:31] and stores the result rA.

In addition, the result of rotating rS by rB[27:31] is also calculated and stored in the MQ register.

This instruction is not part of the PowerPC architecture.

Instruction Encoding:

0 5	6 10	11 15	16 20	21 30	31
0 1 1 1 1 1	S	A	B	0 0 1 0 0 1 1 0 0 1	Rc

S   Source GPR rS

A   Target GPR rA where result of operation is stored

B   Source GPR rB

Rc   Record bit

Shift Left Extended with MQ

POWER • 601

Operation: $r := (rS) \, ⟲ \, rB[27:31]$
$m := \text{Mask}(0, 31 - rB[27:31])$
$rA \Leftarrow (r \ \& \ m) \mid (MQ \ \& \ \sim m)$
$MQ \Leftarrow r$

Syntax:

sleq	rA,rS,rB	(Rc = 0)
sleq.	rA,rS,rB	(Rc = 1)

Condition Register / Fixed-Point Exception Register:

CR Field 0:   LT,GT,EQ,SO updated if Rc = 1, otherwise not affected
CR Fields 1-7:   not affected

XER: not affected

Description:

The **sleq** instruction shifts the contents of rS to the left by the number of bits specified by rB[27:31] and then merges this result with the contents of the MQ register. The rightmost rB[27:31] bits of the result are copied from the corresponding bits of the MQ register instead of from the shifted result. This merged result is stored in rA.

In addition, the result of rotating rS by rB[27:31] is also calculated and stored in the MQ register.

This instruction is not part of the PowerPC architecture.

Instruction Encoding:

0	5	6		10	11		15	16		20	21			30	31
0 1 1 1 1 1		S			A			B			0 0 1 1 0 1 1 0 0 1				Rc

S   Source GPR rS
A   Target GPR rA where result of operation is stored
B   Source GPR rB
Rc   Record bit

Shift Left Immediate with MQ

POWER • 601

Operation: $rA \Leftarrow (rS) \ll n$

$MQ \Leftarrow (rS) \circlearrowleft n$

Syntax:

sliq	r*A*,r*S*,*n*	(Rc = 0)
sliq.	r*A*,r*S*,*n*	(Rc = 1)

Condition Register / Fixed-Point Exception Register:

CR Field 0:   LT,GT,EQ,SO updated if Rc = 1, otherwise not affected

CR Fields 1-7: not affected

XER: not affected

Description:

The **sliq** instruction shifts the contents of rS to the left by the number of bits specified by the immediate value *n* and stores the result rA.

In addition, the result of rotating rS by *n* is also calculated and stored in the MQ register.

This instruction is not part of the PowerPC architecture.

Instruction Encoding:

0 5	6 10	11 15	16 20	21 30	31
0 1 1 1 1 1	S	A	shift	0 0 1 0 1 1 1 0 0 0	Rc

S	Source GPR rS
A	Target GPR rA where result of operation is stored
shift	Number of bits to shift
Rc	Record bit

slliq Shift Left Long Immediate with MQ slliq

POWER • 601

Operation:

$r := (rS) \circlearrowleft n$

$m := \text{Mask}(0, 31\text{-}n)$

$rA \Leftarrow (r \ \& \ m) \mid (MQ \ \& \ {\sim}m)$

$MQ \Leftarrow r$

Syntax:

slliq	rA,rS,n	(Rc = 0)
slliq.	rA,rS,n	(Rc = 1)

Condition Register / Fixed-Point Exception Register:

CR Field 0:   LT,GT,EQ,SO updated if Rc = 1, otherwise not affected
CR Fields 1-7:   not affected

XER: not affected

Description:

The **slliq** instruction shifts the contents of rS to the left by the number of bits specified by the immediate value n and then merges this result with the contents of the MQ register. The rightmost n bits of the result are copied from the corresponding bits of the MQ register instead of from the shifted result. This merged result is stored in rA.

In addition, the result of rotating rS by n is also calculated and stored in the MQ register.

This instruction is not part of the PowerPC architecture.

Instruction Encoding:

0 1 1 1 1 1	S	A	shift	0 0 1 1 1 1 1 0 0 0	Rc

Positions: 0 ... 5 6 ... 10 11 ... 15 16 ... 20 21 ... 30 31

S	Source GPR rS
A	Target GPR rA where result of operation is stored
shift	Number of bits to shift
Rc	Record bit

Operation: $r := (rS) \varnothing rB[27{:}31]$

$m := \text{Mask}(0,31\text{-}rB[27{:}31])$

$\text{if}(rB[26] = 0)$

$\quad rA \Leftarrow (r \mathbin{\&} m) \mid (MQ \mathbin{\&} {\sim}m)$

else

$\quad rA \Leftarrow (MQ \mathbin{\&} m)$

Syntax: **sllq** rA,rS,rB (Rc = 0)

sllq. rA,rS,rB (Rc = 1)

Condition Register / Fixed-Point Exception Register:

CR Field 0:   LT,GT,EQ,SO updated if Rc = 1, otherwise not affected

CR Fields 1-7:   not affected

XER: not affected

Description:

The **sllq** instruction shifts the contents of rS to the left by the number of bits specified by $rB[27{:}31]$ and then merges this result with the contents of the MQ register. The rightmost $rB[27{:}31]$ bits of the result are copied from the corresponding bits of the MQ register instead of from the shifted result. This merged result is stored in rA.

If bit 26 of rB is 1, then the result of this instruction is simply the leftmost 32-$rB[27{:}31]$ bits of the MQ.

This instruction is not part of the PowerPC architecture.

Instruction Encoding:

0					5	6				10	11				15	16				20	21									30	31
0	1	1	1	1	1			S					A					B			0	0	1	1	0	1	1	0	0	0	Rc

S   Source GPR rS

A   Target GPR rA where result of operation is stored

B   Source GPR rB

Rc   Record bit

Shift Left with MQ

POWER • 601

Operation: if(rB[26] = 0)

$\qquad$ rA ⟸ (rS) « rB[27:31]

$\qquad$ else

$\qquad$ rA ⟸ 0

$\qquad$ MQ ⟸ (rS) ϙ rB[27:31]

Syntax:

slq	rA,rS,rB	(Rc = 0)
slq.	rA,rS,rB	(Rc = 1)

Condition Register/Fixed-Point Exception Register:

CR Field 0:   LT,GT,EQ,SO updated if Rc = 1, otherwise not affected

CR Fields 1-7: not affected

XER: not affected

Description:

The **slq** instruction shifts the contents of rS to the left by the number of bits specified by rB[27:31] and then stores this result in rA.

If bit 26 of rB is 1, then it is assumed that the entire contents of rS have been shifted out to the left and a result of 0 is placed in rA.

In addition, the result of rotating rS by rB[27:31] is also calculated and stored in the MQ register.

This instruction is not part of the PowerPC architecture.

Instruction Encoding:

0	5	6	10	11	15	16	20	21	30	31
0 1 1 1 1 1		S		A		B		0 0 1 0 0 1 1 0 0 0		Rc

S	Source GPR rS
A	Target GPR rA where result of operation is stored
B	Source GPR rB
Rc	Record bit

slw

Shift Left Word

slw

POWER • 601 • 603 • PowerPC32/64

Operation: $rA \Leftarrow (rS) \ll rB \left[\frac{26:31}{58:63}\right]$

Syntax:

slw	rA,rS,rB	(Rc = 0)
slw.	rA,rS,rB	(Rc = 1)

Condition Register/Fixed-Point Exception Register:

CR Field 0:   LT,GT,EQ,SO updated if Rc = 1, otherwise not affected
CR Fields 1-7:   not affected

XER: not affected

Description:

The **slw** instruction shifts the low-order word of the source register rS to the left by the number of bits specified in rB [$\frac{26:31}{58:63}$], and places the shifted result into rA. If the shift amount is greater than 31, then the shifted result will be a word of 0's.

On 64-bit PowerPC implementations, the high-order word of the result is simply copied from the high-order word of the source register rS.

Instruction Encoding:

0 5	6 10	11 15	16 20	21 30	31
0 1 1 1 1 1	S	A	B	0 0 0 0 0 1 1 0 0 0	Rc

S   Source GPR rS
A   Target GPR rA where result of operation is stored
B   Source GPR rB
Rc   Record bit

srad   Shift Right Algebraic Doubleword   srad

PowerPC64

Operation: $rA \Leftarrow (rS) \overset{s}{\gg} rB[57:63]$

Syntax:

srad	rA,rS,rB	(Rc = 0)
srad.	rA,rS,rB	(Rc = 1)

Condition Register/Fixed-Point Exception Register:

CR Field 0:   LT,GT,EQ,SO updated if Rc = 1, otherwise not affected
CR Fields 1-7:   not affected

XER[CA]:   always updated
XER[OV,SO]:   not affected

Description:

The **srad** instruction shifts the source register rS to the right by the number of bits specified in rB[57:63], replicating bit 0 of rS as the shift occurs. The result of this operation is stored in rA. Shift amounts greater than 63 result in rA being loaded with 64 sign bits from rS.

The XER[CA] bit is normally set to 0, but is set to 1 if the result is negative and any 1 bits have been shifted out to the right.

This instruction exists on 64-bit PowerPC implementations only.

Instruction Encoding:

0	5	6	10	11	15	16	20	21	30	31
0 1 1 1 1 1		S		A		B		1 1 0 0 0 1 1 0 1 0		Rc

S	Source GPR rS
A	Target GPR rA where result of operation is stored
B	Source GPR rB
Rc	Record bit

sradi   Shift Right Algebraic   sradi
Doubleword Immediate
PowerPC64

Operation: $rA \Leftarrow (rS) \, \mathring{s} \, n$

Syntax:

sradi	rA,rS,n	(Rc = 0)
sradi.	rA,rS,n	(Rc = 1)

Condition Register/Fixed-Point Exception Register:

CR Field 0:   LT,GT,EQ,SO updated if Rc = 1, otherwise not affected
CR Fields 1-7:   not affected

XER[CA]:   always updated
XER[OV,SO]:   not affected

Description:

The **sradi** instruction shifts the source register rS to the right by the number of bits specified by the immediate value n, replicating bit 0 of rS as the shift occurs. The result of this operation is stored in rA. A shift amount of 0 causes rA to be set equal to rS.

The XER[CA] bit is normally set to 0, but is set to 1 if the result is negative and any 1 bits have been shifted out to the right.

This instruction exists on 64-bit PowerPC implementations only.

Instruction Encoding:

0 5	6 10	11 15	16 20	21 29	30	31
0 1 1 1 1 1	S	A	shift - 2	1 1 0 0 1 1 1 0 1	sh	Rc

Note that the shift value is split into 2 fields in the encoding: the high-order bit is stored in *sh* and the low-order bits are stored in *shift-2*. This is necessary because a 5-bit field isn't large enough to hold a 64-bit shift value.

S	Source GPR rS
A	Target GPR rA where result of operation is stored
shift-2	Low-order bits of shift value
sh	High-order bit of shift value
Rc	Record bit

Shift Right Algebraic Immediate with MQ

POWER • 601

Operation: $rA \Leftarrow (rS) \, ? \, n$

$MQ \Leftarrow (rS) \, \circlearrowright \, n$

Syntax:

sraiq	rA,rS,n	(Rc = 0)
sraiq.	rA,rS,n	(Rc = 1)

Condition Register/Fixed-Point Exception Register:

CR Field 0: LT,GT,EQ,SO updated if Rc = 1, otherwise not affected

CR Fields 1-7: not affected

XER[CA]: always updated

XER[OV,SO]: not affected

Description:

The **sraiq** instruction shifts the contents of rS to the right by the number of bits specified by the immediate value *n*, replicating bit 0 of rS as the shift occurs. The result of this operation is stored in rA.

In addition, the result of rotating rS by *n* is also calculated and stored in the MQ register.

Field 0 of the CR is updated to reflect the result of this operation if the instruction's Record (Rc) bit is set. The Carry (CA) bit of the XER is always affected by this instruction.

This instruction is not part of the PowerPC architecture.

Instruction Encoding:

0					5	6				10	11				15	16				20	21									30	31
0	1	1	1	1	1			S					A				shift				1	1	1	0	1	1	1	0	0	0	Rc

S	Source GPR rS
A	Target GPR rA where result of operation is stored
shift	Number of bits to shift
Rc	Record bit

$\mathbb{sraq}$ **Shift Right Algebraic with MQ** $\mathbb{sraq}$

POWER • 601

Operation: if(rB[26] = 0)

   $rA \Leftarrow (rS) \; \S \; rB[27:31]$

else

   $rA \Leftarrow rS[0]$

$MQ \Leftarrow (rS) \; \varphi \; rB[27:31]$

Syntax: **sraq**   rA,rS,rB   (Rc = 0)

   sraq.   rA,rS,rB   (Rc = 1)

Condition Register/Fixed-Point Exception Register:

CR Field 0:   LT,GT,EQ,SO updated if Rc = 1, otherwise not affected

CR Fields 1-7:   not affected

XER[CA]:   always updated

XER[OV,SO]:   not affected

Description:

The **sraq** instruction shifts the contents of rS to the right by the number of bits specified by rB[27:31], replicating bit 0 of rS as the shift occurs. The result of this operation is stored in rA.

If bit 26 of rB is 1, then it is assumed that the entire contents of rS have been shifted out to the right and a word of sign bits from rS is placed in rA.

In addition, the result of rotating rS by rB[27:31] is also calculated and stored in the MQ register.

This instruction is not part of the PowerPC architecture.

Instruction Encoding:

0					5	6				10	11				15	16				20	21									30	31
0	1	1	1	1	1		S					A					B				1	1	1	0	0	1	1	0	0	0	Rc

S   Source GPR rS

A   Target GPR rA where result of operation is stored

B   Source GPR rB

Rc   Record bit

sraw   Shift Right Algebraic Word   sraw

POWER • 601 • 603 • PowerPC32/64

Operation: $rA \Leftarrow (rS) \, \$ \, rB \left[\frac{26:31}{58:63}\right]$

Syntax:

sraw	rA,rS,rB	(Rc = 0)
sraw.	rA,rS,rB	(Rc = 1)

Condition Register/Fixed-Point Exception Register:

CR Field 0:   LT,GT,EQ,SO updated if Rc = 1, otherwise not affected
CR Fields 1-7:   not affected

XER[CA]:   always updated
XER[OV,SO]:   not affected

Description:

The **sraw** instruction shifts the low-order word of source register rS to the right by the number of bits specified in $rB \left[\frac{26:31}{58:63}\right]$, replicating bit 0 of rS as the shift occurs. The result of this operation is stored in rA. Shift amounts greater than 63 result in rA being loaded with 64 sign bits from rS.

The XER[CA] bit is normally set to 0, but is set to 1 if the result is negative and any 1 bits have been shifted out to the right.

On 64-bit PowerPC implementations, the result is copied into the low-order word of the destination register and then sign-extended to fill the entire register.

The archaic POWER mnemonic for this instruction is **sra[.]**.

Instruction Encoding:

0					5	6				10	11				15	16				20	21									30	31
0	1	1	1	1	1		S					A					B				1	1	0	0	0	1	1	0	0	0	Rc

S   Source GPR rS
A   Target GPR rA where result of operation is stored
B   Source GPR rB
Rc   Record bit

srawi   Shift Right Algebraic   srawi
Word Immediate
POWER • 601 • 603 • PowerPC32/64

Operation: $rA \Leftarrow (rS) \mathbin{\overset{s}{\gg}} n$

Syntax:

srawi	rA,rS,n	(Rc = 0)
srawi.	rA,rS,n	(Rc = 1)

Condition Register/Fixed-Point Exception Register:

CR Field 0:   LT,GT,EQ,SO updated if Rc = 1, otherwise not affected
CR Fields 1-7:   not affected

XER[CA]:   always updated
XER[OV,SO]:   not affected

Description:

The **srawi** instruction shifts the low-order word of source register rS to the right by the number of bits specified by the immediate value n, replicating bit 0 of rS as the shift occurs. The result of this operation is stored in rA. A shift amount of 0 causes rA to be set equal to rS.

The XER[CA] bit is normally set to 0, but is set to 1 if the result is negative and any 1 bits have been shifted out to the right.

On 64-bit PowerPC implementations, the result is copied into the low-order word of the destination register and then sign-extended to fill the entire register.

The archaic POWER mnemonic for this instruction is **srai[.]**.

Instruction Encoding:

0					5	6				10	11				15	16			20	21										30	31
0	1	1	1	1	1		S					A					shift			1	1	0	0	1	1	1	0	0	0	Rc

S   Source GPR rS
A   Target GPR rA where result of operation is stored
shift   Number of bits to shift
Rc   Record bit

srd   Shift Right Doubleword   srd

PowerPC64

Operation: $rA \Leftarrow (rS) \gg rB[57:63]$

Syntax:

srd	rA,rS,rB	(Rc = 0)
srd.	rA,rS,rB	(Rc = 1)

Condition Register / Fixed-Point Exception Register:

CR Field 0:   LT,GT,EQ,SO updated if Rc = 1, otherwise not affected
CR Fields 1-7:   not affected

XER: not affected

Description:

The **srd** instruction shifts the source register rS to the right by the number of bits specified in $rB[57:63]$, and places the shifted result into rA. If the shift amount is greater than 63, then the shifted result will be 0.

This instruction exists on 64-bit PowerPC implementations only.

Instruction Encoding:

0 5	6 10	11 15	16 20	21 30	31
0 1 1 1 1 1	S	A	B	1 0 0 0 0 1 1 0 1 1	Rc

S   Source GPR rS
A   Target GPR rA where result of operation is stored
B   Source GPR rB
Rc   Record bit

POWER • 601

Operation: $rA \Leftarrow (rS) \gg rB[27:31]$

               $MQ \Leftarrow (rS) \circlearrowright rB[27:31]$

Syntax: **sre** rA,rS,rB (Rc = 0)

             sre. rA,rS,rB (Rc = 1)

Condition Register / Fixed-Point Exception Register:

CR Field 0:   LT,GT,EQ,SO updated if Rc = 1, otherwise not affected

CR Fields 1-7:   not affected

XER: not affected

Description:

The **sre** instruction shifts the source register rS to the right by the number of bits specified in $rB[27:31]$, and places the shifted result into rA.

In addition, the result of rotating rS by $rB[27:31]$ is also calculated and stored in the MQ register.

This instruction is not part of the PowerPC architecture.

Instruction Encoding:

0					5	6				10	11				15	16				20	21									30	31
0	1	1	1	1	1			S					A					B			1	0	1	0	0	1	1	0	0	1	Rc

     S   Source GPR rS

     A   Target GPR rA where result of operation is stored

     B   Source GPR rB

     Rc   Record bit

Shift Right Extended Algebraic

POWER • 601

Operation: $rA \Leftarrow (rS) \, \$ \, rB[27{:}31]$

$MQ \Leftarrow (rS) \, \circlearrowright \, rB[27{:}31]$

Syntax:

srea	rA,rS,rB	(Rc = 0)
srea.	rA,rS,rB	(Rc = 1)

Condition Register / Fixed-Point Exception Register:

CR Field 0:   LT,GT,EQ,SO updated if Rc = 1, otherwise not affected
CR Fields 1-7:   not affected

XER[CA]:   always updated
XER[OV,SO]:   not affected

Description:

The **sre** instruction shifts the source register rS to the right by the number of bits specified in $rB[27{:}31]$, replicating bit 0 of rS as the shift occurs. The result of this operation is stored in rA.

In addition, the result of rotating rS by $rB[27{:}31]$ is also calculated and stored in the MQ register.

This instruction is not part of the PowerPC architecture.

Instruction Encoding:

0	5	6	10	11	15	16	20	21	30	31
0 1 1 1 1 1		S		A		B		1 1 1 0 0 1 1 0 0 1		Rc

S   Source GPR rS
A   Target GPR rA where result of operation is stored
B   Source GPR rB
Rc   Record bit

POWER • 601

Operation:
$r := (rS) \circlearrowright rB[27:31]$
$m := \text{Mask}(rB[27:31],31)$
$rA \Leftarrow (r \,\&\, m) \mid (MQ \,\&\, \sim m)$
$MQ \Leftarrow r$

Syntax:

sreq	rA,rS,rB	(Rc = 0)
sreq.	rA,rS,rB	(Rc = 1)

Condition Register / Fixed-Point Exception Register:

CR Field 0:   LT,GT,EQ,SO updated if Rc = 1, otherwise not affected
CR Fields 1-7:   not affected

XER: not affected

Description:

The **sreq** instruction shifts the contents of rS to the right by the number of bits specified by r$B[27:31]$, and then merges this result with the contents of the MQ register. The leftmost r$B[27:31]$ bits of the result are copied from the corresponding bits of the MQ register instead of from the shifted result. This merged result is stored in rA.

In addition, the result of rotating rS by r$B[27:31]$ is also calculated and stored in the MQ register.

This instruction is not part of the PowerPC architecture.

Instruction Encoding:

0 5	6 10	11 15	16 20	21 30	31
0 1 1 1 1 1	S	A	B	1 0 1 1 0 1 1 0 0 1	Rc

S   Source GPR rS
A   Target GPR rA where result of operation is stored
B   Source GPR rB
Rc   Record bit

Shift Right Immediate with MQ

POWER • 601

Operation: $rA \Leftarrow (rS) \gg n$

$MQ \Leftarrow (rS) \circlearrowright n$

Syntax:

sriq	rA,rS,n	(Rc = 0)
sriq.	rA,rS,n	(Rc = 1)

Condition Register / Fixed-Point Exception Register:

CR Field 0: LT,GT,EQ,SO updated if Rc = 1, otherwise not affected

CR Fields 1-7: not affected

XER: not affected

Description:

The **sriq** instruction shifts the source register rS to the right by the number of bits specified by the immediate value n, and places the shifted result into rA.

In addition, the result of rotating rS by n is also calculated and stored in the MQ register.

This instruction is not part of the PowerPC architecture.

Instruction Encoding:

0	5	6	10	11	15	16	20	21	30	31
0 1 1 1 1 1		S		A		shift		1 0 1 0 1 1 1 0 0 0		Rc

S	Source GPR rS
A	Target GPR rA where result of operation is stored
shift	Number of bits to shift
Rc	Record bit

srliq Shift Right Long Immediate with MQ srliq

Operation: $r := (rS) \circlearrowright n$
$m := \text{Mask}(n,31)$
$rA \Leftarrow (r \;\&\; m) \mid (MQ \;\&\; \sim m)$
$MQ \Leftarrow r$

Syntax:

srliq	rA,rS,n	(Rc = 0)
srliq.	rA,rS,n	(Rc = 1)

Condition Register / Fixed-Point Exception Register:

CR Field 0:   LT,GT,EQ,SO updated if Rc = 1, otherwise not affected
CR Fields 1-7: not affected

XER: not affected

Description:

The **srliq** instruction shifts the contents of rS to the right by the number of bits specified by the immediate value n, and then merges this result with the contents of the MQ register. The leftmost n bits of the result are copied from the corresponding bits of the MQ register instead of from the shifted result. This merged result is stored in rA.

In addition, the result of rotating rS by n is also calculated and stored in the MQ register.

This instruction is not part of the PowerPC architecture.

Instruction Encoding:

0	5	6	10	11	15	16	20	21	30	31
0 1 1 1 1 1		S		A		shift		1 0 1 1 1 1 1 0 0 0		Rc

S   Source GPR rS
A   Target GPR rA where result of operation is stored
shift   Number of bits to shift
Rc   Record bit

Shift Right Long with MQ

POWER • 601

Operation: $r := (rS) \circ rB[27:31]$

$m := \text{Mask}(rB[27:31],31)$

$\text{if}(rB[26] = 0)$

$\quad rA \Leftarrow (r \, \& \, m) \mid (MQ \, \& \sim m)$

else

$\quad rA \Leftarrow (MQ \, \& \, m)$

Syntax: **srlq** rA,rS,rB (Rc = 0)

srlq. rA,rS,rB (Rc = 1)

Condition Register / Fixed-Point Exception Register:

CR Field 0: LT,GT,EQ,SO updated if Rc = 1, otherwise not affected

CR Fields 1-7: not affected

XER: not affected

Description:

The **srlq** instruction shifts the contents of rS to the right by the number of bits specified by rB[27:31] and then merges this result with the contents of the MQ register. The leftmost rB[27:31] bits of the result are copied from the corresponding bits of the MQ register instead of from the shifted result. This merged result is stored in rA.

If bit 26 of rB is 1, then the result of this instruction is simply the rightmost 32-rB[27:31] bits of the MQ.

This instruction is not part of the PowerPC architecture.

Instruction Encoding:

0					5	6				10	11				15	16				20	21										30	31
0	1	1	1	1	1			S					A					B			1	0	1	1	0	1	1	0	0	0	Rc

S Source GPR rS

A Target GPR rA where result of operation is stored

B Source GPR rB

Rc Record bit

Operation: if($rB[26] = 0$)

           $rA \Leftarrow (rS) \gg rB[27:31]$

     else

         $rA \Leftarrow 0$

    $MQ \Leftarrow (rS) \circlearrowright rB[27:31]$

Syntax: **srq** rA,rS,rB (Rc = 0)

             srq. rA,rS,rB (Rc = 1)

Condition Register/Fixed-Point Exception Register:

CR Field 0:   LT,GT,EQ,SO updated if Rc = 1, otherwise not affected

CR Fields 1-7:   not affected

XER: not affected

Description:

The **srq** instruction shifts the contents of rS to the right by the number of bits specified by $rB[27:31]$ and then stores this result in rA.

If bit 26 of rB is 1, then it is assumed that the entire contents of rS have been shifted out to the right and a result of 0 is placed in rA.

In addition, the result of rotating rS by $rB[27:31]$ is also calculated and stored in the MQ register.

This instruction is not part of the PowerPC architecture.

Instruction Encoding:

0 5	6 10	11 15	16 20	21 30	31
0 1 1 1 1 1	S	A	B	1 0 1 0 0 1 1 0 0 0	Rc

     S   Source GPR rS

     A   Target GPR rA where result of operation is stored

     B   Source GPR rB

     Rc   Record bit

srw Shift Right Word **srw**

POWER • 601 • 603 • PowerPC32/64

Operation: $rA \Leftarrow (rS) \gg rB \left[\frac{26:31}{58:63}\right]$

Syntax:

srw	rA,rS,rB	(Rc = 0)
srw.	rA,rS,rB	(Rc = 1)

Condition Register/Fixed-Point Exception Register:

CR Field 0:   LT,GT,EQ,SO updated if Rc = 1, otherwise not affected
CR Fields 1-7:   not affected

XER: not affected

Description:

The **srw** instruction shifts the source register rS to the right by the number of bits specified in $rB \left[\frac{26:31}{58:63}\right]$, and places the shifted result into rA. If the shift amount is greater than 31, then the shifted result will be 0.

The archaic POWER mnemonic for this instruction is **sr[.]**.

Instruction Encoding:

0					5	6				10	11				15	16				20	21										30	31
0	1	1	1	1	1			S					A					B			1	0	0	0	0	1	1	0	0	0	Rc

S	Source GPR rS
A	Target GPR rA where result of operation is stored
B	Source GPR rB
Rc	Record bit

stb   Store Byte   stb

POWER • 601 • 603 • PowerPC32/64

Operation: Byte $((rA | 0) + `d) \Leftarrow rS \left[\frac{24:31}{56:63}\right]$

Syntax: **stb** $rS,d(rA)$

Condition Register/Fixed-Point Exception Register:

CR Fields 0-7:   not affected

XER: not affected

Description:

The **stb** instruction stores the low-order byte of the source register rS into the byte located at the effective address calculated from $(rA | 0) + `d$.

Instruction Encoding:

0 5	6 10	11 15	16 31
1 0 0 1 1 0	S	A	d

S   Source GPR rS
A   Source GPR rA
d   Signed 16-bit displacement

stbu   Store Byte with Update   stbu

POWER • 601 • 603 • PowerPC32/64

Operation: $\text{Byte } ((rA) + `d) \Leftarrow rS \left[{24:31 \atop 56:63}\right]$

$$rA \Leftarrow (rA) + `d$$

Syntax: **stbu** $rS,d(rA)$

Condition Register/Fixed-Point Exception Register:

CR Fields 0-7:   not affected

XER: not affected

Description:

The **stbu** instruction stores the low-order byte of the source register rS into the byte located at the effective address calculated from $(rA) + `d$.

After the store is performed, the effective address is stored in rA.

If r0 is specified as rA, then the instruction form is invalid. For POWER compatibility, the 601 allows rA to specify r0, but the effective address is calculated from `d, and r0 is not updated with the effective address.

Instruction Encoding:

0 5	6 10	11 15	16 31
1 0 0 1 1 1	S	A	d

S   Source GPR rS
A   Source GPR rA
d   Signed 16-bit displacement

stbux   Store Byte with Update Indexed   stbux

POWER • 601 • 603 • PowerPC32/64

Operation: Byte $((rA) + (rB)) \Leftarrow rS \begin{bmatrix} 24:31 \\ 56:63 \end{bmatrix}$

$rA \Leftarrow (rA) + (rB)$

Syntax: **stbux**   rS,rA,rB

Condition Register/Fixed-Point Exception Register:

CR Fields 0-7:   not affected

XER: not affected

Description:

The **stbux** instruction stores the low-order byte of the source register rS into the byte located at the effective address calculated from $(rA) + (rB)$.

After the store is performed, the effective address is stored in rA.

If r0 is specified as rA, then the instruction form is invalid. For POWER compatibility, the 601 allows rA to specify r0, but the effective address is calculated from (rB), and r0 is not updated with the effective address.

Instruction Encoding:

0	5 6	10 11	15 16	20 21	30 31
0 1 1 1 1 1	S	A	B	0 0 1 1 1 1 0 1 1 1 0	

S   Source GPR rS
A   Source GPR rA
B   Source GPR rB

stbx

stbx

POWER • 601 • 603 • PowerPC32/64

Operation: Byte $((rA\,|\,0) + (rB)) \Leftarrow rS\,\left[\begin{smallmatrix}24:31\\56:63\end{smallmatrix}\right]$

Syntax: **stbx** rS, rA, rB

Condition Register/Fixed-Point Exception Register:

CR Fields 0-7: not affected

XER: not affected

Description:

The **stbx** instruction stores the low-order byte of the source register rS into the byte located at the effective address calculated from $(rA\,|\,0) + (rB)$.

Instruction Encoding:

0	1 1 1 1 1	S	A	B	0 0 1 1 0 1 0 1 1 1	0

0 .... 5 6 .... 10 11 .... 15 16 .... 20 21 .... 30 31

S Source GPR rS
A Source GPR rA
B Source GPR rB

std   Store Doubleword   std

PowerPC64

Operation: Doubleword$((rA \,|\, 0) + `(ds \perp b00)) \Leftarrow rS$

Syntax: **std** $rS,ds(rA)$

Condition Register / Fixed-Point Exception Register:

CR Fields 0-7:   not affected

XER: not affected

Description:

The **std** instruction stores all 64 bits of the source register rS into the doubleword located at the effective address calculated from $(rA \,|\, 0) + `(ds \perp b00)$.

This instruction exists on 64-bit PowerPC implementations only.

Instruction Encoding:

0 5	6 10	11 15	16 29	30 31
1 1 1 1 1 0	S	A	ds	0 0

      S   Source GPR rS
      A   Source GPR rA
      ds   Signed 16-bit displacement

stdcx. Store Doubleword stdcx.
Conditional Indexed
PowerPC64

Operation: if *reservation on ((rA | 0) + (rB))*
$\qquad$ Doubleword((rA | 0) + (rB)) $\Leftarrow$ rS
$\qquad$ CR{0} = b001 $\perp$ XER[SO]
$\quad$ else
$\qquad$ CR{0} = b000 $\perp$ XER[SO]

Syntax: **stdcx.** $\quad$ rS,rA,rB

Condition Register / Fixed-Point Exception Register:
CR Field 0: $\quad$ LT,GT,EQ,SO always updated
CR Fields 1-7: $\quad$ not affected

XER: $\qquad$ not affected

Description:

If a reservation exists for the effective address calculated from (rA | 0) + (rB), the **stdcx.** instruction stores the doubleword in rS into memory starting at that effective address. After the store completes, the reservation is cleared.

If a reservation does not exist for this address, the **stdcx.** instruction does not perform the store operation. A reservation can be placed using the **ldarx** instruction.

The calculated effective address must specify an aligned doubleword (i.e.: it must be a multiple of 8). If the address does not specify an aligned doubleword, the alignment exception handler may be invoked (if the load crosses a page boundary), or the results may be boundedly undefined.

The EQ bit of CR field 0 is updated to indicate whether or not the store operation was performed. This bit is set to 1 if the store was performed and 0 if it was not. The SO bit of CR{0} is copied from XER[SO] and the remaining bits of the field are cleared.

If the address references a *direct-store* storage segment, then a Data Storage interrupt occurs or the results are boundedly undefined.

This instruction exists on 64-bit PowerPC implementations only.

Instruction Encoding:

0 5	6 10	11 15	16 20	21 30	31
0 1 1 1 1 1	S	A	B	0 0 1 1 0 1 0 1 1 0	1

S	Source GPR rS
A	Source GPR rA
B	Source GPR rB

stdu   Store Doubleword with Update   stdu

PowerPC64

Operation: Doubleword $((rA) + \grave{}(ds \perp b00)) \Leftarrow rS$

$rA \Leftarrow (rA) + \grave{}(ds \perp b00)$

Syntax: **stdu** $rS,ds(rA)$

Condition Register/Fixed-Point Exception Register:

CR Fields 0-7:   not affected

XER: not affected

Description:

The **stdu** instruction stores all 64 bits of the source register rS into the doubleword located at the effective address calculated from $(rA) + \grave{}(ds \perp b00)$.

After the store is performed, the effective address is stored in rA.

If r0 is specified as rA, then the instruction form is invalid.

This instruction exists on 64-bit PowerPC implementations only.

Instruction Encoding:

0 5	6 10	11 15	16 29	30 31
1 1 1 1 1 0	S	A	ds	0 1

S   Source GPR rS

A   Source GPR rA

ds   Signed 16-bit displacement

stdux   Store Doubleword   stdux
with Update Indexed
PowerPC64

Operation: Doubleword $((rA) + (rB)) \Leftarrow rS$
              $rA \Leftarrow (rA) + (rB)$

Syntax: **stdux** rS,rA,rB

Condition Register / Fixed-Point Exception Register:
CR Fields 0-7:   not affected

XER: not affected

Description:
The **stdux** instruction stores all 64 bits of the source register rS into the doubleword located at the effective address calculated from $(rA) + (rB)$.

After the store is performed, the effective address is stored in rA.

If r0 is specified as rA, then the instruction form is invalid.

This instruction exists on 64-bit PowerPC implementations only.

Instruction Encoding:

0					5	6				10	11				15	16				20	21									30	31
0	1	1	1	1	1			S					A					B			0	0	1	0	1	1	0	1	0	1	0

      S   Source GPR rS
      A   Source GPR rA
      B   Source GPR rB

stdx   Store Doubleword Indexed   stdx

PowerPC64

Operation: Doubleword $((rA \mid 0) + (rB)) \Leftarrow rS$

Syntax: **stdx** rS,rA,rB

Condition Register / Fixed-Point Exception Register:

    CR Fields 0-7:   not affected

    XER: not affected

Description:

The **stdx** instruction stores all 64 bits of the source register rS into the double-word located at the effective address calculated from $(rA \mid 0) + (rB)$.

This instruction exists on 64-bit PowerPC implementations only.

Instruction Encoding:

0 5	6 10	11 15	16 20	21 30	31
0 1 1 1 1 1	S	A	B	0 0 1 0 0 1 0 1 0 1	0

    S   Source GPR rS
    A   Source GPR rA
    B   Source GPR rB

stfd   Store Floating-Point Double-Precision   stfd

POWER • 601 • 603 • PowerPC32/64

Operation: FP-Double$((rA\,|\,0) + `d) \Leftarrow frS$

Syntax: **stfd** $frS,d(rA)$

Condition Register/Fixed-Point Exception Register:
CR Fields 0-7:   not affected

XER: not affected

Description:
The **stfd** instruction stores the 64-bit double-precision value from the source register frS into the doubleword located at the effective address calculated from $(rA\,|\,0) + `d$.

This instruction affects neither the CR nor the XER.

Instruction Encoding:

0 5	6 10	11 15	16 31
1 1 0 1 1 0	S	A	d

S	Source FPR frS
A	Source GPR rA
d	Signed 16-bit displacement

stfdu   Store Floating-Point   stfdu
Double-Precision with Update
POWER • 601 • 603 • PowerPC32/64

Operation: FP-Double $((rA) + \grave{}d) \Leftarrow frS$
$rA \Leftarrow (rA) + \grave{}d$

Syntax: **stfdu** $frS,d(rA)$

Condition Register/Fixed-Point Exception Register:
CR Fields 0-7:   not affected

XER: not affected

Description:

The **stfdu** instruction stores the 64-bit double-precision value from the source register frS into the doubleword located at the effective address calculated from $(rA) + \grave{}d$.

After the store is performed, the effective address is stored in rA.

If r0 is specified as rA, then the instruction form is invalid. For POWER compatibility, the 601 allows rA to specify r0, but the effective address is calculated from `d, and r0 is not updated with the effective address.

Instruction Encoding:

0	5 6	10 11	15 16	31
1 1 0 1 1 1	S	A	d	

S   Source FPR frS
A   Source GPR rA
d   Signed 16-bit displacement

stfdux   Store Floating-Point Double-   stfdux
Precision with Update Indexed
POWER • 601 • 603 • PowerPC32/64

Operation: FP-Double $((rA) + (rB)) \Leftarrow frS$
$rA \Leftarrow (rA) + (rB)$

Syntax: **stfdux**   frS,rA,rB

Condition Register/Fixed-Point Exception Register:
CR Fields 0-7:   not affected

XER: not affected

Description:

The **stfdux** instruction stores the 64-bit double-precision value from the source register frS into the doubleword located at the effective address calculated from $(rA) + (rB)$.

After the store is performed, the effective address is stored in rA.

If r0 is specified as rA, then the instruction form is invalid. For POWER compatibility, the 601 allows rA to specify r0, but the effective address is calculated from (rB), and r0 is not updated with the effective address.

Instruction Encoding:

0	5	6			10	11		A	15	16		B	20	21											30	31
0 1 1 1 1 1			S					A				B		1 0 1 1 1 1 0 1 1 1													0

S   Source FPR frS
A   Source GPR rA
B   Source GPR rB

stfdx   Store Floating-Point   stfdx
Double-Precision Indexed
POWER • 601 • 603 • PowerPC32/64

Operation: FP-Double $((rA \mid 0) + (rB)) \Leftarrow frS$

Syntax: **stfdx**   frS,rA,rB

Condition Register/Fixed-Point Exception Register:
CR Fields 0-7:   not affected

XER: not affected

Description:
The **stfdx** instruction stores the 64-bit double-precision value from the source register frS into the doubleword located at the effective address calculated from $(rA \mid 0) + (rB)$.

Instruction Encoding:

0 5	6 10	11 15	16 20	21 30	31
0 1 1 1 1 1	S	A	B	1 0 1 1 0 1 0 1 1 1 0	0

S	Source FPR frS
A	Source GPR rA
B	Source GPR rB

stfiwx   Store Floating-Point   stfiwx
as Integer Word
603 • PowerPC32/64

Operation: Word $((rA | 0) + (rB)) \Leftarrow frS[32:63]$

Syntax: **stfiwx**   frS,rA,rB

Condition Register/Fixed-Point Exception Register:
  CR Fields 0-7:   not affected

  XER: not affected

Description:

The **stfiwx** instruction stores the low-order 32 bits of the frS into the word addressed by $((rA | 0) + (rB))$. No conversion of any sort is performed on the data before it is stored.

If the value in frS was derived (either directly or indirectly) from any of the *Load Floating-Point Single-Precision* instructions, any single-precision arithmetic instruction, or the *Floating-Point Round to Single-Precision* instruction, then the value stored in memory is undefined. This gives the designers of PowerPC processors the option of changing the register storage format for single-precision values.

This instruction is an optional part of the PowerPC architecture. It is part of the Graphical group of optional instructions.

Instruction Encoding:

0 5	6 10	11 15	16 20	21 30	31
0 1 1 1 1 1	S	A	B	1 1 1 1 0 1 0 1 1 1 0	0

S	Source FPR frS
A	Source GPR rA
B	Source GPR rB

stfs   Store Floating-Point Single-Precision   **stfs**

POWER • 601 • 603 • PowerPC32/64

Operation: FP-Single $((rA \,|\, 0) + \,`d) \Leftarrow frS$

Syntax: **stfs** $frS,d(rA)$

Condition Register / Fixed-Point Exception Register:

CR Fields 0-7:   not affected

XER: not affected

Description:

The **stfs** instruction takes the 64-bit double-precision value from the source register frS, converts it into a 32-bit single-precision value, and then stores it into the word located at the effective address calculated from $(rA \,|\, 0) + \,`d$.

If the converted value does not fit in single-precision format, then the stored value is undefined.

Instruction Encoding:

0 5	6 10	11 15	16 31
1 1 0 1 0 0	S	A	d

S   Source FPR frS
A   Source GPR rA
d   Signed 16-bit displacement

stfsu

Store Floating-Point
Single-Precision with Update
POWER • 601 • 603 • PowerPC32/64

Operation: FP-Single $((rA) + `d) \Leftarrow frS$
$rA \Leftarrow (rA) + `d$

Syntax: **stfsu** $frS,d(rA)$

Condition Register/Fixed-Point Exception Register:
CR Fields 0-7:   not affected

XER: not affected

Description:
The **stfsu** instruction takes the 64-bit double-precision value from the source register frS, converts it into a 32-bit single-precision value, and then stores it into the word located at the effective address calculated from $(rA) + `d$.

After the store is performed, the effective address is stored in rA.

If r0 is specified as rA, then the instruction form is invalid. For POWER compatibility, the 601 allows rA to specify r0, but the effective address is calculated from `d, and r0 is not updated with the effective address.

If the converted value does not fit in single-precision format, then the stored value is undefined.

Instruction Encoding:

0 5	6 10	11 15	16 31
1 1 0 1 0 1	S	A	d

S   Source FPR frS
A   Source GPR rA
d   Signed 16-bit displacement

stfsux   Store Floating-Point Single-   stfsux
Precision with Update Indexed
POWER • 601 • 603 • PowerPC32/64

Operation: FP-Single $((rA) + (rB)) \Leftarrow frS$
               $rA \Leftarrow (rA) + (rB)$

Syntax: **stfsux**   frS,rA,rB

Condition Register/Fixed-Point Exception Register:
CR Fields 0-7:   not affected

XER: not affected

Description:

The **stfsux** instruction takes the 64-bit double-precision value from the source register frS, converts it into a 32-bit single-precision value, and then stores it into the word located at the effective address calculated from $(rA) + (rB)$.

After the store is performed, the effective address is stored in rA.

If r0 is specified as rA, then the instruction form is invalid. For POWER compatibility, the 601 allows rA to specify r0, but the effective address is calculated from (rB), and r0 is not updated with the effective address.

If the converted value does not fit in single-precision format, then the stored value is undefined.

Instruction Encoding:

0 5	6 10	11 15	16 20	21 30	31
0 1 1 1 1 1	S	A	B	1 0 1 0 1 1 0 1 1 1	0

     S   Source FPR frS
     A   Source GPR rA
     B   Source GPR rB

stfsx

Store Floating-Point
Single-Precision Indexed
POWER • 601 • 603 • PowerPC32/64

Operation: FP-Single $((rA \,|\, 0) + (rB)) \Leftarrow frS$

Syntax: **stfsx**   frS,rA,rB

Condition Register/Fixed-Point Exception Register:

CR Fields 0-7:   not affected

XER: not affected

Description:

The **stfsx** instruction takes the 64-bit double-precision value from the source register frS, converts it into a 32-bit single-precision value, and then stores it into the word located at the effective address calculated from $(rA \,|\, 0) + (rB)$.

If the converted value does not fit in single-precision format, then the stored value is undefined.

Instruction Encoding:

0	5	6	10	11	15	16	20	21	30	31
0 1 1 1 1 1		S		A		B		1 0 1 0 0 1 0 1 1 1 0		

        S   Source FPR frS
        A   Source GPR rA
        B   Source GPR rB

sth

Store Halfword

sth

POWER • 601 • 603 • PowerPC32/64

Operation: $\text{Halfword}((rA \mid 0) + \text{`}d) \Leftarrow rS \left[\frac{16:31}{48:63}\right]$

Syntax: **sth** $rS,d(rA)$

Condition Register/Fixed-Point Exception Register:

CR Fields 0-7:   not affected

XER: not affected

Description:

The **sth** instruction stores the low-order 16 bits of the source register rS into the halfword located at the effective address calculated from $(rA \mid 0) + \text{`}d$.

Instruction Encoding:

0 5	6 10	11 15	16 31
1 0 1 1 0 0	S	A	d

      S   Source GPR rS
      A   Source GPR rA
      d   Signed 16-bit displacement

sthbrx Store Halfword sthbrx
Byte-Reversed Indexed
POWER • 601 • 603 • PowerPC32/64

Operation: Halfword $((rA \mid 0) + (rB)) \Leftarrow rT[24:31] \perp rT[16:23]$

Syntax: **sthbrx**   rS,rA,rB

Condition Register/Fixed-Point Exception Register:
  CR Fields 0-7:   not affected

  XER: not affected

Description:

The **sthbrx** instruction takes the low-order halfword of the source register rS, swaps the two bytes of this halfword, and then stores this *byte-reversed* halfword into the memory halfword addressed by (rA | 0) + (rB).

For some PowerPC implementations, this byte-reversed store instruction may have a greater latency than other store instructions.

Instruction Encoding:

0 5	6 S 10	11 A 15	16 B 20	21 30	31
0 1 1 1 1 1	S	A	B	1 1 1 0 0 1 0 1 1 0 0	0

S   Source GPR rS
A   Source GPR rA
B   Source GPR rB

sthu   Store Halfword with Update   sthu

POWER • 601 • 603 • PowerPC32/64

Operation: Halfword $((rA) + \grave{}d) \Leftarrow rS \left[\frac{16:31}{48:63}\right]$

$rA \Leftarrow (rA) + \grave{}d$

Syntax: **sthu** $rS,d(rA)$

Condition Register/Fixed-Point Exception Register:

CR Fields 0-7:   not affected

XER: not affected

Description:

The **sthu** instruction stores the low-order 16 bits of the source register rS into the halfword located at the effective address calculated from $(rA) + \grave{}d$.

After the store is performed, the effective address is stored in rA.

If r0 is specified as rA, then the instruction form is invalid. For POWER compatibility, the 601 allows rA to specify r0, but the effective address is calculated from $\grave{}d$, and r0 is not updated with the effective address.

Instruction Encoding:

0 5	6 10	11 15	16 31
1 0 1 1 0 1	S	A	d

S   Source GPR rS
A   Source GPR rA
d   Signed 16-bit displacement

sthux

sthux

Store Halfword
with Update Indexed
POWER • 601 • 603 • PowerPC32/64

Operation: $\text{Halfword}\ ((rA) + (rB)) \Leftarrow rS\ \left[\frac{16:31}{48:63}\right]$

$rA \Leftarrow (rA) + (rB)$

Syntax: **sthux**   rS,rA,rB

Condition Register/Fixed-Point Exception Register:
CR Fields 0-7:   not affected

XER: not affected

Description:

The **sthux** instruction stores the low-order 16 bits of the source register rS into the halfword located at the effective address calculated from (rA) + (rB).

After the store is performed, the effective address is stored in rA.

If r0 is specified as rA, then the instruction form is invalid. For POWER compatibility, the 601 allows rA to specify r0, but the effective address is calculated from (rB), and r0 is not updated with the effective address.

Instruction Encoding:

0 5	6 10	11 15	16 20	21 30	31
0 1 1 1 1 1	S	A	B	0 1 1 0 1 1 0 1 1 1	0

     S   Source GPR rS
     A   Source GPR rA
     B   Source GPR rB

sthx　Store Halfword Indexed　sthx

POWER • 601 • 603 • PowerPC32/64

Operation:　Halfword $((rA \mid 0) + (rB)) \Leftarrow rS \left[\frac{16:31}{48:63}\right]$

Syntax:　　**sthx**　　rS,rA,rB

Condition Register / Fixed-Point Exception Register:

CR Fields 0-7:　not affected

XER:　　　　not affected

Description:

The **sthx** instruction stores the low-order 16 bits of the source register rS into the halfword located at the effective address calculated from (rA | 0) + (rB).

Instruction Encoding:

0　　　　　5	6　　　　10	11　　　　15	16　　　　20	21　　　　　　　　　　30	31
0 1 1 1 1 1	S	A	B	0 1 1 0 0 1 0 1 1 1 0	

S　　　　Source GPR rS
A　　　　Source GPR rA
B　　　　Source GPR rB

stmw   Store Multiple Word   stmw

POWER • 601 • 603 • PowerPC32/64

Operation:

$$ea := (rA \mid 0) + \grave{}d$$
$$R := T$$
$$\text{while } (R \leq 31)$$
$$\quad \text{Word } (ea) \Leftarrow rR \, [\tfrac{0:31}{32:63}]$$
$$\quad ea := ea + 4$$
$$\quad R := R + 1$$

Syntax: **stmw** $rS,d(rA)$

Condition Register / Fixed-Point Exception Register:

CR Fields 0-7:   not affected

XER: not affected

Description:

The **stmw** instruction stores words from a set of GPRs into memory. The set of GPRs starts with register rS and continues up to register r31. The address of the first word to be stored is specified by the effective address calculated from $(rA \mid 0) + \grave{}d$. Consecutive registers are stored in consecutive words from this starting point.

On 64-bit PowerPC implementations, only the low-order word of each register is stored into memory.

The calculated effective address must specify an aligned word (i.e., it must be a multiple of 4). If the address does not specify an aligned word, the alignment exception handler may be invoked (if the store crosses a page boundary), or the results may be boundedly undefined.

The preferred form for this instruction is when the effective address and rT are chosen so that the low-order byte from r31 is stored into the last byte of an aligned quadword in memory. It is possible that some PowerPC implementations will execute non-preferred forms more slowly than the preferred forms. On future implementations, this instruction may execute more slowly than a series of instructions that perform the same operation.

The archaic POWER mnemonic for this instruction is **stm**.

Instruction Encoding:

0					5	6				10	11				15	16			31
1	0	1	1	1	1			S				A					d		

S   First source GPR rS to store in memory

A   Source GPR rA

d   Signed 16-bit displacement

stswi   Store String Word Immediate   stswi

POWER • 601 • 603 • PowerPC32/64

Operation: *store nBytes bytes from registers into memory*

Syntax: **stswi**   rS,rA,nBytes

Condition Register / Fixed-Point Exception Register:
CR Fields 0-7:   not affected

XER: not affected

Description:

The **stswi** instruction stores bytes into memory from a set of GPRs. The number of bytes (specified by the immediate *nBytes* value) are stored into memory starting with the address calculated from (rA | 0). The stored data comes from the GPRs starting with r*S* and continuing up toward r31 for as many registers as are needed to produce *nBytes* bytes. The register sequence wraps from r31 to r0 if necessary.

The bytes from each register are stored starting with the leftmost byte in the low-order word and continuing to the rightmost byte of the register. On 64-bit PowerPC implementations, only the low-order word of each register is stored into memory.

If 0 is specified for *nBytes*, then the number of bytes stored is 32.

The operation of this instruction can be summarized as follows:

$$ea := (rA \mid 0)$$
$$R := S - 1$$
$$i := \left[\tfrac{0}{32}\right]$$
$$\text{if}(\ nBytes = 0\ )$$
$$\quad nBytes := 32$$
$$\text{while}(nBytes > 0)$$
$$\quad \text{if}(i = \left[\tfrac{0}{32}\right]\ )$$
$$\qquad R := (R + 1)\ \%\ 32$$
$$\quad \text{Byte}(ea) \Leftarrow rR[i : (i+7)]$$
$$\quad i := i + 8$$
$$\quad \text{if}(i = \left[\tfrac{32}{64}\right]\ )$$
$$\qquad i := \left[\tfrac{0}{32}\right]$$
$$\quad ea := ea + 1$$
$$\quad nBytes := nBytes - 1$$

The preferred form for this instruction is when the starting register rS is r5. It is possible that some PowerPC implementations will execute non-preferred forms more slowly than the preferred forms. Because of the complexity of this instruction, it is also possible that, on some implementations, this instruction may execute slower than a series of instructions that perform the same operation.

Executing this instruction when the processor is operating in *little-endian* byte-order mode will cause the system alignment error handler to be invoked.

The archaic POWER mnemonic for this instruction is **stsi**.

Instruction Encoding:

0 5	6 10	11 15	16 20	21 30	31
0 1 1 1 1 1	S	A	nBytes	1 0 1 1 0 1 0 1 0 1	0

S	First source GPR rS to store in memory
A	Source GPR rA
nBytes	Number of bytes to store

stswx   Store String Word Indexed   stswx

POWER • 601 • 603 • PowerPC32/64

Operation: *store* XER[25:31] *bytes from registers into memory*

Syntax: **stswx**   rS,rA,rB

Condition Register/Fixed-Point Exception Register:

CR Fields 0-7:   not affected

XER: not affected

Description:

The **stswx** instruction stores bytes into memory from a set of GPRs. The number of bytes (specified by bits 25 to 31 of the XER) are stored into memory starting with the address calculated from (rA|0). The stored data comes from the GPRs starting with rS and continuing up toward r31 for as many registers as are needed to produce the required number of bytes. The register sequence wraps from r31 to r0 if necessary.

The bytes from each register are stored starting with the leftmost byte in the low-order word and continuing to the rightmost byte of the register. On 64-bit PowerPC implementations, only the low-order word of each register is stored into memory.

The operation of this instruction can be summarized as follows:

$ea := (rA\,|\,0)+(rB)$
$R := S - 1$
$nBytes := XER[25:31]$
$i := \left[\frac{0}{32}\right]$
$\text{while}(nBytes > 0)$
     $\text{if}(i = \left[\frac{0}{32}\right])$
         $R := (R + 1)\ \%\ 32$
     $\text{Byte}(ea) \Leftarrow rR[i : (i+7)]$
     $i := i + 8$
     $\text{if}(i = \left[\frac{32}{64}\right])$
         $i := \left[\frac{0}{32}\right]$
     $ea := ea + 1$
     $nBytes := nBytes - 1$

If XER[25:31] is 0, then no bytes are stored into memory.

The preferred form for this instruction is when the starting register r*S* is r5 and the total number of registers being loaded is less than or equal to 12. It is possible that some PowerPC implementations will execute non-preferred forms more slowly than the preferred forms. Because of the complexity of this instruction, it is also possible that, on some implementations, this instruction may execute slower than a series of instructions that perform the same operation.

Executing this instruction when the processor is operating in *little-endian* byte-order mode will cause the system alignment error handler to be invoked.

The archaic POWER mnemonic for this instruction is **stsx**.

Instruction Encoding:

0					5	6					10	11					15	16					20	21										30	31
0	1	1	1	1	1			S						A						B			1	0	1	0	0	1	0	1	0	1	0

S	Source GPR rS
A	Source GPR rA
B	Source GPR rB

stw   Store Word   stw

POWER • 601 • 603 • PowerPC32/64

Operation: $\text{Word}((rA \mid 0) + \grave{}d) \Leftarrow rS \left[\frac{0:31}{32:63}\right]$

Syntax: **stw**   rS,d(rA)

Condition Register/Fixed-Point Exception Register:

CR Fields 0-7:   not affected

XER: not affected

Description:

The **stw** instruction stores the low-order 32 bits of the source register rS into the word located at the effective address calculated from (rA | 0) + `d.

Instruction Encoding:

0 5	6 10	11 15	16 31
1 0 0 1 0 0	S	A	d

     S   Source GPR rS
     A   Source GPR rA
     d   Signed 16-bit displacement

stwbrx   Store Word   stwbrx
Byte-Reversed Indexed
POWER • 601 • 603 • PowerPC32/64

Operation: Word $((rA \mid 0) + (rB))$
$$\Leftarrow rT[24:31] \perp rT[16:23] \perp rT[7:15] \perp rT[0:7]$$

Syntax: **stwbrx**   rS,rA,rB

Condition Register/Fixed-Point Exception Register:
CR Fields 0-7:   not affected

XER: not affected

Description:
The **stwbrx** instruction takes the low-order word of the source register rS, reverses the four bytes of this word, and then stores this *byte-reversed* word into the memory word addressed by $(rA \mid 0) + (rB)$.

For some PowerPC implementations, this byte-reversed store instruction may have a greater latency than other store instructions.

Instruction Encoding:

0 5	6 10	11 15	16 20	21 30	31
0 1 1 1 1 1	S	A	B	1 0 1 0 0 1 0 1 1 0 0	0

S   Source GPR rS
A   Source GPR rA
B   Source GPR rB

stwcx. Store Word Conditional Indexed stwcx.

POWER • 601 • 603 • PowerPC32/64

Operation: if *reservation on ((rA | 0) + (rB))*
    Word((rA | 0) + (rB)) ⟸ rS
    CR{0} = b001 ⊥ XER[SO]
else
    CR{0} = b000 ⊥ XER[SO]

Syntax: **stwcx.**   rS,rA,rB

Condition Register/Fixed-Point Exception Register:

CR Fields 0-7:   not affected

XER: not affected

Description:

If a reservation exists for the effective address calculated from (rA | 0) + (rB), the **stwcx.** instruction stores the word in rS into memory starting at that effective address. After the store completes, the reservation is cleared.

If a reservation does not exist for this address, the **stwcx.** instruction does not perform the store operation. A reservation can be placed using the **lwarx** instruction.

The calculated effective address must specify an aligned word (i.e.: it must be a multiple of 4). If the address does not specify an aligned word, the alignment exception handler may be invoked (if the load crosses a page boundary), or the results may be boundedly undefined.

The EQ bit of CR field 0 is updated to indicate whether or not the store operation was performed. This bit is set to 1 if the store was performed and 0 if it was not. The SO bit of CR{0} is copied from XER[SO] and the remaining bits of the field are cleared.

If the address references a *direct-store* storage segment, then a Data Storage interrupt occurs or the results are boundedly undefined.

Instruction Encoding:

0	5 6	10 11	15 16	20 21	30 31
0 1 1 1 1 1	S	A	B	0 0 1 0 0 1 0 1 1 0	1

S   Source GPR rS
A   Source GPR rA
B   Source GPR rB

stwu   Store Word with Update   stwu

POWER • 601 • 603 • PowerPC32/64

Operation: $\text{Word } ((rA) + \grave{}d) \Leftarrow rS \left[\frac{0:31}{32:63}\right]$

$rA \Leftarrow (rA) + \grave{}d$

Syntax: **stwu** $rS,d(rA)$

Condition Register/Fixed-Point Exception Register:

CR Fields 0-7:   not affected

XER: not affected

Description:

The **stwu** instruction stores the low-order 32 bits of the source register rS into the word located at the effective address calculated from $(rA) + \grave{}d$.

After the store is performed, the effective address is stored in rA.

If r0 is specified as rA, then the instruction form is invalid. For POWER compatibility, the 601 allows rA to specify r0, but the effective address is calculated from `d, and r0 is not updated with the effective address.

Instruction Encoding:

0					5	6				10	11				15	16			31
1	0	0	1	0	1			S					A					d	

S   Source GPR rS
A   Source GPR rA
d   Signed 16-bit displacement

stwux   Store Word with Update Indexed   stwux

POWER • 601 • 603 • PowerPC32/64

Operation: Word $((rA \mid 0) + (rB)) \Leftarrow rS \left\lfloor {}^{0:31}_{32:63} \right\rfloor$

$rA \Leftarrow (rA) + (rB)$

Syntax: **stwux**   rS,rA,rB

Condition Register/Fixed-Point Exception Register:

CR Fields 0-7:   not affected

XER: not affected

Description:

The **stwux** instruction stores the low-order 32 bits of the source register rS into the word located at the effective address calculated from (rA | 0) + (rB).

After the store is performed, the effective address is stored in rA.

If r0 is specified as rA, then the instruction form is invalid. For POWER compatibility, the 601 allows rA to specify r0, but the effective address is calculated from (rB), and r0 is not updated with the effective address.

Instruction Encoding:

0 5	6 10	11 15	16 20	21 30	31
0 1 1 1 1 1	S	A	B	0 0 1 0 1 1 0 1 1 1	0

S   Source GPR rS
A   Source GPR rA
B   Source GPR rB

stwx

Store Word Indexed

stwx

POWER • 601 • 603 • PowerPC32/64

Operation: $\text{Word } ((rA\,|\,0) + (rB)) \Leftarrow rS \left[\frac{0:31}{32:63}\right]$

Syntax: **stwx** rS,rA,rB

Condition Register / Fixed-Point Exception Register:

CR Fields 0-7:   not affected

XER: not affected

Description:

The **stwx** instruction stores the low-order 32 bits of the source register rS into the word located at the effective address calculated from $(rA\,|\,0) + (rB)$.

Instruction Encoding:

0 5	6 10	11 15	16 20	21 30	31
0 1 1 1 1 1	S	A	B	0 0 1 0 0 1 0 1 1 1 0	

S   Source GPR rS
A   Source GPR rA
B   Source GPR rB

subf

Subtract From
POWER • 601 • 603 • PowerPC32/64

subf

Operation: $rT \Leftarrow (rB) - (rA)$

Syntax:
subf	rT,rA,rB	(Rc = 0, OE = 0)
subf.	rT,rA,rB	(Rc = 1, OE = 0)
subfo	rT,rA,rB	(Rc = 0, OE = 1)
subfo.	rT,rA,rB	(Rc = 1, OE = 1)

Condition Register/Fixed-Point Exception Register:

CR Field 0:   LT,GT,EQ,SO updated if Rc = 1, otherwise not affected
CR Fields 1-7:   not affected

XER[CA]:   not affected
XER[OV,SO]:   updated if OE=1, otherwise not affected

Description:

The **subf** instruction subtracts the contents of GPR rA from GPR rB and places the result in GPR rT. The operation treats the operand values as signed quantities.

Extended Forms:

There is one extended form for the **subf** instruction which rearranges the operands into a more natural order.

sub[o][.] rT,rA,rB is equivalent to   **subf[o][.]** rT,rB,rA

Instruction Encoding:

0	5	6	10	11	15	16	20	21	22	30	31
0 1 1 1 1 1		T		A		B		OE	0 0 0 1 0 1 0 0 0		Rc

T	Target GPR rT where result of operation is stored
A	Source GPR rA
B	Source GPR rB
OE	Overflow Exception bit
Rc	Record bit

subfc   Subtract From Carrying   subfc

POWER • 601 • 603 • PowerPC32/64

Operation: $rT \Leftarrow (rB) - (rA)$

Syntax:

subfc	rT,rA,rB	(Rc = 0, OE = 0)
subfc.	rT,rA,rB	(Rc = 1, OE = 0)
subfco	rT,rA,rB	(Rc = 0, OE = 1)
subfco.	rT,rA,rB	(Rc = 1, OE = 1)

Condition Register/Fixed-Point Exception Register:

CR Field 0:   LT,GT,EQ,SO updated if Rc = 1, otherwise not affected
CR Fields 1-7:   not affected

XER[CA]:   always updated
XER[OV,SO]:   updated if OE=1, otherwise not affected

Description:

The **subfc** instruction subtracts the contents of GPR rA from GPR rB and places the result in GPR rT, updating the Carry bit of the XER. The operation treats the operand values as signed quantities.

The archaic POWER mnemonic for this instruction is **sf[o][.]**.

Extended Forms:

There is one extended form for the **subfc** instruction which rearranges the operands into a more natural order.

subc[o][.] rT,rA,rB is equivalent to   **subfc[o][.]**rT,rB,rA

Instruction Encoding:

0	5	6	10	11	15	16	20	21	22	30	31
0 1 1 1 1 1		T		A		B		OE	0 0 0 0 1 0 0 0		Rc

T   Target GPR rT where result of operation is stored
A   Source GPR rA
B   Source GPR rB
OE   Overflow Exception bit
Rc   Record bit

subfe   Subtract From Extended   subfe

POWER • 601 • 603 • PowerPC32/64

Operation: $rT \Leftarrow (rB) - (rA) + XER[CA] - 1$

Syntax:

subfe	rT,rA,rB	(Rc = 0, OE = 0)
subfe.	rT,rA,rB	(Rc = 1, OE = 0)
subfeo	rT,rA,rB	(Rc = 0, OE = 1)
subfeo.	rT,rA,rB	(Rc = 1, OE = 1)

Condition Register/Fixed-Point Exception Register:

CR Field 0:   LT,GT,EQ,SO updated if Rc = 1, otherwise not affected
CR Fields 1-7:   not affected

XER[CA]:   always updated
XER[OV,SO]:   updated if OE=1, otherwise not affected

Description:

The **subfe** instruction subtracts the contents of GPR rA from GPR rB, adds the modified Carry bit (XER[CA]-1) of the XER, and then places the result in GPR rT, updating the Carry bit. The operation treats the operand values as signed quantities.

The archaic POWER mnemonic for this instruction is **sfe[o][.]**.

Instruction Encoding:

0 5	6 10	11 15	16 20	21	22 30	31
0 1 1 1 1 1	T	A	B	OE	0 1 0 0 0 1 0 0 0	Rc

T   Target GPR rT where result of operation is stored
A   Source GPR rA
B   Source GPR rB
OE   Overflow Exception bit
Rc   Record bit

subfic Subtract From Immediate Carrying subfic

POWER • 601 • 603 • PowerPC32/64

Operation: $rT \Leftarrow \text{`}s16 - (rA)$

Syntax: **subfic** rT,rA,s16

Condition Register/Fixed-Point Exception Register:

CR Fields 0-7:   not affected

XER[CA]:   always updated
XER[OV,SO]:   not affected

Description:

The **subfic** instruction subtracts the contents of GPR rA from the 32-bit sign-extended quantity specified by *s16*, and places the result in GPR rT, updating the Carry bit.

The archaic POWER mnemonic for this instruction is **sfi**[.].

Instruction Encoding:

0 1 2 3 4 5	6 ... 10	11 ... 15	16 ... 31
0 0 1 0 0 0	T	A	SI

T   Target GPR rT where result of operation is stored
A   Source GPR rA or 0
SI   Signed 16-bit integer

subfme   Subtract From   subfme

Minus One Extended
POWER • 601 • 603 • PowerPC32/64

Operation: $rT \Leftarrow -1 - (rA) + XER[CA] - 1$

Syntax:

subfme	rT,rA	(Rc = 0, OE = 0)
subfme.	rT,rA	(Rc = 1, OE = 0)
subfmeo	rT,rA	(Rc = 0, OE = 1)
subfmeo.	rT,rA	(Rc = 1, OE = 1)

Condition Register / Fixed-Point Exception Register:

CR Field 0:   LT,GT,EQ,SO updated if Rc = 1, otherwise not affected
CR Fields 1-7:   not affected

XER[CA]:   always updated
XER[OV,SO]:   updated if OE=1, otherwise not affected

Description:

The **subfme** instruction subtracts the contents of GPR rA from -1 (0xFFFFFFFF), adds the modified Carry bit (XER[CA]-1), and then places the result in GPR rT, updating the Carry bit in the XER.

The archaic POWER mnemonic for this instruction is **sfme[o][.]**.

Instruction Encoding:

0	5	6	10	11	15	16	20	21	22	30	31
0 1 1 1 1 1		T		A		0 0 0 0 0		OE	0 1 1 1 0 1 0 0 0		Rc

T   Target GPR rT where result of operation is stored
A   Source GPR rA
OE   Overflow Exception bit
Rc   Record bit

subfze Subtract From Zero Extended subfze

POWER • 601 • 603 • PowerPC32/64

Operation: $rT \Leftarrow 0 - (rA) + XER[CA] - 1$

Syntax:

subfze	r*T*,r*A*	(Rc = 0, OE = 0)
subfze.	r*T*,r*A*	(Rc = 1, OE = 0)
subfzeo	r*T*,r*A*	(Rc = 0, OE = 1)
subfzeo.	r*T*,r*A*	(Rc = 1, OE = 1)

Condition Register/Fixed-Point Exception Register:

CR Field 0:	LT,GT,EQ,SO updated if Rc = 1, otherwise not affected
CR Fields 1-7:	not affected
XER[CA]:	always updated
XER[OV,SO]:	updated if OE=1, otherwise not affected

Description:

The **subfze** instruction subtracts the contents of GPR r*A* from 0, adds the modified Carry bit (XER[CA]-1), and then places the result in GPR r*T*, updating the Carry bit in the XER.

The archaic POWER mnemonic for this instruction is **sfze[o][.]**.

Instruction Encoding:

0 5	6 10	11 15	16 20	21	22 30	31
0 1 1 1 1 1	T	A	0 0 0 0 0	OE	0 1 1 0 0 1 0 0 0	Rc

T	Target GPR rT where result of operation is stored
A	Source GPR rA
OE	Overflow Exception bit
Rc	Record bit

sync   Synchronize   sync

POWER • 601 • 603 • PowerPC32/64

Operation: *wait for all previous instructions to complete*

Syntax: **sync**

Condition Register/Fixed-Point Exception Register:

CR Fields 0-7:   not affected

XER: not affected

Description:

The **sync** instruction forces the processor to wait until all of the previous instructions appear to have been completed before initiating the execution of any subsequent instruction.

It is only through the use of the **sync** instruction that a program can be ensured that the effects of all storage accesses have been completed with respect to all other processors and storage access mechanisms.

This instruction is execution synchronizing.

The archaic POWER mnemonic for this instruction is **dcs**.

Instruction Encoding:

0					5	6				10	11				15	16				20	21									30	31
0	1	1	1	1	1	0	0	0	0	0	0	0	0	0	0	0	0	0	0	0	1	0	0	1	0	1	0	1	1	0	0

td   Trap Doubleword   td

PowerPC64

Operation: if (condition is TRUE)
             invoke trap handler

Syntax: **td**   *TO,rA,rB*

Condition Register / Fixed-Point Exception Register:

CR Fields 0-7:   not affected

XER: not affected

Description:

The **td** instruction compares the contents of the two source registers rA and rB and invokes the system trap handler if the condition specified by TO is true.

The *Trap On* (TO) field of the instruction determines the conditions under which the trap is generated. The TO field may be anyone of the following values:

TO					Action
signed		=	unsigned		
<	>		<	>	
0	0	0	0	1	trap if logically greater than
0	0	0	1	0	trap if logically less than
0	0	1	0	0	trap if equal
0	0	1	0	1	trap if logically greater than or equal trap if logically not less than
0	0	1	1	0	trap if logically less than or equal trap if logically not greater than
0	1	0	0	0	trap if greater than
0	1	1	0	0	trap if greater than or equal trap if not less than
1	0	0	0	0	trap if less than
1	0	1	0	0	trap if less than or equal trap if not greater than
1	1	0	0	0	trap if not equal

This instruction exists on 64-bit PowerPC implementations only.

Extended Forms:

The following extended forms are defined for the **td** instruction.

tdeq	r*A*,r*B*	is equivalent to	**td**	4,r*A*,r*B*
tdge	r*A*,r*B*	is equivalent to	**td**	12,r*A*,r*B*
tdgt	r*A*,r*B*	is equivalent to	**td**	8,r*A*,r*B*
tdle	r*A*,r*B*	is equivalent to	**td**	20,r*A*,r*B*
tdlge	r*A*,r*B*	is equivalent to	**td**	5,r*A*,r*B*
tdlgt	r*A*,r*B*	is equivalent to	**td**	1,r*A*,r*B*
tdlle	r*A*,r*B*	is equivalent to	**td**	6,r*A*,r*B*
tdllt	r*A*,r*B*	is equivalent to	**td**	2,r*A*,r*B*
tdlng	r*A*,r*B*	is equivalent to	**td**	6,r*A*,r*B*
tdlnl	r*A*,r*B*	is equivalent to	**td**	5,r*A*,r*B*
tdlt	r*A*,r*B*	is equivalent to	**td**	16,r*A*,r*B*
tdne	r*A*,r*B*	is equivalent to	**td**	24,r*A*,r*B*
tdng	r*A*,r*B*	is equivalent to	**td**	20,r*A*,r*B*
tdnl	r*A*,r*B*	is equivalent to	**td**	12,r*A*,r*B*

Instruction Encoding:

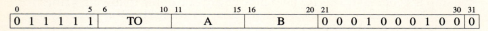

0					5	6			10	11				15	16				20	21									30	31
0	1	1	1	1	1		TO				A					B				0	0	0	1	0	0	0	1	0	0	0

TO	Trap-On condition
A	Source GPR rA
B	Source GPR rB

tdi   Trap Doubleword Immediate   tdi

PowerPC64

Operation: if (condition is TRUE)
               invoke trap handler

Syntax: **tdi**   *TO,rA,s16*

Condition Register/Fixed-Point Exception Register:

CR Fields 0-7:   not affected

XER: not affected

Description:

The **tdi** instruction compares the contents of the source register *rA* and the sign-extended immediate value *s16* and invokes the system trap handler if the condition specified by TO is true.

The *Trap On* (TO) field of the instruction determines the conditions under which the trap is generated. The TO field may be anyone of the following values:

TO					Action
signed		=	unsigned		
<	>		<	>	
0	0	0	0	1	trap if logically greater than
0	0	0	1	0	trap if logically less than
0	0	1	0	0	trap if equal
0	0	1	0	1	trap if logically greater than or equal trap if logically not less than
0	0	1	1	0	trap if logically less than or equal trap if logically not greater than
0	1	0	0	0	trap if greater than
0	1	1	0	0	trap if greater than or equal trap if not less than
1	0	0	0	0	trap if less than
1	0	1	0	0	trap if less than or equal trap if not greater than
1	1	0	0	0	trap if not equal

This instruction exists on 64-bit PowerPC implementations only.

Extended Forms:

The following extended forms are defined for the **tdi** instruction.

tdeqi	r*A*,*s16*	is equivalent to	**tdi**	4,r*A*,*s16*
tdgei	r*A*,*s16*	is equivalent to	**tdi**	12,r*A*,*s16*
tdgti	r*A*,*s16*	is equivalent to	**tdi**	8,r*A*,*s16*
tdlei	r*A*,*s16*	is equivalent to	**tdi**	20,r*A*,*s16*
tdlgei	r*A*,*s16*	is equivalent to	**tdi**	5,r*A*,*s16*
tdlgti	r*A*,*s16*	is equivalent to	**tdi**	1,r*A*,*s16*
tdllei	r*A*,*s16*	is equivalent to	**tdi**	6,r*A*,*s16*
tdllti	r*A*,*s16*	is equivalent to	**tdi**	2,r*A*,*s16*
tdlngi	r*A*,*s16*	is equivalent to	**tdi**	6,r*A*,*s16*
tdlnli	r*A*,*s16*	is equivalent to	**tdi**	5,r*A*,*s16*
tdlti	r*A*,*s16*	is equivalent to	**tdi**	16,r*A*,*s16*
tdnei	r*A*,*s16*	is equivalent to	**tdi**	24,r*A*,*s16*
tdngi	r*A*,*s16*	is equivalent to	**tdi**	20,r*A*,*s16*
tdnli	r*A*,*s16*	is equivalent to	**tdi**	12,r*A*,*s16*

Instruction Encoding:

0 5	6 10	11 15	16 31
0 0 0 0 1 0	TO	A	SI

TO   Trap-On condition
A   Source GPR rA
SI   Signed 16-bit integer

tlbia

TLB Invalidate All

603 • PowerPC32/64

tlbia

Operation: *invalidate all TLB entries*

Syntax: **tlbia**

Condition Register/Fixed-Point Exception Register:
CR Fields 0-7:   not affected

XER: not affected

Description:
The **tlbia** instruction invalidates all of the entries currently in the TLB, regardless of the current setting of the instruction and data translation bits in the MSR (MSR[IT] and MSR[DT].

This is a supervisor-level instruction.

Instruction Encoding:

0					5	6				10	11				15	16				20	21									30	31
0	1	1	1	1	1	0	0	0	0	0	0	0	0	0	0	0	0	0	0	0	0	1	0	1	1	1	0	0	1	0	0

tlbie   TLB Invalidate Entry   tlbie

POWER • 601 • 603 • PowerPC32/64

Operation: *invalidate the specified TLB entry*

Syntax: **tlbie**   r*B*

Condition Register / Fixed-Point Exception Register:

CR Fields 0-7:   not affected

XER: not affected

Description:

The **tlbie** instruction invalidates the TLB entry which corresponds to the effective address stored in r*B*. The invalidation is performed regardless of the current setting of the instruction and data translation bits in the MSR (MSR[IT] and MSR[DT].

This is a supervisor-level instruction.

The archaic POWER mnemonic for this instruction is **tlbi**.

Instruction Encoding:

0					5	6					10	11					15	16					20	21										30	31
0	1	1	1	1	1	0	0	0	0	0		0	0	0	0	0		B						0	1	0	0	1	1	0	0	1	0	0

B   Source GPR rB

tlbsync   TLB Synchronize   tlbsync

603 • PowerPC32/64

Operation: *wait until all previous TLB instructions complete*

Syntax: **tlbsync**

Condition Register/Fixed-Point Exception Register:
CR Fields 0-7:   not affected

XER: not affected

Description:

The **tlbsync** instruction waits until all of the previous TLB instructions (**tlbia** and **tlbie**) have completed execution on this and all other processors.

This is a supervisor-level instruction.

Instruction Encoding:

0					5	6					10	11					15	16					20	21										30	31
0	1	1	1	1	1	0	0	0	0	0	0	0	0	0	0	0	0	0	0	0	0	1	0	0	0	1	1	0	1	1	0	0

tw

Trap Word

tw (right side)

Operation: if (condition is TRUE)
                  invoke trap handler

Syntax: **tw**   *TO,rA,rB*

Condition Register/Fixed-Point Exception Register:
CR Fields 0-7:   not affected

XER: not affected

Description:

The **tw** instruction compares the contents of the two source registers *rA* and *rB* and invokes the system trap handler if the condition specified by TO is true.

The *Trap On* (TO) field of the instruction determines the conditions under which the trap is generated. The TO field may be anyone of the following values:

TO					Action
signed		=	unsigned		
<	>		<	>	
0	0	0	0	1	trap if logically greater than
0	0	0	1	0	trap if logically less than
0	0	1	0	0	trap if equal
0	0	1	0	1	trap if logically greater than or equal trap if logically not less than
0	0	1	1	0	trap if logically less than or equal trap if logically not greater than
0	1	0	0	0	trap if greater than
0	1	1	0	0	trap if greater than or equal trap if not less than
1	0	0	0	0	trap if less than
1	0	1	0	0	trap if less than or equal trap if not greater than
1	1	0	0	0	trap if not equal

Extended Forms:

The following extended forms are defined for the **tw** instruction.

trap		is equivalent to	**tw**	31,r0,r0
tweq	r*A*,r*B*	is equivalent to	**tw**	4,r*A*,r*B*
twge	r*A*,r*B*	is equivalent to	**tw**	12,r*A*,r*B*
twgt	r*A*,r*B*	is equivalent to	**tw**	8,r*A*,r*B*
twle	r*A*,r*B*	is equivalent to	**tw**	20,r*A*,r*B*
twlge	r*A*,r*B*	is equivalent to	**tw**	5,r*A*,r*B*
twlgt	r*A*,r*B*	is equivalent to	**tw**	1,r*A*,r*B*
twlle	r*A*,r*B*	is equivalent to	**tw**	6,r*A*,r*B*
twllt	r*A*,r*B*	is equivalent to	**tw**	2,r*A*,r*B*
twlng	r*A*,r*B*	is equivalent to	**tw**	6,r*A*,r*B*
twlnl	r*A*,r*B*	is equivalent to	**tw**	5,r*A*,r*B*
twlt	r*A*,r*B*	is equivalent to	**tw**	16,r*A*,r*B*
twne	r*A*,r*B*	is equivalent to	**tw**	24,r*A*,r*B*
twng	r*A*,r*B*	is equivalent to	**tw**	20,r*A*,r*B*
twnl	r*A*,r*B*	is equivalent to	**tw**	12,r*A*,r*B*

Instruction Encoding:

0					5	6			10	11			15	16			20	21								30	31
0	1	1	1	1	1	TO				A				B				0	0	0	0	0	0	0	1	0	0	0

TO	Trap-On condition
A	Source GPR rA
B	Source GPR rB

twi   Trap Word Immediate   twi

POWER • 601 • 603 • PowerPC32/64

Operation: if (condition is TRUE)
                invoke trap handler

Syntax: **twi**   *TO,rA,s16*

Condition Register / Fixed-Point Exception Register:

CR Fields 0-7:   not affected

XER: not affected

Description:

The **twi** instruction compares the contents of the source register r*A* and the sign-extended immediate value *s16* and invokes the system trap handler if the condition specified by TO is true.

The *Trap On* (TO) field of the instruction determines the conditions under which the trap is generated. The TO field may be anyone of the following values:

TO					Action
signed		=	unsigned		
<	>		<	>	
0	0	0	0	1	trap if logically greater than
0	0	0	1	0	trap if logically less than
0	0	1	0	0	trap if equal
0	0	1	0	1	trap if logically greater than or equal trap if logically not less than
0	0	1	1	0	trap if logically less than or equal trap if logically not greater than
0	1	0	0	0	trap if greater than
0	1	1	0	0	trap if greater than or equal trap if not less than
1	0	0	0	0	trap if less than
1	0	1	0	0	trap if less than or equal trap if not greater than
1	1	0	0	0	trap if not equal

Extended Forms:

The following extended forms are defined for the **twi** instruction.

tweqi	*rA,s16*	is equivalent to	**twi**	*4,rA,s16*
twgei	*rA,s16*	is equivalent to	**twi**	*12,rA,s16*
twgti	*rA,s16*	is equivalent to	**twi**	*8,rA,s16*
twlei	*rA,s16*	is equivalent to	**twi**	*20,rA,s16*
twlgei	*rA,s16*	is equivalent to	**twi**	*5,rA,s16*
twlgti	*rA,s16*	is equivalent to	**twi**	*1,rA,s16*
twllei	*rA,s16*	is equivalent to	**twi**	*6,rA,s16*
twllti	*rA,s16*	is equivalent to	**twi**	*2,rA,s16*
twlngi	*rA,s16*	is equivalent to	**twi**	*6,rA,s16*
twlnli	*rA,s16*	is equivalent to	**twi**	*5,rA,s16*
twlti	*rA,s16*	is equivalent to	**twi**	*16,rA,s16*
twnei	*rA,s16*	is equivalent to	**twi**	*24,rA,s16*
twngi	*rA,s16*	is equivalent to	**twi**	*20,rA,s16*
twnli	*rA,s16*	is equivalent to	**twi**	*12,rA,s16*

Instruction Encoding:

0	5 6	10 11	15 16	31
0 0 0 0 1 1	TO	A	SI	

TO   Trap-On condition
A   Source GPR rA
SI   Signed 16-bit integer

xor XOR xor

POWER • 601 • 603 • PowerPC32/64

Operation: $rA \Leftarrow (rS) \oplus (rB)$

Syntax:

xor	rA,rS,rB	(Rc = 0)
xor.	rA,rS,rB	(Rc = 1)

Condition Register/Fixed-Point Exception Register:

CR Field 0:   LT,GT,EQ,SO updated if Rc = 1, otherwise not affected
CR Fields 1-7: not affected

XER: not affected

Description:

The **xor** instruction logically XORs the contents of GPR rS and GPR rB and places the result in GPR rA.

Instruction Encoding:

0 5	6 10	11 15	16 20	21 30	31
0 1 1 1 1 1	S	A	B	0 1 0 0 1 1 1 1 0 0	Rc

S   Source GPR rS
A   Target GPR rA where result of operation is stored
B   Source GPR rB
Rc   Record bit

xori   XOR Immediate   xori

POWER • 601 • 603 • PowerPC32/64

Operation: $rA \Leftarrow (rS) \oplus °u16$

Syntax: **xori** $rA,rS,u16$

Condition Register/Fixed-Point Exception Register:

CR Fields 0-7:   not affected

XER: not affected

Description:

The **xori** instruction logically XORs the contents of GPR rS and the value calculated by zero-extending *u16*, and places the result in GPR rA.

The archaic POWER mnemonic for this instruction is **xoril**. (XOR Immediate Lower).

Instruction Encoding:

0 5	6 S 10	11 A 15	16 UI 31
0 1 1 0 1 0	S	A	UI

S   Source GPR rS
A   Target GPR rA where result of operation is stored
UI   Unsigned 16-bit integer

xoris   XOR Immediate Shifted   xoris

POWER • 601 • 603 • PowerPC32/64

Operation: $rA \Leftarrow (rS) \oplus {}^{\circ}(u16 \perp 0x0000)$

Syntax: **xoris**   rA,rS,u16

Condition Register/Fixed-Point Exception Register:

CR Fields 0-7:   not affected

XER: not affected

Description:

The **xoris.** instruction logically XORs the contents of GPR rS and the value calculated by concatenating *u16* with 0x0000, and places the result in GPR rA.

The archaic POWER mnemonic for this instruction is **xoriu**. (XOR Immediate Upper).

Instruction Encoding:

0 5	6 10	11 15	16 31
0 1 1 0 1 1	S	A	UI

S   Source GPR rS
A   Target GPR rA where result of operation is stored
UI   Unsigned 16-bit integer

Complete List of Mnemonics | B

This appendix provides a complete list of the mnemonics for all of the instructions and extended instructions for the POWER and PowerPC processors. This list includes the archaic forms for the POWER mnemonics.

This list is presented in alphabetic order according to the base mnemonic. This means that some mnemonics may appear to be out of order, for example, the instruction addo is not found between addme[o][.] and addze[o][.] entries because it is considered a standard extension to the base mnemonic add[o][.]. Standard mnemonic extensions are: '.', 'a', 'o', and 'l'.

Lines that have a "•" prefix are the standard or preferred instructions for the PowerPC. Lines without a "•" prefix are either archaic mnemonics for valid instructions or obsolete instructions. The mnemonic description will note which case is applicable. The archaic and obsolete forms are included for completeness and historical reasons only; use of the archaic forms is strongly discouraged.

Lines that have a "$_{32}$ •" prefix are defined only for 32-bit implementations of the PowerPC. They will cause an illegal instruction exception on 64-bit implementations.

Lines that have a "64•" prefix are defined only for 64-bit implementations of the PowerPC. They will cause an illegal instruction exception on 32-bit implementations.

Lines that have a "?•" prefix are defined as being optional PowerPC instructions. A PowerPC processor may or may not have these instructions defined. Note that some optional instructions are defined for 64-bit implementations only.

a[o][.]	rT,rA,rB	Add
	archaic form for: addc[o][.] rT,rA,rB	
abs[o][.]	rT,rA	Absolute Value
	This instruction exists on POWER and the 601 only.	
• add[o][.]	rT,rA,rB	Add (without updating Carry)
• addc[o][.]	rT,rA,rB	Add Carrying
• adde[o][.]	rT,rA,rB	Add Extended
• addi	$rT,rA,s16$	Add Immediate
• addic[.]	$rT,rA,s16$	Add Immediate Carrying
• addis	$rT,rA,s16$	Add Immediate Shifted
• addme[o][.]	rT,rA	Add to Minus One Extended
• addze[o][.]	rT,rA	Add to Zero Extended
ae[o][.]	rT,rA,rB	Add Extended
	archaic form for: adde[o][.] rT,rA,rB	
ai[.]	$rT,rA,s16$	Add Immediate
	archaic form for: addic[.] $rT,rA,s16$	
ame[o][.]	rT,rA	Add to Minus One Extended
	archaic form for: addme[o][.] rT,rA	
• and[.]	rA,rS,rB	AND
• andc[.]	rA,rS,rB	AND with Complement
• andi.	$rA,rS,u16$	AND Immediate
andil.	$rA,rS,u16$	AND Immediate Lower
	archaic form for: andi. $rA,rS,u16$	
• andis.	$rA,rS,u16$	AND Immediate Shifted
andiu.	$rA,rS,u16$	AND Immediate Upper
	archaic form for: andis. $rA,rS,u16$	
aze[o][.]	rT,rA	Add to Zero Extended
	archaic form for: addze[o][.] rT,rA	
• b[l][a]	*addr*	Branch
bbf[l][a]	*crbT,addr*	Branch if CR Bit False
	archaic form for: bf[l][a] *crbT,addr*	
	equivalent to: bc[l][a] 0x04,*crbT,addr*	
bbfc[l]	*crbT,addr*	Branch if CR Bit False to CTR
	archaic form for: bfctr[l][a] *crbT*	
	equivalent to: bcctr[l] 0x04,*crbT*	
bbfr[l]	*crbT,addr*	Branch if CR Bit False to LR
	archaic form for: bflr[l] *crbT*	
	equivalent to: bclr[l] 0x04,*crbT*	
bbt[l][a]	*crbT,addr*	Branch if CR Bit True
	archaic form for: bt[l][a] *crbT,addr*	
	equivalent to: bc[l][a] 0x0C,*crbT,addr*	
bbtc[l]	*crbT,addr*	Branch if CR Bit True to CTR
	archaic form for: btctr[l][a] *crbT*	
	equivalent to: bcctr[l] 0x0C,*crbT*	
bbtr[l]	*crbT,addr*	Branch if CR Bit True to LR
	archaic form for: btlr[l] *crbT*	
	equivalent to: bclr[l] 0x0C,*crbT*	
• bc[l][a]	*branchOn,crbT,addr*	Branch Conditional

bcc[l]	*branchOn*, *crbT*	Branch Conditional to CTR
	archaic form for: bcctr[l] *BO*, *crbT*	
• bcctr[l]	*branchOn*, *crbT*	Branch Conditional to CTR
• bclr[l]	*branchOn*, *crbT*	Branch Conditional to LR
bcr[l]	*branchOn*, *crbT*	Branch Conditional to LR
	archaic form for: bclr[l] *BO*, *crbT*	
• bctr[l]		Branch Unconditionally to CTR
	equivalent to: bcctr[l] 0x14,0	
bdn[l][a]	*addr*	Branch if Decremented CTR is Non-zero
	archaic form for: bdnz[l][a] *addr*	
	equivalent to: bc[l][a] 0x10,0,*addr*	
bdneq	cr*T*,*addr*	Branch if Decremented CTR is Non-Zero and Equal
	archaic form for: bdnzt (cr*T**4)+2,*addr*	
	equivalent to: bc 0x08,(cr*T**4)+2,*addr*	
bdnge	cr*T*,*addr*	Branch if Decremented CTR is Non-Zero and Greater Than or Equal
	archaic form for: bdnzf (cr*T**4)+0,*addr*	
	equivalent to: bc 0x00,(cr*T**4)+0,*addr*	
bdngt	cr*T*,*addr*	Branch if Decremented CTR is Non-Zero and Greater Than
	archaic form for: bdnzt (cr*T**4)+1,*addr*	
	equivalent to: bc 0x08,(cr*T**4)+1,*addr*	
bdnle	cr*T*,*addr*	Branch if Decremented CTR is Non-Zero and Less Than or Equal
	archaic form for: bdnzf (cr*T**4)+1,*addr*	
	equivalent to: bc 0x00,(cr*T**4)+1,*addr*	
bdnlt	cr*T*,*addr*	Branch if Decremented CTR is Non-Zero and Less Than
	archaic form for: bdnzt (cr*T**4)+0,*addr*	
	equivalent to: bc 0x08,(cr*T**4)+0,*addr*	
bdnne	cr*T*,*addr*	Branch if Decremented CTR is Non-Zero and Not Equal
	archaic form for: bdnzf (cr*T**4)+2,*addr*	
	equivalent to: bc 0x00,(cr*T**4)+2,*addr*	
bdnns	cr*T*,*addr*	Branch if Decremented CTR is Non-Zero and Not Summary Overflow
	archaic form for: bdnzf (cr*T**4)+3,*addr*	
	equivalent to: bc 0x00,(cr*T**4)+3,*addr*	
bdnr[l]		Branch if Decremented CTR is Not Zero to LR
	archaic form for: bdnzlr[l]	
	equivalent to: bclr[l] 0x10,0	
bdnso	cr*T*,*addr*	Branch if Decremented CTR is Non-Zero and Summary Overflow
	archaic form for: bdnzt (cr*T**4)+3,*addr*	
	equivalent to: bc 0x08,(cr*T**4)+3,*addr*	
• bdnz[l][a]	*addr*	Branch if Decremented CTR is Not Zero
	equivalent to: bc[l][a] 0x10,0,*addr*	

- `bdnzf[l][a]` *crbT,addr*   Branch if Decremented CTR is Not Zero and Condition False

  equivalent to: `bc[l][a] 0x00,`*crbT,addr*
- `bdnzflr[l]` *crbT*   Branch if Decremented CTR is Not Zero and Condition False to LR

  equivalent to: `bclr[l] 0x00,`*crbT*
- `bdnzlr[l]`   Branch if Decremented CTR is Not Zero to LR

  equivalent to: `bclr[l] 0x10,0`
- `bdnzt[l][a]` *crbT,addr*   Branch if Decremented CTR is Not Zero and Condition True

  equivalent to: `bc[l][a] 0x08,`*crbT,addr*
- `bdnztlr[l]` *crbT*   Branch if Decremented CTR is Not Zero and Condition True to LR

  equivalent to: `bclr[l] 0x08,`*crbT*
- `bdz[l][a]` *addr*   Branch if Decremented CTR is Zero

  equivalent to: `bc[l][a] 0x12,0,`*addr*

  `bdzeq` *crT,addr*   Branch if Decremented CTR is Zero and Equal

  archaic form for: `bdzt (`*crT*`*4)+2,`*addr*

  equivalent to: `bc 0x0A,(`*crT*`*4)+2,`*addr*
- `bdzf[l][a]` *crbT,addr*   Branch if Decremented CTR is Zero and Condition False

  equivalent to: `bc[l][a] 0x02,`*crbT,addr*
- `bdzflr[l]` *crbT*   Branch if Decremented CTR is Zero and Condition False to LR

  equivalent to: `bclr[l] 0x02,`*crbT*

  `bdzge` *crT,addr*   Branch if Decremented CTR is Zero and Greater Than or Equal

  archaic form for: `bdzf (`*crT*`*4)+0,`*addr*

  equivalent to: `bc 0x02,(`*crT*`*4)+0,`*addr*

  `bdzgt` *crT,addr*   Branch if Decremented CTR is Zero and Greater Than

  archaic form for: `bdzt (`*crT*`*4)+1,`*addr*

  equivalent to: `bc 0x0A,(`*crT*`*4)+1,`*addr*

  `bdzle` *crT,addr*   Branch if Decremented CTR is Zero and Less Than or Equal

  archaic form for: `bdzf (`*crT*`*4)+1,`*addr*

  equivalent to: `bc 0x02,(`*crT*`*4)+1,`*addr*
- `bdzlr[l]`   Branch if Decremented CTR is Zero to LR

  equivalent to: `bclr[l] 0x12,0`

  `bdzlt` *crT,addr*   Branch if Decremented CTR is Zero and Less Than

  archaic form for: `bdzt (`*crT*`*4)+0,`*addr*

  equivalent to: `bc 0x0A,(`*crT*`*4)+0,`*addr*

  `bdzne` *crT,addr*   Branch if Decremented CTR is Zero and Not Equal

  archaic form for: `bdzf (`*crT*`*4)+2,`*addr*

  equivalent to: `bc 0x02,(`*crT*`*4)+2,`*addr*

bdzns	crT, *addr*	Branch if Decremented CTR is Zero and Not Summary Overflow
	archaic form for: bdzf (crT*4)+3, *addr*	
	equivalent to: bc 0x02, (crT*4)+3, *addr*	
bdzr[l]		Branch if Decremented CTR is Zero to LR
	archaic form for: bdzlr[l]	
	equivalent to: bclr[l] 0x12,0	
bdzso	crT, *addr*	Branch if Decremented CTR is Zero and Summary Overflow
	archaic form for: bdzt (crT*4)+3, *addr*	
	equivalent to: bc 0x0A, (crT*4)+3, *addr*	
• bdzt[l][a]	crbT, *addr*	Branch if Decremented CTR is Zero and Condition True
	equivalent to: bc[l][a] 0x0A, *crbT*, *addr*	
• bdztlr[l]	crbT	Branch if Decremented CTR is Zero and Condition True to LR
	equivalent to: bclr[l] 0x0A, *crbT*	
• beq[l][a]	[crT,]*addr*	Branch if Equal
	equivalent to: bc[l][a] 0x0C, (crT*4)+2, *addr*	
beqc[l]	[crT]	Branch if Equal to CTR
	archaic form for: beqctr[l] [crT]	
	equivalent to: bcctr[l] 0x0C, (crT*4)+2	
• beqctr[l]	[crT]	Branch if Equal CTR
	equivalent to: bcctr[l] 0x0C, (crT*4)+2	
• beqlr[l]	[crT]	Branch if Equal to LR
	equivalent to: bclr[l] 0x0C, (crT*4)+2	
beqr[l]	[crT]	Branch if Equal to LR
	archaic form for: beqlr[l] [crT]	
	equivalent to: bclr[l] 0x0C, (crT*4)+2	
• bf[l][a]	crbT, *addr*	Branch if Condition False
	equivalent to: bc 0x04, *crbT*, *addr*	
• bfctr[l]	crbT	Branch if Condition False to CTR
	equivalent to: bcctr[l] 0x04, *crbT*	
• bflr[l]	crbT	Branch if Condition False to LR
	equivalent to: bclr[l] 0x04, *crbT*	
• bge[l][a]	[crT,]*addr*	Branch if Greater Than or Equal
	equivalent to: bc[l][a] 0x04, (crT*4)+0, *addr*	
bgec[l]	[crT]	Branch if Greater Than or Equal to CTR
	archaic form for: bgectr[l] [crT]	
	equivalent to: bcctr[l] 0x04, (crT*4)+0	
• bgectr[l]	[crT]	Branch if Greater Than or Equal to CTR
	equivalent to: bcctr[l] 0x04, (crT*4)+0	
• bgelr[l]	[crT]	Branch if Greater Than or Equal to LR
	equivalent to: bclr[l] 0x04, (crT*4)+0	
bger[l]	[crT]	Branch if Greater Than or Equal to LR
	archaic form for: bgelr[l] [crT]	
	equivalent to: bclr[l] 0x04, (crT*4)+0	
• bgt[l][a]	[crT,]*addr*	Branch if Greater Than
	equivalent to: bc[l][a] 0x0C, (crT*4)+1, *addr*	

bgtc[l]	[cr*T*]	Branch if Greater Than to CTR

bgtc[l]   [cr*T*]   Branch if Greater Than to CTR
           archaic form for: bgtctr[l] [cr*T*]
           equivalent to: bcctr[l] 0x0C,(cr*T**4)+1

• bgtctr[l] [cr*T*]   Branch if Greater Than to CTR
           equivalent to: bcctr[l] 0x0C,(cr*T**4)+1

• bgtlr[l]   [cr*T*]   Branch if Greater Than to LR
           equivalent to: bclr[l] 0x0C,(cr*T**4)+1

bgtr[l]   [cr*T*]   Branch if Greater Than to LR
           archaic form for: bgtlr[l] [cr*T*]
           equivalent to: bclr[l] 0x0C,(cr*T**4)+1

• ble[l][a] [cr*T*,]*addr*   Branch if Less Than or Equal
           equivalent to: bc[l][a] 0x04,(cr*T**4)+1,*addr*

blec[l]   [cr*T*]   Branch if Less Than or Equal to CTR
           archaic form for: blectr[l] [cr*T*]
           equivalent to: bcctr[l] 0x04,(cr*T**4)+1

• blectr[l] [cr*T*]   Branch if Less Than or Equal to CTR
           equivalent to: bcctr[l] 0x04,(cr*T**4)+1

• blelr[l]   [cr*T*]   Branch if Less Than or Equal to LR
           equivalent to: bclr[l] 0x04,(cr*T**4)+1

bler[l]   [cr*T*]   Branch if Less Than or Equal to LR
           archaic form for: blelr[l] [cr*T*]
           equivalent to: bclr[l] 0x04,(cr*T**4)+1

• blr[l]   Branch Unconditionally to LR
           equivalent to: bclr[l] 0x14,0

• blt[l][a] [cr*T*,]*addr*   Branch if Less Than
           equivalent to: bc[l][a] 0x0C,(cr*T**4)+0,*addr*

bltc[l]   [cr*T*]   Branch if Less Than to CTR
           archaic form for: bltctr[l] [cr*T*]
           equivalent to: bcctr[l] 0x0C,(cr*T**4)+0

• bltctr[l] [cr*T*]   Branch if Less Than to CTR
           equivalent to: bcctr[l] 0x0C,(cr*T**4)+0

• bltlr[l]   [cr*T*]   Branch if Less Than to LR
           equivalent to: bclr[l] 0x0C,(cr*T**4)+0

bltr[l]   [cr*T*]   Branch if Less Than to LR
           archaic form for: bltlr[l] [cr*T*]
           equivalent to: bclr[l] 0x0C,(cr*T**4)+0

• bne[l][a] [cr*T*,]*addr*   Branch if Not Equal
           equivalent to: bc[l][a] 0x04,(cr*T**4)+2,*addr*

bnec[l]   [cr*T*]   Branch if Not Equal to CTR
           archaic form for: bnectr[l] [cr*T*]
           equivalent to: bcctr[l] 0x04,(cr*T**4)+2

• bnectr[l] [cr*T*]   Branch if Not Equal to CTR
           equivalent to: bcctr[l] 0x04,(cr*T**4)+2

• bnelr[l]   [cr*T*]   Branch if Not Equal to LR
           equivalent to: bclr[l] 0x04,(cr*T**4)+2

bner[l]   [cr*T*]   Branch if Not Equal to LR
           archaic form for: bnelr[l] [cr*T*]
           equivalent to: bclr[l] 0x04,(cr*T**4)+2

- **bng[l][a]**   [cr*T*,]*addr*   Branch if Not Greater Than
           equivalent to: **bc[l][a]** 0x04,(cr*T**4)+1,*addr*
  bngc[l]   [cr*T*]   Branch if Not Greater Than to CTR
           archaic form for: **bngctr[l]** [cr*T*]
           equivalent to: **bcctr[l]** 0x04,(cr*T**4)+1
- **bngctr[l]**   [cr*T*]   Branch if Not Greater Than to CTR
           equivalent to: **bcctr[l]** 0x04,(cr*T**4)+1
- **bnglr[l]**   [cr*T*]   Branch if Not Greater Than to LR
           equivalent to: **bclr[l]** 0x04,(cr*T**4)+1
  bngr[l]   [cr*T*]   Branch if Not Greater Than to LR
           archaic form for: **bnglr[l]** [cr*T*]
           equivalent to: **bclr[l]** 0x04,(cr*T**4)+1
- **bnl[l][a]**   [cr*T*,]*addr*   Branch if Not Less Than
           equivalent to: **bc[l][a]** 0x04,(cr*T**4)+0,*addr*
  bnlc[l]   [cr*T*]   Branch if Not Less Than to CTR
           archaic form for: **bnlctr[l]** [cr*T*]
           equivalent to: **bcctr[l]** 0x04,(cr*T**4)+0
- **bnlctr[l]**   [cr*T*]   Branch if Not Less Than to CTR
           equivalent to: **bcctr[l]** 0x04,(cr*T**4)+0
- **bnllr[l]**   [cr*T*]   Branch if Not Less Than to LR
           equivalent to: **bclr[l]** 0x04,(cr*T**4)+0
  bnlr[l]   [cr*T*]   Branch if Not Less Than to LR
           archaic form for: **bnllr[l]** [cr*T*]
           equivalent to: **bclr[l]** 0x04,(cr*T**4)+0
- **bns[l][a]**   [cr*T*,]*addr*   Branch if Not Summary Overflow
           equivalent to: **bc[l][a]** 0x04,(cr*T**4)+3,*addr*
  bnsc[l]   [cr*T*]   Branch if Not Summary Overflow to CTR
           archaic form for: **bnsctr[l]** [cr*T*]
           equivalent to: **bcctr[l]** 0x04,(cr*T**4)+3
- **bnsctr[l]**   [cr*T*]   Branch if Not Summary Overflow to CTR
           equivalent to: **bcctr[l]** 0x04,(cr*T**4)+3
- **bnslr[l]**   [cr*T*]   Branch if Not Summary Overflow to LR
           equivalent to: **bclr[l]** 0x04,(cr*T**4)+3
  bnsr[l]   [cr*T*]   Branch if Not Summary Overflow to LR
           archaic form for: **bnslr[l]** [cr*T*]
           equivalent to: **bclr[l]** 0x04,(cr*T**4)+3
- **bnu[l][a]**   [cr*T*,]*addr*   Branch if Not Unordered
           equivalent to: **bc[l][a]** 0x04,(cr*T**4)+3,*addr*
- **bnuctr[l]**   [cr*T*]   Branch if Not Unordered to CTR
           equivalent to: **bcctr[l]** 0x04,(cr*T**4)+3
- **bnulr[l]**   [cr*T*]   Branch if Not Unordered to LR
           equivalent to: **bclr[l]** 0x04,(cr*T**4)+3
  bnz[l][a]   [cr*T*,]*addr*   Branch if Not Zero
           archaic form for: **bne[l][a]** [cr*T*,]*addr*
           equivalent to: **bc[l][a]** 0x04,(cr*T**4)+2,*addr*
  bnzc[l]   [cr*T*]   Branch if Not Zero to CTR
           archaic form for: **bnectr[l]** [cr*T*]
           equivalent to: **bcctr[l]** 0x04,(cr*T**4)+2

`bnzr[l]`	`[crT]`	Branch if Not Zero to LR

    `bnzr[l]`   `[crT]`   Branch if Not Zero to LR
archaic form for: `bnelr[l]` `[crT]`
equivalent to: `bclr[l] 0x04,(crT*4)+2`

    `br[l]`   Branch Unconditionally to LR
archaic form for: `blr[l]`
equivalent to: `bclr[l] 0x14,0`

• `bso[l][a]`   `[crT,]`*addr*   Branch if Summary Overflow
equivalent to: `bc[l][a] 0x0C,(crT*4)+3,`*addr*

    `bsoc[l]`   `[crT]`   Branch if Summary Overflow to CTR
archaic form for: `bsoctr[l]` `[crT]`
equivalent to: `bcctr[l] 0x0C,(crT*4)+3`

• `bsoctr[l]` `[crT]`   Branch if Summary Overflow to CTR
equivalent to: `bcctr[l] 0x0C,(crT*4)+3`

• `bsolr[l]`   `[crT]`   Branch if Summary Overflow to LR
equivalent to: `bclr[l] 0x0C,(crT*4)+3`

    `bsor[l]`   `[crT]`   Branch if Summary Overflow to LR
archaic form for: `bsolr[l]` `[crT]`
equivalent to: `bclr[l] 0x0C,(crT*4)+3`

• `bt[l][a]`   *crbT*`,`*addr*   Branch if Condition True
equivalent to: `bc 0x0C,`*crbT*`,`*addr*

• `btctr[l]`   *crbT*   Branch if Condition True to CTR
equivalent to: `bcctr[l] 0x0C,`*crbT*

• `btlr[l]`   *crbT*   Branch if Condition True to LR
equivalent to: `bclr[l] 0x0C,`*crbT*

• `bun[l][a]`   `[crT,]`*addr*   Branch if Unordered
equivalent to: `bc[l][a] 0x0C,(crT*4)+3,`*addr*

• `bunctr[l]` `[crT]`   Branch if Unordered to CTR
equivalent to: `bcctr[l] 0x0C,(crT*4)+3`

• `bunlr[l]`   `[crT]`   Branch if Unordered to LR
equivalent to: `bclr[l] 0x0C,(crT*4)+3`

    `bz[l][a]`   `[crT,]`*addr*   Branch if Zero
archaic form for: `beq[l][a]` `[crT,]`*addr*
equivalent to: `bc[l][a] 0x0C,(crT*4)+2,`*addr*

    `bzc[l]`   `[crT]`   Branch if Zero to CTR
archaic form for: `beqctr[l]` `[crT]`
equivalent to: `bcctr[l] 0x0C,(crT*4)+2`

    `bzr[l]`   `[crT]`   Branch if Zero to LR
archaic form for: `beqlr[l]` `[crT]`
equivalent to: `bclr[l] 0x0C,(crT*4)+2`

    `cal`   *rT*`,`*d*`(`*rA*`)`   Compute Address Lower
archaic form for: `addi` *rT*`,`*d*`(`*rA*`)`

    `cau`   *rT*`,`*rA*`,`*u16*   Compute Address Upper
archaic form for: `addis` *rT*`,`*rA*`,`*u16*

    `cax[o][.]` *rT*`,`*rA*`,`*rB*   Compute Address
archaic form for: `add[o][.]` *rT*`,`*rA*`,`*rB*

    `clcs`   *rT*`,`*rA*   Cache Line Compute Size
This instruction exists on POWER and the 601 only.

    `clf`   *rA*`,`*rB*   Cache Line Flush
This instruction exists on POWER only.

	`cli`	rA,rB	Cache Line Invalidate
		This instruction exists on POWER only.	
64 •	`clrldi[.]`	$rA,rS,nBits$	Clear Left Doubleword Immediate
		equivalent to: `rldicl[.]` $rA,rS,0,nBits$	
64 •	`clrlsldi[.]`	$rA,rS,nBits,shift$	Clear Left and Shift Left Doubleword Immediate
		equivalent to: `rldic[.]` $rA,rS,shift,nBits-shift$	
•	`clrlslwi[.]`	$rA,rS,nBits,shift$	Clear Left and Shift Left Word Immediate
		equivalent to: `rlwinm[.]` $rA,rS,shift,nBits-shift,31-shift$	
•	`clrlwi[.]`	$rA,rS,nBits$	Clear Left Word Immediate
		equivalent to: `rlwinm[.]` $rA,rS,0,nBits,31$	
64 •	`clrrdi[.]`	$rA,rS,nBits$	Clear Right Doubleword Immediate
		equivalent to: `rldicr[.]` $rA,rS,0,63-nBits$	
•	`clrrwi[.]`	$rA,rS,nBits$	Clear Right Word Immediate
		equivalent to: `rlwinm[.]` $rA,rS,0,0,31-nBits$	
	`cmp`	crT,rA,rB	Compare
		archaic form for: `cmp` $crT,0,rA,rB$	
•	`cmp`	crT,L,rA,rB	Compare
•	`cmpd`	crT,rA,rB	Compare Doubleword
		equivalent to: `cmp` $crT,1,rA,rB$	
•	`cmpdi`	$crT,rA,s16$	Compare Doubleword Immediate
		equivalent to: `cmpi` $crT,1,rA,s16$	
	`cmpi`	$crT,rA,s16$	Compare Immediate
		archaic form for: `cmpi` $crT,0,rA,s16$	
•	`cmpi`	$crT,L,rA,s16$	Compare Immediate
	`cmpl`	crT,rA,rB	Compare Logical
		archaic form for: `cmpl` $crT,0,rA,rB$	
•	`cmpl`	crT,L,rA,rB	Compare Logical
•	`cmpld`	crT,rA,rB	Compare Logical Doubleword
		equivalent to: `cmpl` $crT,1,rA,rB$	
•	`cmpldi`	$crT,rA,u16$	Compare Logical Doubleword Immediate
		equivalent to: `cmpli` $crT,1,rA,u16$	
	`cmpli`	$crT,rA,u16$	Compare Logical Immediate
		archaic form for: `cmpi` $crT,0,rA,u16$	
•	`cmpli`	$crT,L,rA,u16$	Compare Logical Immediate
•	`cmplw`	crT,rA,rB	Compare Logical Word
		equivalent to: `cmpl` $crT,0,rA,rB$	
•	`cmplwi`	$crT,rA,u16$	Compare Logical Word Immediate
		equivalent to: `cmpli` $crT,0,rA,u16$	
•	`cmpw`	crT,rA,rB	Compare Word
		equivalent to: `cmp` $crT,0,rA,rB$	
•	`cmpwi`	$crT,rA,s16$	Compare Word Immediate
		equivalent to: `cmpi` $crT,0,rA,s16$	
	`cntlz[.]`	rA,rS	Count Leading Zeros
		archaic form for: `cntlzw[.]` rA,rS	
64 •	`cntlzd[.]`	rA,rS	Count Leading Zeros Doubleword
•	`cntlzw[.]`	rA,rS	Count Leading Zeros Word
•	`crand`	$crbT,crbA,crbB$	Condition Register AND
•	`crandc`	$crbT,crbA,crbB$	Condition Register AND with Complement

•	crclr	*crbT*	Condition Register Clear

- **crclr**   *crbT*   Condition Register Clear
  equivalent to: **crxor** *crbT*, *crbT*, *crbT*
- **creqv**   *crbT*, *crbA*, *crbB*   Condition Register Equivalent
- **crmove**   *crbT*, *crbA*   Condition Register Move
  equivalent to: **cror** *crbT*, *crbA*, *crbA*
- **crnand**   *crbT*, *crbA*, *crbB*   Condition Register Not AND
- **crnor**   *crbT*, *crbA*, *crbB*   Condition Register Not OR
- **crnot**   *crbT*, *crbA*   Condition Register Not
  equivalent to: **crnor** *crbT*, *crbA*, *crbA*
- **cror**   *crbT*, *crbA*, *crbB*   Condition Register OR
- **crorc**   *crbT*, *crbA*, *crbB*   Condition Register OR with Complement
- **crset**   *crbT*   Condition Register Set
  equivalent to: **creqv** *crbT*, *crbT*, *crbT*
- **crxor**   *crbT*, *crbA*, *crbB*   Condition Register Exclusive OR
- **dcbf**   *rA*, *rB*   Data Cache Block Flush
- **dcbi**   *rA*, *rB*   Data Cache Block Invalidate
- **dcbst**   *rA*, *rB*   Data Cache Block Store
- **dcbt**   *rA*, *rB*   Data Cache Block Touch
- **dcbtst**   *rA*, *rB*   Data Cache Block Touch for Store
- **dcbz**   *rA*, *rB*   Data Cache Block Zero

   dclst   *rA*, *rB*   Data Cache Line Store
     This instruction exists on POWER only.

   dclz   *rA*, *rB*   Data Cache Line Zero
     archaic form for: **dcbz**

   dcs   Data Cache Synchronize
     archaic form for: **sync**

   div[o][.]   *rT*, *rA*, *rB*   Divide
     This instruction exists on POWER and the 601 only.

64 • **divd[o][.]**   *rT*, *rA*, *rB*   Divide Doubleword
64 • **divdu[o][.]**   *rT*, *rA*, *rB*   Divide Doubleword Unsigned

   divs[o][.]   *rT*, *rA*, *rB*   Divide Short
     This instruction exists on POWER and the 601 only.

- **divw[o][.]**   *rT*, *rA*, *rB*   Divide Word
- **divwu[o][.]**   *rT*, *rA*, *rB*   Divide Word Unsigned

   doz[o][.]   *rT*, *rA*, *rB*   Difference Or Zero
     This instruction exists on POWER and the 601 only.

   dozi   *rT*, *rA*, *s16*   Difference Or Zero Immediate
     This instruction exists on POWER and the 601 only.

? • **eciwx**   *rT*, *rA*, *rB*   External Control Input Word Indexed
? • **ecowx**   *rS*, *rA*, *rB*   External Control Output Word Indexed
- **eieio**   Enforce In-Order Execution of I/O
- **eqv[.]**   *rA*, *rS*, *rB*   Equivalent

64 • **extldi[.]**   *rA*, *rS*, *nBits*, *start*   Extract and Left Justify Doubleword
                                 Immediate
     equivalent to: **rldicr[.]** *rA*, *rS*, *start*, *nBits*−1

- **extlwi[.]**   *rA*, *rS*, *nBits*, *start*   Extract and Left Justify Word Immediate
  equivalent to: **rlwinm[.]** *rA*, *rS*, *start*, 0, *nBits*−1

64 • `extrdi[.]`   r*A*,r*S*,*nBits*,*start*   Extract and Right Justify Doubleword
                                              Immediate
                      equivalent to: `rldicl[.]` r*A*,r*S*,*start*+*nBits*,64−*nBits*

  • `extrwi[.]`   r*A*,r*S*,*nBits*,*start*   Extract and Right Justify Word Immediate
                      equivalent to: `rlwinm[.]` r*A*,r*S*,*start*+*nBits*,32−*nBits*,31

    `exts[.]`   r*A*,r*S*   Extend Sign Halfword
                      archaic form for: `extsh[.]` r*A*,r*S*

  • `extsb[.]`   r*A*,r*S*   Extend Sign Byte
  • `extsh[.]`   r*A*,r*S*   Extend Sign Halfword
64 • `extsw[.]`   r*A*,r*S*   Extend Sign Word
    `fa[.]`   fr*T*,fr*A*,fr*B*   Floating-Point Add
                      archaic form for: `fadd[.]` fr*T*,fr*A*,fr*B*

  • `fabs[.]`   fr*T*,fr*B*   Floating-Point Absolute Value
  • `fadd[.]`   fr*T*,fr*A*,fr*B*   Floating-Point Add
  • `fadds[.]`   fr*T*,fr*A*,fr*B*   Floating-Point Add Single-Precision
64 • `fcfid[.]`   fr*T*,fr*B*   Floating-Point Convert from Integer
                                        Doubleword
  • `fcmpo`   cr*T*,fr*A*,fr*B*   Floating-Point Compare Ordered
  • `fcmpu`   cr*T*,fr*A*,fr*B*   Floating-Point Compare Unordered
64 • `fctid[.]`   fr*T*,fr*B*   Floating-Point Convert to Integer Doubleword
64 • `fctidz[.]` fr*T*,fr*B*   Floating-Point Convert to Integer Doubleword
                                        with Round to Zero
  • `fctiw[.]`   fr*T*,fr*B*   Floating-Point Convert to Integer Word
  • `fctiwz[.]`   fr*T*,fr*B*   Floating-Point Convert to Integer Word with
                                        Round toward Zero
    `fd[.]`   fr*T*,fr*A*,fr*B*   Floating-Point Divide
                      archaic form for: `fdiv[.]` fr*T*,fr*A*,fr*B*

  • `fdiv[.]`   fr*T*,fr*A*,fr*B*   Floating-Point Divide
  • `fdivs[.]`   fr*T*,fr*A*,fr*B*   Floating-Point Divide Single-Precision
    `fm[.]`   fr*T*,fr*A*,fr*C*   Floating-Point Multiply
                      archaic form for: `fmul[.]` fr*T*,fr*A*,fr*C*

    `fma[.]`   fr*T*,fr*A*,fr*C*,fr*B*   Floating-Point Multiply-Add
                      archaic form for: `fmadd[.]` fr*T*,fr*A*,fr*C*,fr*B*

  • `fmadd[.]`   fr*T*,fr*A*,fr*C*,fr*B*   Floating-Point Multiply-Add
  • `fmadds[.]`   fr*T*,fr*A*,fr*C*,fr*B*   Floating-Point Multiply-Add Single-Precision
  • `fmr[.]`   fr*T*,fr*B*   Floating-Point Move Register
    `fms[.]`   fr*T*,fr*A*,fr*C*,fr*B*   Floating-Point Multiply-Subtract
                      archaic form for: `fmsub[.]` fr*T*,fr*A*,fr*C*,fr*B*

  • `fmsub[.]`   fr*T*,fr*A*,fr*C*,fr*B*   Floating-Point Multiply-Subtract
  • `fmsubs[.]`   fr*T*,fr*A*,fr*C*,fr*B*   Floating-Point Multiply-Subtract Single-
                                        Precision
  • `fmul[.]`   fr*T*,fr*A*,fr*C*   Floating-Point Multiply
  • `fmuls[.]`   fr*T*,fr*A*,fr*C*   Floating-Point Multiply Single-Precision
  • `fnabs[.]`   fr*T*,fr*B*   Floating-Point Negative Absolute Value
  • `fneg[.]`   fr*T*,fr*B*   Floating-Point Negate
    `fnma[.]`   fr*T*,fr*A*,fr*C*,fr*B*   Floating-Point Negative Multiply-Add
                      archaic form for: `fnmadd[.]` fr*T*,fr*A*,fr*C*,fr*B*

  • `fnmadd[.]`   fr*T*,fr*A*,fr*C*,fr*B*   Floating-Point Negative Multiply-Add

•	fnmadds[.]	frT,frA,frC,frB	Floating-Point Negative Multiply-Add Single-Precision
	fnms[.]	frT,frA,frC,frB	Floating-Point Negative Multiply-Subtract
		archaic form for: fnmsub[.] frT,frA,frC,frB	
•	fnmsub[.]	frT,frA,frC,frB	Floating-Point Negative Multiply-Subtract
•	fnmsubs[.]	frT,frA,frC,frB	Floating-Point Negative Multiply-Subtract Single-Precison
?•	fres[.]	frT,frB	Floating-Point Reciprocal Estimate Single-Precision
•	frsp[.]	frT,frB	Floating-Point Round to Single-Precision
?•	frsqrte[.]	frT,frB	Floating-Point Reciprocal Square Root Estimate
	fs[.]	frT,frA,frB	Floating-Point Subtract
		archaic form for: fsub[.] frT,frA,frB	
?•	fsel[.]	frT,frA,frC,frB	Floating-Point Select
?•	fsqrt[.]	frT,frB	Floating-Point Square Root
?•	fsqrts[.]	frT,frB	Floating-Point Square Root Single-Precision
•	fsub[.]	frT,frA,frB	Floating-Point Subtract
•	fsubs[.]	frT,frA,frB	Floating-Point Subtract Single-Precision
•	icbi	rA,rB	Instruction Cache Block Invalidate
	ics		Instruction Cache Synchronize
		archaic form for: isync	
•	inslwi[.]	rA,rS,nBits,start	Insert from Left Word Immediate
		equivalent to: rlwimi[.] rA,rS,32-start,start,(start+nBits)-1	
64•	insrdi[.]	rA,rS,nBits,start	Insert from Right Doubleword Immediate
		equivalent to: rldimi[.] rA,rS,64-(start + nBits),start	
•	insrwi[.]	rA,rS,nBits,start	Insert from Right Word Immediate
		equivalent to: rlwimi[.] rA,rS,32-end,start,end-1	
		where end = (start + nBits)	
•	isync		Instruction Cache Synchronize
	l	rT,d(rA)	Load
		archaic form for: lwz rT,d(rA)	
•	la	rT,d(rA)	Load Address
		equivalent to: addi rT,rA,d	
•	la	rT,symbol	Load Address
		equivalent to: addi rT,rN,dSymbol	
		where dSymbol is the offset from rN to symbol and rN has been specified using the .using assembler directive	
	lbrx	rT,rA,rB	Load Byte-Reversed Indexed
		archaic form for: lwbrx rT,rA,rB	
•	lbz	rT,d(rA)	Load Byte and Zero
•	lbzu	rT,d(rA)	Load Byte and Zero with Update
•	lbzux	rT,rA,rB	Load Byte and Zero with Update Indexed
•	lbzx	rT,rA,rB	Load Byte and Zero Indexed
64•	ld	rT,ds(rA)	Load Doubleword
64•	ldarx	rT,rA,rB	Load Doubleword and Reserve Indexed
64•	ldu	rT,ds(rA)	Load Doubleword with Update
64•	ldux	rT,rA,rB	Load Doubleword with Update Indexed
64•	ldx	rT,rA,rB	Load Doubleword Indexed

• lfd	frT,d(rA)	Load Floating-Point Double-Precision
• lfdu	frT,d(rA)	Load Floating-Point Double-Precision with Update
• lfdux	frT,rA,rB	Load Floating-Point Double-Precision with Update Indexed
• lfdx	frT,rA,rB	Load Floating-Point Double-Precision Indexed
• lfs	frT,d(rA)	Load Floating-Point Single-Precision
• lfsu	frT,d(rA)	Load Floating-Point Single-Precision with Update
• lfsux	frT,rA,rB	Load Floating-Point Single-Precision with Update Indexed
• lfsx	frT,rA,rB	Load Floating-Point Single-Precision Indexed
• lha	rT,d(rA)	Load Halfword Algebraic
• lhau	rT,d(rA)	Load Halfword Algebraic with Update
• lhaux	rT,rA,rB	Load Halfword Algebraic with Update Indexed
• lhax	rT,rA,rB	Load Halfword Algebraic Indexed
• lhbrx	rT,rA,rB	Load Halfword Byte-Reversed Indexed
• lhz	rT,d(rA)	Load Halfword and Zero
• lhzu	rT,d(rA)	Load Halfword and Zero with Update
• lhzux	rT,rA,rB	Load Halfword and Zero with Update Indexed
• lhzx	rT,rA,rB	Load Halfword and Zero Indexed
• li	rT,s16	Load Immediate

equivalent to: `addi` rT,0,s16

lil	rT,s16	Load Immediate Lower

archaic form for: `li` rT,s16

equivalent to: `addi` rT,0,s16

• lis	rT,s16	Load Immediate Shifted

equivalent to: `addis` rT,0,s16

liu	rT,u16	Load Immediate Upper

archaic form for: `lis` rT,s16

equivalent to: `addis` rT,0,u16

lm	rT,d(rA)	Load Multiple

archaic form for: `lmw` rT,d(rA)

• lmw	rT,d(rA)	Load Multiple Word
lscbx[.]	rT,rA,rB	Load String and Compare Byte Indexed

This instruction exists on POWER and the 601 only.

lsi	rT,rA,nBytes	Load String Immediate

archaic form for: `lswi` rT,rA,nBytes

• lswi	rT,rA,nBytes	Load String Word Immediate
• lswx	rT,rA,rB	Load String Word Indexed
lsx	rT,rA,rB	Load String Indexed

archaic form for: `lswx` rT,rA,rB

lu	rT,d(rA)	Load with Update

archaic form for: `lwzu` rT,d(rA)

lux	rT,rA,rB	Load with Update Indexed

archaic form for: `lwzux` rT,rA,rB

64 • lwa	rT,ds(rA)	Load Word Algebraic
• lwarx	rT,rA,rB	Load Word and Reserve Indexed

64 •	lwaux	rT,rA,rB	Load Word Algebraic with Update Indexed
64 •	lwax	rT,rA,rB	Load Word Algebraic Indexed
•	lwbrx	rT,rA,rB	Load Word Byte-Reversed Indexed
•	lwz	$rT,d(rA)$	Load Word and Zero
•	lwzu	$rT,d(rA)$	Load Word and Zero with Update
•	lwzux	rT,rA,rB	Load Word and Zero with Update Indexed
•	lwzx	rT,rA,rB	Load Word and Zero Indexed
	lx	rA,rS,rB	Load Indexed

archaic form for: lwzx rA,rS,rB

	maskg[.]	rA,rS,rB	Mask Generate

This instruction exists on POWER and the 601 only.

	maskir[.]	rA,rS,rB	Mask Insert from Register

This instruction exists on POWER and the 601 only.

•	mcrf	crT,crS	Move Condition Register Fields
•	mcrfs	crT,crS	Move to Condition Register from FPSCR
•	mcrxr	crT	Move to Condition Register from XER
64 •	mfasr	rT	Move from Address Space Register

equivalent to: mfspr $rT,280$

•	mfcr	rT	Move from Condition Register
•	mfctr	rT	Move from Count Register

equivalent to: mfspr $rT,9$

•	mfdar	rT	Move from Data Address Register

equivalent to: mfspr $rT,19$

•	mfdbatl	rT,n	Move from Data Block-Address Translation Register n Lower

equivalent to: mfspr $rT,537+2*n$

•	mfdbatu	rT,n	Move from Data Block-Address Translation Register n Upper

equivalent to: mfspr $rT,536+2*n$

•	mfdec	rT	Move from Decrement Register

equivalent to: mfspr $rT,22$

Note: on POWER, the SPR encoding for the DEC Register was 6 instead of 22; the MPC601 accepts either encoding.

•	mfdsisr	rT	Move from Data Storage Interrupt Status Register

equivalent to: mfspr $rT,18$

•	mfear	rT	Move from External Access Register

equivalent to: mfspr $rT,282$

•	mffs[.]	frT	Move from FPSCR
•	mfibatl	rT,n	Move from Instruction Block-Address Translation Register n Lower

equivalent to: mfspr $rT,529+2*n$

•	mfibatu	rT,n	Move from Instruction Block-Address Translation Register n Upper

equivalent to: mfspr $rT,528+2*n$

•	mflr	rT	Move from Link Register

equivalent to: mfspr $rT,8$

mfmq	rT	Move from MQ Register

This extended form is defined on POWER and the 601 only.
equivalent to: `mfspr rT,0`

- mfmsr   rT   Move from Machine State Register
- mfpvr   rT   Move from Processor Version Register

equivalent to: `mfspr rT,287`

  mfrtcl   rT   Move from Real Time Counter Lower

This extended form is defined on POWER and the 601 only.
equivalent to: `mfspr rT,5`

  mfrtcu   rT   Move from Real Time Counter Upper

This extended form is defined on POWER and the 601 only.
equivalent to: `mfspr rT,4`

- mfsdr1   rT   Move from Storage Description Register 1

equivalent to: `mfspr rT,25`

- mfspr   rT,SPR   Move from Special Purpose Register
- mfsprg   rT,n   Move from SPR G0-G3

equivalent to: `mfspr rT,272+n`

32 • mfsr   rT,SR   Move from Segment Regster

  mfsri   rT,rA,rB   Move from Segment Register Indirect

archaic form for: `mfsrin rT,rB`

Note that A must equal 0 for `mfsrin` to replace `mfsri` and that the
     instruction encoding is different for these instructions.

32 • mfsrin   rT,rB   Move from Segment Register Indirect
- mfsrr0   rT   Move from Save/Restore Register 0

equivalent to: `mfspr rT,26`

- mfsrr1   rT   Move from Save/Restore Register 1

equivalent to: `mfspr rT,27`

- mftb   rT,TBR   Move from Time Base Register
- mftb   rT   Move from Time Base Lower

equivalent to: `mftb rT,268`

- mftbu   rT   Move from Time Base Upper

equivalent to: `mftb rT,269`

- mfxer   rT   Move from Fixed-Point Exception Register

equivalent to: `mfspr rT,1`

- mr[.]   rA,rS   Move Register

equivalent to: `or[.] rA,rS,rS`

64 • mtasr   rS   Move to Address Space Register

equivalent to: `mtspr 280,rS`

  mtcr   rS   Move to Condition Register

equivalent to: `mtcrf 0xFF,rS`

- mtcrf   crMask,rS   Move to Condition Register Fields
- mtctr   rS   Move to Count Register

equivalent to: `mtspr 9,rS`

- mtdar   rS   Move to Data Address Register

equivalent to: `mtspr 19,rS`

- mtdbatl   n,rS   Move to Data Block-Address Translation
                                    Register n Lower

equivalent to: `mtspr 537+2*n,rS`

- `mtdbatu` n, rS Move to Data Block-Address Translation Register n Upper
  equivalent to: `mtspr 536+2*n,rS`
- `mtdec` rS Move to Decrement Register
  equivalent to: `mtspr 22,rS`
- `mtdsisr` rS Move to Data Storage Interrupt Status Register
  equivalent to: `mtspr 18,rS`
- `mtear` rS Move to External Access Register
  equivalent to: `mtspr 282,rS`
- `mtfs[.]` frB Move to FPSCR
  equivalent to: `mtfsf[.] 0xFF,frB`
- `mtfsb0[.]` $crbT$ Move to FPSCR Bit 0
- `mtfsb1[.]` $crbT$ Move to FPSCR Bit 1
- `mtfsf[.]`   *fpscrMask*, `frB`   Move to FPSCR Fields
- `mtfsfi[.]`   *fpscrfT*, *fieldVal*   Move to FPSCR Field Immediate
- `mtibatl` n, rS Move to Instruction Block-Address Translation Register n Lower
  equivalent to: `mtspr 529+2*n,rS`
- `mtibatu` n, rS Move to Instruction Block-Address Translation Register n Upper
  equivalent to: `mtspr 528+2*n,rS`
- `mtlr` rS Move to Link Register
  equivalent to: `mtspr 8,rS`
- `mtmq` rS Move to Multiply Quotient Register
  This extended form is defined on POWER and the 601 only.
  equivalent to: `mtspr 0,rS`
- `mtmsr` rS Move to Machine State Register
- `mtsdr1` rS Move to Storage Description Register 1
  equivalent to: `mtspr 25,rS`
- `mtspr` SPR, rS Move to Special Purpose Register
- `mtsprg` n, rS Move to SPR G0-G3
  equivalent to: `mtspr 272+n,rS`
- ₃₂ `mtsr` SR, rS Move to Segment Register

  `mtsri` rS, rA, rB Move to Segment Register Indirect
  archaic form for: `mtsrin` rS, rB
  Note that A must equal 0 for `mtsrin` to replace `mtsri`.
- ₃₂ `mtsrin` rS, rB Move to Segment Register Indirect
- `mtsrr0` rS Move to Save/Restore Register 0
  equivalent to: `mtspr 26,rS`
- `mtsrr1` rS Move to Save/Restore Register 1
  equivalent to: `mtspr 27,rS`

  `mttb` TBR, rS Move to Time Base Register
  This instruction was originally intended to provide write access to the Time Base Register, but it has since been removed from the PowerPC Architecture specification.
- `mttbl` rS Move to Time Base Lower
  equivalent to: `mtspr 284,rS`
- `mttbu` rS Move to Time Base Upper
  equivalent to: `mtspr 285,rS`

• `mtxer`	`rS`		Move to Fixed-Point Exception Register
		equivalent to: `mtspr 1,rS`	
`mul[o][.]`	`rT,rA,rB`		Multiply
		This instruction exists on POWER and the 601 only.	
64 • `mulhd[.]`	`rT,rA,rB`		Multiply High Doubleword
64 • `mulhdu[.]`	`rT,rA,rB`		Multiply High Doubleword Unsigned
• `mulhw[.]`	`rT,rA,rB`		Multiply High Word
• `mulhwu[.]`	`rT,rA,rB`		Multiply High Word Unsigned
`muli`	`rT,rA,s16`		Multiply Immediate
		archaic form for: `mulli rT,rA,s16`	
64 • `mulld[o][.]`	`rT,rA,rB`		Multiply Low Doubleword
• `mulli`	`rT,rA,s16`		Multiply Low Immediate
• `mullw[o][.]`	`rT,rA,rB`		Multiply Low Word
`muls[o][.]`	`rT,rA,rB`		Multiply Short
		archaic form for: `mullw rT,rA,rB`	
`nabs[o][.]`	`rT,rA`		Negative Absolute Value
		This instruction exists on POWER and the 601 only.	
• `nand[.]`	`rA,rS,rB`		NAND
• `neg[o][.]`	`rT,rA`		Negate
• `nop`			No-op
		equivalent to: `ori r0,r0,0`	
• `nor[.]`	`rA,rS,rB`		NOR
• `not[.]`	`rA,rS`		NOT
		equivalent to: `nor[.] rA,rS,rS`	
• `or[.]`	`rA,rS,rB`		OR
• `orc[.]`	`rA,rS,rB`		OR with Complement
• `ori`	`rA,rS,u16`		OR Immediate
`oril`	`rA,rS,u16`		OR Immediate Lower
		archaic form for: `ori rA,rS,u16`	
• `oris`	`rA,rS,u16`		OR Immediate Shifted
`oriu`	`rA,rS,u16`		OR Immediate Upper
		archaic form for: `oris rA,rS,u16`	
`rac[.]`	`rT,rA,rB`		Real Address Compute
		This instruction exists on POWER only.	
• `rfi`			Return from Interrupt
`rfsvc`			Return from SVC
		This instruction exists on POWER only.	
64 • `rldcl[.]`	`rA,rS,rB,mb64`		Rotate Left Doubleword then Clear Left
64 • `rldcr[.]`	`rA,rS,rB,me64`		Rotate Left Doubleword then Clear Right
64 • `rldic[.]`	`rA,rS,shift64,mb64`		Rotate Left Doubleword Immediate then Clear
64 • `rldicl[.]`	`rA,rS,shift64,mb64`		Rotate Left Doubleword Immediate then Clear Left
64 • `rldicr[.]`	`rA,rS,shift64,me64`		Rotate Left Doubleword Immediate then Clear Right
64 • `rldimi[.]`	`rA,rS,shift64,mb64`		Rotate Left Doubleword Immediate then Mask Insert
`rlimi[.]`	`rA,rS,shift,mb,me`		Rotate Left Immediate then Mask Insert
		archaic form for: `rlwimi[.] rA,rS,shift,mb,me`	

`rlinm[.]`	rA,rS,*shift*,*mb*,*me*	Rotate Left Immediate then AND with Mask	
	archaic form for: `rlwinm[.]` rA,rS,*shift*,*mb*,*me*		
`rlmi[.]`	rA,rS,rB,*mb*,*me*	Rotate Left then Mask Insert	
	This instruction exists on POWER and the 601 only.		
`rlnm[.]`	rA,rS,rB,*mb*,*me*	Rotate Left then AND with Mask	
	archaic form for: `rlwnm[.]` rA,rS,rB,*mb*,*me*		

- `rlwimi[.]` rA,rS,*shift*,*mb*,*me*   Rotate Left Word Immediate then Mask Insert
- `rlwinm[.]` rA,rS,*shift*,*mb*,*me*   Rotate Left Word Immediate then AND with Mask
- `rlwnm[.]` rA,rS,rB,*mb*,*me*   Rotate Left Word then AND with Mask
- 64 `rotld[.]` rA,rS,rB Rotate Left Doubleword
  - equivalent to: `rldcl[.]` rA,rS,rB,0
- 64 `rotldi[.]` rA,rS,*nBits*   Rotate Left Doubleword Immediate
  - equivalent to: `rldicl[.]` rA,rS,*nBits*,0
- `rotlw[.]` rA,rS,rB Rotate Left Word
  - equivalent to: `rlwnm[.]` rA,rS,rB,0,31
- `rotlwi[.]` rA,rS,*nBits*   Rotate Left Word Immediate
  - equivalent to: `rlwinm[.]` rA,rS,*nBits*,0,31
- 64 `rotrdi[.]` rA,rS,*nBits*   Rotate Right Doubleword Immediate
  - equivalent to: `rldicl[.]` rA,rS,64−*nBits*,0
- `rotrwi[.]` rA,rS,*nBits*   Rotate Right Word Immediate
  - equivalent to: `rlwinm[.]` rA,rS,32−*nBits*,0,31

`rrib[.]`	rA,rS,rB	Rotate Right and Insert Bit	
	This instruction exists on POWER and the 601 only.		

- `sc`   System Call

`sf[o][.]`	rT,rA,rB	Subtract From	
	archaic form for: `subf[o][.]` rT,rA,rB		
`sfe[o][.]`	rT,rA,rB	Subtract From Extended	
	archaic form for: `subfe[o][.]` rT,rA,rB		
`sfi`	rT,rA,*s16*	Subtract From Immediate	
	archaic form for: `subfic` rT,rA,*s16*		
`sfme[o][.]`	rT,rA	Subtract From Minus One Extended	
	archaic form for: `subfme[o][.]` rT,rA		
`sfze[o][.]`	rT,rA	Subtract From Zero Extended	
	archaic form for: `subfze[o][.]` rT,rA		
`si[.]`	rT,rA,*s16*	Subtract Immediate	
	equivalent to: `addic[.]` rT,rA,−*s16*		
`sl[.]`	rA,rS,rB	Shift Left	
	archaic form for: `slw[.]` rA,rS,rB		

- ? `slbia`   SLB Invalidate All
- ? `slbie` rB SLB Invalidate Entry

`slbiex`	rB	SLB Invalidate Entry by Index	
	This instruction was originally intended as an optional instruction for 64-bit PowerPC implementations, but it has since been removed from the PowerPC Architecture specification.		

- 64 `sld[.]` rA,rS,rB Shift Left Doubleword
- 64 `sldi[.]` rA,rS,*nBits*   Shift Left Doubleword Immediate
  - equivalent to: `rldicr[.]` rA,rS,*nBits*,63−*nBits*

| `sle[.]` | `rA,rS,rB` | Shift Left Extended |
| | This instruction exists on POWER and the 601 only. | |

`sle[.]` `rA,rS,rB` Shift Left Extended
This instruction exists on POWER and the 601 only.

`sleq[.]` `rA,rS,rB` Shift Left Extended with MQ
This instruction exists on POWER and the 601 only.

`sliq[.]` `rA,rS,`*shift* Shift Left Immediate with MQ
This instruction exists on POWER and the 601 only.

`slliq[.]` `rA,rS,`*shift* Shift Left Long Immediate with MQ
This instruction exists on POWER and the 601 only.

`sllq[.]` `rA,rS,rB` Shift Left Long with MQ
This instruction exists on POWER and the 601 only.

`slq[.]` `rA,rS,rB` Shift Left with MQ
This instruction exists on POWER and the 601 only.

• `slw[.]` `rA,rS,rB` Shift Left Word

• `slwi[.]` `rA,rS,`*nBits* Shift Left Word Immediate
equivalent to: `rlwinm[.]` `rA,rS,`*nBits*`,0,31-`*nBits*

`sr[.]` `rA,rS,rB` Shift Right
archaic form for: `srw[.]` `rA,rS,rB`

`sra[.]` `rA,rS,rB` Shift Right Algebraic
archaic form for: `sraw[.]` `rA,rS,rB`

64 • `srad[.]` `rA,rS,rB` Shift Right Algebraic Doubleword

64 • `sradi[.]` `rA,rS,`*shift64* Shift Right Algebraic Doubleword Immediate

`srai[.]` `rA,rS,`*shift* Shift Right Algebraic Immediate
archaic form for: `srawi[.]` `rA,rS,`*shift*

`sraiq[.]` `rA,rS,`*shift* Shift Right Algebraic Immediate with MQ
This instruction exists on POWER and the 601 only.

`sraq[.]` `rA,rS,rB` Shift Right Algebraic with MQ
This instruction exists on POWER and the 601 only.

• `sraw[.]` `rA,rS,rB` Shift Right Algebraic Word

• `srawi[.]` `rA,rS,`*shift* Shift Right Algebraic Word Immediate

64 • `srd[.]` `rA,rS,rB` Shift Right Doubleword

64 • `srdi[.]` `rA,rS,`*nBits* Shift Right Doubleword Immediate
equivalent to: `rldicl[.]` `rA,rS,64-`*nBits*`,`*nBits*

`sre[.]` `rA,rS,rB` Shift Right Extended
This instruction exists on POWER and the 601 only.

`srea[.]` `rA,rS,rB` Shift Right Extended Algebraic
This instruction exists on POWER and the 601 only.

`sreq[.]` `rA,rS,rB` Shift Right Extended with MQ
This instruction exists on POWER and the 601 only.

`sriq[.]` `rA,rS,`*shift* Shift Right Immediate with MQ
This instruction exists on POWER and the 601 only.

`srliq[.]` `rA,rS,`*shift* Shift Right Long Immediate with MQ
This instruction exists on POWER and the 601 only.

`srlq[.]` `rA,rS,rB` Shift Right Long with MQ
This instruction exists on POWER and the 601 only.

`srq[.]` `rA,rS,rB` Shift Right with MQ
This instruction exists on POWER and the 601 only.

• `srw[.]` `rA,rS,rB` Shift Right Word

• `srwi[.]` `rA,rS,`*nBits* Shift Right Word Immediate
equivalent to: `rlwinm[.]` `rA,rS,32-`*nBits*`,`*nBits*`,31`

	st	rS,d(rA)	Store
		archaic form for: stw rT,d(rA)	
•	stb	rS,d(rA)	Store Byte
	stbrx	rS,rA,rB	Store Byte-Reversed Indexed
		archaic form for: stwbrx rT,rA,rB	
•	stbu	rS,d(rA)	Store Byte with Update
•	stbux	rS,rA,rB	Store Byte with Update Indexed
•	stbx	rS,rA,rB	Store Byte Indexed
64 •	std	rS,ds(rA)	Store Doubleword
64 •	stdcx.	rS,rA,rB	Store Doubleword Conditional Indexed
64 •	stdu	rS,ds(rA)	Store Doubleword with Update
64 •	stdux	rS,rA,rB	Store Doubleword with Update Indexed
64 •	stdx	rS,rA,rB	Store Doubleword Indexed
•	stfd	frS,d(rA)	Store Floating-Point Double
•	stfdu	frS,d(rA)	Store Floating-Point Double with Update
•	stfdux	frS,rA,rB	Store Floating-Point Double with Update Indexed
•	stfdx	frS,rA,rB	Store Floating-Point Double Indexed
? •	stfiwx	frS,rA,rB	Store Floating-Point as Integer Word
•	stfs	frS,d(rA)	Store Floating-Point Single
•	stfsu	frS,d(rA)	Store Floating-Point Single with Update
•	stfsux	frS,rA,rB	Store Floating-Point Single with Update Indexed
•	stfsx	frS,rA,rB	Store Floating-Point Single Indexed
•	sth	rS,d(rA)	Store Halfword
•	sthbrx	rS,rA,rB	Store Halfword Byte-Reversed Indexed
•	sthu	rS,d(rA)	Store Halfword with Update
•	sthux	rS,rA,rB	Store Halfword with Update Indexed
•	sthx	rS,rA,rB	Store Halfword Indexed
	stm	rS,d(rA)	Store Multiple
		archaic form for: stmw rT,d(rA)	
•	stmw	rS,d(rA)	Store Multiple Word
	stsi	rS,rA,nBytes	Store String Immediate
		archaic form for: stswi rT,rA,nBytes	
•	stswi	rS,rA,nBytes	Store String Word Immediate
•	stswx	rS,rA,rB	Store String Word Indexed
	stsw	rS,rA,rB	Store String Indexed
		archaic form for: stswx rT,rA,rB	
	stu	rS,d(rA)	Store with Update
		archaic form for: stwu rT,d(rA)	
	stux	rS,rA,rB	Store with Update Indexed
		archaic form for: stwux rT,rA,rB	
•	stw	rS,d(rA)	Store Word
•	stwbrx	rS,rA,rB	Store Word Byte-Reversed Indexed
•	stwcx.	rS,rA,rB	Store Word Conditional Indexed
•	stwu	rS,d(rA)	Store Word with Update
•	stwux	rS,rA,rB	Store Word with Update Indexed
•	stwx	rS,rA,rB	Store Word Indexed

stx	rS,rA,rB	Store Indexed
	archaic form for: stwx rT,rA,rB	
• sub[o][.]	rT,rA,rB	Subtract
	equivalent to: subf[o][.] rT,rB,rA	
• subc[o][.]	rT,rA,rB	Subtract Carrying
	equivalent to: subfc[o][.] rT,rB,rA	
• subf[o][.]	rT,rA,rB	Subtract From
• subfc[o][.]	rT,rA,rB	Subtract From Carrying
• subfe[o][.]	rT,rA,rB	Subtract From Extended
• subfic	rT,rA,s16	Subtract From Immediate Carrying
• subfme[o][.]	rT,rA	Subtract From Minus One Extended
• subfze[o][.]	rT,rA	Subtract From Zero Extended
• subi	rT,rA,s16	Subtract Immediate
	equivalent to: addi rT,rA,−s16	
• subic[.]	rT,rA,s16	Subtract Immediate Carrying
	equivalent to: addic[.] rT,rA,−s16	
• subis	rT,rA,s16	Subtract Immediate Shifted
	equivalent to: addis rT,rA,−s16	
svc		Supervisor Call
	This instruction exists on POWER only.	
svca	SV	Supervisor Call Absolute
	archaic form for: sc	
	Note that SV must equal 0 for sc to replace svca.	
svcl		Supervisor Call with Link
	This instruction exists on POWER only.	
svcla	SV	Supervisor Call Absolute with Link
	This instruction exists on POWER only.	
• sync		Synchronize
t	trapOn,rA,rB	Trap
	archaic form for: tw trapOn,rA,rB	
64 • td	trapOn,rA,rB	Trap Doubleword
64 • tdeq	rA,rB	Trap Doubleword if Equal
	equivalent to: td 4,rA,rB	
64 • tdeqi	rA,s16	Trap Doubleword if Equal Immediate
	equivalent to: tdi 4,rA,s16	
64 • tdge	rA,rB	Trap Doubleword if Greater Than or Equal
	equivalent to: td 12,rA,rB	
64 • tdgei	rA,s16	Trap Doubleword if Greater Than or Equal Immediate
	equivalent to: tdi 12,rA,s16	
64 • tdgt	rA,rB	Trap Doubleword if Greater Than
	equivalent to: td 8,rA,rB	
64 • tdgti	rA,s16	Trap Doubleword if Greater Than Immediate
	equivalent to: tdi 8,rA,s16	
64 • tdi	rapOn,rA,s16	Trap Doubleword Immediate
64 • tdle	rA,rB	Trap Doubleword if Less Than or Equal
	equivalent to: td 20,rA,rB	

64 • `tdlei`	`rA,s16`	Trap Doubleword if Less Than or Equal Immediate
	equivalent to: `tdi 20,rA,s16`	
64 • `tdlge`	`rA,rB`	Trap Doubleword if Logically Greater Than or Equal
	equivalent to: `td 5,rA,rB`	
64 • `tdlgei`	`rA,s16`	Trap Doubleword if Logically Greater Than or Equal Immediate
	equivalent to: `tdi 5,rA,s16`	
64 • `tdlgt`	`rA,rB`	Trap Doubleword if Logically Greater Than
	equivalent to: `td 1,rA,rB`	
64 • `tdlgti`	`rA,s16`	Trap Doubleword if Logically Greater Than Immediate
	equivalent to: `tdi 1,rA,s16`	
64 • `tdlle`	`rA,rB`	Trap Doubleword if Logically Less Than or Equal
	equivalent to: `td 6,rA,rB`	
64 • `tdllei`	`rA,s16`	Trap Doubleword if Logically Less Than or Equal Immediate
	equivalent to: `tdi 6,rA,s16`	
64 • `tdllt`	`rA,rB`	Trap Doubleword if Logically Less Than
	equivalent to: `td 2,rA,rB`	
64 • `tdllti`	`rA,s16`	Trap Doubleword if Logically Less Than Immediate
	equivalent to: `tdi 2,rA,s16`	
64 • `tdlng`	`rA,rB`	Trap Doubleword if Logically Not Greater Than
	equivalent to: `td 6,rA,rB`	
64 • `tdlngi`	`rA,s16`	Trap Doubleword if Logically Not Greater Than Immediate
	equivalent to: `tdi 6,rA,s16`	
64 • `tdlnl`	`rA,rB`	Trap Doubleword if Logically Not Less Than
	equivalent to: `td 5,rA,rB`	
64 • `tdlnli`	`rA,s16`	Trap Doubleword if Logically Not Less Than Immediate
	equivalent to: `tdi 5,rA,s16`	
64 • `tdlt`	`rA,rB`	Trap Doubleword if Less Than
	equivalent to: `td 16,rA,rB`	
64 • `tdlti`	`rA,s16`	Trap Doubleword if Less Than Immediate
	equivalent to: `tdi 16,rA,s16`	
64 • `tdne`	`rA,rB`	Trap Doubleword if Not Equal
	equivalent to: `td 24,rA,rB`	
64 • `tdnei`	`rA,s16`	Trap Doubleword if Not Equal Immediate
	equivalent to: `tdi 24,rA,s16`	
64 • `tdng`	`rA,rB`	Trap Doubleword if Not Greater Than
	equivalent to: `td 20,rA,rB`	
64 • `tdngi`	`rA,s16`	Trap Doubleword if Not Greater Than Immediate
	equivalent to: `tdi 20,rA,s16`	

64 •	`tdnl`	*rA*,*rB*	Trap Doubleword if Not Less Than
			equivalent to: `td 12,`*rA*`,`*rB*
64 •	`tdnli`	*rA*,*s16*	Trap Doubleword if Not Less Than Immediate
			equivalent to: `tdi 12,`*rA*`,`*s16*
	`ti`	*trapOn*,*rA*,*s16*	Trap Immediate
			archaic form for: `twi` *trapOn*,*rA*,*s16*
	`tlbi`	*rA*,*rB*	TLB Invalidate Entry
			archaic form for: `tlbie` *rB*
			Note that *A* must equal 0 for `tlbie` to replace `tlbi`.
? •	`tlbia`		TLB Invalidate All
? •	`tlbie`	*rB*	TLB Invalidate Entry
	`tlbiex`	*rB*	TLB Invalidate Entry by Index

This instruction was originally intended as an optional instruction for PowerPC implementations, but it has since been removed from the PowerPC Architecture specification.

? •	`tlbsync`		TLB Synchronize
•	`trap`		Trap Unconditionally
			equivalent to: `tw 31,r0,r0`
•	`tw`	*trapOn*,*rA*,*rB*	Trap Word
•	`tweq`	*rA*,*rB*	Trap Word if Equal
			equivalent to: `tw 4,`*rA*`,`*rB*
•	`tweqi`	*rA*,*s16*	Trap Word if Equal Immediate
			equivalent to: `twi 4,`*rA*`,`*s16*
•	`twge`	*rA*,*rB*	Trap Word if Greater Than or Equal
			equivalent to: `tw 12,`*rA*`,`*rB*
•	`twgei`	*rA*,*s16*	Trap Word if Greater Than or Equal Immediate
			equivalent to: `twi 12,`*rA*`,`*s16*
•	`twgt`	*rA*,*rB*	Trap Word if Greater Than
			equivalent to: `tw 8,`*rA*`,`*rB*
•	`twgti`	*rA*,*s16*	Trap Word if Greater Than Immediate
			equivalent to: `twi 8,`*rA*`,`*s16*
•	`twi`	*trapOn*,*rA*,*s16*	Trap Word Immediate
•	`twle`	*rA*,*rB*	Trap Word if Less Than or Equal
			equivalent to: `tw 20,`*rA*`,`*rB*
•	`twlei`	*rA*,*s16*	Trap Word if Less Than or Equal Immediate
			equivalent to: `twi 20,`*rA*`,`*s16*
•	`twlge`	*rA*,*rB*	Trap Word if Logically Greater Than or Equal
			equivalent to: `tw 5,`*rA*`,`*rB*
•	`twlgei`	*rA*,*s16*	Trap Word if Logically Greater Than or Equal Immediate
			equivalent to: `twi 5,`*rA*`,`*s16*
•	`twlgt`	*rA*,*rB*	Trap Word if Logically Greater Than
			equivalent to: `tw 1,`*rA*`,`*rB*
•	`twlgti`	*rA*,*s16*	Trap Word if Logically Greater Than Immediate
			equivalent to: `twi 1,`*rA*`,`*s16*
•	`twlle`	*rA*,*rB*	Trap Word if Logically Less Than or Equal
			equivalent to: `tw 6,`*rA*`,`*rB*

- `twllei` $rA, s16$ Trap Word if Logically Less Than or Equal
                                    Immediate
             equivalent to: `twi 6,rA,s16`
- `twllt` rA, rB Trap Word if Logically Less Than
             equivalent to: `tw 2,rA,rB`
- `twllti` $rA, s16$ Trap Word if Logically Less Than Immediate
             equivalent to: `twi 2,rA,s16`
- `twlng` rA, rB Trap Word if Logically Not Greater Than
             equivalent to: `tw 6,rA,rB`
- `twlngi` $rA, s16$ Trap Word if Logically Not Greater Than
                                    Immediate
             equivalent to: `twi 6,rA,s16`
- `twlnl` rA, rB Trap Word if Logically Not Less Than
             equivalent to: `tw 5,rA,rB`
- `twlnli` $rA, s16$ Trap Word if Logically Not Less Than
                                    Immediate
             equivalent to: `twi 5,rA,s16`
- `twlt` rA, rB Trap Word if Less Than
             equivalent to: `tw 16,rA,rB`
- `twlti` $rA, s16$ Trap Word if Less Than Immediate
             equivalent to: `twi 16,rA,s16`
- `twne` rA, rB Trap Word if Not Equal
             equivalent to: `tw 24,rA,rB`
- `twnei` $rA, s16$ Trap Word if Not Equal Immediate
             equivalent to: `twi 24,rA,s16`
- `twng` rA, rB Trap Word if Not Greater Than
             equivalent to: `tw 20,rA,rB`
- `twngi` $rA, s16$ Trap Word if Not Greater Than Immediate
             equivalent to: `twi 20,rA,s16`
- `twnl` rA, rB Trap Word if Not Less Than
             equivalent to: `tw 12,rA,rB`
- `twnli` $rA, s16$ Trap Word if Not Less Than Immediate
             equivalent to: `twi 12,rA,s16`
- `xor[.]` rA, rS, rB Exclusive OR
- `xori` $rA, rS, u16$ Exclusive OR Immediate
  `xoril` $rA, rS, u16$ Exclusive OR Immediate Lower
             archaic form for: `xori rA,rS,u16`
- `xoris` $rA, rS, u16$ Exclusive OR Immediate Shifted
  `xoriu` $rA, rS, u16$ Exclusive OR Immediate Upper
             archaic form for: `xoris rA,rS,u16`

Register Bit Definitions | C

C.1 Condition Register (CR)

The Condition Register is divided into eight 4-bit fields as described in Table C-1. The interpretation of the bits within these fields depends on how the bit field was originally updated. Table C-2 through Table C-5 describes the bit interpretations for the commonly performed CR field operations.

Table C-1 Condition Register

Bit #	Description
0-3	*CR field 0* This field is implicitly updated by some fixed-point instructions.
4-7	*CR field 1* This field is implicitly updated by some floating-point instructions.
8-11	*CR field 2*
12-15	*CR field 3*
16-19	*CR field 4*
20-23	*CR field 5*
24-27	*CR field 6*
28-31	*CR field 7*

If CR field 0 is updated by a fixed-point instruction with the record bit set, then the CR bits will be updated as described in Table C-2.

Table C-2 CR Bit Field Settings from Fixed-Point Instructions

Bit #	Name	Description
0	LT	*Less Than, or Negative* Set if the result is negative.
1	GT	*Greater Than, or Positive* Set if the result is positive.
2	EQ	*Equal, or Zero* Set if the result is zero.
3	SO	*Summary Overflow* Copied from XER[SO] after the instruction is complete.

If CR field 1 is updated by a floating-point instruction with the record bit set, then the CR bits will be updated as described in Table C-3.

Table C-3 CR Bit Field Settings from Floating-Point Instructions

Bit #	Name	Description
0	FX	*Floating-Point Exception Summary* Copied from FPSCR[FX] after the instruction is complete.
1	FEX	*Floating-Point Enabled Exception Summary* Copied from FPSCR[FEX] after the instruction is complete.
2	VX	*Floating-Point Invalid Operation Exception Summary* Copied from FPSCR[VX] after the instruction is complete.
3	OX	*Floating-Point Overflow Exception* Copied from FPSCR[OX] after the instruction is complete.

Fixed-point compare instructions update the target CR field as summarized in Table C-4.

Table C-4 CR Bit Field Settings from Fixed-Point Compare Instructions

Bit #	Name	Description
0	LT	*Less Than* Set if (rA) < s16 or if (rA) < (rB).
1	GT	*Greater Than* Set if (rA) > s16 or if (rA) > (rB).
2	EQ	*Equal* Set if (rA) = s16 or if (rA) = (rB).
3	SO	*Summary Overflow* Copied from XER[SO] after the instruction is complete.

Floating-point compare instructions update the target CR field as summarized in Table C-5.

Table C-5 CR Bit Field Settings from Floating-Point Compare Instructions

Bit #	Name	Description
0	FL	*Floating-Point Less Than* Set if (frA) < (frB).
1	FG	*Floating-Point Greater Than* Set if (frA) > (frB).
2	FE	*Floating-Point Equal* Set if (frA) = (frB).
3	FU	*Floating-Point Unordered* Set if one or both of (frA) and (frB) is NaN.

C.2 Machine State Register (MSR)

The MSR contains a large number of flags which describe the current processor state. The bits of the MSR are summarized in Table C-6. Note that not all of the bits are implemented on all processors.

Table C-6 MSR Bit Settings

Bit # 32-bit	Bit # 64-bit	Bit Name	Description	
-	0	SF	*64-bit mode*	
			0	The processor is running in 32-bit mode.
			1	The processor is running in 64-bit mode.
0	1-32	-	*Reserved*: These bits are saved in SRR1 during interrupts.	
1-4	33-36	-	*Reserved*	
5-9	37-41	-	*Reserved*: These bits are saved in SRR1 during interrupts.	
10-12	42-44	-	*Reserved*	
13	45	POW	*Power Management Enable*: Not all processors have power management facilities. On the 601, this bit is unused.	
			0	The power management facilities are disabled.
			1	The power management facilities are enabled.
14	46	-	*Implementation-Dependent Function*: Interpretation of this bit depends on the implementation. On the 601, this bit is unused.	
15	47	ILE	*Interrupt Little-Endian Mode*: On the 601, this bit is unused.	
			0	The processor should execute interrupts in big-endian mode.
			1	The processor should execute interrupts in little-endian mode.
16	48	EE	*External Interrupt Enable*:	
			0	The processor is disabled against accepting External or Decrementer interrupts.
			1	The processor is enabled to accept External or Decrementer interrupts.
17	49	PR	*Problem State*: This bit is sometimes referred to as the "privilege level" bit.	
			0	The processor is allowed to execute both user-level and privileged instructions.
			1	The processor is allowed to execute user-level instructions only.

18	50	FP		*Floating-Point Available*:
			0	The processor is not allowed to execute floating-point instructions (including loads, stores and moves).
			1	The processor is allowed to execute floating-point instructions.
19	51	ME		*Machine Check Enable*:
			0	Machine Check interrupts are disabled. On the 601, a Machine Check interrupt will be taken if HID0[CE] or HID0[EM] is cleared.
			1	Machine Check interrupts are enabled.
20	52	FE0		*Floating-Point Exception Mode 0*: This bit, along with FE1, controls the current Floating-Point Exception Mode. See Table C-7.
21	53	SE		*Single-Step Trace Enable*: This feature may not be present on all implementations.
			0	Instructions are executed normally.
			1	The processor should generate a Single-Step type Trace interrupt after the successful execution of an instruction.
22	54	BE		*Branch Trace Enable*: This feature may not be present on all implementations. On the 601, this bit is unused.
			0	Instructions are executed normally.
			1	The processor should generate a Branch type Trace interrupt after the successful execution of a branch instruction (whether or not the branch is taken)
23	55	FE1		*Floating-Point Exception Mode 1*: This bit, along with FE0, controls the current Floating-Point Exception Mode. See Table C-7.
24	56	(AL)		*Reserved*: This bit is not used by PowerPC processors but is reserved for POWER compatibility. It corresponds to the Alignment Check (AL) bit and should be set if POWER compatibility is required. This bit is saved in SRR1 during interrupts.
			0	Alignment checking is off and low-order bits of address are ignored.
			1	Alignment checking is on and the processor should generate alignment interrupts if it is unable to handle a requested unaligned access.
25	57	IP		*Interrupt Prefix*: This bit is sometimes referred to as the Exception Prefix (EP) bit.
			0	Interrupts are vectored through the real address calculated by prepending 0x0s to the interrupt offset.
			1	Interrupts are vectored through the real address calculated by prepending 0xFs to the interrupt offset.
26	58	IR		*Instruction Relocate*: This bit is sometimes referred to as the Instruction Address Translation (IT) bit.
			0	Instruction address translation is disabled.
			1	Instruction address translation is enabled.
27	59	DR		*Data Relocate*: This bit is sometimes referred to as the Data Address Translation (DT) bit.
			0	Data address translation is disabled.
			1	Data address translation is enabled.
28-29	60-61	-		*Reserved*: These bits are saved in SRR1 during interrupts.
30	62	RI		*Recoverable Interrupt*: On the 601, this bit is unused.
			0	The interrupt is not recoverable.
			1	The interrupt is recoverable.

				Little-Endian Mode: On the 601, this bit is unused.	
31	63	LE	0	The processor is running in big-endian mode.
			1	The processor is running in little-endian mode.

The FE0 and FE1 bits of the MSR combine to determine the current floating-point exception mode. These bits are interpreted as shown in Table C-7.

Table C-7 Floating-Point Exception Modes

FE0	FE1	Floating-Point Exception Mode
0	0	Floating-point interrupts disabled
0	1	Imprecise, non-recoverable interrupts enabled
1	0	Imprecise, recoverable interrupts enabled
1	1	Precise interrupts enabled

C.3 Floating-Point Status and Control Register (FPSCR)

The FPSCR contains a variety of flags that control the operation of floating-point instructions and addtional flags that indicate exceptional conditions that may have arisen during the execution of floating-point instructions.

Table C-8 FPSCR Bit Settings

Bit #	Bit Name	Description
0	FX	Floating-Point Exception Summary
1	FEX	Floating-Point Enabled Exception Summary
2	VX	Floating-Point Invalid Operation Exception Summary
3	OX	Floating-Point Overflow Exception
4	UX	Floating-Point Underflow Exception
5	ZX	Floating-Point Zero Divide Exception
6	XX	Floating-Point Inexact Exception
7	VXSNAN	Floating-Point Invalid Operation Exception (SNaN)
8	VXISI	Floating-Point Invalid Operation Exception ($\infty - \infty$)
9	VXIDI	Floating-Point Invalid Operation Exception ($\infty + \infty$)
10	VXZDZ	Floating-Point Invalid Operation Exception ($0 + 0$)
11	VXIMZ	Floating-Point Invalid Operation Exception ($\infty \times 0$)
12	VXVC	Floating-Point Invalid Operation Exception (Invalid Compare)
13	FR	Floating-Point Fraction Rounded
14	FI	Floating-Point Fraction Inexact

FPRF	FPCC	Bit	Name	Description
				Floating-Point Result Flags
		15	C	Floating-Point Result Class Descriptor
				Floating-Point Condition Code
		16	FL	Floating-Point Less Than or Negative
		17	FG	Floating-Point Greater Than or Positive
		18	FE	Floating-Point Equal or Zero
		19	FU	Floating-Point Unordered or NaN
		20	-	Reserved
		21	VXSOFT	Floating-Point Invalid Operation Exception (Software Request)
		22	VXSQRT	Floating-Point Invalid Operation Exception (Invalid Square Root)
		23	VXCVI	Floating-Point Invalid Operation Exception (Invalid Integer Convert)
		24	VE	Floating-Point Invalid Operation Exception Enable
		25	OE	Floating-Point Overflow Exception Enable
		26	UE	Floating-Point Underflow Exception Enable
		27	ZE	Floating-Point Zero Divide Exception Enable
		28	XE	Floating-Point Inexact Exception Enable
		29	NI	Floating-Point Non-IEEE Mode
		30-31	RN	Floating-Point Rounding Control
				00 — Round to Nearest
				01 — Round toward 0
				10 — Round toward +∞
				11 — Round toward -∞

C.4 Fixed-Point Exception Register (XER)

The XER contains bits that are updated by some fixed-point instructions to indicate Carry and Overflow conditions. In addition, there are also extra fields that are used by some of the *Load* and *Store String* instructions.

Table C-9 XER Bit Settings

Bit #	Bit Name	Description
0	SO	*Summary Overflow* This bit is set whenever any instruction sets the OV bit. This bit is only cleared by the `mtxer` and `mcrxr` instructions.
1	OV	*Overflow* This bit is set when an instruction has an overflow condition. This bit is updated only if the Overflow Enable (OE) bit of the instruction is set.
2	CA	*Carry* This bit is set whenever there is a carry out of bit 0 during the instruction execution. Only the Add Carrying, Subtract From Carrying, Add Extended, Subtract From Extended and Shift Right Algebraic instructions update the carry bit.
3-15	-	Reserved

16-23	-	This 8-bit field contains the compare byte that is used by the `lscbx` instruction. Since the `lscbx` instruction is not part of the PowerPC architecture and exists only on the 601, this field is used only on the 601.
24	-	*Reserved*
25-31	-	This 7-bit field contains the number of bytes that should be transferred by the `lswx`, `stswx` or `lscbx` instructions.

PowerPC 601 Optimization Summary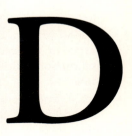

The following list provides a basic "rule of thumb" summary of the techniques that should be used to minimize the number of pipeline stalls in PowerPC programs executing on the 601 processor. This is not intended to be a complete list of all optimization techniques, but is rather a overview of the most important techniques to be aware of.

- Place at least **three** independent fixed-point instructions between a *compare* instruction and a *branch* dependent on that compare. As long as a previous instruction doesn't cause the compare to stall, this will guarantee that the branch is not dispatched until the compare results are available.

- Place at least **four** independent fixed-point instructions between a *fixed-point* instruction with the Record bit set and a *branch* dependent on the results of that instruction. As long as a previous instruction doesn't cause the fixed-point instruction to stall, this will cause the branch to be executed at the same time as the fixed-point instruction is writing its results to the CR. Multi-cycle fixed-point instructions will require additional instructions to be inserted.

- Place at least **four** independent fixed-point instructions between a `mtlr` or `mtctr` instruction and a *branch* dependent on the SPR. As long as a previous instruction doesn't cause the *Move to SPR* instruction to stall, this will cause the branch to be executed at the same time as the SPR is being updated.

- For each conditional *branch*, make sure that there is a fixed-point instruction within **three** instructions before the branch. This insures that the branch has an instruction to tag and prevents it from generating a bubble. This is expecially important for series of conditional branches which are not taken – each branch instructions needs its own fixed-point instruction to tag. Alternating branches and fixed-point instructions is a common way of addressing this problem.

- Between two *branch* instructions that are taken, up to **two** fixed-point instructions can be inserted. If the first branch jumped directly to the second branch, there would be a stall in the integer pipe while the target of the second branch was being fetched. Inserting the two instructions allows the processor to perform useful work during this time.

- For a *floating-point* instruction with the Record bit set and a *branch* dependent on the results of that instruction, place at least **three** independent fixed-point instructions *before* the floating-point instruction and at least and **five** independent fixed- or floating-point instructions *between* the floating-point and branch instructions. This will guarantee that the results of the floating-point instruction are available when the branch is executed.

- Place at least **one** independent fixed-point instruction between a *load* of a GPR and an instruction which *uses* the loaded register value. This extra instruction will cover the delay assuming a cache hit. More independent instructions are necessary to cover the delay due to a cache miss.

- Place at least **three** independent floating-point instructions between an instruction which *updates* the FPR and an instruction which *uses* the updated value. This will prevent the FPU from stalling until the data is available. Multi-cycle floating-point instructions will require additional instructions to be inserted.

References & Further Reading

[Apple94]   *Inside Macintosh: PowerPC System Software*, Addison-Wesley, Reading, Massachusetts, ISBN 0-201-49727-2, QA76.8.M31528, 1994.

[Dowd93]   Dowd, K., *High Performance Computing*, O'Reilly & Associates, Inc., Sebastopol, California, ISBN 1-56592-032-5, 1993.

[Gircys88]   Gircys, G.R., "Understanding and Using COFF," O'Reilly & Associates, Inc., Sebastopol, California, ISBN 0-937175-31-5, 1988.

[Grohoski90a]   Grohoski, G.F., "Machine Organization of the IBM RISC System/6000 Processor," *IBM J. Res. & Develop.*, Vol. 34 #1, pp. 37-58, IBM Corporation, G322-0169-00, January 90.

[Grohoski90b]   Grohoski, G.F., Kahle, J.A., Thatcher, L.E., Moore, C.R., "Branch and Fixed-Point Instruction Execution Units," *IBM RISC System/6000 Technology*, pp. 24–32, IBM Corporation, SA23-2619, 1990.

[IBM91]   Course Outline Notes from "RISC System/6000 Hardware Architecture," IBM Corporation, IBM966-8211, 9 January 1991.

[IBM93a]   *AIX Version 3.2 Assembler Language Reference, Third Edition*, IBM Corporation, SC23-2197-02, October 1993.

[IBM93b]   *PowerPC Architecture, First Edition*, IBM Corporation, 52G7487, May 1993.

[Kim92]   Kim, J-H., Huang, W., "The AIX Binder System," *AIXpert,* pp. 29–36, IBM Corporation, August 1992.

[Motorola93a]   *PowerPC™ 601 RISC Microprocessor User's Manual,* Motorola, MPC601UM/AD Rev 1, 1993.
                 (also listed under IBM document #52G7484 or MPR601UMU-02)

[Motorola93b]   *Technical Summary: PowerPC 603™ RISK Microprocessor,* Motorola, MPC603/D Rev 1, 1993.

[Motorola94]   *PowerPC™ 603 RISK Microprocessor User's Manual,* Motorola, MPC603UM/AD, 1994.
                 (also listed under IBM document #MPR603UMU-01)

[Oehler92]   Oehler, R.R., Outline Notes from *PowerPC Architecture,* IBM Corporation, IBM966K-3635, 27 February 1992.

[Patterson90]   Patterson, D.A., Hennessy, J.L., *Computer Architecture: A Quantitive Approach,* Morgan Kaufmann Publishers, San Mateo, California, ISBN 1-55880-069-8, QA76.9.A73P377, 1990.

[Patterson94]   Patterson, D.A., Hennessy, J.L., *Computer Organization and Design: The Hardware/Software Interface,* Morgan Kaufmann Publishers, San Mateo, California, ISBN 1-55860-281-X, QA76.9.C643P37, 1994.

[Przybylski90]   Przybylski, S.A., *Cache and Memory Hierarchy Design: A Performance-Directed Approach,* Morgan Kaufmann Publishers, San Mateo, California, ISBN 1-55860-136-8, TK7895.M4P79, 1990.

[Warren91]   Warren, H.S., Jr., *Predicting Execution Time on the IBM RISC System/6000,* IBM Corporation, GG24-3711-00, July 1991.

Index

ASR, 22
  64-bit mode, 25
  instructions, 167-168
associativity (cache), 179
  fully associative, 180
  n-way set associative, 181

B

b[l][a], 36
BAT area, 192
bc[l][a], 36
  extended forms, 38-41
bcctr[l], 36
  extended forms, 45-47
bclr[l], 36
  extended forms, 41-45
BE (BPU stage), 213
BE (MSR), 18, C672
biased exponent, 137
big-endian, 11
binary point, 136
bit numbering, 11
block (cache), 178
block (for BAT), 192
block address translation, 192, **195-196**
boolean instructions, 86-88
  timing, 220
BPU, 12, 13, 205, **207**, 212-213
  conflicts, 312-314
  pipeline stages
    BE, 213
    BW, 213
    MR, 213
branch
  condition encoding, 37
  instruction, 35-47
  instruction timing
    conditional, 233-238
    non-conditional, 228-230
  prediction, 47-50, 234-238
    PowerPC 601, 49
    dynamic, 48
    hints, 49
    static, 48
  tags, 230-233
Branch Execute (BPU/BE), 213
Branch Processor Unit (BPU), 12, 13, 205, **207**, 212-213

Branch Trace Enable (MSR[BE]), 18, C672
Branch Writeback (BPU/BW), 213
bubble, 230-231
BW (BPU stage), 213
byte
  data type, 10
  ordering, 11

C

C (FPSCR), C674
CA (XER), 16, C674
CACC (CAU stage), 208, 216
cache
  associativity, 179
  block, 178
  coherency, 183-185
  dependencies, 335-336
  description, 174
  direct-mapped, 179
  disk cache , 175
  fully associative, 180
  hit, 176
    timing, 238-239
  line, 178
  memory cache, 174
  miss, 176
    timing, 239-240, 250
  multiple level, 183
  sector, 178
  split, 182
  sub-block, 178
  tag, 178
  timings
    access, 238-240
    instruction, 224
  unified, 182
Cache Access (CAU/CACC), 208, 216
Cache Access Unit, 205-206, **208**, 210-211
Cache Arbitration (CAU/CARB), 208, 216
Caching Inhibited (I), 197
CARB (CAU stage), 208, 216
Carry
  CA (XER), 16, C674
CAU, 205-206, **208**, 210-211
  conflicts, 307

F

F1 (FPU stage), 211-212
FA (FAU stage), 208
`fabs[.]`, 149
`fadd[s][.]`, 150
FAU, 205-206, **207-208**
    conflicts, 307
    pipeline stages
        FA, 208
`fcfid[.]`, 153
`fcmpo`, 151
`fcmpu`, 151
`fctid[z][.]`, 153
`fctiw[z][.]`, 153
FD (FPU stage), 211-212, 224
`fdiv[s][.]`, 150
FE (CR), 15, 151, C671
FE (FPSCR), C674
FE0 (MSR), 18, 144, C672-C673
FE1 (MSR), 18, 144, C672-C673
feed-forwarding, **204**, 315
Fetch Arbitrate (FAU/FA), 208
Fetch Arbitration Unit (FAU), 205-206, **207-208**
FEX (CR), 16, 148, C670
FEX (FPSCR), 17, 149, C673
FG (CR), 15, 151, C671
FG (FPSCR), C674
FI (FPSCR), 17, 145, C673
Fixed-Point Exception Register (XER), 12, **16**, C674
Fixed-Point Unit (IU), 12, 205-207, **209-211**
FL (CR), 15, 151, C671
FL (FPSCR), C674
floating-point
    arithmetic, 149-151
    comparison, 151-152
    conversion instructions, 152-153
    conversion algorithms, 155-158
        doubleword to FP double, 157-158
        FP double to doubleword, 157
        FP double to FP single, 155
        FP double to integer, 155-156
        FP single to FP double, 155
        integer to FP double, 156-157
    data representation, 135-142
    double-precision, 10
    instruction timing, 225-228

floating-point *(continued)*
    optional instructions, 153-154
    register (FPR), 14
    single-precision, 10
    tags, 240
    timings
        instruction, 225-228
        precise exceptions, 241-242
Floating-Point Add (FPU/FPA), 211-212
Floating-Point Arithmetic Writeback (FPU/FWA), 211-212
Floating-Point Available (MSR[FP]), 18, C672
Floating-Point Condition Code (FPSCR[FPCC]), C674
Floating-Point Decode (FPU/FD), 211-212, 224
Floating-Point Enabled Exception Summary (CR[FEX]), 16, 148, C670
Floating-Point Enabled Exception Summary (FPSCR[FEX]), 17, 149, C673
Floating-Point Equal (CR[FE]), 15, 151, C671
Floating-Point Equal (FPSCR[FE]), C674
Floating-Point Exception Mode 0 (MSR[FE0]), 18, 144, C672-C673
Floating-Point Exception Mode 1 (MSR[FE1]), 18, 144, C672-C673
Floating-Point Exception Summary (CR[FX]), 16, 148, C670
Floating-Point Exception Summary (FPSCR[FX]), 17, 149, C673
Floating-Point Fraction Inexact (FPSCR[FI]), 17, 145, C673
Floating-Point Fraction Rounded (FPSCR[FR]), 17, 145, C673
Floating-Point Greater Than (CR[FG]), 15, 151, C671
Floating-Point Greater Than (FPSCR[FG]), C674
Floating-Point Inexact Exception (FPSCR[XX]), 17, 147, C673
Floating-Point Inexact Exception Enable (FPSCR[XE]), 17, C674
Floating-Point Instruction Queue (FPU/F1), 211-212
Floating-Point Invalid Operation Exception ($\infty - \infty$) (FPSCR[VXISI]), 17, C673

M

Machine Check Enable (MSR[ME]), 18, C672

Machine State Register (MSR), 18, C671-C673

mask instructions, 129-130

    timing, 220

`maskg[.]`, 130

`maskir[.]`, 130

`mcrf`, 161

`mcrfs`, 162

`mcrxr`, 162

ME (MSR), 18, C672

Memory Coherence (M), 197

MESI, 185

`mfcr`, 161

`mffs[.]`, 162

`mfmsr`, 164

`mfspr`, 164

    extended forms, 164-170

`mfsr`, 171

`mfsrin`, 171

`mftb`, 170

    extended forms, 170

Mispredict Recovery (BPU / MR), 213

mixed cache, 182

MQ, 22

    dependencies, 329

    instructions, 166

MR (BPU stage), 213

msb (most significant bit), **11**, 13

MSR, 18, C671-C673

    64-bit mode, 24

    bits

        AL, C672

        BE, 18, C672

        DR, 18, C672

        DT, C672

        EE, 18, C671

        EP, C672

        FE0, 18, 144, C672-C673

        FE1, 18, 144, C672-C673

        FP, 18, C672

        ILE, 18, C671

        IP, 18, C672

        IR, 18, C672

        IT, C672

        LE, 18, C673

MSR *(continued)*

    bits *(continued)*

        ME, 18, C672

        POW, 18, C671

        PR, 18, C671

        RI, 18, C672

        SE, 18, C672

        SF, 18, C671

    instructions, 163-164

`mtcrf`, 162

    extended forms, 162

`mtfsb0[.]`, 163

`mtfsb1[.]`, 163

`mtfsf[.]`, 163

    extended forms, 163

`mtfsfi[.]`, 163

`mtmsr`, 164

`mtspr`, 164

    extended forms, 164-170

`mtsr`, 172

`mtsrin`, 172

`mul[o][.]`, 89

`mulhd[u][.]`, 81

`mulhw[u][.]`, 80

    timing, 220

`mulld[o][.]`, 80

`mulli`, 81

    timing, 219

`mullw[o][.]`, 80

multiplication

    integer instructions, 80-81

    obsolete instructions, 89

    timing

        floating-point, 226

        integer, 219-220

    using left shifts, 346-347

Multiply-Quotient Register (MQ), 22

N

`nabs[o][.]`, 90

NaN, 12, 139, **142**

`nand[.]`, 86

`neg[o][.]`, 83

    timing, 219

negate, 83

Negative (CR[LT]), 15, C670

NI (FPSCR) , C674

non-speculative instructions, 232

Z